WITHDRAWN

KT-173-557

1940

8 MARCH In Finland, Viipuri falls to Red Army, but Stalin refuses an armistice.

9–11 APRIL German troops invade Norway and Denmark. Denmark surrenders. First British troops dispatched to Norway.

10 MAY Hitler launches invasion of the Low Countries and France, engaging French and British forces.

4 JUNE Last British evacuation ship leaves Dunkirk.

4 AUGUST Italians invade British Somaliland in East Africa.

20 SEPTEMBER – 29 OCTOBER Chinese attack Japanese lines, repelling them into Indochina.

25 OCTOBER Hostilities end in German-occupied France.

28 OCTOBER Italian troops invade Greece from occupied Albania.

---

5 APRIL Allies inform Norway and Sweden that they will begin mining Norwegian waters.

10 APRIL Major naval engagements between British and German ships. German cruiser *Königsberg* sunk by British dive-bombing attack.

17 JUNE Japan starts a blockade to stop military supplies reaching China.

3 JULY The Royal Navy attacks French fleet at Oran and Mers-el-Kebir to prevent ships from falling into German hands.

6 JULY First U-boat base in France opens at Lorient on the Atlantic coast.

9 JULY First battle between British and Italian naval forces in Mediterranean.

17–20 OCTOBER U-boats sink 32 ships from convoys SC-7 and HX-79.

---

31 JANUARY RAF Coastal Command planes enter service with ASV (Air to Surface Vessel) radar, which could detect surfaced submarines at a range of up to 36 miles (58km).

11 JUNE Italian aircraft bomb British bases at Malta, Aden and Port Sudan.

30 JULY First phase of Battle of Britain ends.

7 SEPTEMBER London subjected to massive bombing as *Luftwaffe* begins move to night *Blitz* attacks.

14/15 NOVEMBER Air raid on Coventry causes severe damage and marks commencement of heavy attacks on British industrial cities.

4/5 DECEMBER The RAF bombs Turin and Dusseldorf.

---

12 MARCH Peace agreement between USSR and Finland signed in Moscow.

27 APRIL Germany declares war on Norway.

8 MAY Neville Chamberlain resigns as British Prime Minister. Winston Churchill replaces him.

28 MAY King Leopold of Belgium orders his army to surrender to Germany.

10 JUNE Norway surrenders to Germany.

22 JUNE Armistice signed between France and Germany.

16 SEPTEMBER US introduces conscription.

27 SEPTEMBER Japan signs tripartite pact with Germany and Italy.

1941

22 JANUARY Tobruk falls to the British.

7 MARCH British and Commonwealth troops land in Greece. Within two months they have evacuated.

6 APRIL Axis forces invade Yugoslavia.

22 JUNE Germans launch Operation Barbarossa, the invasion of the USSR.

26–27 JUNE Finland and Hungary declare war on the USSR.

4 SEPTEMBER Leningrad comes under German sieg[e]

23 NOVEMBER German troops advance to w[ithin] 30 miles (48km) of Moscow.

7 DECEMBER Japanese troops invade Bri[tish]

15 DECEMBER Japanese troops ente[r]

---

19 MARCH Churchill forms Battle of the Atlantic Committee to coo[rdinate] British efforts against U-boats.

27 MAY First convoy to enjoy protection of continuous escort sails from Canada. *Bismarck* sunk by the battleships *King George* V and *Rodney*.

4 SEPTEMBER A German U-boat is engaged by US destroyer USS *Greer*.

26 SEPTEMBER First Arctic convoy carrying war material to the USSR leaves Britain.

31 OCTOBER Torpedo attack by U-boat sinks destroyer USS *Reuben James*.

10/11 MAY Last night of *Blitz* on Britain sees heaviest attack of the war on London.

1 AUGUST Soviet TB-3 bomber successfully employs dive-bombing technique in attack on German forces in Romania.

14 SEPTEMBER German heavy transport gliders are used for first time in assault on Baltic islands.

07 DECEMBER Japanese aircraft from aircraft carriers attack the US fleet and airfields at Pearl Harbor, Hawaii, destroying hundreds of planes, but failing to sink any aircraft carriers.

10 DECEMBER British warships HMS *Repulse* and *Prince of Wales* sunk by Japanese air attack off the coast of Malaya.

---

13 APRIL Japanese-Soviet non-aggression treaty signed.

17 APRIL Yugoslavia surrenders.

9–12 AUGUST Churchill and Roosevelt produce the Atlantic Charter.

2 SEPTEMBER Through the Lend-Lease Act, the US begins to send aid to the USSR and supplies 50 destroyers to the UK.

13 NOVEMBER USA repeals Neutrality Act.

5 DECEMBER Britain declares war on Finland, Hungary and Romania.

11 DECEMBER Germany declares war on US.

FOR 1942–45 SEE INSIDE BACK COVER

GREAT BATTLES
OF WORLD WAR II

General Editor: Dr. Chris Mann

Bath · New York · Singapore · Hong Kong · Cologne · Delhi · Melbourne

First published by Parragon in 2008
Parragon
Queen Street House
4 Queen Street
Bath BA1 1HE, UK

Copyright © Parragon Books Ltd 2008

All illustrations and maps © Art-Tech Ltd.

ISBN: 978-1-4075-2512-9

Editorial and design by
Amber Books Ltd
Bradley's Close
74–77 White Lion Street
London N1 9PF
United Kingdom
www.amberbooks.co.uk

Project Editor: Michael Spilling
Design: Graham Beehag
Picture Research: Terry Forshaw
Text: Rupert Butler, Martin J. Dougherty,
Michael E. Haskew, Christer Jorgensen,
Chris Mann and Chris McNab

All rights reserved.
No part of this publication may be reproduced, stored in a retrieval
system, or transmitted, in any form or by any means, without the prior
written permission of the copyright holder.

Printed in China

PICTURE CREDITS

Alcaniz Fresno's S.A.: 29(t); 30(b); 71(b); 135(b); 143(t); 169(t); 179(b); 201(b); 224(b)

Art-Tech/Aerospace: 10/11; 12(t); 20(t); 21(both); 28; 29(b); 30(t); 36; 36/37; 44(both); 45(t); 46; 47(b);
50/51; 52(both); 53(b); 54–55(all); 60(b); 61; 63(t); 68; 69(r); 70(b); 71(t); 76(both); 77(b); 87(both);
95(all); 96/97; 97; 102–103(all); 105(t); 110(t); 111(t); 112(t); 118(b); 121(b); 126; 129(t); 137(t); 144(l);
151(b); 152(b); 156/157; 158; 160(t); 161(b); 171(b); 174/175; 178(t); 179(t); 184(t); 185;
193(t); 198/199; 203(b); 208–210(all); 211(t); 216(b); 217(b); 232(t); 233(b); 234(t)

Art-Tech/MARS: 20(b); 22; 34/35; 69(l); 70(t); 92/93; 94(t); 96; 104; 150; 164/165; 170(b); 177(b); 186(b);
187; 200; 202(t); 217(t); 219; 225; 232(b); 233(t); 235(b)

Cody Images: 12(b); 13; 14(t); 15(both); 58/59; 60(t); 62; 63(b); 84/85; 86(b); 88(t); 105(b); 108/109; 110(b); 113(both);
118(t); 120; 121(t); 142(b); 151(t); 152(t); 153(b); 159(both); 160(b); 161(t); 170(t); 176; 177(t); 192; 202(b); 203(t)

Corbis: 31(t); 86(t); 111(b); 119(both); 182/183; 184(b); 186(t); 193(b); 214/215

Nik Cornish: 140/141

Getty Images: 14(b); 18/19; 23(both); 26/27; 31(b); 37(b); 38–39(all); 53(t); 79; 94(b); 153(t); 190/191; 194(t);
195(both); 211(b); 226(t)

Photos.com: Endpapers (bm)

Photos.12: 8/9

Suddeutscher Verlag: 66/67; 124/125; 132/133; 136(b); 206/207

Topfoto: 166/167

Ukrainian State Archive: 74/75; 77(t); 78(both); 127–128(all); 129(b); 134; 135(t); 136(t); 137(b); 142(t);
143(b); 144(r); 145; 194(b); 222/223; 224(t); 226(b); 227(both)

U.S. Department of Defense: Endpapers (t, tm, b); 3–7; 42/43; 45(b); 47(t); 82/83; 88(b); 89; 100/101; 112(b);
116/117; 148/149; 168; 169(b); 171(t); 178(b); 201(t); 216(t); 218; 230/231; 234(b); 235(t)

CONTENTS

INTRODUCTION

World War II was the most destructive conflict in human history. We tend to trace its progress through the milestones of the major engagements between the combatants. This is perfectly understandable, as the course of military history is marked by decisive battles.

This conforms to Western military philosophy, as propounded by Carl Von Clausewitz (1780–1831), that it is job of the military commander to seek out and attack that which will defeat the enemy, his 'centre of gravity'. At the operational level, this centre is the army, and thus it is important to bring an opponent to battle and to win decisively.

Yet in the twentieth century's two world wars, decisive victory proved elusive. Many of the battles or campaigns examined in this work were the result of seeking the decisive blow. Pearl Harbor, the Battle of Britain, Operation *Barbarossa*, Monte Cassino and *Market Garden* are good examples. Yet the knock-out blow was rarely achieved. The breakthrough at Sedan is perhaps the only case where a campaign was virtually decided in a single battle. Rather,

LEADERS IN VICTORY: *British Prime Minister Winston Churchill (left), US President Franklin Roosevelt (centre) and Soviet premier Joseph Stalin (right) meet at the Yalta Conference, February 1945. At this tripartite conference, the fate of millions of people was decided by agreements made about the postwar reorganization of Europe.*

these battles mark significant moments or turning points over longer, drawn-out campaigns. The battles were building blocks on the way to final victory or defeat. They moved front lines, wore down the enemy's strength and set up the next major clash. Such was the nature of Total War between industrialized nations.

Thus the battles examined in this collection follow the process as the Allies and Axis sought to impose their will on each over the course of six long years of war. The myth of early German invincibility is challenged by some of the battles from the early period of the war. Whilst Sedan, Dunkirk, Crete and the opening phases of Barbarossa demonstrate the German mastery of combined arms warfare, Westerplatte, Narvik and Leningrad show that the Allies were capable of checking the *Wehrmacht*.

As the prospect of immediate victory faded, the battles of the middle phase of the war took on a more attritional aspect. El Alamein, Stalingrad, Kursk, Imphal and Cassino were all grinding, drawn-out and costly struggles, in which Allied grit and material strength were key to victory. Naval and amphibious warfare was similarly attritional and the battles of Midway and Guadalcanal were more about wearing down Japanese strength than achieving rapid victory. Yet the Germans and Japanese were remarkably skilled and resilient opponents, and even as the tide turned irrevocably they put up extraordinary resistance in Normandy and Arnhem and on the islands of Iwo Jima and Okinawa.

It is the job of armies and their commanders to fight these battles and campaigns. The nature of the political leaderships of the major protagonists goes some way to explain the ferocity and longevity of the conflict. This is particularly the case with regards to the rulers of the totalitarian states, Nazi Germany's Adolf Hitler, the Soviet Union's Joseph Stalin and the military leaders of Japan, whose expansionist goals and uncompromising war aims did much to prolong the fighting. Yet they were also matched in determination by the leaders of democracies, Britain's Winston Churchill and the United States' Franklin Roosevelt.

The determination of the political leaders to fight to the bitter end was made possible only by the efforts of ordinary people. In a long, drawn-out war of attrition, the willingness of the populations to produce the matériel necessary, provide the manpower and endure, for the first time in history, the deliberate, large-scale targeting of civilians by aerial bombardment was absolutely crucial.

Ultimately, the 'Total War' of World War II was brought to a close only by the capture of the German capital, Berlin, and the use of a new and terrible weapon, the atomic bomb, against Japan.

Dr. Chris Mann, General Editor

THREE CHILDREN WAIT amongst the wreckage of a bomb-damaged street in London following a German air raid, September 1940.

THE GERMAN FÜHRER Adolf Hitler shares words with his Italian counterpart, Benito Mussolini, in a cavalcade through Munich, June 1940.

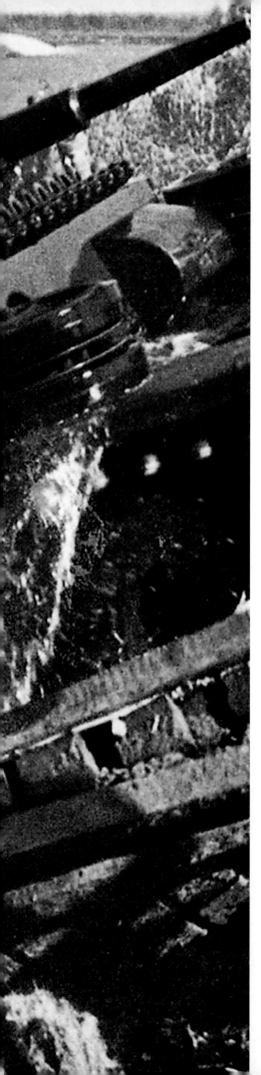

THE EARLY YEARS

The opening campaigns of World War II were marked by German victory after German victory. Superior use of modern weapons systems such as tanks and aircraft, sound doctrine and bold leadership swept aside more minor powers and even lead to impressive victories against broadly numerically, technologically equal and, sometimes, superior powers such as Britain, France and the Soviet Union.

Yet despite the achievements of the German military, the final crushing victory proved elusive and Allied victories in the skies of southern England and outside the gates of Moscow meant Germany was committed to a long-term attritional struggle.

A GERMAN PANZER III tank crosses a river in Belorussia following the invasion of the Soviet Union in June 1941. German armour proved invincible in the early years of the war, primarily due to superior tactics.

WESTERPLATTE 1939

Gdansk's Westerplatte peninsula was the site of the official start of World War II. A small forested island separated from Gdansk by the harbour channel, Westerplatte was established as a Polish military outpost during the interwar period.

The Poles were equipped with one 75mm (3in) field gun, two 37mm (1.5in) antitank guns, four mortars and several medium machine guns, but lacked any true fortifications. By the autumn of 1939, the Polish garrison occupying Westerplatte comprised 182 soldiers, who were expected to withstand any attack for 12 hours. The Versailles treaty made the city of Danzig (Gdansk) a free city state under the protection of the League of Nations, where Poland had a post office, special harbour rights and from 1924 the right to have a 'protected' depot. The site of the railway depot was the small, flat sandy peninsula of Westerplatte, which covered about half a square kilometre of land.

When Hitler took power in January 1933, the Poles set out to reinforce their defences at Westerplatte. They built bunkers, officially designated as

WESTERPLATTE FACTS

Who: Major Henryk Sucharski (1898–1946) led the small Polish garrison's resistance during a week of fighting against superior German naval and military police forces under the respective commands of Rear-Admiral Gustav Kleikamp and Police General Friedrich Eberhardt.

What: Westerplatte's unexpectedly fierce resistance delayed the German occupation of the narrow Polish coastline, thereby indirectly saving the Polish Navy and embarrassing the Germans.

Where: The semi-fortified supply depot on the Westerplatte peninsula at the mouth of the Vistula river north of Danzig (Gdaƒsk).

When: 1–7 September 1939

Why: Hitler was determined, despite the existence of a non-aggression pact from 1934, to destroy Poland.

Outcome: The attack on Westerplatte on the morning of 1 September unleashed World War II.

JUST BEFORE THE GERMAN ONSLAUGHT: *Polish troops with a light field piece on army manoeuvres, led by an officer wearing the characteristic four-cornered peaked cap.*

'Guardhouses', while making concrete reinforced shelters at the bottom of the barracks and the NCOs' villa. In addition, the Poles created seven field works (*placówka*), two of which blocked access across the vulnerable land-bridge to the mainland. From March 1939, when Hitler made his demands on Poland, the garrison was on full alert and had completed the construction of the fieldworks by late August. The number of troops was also increased from the stipulated 88 men to 210 by 31 August. The commandant was Henryk Sucharski (1898–1946) and his deputy Captain Dabrowski.

PREPARATIONS

On the German side, the fighting would be done by the *SS-Heimwehr* force of 1500 men led by Police General Friedrich Eberhardt. He had some 225 crack German Marines, under Lieutenant Henningsen, to spearhead any attack on the depot. Overall command would rest with Rear-Admiral Gustav Kleikamp whose flagship *Schleswig-Holstein*, built in 1908, was officially on a

LEFT: A GERMAN MARINE in full white summer uniform as war breaks out in September 1939.

courtesy visit in Danzig. It had anchored on the southern embankment of the Harbour canal at Neufahrwasser during the morning of 25 August – only 150m (164 yards) away. Sucharski put his garrison on heightened alert and ordered that all defensive work was to be conducted during the night, since the Germans could use the tall warehouses along the quays to observe the peninsula during daytime. Kleikamp moved his ship further upstream on 26 August, to be in a better position to open fire on Westerplatte.

FRIDAY 1 SEPTEMBER

At 4.48 a.m. on Friday 1 September, the massive guns of the *Schleswig-Holstein* fired eight grenades at the southeast sector of Westerplatte. World War II had erupted and Sucharski radioed to Hel Peninsula, 'SOS: I'm under fire.'

Three large holes had been created in the perimeter wall while warehouses with oil were blazing away. Eight minutes later, Henningsen's marines attacked in formation of three platoons while his pioneers managed to blow up the railway gate in the perimeter fence cutting across the land bridge. But then things went wrong for the Germans.

First the Poles counterattacked, knocking out the machine-gun nest at the German *Schupo* (security police) post, for the loss of three men. Then Polish commander Lieutenant Leon Pajak opened intense howitzer fire on the advancing Germans, who faltered and stopped their attack. Sucharski ordered his artillery to fire on the German sniper machine-gun nests on top of the warehouses across the canal. It had the desired effect: there was no more shooting from that direction. Then the same battery almost knocked out *Schleswig-Holstein*'s command post, but finally the ship's guns managed to knock out the battery.

BELOW: AS THE FIGHTING INTENSIFIES, Westerplatte's oil tanks and buildings burn fiercely in the darkness of the night.

STILL PULLING A FIERCE PUNCH for an old lady: the Schleswig-Holstein opens fire with her main guns.

At 6.22 a.m., the Marines radioed frantically to the ship: *'Verluste zu gross, gehen zurück'* ('Heavy losses, we're leaving'). At the other end of the Westerplatte, the Danzig police had tried to seize control of the harbour but armed civilians and the garrison had defeated this surprise attack. A total of 50 Germans lay dead while the Poles had lost only eight men. Kleikamp, who had expected to take the depot through a lightning strike, now had a real battle on his hands. Reinforced by 60 *SS-Heimwehr* troops, the marines attacked again at 8.55 a.m., led by Henningsen. They got through the perimeter wall, which lay in ruins, but they were halted by mines, fallen trees, barbed wire and intense Polish fire. By noon, the fighting was still continuing, but the demoralized SS men fled. Henningsen was mortally wounded, and half an hour later the marines had had enough as well.

The fighting had cost the Germans 82 lives and Westerplatte was still holding out. The only consolation for the Germans was that they had massacred the Polish defenders of the post office in Danzig city. The German strike against Westerplatte had been an utter fiasco.

THE LULL: 2–5 SEPTEMBER

In the ensuing days, the Germans claimed they were not making any serious moves on the armed depot, while to the tired, hungry and harassed defenders there seemed to be no end to the German attacks.

Eberhardt convinced the German Commander General Fedor von Bock (1880–1945) that a land attack was not possible. Bock agreed, having witnessed the fiasco of 1 September. The following day, the *Luftwaffe* attacked the garrison with 60 bombers, dropping more than100 bombs. No 5 bunker sustained a direct hit, killing all but three of its occupants while the kitchen, food supplies and the radio station were knocked out.

urged that Westerplatte was to surrender. An angered Dabrowski adamantly opposed such defeatism and stormed out. Sucharski ordered his men to fight on with the same dogged and brave fashion as before.

FIRETRAIN ATTACK: 6 SEPTEMBER

The Germans had no inkling that the Poles were contemplating capitulation. Every day that Westerplatte held out was superb propaganda for Poland and a humiliation for Hitler who fumed at the setbacks. A Polish agent working for the Germans pointed out that Westerplatte had no deep bunker defences.

At 3 a.m. on 6 September, the Germans sent a fire-train against the land-bridge but it was de-coupled too early by the terrified engine driver and failed to reach the oil cistern inside the Polish perimeter. If it had succeeded, it would have set the forest alight and destroyed its valuable cover for the defenders. The blazing wagons gave the

LEFT: TESTED IN SPAIN IN 1938, the Stuka was used to terrorize both military and civilians in dive bombing operations in Poland.

Now the garrison faced hunger, total isolation and the prospect of renewed attacks. Westerplatte had no anti-aircraft (AA) defences at all and this made the aerial attack on 2 September destructive to the troops' plummeting morale.

During the night of 3/4 September, the Germans attacked the Polish outposts but these were repelled. On 4 September, a German torpedo boat (T-196) made a surprise attack on the peninsula from the sea side. At the same time, the forward post of 'Wal' had been abandoned and this seemed to invite a German attack along the northern side of Westerplatte – only the 'Fort' position prevented this. At the same time, there was no hot food and the number of wounded was piling up.

On 5 September, Sucharski called a war council in the food stores where he

RIGHT: FINALLY, AFTER A WEEK of fierce fighting, the German Reichsflagge is raised above Westerplatte following the capture of the outpost.

THE SCHLESWIG-HOLSTEIN

Built between 1905 and 1908, the old battlecruiser was retained in service after 1919, when most of the German Navy was sunk, and modernized in 1925–6, 1930–31 and 1936. She was used as a cadet training ship and a floating battery. Her displacement was 13,454 tonnes (14,830 tons), her dimensions 126m (413ft) long and 22.2m (73ft) broad, while her draught (the depth of water needed in order to float) was 8.25m (27ft). The *Schleswig-Holstein* was armed with four 280mm (11in), ten 150mm (6in) and four 88mm (3.46in) naval guns as well as four 200mm (8in) AA guns. Her crew was reinforced with 225 Marines and 60 AA artillery troops when facing the indomitable Poles of Westerplatte. The ordinary crew numbered 907 men, but with all the troops this had grown to a total of 1197 by 25 August 1939.

Poles a perfect field of fire and the Germans suffered heavy casualties as a consequence. A second fire-train attack came in the afternoon but it failed too.

7 SEPTEMBER: THE LAST ASSAULT

Sucharski held a second council of war in the evening and he had by then made up his mind not to continue fighting. After all, the German Army was now outside Warsaw and the first cases of gangrene had appeared among the wounded.

At 4.30 a.m., the Germans opened intense fire upon Westerplatte, which continued until 7 a.m., when there was a final rolling barrage followed by German storm columns. Despite the use of flamethrowers, the Poles repelled the assault. But Bunker 2 was now destroyed and Numbers 1 and 4 badly damaged.

At 9.45 a.m. the white flag appeared, and at 11.00 a.m. Sucharski surrendered the post to Kleikamp who allowed the valiant commandant to keep his sword. The German troops paraded in full order when the haggard and exhausted Polish garrison marched out of Westerplatte at 11.33 a.m.

The White Eagle of Poland had surrendered at last but not without a truly heroic struggle.

LED BY THEIR OFFICER, Polish soldiers are escorted from the fighting – still erect and proud despite their defeat.

WESTERPLATTE

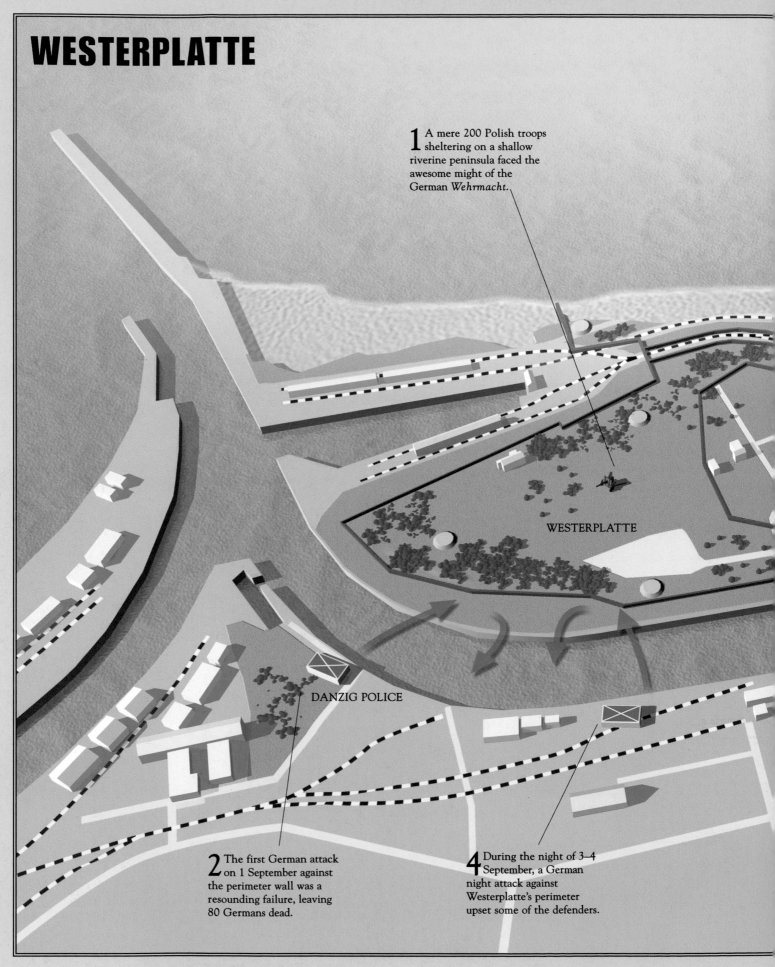

1 A mere 200 Polish troops sheltering on a shallow riverine peninsula faced the awesome might of the German *Wehrmacht*.

WESTERPLATTE

DANZIG POLICE

2 The first German attack on 1 September against the perimeter wall was a resounding failure, leaving 80 Germans dead.

4 During the night of 3–4 September, a German night attack against Westerplatte's perimeter upset some of the defenders.

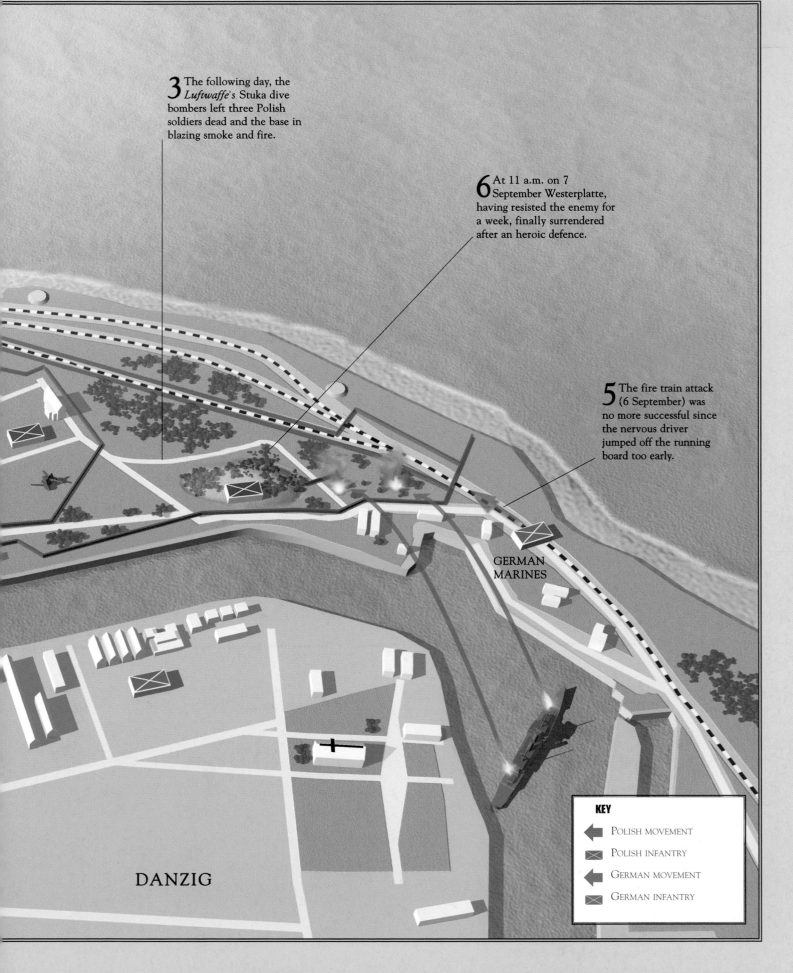

3 The following day, the *Luftwaffe's* Stuka dive bombers left three Polish soldiers dead and the base in blazing smoke and fire.

6 At 11 a.m. on 7 September Westerplatte, having resisted the enemy for a week, finally surrendered after an heroic defence.

5 The fire train attack (6 September) was no more successful since the nervous driver jumped off the running board too early.

GERMAN MARINES

DANZIG

KEY

← POLISH MOVEMENT

✕ POLISH INFANTRY

← GERMAN MOVEMENT

✕ GERMAN INFANTRY

NARVIK 1940

In early April 1940, the race was on to see which of the warring powers – Britain or Germany – would be first to seize the strategically vital port of Narvik in northern Norway. General Eduard Dietl, the commander of the German expeditionary force of 2000 mountain troops, made an unopposed landing at Narvik on 9 April.

The Germans' entry onboard 10 modern German cruisers had been blocked by two ancient Norwegian ironclads that were promptly sunk by torpedoes. Berlin had told Dietl and his men that they would be treated as 'liberators' by the Norwegians. To give credence to this fantasy, the local commander Colonel Konrad Sundlo (1881–1965) promptly capitulated. His deputy, Major Spjeldnes, took his 209 troops out of town right under the noses of the puzzled Germans whom he greeted with a cheerful '*Guten Morgen*' (Good Morning). Upon hearing this, Dietl gave orders that all Norwegians were to be disarmed. Otherwise Narvik fell without a shot being fired in anger.

NARVIK FACTS

Who: The German and Austrian mountain troopers were led by Hitler's favourite general, Eduard Dietl (1890–1944). He faced a superior allied force commanded first by General Pierse Mackesy (1883–1956) and general Field-Marshal Claude Auchinleck (1884–1981). The French were under the command of General Antoine Béthouart (1889–1982).

What: Narvik, recaptured by the Allies by 28 May, was Germany's first military defeat in World War II.

Where: The iron-ore port of Narvik in the semi-Arctic north of Norway.

When: 9 April–7 June 1940

Why: Hitler wanted Norway's strategically valuable coastline, ports and airfields in his war against Britain.

Outcome: The belated Allied recapture of Narvik could not change the outcome of the battle for Norway or the catastrophic fortunes of the Allies on the continent after Hitler's invasion of the Low Countries on 10 May 1940.

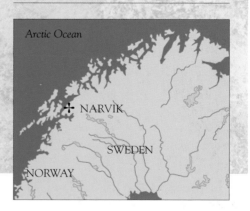

A VILLAGE OUTSIDE NARVIK is swept up in the fighting as it burns after an Allied naval bombardment in May 1940.

LEFT: *MERCHANT SHIPS IN NARVIK HARBOUR in various stages of burning and sinking after the unexpected Allied attack.*

At dawn the following day, four British destroyers led by RN commander Bernard Warburton-Lee (1895–1940) steamed into the port. Lee's ships sank two German destroyers, the captain of one of which was thrown up in the air with the ship but survived. Lee's own ship went straight into a nearby cliff, earning him a posthumous VC.

Three days later, Lee was avenged when the RN returned and sank the remaining eight destroyers. The First Lord of the Admiralty, Churchill, was delighted but in Berlin Hitler was apoplectic at the news. Dietl's force was now completely cut off and Hitler wanted to pull him back.

Dietl had not been idle. He equipped the redundant 2500 sailors with captured Norwegian arms and built a powerful defensive perimeter around Narvik and along the Ofot railway into Sweden. The 'neutral' Swedes were to keep him generously supplied and informed.

LOST OPPORTUNITY

On 16 April, the lacklustre British commander, General Pierse Mackesy (1883–1956), wired London telling the Cabinet that he could not advance on Narvik. The following day, Hitler cancelled the order to evacuate Dietl, and the Allies concentrated on holding southern Norway

BELOW: *GERMANS AND AUSTRIANS served in the Gebirgs or mountain troops, shown here being flown in a German transport plane (Junkers Ju-52) to Narvik.*

instead of throwing Dietl's isolated garrison out of Narvik. Thanks to the 'neutral' Swedes, Dietl received 24 waggon-loads of supplies (including much needed ammunition) and three troops disguised as 'medical' staff.

Nevertheless by late April the Allied Expeditionary Force (AEF) under Admiral Lord Cork (1873–1967) numbered 30,000, including four battalions of *Chasseurs Alpins* (Alpine Hunters) and Polish mountain troops and two battalions of Foreign legionnaires.

FIRST ALLIED OFFENSIVE: 12 MAY

On 28 April, General Antoine Béthouart (1889–1982) landed at Harstad – the Allied GHQ – to be told by Mackesy that Narvik should be taken by a three-pronged attack. Béthouart wanted none of that. His *Chasseurs Alpins*, together with Norwegian ski troops, would seize the Oyjord peninsula as a bridgehead for the final assault upon Narvik.

At midnight on 12 May in brilliant sunshine and glittering snow, the Allied flotilla opened fire on Bjerkvik, north of Narvik and held by the *Windisch* Group. The Foreign legionnaires landed and advanced in the face of heavy enemy fire. Bjerkvik was an inferno, in which the civilian population was massacred in the crossfire. It took two hours to clear the village.

At Meby, the German resistance was crushed by the guns of HMS *Effingham*, two French Renault tanks and the 2nd Battalion of the Legion. By 7.30 a.m., after three hours of intense fighting, the Legion captured Elve-gaardsmoen and a mountain of German supplies, including Dietl's correspondence, fell into French hands. Béthouart sent the Poles and his tanks to chase down the Oyjord peninsula. The Germans fled.

The German army had invaded the Low

LEFT: THE CHASSEURS ALPINS were specially trained and equipped for fighting in mountainous, cold and snowy terrain.

ABOVE: A GERMAN NAVAL OFFICER *of the* Kriegsmarine *addresses naval marines and mountain troops on board a German transport ship following operations at Narvik.*

Countries on 10 May, the same day Churchill was made British Prime Minister. They also controlled the whole of Norway south of Mosjoen, with the aim of relieving Dietl at Narvik. Time was not on the Allies' side. On 20 May, Churchill complained that the AEF was tying up much needed resources in a sideshow campaign.

HOLLOW VICTORY

The British commander Field-Marshal Claude Auchinleck (1884–1981) and Béthouart agreed to take Narvik in a four-pronged attack on the Germans.

At 11.45 p.m. on 27 May, the Allied Fleet opened up a withering bombardment of the landing beaches. Shells plastered Narvik town, Ankenes, Fagernes and the entire shoreline until wooden houses along the shore were burning like torches and the coastline was enveloped in thick smoke.

At 12.15 a.m., the legionnaires landed right into the lap of Naval Artillery Company Nöller, numbering 50 troops, and engaged them in savage hand-to-hand fighting. The heavily outnumbered sailors retreated to the railway embankment, closely followed up the slope by the legionnaires who took control of the railway area despite fierce resistance. A German gun was firing out of the nearby tunnel. The legionnaires pulled up by hand a French gun and fired at the mouth of the tunnel until the German battery was silenced for good.

A Norwegian battalion landed at Orneset and combined with the legionnaires to attack Hill 457, where the German *Gebirgsjägers* and sailors had entrenched themselves. They offered heavy resistance and the advancing Allied troops suffered heavy casualties. By four in the morning, the Poles were under heavy German fire at Ankenes while the Legion's 2nd Battalion had not landed across Rombaksfjord.

Half an hour later, German bombers attacked the Allied Fleet, forcing it back and denying the AEF supportive fire.

Two German companies immediately attacked down the slope of Hill 457, forcing the faltering Allies back and putting their precarious bridgehead in peril. At Ankenes, the Polish left flank was under threat. At sea, Béthouart's chief of staff was killed by German fire while two landing craft were sunk. Things were not looking good.

At 6 a.m., British Hurricanes flew over the battlefield, chasing away the *Luftwaffe* while the 2nd Battalion finally landed at Taraldsvik. The legionnaires and the Norwegians drove back the enemy. They gained the upper hand at Hill 457, which was now pockmarked with craters and littered with corpses.

Meanwhile the 2nd Battalion and the Norwegians pushed back the Germans along the Ofoten railway, while on the northern side of Rombaksfjord the *Chasseurs Alpins* and Norwegians drove back the Germans towards Hundal. The 2nd Polish Battalion took Nybord, from where it could fire on Ankenes.

Escorted by a Royal Navy destroyer, British troops in life vests are transported to the far north in April 1940.

At Narvik, Major Häussel and his mixed force of 400 sailors and mountain troops had no reserves, were running low on ammunition and had no communications with Dietl's HQ. Häussel decided to evacuate Narvik, taking his force along the still open Beisfjord road. That left small pockets of Germans still fighting at Hill 457 and Fagernes. By the afternoon, the Allied troops led by Béthouart made a triumphant entry into the newly liberated Narvik.

FRENCH TROOPS DISEMBARK somewhere in the vicinity of Narvik, prior to their successful capture of the port.

It did not last. On 7 June, the Allies sailed out of Narvik, taking the Norwegian King and Government to Britain in exile. By 1941, Narvik was supplying the Germans with 612,000 tonnes (674,615 tons) of iron ore. It had all been in vain.

THE NORWEGIAN ARMED FORCES (1940)

On paper, the mobilized Norwegian army was to number 100,000 men organized in six territorial divisions, one of which was to be under the command of General Carl Fleischer (1883–1942) at Harstad. The troops were equipped with green uniforms dating from 1912 and armed with 1894 Krag-Jorgensen rifles.

The army had no tanks, a handful of armoured cars, few heavy machine guns and no real professional core. The tiny Norwegian airforce numbered 76 planes (mostly Gloucester Gladiators) and 940 men – it was knocked out on 9 April. The Navy had 113 vessels including two armoured cruisers, *Eidsvold* and *Norge*.

GLUM NORWEGIAN SOLDIERS surrender to the Germans knowing a harsh occupation awaits their country.

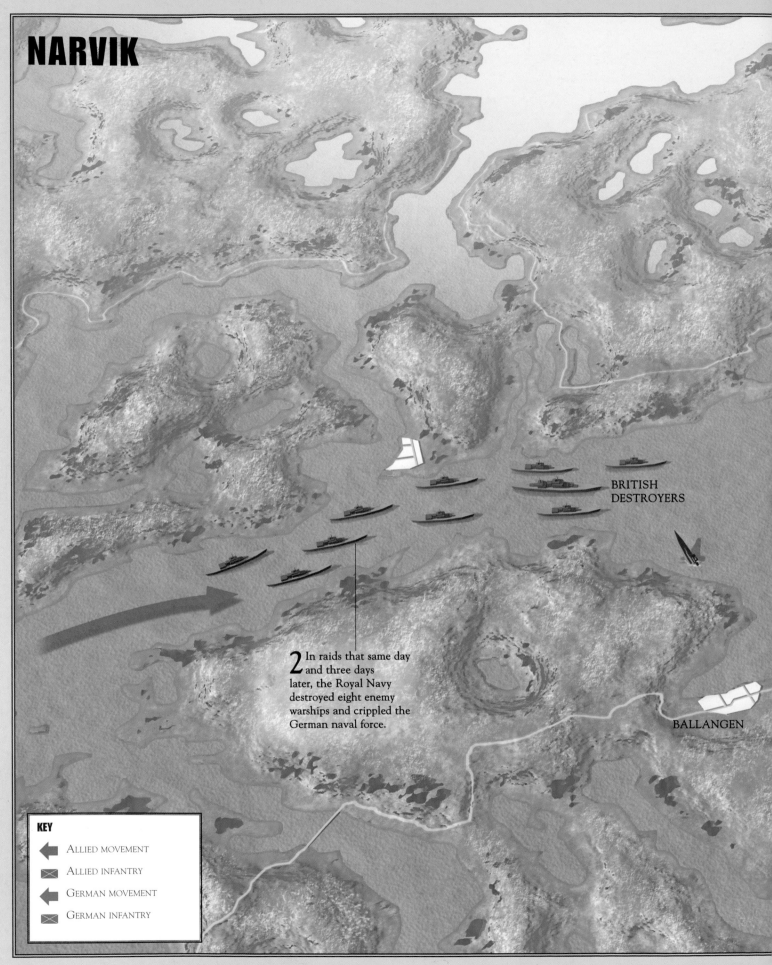

NARVIK

BRITISH
DESTROYERS

2 In raids that same day and three days later, the Royal Navy destroyed eight enemy warships and crippled the German naval force.

BALLANGEN

KEY

← ALLIED MOVEMENT

⊠ ALLIED INFANTRY

← GERMAN MOVEMENT

⊠ GERMAN INFANTRY

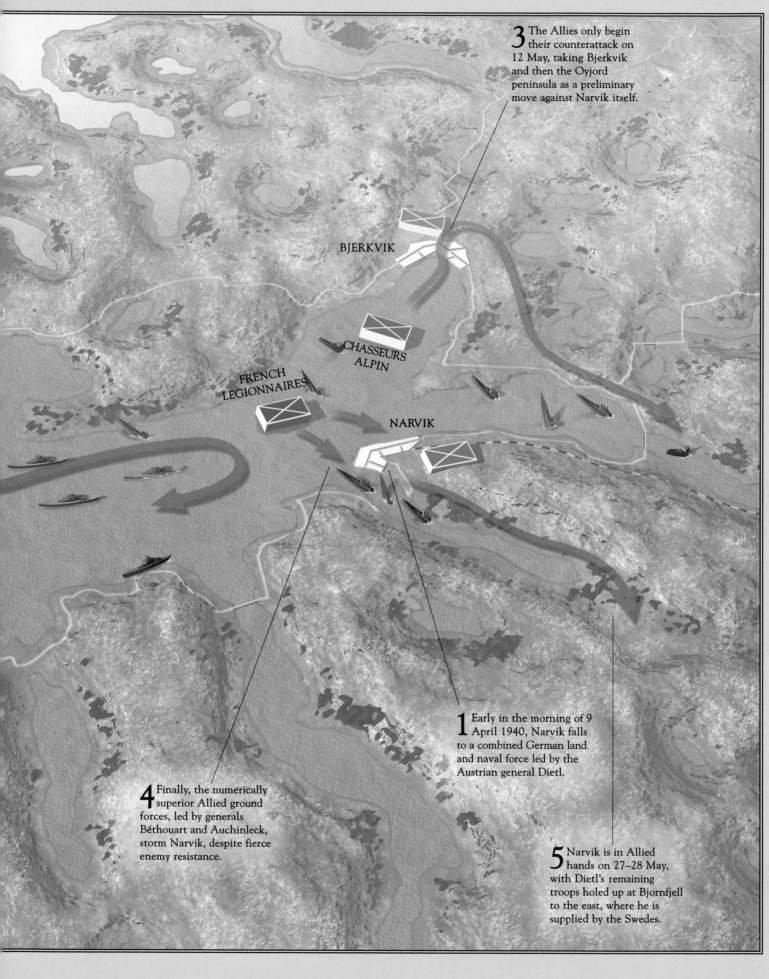

3 The Allies only begin their counterattack on 12 May, taking Bjerkvik and then the Oyjord peninsula as a preliminary move against Narvik itself.

BJERKVIK

CHASSEURS ALPIN

FRENCH LEGIONNAIRES

NARVIK

1 Early in the morning of 9 April 1940, Narvik falls to a combined German land and naval force led by the Austrian general Dietl.

4 Finally, the numerically superior Allied ground forces, led by generals Béthouart and Auchinleck, storm Narvik, despite fierce enemy resistance.

5 Narvik is in Allied hands on 27–28 May, with Dietl's remaining troops holed up at Bjornfjell to the east, where he is supplied by the Swedes.

INVASION OF FRANCE – SEDAN 1940

The conquest of France and the Netherlands during the summer of 1940 was a conspicuous triumph for Germany's Army and Air Force, leading to the defeat of the French, Dutch and Belgian armies. After the successful Polish campaign the previous September, Hitler relished the the triumph of his original Blitzkrieg (Lightning War), codenamed Fall Gelb (Case Yellow), with its emphasis on mobility and fluidity.

However, bad weather, equipment deficiencies and the need for fresh training led to further postponements. Major General Erich von Manstein (1887–1973), Chief-of-Staff in Field-Marshal Gerd von Rundstedt's (1875–1953) Army Group A, urged a giant armoured sweep through the thickly

INVASION OF FRANCE – SEDAN FACTS

Who: Gerd von Rundstedt (1875–1953) and his Chief-of-Staff Erich von Manstein (1887–1973) commanded Army Group A. Heinz Guderian (1888–1954), key in developing the concept of mass tank divisions, versus General Maurice Gamelin (1872–1958), French Commander-in-Chief, and his eventual successor Maxime Weygand (1867–1965).

What: The tactics of *Blitzkrieg* – panzers working in close coordination with artillery and dive bombers (Stukas) – achieved conspicuous successes.

Where: Germany's area of victories extended from the 'impregnable' French Maginot line to Belgium, the edge of the English Channel and the Netherlands to the north.

When: 10–28 May 1940

Why: Hitler wished to turn his attentions to a decisive assault on the Soviet Union.

Outcome: French forces in the Allied line's vital centre were shattered. In the north, Dutch armed forces were all but destroyed.

MAY 1940: A GERMAN ARMOURED COLUMN *of Panzer II tanks passes French anti-tank barriers in Sedan, following the evacuation of the town by the French Army.*

A Young German soldier poses for the camera in the advance towards Dunkirk. He is armed with a Kar-98 rifle and has a grenade tucked in his belt.

was considered impregnable. The Belgians shared the belief in the Maginot Line, the elaborate system of fortifications running along France's eastern frontier. Fast-moving German armies had no trouble in outflanking it. Seven panzer divisions totalling 2270 tanks, self-propelling guns and armoured vehicles drove unopposed through Luxembourg and into the wooded hills and densely forested plateau of the Belgian Ardennes. The area was only lightly screened by French cavalry, in the belief that the narrow roads of the region could not accommodate a large armoured force.

In the early hours, the tanks of General Erwin Rommel (1891–1944), the recently appointed commander of 7th Panzer Division, crossed the southern end of the Belgian frontier, heading for the Meuse at Dinant 105km (65 miles) away. Simultaneously Hitler's panzers rolled over the Luxembourg frontier.

General Heinz Guderian (1888–1954), the spearhead commander, had spelt out to his men the prime objective – the Channel. His superior, General Ewald von Kleist (1881–1954), had command of the principal panzer forces in the *Sichelschnitt* (Sickle Stroke) plan, scything through the Allied front's centre to the English Channel, trapping the British Expeditionary Force and the First and Seventh French Armies against the sea. A gigantic phalanx of armour and vehicles, enjoying the added protection of the *Luftwaffe*, stretched back for 160km (100 miles), with its rear rank lying 80km (50 miles) east of the Rhine. Due to intelligence disregarded by the *Deuxième Bureau*, all areas were virtually undefended.

PANZER THRUST

French forces, many on leave, were hastily recalled following an order from General Maurice Gamelin (1872–1958), the Commander-in-Chief. Two Corps on the left of the Ninth Army under France's General André Corap (1873–1953) took up positions on the Meuse between

wooded Ardennes, which the French considered impassable. It was planned that the Germans would then cross the river Meuse just north of the French frontier town of Sedan and break out into the open country, with a race to the Channel at Abbeville. After slicing through the French at Sedan, there would be a heading west along the Somme's north bank to the Channel, entrapping the bulk of major Anglo-French forces.

ATTACK ON THE LOW COUNTRIES

As dawn broke on 10 May, a special force of 424 men and a swarm of gliders swooped down to destroy the heavily armoured fort of Eben Emael, a key Belgian defence, which

THE THICK ARMOURED French Char B1 bis tank required costly maintainance and constant refuelling and faced frequent breakdowns.

Namur and Givet, crossing the water to clash with von Rundstedt, approaching through the Ardennes.

On 12 May, Guderian's corps had captured Bouillon in the western part of the Belgian province of Luxembourg, crossing the French frontier just north of Sedan, where the Belgians had left many road blocks undefended. Keen to press his advantage, Guderian persuaded von Kleist to let him unleash his three panzer divisions across the Meuse near Sedan without waiting for rear guard infantry protection. Howling Junkers JU 87 Stuka bombers rained down on the French artillery while high velocity 88mm (3.46in) 'ack-ack' guns

A BREAK ON THE GERMAN advance through the Ardennes – triumphant despite the Allied belief that swift movement was impossible in such terrain.

sprayed the enemy bunkers. Infantry of the crack Infantry regiment *Grossdeutschland*, thrusting through Luxembourg into Belgium towards the Meuse, were ferried over to attack the French positions. Within hours, *Grossdeutschland* gained a river line that the French believed would hold. A gap was smashed between Second and Ninth French armies; Guderian's Panzer Corps, driving through the breach, wheeled and positioned on line direct to the English Channel.

Further German advances revealed insufficient coordination between French tanks and infantry. Nevertheless 6th and 8th Panzer Divisions had to contend with ripostes of machine-gun fire, which also hampered the work of engineers building pontoons across the river at the village of Monthermé, within some of the most rugged territory in the Ardennes. Regrouped German armour secured the position after a fierce engagement. Two French

Divisions, 55th and 71st, faced annihilation. Rommel's 7th Panzer Division had reached the Meuse below the city of Dinant but encountered French heavy artillery shelling and small arms fire from troops on the left bank. Rommel's attention fastened on the plight of his motorized infantry attempting to cross the river in its inflatable boats. To screen the crossings, he ordered buildings on the German side to be set alight. The resulting smoke drifted across the river. Rommel's assault troops were able to establish a bridgehead; French reservists were too stunned to fight back.

At Sedan, the entire 1st Panzer Brigade crossed the Meuse on a hastily constructed pontoon bridge. *Luftwaffe* fighters fended off enemy assaults while to the south Guderian's forces deepened their bridgehead, by evening 48km (30 miles) wide. On 14 May also, Allied forces had their first encounter with the Germans sweeping through Belgium. Guderian's rapid advance caused anxiety in Berlin that, deprived of infantry, he could be cut off by any counterattack. But, in fact, the Allies were in danger of being outflanked.

ROAD TO PARIS

The British Prime Minister Winston Churchill (1874–1965) next day received a despairing telephone call from the French premier Paul Reynaud (1878–1966) declaring, 'We are beaten … The road to Paris is open'. With forces hastily assembled near the town of Montcornet, north of Paris, Colonel Charles de Gaulle (1890–1970) launched three

LEFT: THIS CORPORAL SERVED *with 1st Panzer Regiment, one of the many Panzer units involved in the breakthrough at Sedan.*

BELOW: AN EFFECTIVE LIGHT *medium tank with mounted assault, antitank and anti-aircraft armament, the Pz 38t was Czech manufactured throughout the war. This example fought with the 2nd Panzer Division.*

offensive actions, all but reaching Guderian's advanced headquarters, only to be repulsed. A shaky defensive perimeter, to where the British and French could retreat, was assembled around Dunkirk. The situation in Europe deteriorated still further. The concern was how British and French forces could escape annihilation at Dunkirk. Nevertheless on 21 May four battalions clashed with 7th Panzer and the Waffen SS *Totenkopf* Division near Arras, costing the Germans 700 casualties and the loss of 20 tanks. But two days later the German armoured divisions had penetrated to the coast. The BEF was cut off, communications severed and ammunition short. To make matters worse, on 28 May the Belgian army capitulated.

AFTERMATH

Many reasons have been cited for Hitler's order to Guderian to halt his forces at Dunkirk. It might have been advice that the boggy terrain near the coast was unsuitable for tanks, or maybe it was the setback at Arras – or perhaps von Rundstedt's wish to regroup forces for the assault on Paris. Churchill was determined to keep France in the war and sent what reinforcements he could, landing at Cherbourg and Brest, but progress in all areas was hopeless in the face of the panzers and Stukas. On 14 June, the unstoppable juggernaut of the *Wehrmacht* entered the undefended French capital. Within months, Hitler's interest was turning to the east.

PANZER IIIS AND IVS roll down the main street of a town somewhere in northern France. Notably, Panzer IV was the sturdy warhorse throughout, more than holding its own against Allied opponents.

ERICH VON MANSTEIN

Erich Von Manstein (1887–1973), the architect of *Blitzkreig*, achieved promotion to general field marshal on 19 July 1940, after France fell. In 1941–42, he conducted Eleventh Army's conquest of the Crimea, while his Caucasian counteroffensive saved Army Group Don from destruction after Germany's devastating defeat at Stalingrad at the end of 1942. He clashed increasingly with Hitler as the military situation on the Eastern Front declined. This served to fuel Hitler's distrust – probably influenced by Manstein's Jewish origins. Hitler sacked him in 1944, but he proved a tough survivor despite a flirtation with the anti-Nazi resistance movement. In 1948, he was arraigned as a war criminal, imprisoned and then released in 1953. He was subsequently consultant to the West German government on military matters, dying near Munich on 1 June 1973, aged 85.

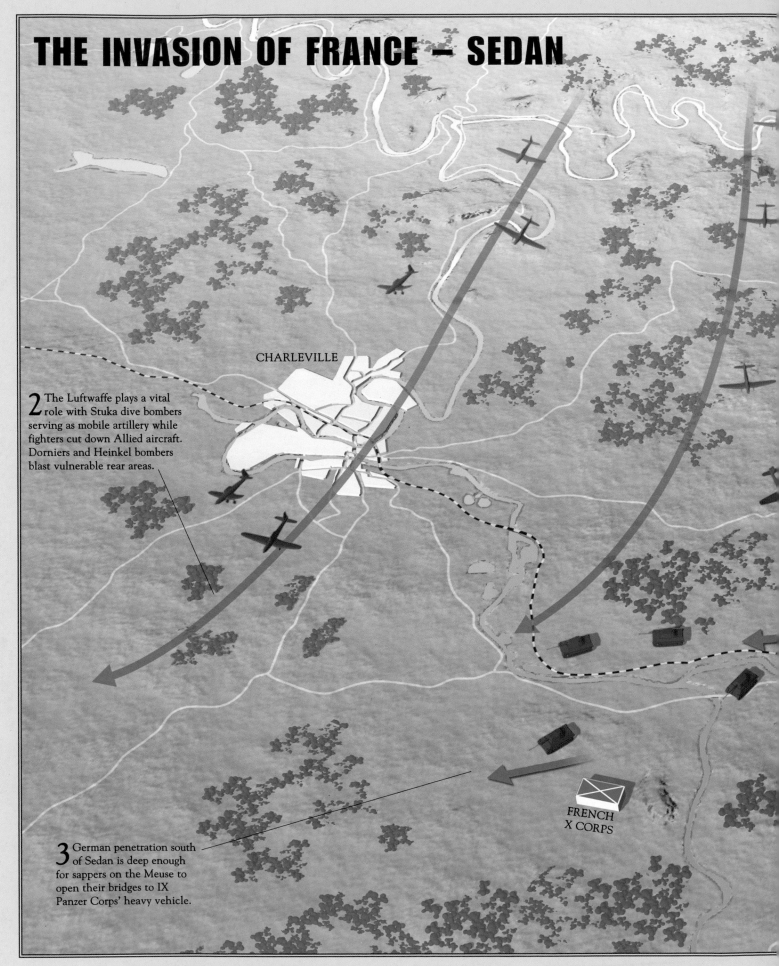

THE INVASION OF FRANCE – SEDAN

CHARLEVILLE

2 The Luftwaffe plays a vital role with Stuka dive bombers serving as mobile artillery while fighters cut down Allied aircraft. Dorniers and Heinkel bombers blast vulnerable rear areas.

3 German penetration south of Sedan is deep enough for sappers on the Meuse to open their bridges to IX Panzer Corps' heavy vehicle.

FRENCH X CORPS

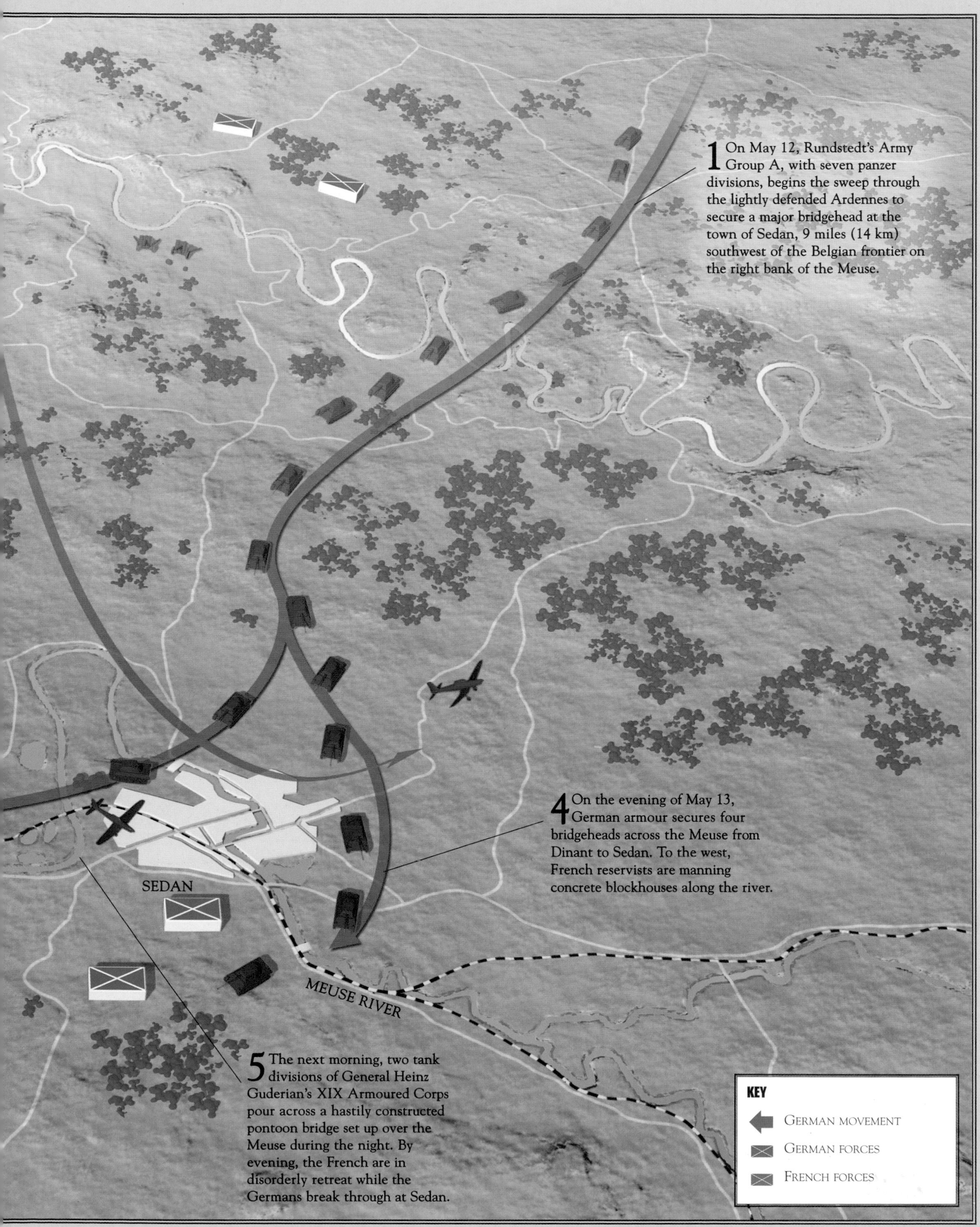

1 On May 12, Rundstedt's Army Group A, with seven panzer divisions, begins the sweep through the lightly defended Ardennes to secure a major bridgehead at the town of Sedan, 9 miles (14 km) southwest of the Belgian frontier on the right bank of the Meuse.

4 On the evening of May 13, German armour secures four bridgeheads across the Meuse from Dinant to Sedan. To the west, French reservists are manning concrete blockhouses along the river.

SEDAN

MEUSE RIVER

5 The next morning, two tank divisions of General Heinz Guderian's XIX Armoured Corps pour across a hastily constructed pontoon bridge set up over the Meuse during the night. By evening, the French are in disorderly retreat while the Germans break through at Sedan.

KEY

← GERMAN MOVEMENT

GERMAN FORCES

FRENCH FORCES

DUNKIRK 1940

During the opening weeks of World War II in the West, thousands of soldiers of the British Expeditionary Force and the French First Army, with their backs to the sea, were evacuated from the European continent in nine desperate days of fighting on the coast of the English Channel.

The rescue itself was deemed a 'miracle' as a hastily assembled flotilla of military and civilian vessels of every description ran a gauntlet of air attacks by the German *Luftwaffe* to ferry the troops to safety.

For eight months, the opposing armies had only watched one another warily. Then, on 10 May 1940, the *Sitzkrieg* ('Phoney War') was shattered with the German invasion of France and the Low Countries. In the north, 30 divisions of Army Group B advanced across the frontiers of The Netherlands and Belgium on a 322km (200-mile) front. Further south, 45 divisions of Army Group A slashed through the Ardennes Forest and skirted the defences of the Maginot Line. Led by one of the world's foremost proponents of mobile warfare, General Heinz Guderian

DUNKIRK FACTS

Who: The British Expeditionary Force, French, Belgian and Dutch armed forces, with the British under Field-Marshal John, Lord Gort (1886–1946) versus German Army Group A under General Gerd von Rundstedt (1875–1953).

What: The Germans forced the evacuation of the British and other Allied troops from the European Continent but failed to deliver the devastating blow that might have altered the course of World War II inexorably in their favour.

Where: The port city of Dunkirk and environs on the coast of the English Channel in northwest France.

When: 26 May– 4 June 1940

Why: The Germans sought to occupy Western Europe with the conquest of France and the Low Countries.

Outcome: The Allied forces lost thousands of prisoners along with vast quantities of war matériel; however, 338,226 soldiers were evacuated to England.

WOUNDED BRITISH AND FRENCH *soldiers file from the beach at Dunkirk. Within days of the German offensive launched on 10 May 1940, the British Expeditionary Force and remnants of the French Army were forced to evacuate the European continent.*

(1888–1954), German tanks and motorized infantry swept relentlessly northwest in a great arc, reaching the coast in only 10 days.

BLITZKRIEG

The startling swiftness of the German offensive threatened to trap all Allied troops north of the thrust by Army Group A as Guderian sent three panzer divisions racing towards the Channel ports of Boulogne, Calais and Dunkirk. Three key positions, the French at Lille, Belgian Army units along the Lys river and the British at Calais, offered resistance to the German onslaught. Within 72 hours of reaching Abbeville, the Germans captured both Boulogne and Calais, and elements of the 1st Panzer Division had advanced to within 19km (12 miles) of Dunkirk, the sole remaining avenue of

escape for Allied forces in northern France and Belgium. Although he had been ordered to mount a counterattack in support of the French, Field-Marshal John, Lord Gort (1886–1946), commander of the British Expeditionary Force, chose instead to concentrate his troops in the vicinity of Dunkirk in order to evacuate as many soldiers as possible to the relative safety of England. The heroic defence of Lille by the French, of Boulogne by the 2nd Battalion Irish Guards and a battalion of the Welsh Guards, and Calais by the British 30th Infantry Brigade, bought precious time for Gort to prepare a defensive perimeter around Dunkirk. But the effort appeared to be in vain as German tank commanders peered at the town's church spires through binoculars.

THE PANZERS PAUSE

Quite unexpectedly, the greatest assistance to the Allied evacuation plan came from Hitler himself. On 24 May the *Führer* visited the headquarters of General Gerd von Rundstedt (1875–1953), commander of Army Group A, at Charleville. Influenced by *Reichsmarschall* Hermann Göring (1893–1946) to allow his *Luftwaffe* to deliver the death blow to the enemy at Dunkirk, Hitler directed Rundstedt to halt the tanks of six panzer divisions along the Aa canal.

THE INDOMITABLE 'TOMMY'

His trusty Lee-Enfield rifle slung across his shoulder and the distinctive helmet secured by its sturdy chinstrap, a soldier of the British Expeditionary Force (BEF), affectionately known as a 'Tommy', manages a cheerful expression during the dark days of 1940. As the threat of war with Nazi Germany increased, conscription rapidly raised the strength of the British Army, and in 1939 alone the size of the force grew by a million men.

At the time of the German spring offensive in 1940, the BEF comprised 10 divisions deployed on the European continent. During the evacuation of the BEF from Dunkirk, codenamed Operation *Dynamo*, more than 218,000 British and 120,000 French soldiers were evacuated to safety in Britain by a seaborne effort that included many civilian craft.

ABOVE: THOUSANDS OF ALLIED SOLDIERS *waiting for rescue at Dunkirk while German armour and infantry continue to pressure a shrinking perimeter.*

Guderian was rendered 'utterly speechless' by the order. For nearly 48 hours the German ground assault abated and the Allied troops around Dunkirk were pummelled by screeching Stukas and strafed by *Luftwaffe* fighters. On 26 May, the ground attack resumed but the reprieve allowed Gort to patch together the tenuous defence of a 48km (30-mile) stretch of beach from Gravelines in the south to Nieuport, Belgium, in the north. Two days later, Belgian King Léopold III (1901–1983) ordered his forces to surrender, and the Allied defensive perimeter continued to contract. Eventually the Allies were squeezed into a pocket only 11km (7 miles) wide.

OPERATION DYNAMO

As early as 20 May, while the Allied debacle on the Continent was unfolding, British Prime Minister Winston Churchill (1874–1965) authorized the preparation of

RIGHT: UNDER CONSTANT THREAT *of Luftwaffe air attack, soldiers of the British Expeditionary Force queue up for the next watercraft that will transport them from Dunkirk to safety.*

Operation *Dynamo*, the evacuation of the British Expeditionary Force from France.

The hard-pressed Royal Navy could not possibly supply the number of vessels needed for the rescue, and Vice-Admiral Bertram Ramsay (1883–1945) called for boats in excess of 9.3m (30ft) in length to assemble at ports in England. Cabin cruisers, ferries, sailing schooners and their civilian crews joined Royal Navy destroyers in the treacherous 88km (55-mile) journey through a maze of German contact mines sown in the Channel, under continuous air attack and often within range of fire from German heavy artillery.

AIR RAIDS

Luftwaffe bombing had set the town of Dunkirk ablaze and wrecked the port facilities. Rescue vessels were compelled to risk running aground in the shoals along the beaches or to tie up at one of two 'moles' – rocky breakwaters covered with planking wide enough for men to stand three abreast – in order to take soldiers aboard. Countless acts of heroism occurred as vessels made numerous shuttle runs. One 19m

AS A PALL of smoke from a Luftwaffe air strike rises in the background, a British soldier lying on his back takes aim at a low flying German plane.

(60ft) yacht, the *Sundowner*, carried 130 soldiers to safety, while close to a hundred perished aboard the paddlewheel steamer *Fenella* when a German bomb ripped through its deck and detonated. Nearly one-third of the 693 boats involved were destroyed, but from 26 May until the final rescue run in the pre-dawn hours of 4 June, a total of 338,226 Allied soldiers reached England.

When the battered and exhausted Allied troops arrived, they were welcomed as heroes. Townspeople poured out of their homes with food and drink for the famished soldiers. Virtually all of their heavy equipment had been abandoned on the Dunkirk beaches, thousands of their comrades were killed or captured, and the armed forces of Britain and France had suffered one of the greatest military defeats in their history.

Yet these men had survived. Amid the celebration Churchill groused, 'Wars are not won by evacuation.' He later wrote, 'There was a white glow, overpowering, sublime,

RIGHT: THEIR VESSEL SUNK by German aircraft, dazed French soldiers and sailors of the Royal Navy are plucked from the waters of the English Channel during Operation Dynamo.

which ran through our Island from end to end … and the tale of the Dunkirk beaches will shine in whatever records are preserved of our affairs.'

AFTERMATH

Historians have debated Hitler's reasons for halting the panzers. Some assert that the focus of the Germans was already on the complete defeat of France and the capture of Paris. Others say that Hitler was concerned about the marshy terrain in Flanders, which was less than ideal for the manoeuvring of tanks. The tanks themselves had been driven rapidly and engaged for some time. Many of them undoubtedly needed refitting and some of their precious number would have been lost in an all-out attack on the Allied defences. Göring had argued that the *Luftwaffe* was certainly more loyal and fervently Nazi than the leadership of the German Army; therefore, his air arm should be given the honour of annihilating the enemy.

In the end, the *Luftwaffe* had failed to force an Allied capitulation. Thousands of Allied soldiers had escaped death or capture. The miracle of Dunkirk stands as a stirring moment in military history, and Hitler's decision to halt his panzers as one of the great 'what ifs' of World War II.

BELOW: CAPTURED BRITISH AND FRENCH soldiers await disposition following the German occupation of Dunkirk. The Luftwaffe had failed to annihilate the Allied force, and those who were rescued fought another day.

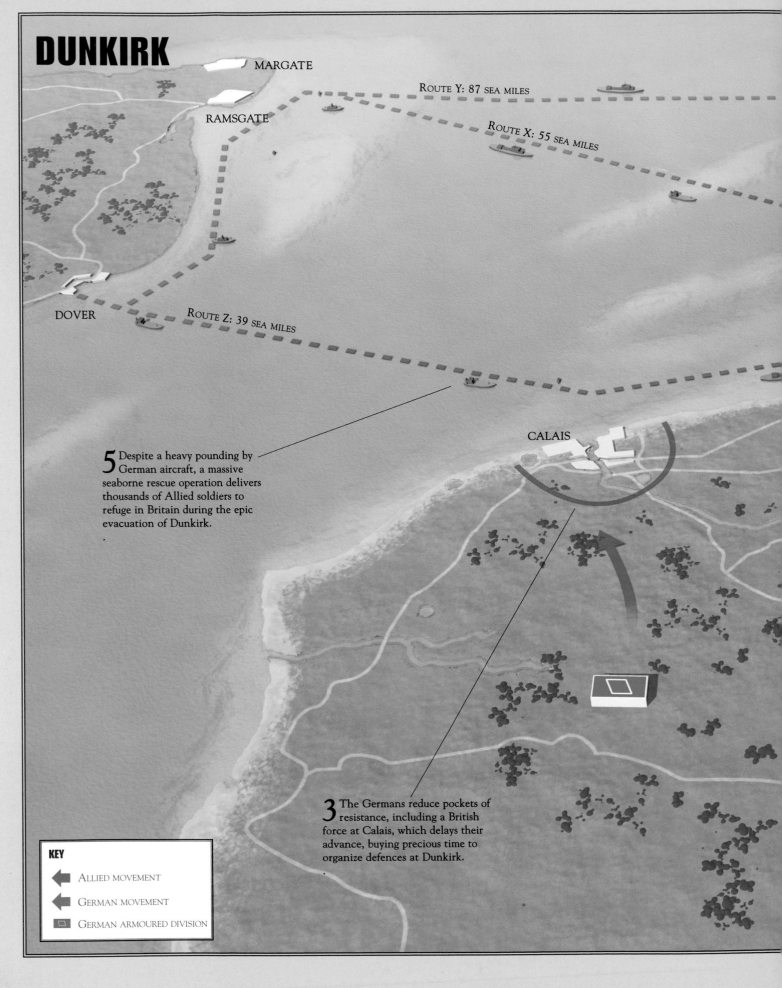

DUNKIRK

MARGATE

ROUTE Y: 87 SEA MILES

RAMSGATE

ROUTE X: 55 SEA MILES

DOVER

ROUTE Z: 39 SEA MILES

5 Despite a heavy pounding by German aircraft, a massive seaborne rescue operation delivers thousands of Allied soldiers to refuge in Britain during the epic evacuation of Dunkirk.

CALAIS

3 The Germans reduce pockets of resistance, including a British force at Calais, which delays their advance, buying precious time to organize defences at Dunkirk.

KEY

← ALLIED MOVEMENT

← GERMAN MOVEMENT

▣ GERMAN ARMOURED DIVISION

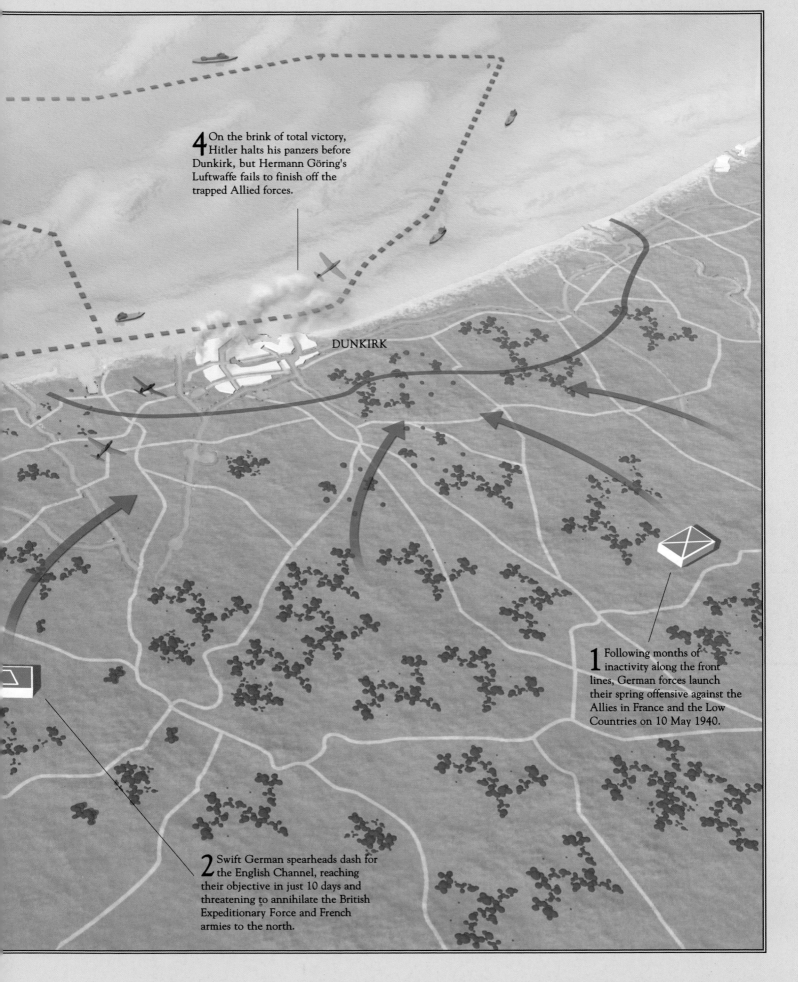

4 On the brink of total victory, Hitler halts his panzers before Dunkirk, but Hermann Göring's Luftwaffe fails to finish off the trapped Allied forces.

DUNKIRK

1 Following months of inactivity along the front lines, German forces launch their spring offensive against the Allies in France and the Low Countries on 10 May 1940.

2 Swift German spearheads dash for the English Channel, reaching their objective in just 10 days and threatening to annihilate the British Expeditionary Force and French armies to the north.

BATTLE OF BRITAIN

1940

The German conquest of France and the Low Countries had been accomplished with astonishing speed. During the opening months of World War II in Europe, Nazi Germany had emerged victorious across the Continent. As German troops paraded down the Champs Elysées, Führer Adolf Hitler and his generals planned for the invasion of Great Britain.

German officers and soldiers had gazed from the French coastline across the 32km (20 miles) of the English Channel which separated them from their enemy. To a man, they knew that the conquest of Great Britain would be their greatest challenge to date. However, they were brimming with confidence.

BATTLE OF BRITAIN FACTS

Who: The German *Luftwaffe* commanded by *Reichsmarschall* Hermann Göring (1893–1946) versus Royal Air Force Fighter Command under Air Chief Marshal Hugh Dowding (1882–1970).

What: The *Luftwaffe* attempted to destroy the Royal Air Force and later to raze British cities.

Where: The skies above Britain and the English Channel.

When: 10 July 1940–10 May 1941

Why: Initially, the Germans needed control of the skies to cover Operation *Sea Lion*, the invasion of Great Britain. Later, the Blitz raids were primarily terror attacks.

Outcome: The *Luftwaffe* failed to subdue the RAF and break the will of the British people. Operation *Sea Lion* was cancelled.

FROM HIS ROOFTOP *vantage point, an air raid warden scans the skies above London for Luftwaffe bombers. The dome of St. Paul's Cathedral rises in the background.*

ABOVE: BRITISH PRIME MINISTER WINSTON CHURCHILL visits coastal defences on the southern coast of England, August 1940.

Operation *Sea Lion*, as the invasion was codenamed, would involve the marshalling of troops and matériel, as well as the rounding up of enough barges suitable for transporting the most formidable fighting machine in the world across the narrow expanse of the Channel. Still, all of the victories thus far, all of the planning and all of the *Führer's* bold rhetoric meant far less without mastery of the skies. Control of the air was a prerequisite to any successful invasion.

KANALKAMPF

Its opening phase was known as *Kanalkampf*, or the Channel Battle, to the Germans. For the rest of the world, the aerial conflict which began on 10 July 1940 and lasted fully 10 months was known collectively as the Battle of Britain. Less than three weeks after the Fall of France, *Reichsmarschall* Hermann Göring (1893–1946) and his *Luftwaffe* began the effort to take control of the skies above Britain. Hitler had initially set the date for the invasion as 15 August, and the German planes were to pound British harbours and shipping.

Göring had gathered more than 750 fighters, including the nimble but short-range Messerschmitt Me-109 and the twin-engine Me-110, to escort more than 1300 Heinkel He-111 and Dornier Do-17 bombers along with 300 of the infamous Junkers Ju-87 Stuka dive bombers which had sown destruction in Poland and France. Air Chief Marshal Hugh Dowding (1882–1970), chief of Royal Air Force Fighter Command, could muster few more than 700 frontline Supermarine Spitfire and Hawker Hurricane fighters and other obsolescent types in defence. During the ensuing four weeks, dogfights raged daily, a number of merchant ships were sunk by the marauding Germans and the Royal Navy

LEFT: UNIFORMED IN HIS flight suit, a Luftwaffe bomber pilot proceeds to a pre-mission briefing.

ABOVE: CONCEIVED AS A commercial airliner, the Heinkel He-111 was easily converted to a bomber.

relocated most of its ships and personnel to Portsmouth from Dover. The *Luftwaffe* failed, however, to sufficiently erode the strength of the Royal Air Force.

Early in the battle the British came fully to appreciate the value of accurate intelligence and a new early warning device called radar, both of which provided advance notice to them of incoming German air raids. It was also quickly determined that the lumbering Stukas were unfit for air-to-

BELOW: COURAGEOUS MEMBERS OF the London Fire Brigade wrestle a hose into position to combat a fire ignited by Luftwaffe incendiary bombs.

air combat, easy prey for RAF fighters. Although they had lost 300 planes, while half that number of British aircraft had fallen, the Germans considered their initial operations sufficiently effective to begin round two of the aerial preparations for invasion.

DER ADLERTAG

Still confident of victory, German airmen often sang a jaunty tune with the lyric, '*Wir fliegen gegen England*' ('We are flying against England'). Göring scheduled *Adlertag*, or

THE MESSERSCHMITT ME-109 was the premiere Luftwaffe *fighter aircraft of World War II. It was heavily armed and skilfully piloted, but its limited range allowed only 20 minutes of fighting time in hostile airspace over Britain.*

Eagle Day, for 13 August 1940. The second phase of the Battle of Britain was intended to bring the RAF to its knees, through the systematic bombing of its airfields in southern and central England; the destruction of the 93m (300ft) towers and installations which comprised the early warning radar stations strung along the English coastline; and, finally, the elimination of the planes and pilots of Fighter Command.

On Eagle Day, the Germans lost 46 planes, and the RAF 13. However, a week of nearly continuous daylight aerial combat followed. Citizens below could see the swirling vapour trails of the dogfighting planes. Occasionally they saw the puff of an exploding aircraft or the long, black trail of a burning machine as it hurtled towards the ground. At times, it actually seemed to be raining spent cartridges from British and German machine guns and cannon. Though its actual losses may have been fewer than those of the *Luftwaffe*, Fighter Command was being stretched to breaking point. Young pilots were often thrown into combat

with only a few hours of flying time, facilities had been bombed and strafed, and the rigours of combat had taken their toll on the remaining airworthy planes.

A CHANCE REPRIEVE

In concert with daylight raids, Göring also instructed his pilots to fly nocturnal bombing missions against military targets in Britain. Major cities, particularly London, had not been targeted due to the probability of retaliation by RAF bombers against German cities. However, on the night of 24 August 1940 a few *Luftwaffe* bombers strayed off course and dropped their ordnance on the city of London. The next night RAF bombers hit Berlin. Enraged, the *Führer* vowed to lay waste to British cities.

On 7 September 1940, Hitler authorized a change in strategy. The *Luftwaffe* was to bomb London into submission. A week later, however, he postponed Operation Sea Lion indefinitely. On the first night of the Blitz, more than 2000 Londoners were killed or wounded. The sacrifice of the civilian population proved to be the salvation of Fighter Command, which was given time to rest and refit. London was not the only city ravaged by German bombs in the months to come. On the night of 14 November 1940, Coventry was assailed by more than 400 *Luftwaffe* bombers, killing 568 civilians and injuring more than 1200 others. Birmingham, Liverpool and Manchester were hit. But the turning point had come with the change in German strategy and the refusal of the British people to buckle. The last *Luftwaffe* raids of the Blitz struck London on the night of 10 May 1941.

AN EASTWARD GAZE

Hitler's frustration with Göring's failure to destroy the RAF was tempered by his preoccupation with preparations for Operation *Barbarossa*, the invasion of the Soviet Union, which was scheduled for 22 June 1941. Some historians argue that the *Führer* had been reluctant to continue fighting the British, hoping that the fellow Anglo-Saxons might join in the war against the Soviet communists. At any rate, as early as the autumn of 1940 Hitler had concluded that the Battle of Britain could not be won. The opportunity for victory had been squandered and *Luftwaffe* losses continued to mount. British cities burned, but he RAF remained a potent force.

Prime Minister Winston Churchill (1874–1965) hailed the spirit of the British people and called the time of peril and suffering 'their finest hour'. On 20 August 1940, Churchill rose to address the House of Commons, praising the courage of the intrepid Royal Air Force pilots. 'Never in the field of human conflict,' he declared, 'has so much been owed by so many to so few.'

LONDONERS GAZE SKYWARD for any sign of approaching German aircraft as crews man antiaircraft guns positioned in Hyde Park. Hitler and Luftwaffe chief Hermann Göring believed that the Blitz could bring Great Britain to its knees.

SUPERMARINE SPITFIRE

Originally conceived in the 1930s by British aircraft designer Reginald Mitchell, the Supermarine Spitfire flew for the first time on 5 March 1936. Production began two years later. Powered by the Rolls-Royce Merlin engine and initially armed with a pair of 20mm (0.78in) cannon and four .303 Browning machine guns, the Spitfire represented the leading edge of technology deployed by the Royal Air Force during the Battle of Britain.

The superior performance of the Spitfire made it a worthy adversary of the German Messerschmitt Me-109. However, it was available in limited numbers compared to the older Hawker Hurricane. Therefore, the RAF instructed Spitfire squadrons to engage the German fighters, while the Hurricanes attacked the slower bomber formations. The aircraft depicted is a Spitfire Mk 1 of No. 66 Squadron.

BATTLE OF BRITAIN

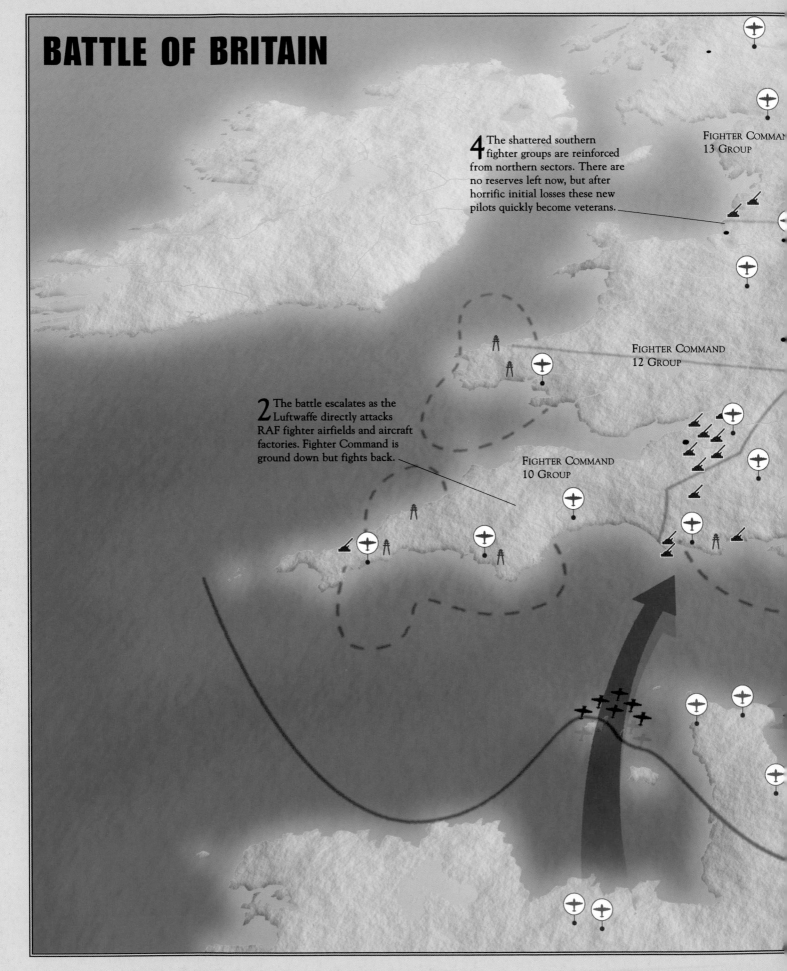

4 The shattered southern fighter groups are reinforced from northern sectors. There are no reserves left now, but after horrific initial losses these new pilots quickly become veterans.

FIGHTER COMMAND
13 GROUP

FIGHTER COMMAND
12 GROUP

2 The battle escalates as the Luftwaffe directly attacks RAF fighter airfields and aircraft factories. Fighter Command is ground down but fights back.

FIGHTER COMMAND
10 GROUP

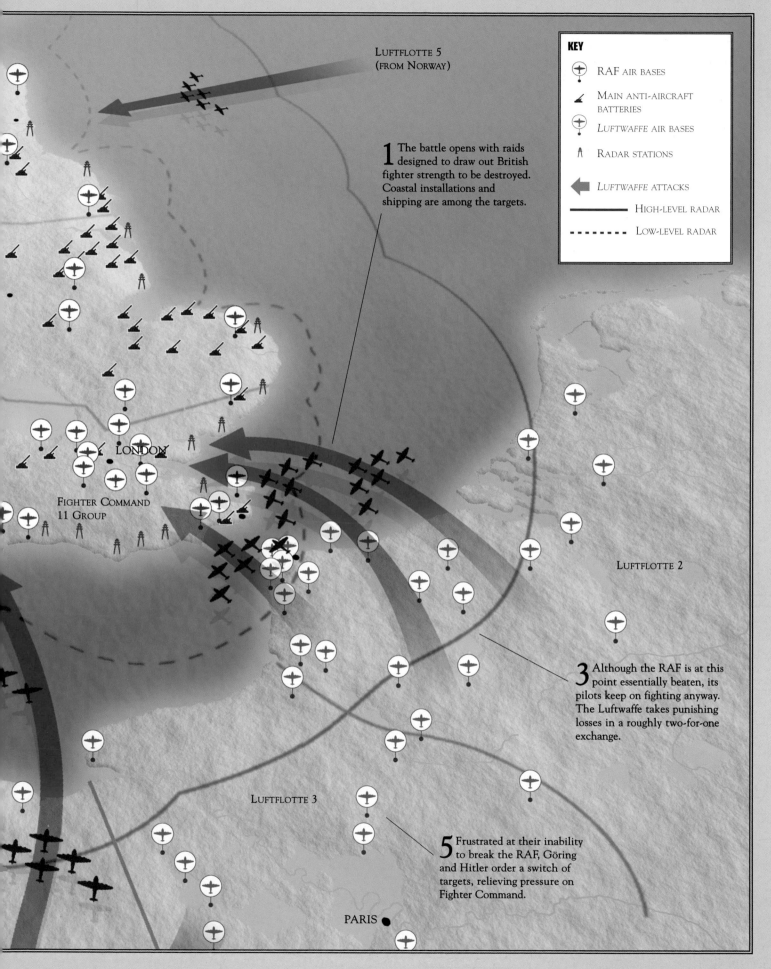

LUFTFLOTTE 5
(FROM NORWAY)

KEY

✈ RAF AIR BASES

⚔ MAIN ANTI-AIRCRAFT
BATTERIES

✈ *LUFTWAFFE* AIR BASES

🗼 RADAR STATIONS

⬅ *LUFTWAFFE* ATTACKS

──────── HIGH-LEVEL RADAR

- - - - - - - LOW-LEVEL RADAR

1 The battle opens with raids
designed to draw out British
fighter strength to be destroyed.
Coastal installations and
shipping are among the targets.

LONDON

FIGHTER COMMAND
11 GROUP

LUFTFLOTTE 2

3 Although the RAF is at this
point essentially beaten, its
pilots keep on fighting anyway.
The Luftwaffe takes punishing
losses in a roughly two-for-one
exchange.

LUFTFLOTTE 3

5 Frustrated at their inability
to break the RAF, Göring
and Hitler order a switch of
targets, relieving pressure on
Fighter Command.

PARIS ●

49

BATTLE FOR CRETE

1941

The German airborne assault of Crete, although successful in terms of conquest, came at a terrific cost in lives, and led to the sharp decline of the Luftwaffe's parachute arm as a surprise weapon. German airborne forces were never to launch an operation of this scale again.

Crete, a mountainous island 260km (160-mile) long, some 100km (60 miles) from mainland Greece and lying in the eastern Mediterranean, was from late April 1941 the sole piece of Greek territory left in Allied hands. One of the threats posed by Crete to the Germans was its key resource for the formidable presence of the Royal Navy at Suda Bay, to the east of the then capital, Khania. It was one of the Mediterranean's largest natural harbours and vital as a refuelling centre. British aircraft could also block naval convoys crossing the Mediterranean to supply Rommel's forces in North Africa. In addition, Hitler foresaw Crete as a

BATTLE FOR CRETE FACTS

Who: Overall commander of the 'Creforce' garrison, Major-General Bernard Freyberg VC (1889–1963) versus General Kurt Student (1890–1978), Commander of XI *Flieger* Corps, the *Luftwaffe's* elite airborne troops.

What: The Germans landed in Crete from the Greek mainland and in 10 days of fierce fighting drove out the bulk of Allied troops.

Where: Crete, the largest island in Greece and the second largest in the eastern Mediterranean.

When: The main German attack on Greece took place between 20 May and 2 June 1941.

Why: The Germans urgently sought a free gateway to the East and Crete posed a major threat to their operations, especially

the naval convoys crossing the Mediterranean to replenish Rommel's forces in North Africa.

Outcome: German forces occupied Crete until the end of 1944 when, along with Greece and Albania, the island was abandoned and Hitler ordered a major retreat from the Balkans.

GLIDER-BORNE TROOPS LANDED AS *part of the airborne invasion of Crete, enjoy a rest and a meal of wurst.*

potentially valuable fortress guarding the Balkan flank of his projected Operation *Barbarossa*, the invasion of the Soviet Union. Hitler ordered the invasion of Crete on 25 April to be designated Operation *Merkur* (Mercury). However, due to logistical problems, the date was postponed to 20 May.

PARATROOP WARFARE

General Kurt Student, begetter of the *Fallschirmjäger* ('Hunters from the sky'), was a strong advocate of aerial warfare and had pressed the case vigorously for an airborne assault on Crete. But Hitler had considered an air campaign too dangerous and had predicted an unacceptably heavy toll of casualties. However, following pressure from the *Luftwaffe* chief Hermann Göring (1893–1946) he had yielded.

In anticipation of invasion, Commonwealth forces in Crete were, in May 1941, organized in five widely separated defence areas along the north coast – around the three airfields at Heraklion, Rethymnon and Maleme, as well as at Suda Bay and the port of Khania. At dawn on 20 May, the island's defence garrison of Anzac (Australian, New

LEFT: *ELITE GLIDER-BORNE FORCES of German* Gebirgsjäger *(mountain troops) from the Greek mainland poised to land on Crete.*

BELOW: *JU 52s CARRYING AIRBORNE forces landed on key airports on the second day of the invasion, beginning with the capture of Maleme airport.*

GENERAL KURT STUDENT

General Kurt Student (1890–1978, pictured right) was a World War I fighter pilot, chosen by Göring in 1938 to form a parachute infantry force, which later expanded to around 4500 men. After the evacuation from Crete, Student's troops fought mainly as infantry. Student received no decoration for his services and his personal access to Hitler came to an end. Though he claimed little interest in Nazism, he was brought before an Allied military tribunal in 1947 on eight charges of war crimes in Crete, including sanctioning the execution of British prisoners of war. He was acquitted on certain counts but sentenced to five years in prison. The Greeks requested his extradition from Germany for war crimes but he was never handed over, and died at the age of 88.

EVERY SURVIVING MEMBER of Student's forces received an Iron Cross, but after such losses, he said: 'Crete was the grave of the German paratroops'.

Zealand), British and local troops was subjected to familiar heavy bombing and the scream of Stukas.

What followed a few hours later was a major invasion by elite airborne forces. The assault was in two waves: the first launched against Maleme and Khania to the west, the second against Rethymnon and Heraklion, further to the east. This consisted of transport and 100 gliders, launched from bases on the Greek mainland. These delivered 6000 paratroopers and airborne infantry on and around Maleme with bombers pounding New Zealand troop positions.

General Student divided his forces into three battle groups: West, Centre and East, concentrating particularly on Khania and the prominent hunk of the Akrotiri peninsula. He would thus be given both an airfield and harbour where the battle line could be reinforced, the main object being the capture of the capital.

With more than 40,000 defenders – ANZAC and British troops, Greek and Cretan irregulars – was the 'Creforce' Commander, Major-General Bernard Freyberg, a VC from World War I. He faced serious problems: tired and demoralized troops, battered tanks from North Africa, no air cover and paucity of communications. But Freyberg was receiving intelligence from deciphered German codes alerting him to Student's intentions. He also had the support of a fiercely loyal local population.

BRIDGEHEADS ESTABLISHED

Although many of the Germans paras presented easy targets as they drifted down over New Zealand positions, many survived to regroup and fight fiercely, on Maleme. A severe

A MEMBER OF 7TH FLIEGER DIVISION (7th Air Division) of the Fallschirmjäger units, consisting of airborne light infantry which made a drop during the battle of Crete.

blow on the first day was the loss of a small hill known to the military as Hill 107, commanding the Maleme airfield from the south. The area around the airfield and hill was made up of 5 square kilometres (2 square miles) of rough territory, much of it giving poor visibility. There was a significant buildup of German forces, notably paratrooper battalions and dive bombers forming up to the southeast of the airfield. Lieutenant-Colonel Les Andrew, the area's New Zealand commander, was determined to go on the offensive.

Receiving no extra support, he attacked the invaders on his own initiative but could not contend with the overwhelming superiority of the paratroopers holding the hill. His small force was soon beaten back and his tanks immobilized. A promise of reinforcements came to nothing and Andrew was given permission to withdraw. Hill 107 was taken unopposed and control of the airfield passed to the Germans.

Student, more determined than ever to consolidate the Maleme bridgehead, flew in over the next two days a total of 3200 mountain troops and paras. He encountered fierce local resistance. But the Germans beat it off and the Stukas went in. On 25 May, the New Zealanders under Colonel Howard Kippenberger had some success with a counterattack near Galatas, lying to the southwest of Khania. But this simply delayed the German advance and Kippenberger had no resources to recover.

FLIMSY CANVAS AND WOOD-BUILT German gliders were vulnerable targets. Many crashed into olive trees or were shattered on landing, their fleeing crews cut down by the defenders.

The remainder of the Maleme position had to be yielded in the face of the presence of 2000 additional German mountain troops. The defenders retreated to Khania, which fell on 27 May. Resistance to the overwhelming air and eventually land power of the Germans became impossible, not least through lack of ammunition which severely weakened the Allied divisions. All was now set for a general evacuation.

Withdrawal from Suda Bay was covered by flown-in British commandos, while between 28 May and 1 June Britain's Mediterranean Fleet took off around 17,000 men, from Sphakia on the island's south coast, mostly from open beaches during a few short hours of darkness. Nine ships were sunk by the *Luftwaffe*. Back on land, 5000 men had to be left behind after being separated from their units. The Germans lost 1990 killed in action, while British and Commonwealth forces lost 1742. For the Allies, the debacle of Crete was complete.

ABOVE: GERMAN PARATROOPERS *move forward past the bodies of Allied soldiers after their successful air invasion of Crete.*

AFTERMATH

Hitler, severely shaken by figures for casualties in Crete, informed Student that he considered the days of the parachutist over, since its arm was no longer a surprise weapon. During the battle for Crete, over 1700 ANZAC and British troops had died, a similar number were wounded and around 12,000 were taken prisoners. The full extent of German losses differ, one of the highest figures being 3986 killed and missing with about 2000 having perished in the parachute drop alone.

Subsequent airborne operations by the Germans were strictly limited. As it turned out, the occupation of Crete proved a mixed blessing. The Cretans put up unremitting guerrilla resistance, forcing the Germans to garrison more troops than they wished, thereby making them unavailable elsewhere.

LEFT: ALTHOUGH MANY BRITISH 'TOMMIES', *such as these on Suda Bay, were forced to surrender, others escaped in small craft or fled into the mountains to fight with partisans.*

BATTLE FOR CRETE

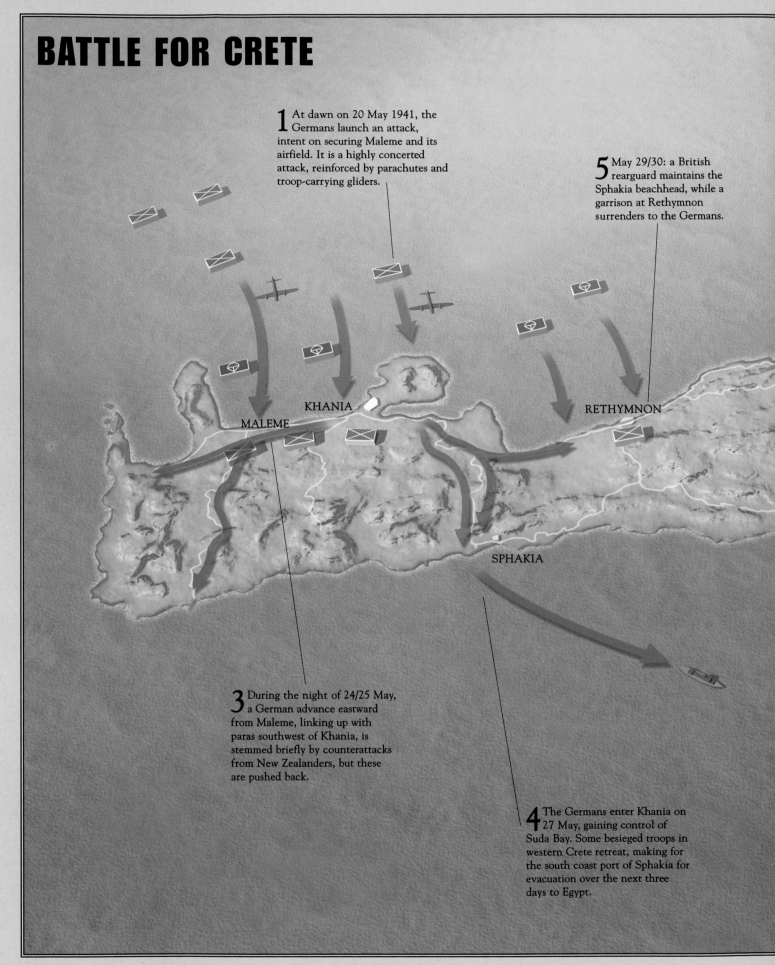

1 At dawn on 20 May 1941, the Germans launch an attack, intent on securing Maleme and its airfield. It is a highly concerted attack, reinforced by parachutes and troop-carrying gliders.

5 May 29/30: a British rearguard maintains the Sphakia beachhead, while a garrison at Rethymnon surrenders to the Germans.

KHANIA

MALEME

RETHYMNON

SPHAKIA

3 During the night of 24/25 May, a German advance eastward from Maleme, linking up with paras southwest of Khania, is stemmed briefly by counterattacks from New Zealanders, but these are pushed back.

4 The Germans enter Khania on 27 May, gaining control of Suda Bay. Some besieged troops in western Crete retreat, making for the south coast port of Sphakia for evacuation over the next three days to Egypt.

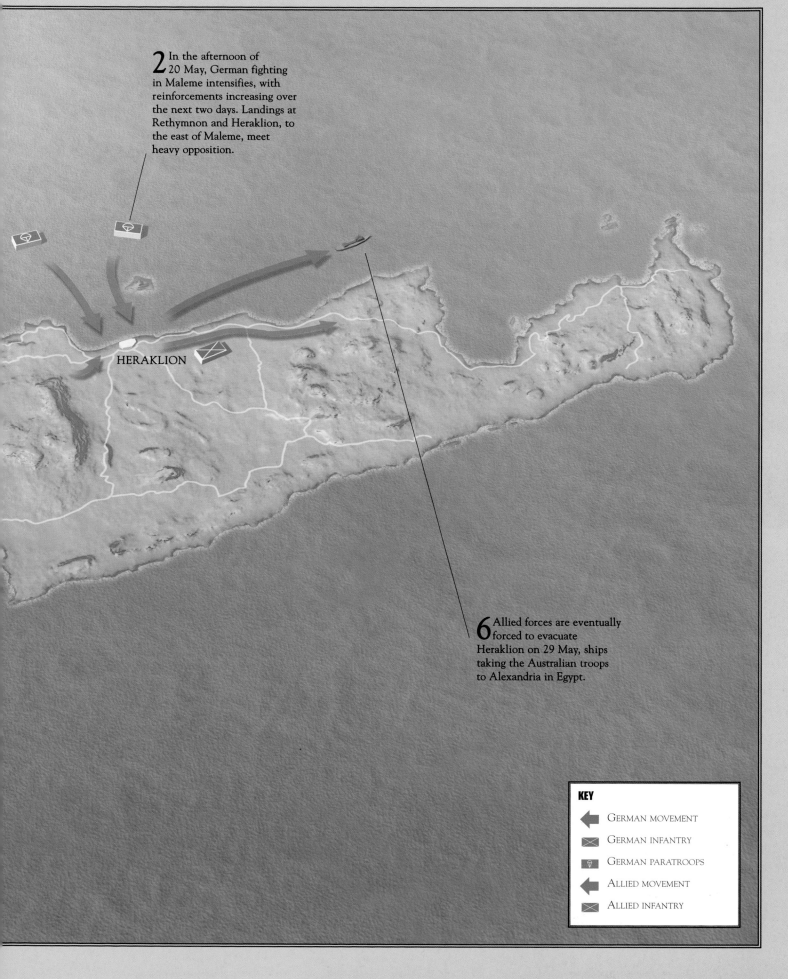

2 In the afternoon of 20 May, German fighting in Maleme intensifies, with reinforcements increasing over the next two days. Landings at Rethymnon and Heraklion, to the east of Maleme, meet heavy opposition.

HERAKLION

6 Allied forces are eventually forced to evacuate Heraklion on 29 May, ships taking the Australian troops to Alexandria in Egypt.

KEY

←	GERMAN MOVEMENT
⊠	GERMAN INFANTRY
⊡	GERMAN PARATROOPS
←	ALLIED MOVEMENT
⊠	ALLIED INFANTRY

HUNT FOR THE BISMARCK 1941

By the summer of 1941, the Battle of the Atlantic had become a struggle for the survival of Great Britain. Not only were Nazi U-boats ravaging convoys and sinking merchant vessels laden with precious cargoes, but surface raiders of the Kriegsmarine (German Navy) also posed a significant threat.

From January to April, more than 610,000 tonnes (672,410 tons) of Allied shipping were lost. Then in May the worst fears of the British Admiralty were realized. The massive 42,800-tonne (47,200-ton) battleship *Bismarck* had weighed anchor and Operation *Rheinübung* (Rhine Exercise) was under way. In company with the heavy cruiser *Prinz Eugen*, the great battleship might wreak havoc on Allied merchant shipping with its eight 380mm (15in) guns.

HUNT FOR THE BISMARCK FACTS

Who: Elements of the British Royal Navy under Admiral John Tovey (1885–1971) versus the German battleship Bismarck and cruiser *Prinz Eugen*, under Admiral Günther Lütjens (1889–1941).

What: The *Bismarck* and *Prinz Eugen* tried to attack Allied shipping but were confronted by the Royal Navy.

Where: The North Atlantic near Allied convoy routes.

When: 18–27 May 1941

Why: The Germans hoped to inflict substantial losses on Allied merchant shipping, thereby strangling the supply line to Great Britain.

Outcome: During an epic chase, the Royal Navy sank the *Bismarck*. The *Kriegsmarine* mounted no more serious surface threats to Allied shipping in the Atlantic.

FAIREY SWORDFISH TORPEDO PLANES, the flying anachronisms that slowed the German battleship Bismarck, *are lashed to the flight deck of the aircraft carrier HMS Victorious amid an angry sea.*

Admiral Günther Lütjens, commander of the Kriegsmarine *task force which included the battleship* Bismarck *and the heavy cruiser* Prinz Eugen, *wearing his Knight's Cross.*

Recognizing the imminent danger, Admiral John Tovey (1885–1971), commander of the British Home Fleet at Scapa Flow, began to marshal his scattered surface assets to find and sink the Bismarck. Meanwhile Admiral Günther Lütjens (1889–1941), at sea aboard the German behemoth, knew that his movements during daylight hours had been observed by the Swedish cruiser *Gotland* and patrol planes from the neutral country. On 21 May, the battleship was photographed by a British reconnaissance aircraft.

BREAKOUT AND PURSUIT

Lütjens was determined to break out into the open sea and chose the Denmark Strait, one of three options, as his avenue of approach. Shadowed by a pair of British cruisers (*Suffolk* and *Norfolk*), the *Bismarck* and *Prinz Eugen* were engaged in the pre-dawn darkness of 24 May by the brand new battleship HMS *Prince of Wales* and the venerable battlecruiser HMS *Hood*. Launched in 1918, the *Hood* was equal in firepower to the *Bismarck* but it was vulnerable to the enemy's heavy guns, its designers having sacrificed armour protection for speed more than 20 years earlier.

Seconds into the fight, a German shell penetrated the *Hood's* thin armour and detonated an ammunition magazine. A gigantic explosion enveloped the warship and the pride of the Royal Navy was gone. Only three of the battle-cruiser's 1421 sailors survived. The *Prince of Wales* was seriously damaged, one German shell wrecking her bridge. Although the *Bismarck* sustained only three hits, one of these gashed her forecastle and tonnes of seawater poured in. Another ruptured a fuel tank and precious oil leaked in a telltale slick. Urged by the *Bismarck's* captain, Ernst Lindemann, to head back to Germany, Lütjens instead dispatched the *Prinz Eugen* to continue prowling for merchantmen and turned his wounded battleship towards the French port of Brest. En route, he hoped that U-boats might offer protection and air cover from planes based in France might soon appear.

THE BISMARCK

Named in honour of the Iron Chancellor of a unified Germany, the battleship *Bismarck* undertook Operation Rhine Exercise on 18 May 1941. Displacing nearly 43,000 tons, the warship posed a major threat to Allied shipping in the Atlantic. The *Bismarck's* main armament consisted of eight 380mm (15in) guns.

Capable of achieving speed in excess of 30 knots, the *Bismarck* was relentlessly pursued by heavy units of the Royal Navy. It was disabled by Swordfish torpedo planes and was eventually sunk on 27 May. However, the battleship and her consort, the heavy cruiser *Prinz Eugen*, had previously achieved a great success: the sinking of the battlecruiser HMS *Hood*, the pride of the Royal Navy.

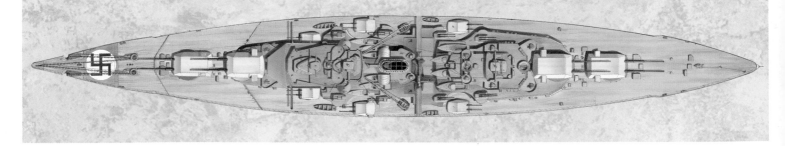

SAILORS OF THE German Navy, or Kriegsmarine, stand at attention during an inspection by officers prior to their departure from an anchorage on the Baltic Sea.

PERSEVERANCE AND LUCK

Devastated by the loss of the *Hood*, the British nevertheless continued their pursuit of the *Bismarck*. The Germans gave the shadowing cruisers the slip on the night of the 24 May after beating back an attack by Fairey Swordfish torpedo lauched planes from the aircraft carrier *Victorious*. Lütjens then inexplicably began to broadcast a lengthy radio message to Berlin, unaware that he had temporarily shaken the British off his trail. The British picked up the signal, corrected a navigational error which had sent them steaming in the wrong direction and locked on to their quarry once again.

SAILING IN LINE ASTERN, the Bismark *as seen from the rear of the* Prinz Eugen *as they head out into the North Atlantic.*

On the morning of 26 May, a Consolidated PBY Catalina flying boat spotted the *Bismarck* less than 1300km (800 miles) from the French coast and nearing the range of a protective *Luftwaffe* air umbrella. Several of the Royal Navy warships initially engaged in the chase were obliged to turn for home as fuel ran low. The battleship HMS *King George V*, with Tovey aboard, ploughed ahead. Detached from convoy duty, the battleship HMS *Rodney* joined the pursuit, as did Gibraltar-based Force H, under Admiral James Somerville (1882–1949). The British had lost critical time and distance, though. The *Bismarck* might still escape.

SWORDFISH AT SUNSET

Tovey had one more card to play. The Fairey Swordfish was a flying anachronism, a biplane constructed primarily of wood, canvas and wire. Fifteen of these planes, with torpedoes slung beneath their bellies, took off from the pitching deck of the Force H aircraft carrier HMS *Ark Royal* on the afternoon of the 26 May. Several mistakenly attacked the cruiser HMS *Sheffield* and luckily did not score a hit.

In the gathering twilight, the remaining 'Stringbags' pressed home their attacks through a curtain of withering anti-aircraft fire. Two torpedoes struck home. One of these hits was inconsequential. The other was catastrophic for the Germans. Flying only 15.5m (50ft) above the water and in gale force winds, Sub-Lieutenant John Moffat released his plane's weapon, which slammed into the *Bismarck*'s stern and jammed her rudders 15° to port. As a result, the great ship was able to steer only one course, northwest towards the assembling might of the vengeful Royal Navy.

TORRENT OF SHELLS

Every sailor aboard the *Bismarck* now knew that the fate of their ship was sealed. Lindemann ordered the storage areas open and allowed the men to take what provisions they could. A cable from Hitler – 'The whole of Germany is with you' – seemed a forlorn hope. The Royal Navy would come with morning light and the death struggle would follow.

At 8.47 a.m. on 27 May, the 406mm (16in) guns of the *Rodney* barked from a range of 19km (12 miles). The *King George V* joined in. The crew of the *Bismarck* fought valiantly, but repeated hits seriously damaged her fire control system and disabled her main armament. The British battleships closed to less than 3.2km (2 miles) and bodies of dead and wounded sailors littered the *Bismarck's* decks. By 11 a.m., the ship was still afloat but blazing from bow to stern and unable to fight back. Shortly afterwards, the battleship rolled to port and sank stern first.

LINGERING CONTROVERSY

Three torpedo hits from the cruiser HMS *Dorsetshire* have long been credited with administering the *coup de grâce*. However, survivors of the *Bismarck* have insisted that they opened the vessel's seacocks and scuttled the ship. Exploration of the wreckage tends to support their claim but remains inconclusive. Only 110 of the *Bismarck's* complement of more than 2000 sailors were pulled from the chilly waters of the Atlantic. More might have been rescued, but a U-boat alarm sounded and the British were forced to abandon many sailors to the sea.

ABOVE: FAIREY SWORDFISH BIPLANES, torpedoes slung beneath their fuselages, in flight. Constructed primarily of wood and canvas, the Swordfish proved effective against the Bismarck.

The epic *Bismarck* chase resonates through history as a classic tale of naval warfare. In a practical sense, the loss of the great warship effectively ended the threat of the *Kriegsmarine* surface fleet to Allied merchant shipping in the Atlantic. Hitler simply became unwilling to risk his few capital ships in such an endeavour. Far to the north, German warships, including another giant, the battleship *Tirpitz*, menaced Allied convoys to the ports of Murmansk and Archangel in the Soviet Union. However, the Atlantic was to be the domain of the U-boats until they too were defeated.

BELOW: DAMAGED AND DOWN by the bow, the Bismarck ploughs through the waters of the Atlantic prior to its deadly rendezvous with the Royal Navy, principally the battleships King George V and Rodney.

HUNT FOR THE BISMARCK

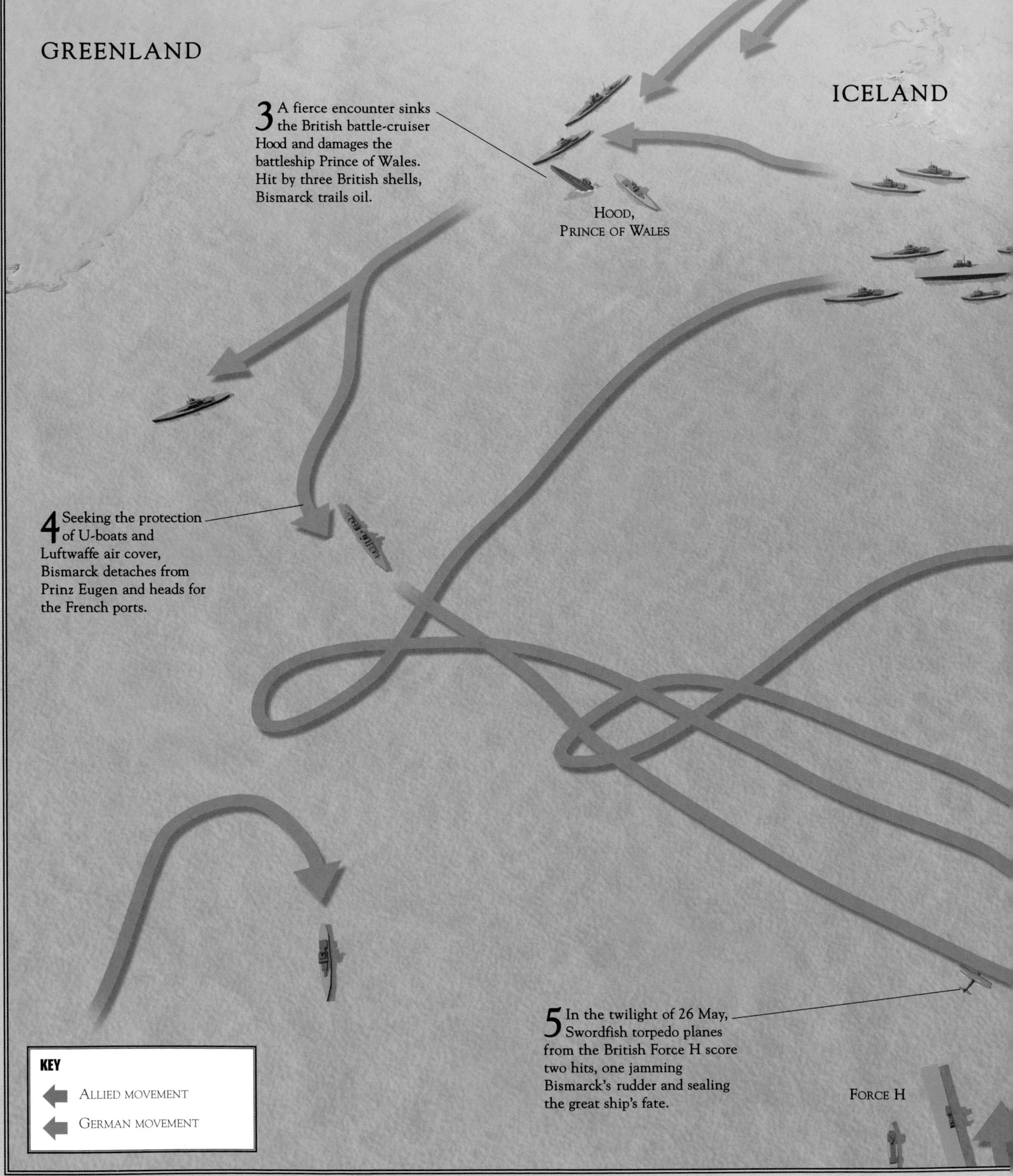

GREENLAND

ICELAND

3 A fierce encounter sinks the British battle-cruiser Hood and damages the battleship Prince of Wales. Hit by three British shells, Bismarck trails oil.

HOOD,
PRINCE OF WALES

4 Seeking the protection of U-boats and Luftwaffe air cover, Bismarck detaches from Prinz Eugen and heads for the French ports.

5 In the twilight of 26 May, Swordfish torpedo planes from the British Force H score two hits, one jamming Bismarck's rudder and sealing the great ship's fate.

FORCE H

KEY	
←	ALLIED MOVEMENT
←	GERMAN MOVEMENT

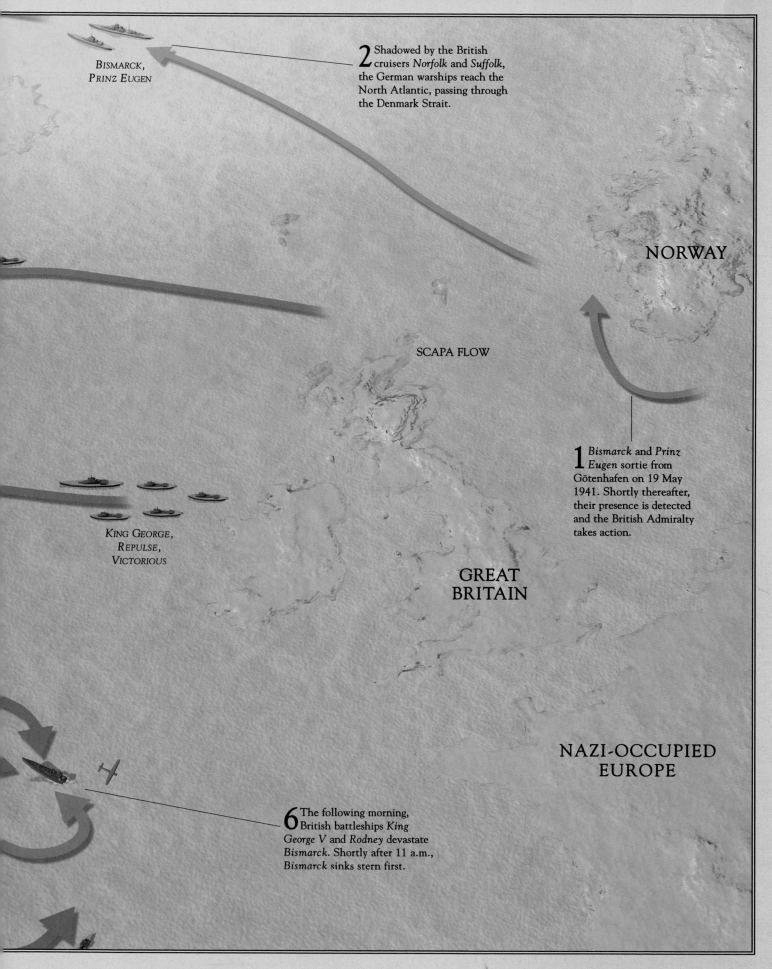

2 Shadowed by the British cruisers *Norfolk* and *Suffolk*, the German warships reach the North Atlantic, passing through the Denmark Strait.

BISMARCK, PRINZ EUGEN

NORWAY

SCAPA FLOW

1 *Bismarck* and *Prinz Eugen* sortie from Götenhafen on 19 May 1941. Shortly thereafter, their presence is detected and the British Admiralty takes action.

KING GEORGE, REPULSE, VICTORIOUS

GREAT BRITAIN

NAZI-OCCUPIED EUROPE

6 The following morning, British battleships *King George V* and *Rodney* devastate *Bismarck*. Shortly after 11 a.m., *Bismarck* sinks stern first.

OPERATION BARBAROSSA 1941

A massive German army of 3.3 million men supported by over 3000 tanks and almost as many aircraft invaded the Soviet Union on 22 June 1941. The huge invasion force was to capture Moscow, the Ukraine and Leningrad in short order.

The largest military operation of all time, codenamed *Barbarossa* ('Red Beard'), was under way. It would see the German *Wehrmacht* achieve its most spectacular victories. It did not lead to ultimate victory, however, and the Red Army would storm Berlin four years later.

Hitler had placed the greatest emphasis in his plans for the capture of Leningrad – the USSR's second city and primary naval base – and the clearing of the Baltic States. Yet he had allocated the least number of troops, some 26 divisions to Army Group North under Marshal von Leeb (1876–1956). As a consequence,

OPERATION BARBAROSSA FACTS

Who: Three German Army Groups (North, Centre and South) led respectively by Marshals Ritter von Leeb (1876–1956), Fedor von Bock (1880–1945) and Gerd von Rundstedt (1875–1953) were charged by Hitler to destroy the Red Army in two months.

What: Barbarossa was the decisive turning point of the war. If the Soviet Union survived the German onslaught, Hitler's Reich would face a two-front war.

Where: By July 1941, when Finland had joined the German onslaught in the north, the Eastern Front would eventually stretch from the Black Sea to the Arctic North and the Germans would almost reach the gates of Moscow.

When: 22 June–5 December 1941

Why: Undaunted by his failure to subdue Britain during the summer of 1940, Hitler gambled that his *Wehrmacht* would be able to knock out the Soviet Union before the United States eventually intervened in the war on the side of Britain.

Outcome: Ultimately the outcome of *Barbarossa* would decide the outcome of World War II.

A CZECH-BUILT 35(T) TANK PASSES a burning manor house in White Russia in early June 1941 as the blitzkrieg rips through Soviet territory.

Leeb's advance was slow and it was not until September that his exhausted troops managed to cut off Leningrad from the rest of the USSR. And instead of a swift capture of the great city, a long and ultimately fatal siege ensued.

UKRAINIAN VICTORIES, ROSTOV SETBACK

Marshal Gerd von Rundstedt's (1875–1953) Army Group South – 41 divisions, including five panzer and 14 Romanian divisions – were entrusted with the vital task of taking the Ukraine. With its abundant grain fields and the industrial might of the Donbass region, it was a prize that was much needed.

Unfortunately for Rundstedt, however, the Southwestern Front, the strongest of the Soviet army groups, offered fierce

HISTORY TENDS TO SEE THE GERMAN ARMY as a fast-moving, motorized force. However, the reality was that a great deal of equipment was moved by horse power – 750,000 horses were used in the invasion of the Soviet Union.

resistance, led ably by its commander General Mikhail Kirponos (1892–1941). As a result, Army Group South was able to advance only slowly and deliberately. Nevertheless, the panzer forces of Army Group Centre intervened, converging on 10 September with those of Rundstedt's panzers east of Kiev.

Three massive Soviet armies (Fifth, Twenty-Sixth and Thirty-Seventh) were now trapped in and around Kiev. Kirponos died trying to escape the German trap and a staggering 665,000 of his men were captured.

THE 'LIBERATOR' SOON turned to savage oppressor: a German landser (infantryman) with a burning Russian cottage in the background.

On 30 September, the 1st Panzer Group attacked and had, by 6 October, trapped much of the Soviet Southern Front in a large pocket in southeast Ukraine. Two armies (the Ninth and Eighteenth) were destroyed, yielding 100,000 prisoners.

The German advance continued towards Rostov on the Don river, which was captured on 20 November. However, the Soviet High Command (*Stavka*) launched a vigorous counterattack with three armies against the by now overextended German lines. By 29 November, this strategically located city was back in Soviet hands and the Germans had narrowly escaped an early version of Stalingrad.

ADVANCE OF ARMY GROUP CENTRE

When Napoleon had invaded Russia in 1812, he ultimately reached Moscow but still did not achieve victory. Hitler's generals – especially Fedor von Bock (1880–1945), the commander of Army Group Centre – believed that the Soviet Union would collapse if Moscow was captured. Here, as in the south, the Germans scored some major successes. A string of armies were trapped inside the Bialystok salient and in a vast pocket west of Minsk, yielding 300,000 prisoners. Stalin had the Western Front's commander, General Dimitri Pavlov (1897–1941), fired and shot upon his return to Moscow for his failures. His place was taken by Marshal Simeon Timoshenko (1883–1973), an experienced and hard-headed commander.

The Red Army continued to suffer catastrophic reverses, however. Smolensk, the gateway to Moscow, fell on 16 July. Stalin was now determined to block the German advance, and a series of counterattacks were launched by the Western Front armies, costing them yet another 300,000 men and 3000 tanks. Among the Germans, the feeling spread that

GENERAL HEINZ GUDERIAN

Heinz Guderian (1888–1954) was Hitler's most successful tank commander, who combined brilliant brains with outstanding abilities as a practical and hard-headed field commander. He was made head of the 2nd Panzer Division in 1935, took part in the Polish campaign (September 1939) and broke through at Sedan on 14 May 1940. During the *Barbarossa* campaign, Guderian was in command of the 2nd Panzer Group, renamed simply 'Guderian'. He was set to march on Moscow, having taken Smolensk in July when his panzer forces were diverted south. Guderian was called '*Schneller Heinz*' (Hurrying Heinz) by his hard-pressed but admiring troops. During Operation *Typhoon*, Guderian held command of the Second Panzer Army but was fired on 25 December and remained without a command until 1943.

with each success they were no closer to victory and that the Red Army's reserves were inexhaustible.

Hitler, who did not share his generals' views, diverted most of Army Group Centre's panzer divisions to take part in the battle for Kiev. For more than a month, the Central Front of 800km (496 miles) remained unchanged, giving the Red Army invaluable time to prepare its defences. General Andrei Yeremenko (1892–1970) had three armies (30 divisions) at Bryansk, and Timoshenko had six armies with 55 divisions at Vyazma. Incredibly, all these forces had been either wiped out or captured by October.

BELOW: A GERMAN PAK-36 team knocks out a light Soviet tank during the fighting of the summer of 1941.

LEFT: AS RUSSIA FACES yet another savage invasion, these Ukrainians dig antitank ditches during the late summer of 1941.

The march on Moscow, codenamed Operation *Typhoon*, was unleashed early in the morning of 2 October in brilliant sunshine. Army Group Centre numbered a million men in 77 divisions with 1700 tanks and almost a thousand planes.

Five days later, General Höppner's Fourth Panzer Group co-operating with General Hermann Hoth's (1885–1971) Third Panzer Group had trapped Timoshenko's six armies in a massive pocket in and around Vyazma.

THE BATTLE FOR MOSCOW

On 9 October, Hoth and Hoeppner linked up with Guderian's panzer forces, trapping the Third, Thirteenth and Fiftieth Soviet armies north and south of Bryansk. Leaving only a minimum of troops to seal up the pockets at Vyazma and Bryansk, the Army Group's panzer groups aimed for Mozhaiska and Tula. These pockets were eliminated by 14 and 20 October respectively, leaving eight armies destroyed. The yield was as massive as at Kiev – some 673,000 prisoners, more than 1000 tanks and 5000 guns.

Despite torrential rains that turned the roads into quagmires, the Germans had covered two-thirds of the distance to Moscow by the middle of the month. Finally, Soviet morale snapped. On 16 October, law and order collapsed in the capital, a million of its citizens fleeing for their lives in the 'Great Flight'. Only a policy of shooting to kill by the NKVD (Soviet Secret Police) stemmed the panic and prevented further looting and chaos.

In early November, the weather turned colder, enabling the Germans to advance again across frozen and hard roads. But it was soon too cold with temperatures of -21°C (-6°F),

RIGHT: OCTOBER 1941 – Soviet propaganda trying to show a united nation rallying to the defence of the capital. In reality, there was oppression, corruption and defeatism before the onset of winter.

and a new commander had appeared on the Soviet side, General Georgi Zhukov (1896–1974), who had already saved Leningrad and was now planning a counterattack against the exhausted Germans. By 18 November, Zhukov had 21 rested, fully equipped and battle-hardened Siberian divisions ready to be unleashed against Bock's army.

The German plan was for a frontal assault with 36 divisions while the three panzer groups encircled the Soviet defenders around Moscow. On 27 November, 2nd Panzer Division was just 22km (14 miles) from the capital and could see the spires of the Kremlin palaces through the haze.

Bock's Army Group now held a front almost 1000km (600 miles) long with a mere 60 divisions. The crawling offensive came to a halt on 5 December when temperatures plunged to a bone-chilling -35°C (-31°F). That same day Zhukov ordered General Ivan Konev's (1897–1973) Kalinin Front to attack, and the following day his own Western Front went on to the offensive.

The attack took the Germans completely by surprise, and over the next two months the Red Army held the initiative on the Central Front. Hitler gave orders that there was to be no retreat and this probably saved Army Group Centre from a complete collapse.

The failure of *Typhoon* spelled the defeat of *Barbarossa*. In the long run, the Soviet counterattack sounded the death-knell to the German Nazi Reich as well. Two days after Zhukov began his offensive, the United States entered the war, and Hitler's defeat was now only a question of time.

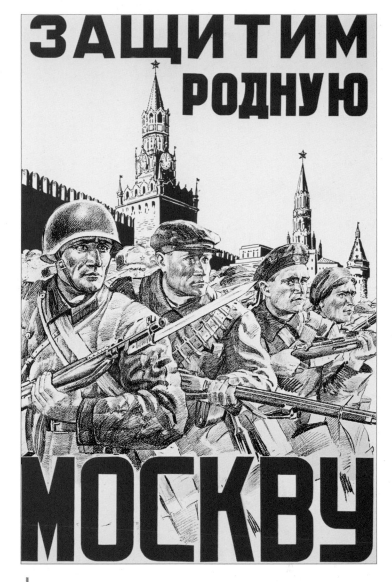

ЗАЩИТИМ РОДНУЮ МОСКВУ

BELOW: THE PANZER MK III (this model belonging to the 2nd Panzer Division) was the sturdy workhorse of the German Panzer forces but was no match for the Soviet T-34.

OPERATION BARBAROSSA

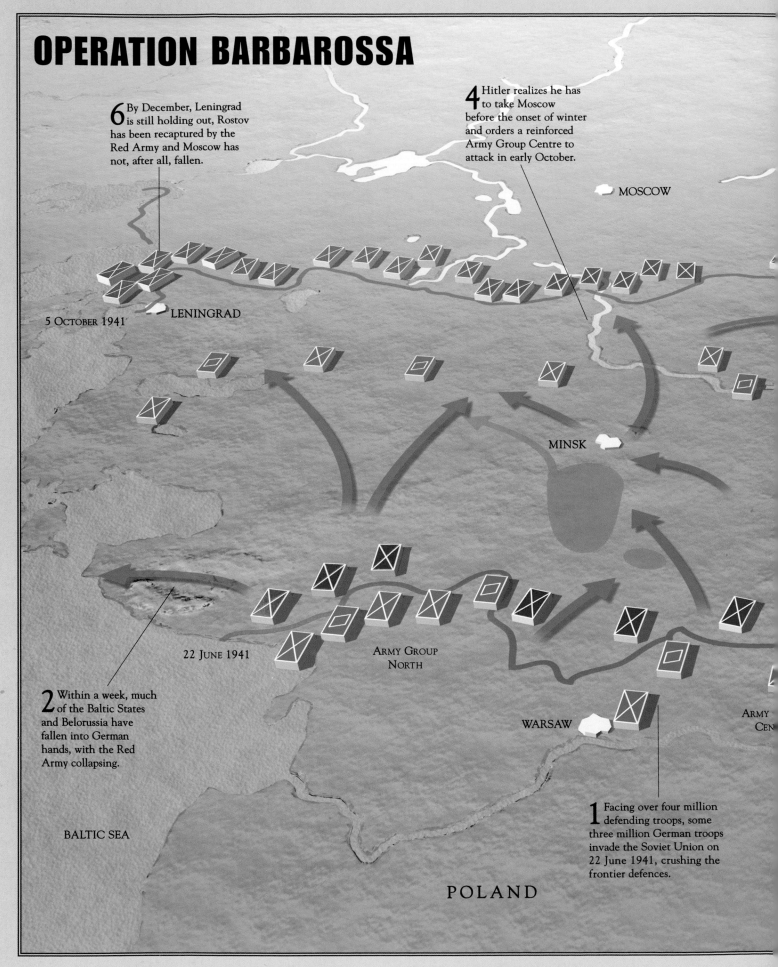

6 By December, Leningrad is still holding out, Rostov has been recaptured by the Red Army and Moscow has not, after all, fallen.

4 Hitler realizes he has to take Moscow before the onset of winter and orders a reinforced Army Group Centre to attack in early October.

MOSCOW

5 OCTOBER 1941   LENINGRAD

MINSK

2 Within a week, much of the Baltic States and Belorussia have fallen into German hands, with the Red Army collapsing.

22 JUNE 1941   ARMY GROUP NORTH

WARSAW   ARMY CEN

1 Facing over four million defending troops, some three million German troops invade the Soviet Union on 22 June 1941, crushing the frontier defences.

BALTIC SEA

POLAND

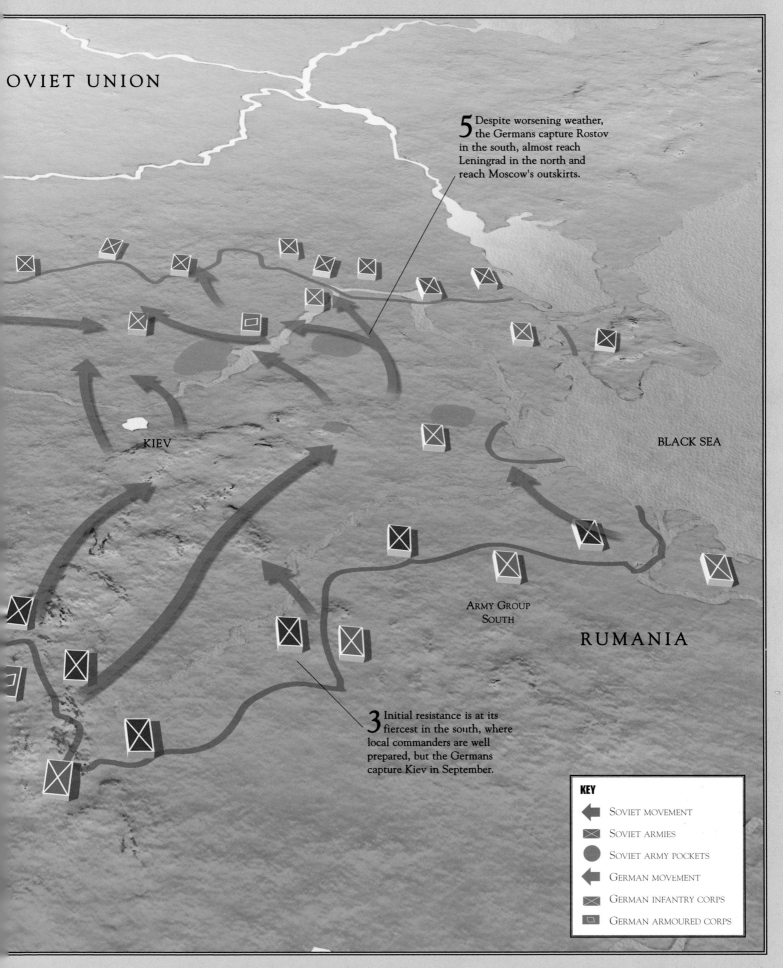

SOVIET UNION

5 Despite worsening weather, the Germans capture Rostov in the south, almost reach Leningrad in the north and reach Moscow's outskirts.

KIEV

BLACK SEA

ARMY GROUP SOUTH

RUMANIA

3 Initial resistance is at its fiercest in the south, where local commanders are well prepared, but the Germans capture Kiev in September.

KEY

← SOVIET MOVEMENT

⊠ SOVIET ARMIES

● SOVIET ARMY POCKETS

← GERMAN MOVEMENT

⊠ GERMAN INFANTRY CORPS

⊡ GERMAN ARMOURED CORPS

SIEGE OF LENINGRAD 1941–44

The siege of Leningrad was a ghastly epic of endurance that cost the lives of up to 1.5 million people, both soldiers and civilians. In total, it ran for nearly 900 days.

On 22 June 1941, German forces surged across the Soviet border in Operation *Barbarossa*. The *Wehrmacht* was split into three major formations – Army Groups North, Centre and South – each with its own objectives. Army Group North under the command of Field-Marshal Wilhelm von Leeb (1876–1956), had Leningrad as its goal, a large urban zone of a million souls located on the Gulf of Finland. Von Leeb's forces, as with the other elements of *Barbarossa,* made vigorous progress, pushing on through the Baltic states and breaking across the Luga river just 120km (75 miles) south of Leningrad on 9 August.

SIEGE OF LENINGRAD FACTS

Who: The German Army Group North under several commanders versus the Soviet Volkhov and Leningrad Fronts, commanded by General Kirill Meretskov (1897–1968) and Marshal Leonid Govorov (1897–1955) respectively.

What: A partial blockade of Leningrad by Army Group North reduced Leningrad to starvation conditions, the blockade being broken only by a succession of Soviet offensives over nearly three years.

Where: Leningrad (now renamed St Petersburg), a city in the far north of Russia, nestling on the Gulf of Finland.

When: The siege effectively ran from September 1941 to January 1944.

Why: Leningrad was an early target of Hitler's Operation *Barbarossa*, but by the end of 1943 the German operations there had little military function besides maintaining the overall German frontline.

Outcome: A million civilians died from starvation, bombing and shelling, but the ultimate defeat of the Germans was a key ingredient in the German Army's defeat on the Eastern Front.

A RED ARMY UNIT makes a characteristic attack in the Leningrad sector, winter 1943 – a simple charge backed by heavy machine-gun support.

ABOVE: *JU-87 STUKA DIVE-BOMBERS were used intensively as 'flying artillery' to intercept Soviet supply runs into Leningrad from across Lake Ladoga.*

SAVED FOR A SIEGE

The fate of the city seemed assured, not least because German-allied Finnish forces were fighting down from the north between Lake Ladoga and the sea. Important road and rail links into Leningrad fell to the Germans one by one – Novgorod on 16 August, Chudovo on the 20th – and by 1 September the German artillery shells were dropping into the city itself. The inhabitants of Leningrad prepared themselves for a battle for survival. From 9 September, the esteemed Soviet General Georgi Zhukov (1896–1974) was in the city, transforming it from a beautiful northern city into a massive fortress ringed by defensive positions, pillboxes and trenches. Yet the direct German assault on Leningrad did not come. On 6 September, Hitler switched the priority of *Barbarossa* to objectives further south and drew off much of von Leeb's panzer strength to support the offensive. Therefore Leningrad would have to be defeated by siege and bombardment.

Throughout September and October, the strategic situation for Leningrad worsened considerably. The major railway stations at Schlisselburg and Mga to the east

fell into German hands, and in October von Leeb began an offensive towards the vital railway centre at Tikhvin, which fell on 8 November. A ring of steel was closing around Leningrad, but the fighting was far from easy for the Germans. The offensive had grossly overstretched an already weakened Army Group North and it faced pressing resistance from the armies of the Volkhov Front commanded by General Kirill Meretskov (1897–1968).

By 10 December 1941, Tikhvin was back in Soviet hands following a huge but crudely handled Red Army offensive and by early January the Germans were forced to re-establish their frontlines further west. Only

LEFT: *A WELL-EQUIPPED Red Army infantryman, seen here in the autumn of 1941, armed with the Tokarev SVT-40, an early Soviet semi-automatic rifle.*

ABOVE: THE LIFELINE – A TRUCK CONVOY moves across a frozen Lake Ladoga. Under such conditions, up to 400 trucks a day were able to make the journey.

the narrowest of supply corridors, however, remained for Leningrad's already desperate people.

STARVATION AND RESISTANCE

As the German and Soviet armies outside Leningrad battled for dominance, a horrifying battle against starvation was under way within the city itself. In an especially bitter winter, the citizens of Leningrad were beginning to starve in their thousands, their predicament worsened by a collapse in fuel supplies for warmth.

By the end of November, people were trying to survive on a daily ration of less than 250g (9oz) of bread. Bodies littered

RIGHT: GERMAN INFANTRY BATTLE the Russian winter, late 1941. As elsewhere, the harsh Russian climate hampered German mobility on the Leningrad Front.

every street – people would literally died on their feet or curled up in doorways. On one day alone, 13,500 deaths occurred. Film footage of the period shows old people scraping out refuse bins with spoons and putting what they found into their mouths. Cannibalism became one way of surviving, and disturbing-looking meat appeared on sale by some street vendors. Every animal, wild or domestic, was killed for food, and other items such as linseed oil and tallow candles found their way on to the menu. Against this horrifying backdrop was the constant German air and artillery bombardment.

The main lifeline to the city was Lake Ladoga, though it was hardly adequate. Supplies were moved by land to Tikhvin, then to disembarkation points such as Novaya Ladoga and Lednevo. Small boats of every military and civilian variety sailed the waters in the non-winter months, frequently under heavy German air assault, to dock in Osinovets, northeast of Leningrad. When Lake Ladoga froze over, up to 400 trucks a day shuttled supplies straight across the ice and took back refugees on the return

ABOVE: LENINGRAD CIVILIANS GATHER *in a small group to distribute what meagre supplies are available, transporting them across icy streets on sledges.*

BELOW: THE T34/76 TANK WAS *the primary Soviet armoured fighting vehicle of the Leningrad Front, and its numbers were critical in breaking the German siege in 1944.*

journey. Conditions for the supply convoys were grim: many truck crews, ship crews and refugees found their graves at the bottom of Ladoga. However, in the spring of 1942 fuel and electricity pipelines were laid across the river, bringing power for cooking and heating. Yet although conditions had improved by the end of 1942 blockade conditions existed for nearly 900 days, during which time about one million people died out of a population of 2.5 million. Some sources put the death toll as high as 1.5 million.

BREAKING THE SIEGE

In 1942, the Soviets looked to make further gains. In January, a large offensive by the Volkhov Front between Novgorod (just north of Lake Ilmen) and Spasskaya Polist made a 60km (37-mile) salient in the German frontline, but the offensive had stalled by March, leaving the Germans to nip out of the salient and completely destroy the Soviet Second Shock Army. Nevertheless, the Soviet attack had alarmed Hitler enough for him to replace von Leeb as commander of the Army Group North (von Leeb had requested a tactical withdrawal in the face of the offensive) with Field-Marshal Georg von Küchler (1881–1968). Küchler himself would go in August 1942 after he resisted Hitler's idea for a general offensive to crush Leningrad, codenamed *Northern Lights*. Manstein then took what was proving to be a poisoned chalice for German commanders.

Between 27 August and 25 September 1942, there was considerable movement around Leningrad. An offensive by Meretskov against the bottleneck was eventually stopped by Manstein, but his counteroffensive also ground to a halt against the Soviet defence. The critical change in fortunes, however, came in January 1943. The Soviet Leningrad Front under Marshal Leonid Govorov (1897–1955), four armies strong, launched a combined offensive with the Volkhov Front against the German forces in the bottleneck. The sheer weight of men and armour was irresistible and Schlisselburg was back in Soviet hands by 19 January. By early February, the Soviets were running direct rail journeys into Leningrad, albeit ones under constant German bombardment – the corridor secured by the Red Army was only 10km (6.2 miles) wide.

SIEGE OVER

The worst of the siege was over but the partial blockade ran until January 1944. The Germans held their lines even as they were weakened by Hitler's redeployment of forces for his 1943 offensives in the Ukraine. On 14 January 1944, an overwhelming Soviet offensive by both Red Army fronts flooded over the German defences and put the *Wehrmacht* troops on the retreat. On 27 January, with the recapture of the Leningrad–Moscow rail line, Stalin officially declared the siege of Leningrad over.

THE BETRAYAL OF LENINGRAD

The siege of Leningrad became iconic in the years following its liberation, with artists, writers, musicians and historians enshrining the resistance in their work. This publicity soon fuelled Stalin's paranoia – he had long suspected that Leningrad (as Russia's second city) could produce a rival power base to his own. In 1946, he acted against the figures behind Leningrad's resistance, arresting them on false charges. The Leningrad Party Organization was purged and some 2000 people were executed, imprisoned or exiled between 1946 and 1950, including Pyotr Popkov, Aleksei Kuznetsov and Nikolai Voznesensky, important players in Leningrad's survival and attempted post-war renaissance.

LOCAL PEOPLE MARK the fiftieth anniversary of the end of the siege of Leningrad at the St Petersburg Cemetery, 1994.

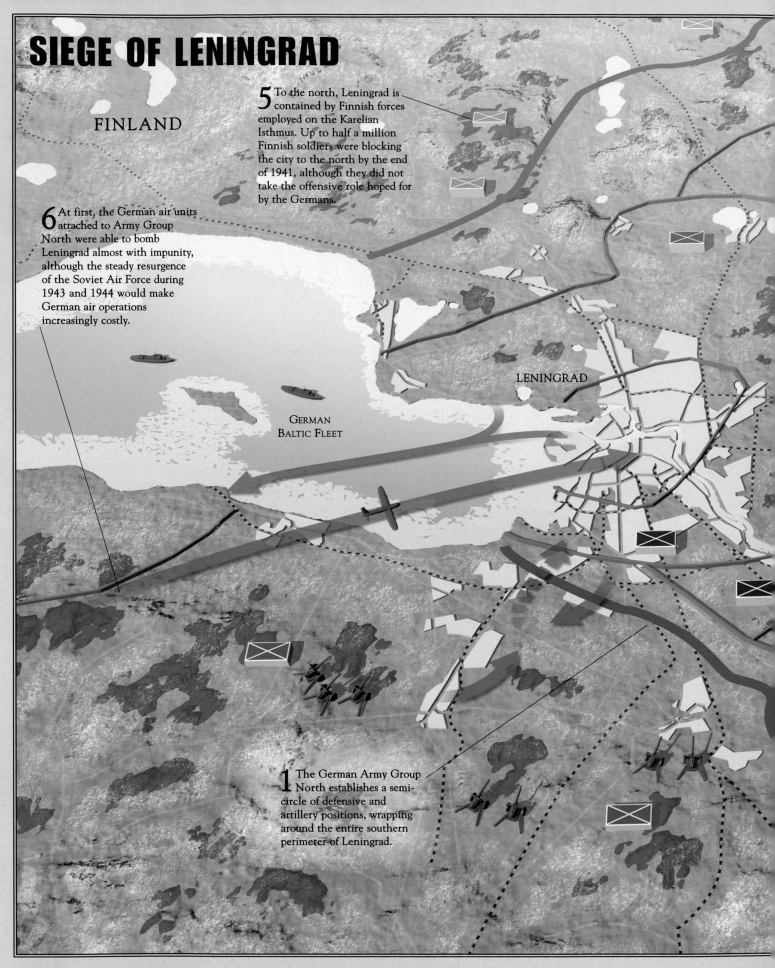

SIEGE OF LENINGRAD

FINLAND

5 To the north, Leningrad is contained by Finnish forces employed on the Karelian Isthmus. Up to half a million Finnish soldiers were blocking the city to the north by the end of 1941, although they did not take the offensive role hoped for by the Germans.

6 At first, the German air units attached to Army Group North were able to bomb Leningrad almost with impunity, although the steady resurgence of the Soviet Air Force during 1943 and 1944 would make German air operations increasingly costly.

GERMAN
BALTIC FLEET

LENINGRAD

1 The German Army Group North establishes a semi-circle of defensive and artillery positions, wrapping around the entire southern perimeter of Leningrad.

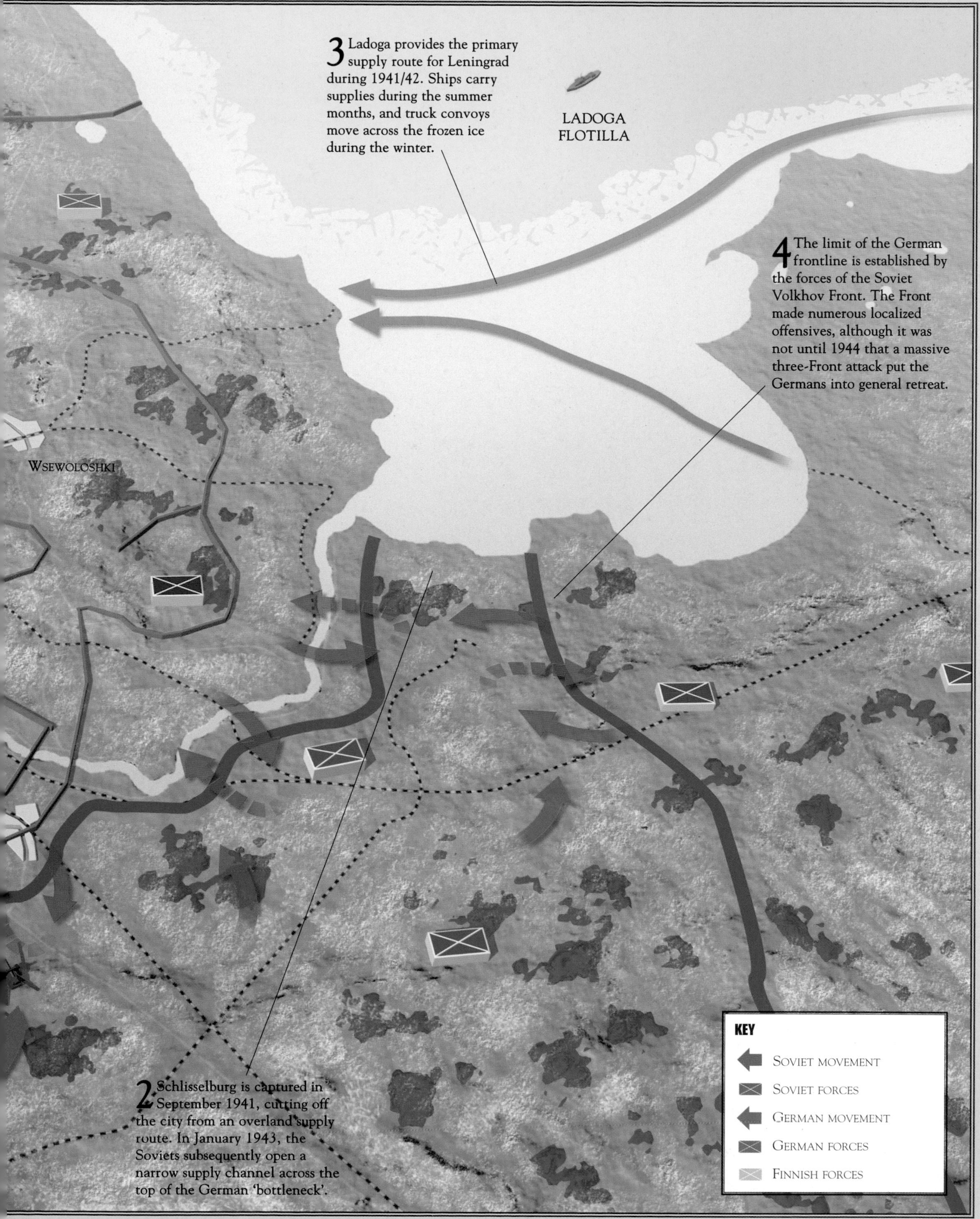

3 Ladoga provides the primary supply route for Leningrad during 1941/42. Ships carry supplies during the summer months, and truck convoys move across the frozen ice during the winter.

LADOGA FLOTILLA

4 The limit of the German frontline is established by the forces of the Soviet Volkhov Front. The Front made numerous localized offensives, although it was not until 1944 that a massive three-Front attack put the Germans into general retreat.

WSEWOLOSHKI

2 Schlisselburg is captured in September 1941, cutting off the city from an overland supply route. In January 1943, the Soviets subsequently open a narrow supply channel across the top of the German 'bottleneck'.

KEY

←	SOVIET MOVEMENT
⊠	SOVIET FORCES
←	GERMAN MOVEMENT
⊠	GERMAN FORCES
⊠	FINNISH FORCES

IN THE BALANCE

With the entry of the United States into the war in December 1941, Winston Churchill famously 'slept the sleep of the saved and the thankful' because 'there was no more doubt about the end.' Yet Germany remained ascendent and Japan was rampaging through the Far East. American power would take time to deploy decisively and the war was by no means won.

It took desperate and bloody battles at El Alamein in the Western Desert and on a far greater scale at Stalingrad and Kursk on the Eastern Front to turn the tide against the Germans, and at Midway, Guadalcanal and Imphal to do the same against the Japanese in the Pacific theatre.

US Marines take cover amidst landing operations in the Solomon Islands, 30 June 1943. The crucial battles at Midway and Guadalcanal proved to be the turning point in the war in the Pacific.

PEARL HARBOR 1941

When Japanese warplanes swept in to attack the US naval base at Pearl Harbor and other installations on the Hawaiian island of Oahu on 7 December 1941, the act was the culmination of years of growing tension between the two countries. Japan, seeking preeminence in Asia and the Pacific, required land and other natural resources to sustain its growing population and fuel its formidable military machine.

In 1931, Japan's army had invaded Manchuria, and a decade of fighting in China followed. By 1941, Japan had occupied all of Indochina. Recognizing the US and the traditional European powers as the chief impediments to the establishment of its 'Greater East Asia Co-Prosperity Sphere', Japan prepared for a war that its militaristic leaders considered inevitable.

In response to the growing threat, President Franklin D. Roosevelt (1882–1945) utilized political and economic pressure to curb Japanese ambitions. In May 1940, he ordered the US Pacific Fleet, already in Hawaiian waters for

PEARL HARBOR FACTS

Who: The Japanese Combined Fleet under strategic command of Admiral Isoroku Yamamoto (1884–1943) and tactical command of Vice-Admiral Chuichi Nagumo (1887–1944) versus the US Pacific Fleet under Admiral Husband Kimmel (1882–1968) and US Army forces under General Walter Short (1880–1949).

What: The Japanese Combined Fleet assembled six fleet carriers to launch an audacious attack on the US Pacific Fleet base of Pearl Harbor 5472km (3400 miles) away.

Where: Pearl Harbor and US military facilities on the Hawaiian island of Oahu.

When: 7 December 1941

Why: In the face of US and British sanctions, Japan needed to neutralize US naval power in the Pacific, at least temporarily, in order to seize British and Dutch resources in the region, especially oil.

Outcome: Tactically Japan caused considerable damage at little cost to itself, but, in the words of Vice-Admiral Nagumo, it managed only 'to awaken a sleeping giant and fill her with a terrible resolve'.

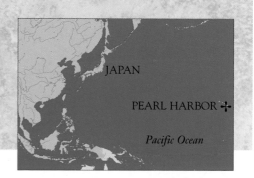

STRUCK BY SEVERAL JAPANESE *torpedoes, the battleship USS* West Virginia *burns and settles to the shallow bottom of Pearl Harbor. In the foreground, sailors pull a survivor from the water.*

85

LEFT: JAPANESE PREMIER HIDEKI TOJO led his nation to war with the United States. After the war, Tojo survived a suicide attempt. He was later tried, convicted, and executed for war crimes.

exercises, to remain on station at Pearl Harbor rather than return to its home port of San Pedro, California. In the summer of 1940, he prohibited the export of strategic minerals, chemicals and scrap iron to Japan. On 26 July 1941, in retaliation for Japan's occupation of Indochina, he imposed an embargo on oil, nationalized the Filipino Army and froze Japanese assets in the United States.

WAR WARNINGS

Admiral Isoroku Yamamoto (1884–1943), Commander-in-Chief of the Combined Fleet, was reluctant to go to war with the United States. Nevertheless he became the architect of what was conceived as a crippling blow to American military power in the Pacific, a pre-emptive strike by carrier-based aircraft against the US Pacific Fleet anchored at Pearl Harbor. For months, the Japanese pilots trained in secret. Then, on 26 November 1941, the powerful

BELOW: THE ENGINES OF JAPANESE Mitsubishi Zero fighters roar to life aboard the aircraft carrier Shokaku. The Zeroes provided air cover for the attackers at Pearl Harbor.

armada sailed from Hittokapu Bay in the Kurile islands. Two battleships, three cruisers, nine destroyers and three submarines escorted the heart of the strike force, six aircraft carriers, *Akagi, Kaga, Soryu, Hiryu, Shokaku* and *Zuikaku*.

American military leaders and diplomats acknowledged that war with Japan was imminent. However, they were convinced that the first blow would fall in the Philippines or Southeast Asia. The day after the Japanese fleet sailed, US commanders across the Pacific received a war warning. But the commander of the US Pacific Fleet, Admiral Husband Kimmel (1882–1968), and his Army counterpart, General Walter Short (1880–1949), were preoccupied with safeguarding installations and equipment from sabotage. They also fell victim to a series of communication failures.

EARLY WARNINGS IGNORED

In the pre-dawn hours of 7 December, the Japanese strike force had reached its appointed station 370km (230 miles) north of the island of Oahu. At 3.30 a.m. Pacific time, US cryptanalysts in Washington DC intercepted the last of a 14-part message from Tokyo to its emissaries there. The message seemed to indicate the opening of hostilities by Japan within a matter of hours.

At 3.45 a.m., the minesweeper USS *Condor*, on routine patrol, sighted what appeared to be a submarine periscope in

A JAPANESE PILOT wearing leather headcover, goggles and flight suit, strides towards his waiting aircraft. At the time of Pearl Harbor, many Japanese fliers had combat experience, gained in China.

a restricted area near the entrance to Pearl Harbor. The sighting was probably one of five Japanese midget submarines which were tasked with entering the harbour and firing torpedoes at American warships. Although the submarines failed in their assigned task, their two-man crews were lionized as heroes in Japan – with one notable exception. After his disabled midget submarine was beached, Ensign Kazuo Sakamaki was captured and became the first Japanese prisoner of war in World War II.

As streaks of daylight brightened the eastern sky, 183 Japanese planes of the first attack wave were being launched from the decks of the carriers. At 6.40 a.m., the destroyer USS *Ward*, patrolling the entrance to Pearl Harbour sighted and attacked one of

THE VERSATILE 'VAL'

Designed in 1935 as the Dive Bomber Type 99 Model 11, the Aichi D3A1 was the primary dive bomber of the Imperial Japanese Navy until 1942. Designated the 'Val' by the Allies, this aircraft was utilized in large numbers during the attack on Pearl Harbor, 7 December, 1941.

In the hands of a skilled pilot, the Val proved a highly accurate platform for the delivery of ordnance, achieving a success rate of greater than 80 per cent at its peak. However, following severe losses of veteran airmen, particularly at the battles of the Coral Sea and Midway and during the prolonged actions in the vicinity of the Solomons, the combat efficiency of the Val suffered.

the midget submarines. The destroyer's second 76mm (3in) shell struck the conning tower of the craft, which sank immediately. The *Ward*'s message concerning hostile contact was dismissed as another phantom sighting. Just 20 minutes later, the US Army's Opana radar station at Point Kahuku on Oahu picked up and reported an unidentified formation of aircraft. This warning was also discounted. By 7.30 a.m., the 170-planes of the Japanese second wave were airborne.

TORA, TORA, TORA!

Unmolested by US fighters or antiaircraft defences, the bombers of Lieutenant-Commander Mitsuo Fuchida (1902–1976) cleared the mountains west of Pearl Harbor. When it was apparent that the attackers had achieved complete surprise, Fuchida transmitted the message, '*Tora, Tora, Tora!*' to the Japanese fleet. The first bombs fell on Ford Island at 7.55 a.m.; Kaneohe Naval Air Station, Wheeler Field, Bellows Field, Hickam Field and Ewa Marine Corps Air Station came under attack from bombers and strafing fighters, destroying most American aircraft on the ground.

Moored along Battleship Row southeast of Ford Island, the pride of the US Pacific Fleet lay at anchor. Seven battleships – *Nevada, Arizona, West Virginia, Tennessee, Oklahoma, Maryland* and *California* – represented easy targets for screeching dive bombers and torpedo planes, which skimmed the harbour at barely 15.5m (50ft) to launch their deadly weapons. The flagship of the fleet, the battleship USS *Pennsylvania*, lay in a nearby drydock.

ABOVE: EDGY AMERICAN SOLDIERS, *one with a pair of binoculars, scan the skies above Pearl Harbor following the Japanese attack. Their weapons are Browning 7.62mm (0.3in) machine guns.*

BELOW: WITH THE SMOKE *from the effects of the Japanese attack blackening the sky, the USS Shaw explodes with spectacular consequences during the Japanese raid on Pearl Harbor.*

Within minutes, Pearl Harbor was ablaze. Four battleships were sunk. The *West Virginia* was hit by seven torpedoes and two bombs. The *California* took two torpedoes and a bomb. The *Oklahoma* was hit by at least five torpedoes and capsized, trapping many sailors below decks. A bomb fashioned from a modified 355mm (14in) shell originally intended for a naval cannon penetrated the deck of the *Arizona* and ignited a catastrophic explosion that shattered the ship and took the lives of 1177 men. The *Pennsylvania*, *Maryland*, *Nevada* and *Tennessee* were heavily damaged. The cruisers *Helena*, *Raleigh* and *Honolulu*; the destroyers *Cassin*, *Downes* and *Shaw*; the seaplane tender *Curtiss* and the repair ship *Vestal* were damaged, and the target ship *Utah* and minelayer *Oglala* were sunk.

THE WAKES OF JAPANESE torpedoes reach out toward Battleship Row at Pearl Harbor on 7 December 1941, while the shock waves of prior hits and oil haemorrhaging into the harbour are also visible.

STUNNING BLOW

In little more than two hours, Japan had altered the balance of power in the Pacific. The bold attack had taken the lives of 2403 Americans. Eighteen of 96 vessels at Pearl Harbor were sunk or damaged heavily. A total of 165 US aircraft were destroyed and 128 others damaged. In exchange, the Japanese lost 29 aircraft, five midget submarines, one fleet submarine and 185 dead.

Although they had achieved a great victory, the Japanese failed to achieve two major goals. The US aircraft carriers, their primary objective, were at sea and thus spared the attack. The marauding planes had also neglected nearly 23 million litres (5 million gallons) of fuel oil stored in tanks around Pearl Harbor and barely touched repair facilities, which would prove essential to future operations. The day after the attack, President Roosevelt asked a joint session of Congress for a declaration of war and called 7 December 1941 'a date which will live in infamy'.

PEARL HARBOR

3 At 7.55 a.m., 'Kate' torpedo bombers target ships to the northwest of Ford Island. This was where the missing carriers were normally berthed.

MIDDLE LOCH

6 The USS Nevada attempted to make for the safety of open water, but was attacked by wave after wave of torpedo and dive bombers.

FORD ISLAND NAVAL AIR STATION

USS CALIFORNIA

US NAVY YARD

5 Attacked by both the first and second waves, Hickam Field suffers the heaviest damage of Oahu's airbases.

SOUTHEAST LOCH

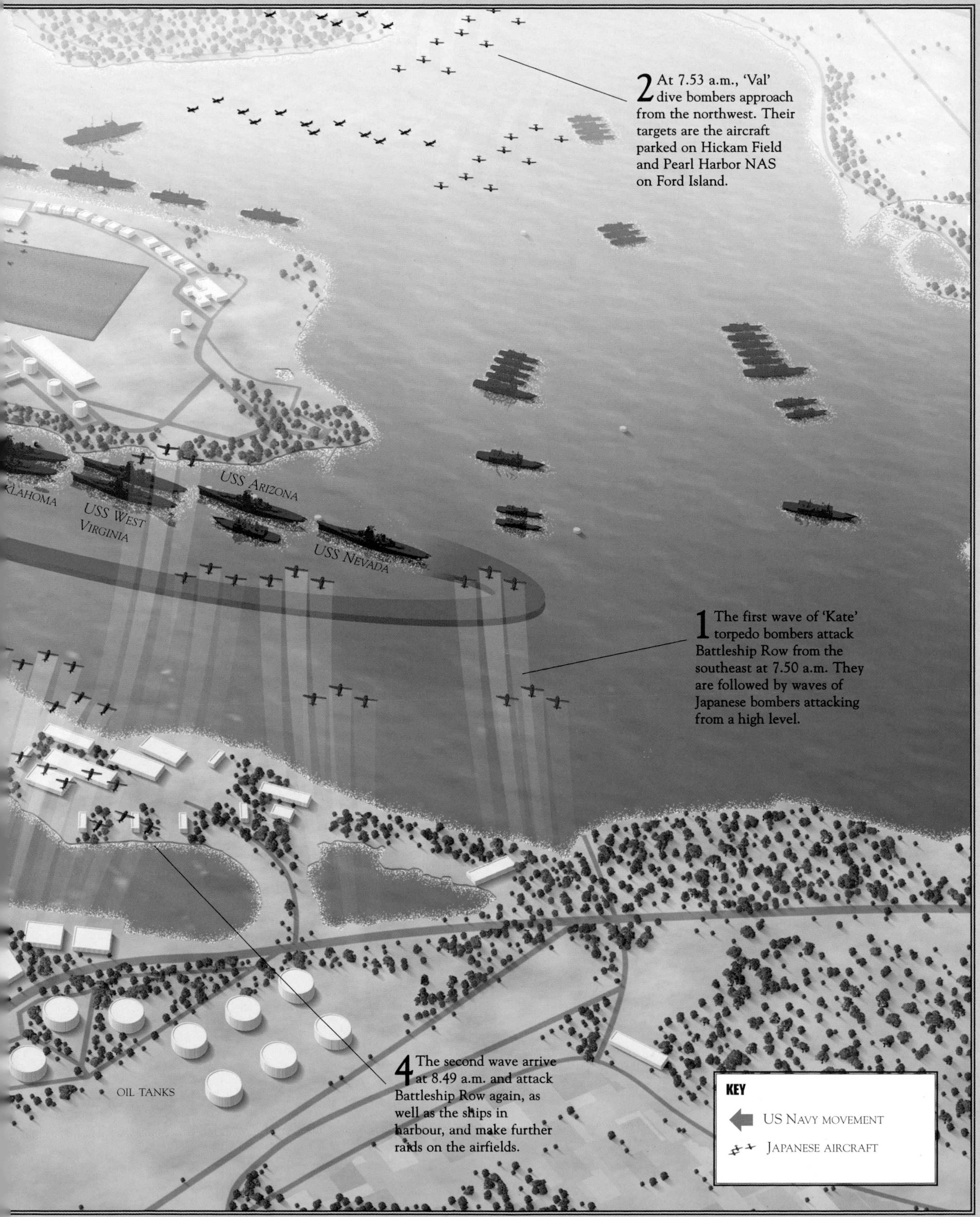

2 At 7.53 a.m., 'Val' dive bombers approach from the northwest. Their targets are the aircraft parked on Hickam Field and Pearl Harbor NAS on Ford Island.

OKLAHOMA

USS WEST
VIRGINIA

USS ARIZONA

USS NEVADA

1 The first wave of 'Kate' torpedo bombers attack Battleship Row from the southeast at 7.50 a.m. They are followed by waves of Japanese bombers attacking from a high level.

4 The second wave arrive at 8.49 a.m. and attack Battleship Row again, as well as the ships in harbour, and make further raids on the airfields.

OIL TANKS

KEY

← US NAVY MOVEMENT

✈✈ JAPANESE AIRCRAFT

BATTLE OF MIDWAY

1942

Reluctant to go to war in the first place, Admiral Isoroku Yamamoto (1884–1943), Commander-in-Chief of the Japanese Combined Fleet, had warned prior to the attack on Pearl Harbor, 'For six months, I will run wild in the Pacific. After that, I make no guarantees.'

Yamamoto was familiar with the United States, having attended Harvard University and served as a naval attaché in Washington DC. He recognized the huge industrial might of the United States and was convinced that a series of rapid victories and the destruction of the US Pacific Fleet were Japan's only hope of winning the war.

Although the Pearl Harbor attack had been a success, the American aircraft carriers had been at sea and were not destroyed. Yamamoto realized that he had

BATTLE OF MIDWAY FACTS

Who: Japanese naval forces under Admiral Isoroku Yamamoto (1884–1943) and Admiral Chuichi Nagumo (1887–1944) versus the US Pacific Fleet under Admirals Chester Nimitz (1885–1966), Frank Jack Fletcher (1885–1973) and Raymond Spruance (1886–1969).

What: A Japanese armada of four aircraft carriers carrying 256 aircraft, 11 battleships and numerous smaller vessels opposed an American force that included three aircraft carriers, 234 carrier- and land-based planes, and a variety of smaller craft.

Where: The central Pacific west of Hawaii and the northern Pacific near the Aleutians.

When: 4–7 June 1942

Why: The Japanese attempted to capture Midway atoll and occupied the islands of Attu and Kiska in the Aleutians.

Outcome: A turning point in the Pacific War, the battle was a devastating defeat for Japan. Four aircraft carriers were sunk and the invasion of Midway was cancelled.

CREWMEN ABOARD THE aircraft carrier USS Yorktown tend planes on the ship's flight deck. Damaged at Coral Sea, the Yorktown was repaired within 72 hours of returning to Pearl Harbor.

ABOVE: THE CREWMEN OF *the American search plane that located the Japanese invasion force headed for Midway atoll pose beside their Consolidated PBY Catalina flying boat.*

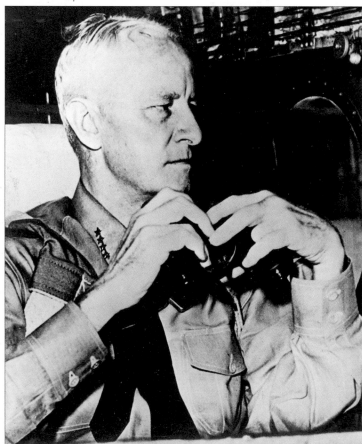

unfinished business. It was still necessary to engage the bulk of the US warships in a decisive battle. Despite the setback at Coral Sea in May, he forged ahead in the first week of June 1942 with plans for the capture of Midway, a tiny atoll less than 1930km (1200 miles) west of Hawaii and composed of two small islands, Sand and Eastern. With Midway in Japanese hands, the defensive perimeter of the Empire would be extended considerably. Hawaii itself might be open to invasion. In the process, Yamamoto would annihilate what remained of the US Pacific Fleet.

READING ENEMY MAIL

Yamamoto was unaware, however, that US Navy cryptanalysts based at Pearl Harbor had cracked the Japanese naval code, JN 25, and that Admiral Chester Nimitz (1885–1966), Commander-in-Chief of the US Pacific Fleet, was planning to counter the Midway operation. Nimitz ordered the aircraft carriers USS *Enterprise* and USS *Hornet* and their escorts to join the

LEFT: ADMIRAL CHESTER W. NIMITZ *became the Commander of the Pacific Fleet after Pearl Harbor. Aggressive and willing to take risks, he played decisive roles in the American victories at the battles of Coral Sea and Midway.*

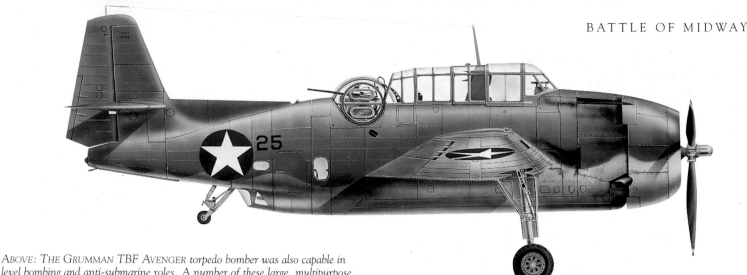

ABOVE: THE GRUMMAN TBF AVENGER *torpedo bomber was also capable in level bombing and anti-submarine roles. A number of these large, multipurpose aircraft were present at Midway.*

USS *Yorktown* – seriously damaged at Coral Sea but returned to service following a Herculean 72-hour repair effort at Pearl Harbor – northeast of Midway, to lie in wait for the Japanese. Admiral Frank Jack Fletcher (1885–1973), aboard the *Yorktown*, was to assume overall command of the American naval force, while Admiral Raymond Spruance (1886–1969) operated with a great deal of autonomy in command of the *Enterprise* and *Hornet*.

Yamamoto, meanwhile, stuck to his penchant for complex operations and formulated a plan that would initially involve a feint against the islands of Attu and Kiska in the Aleutian Islands far to the north. He further divided his forces into a powerful surface fleet formed around the super battleship *Yamato*, an invasion force transporting 500 soldiers to capture Midway and a carrier force consisting of four aircraft carriers, *Akagi*, *Kaga*, *Soryu* and *Hiryu*, which together transported 234 combat aircraft. Yamamoto himself sailed aboard the *Yamato*, while Admiral Chuichi Nagumo (1887–1944) commanded the carrier force.

BELOW: THE DOUGLAS SBD DAUNTLESS *dive bomber was responsible for inflicting the lethal damage against four aircraft carriers of the Imperial Japanese Navy during the Battle of Midway.*

BATTLE JOINED

On the morning of 3 June, a US search plane spotted the Japanese invasion force, but subsequent attacks by aircraft based at Midway failed to achieve any success. The next day, the Japanese carrier force emerged from dense fog and rain as Nagumo launched more than 100 planes to strike Midway

BELOW: THE LAST SURVIVOR *of the Japanese battle fleet at Midway, Hiryu was struck by SBD Dauntless dive bombers late on 4 June 1942. Burning fiercely, the carrier was abandoned and scuttled some 12 hours later.*

in an effort to render its airstrip unusable and soften up the atoll's defences.

The attack was only partially effective and Nagumo faced a dilemma. A portion of his aircraft had been retained and armed with torpedoes to hit the American carriers if and when they were sighted. A second attack on Midway would require that these planes have their torpedoes exchanged for bombs, a hazardous and time-consuming process. The need for a second attack on Midway was confirmed by the appearance of American land-based bombers overhead. Although they scored no hits, Nagumo ordered planes not returning from the first Midway raid to be rearmed with bombs.

Moments later, however, Nagumo's resolve was again tested when a Japanese reconnaissance aircraft reported 10 US ships, including a carrier, steaming just over 320km (200 miles) to the northeast. Nagumo considered ordering the planes already rearmed with bombs to take off against Midway while those still carrying torpedoes attacked the American ships.

To complicate matters, the planes returning from the first Midway attack and the Zero fighters flying protective combat air patrol above his ships were low on fuel and needed to land. Finally, Nagumo decided to recover planes that were airborne and to equip with torpedoes the bombers which had been withheld. In their haste to land and refuel

BELOW: BADLY DAMAGED IN A collision with its sister ship, Mogami, *and by repeated US air attacks, the Japanese heavy cruiser* Mikuma *drifts prior to sinking on 6 June 1942.*

BELOW: DISPLACING 19,800 TONS and carrying 71 aircraft, the Japanese carrier Soryu (Green Dragon) *was a veteran of Pearl Harbor. Hit by three American bombs at Midway,* Soryu *was turned into a blazing inferno and sunk.*

aircraft while rearming others, Japanese crewmen stretched fuel lines across the carrier decks and stacked bombs below without properly securing them. For a dangerously long time, the Japanese aircraft carriers were as vulnerable as they could possibly be. Fletcher and Spruance swung into action when a search plane located the enemy carrier force at about 5.30 a.m. on 4 June. Near the limits of their range, more than 150 dive bombers, torpedo bombers and fighters took off from the *Hornet*, *Enterprise* and *Yorktown*.

FATAL MISCALCULATION

Some of the formations drifted off course and the opportunity for a coordinated attack was lost. In a twist of fate, however, this worked to the advantage of the Americans. The slow, obsolete torpedo bombers found the Japanese first but were decimated by anti-aircraft fire and the covering Zeros.

Nearly every one was lost without scoring a single hit. Shortly after 10 a.m., the Japanese carriers began the launch of their own planes. As the first aircraft roared down the flight decks, lookouts shouted the warning. Unmolested by the fighters, which were off chasing the last of the torpedo planes, 50 American dive bombers pressed home their attacks. In a flash, the course of the Pacific War was changed. Bombs exploded among aircraft waiting to take off and amid the ordnance stacked below decks. *Akagi*, *Kaga* and *Soryu*, engulfed in flames, were doomed.

The lone surviving Japanese carrier, the *Hiryu*, had been steaming in a rain squall some distance away and managed to launch a strike against *Yorktown*, seriously damaging the veteran of the Coral Sea fight. Although damage control parties worked to save the ship, *Yorktown* was spotted by a Japanese submarine and sunk along with the destroyer USS *Hammann* on 7 June. The *Hiryu*, however, did not outlive her sisters for long. US dive bombers scored four hits on the afternoon of 4 June, turning the last Japanese carrier into a blazing hulk.

AN EMPIRE SHATTERED

The action in the waters around Midway on 4 June 1942 turned the tide of World War II in the Pacific. The loss of four aircraft carriers, a cruiser, 332 aircraft and more than

ADMIRAL ISOROKU YAMAMOTO

Admiral Isoroku Yamamoto, Commander-in-Chief of the Japanese Combined Fleet, conceived of the attack on Pearl Harbor and the bold stroke against Midway. Before the war, Yamamoto had attended Harvard University and served as a naval attaché in Washington, DC. As a young officer, he had been seriously wounded at the great battle of Tsushima during the Russo-Japanese War. Yamamoto's penchant for gambling may have betrayed him in the planning for the Midway operation. The admiral was killed in April 1943, when the bomber carrying him on an inspection tour was shot down by American P-38 Lightning fighters.

2000 men was a crippling blow from which the Japanese never recovered. In contrast, the US lost one carrier, a destroyer, 137 planes and 307 men.

Yamamoto briefly entertained the prospect of bringing his overwhelming superiority in battleships and cruisers to bear in a surface engagement against the Americans. Spruance would have none of it. He had recognized a great victory, remembered the admonition of Nimitz to employ the 'principle of calculated risk' and retired out of harm's way. The invasion of Midway was cancelled. The defeated Japanese retreated and for the remainder of the war were obliged to fight defensively.

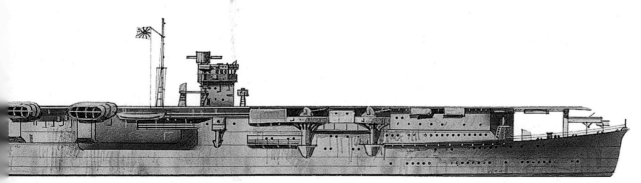

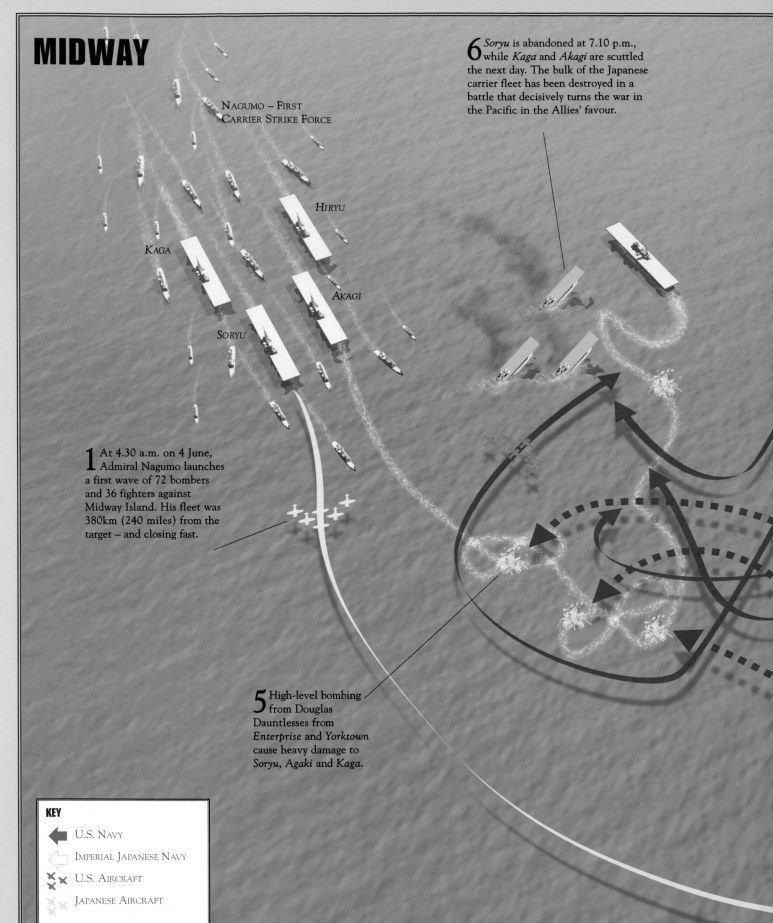

MIDWAY

NAGUMO – FIRST
CARRIER STRIKE FORCE

HIRYU

KAGA

AKAGI

SORYU

6 *Soryu* is abandoned at 7.10 p.m.,
while *Kaga* and *Akagi* are scuttled
the next day. The bulk of the Japanese
carrier fleet has been destroyed in a
battle that decisively turns the war in
the Pacific in the Allies' favour.

1 At 4.30 a.m. on 4 June,
Admiral Nagumo launches
a first wave of 72 bombers
and 36 fighters against
Midway Island. His fleet was
380km (240 miles) from the
target – and closing fast.

5 High-level bombing
from Douglas
Dauntlesses from
Enterprise and *Yorktown*
cause heavy damage to
Soryu, Agaki and *Kaga*.

KEY

← U.S. NAVY

⇐ IMPERIAL JAPANESE NAVY

✕✕ U.S. AIRCRAFT

✕✕ JAPANESE AIRCRAFT

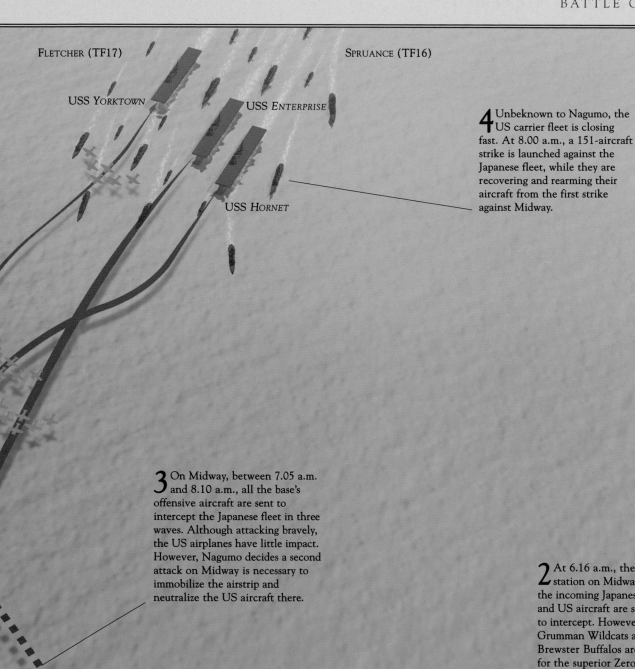

FLETCHER (TF17)

SPRUANCE (TF16)

USS YORKTOWN

USS ENTERPRISE

USS HORNET

4 Unbeknown to Nagumo, the US carrier fleet is closing fast. At 8.00 a.m., a 151-aircraft strike is launched against the Japanese fleet, while they are recovering and rearming their aircraft from the first strike against Midway.

3 On Midway, between 7.05 a.m. and 8.10 a.m., all the base's offensive aircraft are sent to intercept the Japanese fleet in three waves. Although attacking bravely, the US airplanes have little impact. However, Nagumo decides a second attack on Midway is necessary to immobilize the airstrip and neutralize the US aircraft there.

2 At 6.16 a.m., the radar station on Midway detects the incoming Japanese aircraft and US aircraft are scrambled to intercept. However, the slow Grumman Wildcats and Brewster Buffalos are no match for the superior Zeros.

MIDWAY ISLAND

CONVOY PQ-17 1942

Convoy PQ-17 was in some ways a triumph for the heavy surface raiders, even though they played no part in the actual attacks. The threat that a battleship was at large was enough to force the convoy to scatter, at which point its fate was sealed.

At the outbreak of World War II, the *Kriegsmarine* possessed a handful of powerful heavy cruisers and capital ships. These were not enough to threaten the Royal Navy but they did affect the course of the war.

The strategy of a 'fleet in being' meant that rather than coming out to fight a battle that they would certainly lose, the German major units tied down, merely through their existence, large segments of the Allied fleet that could be used elsewhere such as in the Mediterranean or the Pacific.

Traditionally, weaker naval powers have resorted to 'cruiser warfare' – ie, raiding the sea traffic of their enemies. While this is normally the province of cruisers and submarines, a capital ship could swiftly slaughter a convoy and its escorts.

CONVOY PQ-17 FACTS

Who: An Allied convoy of 33 ships with an escort of four cruisers, three destroyers and two Royal Navy submarines sailing to the Soviet Union, versus 10 submarines, aircraft based on the Norwegian mainland and the threat of surface attack.

What: A gradual massacre of the merchant ships and their escorts.

Where: North of Norway in the Arctic Sea, close to the island of Spitzbergen.

When: June–July 1942

Why: The convoy scattered in response to a supposed surface threat.

Outcome: Massive casualties among the Allied merchant ships, with only 11 ships arriving at their destination. Shortly afterwards, the Allies suspended Arctic convoys because of the heavy losses.

DEPTH CHARGES EXPLODE *in the Arctic twilight. Whether or not the submarine was destroyed, aggressive depth-charging could prevent it from making a successful attack while the convoy moved on. The submarines of the period were too slow to catch up with most convoys once they were past.*

THE TYPE IX U-BOAT was capable of long-range operations, though it had to travel mostly on the surface. These boats could strike anywhere on a convoy route and remain at sea for long periods waiting for a suitable target.

The big surface raiders of the German Navy were thus a serious threat to Allied supply lines. Although raiding cruises by the heavy ships had not achieved as much as might have been hoped, an attack on a concentrated high-value target such as a major convoy could achieve results of strategic importance.

Much effort was expended on keeping the major units of the *Kriegsmarine* bottled up, especially when a critical convoy was under way. Some convoys were protected by old battleships or given distant heavy covering forces that could counter a sortie by the major raiders. However, some areas were simply too hazardous for capital ships. One such was the Arctic passage to Murmansk.

The German attack on Russia in 1941 brought the Soviet Union into the war on the side of the Allies and ultimately doomed the Axis to defeat. However, there was a time when the situation in Russia was desperate and the new allies needed to send support. The only practicable way was to ship vast quantities of tanks, vehicles, artillery, aircraft and other war matériel into Russian ports, and the only available route was through the Arctic Ocean, around the north of Norway and into the Kola Inlet on the White Sea.

ARCTIC CONVOYS

Arctic convoys were difficult enough without enemy interference. Ice was a constant hazard – not just in the water but forming on ships. It jammed turrets and winches and, more dangerously, increased topweight so that ships rolled more and could become unstable. Ice clearance was a constant task. The Arctic ocean largely freezes in the

winter; pack ice advances far south. This requires ships making the passage to travel relatively close to the northern coastline of Norway, which was at the time occupied by German forces. Aircraft and submarines based there not only had less far to travel to find the convoy but also a smaller area to search in.

However, winter convoys were at least covered by darkness – that far north, there were months of night in which the sun barely rose above the horizon. In the summer, convoys could take a more northerly route, putting some

U-BOATS WERE VULNERABLE to aircraft and surface vessels, so maintaining a good lookout was essential. This was a miserable job in rough weather, as the top of the conning tower was constantly lashed with icy spray.

distance between the ships and their enemies, but the constant daylight offset this defensive advantage.

Convoys were given a code name and number that indicated, to those who knew the system, their route and sometimes composition or speed. 'Fast' convoys received a different designation to those that could make a relatively low average speed. Each route had its own pair of code

TYPE VIIC U-BOAT

Coming into service in 1941, just as the 'happy time' for U-boats was ending, the Type VIIC was smaller than the Type IX and had a shorter range as well as a smaller torpedo load. It was the mainstay of the German U-boat service for the remainder of the war and several hundred were built.

Although the tide was slowly turning against the U-boats, the Type VIIC was highly successful in combat. Many received *Schnorkels* from 1944 onwards, increasing their underwater endurance. Others were modified into flak boats to counter air attacks near the U-boat bases in the Bay of Biscay.

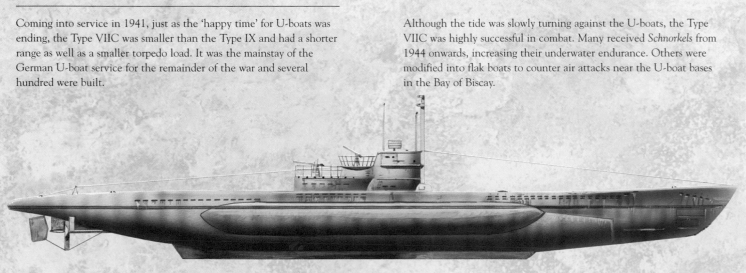

POOR VISIBILITY WAS a mixed blessing for the arctic convoys. It helped them to avoid submarine and air attack but also concealed the U-boats that did find the convoy as they closed in to make their attack.

letters. Arctic convoys to Russia were designated PQ, with returning convoys labelled QP.

PQ convoys began with PQ-1, which assembled in Iceland and set sail on 29 September 1941. Only one ship was lost among the 103 that set out before the spring of 1941, but the sinking of a destroyer by a U-boat on January 1942 warned of things to come. Losses mounted, with increasing pressure from air and submarine units. PQ-16 lost five of its 30 merchant ships, four others arriving damaged.

CONVOY PQ-17

It was with the expectation of a tough passage that PQ-17 formed up. It was the largest convoy thus far, with 36 merchant ships. The close escort consisted of four destroyers, 10 lighter craft (mostly armed trawlers) and two anti-aircraft ships. Distant cover was provided by four cruisers and four destroyers. A heavy force containing two battleships, two cruisers and an aircraft carrier was available for the first part of the route but could not be risked past the North Cape.

German high command considered breaking the Arctic convoy route to be of great importance and had made plans for heavy air and submarine attacks plus a possible sortie by heavy surface units. The Allies were aware that this was a prospect, though they could not know whether an attack was planned.

The convoy sailed on 27 June 1942. It took a very northerly route, passing close to the Svalbard archipelago, to keep as much distance between it and the enemy's northern bases as possible. This meant struggling through sea ice at times and some ships were damaged. One had to be sent back to join another that had turned back just after leaving Iceland.

Despite this and being spotted first by U-boats and later by aircraft, the convoy suffered no losses until 4 July. Two ships were sunk after three days of intermittent air attack. However, something much more serious happened that day. The Allies received word that the battleship *Tirpitz* was out.

Tirpitz was the most powerful ship in the German fleet. Modern and well-designed, she was quite probably capable of defeating a single Allied battleship if she met one; the convoy escorts and cruisers would stand no chance. *Tirpitz* was fast enough to destroy the escorting cruisers and then chase down the slow merchant ships; if she got into range of the convoy, it would be a massacre. Worse, she was reported as sailing in company with two heavy cruisers and several destroyers. The only chance to save any of the convoy was to scatter it and to hope that the heavy raiders found only some of the ships.

The British intelligence service was subsequently able to establish that this was not a sortie against PQ-17 but merely a redeployment. The damage had been done, though. The order to scatter was sent and the covering force was pulled back. Many of the warship crews were sickened by what they heard on the radio. Unable to help, they heard the scattered merchant ships struggling on under submarine and air attack – vessels calling for help and then going off the air.

Many of the escort crews met a hostile reception in the bars of their home ports. Challenged by other sailors for 'abandoning' PQ-17, they gave vent to their own bitter emotions. There were many fights, and several men were killed. The 'stigma' of PQ-17 took a long time to erase, even though none of what happened was the sailors' fault: the Admiralty ordered the convoy to scatter and the ship captains were bound to obey.

On 5 July, the convoy came under heavy attack from aircraft and lost six ships, while submarines accounted for six more. The remaining close escorts did what they could for nearby vessels, but without an organized convoy the merchants were desperately vulnerable, especially to submarines. With no destroyer force to counter them, U-boats could make their attacks at leisure and consequently were very effective.

Similarly, the *Luftwaffe* was able to press home its attacks with great precision, since there was little anti-aircraft fire.

This, too, increased the effectiveness of the sorties. As a consequence, nine more ships were sunk over the following five days. The survivors began to arrive in Russia on 10 July. Eleven ships straggled in over the next week. More than half the convoy had been destroyed by aircraft and submarines. Some of the ships would have been sunk whether or not the full escort had been available. However, the circumstances leading to the destruction of PQ-17 were brought about just by the threat of attack. The very existence of the 'fleet in being' brought ruin upon the Arctic convoy route.

AFTERMATH

The effect of the 'abandonment' on the psyche of the escort crews is summed up by a statement made by one of the captains involved. During Operation *Pedestal*, a convoy to Malta facing heavy opposition, this officer said: 'I don't care what signals I get from whom, so long as there's a merchant afloat I'm putting my ship alongside her and we're going to Malta.' His was one of three destroyers that rescued the crippled tanker *Ohio* and somehow got her into Grand Harbour, quite probably changing the course of the war.

ABOVE: A ROYAL NAVY OFFICER dressed for Arctic convoy service. The cold was a deadly enemy; men keeping watch or venturing above decks risked hypothermia, and falling overboard was a death sentence.

LEFT: CAPTAIN HEINZ BEILFELD of U-703 is congratulated by a superior officer after the successful raid against convoy PQ-17.

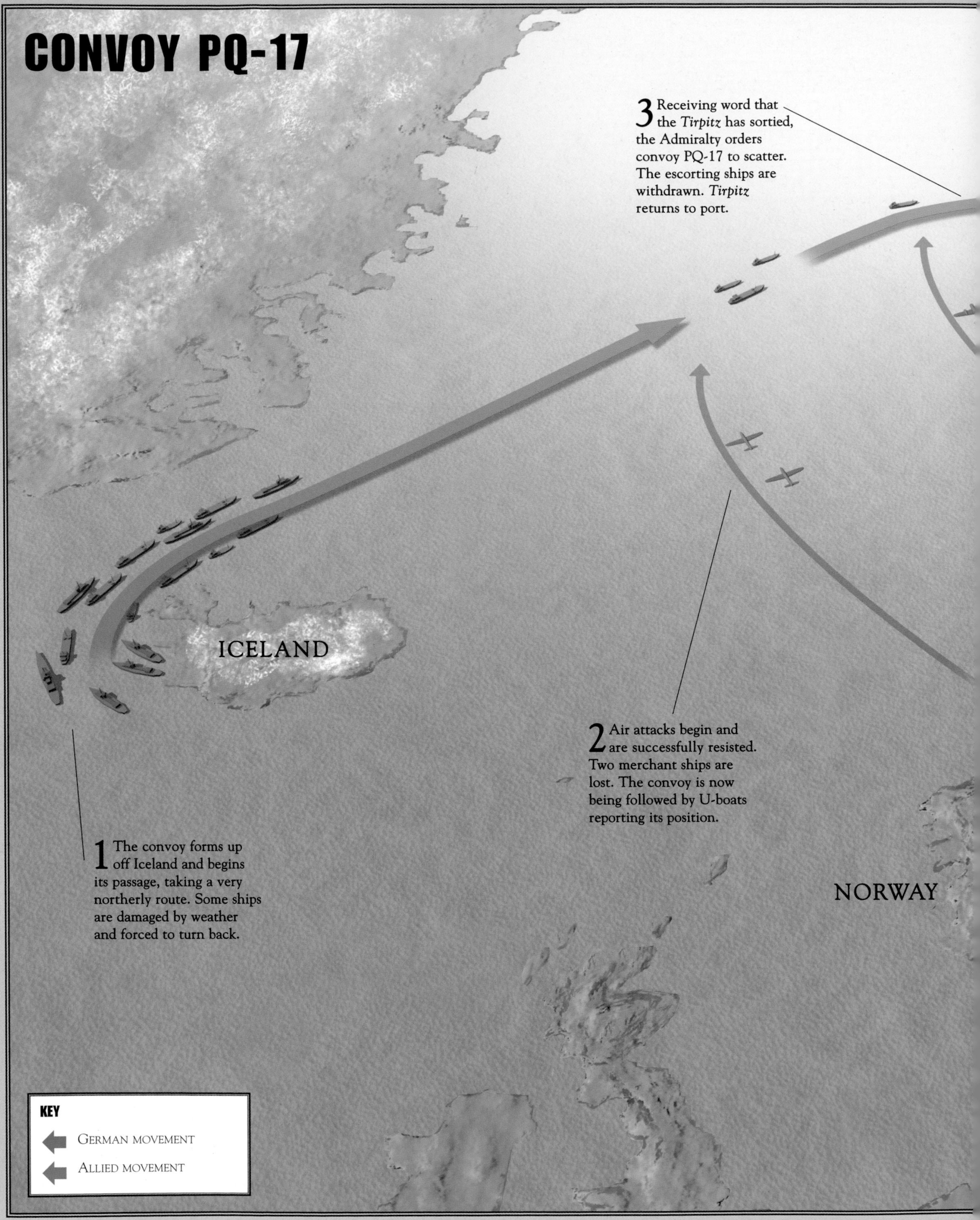

CONVOY PQ-17

3 Receiving word that the *Tirpitz* has sortied, the Admiralty orders convoy PQ-17 to scatter. The escorting ships are withdrawn. *Tirpitz* returns to port.

2 Air attacks begin and are successfully resisted. Two merchant ships are lost. The convoy is now being followed by U-boats reporting its position.

ICELAND

NORWAY

1 The convoy forms up off Iceland and begins its passage, taking a very northerly route. Some ships are damaged by weather and forced to turn back.

KEY

← GERMAN MOVEMENT

← ALLIED MOVEMENT

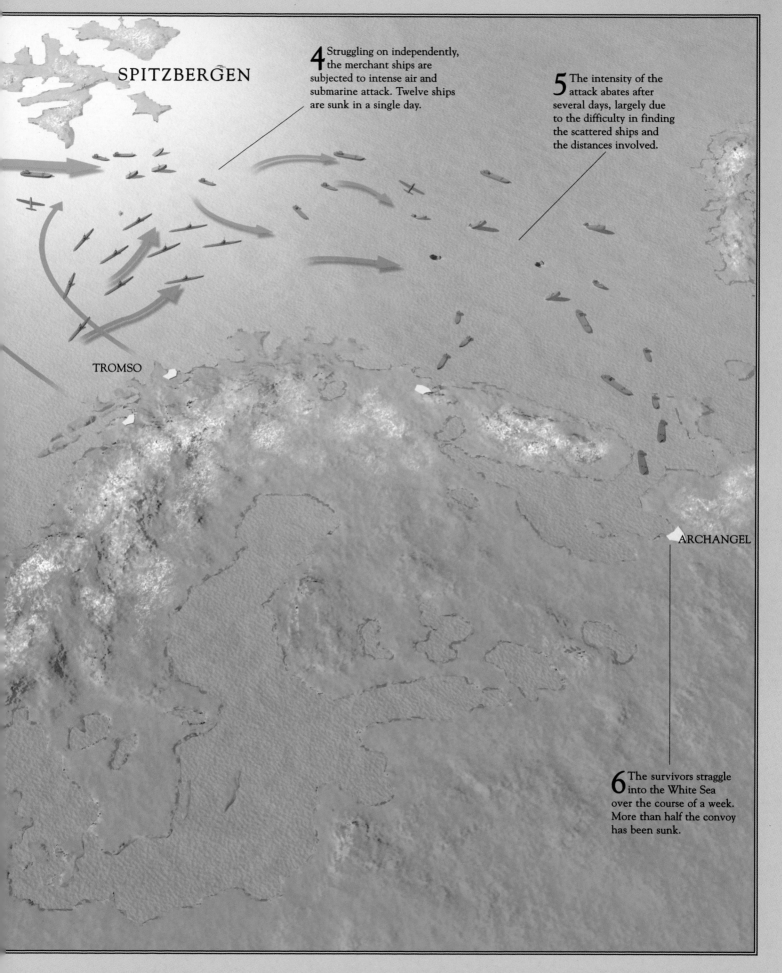

SPITZBERGEN

4 Struggling on independently, the merchant ships are subjected to intense air and submarine attack. Twelve ships are sunk in a single day.

5 The intensity of the attack abates after several days, largely due to the difficulty in finding the scattered ships and the distances involved.

TROMSO

ARCHANGEL

6 The survivors straggle into the White Sea over the course of a week. More than half the convoy has been sunk.

EL ALAMEIN 1942

The Battle of El Alamein, 23 October–4 November 1942, taking its name from an Egyptian railway halt west of Alexander, marked a turning point in the war in North Africa. The British Prime Minister Winston Churchill (1874–1965) claimed that, 'Before Alamein we never had a victory. After Alamein we never had a defeat.'

Although Churchill's pronouncement was something of an exaggeration, the German–Italian army was forced into full-scale retreat and its position worsened considerably after the Allied landings in French North Africa on 8 November. However, for the Commonwealth army the battle also had the psychological effect of finally breaking the myth of German invincibility.

The war in the Western Desert had swung back and forth over the course of nearly two years. Field-Marshal Erwin Rommel's (1891–1944) German–Italian Panzer Army Africa had driven the British back past the Egyptian border, where it

EL ALAMEIN FACTS

Who: The Commonwealth Eighth Army (British, Australian, New Zealand, Indian and South African troops) led by Lieutenant-General Bernard Montgomery (1887–1976) faced Field Marshal Erwin Rommel's (1891–1944) Panzer Army Africa, renamed the German–Italian Panzer Army on 25 October 1942.

What: Operation Lightfoot was a carefully planned and prepared set-piece offensive launched by Montgomery on the Axis forces, who had shifted to the defensive after being defeated at Alam Halfa in September.

Where: El Alamein, a small Egyptian railway halt, 95 kilometres (60 miles) west of Alexandria.

When: 23 October to 4 November 1942

Why: Growing British material strength allowed Montgomery to shift decisively to the offensive against Rommel's over-extended forces and finally ensure the safety of the Suez Canal and the Middle Eastern oil fields.

Outcome: Although Rommel was able to escape with a large proportion of his army, El Alamein marked a clear turning point in the Western Desert Campaign with the initiative shifting decisively to the Allies.

A PROBABLY STAGED photograph of troops of the 51st Highland Division running past a knocked-out German Panzer Mark III at El Alamein.

ABOVE: *FIELD MARSHAL ERWIN ROMMEL, the charismatic, energetic commander of German and Italian forces in the Western Desert.*

BELOW: *BRITISH ARTILLERY BOMBARDS German positions during the buildup to the offensive at El Alamein, Operation* Lightfoot.

was stopped by General Claude Auchinleck's (1884–1981) Eighth Army between 1 and 4 July 1942, at the first battle of El Alamein. By the time Rommel was ready to try again, Auchinleck had been replaced as Army Commander by Lieutenant General Bernard Law Montgomery (1887–1976). Montgomery was a meticulous planner and superb trainer of men, and set about rebuilding the Eighth Army, both in terms of matériel and confidence.

When Rommel attacked in September at Alam Halfa, the British were well prepared and he was soundly defeated. At the end of a long logistical chain, plagued by shortages of fuel and facing an increasingly strong Commonwealth Army, Rommel, debilitated by ill health, shifted to the defensive. The Germans and Italians set about establishing a system of strong points set among deep minefields. Rommel's mobile troops were held back behind his infantry to counter any breakthrough, but the desperate lack of fuel meant they were held closer to the front than normal. In the north, he placed 15th Panzer, 90th Light and the Italian *Littorio* armoured divisions; and in the south, 21st Panzer and *Ariete*.

SET-PIECE BATTLE

Montgomery refused to be pushed by Churchill into attacking before he believed he was ready. He would launch his offensive only when he was sure his men were trained to the peak of perfection and completely in his grip, ready to do exactly what he wanted of them. Unlike so many previous desert battles, Alamein would be a set-piece affair, with both

RIGHT: A PRIVATE FROM THE 9TH Australian Division with his Short Magazine Lee Enfield Rifle. He is well wrapped-up to withstand the rigours of the desert at night.

flanks soundly anchored by the Mediterranean to the north and the impassable Qattara Depression to the south. Montgomery could muster 195,000 men to Rommel's 105,000, of whom 53,000 were German. He fielded 1000 tanks to the enemy's 500 and roughly double the amount of aircraft.

The Commonwealth forces, broadly speaking, held a two-to-one advantage in most weapon systems. Montgomery's plan was that four infantry divisions of Lieutenant-General Oliver Leese's (1884–1978) XXX Corps would clear a path through the German positions in the north to allow the two armoured divisions of Lieutenant-General Herbert Lumsden's (1897–1945) X Corps to push through and take defensive positions in the west. Then the infantry would break up the German line to the north and south – 'crumbling' as Montgomery called it. Brian Horrocks's (1895–1985) XIII Corps would make strong representations to the south.

THE OFFENSIVE OPENS

Operation *Lightfoot*, a codename in somewhat poor taste given the 445,000 German mines, opened with a massive barrage on the evening of 23 October. It took the Germans by surprise and seriously disrupted Axis communications. General George Stumme (1886–1942), commanding in Rommel's absence on sick leave, died of a heart attack going forward to find out what was happening. The battle started well but resistance began to stiffen quickly, particularly in the 51st Highland Division's sector. The northernmost 9th Australian Division took all its objectives, but the armour

RIGHT: A HEAVILY DECORATED GERMAN tanker swigs from his water, standing atop of his Panzer Mark III.

was to advance through the Highlanders and the 2nd New Zealand Division, where more difficulties had been encountered and heavy casualties suffered. The Commonwealth forces had failed to reach their first day objectives. Bitter fighting continued over the next couple of days and, although progress was slow, a couple of serious German counterattacks were repulsed. Rommel returned on 26 October and concentrated what armour he could muster after the attritional fighting of the previous few days to counterattack a salient created by British 1st Armoured Division on the slight rise of Kidney Ridge. Both 21st Panzer and 90th Light Divisions were stopped dead by well-served antitank guns, artillery and air power. Meanwhile, Montgomery's forces slowly reduced the Axis positions, although progress was much slower than expected.

SUPERCHARGE LAUNCHED

The failure to make much headway forced Montgomery to come up with another plan. Operation *Supercharge* shifted the weight of the offensive away from the north to the Kidney Ridge area on the night of 1 November. Led by Lieutenant-General Bernard Freyberg's (1889–1963) New Zealanders, bolstered by three British brigades, *Supercharge*

The US-built M3 Medium Tank (known to the British as the Lee or Grant) first saw service in the Western Desert in early 1942. Although it had a number of flaws, the British appreciated the fire power provided by its hull-mounted 75mm (2.95in) gun.

T24203

penetrated deep into the Axis position and convinced Rommel that the battle was lost.

On 3 November, he began to pull back his armoured forces and ordered the rest of his men to disengage. The New Zealanders and 1st Armoured Division, then 7th Armoured Division threatened to cut off the escape, which was in itself hampered by Hitler ordering Rommel to stand fast. Rommel managed to extricate large numbers of his forces, although 30,000 – about a third of them German – were taken prisoner. The Battle of El Alamein was over and had cost the Allies 13,560 casualties, Major-General Douglas Wimberley's (1896–1983) inexperienced

51st Highland Division taking the brunt, with the other infantry divisions also suffering heavily.

PURSUIT AND DEFENCE

Montgomery was hesitant in the pursuit and Rommel was able to retreat westwards about 1000km (620 miles) before turning to make a serious stand in January 1943. By then, the strategic situation had worsened even further for the Axis, as on 8 November US and British forces landed in French North Africa seriously threatening Rommel's rear. The remorseless logic of a two-front campaign doomed the Axis presence in Africa.

GENERAL BERNARD MONTGOMERY

Bernard Montgomery combined undeniable charisma and flair for showmanship with a single-minded dedication to the profession of arms. He proved to be a superb trainer of men and meticulous planner, who did much to banish the myth of German invincibility. He was seriously wounded in World War I, but by the outbreak of World War II he commanded 3rd Division, which he led with distinction through the French campaign of 1940.

Corps and Area commands in Britain followed. Then, in August 1942, the death of Lieutenant-General William Gott, Churchill's first choice as commander for the Eighth Army, gave Montgomery his opportunity.

ABOVE: A GERMAN TANK MAN *surrenders to Commonwealth infantry in another probably staged photo from the period.*

El Alamein was the climax of the campaign in the Western Desert and the turning point in the war in North Africa. Montgomery had approached the battle with determination and a hard-headed will to succeed. He had also proved flexible enough – although he would never admit it – to change his plan midway through the battle. More importantly, he had proved himself to be a general capable of defeating the Germans. This was vital for the morale of the Eighth Army, vital for Churchill, who was under political pressure at home, and vital for the British nation as a whole.

LEFT: THE MARK II MATILDA *had been a mainstay of British tanks forces in the early part of the desert war, but by El Alamein it was obsolescent.*

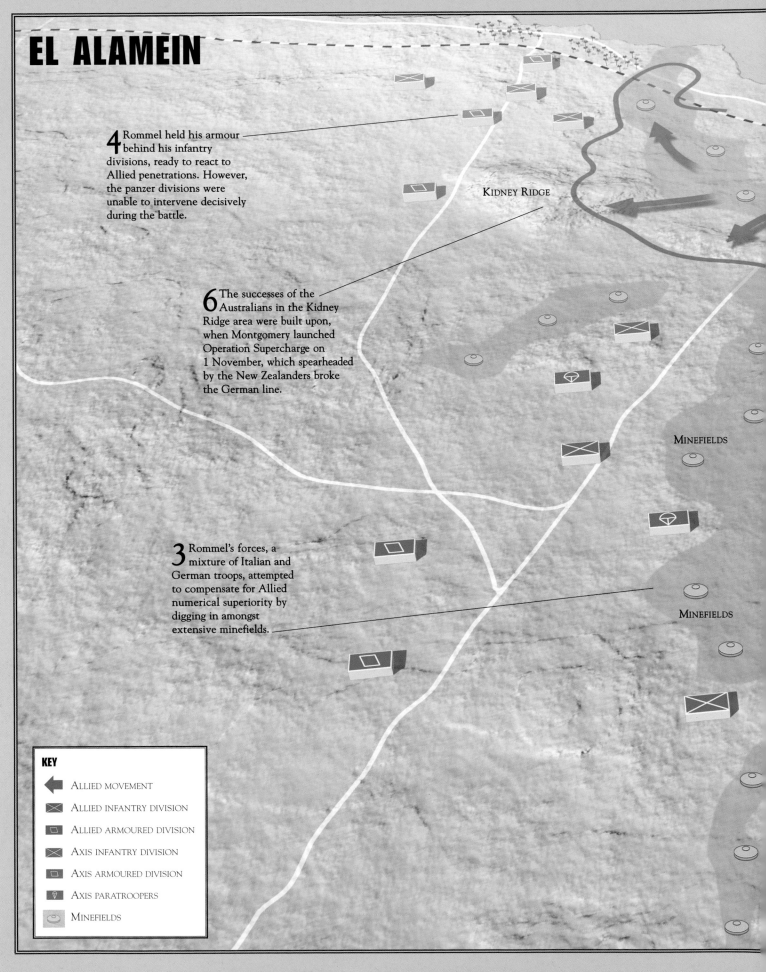

EL ALAMEIN

4 Rommel held his armour behind his infantry divisions, ready to react to Allied penetrations. However, the panzer divisions were unable to intervene decisively during the battle.

KIDNEY RIDGE

6 The successes of the Australians in the Kidney Ridge area were built upon, when Montgomery launched Operation Supercharge on 1 November, which spearheaded by the New Zealanders broke the German line.

MINEFIELDS

3 Rommel's forces, a mixture of Italian and German troops, attempted to compensate for Allied numerical superiority by digging in amongst extensive minefields.

MINEFIELDS

KEY

◄ ALLIED MOVEMENT

⊠ ALLIED INFANTRY DIVISION

▭ ALLIED ARMOURED DIVISION

⊠ AXIS INFANTRY DIVISION

▭ AXIS ARMOURED DIVISION

▽ AXIS PARATROOPERS

⬯ MINEFIELDS

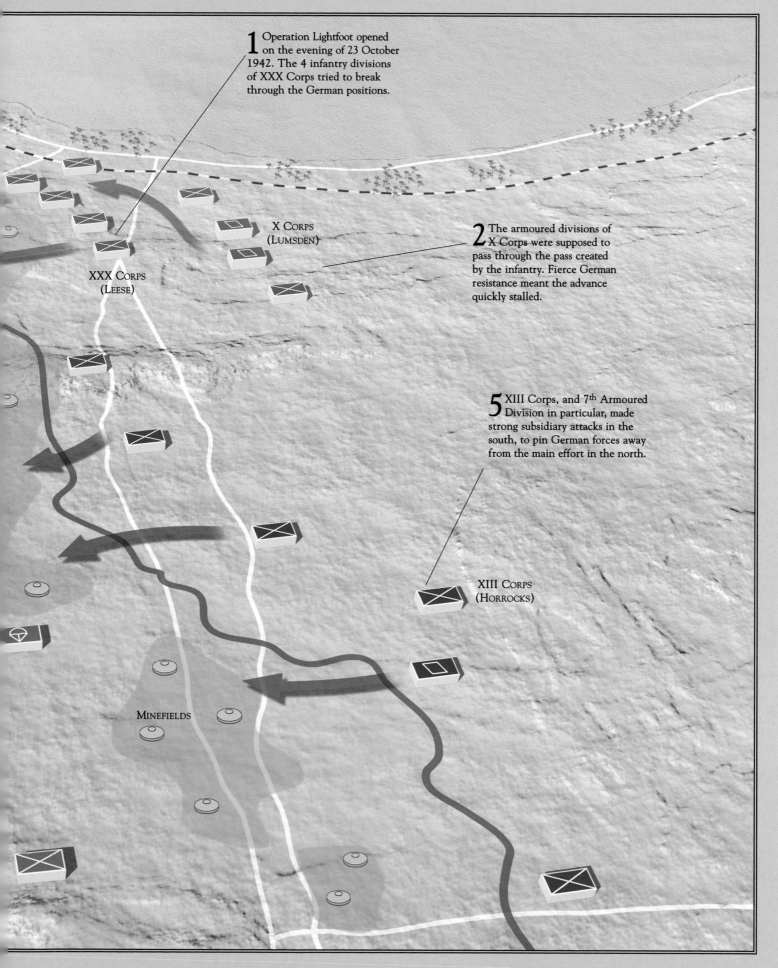

1 Operation Lightfoot opened on the evening of 23 October 1942. The 4 infantry divisions of XXX Corps tried to break through the German positions.

X CORPS
(LUMSDEN)

2 The armoured divisions of X Corps were supposed to pass through the pass created by the infantry. Fierce German resistance meant the advance quickly stalled.

XXX CORPS
(LEESE)

5 XIII Corps, and 7th Armoured Division in particular, made strong subsidiary attacks in the south, to pin German forces away from the main effort in the north.

XIII CORPS
(HORROCKS)

MINEFIELDS

BATTLE OF GUADALCANAL 1942–3

After defeating the Imperial Japanese Navy at the Battle of Midway in June 1942, the Allies set about clearing Japanese bases from the Solomon Islands. This required amphibious operations against several islands – including Tulagi, where a seaplane base needed removing, and Guadalcanal, where a major airbase was being constructed.

The Allies assembled an invasion force at Fiji under US Vice-Admiral Frank Fletcher (1885–1973), with ground forces led by Major-General Alexander Vandegrift (1887–1973), commander of the US 1st Marine Division, which provided most of the ground forces.

BATTLE OF GUADALCANAL FACTS

Who: Allied forces from the United States, Australia and New Zealand versus Japanese ground, air and naval forces.

What: The battle of Guadalcanal was a drawn-out fight lasting several months and involving land, naval and air forces. Allied forces captured the island and held it against determined attack.

Where: Guadalcanal in the Solomon Islands, in the South Pacific.

When: August 1942–February 1943

Why: The island was important to both sides as a base for future operations.

Outcome: With its eventual success, the Allies won their first major ground victory against the Japanese. Despite heavy losses on both sides, the island was held by the Allies and used as a forward base.

US MARINES GO ASHORE *in August 1942. There was little opposition to the initial landings on Guadalcanal, though later the island was bitterly contested until the Japanese finally gave up.*

LEFT: A US DESTROYER off the coast of Guadalcanal. Although the fate of the island was decided on land, naval power greatly influenced the battle by limiting Japanese reinforcements and supply runs.

This was met by carrier-based fighters, with casualties on both sides. Some attacks got through and caused damage to transport ships not yet unloaded. Soon afterwards, the carrier force had to withdraw for lack of fuel.

An attack by a powerful Japanese cruiser force under Vice-Admiral Gunichi Mikawa (1888–1981) resulted in heavy losses to Allied cruisers off Savo island, and the decision was taken to withdraw the surviving naval vessels from the area. This meant it became necessary to pull the half-unloaded transports out as well – they were too vulnerable to air attack without carrier cover and surface ships without cruisers to protect them.

The forces ashore on Guadalcanal at this point comprised some 11,000 marines, but much of their heavy equipment was still aboard the transports steaming away towards safety. Nevertheless they proceeded with the plan and finished building the airfield the Japanese had started, naming it Henderson Field.

Approaching under cover of bad weather, the assault force went ashore on 7 August 1942. The main objective was the capture of Guadalcanal itself and the airbase there. Other forces were tasked with capturing Tulagi and other smaller islands in the group.

On Guadalcanal itself, things went very well. The terrain, which was mostly jungle, proved more of a problem than enemy resistance for the first day, and by the end of the second the airfield was in Allied hands, along with stores, supplies and construction equipment abandoned there.

Although heavily outnumbered, the Japanese troops on the other islands put up a stiff fight and had to be eliminated almost to a man. This sort of fanatical resistance became familiar as the war went on and resulted in heavy casualties for the Allies, even when dealing with quite small outposts.

Meanwhile, the Allies came under attack from aircraft out of Rabaul on the island of New Britain in New Guinea.

SECURING THE ISLAND

Some Japanese forces had dispersed around the island after the Allied landings, and these were reinforced by a small number landed by destroyer. Patrols and expeditions were launched to locate and remove these holdouts, and though success was mixed the enemy was largely kept away from the airfield, which received its first aircraft – a mix of fighters and dive bombers.

The island was harassed by air attacks more or less constantly, but the Japanese commanders were not satisfied: they wanted the Allies driven off Guadalcanal and the rest of the Solomons, and so planned an

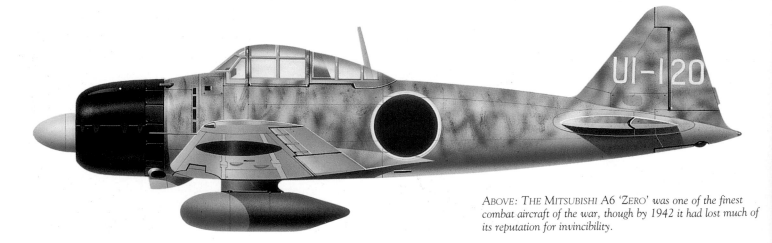

ABOVE: THE MITSUBISHI A6 'ZERO' was one of the finest combat aircraft of the war, though by 1942 it had lost much of its reputation for invincibility.

ABOVE: US MARINE GENERAL VANDERGRIFT and US Navy Admiral Kelly were in command of the land and naval components of the operation respectively. Amphibious operations of this kind required close cooperation between services.

amphibious attack of their own. The task fell to Seventeenth Army, which was already heavily committed to the battles for New Guinea.

Some elements of Seventeenth Army were available for an operation against Guadalcanal but they arrived in piecemeal fashion. The first assault force was a contingent of about 1000 men of the 28th Infantry Regiment under Colonel Kiyonao Ichiki (1892–1942). This inadequate force was landed from destroyers and immediately moved west to engage the defenders.

Although it was outnumbered more than ten to one Ichiki's force attacked towards Henderson Field under cover of darkness. Japanese casualties were extremely high and the attack achieved nothing. A subsequent marine counterattack scattered the survivors after Ichiki himself was killed.

A second force, about 2000 strong, was also on its way and its approach was covered by Japanese naval forces, including three carriers. This resulted in the Battle of the Eastern Solomons as the Allied carrier forces engaged the Japanese fleet. Amid this action, aircraft out of Henderson field attacked the Japanese troop transports and caused heavy casualties. The survivors were eventually landed from destroyers.

During this period, the Allied forces on Guadalcanal were reinforced with additional aircraft, steadily increasing the strength of the island's air group despite losses in combat. Guadalcanal became a big threat to Japanese intentions in the area and both sides knew that a major operation to eliminate Henderson Field and its air group was going to be launched.

General Vandergrift set his marines, now reinforced, to improving their positions. Units were redeployed to create a better overall defence while minor operations were undertaken against the increasing Japanese forces on the island. Dysentery was a serious problem for the garrison, with as much as 20 per cent of the force down at any given time, and the island's terrain also made offensive operations difficult.

THE TOKYO EXPRESS

After losing many transports to air attack, Japanese commanders decided that a traditional amphibious operation was not feasible and instead implemented what became known as the Tokyo Express, whereby destroyers and light cruisers dashed in under cover of night to land relatively small forces and re-supply them.

The Tokyo Express was a clever solution to the problem of getting troops on to Guadalcanal, but it had its limitations. Small warships could not carry heavy equipment or artillery and ships engaged in these operations were not available for war-fighting missions elsewhere. Nevertheless the Tokyo Express ran several thousand Japanese troops into Guadalcanal over the next few weeks until sufficient forces had been built up for an attack.

RIGHT: THE JAPANESE DEPLOYED large numbers of naval infantry personnel to defend the Pacific islands. Marines by any other name, these troops put up a determined fight on Guadalcanal and elsewhere.

THE M3 STUART was too light for anything but reconnaissance duty in the European theatre, but in the Pacific island terrain the light tank really came into its own.

On 31 August, General Kawaguchi arrived to take command of all Japanese forces on Guadalcanal, and on 7 September he gave the order for an assault on Henderson Field. A raid by US Marines hit the supply base of one of these groups the next day, giving an indication that a large force was on the island and an attack was imminent.

JAPANESE ATTACKS

The Japanese plan was to attack at night, in three groups from the east, west and south. However, the Allies were forewarned and had posted troops on a rise to the south of Henderson Field. This later became known as Edson's Ridge after Lieutenant-Colonel Merritt Edson (1897–1955), who led the defence. They were right in the path of the main Japanese force when the attack went in on 12 September.

Fighting on the ridge was heavy and the defenders, who were outnumbered more than three to one, were eventually pushed on to a central high point. There they resisted several assaults, but were unable to prevent other Japanese troops bypassing them. Those who got past Edson's Ridge ran into other defenders, who were able to hold and eventually repel them. Attacks in other sectors were likewise halted. Finally, after two days of intense fighting, the Japanese pulled back to regroup.

Both sides rebuilt their forces and defences as best they could. More Allied troops were brought in, although the sea routes were hotly contested. The US carrier *Wasp* was sunk during this operation. General Vandergrift reorganized his forces and promoted some men, including Edson.

After a period of bad weather, the air battle resumed on 27 September, with even greater intensity as both sides had been reinforced. On the ground, more Japanese troops arrived while US forces tried to drive the scattered survivors of previous attacks away from their defences and prevent the new arrivals from establishing themselves close to the airfield. The result was several clashes in late September and early October which disrupted Japanese offensive preparations.

However, the island's defenders were under pressure from the air and the Japanese buildup was causing concern. Reinforcements were requested and in due course set sail.

The timing was fortuitous. US naval units covering the reinforcement convoy ran into a major Japanese force shipment that included vessels tasked to bombard Henderson Field. In the resulting Battle of Cape Esperance, the US vessels inflicted a heavy defeat on the Japanese navy, though the associated Tokyo Express convoy got through and unloaded on Guadalcanal.

Another bombardment was ordered for 13 October while yet more troops were brought in. This time, the attack included two battleships and did major damage to the airfield, which nevertheless was restored to minimal function in time to launch strikes against the Japanese troop transports.

By the middle of October, the Japanese had brought several thousand troops on to Guadalcanal and had repeatedly shelled the airfield. Ground forces began to move into position for the assault. Some 20,000 Japanese troops were available, the main attack coming in from the south with additional flanking operations. The attack was dislocated by delays in preparation, and communication problems meant that some forces attacked on 23 October and some the day after. The assault was sustained, and in

DESPITE GREAT DETERMINATION, many of the Japanese attacks on US positions were ill-advised given the tactical situation. Heavy casualties were inevitable.

some places the Japanese got through the outer defences despite heavy casualties. A handful of tanks were used but were easily disabled by the defenders.

Although under pressure, the defenders held out on the ground while the air forces fought off air and naval attacks. Repeated frontal charges were cut up by infantry weapons and artillery firing over open sights. Finally, on 26 October, the assault was called off, and the Japanese retreated.

ENDGAME

Land warfare in the Pacific was heavily influenced by the situation at sea. Whichever side had sea control could bring in supplies and reinforcements, tipping the balance of the land engagement. Thus the naval actions off Guadalcanal were vital to the land campaign. Several battles were fought at sea in the vicinity of Guadalcanal, including the Battles of Savo Island and Cape Esperance. On 13 November 1942, a Japanese force attempting to bring reinforcements to the islands and to bombard Henderson Field clashed with US ships in a close-range brawl that cost both sides dearly and left the US Navy very short of ships to defend Guadalcanal when the Japanese Navy came back to try again.

Further Japanese attempts to reinforce their presence on the island were unsuccessful and US forces began taking the offensive, pushing the enemy away from the airfield. Cut off from re-supply and being ground down, the remaining Japanese forces were evacuated in early February, ending the campaign. Guadalcanal was the first clear-cut land victory

over the Japanese and did much to restore Allied confidence. It also deprived the Japanese of an important forward base. The battle had a wider significance too.

After the failure of the first big attack, Japanese commanders realized that the struggle for Guadalcanal was a battle of real strategic significance and gave it great prominence. One consequence of this was that forces advancing on Port Moresby in New Guinea were pulled back and denied reinforcements. Thus the fighting on Guadalcanal indirectly assisted the Allied cause elsewhere.

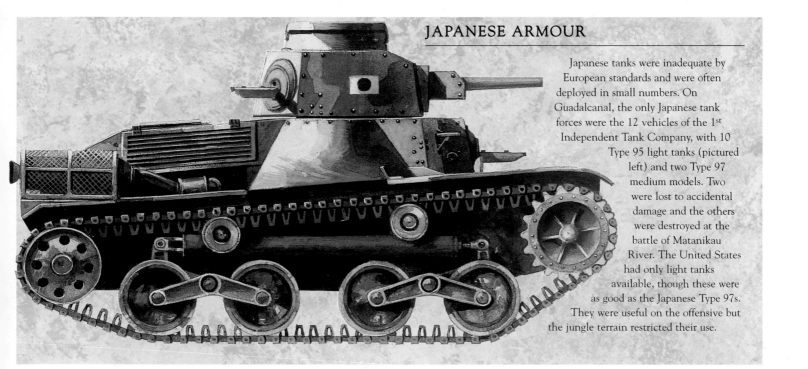

JAPANESE ARMOUR

Japanese tanks were inadequate by European standards and were often deployed in small numbers. On Guadalcanal, the only Japanese tank forces were the 12 vehicles of the 1st Independent Tank Company, with 10 Type 95 light tanks (pictured left) and two Type 97 medium models. Two were lost to accidental damage and the others were destroyed at the battle of Matanikau River. The United States had only light tanks available, though these were as good as the Japanese Type 97s. They were useful on the offensive but the jungle terrain restricted their use.

GUADALCANAL

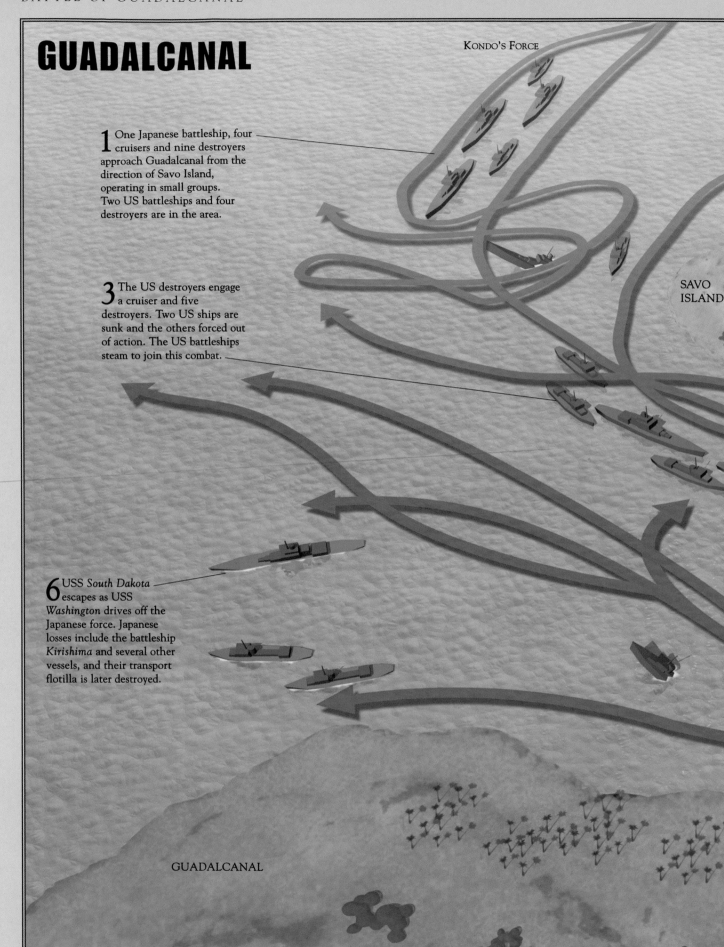

KONDO'S FORCE

1 One Japanese battleship, four cruisers and nine destroyers approach Guadalcanal from the direction of Savo Island, operating in small groups. Two US battleships and four destroyers are in the area.

3 The US destroyers engage a cruiser and five destroyers. Two US ships are sunk and the others forced out of action. The US battleships steam to join this combat.

SAVO ISLAND

6 USS *South Dakota* escapes as USS *Washington* drives off the Japanese force. Japanese losses include the battleship *Kirishima* and several other vessels, and their transport flotilla is later destroyed.

GUADALCANAL

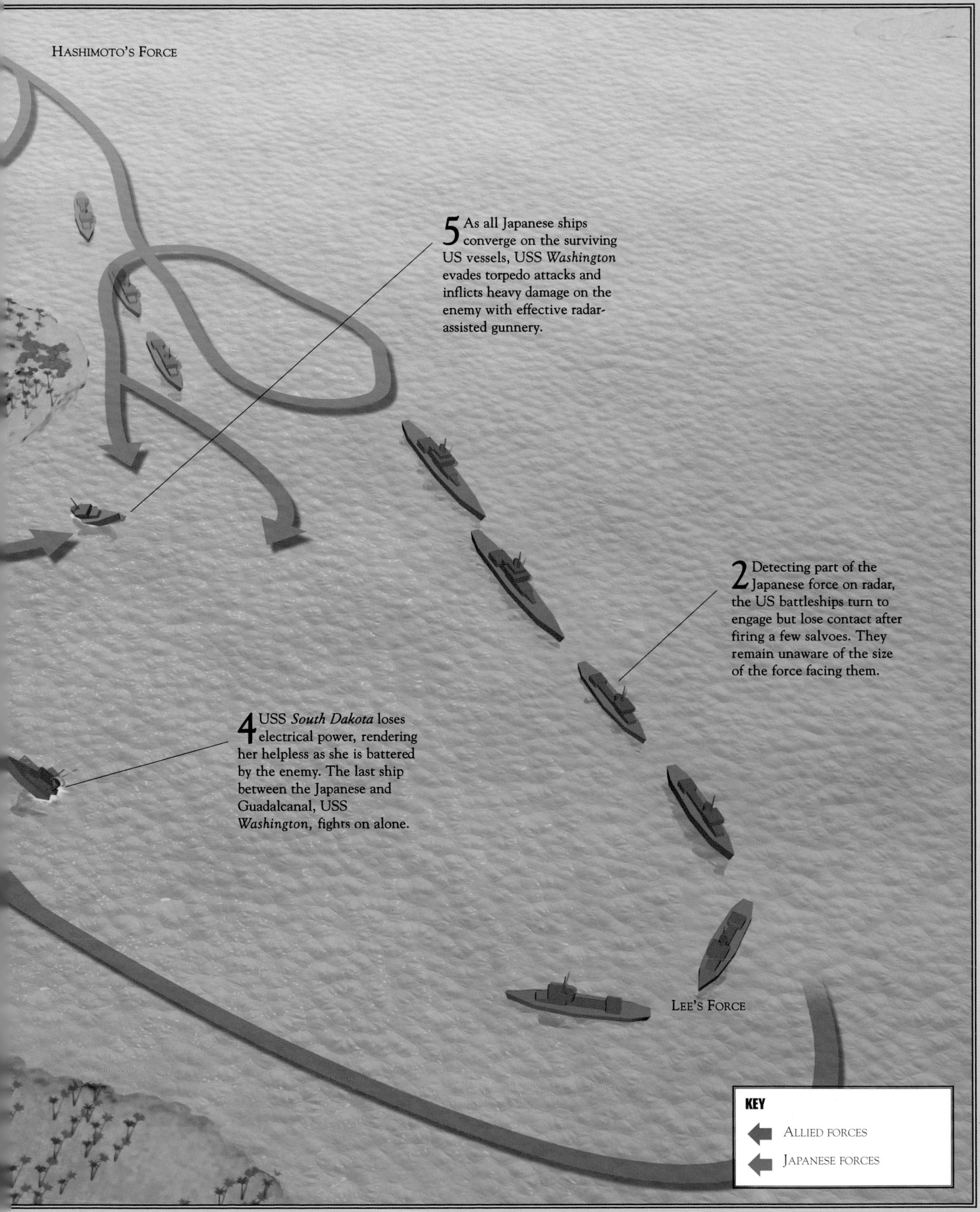

HASHIMOTO'S FORCE

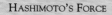

5 As all Japanese ships converge on the surviving US vessels, USS *Washington* evades torpedo attacks and inflicts heavy damage on the enemy with effective radar-assisted gunnery.

2 Detecting part of the Japanese force on radar, the US battleships turn to engage but lose contact after firing a few salvoes. They remain unaware of the size of the force facing them.

4 USS *South Dakota* loses electrical power, rendering her helpless as she is battered by the enemy. The last ship between the Japanese and Guadalcanal, USS *Washington*, fights on alone.

LEE'S FORCE

KEY

◄ ALLIED FORCES

◄ JAPANESE FORCES

STALINGRAD 1942–43

Stalingrad changed the face of World War II. In a cataclysmic struggle, the Wehrmacht experienced its first major army-sized defeat and the strategic advantage on the Eastern Front began to shift to the Red Army.

As the crushing Russian winter of 1941–42 ran its course, Adolf Hitler was faced with a critical strategic decision. His *Barbarossa* campaign to smash the Soviet Union, which began in June 1941, had stalled before Moscow and was even put into temporary retreat by a Soviet counteroffensive on 5–6 December. Only the late spring would return the *Wehrmacht* to mobility and Hitler decided to apply this mobility in a new direction. Instead of renewing the Moscow offensive, much as the Soviets expected, Hitler ordered Operation *Blue* – a massive offensive by his Army Group South through the Ukraine and into the Crimea towards the Caucasus. The ultimate objective was to capture the Soviet oilfields of the Caucasus, oilfields upon which Germany relied to power its war machine.

STALINGRAD FACTS

Who: The German Sixth Army under General Friedrich Paulus (1890–1957), along with elements of the Fourth Panzer Army under General Hermann Hoth (1885–1971), versus the Red Army's Stalingrad Front, principally the Sixty-Second Army under Major-General Vasily Chuikov (1900–1982).

What: German forces nearly succeeded in conquering Stalingrad, but with massive losses. A Soviet counteroffensive trapped 250,000 Germans within the city. About 100,000 of these men were killed and 110,000 went to almost certain death in Soviet captivity.

Where: The city of Stalingrad, set on the Volga river.

When: 14 September 1942 to 2 February 1943

Why: The Stalingrad battle was part of a German campaign to occupy the Soviet Union's southern oilfields in the Caucasus. Stalingrad needed securing to protect the German left flank.

Outcome: Stalingrad marked the beginning of the German defeat on the Eastern Front, with the Red Army maintaining an offensive drive for the rest of the war.

AMIDST THE DEVASTATION OF STALINGRAD, *a heavily armed German platoon prepares to make yet another assault on Soviet positions.*

A TWO-MAN GERMAN MG34 machine-gun team occupies a shell-hole in the ruined Stalingrad suburbs, September 1942.

Operation *Blue* began on 28 June, consisting of 1.3 million men (including 300,000 German allies, principally Romanians and Italians) and 1500 aircraft. Army Group South was divided into Army Groups A and B, and the plan was for both groups to converge on the city of Stalingrad on the banks of the Volga, at which point Army Group B would remain on the Don and Volga rivers to provide flank protection for Army Group A's assault into the Caucasus. As with the *Wehrmacht* operations of the previous spring/summer, the Germans made good headway, and by mid-July the Sixth Army under General Friedrich Paulus (1890–1957) – the main component of Army Group B – was closing in on Stalingrad.

On 23 July, Hitler gave the order to take the city itself. General Hermann Hoth's (1885–1971) Fourth Panzer Army was deployed south of Stalingrad to assist in the assault. On the same day, Stalin issued his own directive stating that Stalingrad

RIGHT: GENERAL VASILY CHUIKOV, commander of the Soviet Sixty-Second Army, seen here (centre) in his command post at Stalingrad.

RIGHT: GENERAL VASILY CHUIKOV, commander of the Soviet Sixty-Second Army, seen here (centre) in his command post at Stalingrad.

would be defended to the last. Soviet forces in the newly designated Stalingrad Front consisted of the Sixty-Second, Sixty-Third and Sixty-Fourth Armies. Although Stalingrad was an important industrial centre, the fact that it bore Stalin's name gave the Soviet leader a definite psychological imperative to see that it did not fall.

STREET BATTLE

The prelude to fighting within the city was a heavy air bombardment by *Luftlotte* 4, which reduced much of the city to rubble and killed more than 30,000 people. By 12 September, German troops were already pushing into the city's suburbs, where they faced a defence of almost psychotic vigour from the troops of Chuikov's Sixty-Second Army within the city. Chuikov, a rough-edged commander in contrast to the urbane Paulus, had a numerical disadvantage within the city compared to the Germans (roughly 54,000 Soviets to 100,000 Germans).

Yet the battle for Stalingrad was to be pure street fighting, a form of warfare depriving the Germans of the mobility that was their accustomed route to success in battle. Moreover, Chuikov deliberately pushed his troops into extreme close-quarters battle, ordering them to 'hug' the German troops and thus limit enemy use of air bombardment and heavy artillery fire, both of which would

risk the danger of 'friendly fire' casualties. The effect was that every building, and every room in every building, became a battleground, the Germans paying for each yard with blood.

By the end of September, Paulus and Hoth had taken around two-thirds of Stalingrad. An offensive launched on 14 September by LI Corps penetrated deep inside the city, taking the Mamayev Kurgan heights (a salient feature of the

BELOW: ALL AVAILABLE SOVIET personnel were used in the defence of Stalingrad – this group includes sailors and civilians.

ABOVE: TROOPS AND ARMOUR of the Soviet Twenty-First Army advance during Operation Uranus, the two-pronged offensive designed to trap German forces in Stalingrad.

minute reinforcements from Major-General Aleksandr Rodimtsev's (1905–1977) 13th Guards Division meant that the station changed hands 15 times before it finally fell to the Germans. Hoth's Fourth Panzers coming up from the south had a similar harrowing experience but made better progress, reaching the river by 13 October.

Between mid-October and mid-November, the Germans slowly squeezed the Soviets back, battling through the factory district at appalling cost (major battlegrounds were the Barrikady, Krasny Oktyabr and Tractor factories). Stalingrad was by now utterly destroyed, but the rubble created by German firepower actually made a convoluted landscape that was easier to defend and harder to attack. By 18 November, the Soviets held only a thin broken strip of territory on the Volga, little more than 10 per cent of the city. Winter was beginning, however, and the Germans were shattered and depleted from the last weeks of fighting.

city) and driving through towards the No 1 Railway station. The aim was to reach the Volga and destroy the Soviet landing stages, which were receiving resupply and reinforcements boated across the river (a harrowing experience for boat crews and passengers, who were bombed remorselessly by German attack aircraft). However, last-

BELOW: THE ITALIAN EIGHTH ARMY begins its long retreat from positions on the left flank of the German Sixth Army, December 1942.

THE SOVIET OFFENSIVE

On 19 November, Soviet forces around Stalingrad played their masterstroke, a counteroffensive planned by General Georgy Zhukov (1896–1974). North of Stalingrad, the Soviet Southwest Front and Don Front launched a six-army push southwards across the Don, smashing weak Romanian resistance. The next day, the Stalingrad Front attacked north from positions south of Stalingrad, once again overcoming weak German flank protection. On 23 November, the two

A YAK 1B of the 37th Guards IAP. The Soviets had a total of about 1400 aircraft at Stalingrad, flying about 500 sorties a day.

'pincers' met behind Stalingrad, trapping the Sixth Army and much of the Fourth Army – more than 250,000 men – within the city. A German disaster was unfolding.

In the early days of the offensive, a German breakout was possible but it was refused by Hitler. Instead, he opted for one of Hermann Göring's wildly optimistic aerial resupply plans, which was never realistic, and then for a relief offensive by Manstein's Eleventh Army. This offensive – Operation *Winter Storm* – was launched on 12 December and made some progress but was eventually battered to a standstill 48km (30 miles) from Stalingrad. Two weeks later, Manstein's forces were in retreat from fresh Soviet offensives, leaving the German soldiers in Stalingrad to a ghastly fate.

Horrific fighting continued in Stalingrad for over a month as the Soviets steadily crushed the German occupiers. Although 34,000 Germans were evacuated by air before the final airfield fell on 25 January, more than 100,000 *Wehrmacht* troops were killed in this period. Finally, between 31 January and 2 February, Paulus and some 110,000 German survivors surrendered, destined for Soviet labour camps from which only 5000 men would emerge alive.

THE BEGINNING OF THE END

The German defeat at Stalingrad tilted the balance of the war both strategically and psychologically. Strategically, it put paid to Operation *Blue* and began, in effect, the German retreat that would end in Berlin in 1945. Psychologically it gave the Soviets an enormous boost of confidence and showed that they could compete with the Germans on both tactical and strategic levels. For the Germans, it was an undeniable sign that they could be defeated – the glory days of 1939–40 were now forgotten.

FIELD-MARSHAL FRIEDRICH PAULUS

Friedrich Paulus (1890–1957) cut his military teeth as an army captain during World War I and showed the ability and ambition that enabled him to rise to the rank of general by 1939. He subsequently served as deputy to General Franz Halder, the German Chief of Staff, before taking his most infamous command, that of the Sixth Army, in 1941. Paulus was an urbane 'old school' officer whose loyalty to the military led him, initially, to obey Hitler's ludicrous 'to the last man' defence orders at Stalingrad. On 31 January 1942, Hitler made Paulus a field-marshal, knowing that no field-marshal in German history had ever surrendered or been captured alive. (Hitler was in effect requesting his suicide.) At this point, however, Paulus chose to ignore the precedent and surrendered, going on to be a vocal critic of the Nazi regime while in captivity. His last career posting was as an adviser to the East German Army in the mid-1950s.

FIELD-MARSHAL PAULUS (left) and his chief-of-staff Arthur Schmidt (right) seen after their surrender in early 1943.

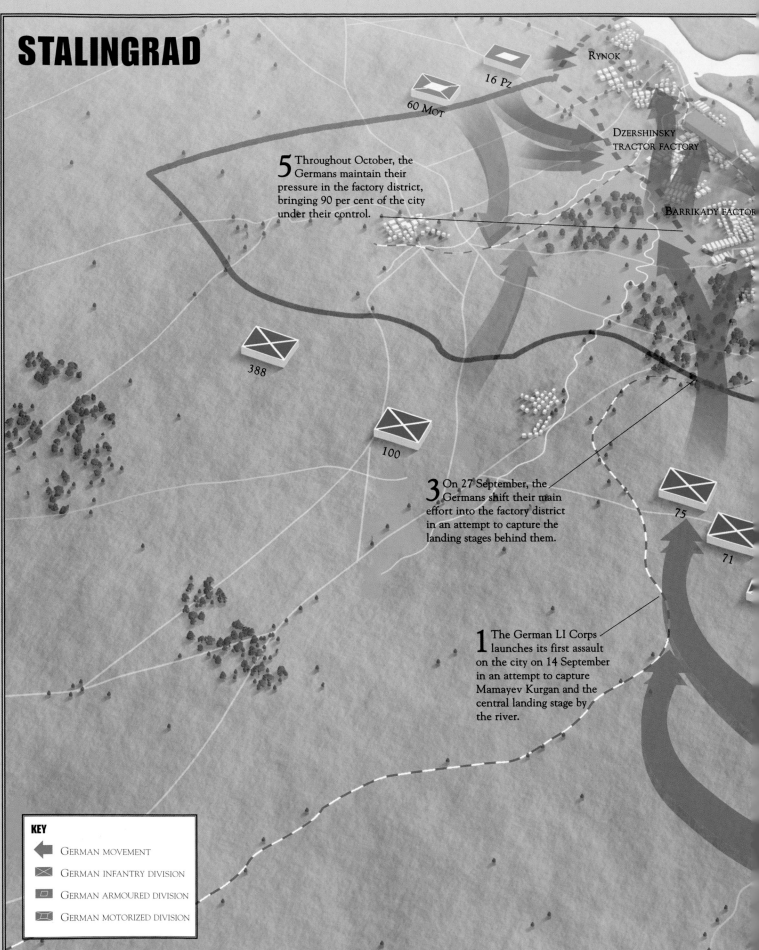

STALINGRAD

RYNOK

16 PZ

60 MOT

DZERSHINSKY
TRACTOR FACTORY

BARRIKADY FACTORY

5 Throughout October, the Germans maintain their pressure in the factory district, bringing 90 per cent of the city under their control.

388

100

3 On 27 September, the Germans shift their main effort into the factory district in an attempt to capture the landing stages behind them.

75

71

1 The German LI Corps launches its first assault on the city on 14 September in an attempt to capture Mamayev Kurgan and the central landing stage by the river.

KEY

⬅ GERMAN MOVEMENT

✉ GERMAN INFANTRY DIVISION

▭ GERMAN ARMOURED DIVISION

▭ GERMAN MOTORIZED DIVISION

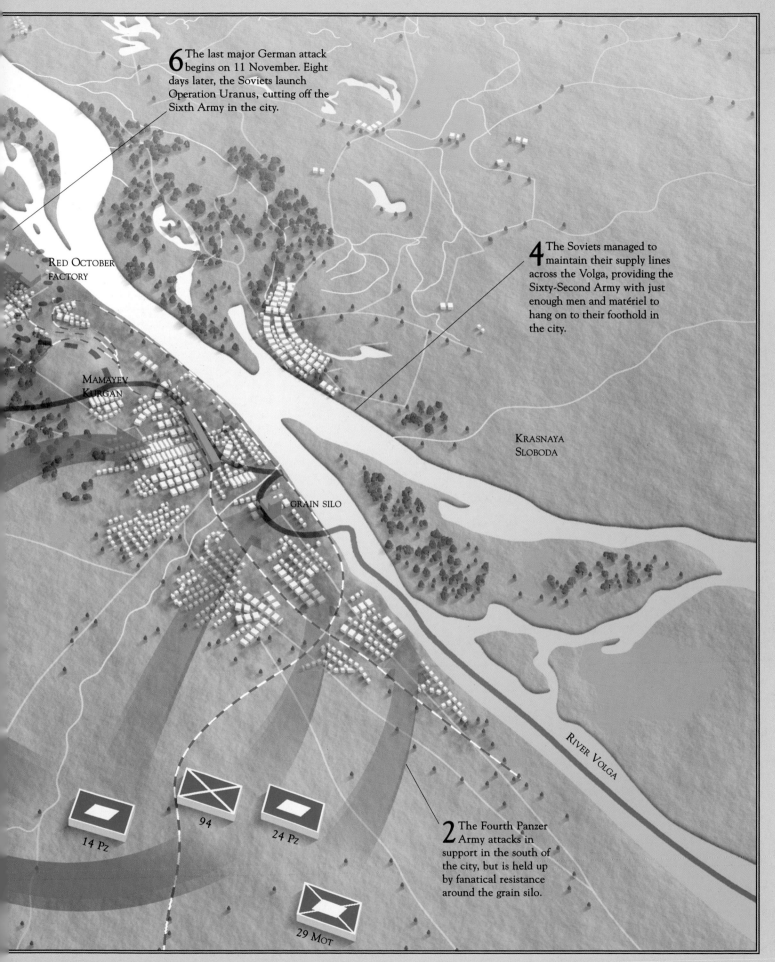

6 The last major German attack begins on 11 November. Eight days later, the Soviets launch Operation Uranus, cutting off the Sixth Army in the city.

4 The Soviets managed to maintain their supply lines across the Volga, providing the Sixty-Second Army with just enough men and matériel to hang on to their foothold in the city.

RED OCTOBER FACTORY

MAMAYEV KURGAN

GRAIN SILO

KRASNAYA SLOBODA

RIVER VOLGA

94

14 PZ

24 PZ

29 MOT

2 The Fourth Panzer Army attacks in support in the south of the city, but is held up by fanatical resistance around the grain silo.

THIRD BATTLE OF KHARKOV 1943

The Third Battle of Kharkov is generally considered to be the last German victory on the Eastern Front. It stands as a classic example of armoured manoeuvre tactics executed under difficult conditions against a well-prepared and numerically superior enemy.

When Hitler ordered the invasion of the Soviet Union in 1941, he did not envisage a long war. There was a time when a knockout blow might have been achieved, but the Soviets averted defeat long enough for the weather to close in. This granted some time to prepare and allowed renewed German offensives to be halted.

The German army tried again in 1942 and then 1943, but decisive victory proved elusive and all the time Soviet strength was increasing. The odds became

THIRD BATTLE OF KHARKOV FACTS

Who: 160,000 German troops led by Field Marshal Erich von Manstein (1887–1973) versus approximately 300,000 Soviet troops of the Bryansk, Volkhov and South Western Fronts led by generals Golikov and Vatutin (1901–1944).

What: Committed to the operation by the Red Army were the Bryansk, Voronezh and the South Western Fronts. These included the Fortieth, Sixty-Ninth and Third Tank armies. The Germans' counteroffensive was led by the Fourth Panzer Army and included the II SS Panzer Corps, comprising the *Leibstandarte Adolf Hitler* and *Das Reich* divisions.

Where: The city of Kharkov in the Ukraine.

When: February–March 1943

Why: The city was important politically and as a transport nexus.

Outcome: The city was captured by the Germans but was lost again in August to a Soviet offensive.

PANZERGRENADIERS OF THE SS DIVISION Das Reich *ride into Kharkov on the engine deck of a Panzer III. Early 1943 was the last period in which the war on the Eastern Front was winnable for Germany.*

slimmer each year, but there was no choice: Germany had to attack and defeat the enemy its leader had chosen.

By the beginning of 1943, the tide was turning against Germany. Defeats in North Africa had dealt a serious blow to German prestige. Her allies were reconsidering their position and there seemed little prospect of persuading others – such as Turkey – to join the fight. Meanwhile at home there were economic problems and social unrest.

SOVIET SUCCESSES

The fall of Stalingrad after months of bitter fighting was a serious blow to German morale and prestige while their opponents were riding a wave of success. The Red Army began advancing, urged on by a jubilant Stalin, who believed that he could sweep the invaders out of Russia with a headlong offensive. Leningrad was relieved and the threat to Moscow greatly diminished. In the south, Soviet troops were making gains against the tired and depleted Germans.

There was a danger that the German Army Group South might be cut off and forced to surrender and matters were not helped by a catastrophic defeat in Stalingrad. However, the German commander Field-Marshal Von Manstein (1887–1973) ignored his orders to die in place and organized a fighting retreat that not only got his army out

T-34 TANKS IN *Dzerzhinsky Square, Kharkov. After the fall of Stalingrad, it seemed that the Germans could be swiftly pushed out of Soviet Russia, but their recapture of Kharkov challenged that assumption.*

of the trap in condition to fight on but also bought time for reinforcements to arrive.

The Soviets were running ahead of their logistics capability and beginning to falter, but were forced to push on by Stalin's urgings. The Soviet high command did not believe that the battered German army could do anything but retreat westwards, putting up local resistance. A counterattack was obviously out of the question.

REINFORCEMENTS ARRIVE

In fact, the German army did possess the capability to counterattack. Reinforcements had begun to arrive. In some cases, these were damaged units pushed back into the line after receiving some replacement personnel and equipment and were in little better shape than the line formations. However, some very powerful units were placed at Manstein's disposal.

Most significantly Manstein was given control of I SS Panzer Corps. This comprised the SS *Totenkopf*, *Liebstandarte* and *Das Reich* divisions, all of which had been

THESE WAFFEN-SS SOLDIERS show the benefits of their period of rest and refitting. Their good morale and better supply situation enabled them to defeat a larger number of Soviet troops in the battle for Kharkov.

refitting and were well rested. More importantly perhaps, they were equipped with the new Panzer VI Tiger tank armed with a formidable 88mm (3.46in) gun. Much of the divisions' tank strength was made up of lesser vehicles but the Tigers made a potent spearhead.

The first arrivals were formed into a battle group and pushed into the line to halt the Soviet advance. Remnants of German and Italian units retreated past them, but despite heavy Soviet attacks the battle group was able more or less to hold its positions. A period of repositioning then followed as the German army tried to establish defences that would prevent the strategic city of Kharkov being encircled.

Although the Soviets were suffering severe ammunition shortages and were becoming disorganized, they pushed forward faster than expected. It became obvious that an attack on Kharkov could not be prevented by defensive measures. The SS troops were ordered to attack.

The Soviet advance on Kharkov took the form of a pincer movement, in which the southern arm was much more powerful. The advancing Soviets were hit from the flank with armoured units and dive-bombers savaging their rear echelon support units before falling on the disorganized combat formations.

The attack was a success and halted the advance for a time. However, the Soviets were still able to drive forwards and despite inflicting heavy casualties the SS troops were pushed back. Again the German force was threatened with encirclement. The SS commander Paul Hausser (1880–1972) asked for permission to retreat.

Although Hitler himself refused permission to retreat and commanded the SS troops to hold at all costs, Hausser decided to ignore this order. He launched a local counter-

T-34/76: THE GREATEST TANK OF WORLD WAR II?

The T-34 was among the most important weapons systems in the Red Army in World War II. At the time it was first fielded in 1940, it was easily the finest tank design in the world. Individually, T-34s were workmanlike rather than excellent combat vehicles. They were well protected, mobile, and possessed a good gun that could knock out enemy tanks at a respectable range. However, they were also prone to mechanical problems, especially with the transmission.

One for one, German tanks were generally better, but the phrase 'all things being equal' never applies in warfare. Tanks did not fight one on one but as part of a military/technical/industrial partnership in which the fighting capabilities of the vehicle were only one aspect. The ability to repair or replace breakdowns and get tanks back into the fight was also critical, as was the capacity to manufacture them in large enough numbers to make a difference. It was in this context that the T-34 was a world-beater.

attack with tanks to blunt the Soviet offensive and pulled his force back on 15 February. Disregarding renewed orders to stand his ground, Hausser was able to bring his force out in reasonably good order despite large Soviet forces entering the city.

Hitler was enraged and ordered Manstein to use Hausser's command as the spearhead of an attack to retake the city of Kharkov. This suited Manstein. A deep salient had appeared in the battle front where the Soviets had pushed forwards. This created an ideal opportunity for a double envelopment against the shoulders of the salient, pincering off and encircling the advancing Soviets for destruction.

Plans were made while the SS troops reorganized themselves, amalgamating their depleted tanks and other assets into scratch battalions. This method of creating effective battle groups from the remains of heavily damaged units was a hallmark of the German forces during World War II and allowed the shrinking formations to go on fighting long after the individual units they were created from had ceased to be useful.

ABOVE: A MACHINE-GUN TEAM of the SS Division Liebstandarte. In close-quarters urban fighting, the observer's submachinegun and grenade might prove more useful than the support weapon.

MANSTEIN'S COUNTERATTACK

Manstein's counterattack went in on 19 February 1943. The SS formations spearheaded the northern half of the pincer attack while regular Panzer units led the southern arm. Despite minefields and foul weather that included both snow and fog, the SS troops advanced to contact and hit the enemy flank. Early successes included cutting the main road link to the River Dnieper, hampering Soviet movements.

Renewing the advance, the SS force fought several small but sharp encounter battles with Soviet units moving up to the front, capturing the town of Pavlograd on 24 February.

Elsewhere, the flanking movements had thrown the Soviets into confusion and their advance to the Dnieper was brought to a halt then pushed back. The way to Kharkov was now open and the Das Reich division led the way

ABOVE: GENERAL PAUL HAUSSER defied Hitler's orders to fight to the last and instead pulled his troops out of a bad position, creating the opportunity for a successful counterattack.

towards the city. The Soviet high command issued 'hold at all costs' orders. Reinforcements were rushed into Kharkov and attacks made elsewhere to try to divert German resources. This measure failed. The strategic rail junctions at Lasovaya were taken by the *Das Reich* and *Totenkopf* divisions.

Still Soviet reinforcements continued to arrive. The Third Tank Army (equivalent to a Panzer corps) managed to get between the *Das Reich* and *Liebstandarte* divisions. This was a perilous situation – or a great opportunity to smash it from both sides, depending on your viewpoint.

Hausser took the latter view and launched an attack that became a three-day slogging match. Despite appalling weather, the landscape rapidly turning into a sea of mud and critical supply shortages, the SS troops gradually came out on top. By the time it was over, three Soviet tank brigades, three infantry divisions and an entire corps of cavalry were shattered or captured.

Under this punishing onslaught, the Soviet forces pulled back in some areas, and on 11 March a battle group of SS troops established itself within the city limits. On 12 March, the battle for the city began. Despite extremely stubborn resistance, notably around the railway station and the industrial district, the Soviets were gradually pushed out of the city.

By now, the Soviets were in a state of confusion and thoroughly demoralized. Driving ever eastwards, the SS divisions, though heavily depleted, smashed up two Guards Tank Corps and four infantry divisions. The last organized resistance was around a tractor factory outside the city. Once this was taken, Kharkov was firmly in German hands.

Subsequent operations cleared Soviet forces out of the immediate area and stabilized the front before the spring

BELOW: COSSACK CAVALRY WERE more often used for scouting operations, but if they achieved surprise and got in among enemy infantry, their sabres and pistols were highly effective.

RIGHT: AN NCO OF THE SS DAS REICH division bundled up warmly against the cold. Heavy gloves could interfere with operating a weapon, so some troops sawed the trigger guard off.

thaw turned everything to mud and brought a halt to offensive operations on both sides.

AFTERMATH

Hitler remained angry at Hausser for ignoring his orders and refused to decorate him even though his troops had performed brilliantly in the battle for the city. His command did receive considerable replacements and much of its artillery was upgraded to self-propelled guns. The formation was re-designated II SS Panzer Corps.

In the wake of the victory at Kharkov, plans were formulated to launch a new offensive in the summer. Codenamed Operation *Citadel*, it would smash the Soviet forces facing Army Group South and tip the balance of the war back in the direction of Germany – if it succeeded. The stage was thus set for the Battle of Kursk; the greatest armoured clash of all time.

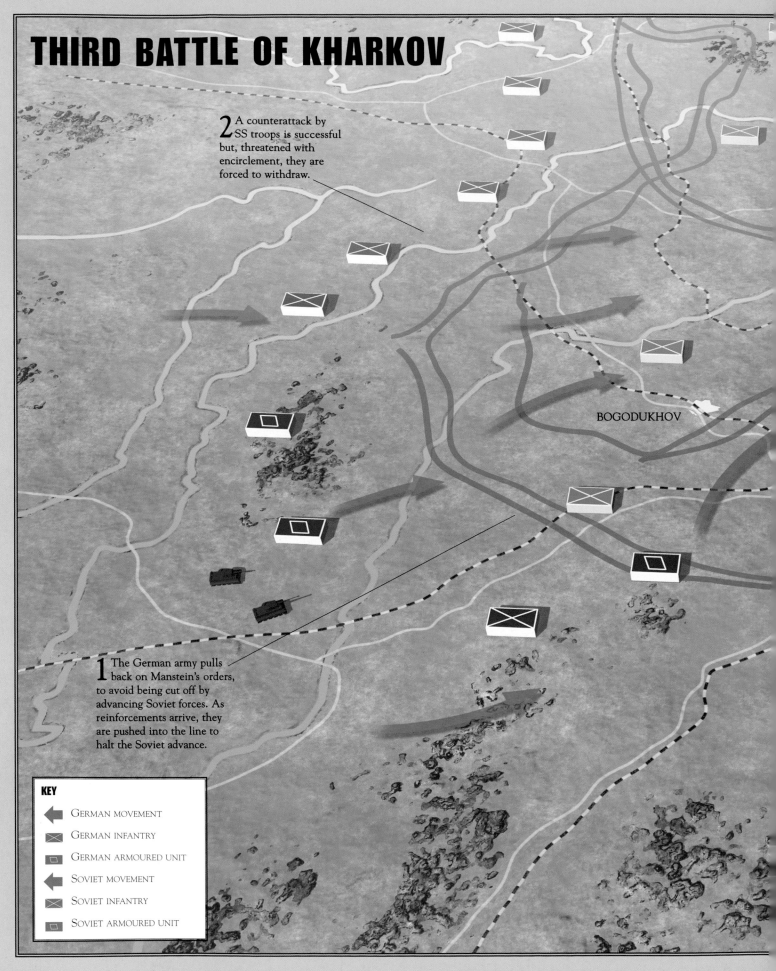

THIRD BATTLE OF KHARKOV

2 A counterattack by SS troops is successful but, threatened with encirclement, they are forced to withdraw.

BOGODUKHOV

1 The German army pulls back on Manstein's orders, to avoid being cut off by advancing Soviet forces. As reinforcements arrive, they are pushed into the line to halt the Soviet advance.

KEY

← GERMAN MOVEMENT

⊠ GERMAN INFANTRY

▱ GERMAN ARMOURED UNIT

← SOVIET MOVEMENT

⊠ SOVIET INFANTRY

▱ SOVIET ARMOURED UNIT

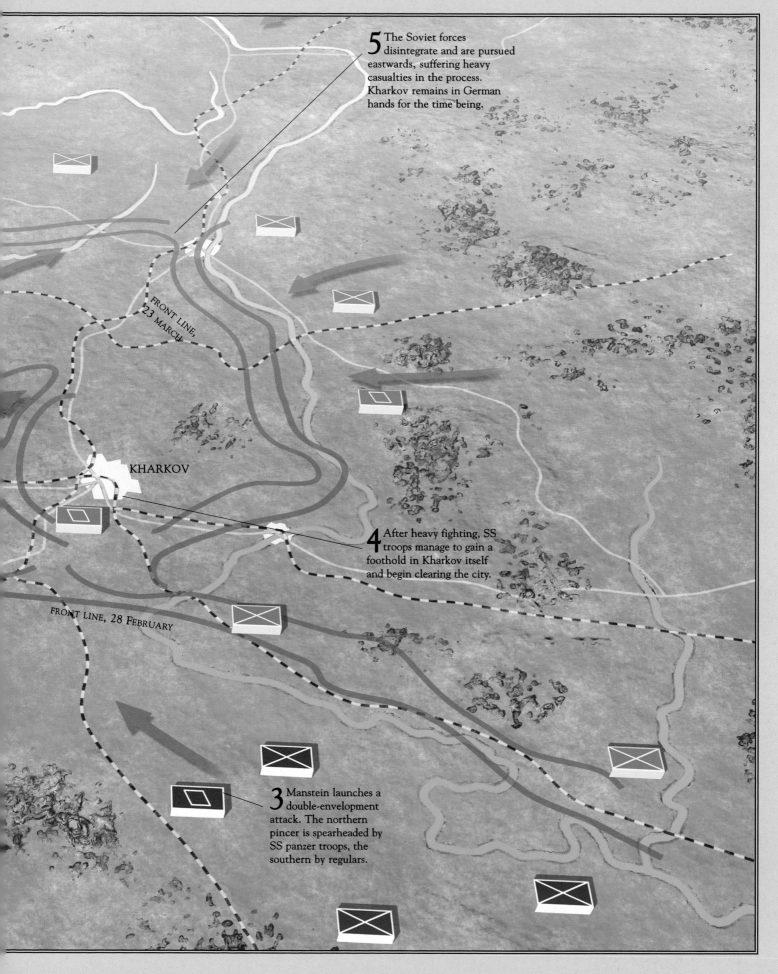

5 The Soviet forces disintegrate and are pursued eastwards, suffering heavy casualties in the process. Kharkov remains in German hands for the time being.

FRONT LINE, 23 MARCH,

KHARKOV

4 After heavy fighting, SS troops manage to gain a foothold in Kharkov itself and begin clearing the city.

FRONT LINE, 28 FEBRUARY

3 Manstein launches a double-envelopment attack. The northern pincer is spearheaded by SS panzer troops, the southern by regulars.

KURSK

The July 1943 Battle of Kursk was the greatest clash of armoured forces yet seen in warfare. The origins of this German offensive – Operation Citadel – lay in the disastrous start to 1943, when Soviet counterattacks not only destroyed the Sixth Army in Stalingrad but also imperilled Field-Marshal Erich von Manstein's Army Group Don.

However, between 18 February and 18 March von Manstein's effective counteroffensive destroyed the Soviet spearheads and subsequently a pause descended over the Eastern Front as the exhausted combatants rebuilt their shattered forces for the looming summer campaign. These battles left a large Soviet-held salient jutting west into the German lines around Kursk. Hitler ordered his forces to launch a double-pincer attack across the base of this salient to surround and destroy the sizable Soviet force trapped within. Such an offensive would accomplish this encirclement within a restricted geographical area, a sensible plan that reflected the *Wehrmacht*'s dwindling operational mobility. For

KURSK FACTS

Who: Elements of Field Marshal Günther von Kluge's (1882–1944) Army Group Centre and Field Marshal Erich von Manstein's (1887–1973) Army Group South faced Marshal Konstantin Rokossovsky's (1896–1968) Central Front and Marshal Nikolai Vatutin's (1901–1944) Voronezh Front under the direction of Supreme Commander-in-Chief Marshal Georgi Zhukov (1896–1974).

What: The German strategic offensive of 1943, aimed at eliminating the Soviet salient centred around Kursk.

Where: The area around Kursk in the Ukraine, an important rail junction 800km (497 miles) south of Moscow.

When: 4 to 13 July 1943

Why: Only having resources for a limited offensive in the east and needing a victory to reassure wavering allies, the Kursk salient provided the Germans with an apparently manageable strategic objective.

Outcome: The German offensive failed and the Soviet counterattack provided a launching point for further Soviet operations in 1943. The strategic balance in the East had shifted in favour of the Soviets for good.

A RARE PHOTOGRAPH of a Churchill tank from Fifth Guards Army, a unit equipped with a number of Lend-Lease vehicles from the Western Allies. It is passing a knocked-out German Sd Kfz 232.

ABOVE: A HEAVY PANZER BATTALION, equipped with Tiger Mark Is, deploys prior to the Battle of Kursk. Much hope was placed by the Germans on their new generation of armour.

Citadel, therefore, the Germans achieved a massive concentration of force by assembling 17 panzer/panzergrenadier divisions across a total attack frontage of just 164km (102 miles).

BELOW: FIELD MARSHAL MODEL (centre, with goggles on cap) addresses some of his soldiers in the build-up to the battle of Kursk.

DELAYS AND POSTPONEMENTS

The Germans set Citadel to begin in early May, but Hitler repeatedly postponed the offensive so that small numbers of Germany's latest weapons could reach the front. Hitler believed that with these 340 new 'war-winning' weapons – 250 Panther medium and 90 Tiger heavy tanks – the massive German forces committed to Citadel could smash any resistance the Soviets offered, however powerful. Yet the Germans proved unable to exploit their concentration of

PANZER V 'PANTHER' TANK

The Panther was built as a direct response to encountering the Soviet T-34 during 1941. The T-34 outclassed the current generation of German tanks and thus a counter was required. The MAN-produced Panther owed its sloping armour to the Soviet design, but maintained the German tradition of superbly designed, expensive and complex engineering. Its high velocity 75mm (2.95in) gun had excellent armour-piercing capabilities and proved very well protected.

A prototype was ready by September 1942 and the first production models by December. It was deployed for the first time at Kursk, although these early models were plagued with automotive problems.

force. The obvious German preparations for *Citadel* cast aside any element of surprise while Hitler's repeated postponements gave the Soviets sufficient time to construct the most powerful defensive system yet seen in the war. The Germans remained partially ignorant of the strength of these Soviet defences, thanks to the latter's skill at concealment and deception. Either that or they dismissed this strength; all it would mean was a bigger 'prize' when the German offensive successfully encircled the salient. Indeed, when *Citadel*

commenced on 4/5 July the Germans were outnumbered by the Soviets – astonishing given that the offensive was of the Germans' choosing in timing, location and method.

PINCER MOVEMENT

The Germans deployed two main groupings for *Citadel*: in the north, elements of Field-Marshal Günther von Kluge's (1882–1944) Army Group Centre; and in the south, forces from von Manstein's Army Group South. In the north,

SOVIET INFANTRYMEN deploy their 14.5mm (0.57in) Simov PTRS Rifle. By 1943, the antitank rifle was obsolescent and would struggle to pierce German armour from most angles, but it remained in service due to lack of anything else.

LEFT: A GROSSDEUTSCHLAND NCO in his black Panzerwaffe overalls. Grossdeutschland was one of the most elite, lavishly equipped German formations and was expanded to divisional status in time for Kursk.

General Walter Model's (1891–1945) Ninth Army had at its disposal six panzer/panzergrenadier and 14 infantry divisions. In the south, Colonel-General Hermann Hoth's (1885–1971) Fourth Panzer Army and General Franz Kempf's (1886–1964) Army Detachment put into the field 11 panzer/panzergrenadier and 10 infantry divisions. The offensive commenced on 4 July, when von Manstein's forces initiated preliminary attacks from the salient's southern shoulder. At dawn the next day, 10 of Model's divisions assaulted the first Soviet defence line. By evening Model's forces had only managed painfully slow advances – at most, 10km (six miles) along a front some 40km (25 miles) long.

Meanwhile that same day, Hoth and Kempf's forces initiated their main assaults along the southern shoulder. By dusk, Hoth's forces had advanced only 10km (six miles) south to penetrate the first Soviet defensive line. Further east, Kempf's forces failed even to smash through the first Soviet defensive line. During the next day, Model's forces in the north attacked the Soviet second defence line, aiming to capture the Olkhovtka Ridge, from where they could surge through the open plain to the south. Though the repeated German attacks made some progress, intense Soviet counterattacks prevented the capture of Ponyri.

Between 7 and 9 July, both sides threw in their reserves as Model repeatedly attempted to capture this village in the face of fanatical resistance that included powerful counterattacks. Finally, between 10 and 11 July, these Soviet counterattacks halted Model's advance. The northern German thrust had proven a dismal failure: despite a week of intense and costly attacks, it had managed to advance just 15km (9 miles).

ABOVE: MARSHAL KONSTANTIN ROKOSSOVSKY was one of the new breed of successful Soviet commanders coming to the fore after the disasters of 1941–42. He commanded the Central Front at Kursk.

In the south, on 6 July, Hoth's XXXXVIII Panzer Corps pushed north towards the second Soviet defence line near Oboyan despite counterattacks by fresh Soviet armoured reserves. Further east, II SS Panzer Corps drove the defenders north towards the village of Prokhorovka. Over the next four days, these two panzer corps inched their way north towards Oboyan and Prokhorovka in the face of bitter Soviet resistance sustained by freshly arrived reserves. Between 10 and 11 July, German forces successfully pierced the third Soviet defensive line in an attempt to outflank the Soviet units located further west around Oboyan. Sensing the danger in this success, the Soviets redeployed the Fifth Guards Tank Army to the area north of Prokhorovka.

THE GREATEST TANK BATTLE

On 12 July, the climax to *Citadel* occurred – the titanic clash of armour at Prokhorovka, into which the Soviets committed Fifth Guards Tank Army. With 800 Soviet tanks engaging 600 panzers, this action was the largest armoured battle of the war. For eight hours, the battle raged back and forth with the tanks throwing up vast clouds of dust that limited visibility to just a few yards.

The Soviets exploited these conditions, closing the range so that the Germans could not benefit from their lethal long-range guns. Tactically the battle was a draw, but strategically it was a German disaster: the Germans spent their armoured strength – whereas sizable Soviet armoured reserves remained available – and lost the initiative to the Red Army, an opportunity the latter then ruthlessly exploited.

Prokhorovka convinced Hitler that *Citadel* could not succeed and on 13 July he cancelled the offensive. Between 15 and 25 July, the German assault forces conducted a slow fighting withdrawal back to their starting positions in the face of ferocious Soviet attacks. On 12 July, moreover, the Soviets had also launched an offensive against the German units that protected the northern flank of Model's forces. Catching the Germans by surprise, the Soviets gradually drove them back 120km (80 miles).

Then, on 3 August, the Soviets attacked the German forces concentrated along the southern shoulder of the erstwhile Kursk salient. This new Soviet attack swiftly eliminated the German-held bulge to the south of the former salient. After securing rapid success with these two counterattacks, the Soviets escalated their operations into a general strategic counteroffensive across the entire centre and south of the Eastern Front. During the remainder of 1943, this general counteroffensive west drove the Germans back to the river Dnieper and beyond.

AFTERMATH

All things considered, *Citadel* was a dire German strategic defeat. Despite their huge concentration of force, all the Germans gained was an advance never deeper than 40km (25 miles) and through insignificant terrain, for the heavy price of 52,000 casualties and 850 AFVs. Indeed, all *Citadel* accomplished was to shatter the German strategic armoured reserves, thus making it easier for the Soviets to achieve rapid operational successes with their counterattacks. In fact, Kursk – rather than Stalingrad – was probably the key turning point of the war, which ensured Germany would be defeated in 1945.

THE CREW OF A SOVIET T-34 tank surrender to an SS soldier, presumably during the fighting on the southern side of the Kursk salient.

KURSK

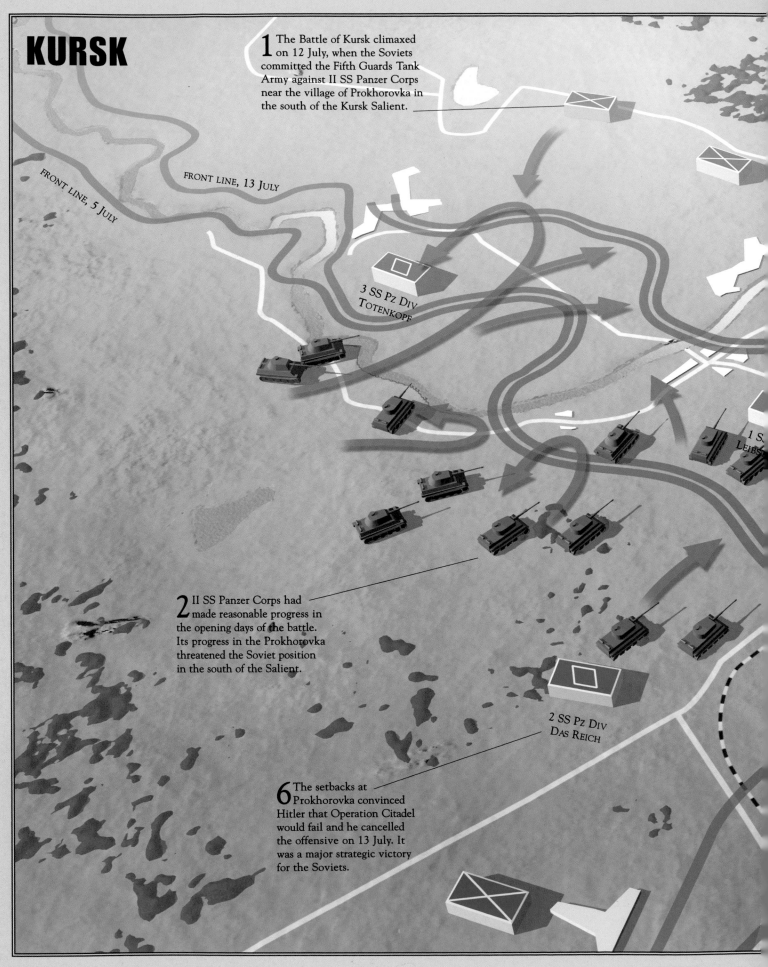

1 The Battle of Kursk climaxed on 12 July, when the Soviets committed the Fifth Guards Tank Army against II SS Panzer Corps near the village of Prokhorovka in the south of the Kursk Salient.

FRONT LINE, 5 JULY

FRONT LINE, 13 JULY

3 SS Pz Div TOTENKOPF

1 S... LEIBS...

2 II SS Panzer Corps had made reasonable progress in the opening days of the battle. Its progress in the Prokhorovka threatened the Soviet position in the south of the Salient.

2 SS Pz Div DAS REICH

6 The setbacks at Prokhorovka convinced Hitler that Operation Citadel would fail and he cancelled the offensive on 13 July. It was a major strategic victory for the Soviets.

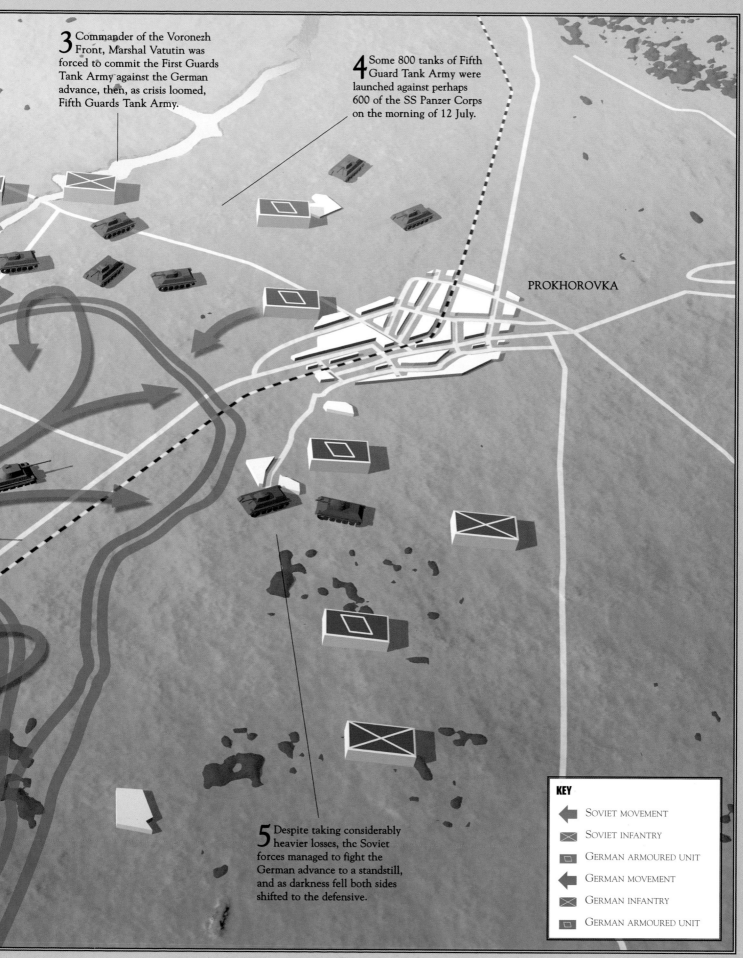

3 Commander of the Voronezh Front, Marshal Vatutin was forced to commit the First Guards Tank Army against the German advance, then, as crisis loomed, Fifth Guards Tank Army.

4 Some 800 tanks of Fifth Guard Tank Army were launched against perhaps 600 of the SS Panzer Corps on the morning of 12 July.

PROKHOROVKA

5 Despite taking considerably heavier losses, the Soviet forces managed to fight the German advance to a standstill, and as darkness fell both sides shifted to the defensive.

KEY

←	SOVIET MOVEMENT
⊠	SOVIET INFANTRY
▱	GERMAN ARMOURED UNIT
←	GERMAN MOVEMENT
⊠	GERMAN INFANTRY
▱	GERMAN ARMOURED UNIT

BATTLE OF IMPHAL AND KOHIMA 1944

The Battle of Imphal and the action at Kohima represented the high water mark of Japanese aspirations in Burma and India. However, after some initial successes, the defeated Japanese fell back into Burma and were subsequently driven back the way they had come.

The Japanese advance in the early months of World War II seemed unstoppable. Allied forces were driven down the Malay Peninsula to the 'fortress island' of Singapore and forced to surrender there. Other formations were pushed back through Burma towards India. A determined rearguard action slowed the Japanese advance and the monsoon brought it to a halt.

This gave the Allies a chance to regroup and mount a defence, which the terrain favoured. The jungle and hills of the Burmese–Indian border region would

BATTLE OF IMPHAL FACTS

Who: British and Indian troops opposed by Japanese forces and elements of the anti-British Indian National Army.

What: Japanese forces encircled the city of Imphal but were driven off and then counterattacked.

Where: The city of Imphal, the capital of the state of Manipur in northeast India.

When: 8 March–3 July 1944

Why: The Japanese wished to invade India and 'liberate' it from the British. This was their last chance of launching a major land invasion against British India, since their military resources were being rapidly used up against the United States in the Pacific.

Outcome: The Japanese were decisively defeated and never again threatened British India with invasion.

THE WIDE IRRAWADDY RIVER *was a serious obstacle to the logistics services of armies operating in the region. This makeshift barge turns a disadvantage into an asset, using the river to transport a truck.*

LIGHT UTILITY VEHICLES like these British Universal Carriers (Bren Carriers) were invaluable in keeping the supply lines open. As the name suggests, they could carry almost anything over rough terrain or on roads.

funnel an advance into corridors that could be defended with relative ease. The city of Imphal provided a base and logistics centre for the allies while the Japanese would have to operate at the end of a long supply line that ran through difficult terrain.

Breaking the Allied positions around Imphal would be a major undertaking, requiring resources that might be better used elsewhere. Thus the pressure dropped off considerably, allowing the Allies to build up their strength for an offensive back into Burma. Raids, including the famous exploits of the Chindits, were launched into Japanese territory.

This required some kind of countermeasure, and Japanese commanders decided that since it would require as much manpower to mount a proper defence of Burma as to drive the Allies out of Imphal, the offensive option was the most suitable.

THE JAPANESE ATTACK AT IMPHAL

Japanese forces in the region gained a new and aggressive commander, Lieutenant-General Masakazu Kawabe (1886–1965), who thought an attack on Imphal was practicable. There were several benefits to a victory there. As well as countering the Chindit raids, elimination of the logistics base at Imphal would cut off Allied supplies going

to Chinese Nationalist forces that were still fighting the Japanese to the North. More importantly, it would open the way to attack India.

India was extremely important to the British Empire, supplying large numbers of troops to the Imperial forces. However, there was a movement towards independence and the Japanese believed that India might be induced to break away, depriving the Allies of a vast amount of manpower. For this reason, the coming offensive was to include elements of the Indian National Army, a force raised from Indian prisoners taken by the Japanese during the Malaya campaign and who were willing to fight against the British in the name of Indian independence.

The Allies had occupied several forward positions in preparation for their own offensive into Burma. The Japanese plan was to encircle and eliminate these quickly before advancing on Imphal and driving off the defenders. This was by no means as easy as it sounded, since the attack would have to be made through difficult country at the end of a long supply chain. Some of the senior officers involved had grave doubts about the plan, especially the logistical elements.

Nevertheless the campaign opened on 8 March 1944, at which point the Allies began to withdraw their forward units. Some managed this without undue difficulty, but others had to fight their way out with the aid of the few available reserves. By the beginning of April, the Allies had pulled back to the Imphal plain and were receiving reinforcements by air.

Japanese troops then converged on Imphal along several roads. They were travelling light, having left much of their artillery and heavy equipment behind. One reason for this was the conviction that the terrain was unsuitable for tanks and so antitank weapons would not be needed. Ironically, it was exactly the same misconception that allowed Japanese tanks to do so much damage to the Allies in Malaya at the beginning of the war.

The Allies were using US-supplied M3 Lee light tanks, which could cope with the difficult terrain. Although far too light for anything

EXPECTING TO FIGHT ONLY INFANTRY, *the Japanese forces brought along anti-personnel support weapons like this light machinegun but left most of their antitank weaponry behind as they advanced on Imphal.*

but armoured reconnaissance elsewhere in the world, the Lees were more than capable of cutting up infantry, with little in the way of antitank equipment.

There were other serious problems too. The Japanese needed to capture Allied supplies or at least airfields suitable to fly them into before their supplies ran out. Inventive solutions, such as bringing herds of buffalo along behind the combat formations as rations 'on the hoof', had failed, and the situation was becoming serious. Foraging parties were able to obtain some supplies at a cost of diluting the combat effectiveness of the units involved.

Repeated attacks were put in against Imphal, but they grew steadily weaker and never really had a chance of success. Conversely, although the Allies were themselves getting short of supplies and ammunition their defence became increasingly aggressive, launching local counterattacks to harass the Japanese positions.

MERILL'S MARAUDERS

Named after its commander, Brigadier-General Frank Merrill (1903–55), the 5307th Composite Unit (Provisional) became better known as Merrill's Marauders during its long-range raiding exploits in the China-Burma theatre.

After training with the highly successful Chindits, the all-volunteer Marauders embarked on a campaign of harassment deep within Japanese territory. Despite heavy casualties and sickness caused by the harsh jungle conditions, they were able to cut Japanese supply lines and inflict serious losses on their opponents in dozens of actions.

At the end of the war, every member of the Marauders was awarded the Bronze Star and the unit was honoured with a Distinguished Unit Citation for its contribution to the Burma campaign.

ABOVE: THE ROUGH TERRAIN of the Imphal region could in many places be crossed only on foot, and slowly at that. This severely restricted the offensive capabilities of both sides.

BELOW: WHERE THE TERRAIN was more open, light vehicles and tanks such as these Lee-Grants were able to operate. Lacking antitank weapons, the Japanese could do little about them.

The Allies were able to fly supplies into Imphal, as they had during the battle of the Admin Box a few months earlier. Where similar attempts had failed, such as the German 'air bridge' at Stalingrad, the position at Imphal was such that the besieging Japanese forces ran short before the Allies did.

OPERATIONS AGAINST KOHIMA

Meanwhile, the Japanese had tried for two weeks in early April to capture the Kohima ridge, which would allow them to control the main supply route into Imphal. The ridge was to have been seized early in the campaign, but stubborn defence by Allied troops encountered in the advance delayed the arrival of the Japanese at their objective. This bought time for a defence to be put in place.

The defenders at Kohima came under increasing pressure due to heavy shelling interspersed with infantry assaults. They held out in a shrinking perimeter, and by 17 April the situation was desperate. However, the position was relieved the next day by troops moving up from India. The attacks continued unabated, but the chances of success were ever decreasing.

By early May, more Allied troops had joined the fight at Kohima, and the Japanese, now very short of supplies, came under air attack as well as increasing bombardment. The ridge was partially cleared of Japanese defenders after a very stubborn fight, but as late as mid-May some high points were still stubbornly held.

However, with Allied troops across their supply line and almost out of ammunition, the starving Japanese were forced to pull back and leave the ridge to the Allies. Not that there was much left of it or the villages there – Kohima has been referred to as the Stalingrad of the East, and with good reason.

ABOVE: COOPERATION BETWEEN BRITISH *and Indian formations allowed the Allies to go over to the offensive after the Imphal-Kohima road was reopened. Field conferences like this one were essential to maintain coordination.*

At the end of May, the Japanese pulled back from Kohima entirely. Many units broke up, straggling east and south in search of food. They were unable to play any further part in the campaign. Meanwhile, with the road now open, the British began to push through to Imphal.

THE ALLIES COUNTERATTACK AT IMPHAL

Japanese attacks on Imphal itself wound down by 1 May. A siege continued, but there was no longer any real chance of a successful assault. As the Japanese supply situation worsened, the Allies were re-supplied by airdrops at both Imphal and Kohima. This was a difficult and hazardous undertaking, especially at Kohima, but it enabled the Allies to establish superiority over their weakening opponents.

This took time due to poor weather and the stubbornness of the Japanese troops. Even desperately short of food and ammunition, they were difficult to shift from their positions. Although the Japanese commanders on the spot knew they could not win this battle, a final effort was ordered. A few reinforcements had arrived and these allowed the assault to achieve some limited success. Nevertheless by 22 June the road through to Kohima was opened and the siege was effectively over.

The Japanese divisions around Imphal were at the end of their tether and more or less ignored orders from above to make a new assault. Bowing to the inevitable, the order was given for a retreat and on 3 July the divisions began pulling back. Many of these formations were debilitated by disease and starvation and were able to do little more than shamble eastwards, leaving their remaining heavy equipment and artillery behind.

AFTERMATH

The ill-advised advance on Imphal was the turning point of the campaign. From then on the Japanese were on the defensive and were steadily pushed back. For the Allies, the dark days of shambolic retreat were long over and they returned to Burma confident that they could take on and beat the Imperial Japanese Army.

ABOVE: INDIAN TROOPS WAIT IN A CLEARING. *The thick vegetation was a serious obstacle to troop movements and tended to funnel units into predictable lines of advance.*

BATTLE OF IMPHAL AND KOHIMA

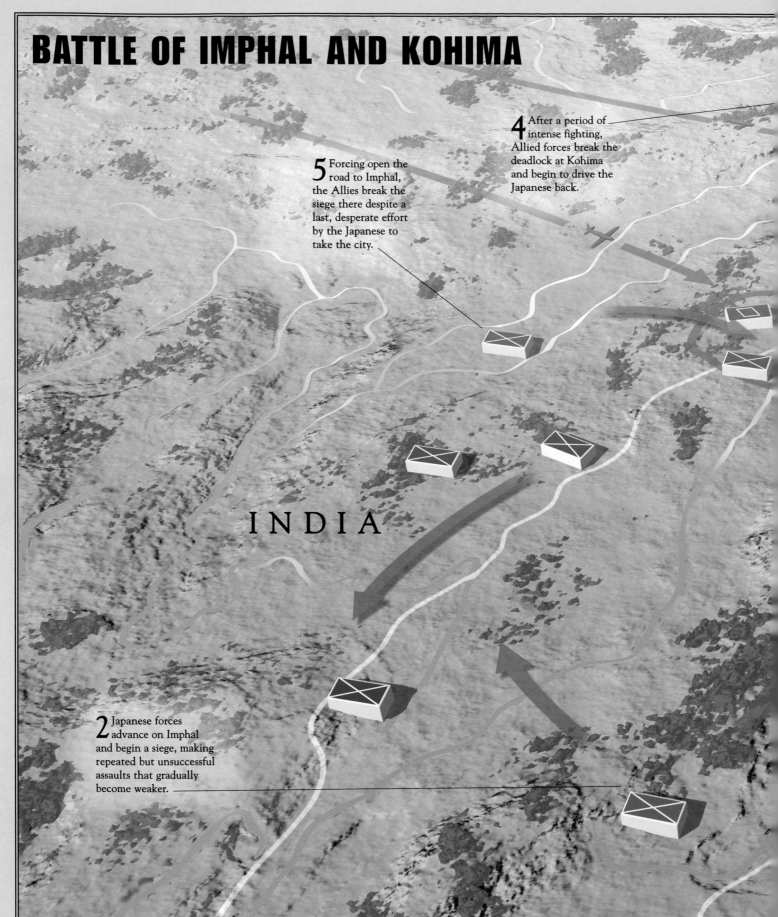

4 After a period of intense fighting, Allied forces break the deadlock at Kohima and begin to drive the Japanese back.

5 Forcing open the road to Imphal, the Allies break the siege there despite a last, desperate effort by the Japanese to take the city.

INDIA

2 Japanese forces advance on Imphal and begin a siege, making repeated but unsuccessful assaults that gradually become weaker.

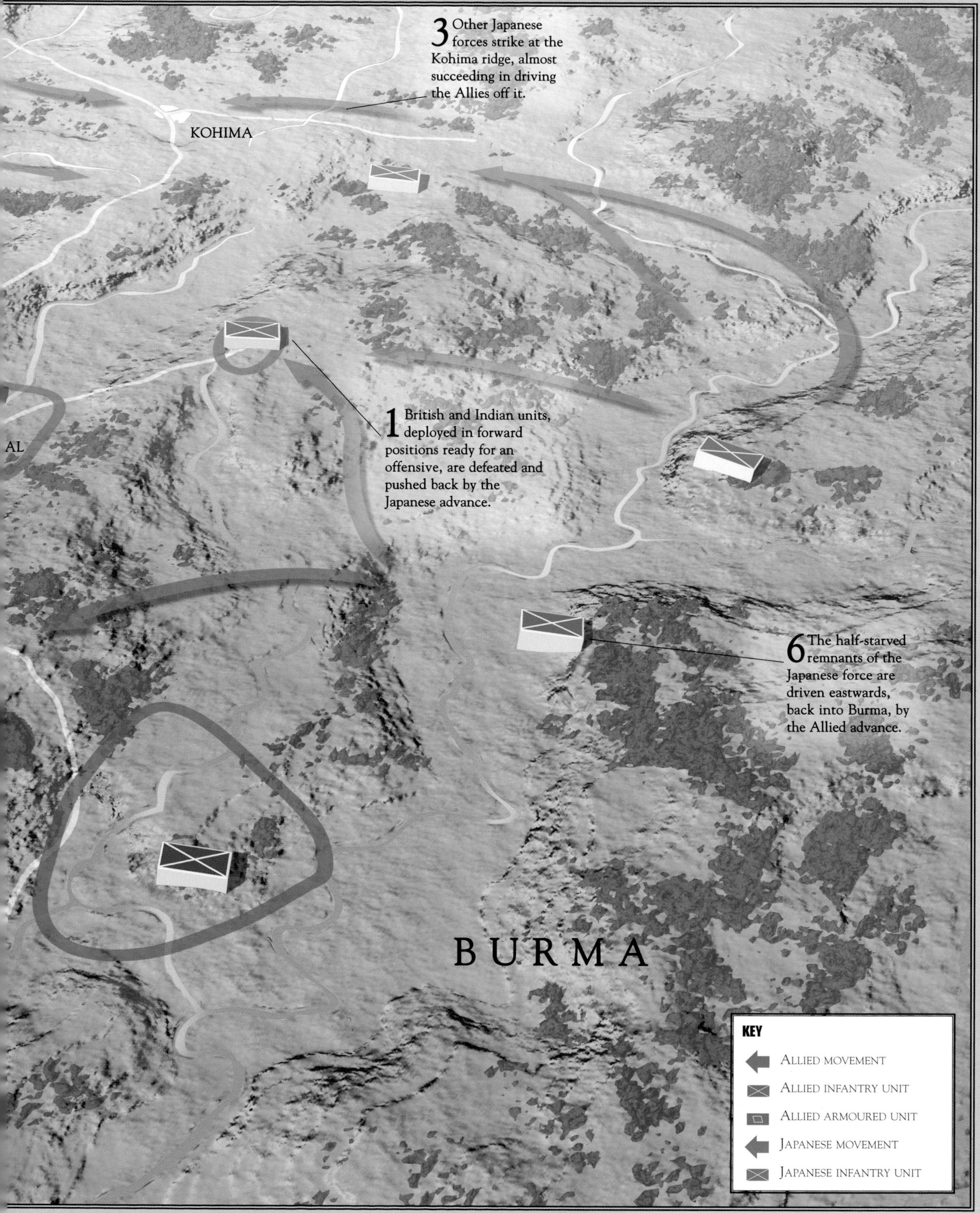

3 Other Japanese forces strike at the Kohima ridge, almost succeeding in driving the Allies off it.

KOHIMA

1 British and Indian units, deployed in forward positions ready for an offensive, are defeated and pushed back by the Japanese advance.

AL

6 The half-starved remnants of the Japanese force are driven eastwards, back into Burma, by the Allied advance.

BURMA

KEY

← ALLIED MOVEMENT

⬒ ALLIED INFANTRY UNIT

▱ ALLIED ARMOURED UNIT

← JAPANESE MOVEMENT

⬒ JAPANESE INFANTRY UNIT

MONTE CASSINO 1944

The Battles of Monte Cassino between January and May 1944 represented something of an anomaly in the conduct of the war in Europe. In an unusually static period of warfare, the Allies took five months and four separate battles to break through the German Gustav Line, anchored around the position at Monte Cassino.

It cost the Allies – including the fighting at Anzio – 105,000 casualties and the Germans at least 80,000. Despite the breakthrough, the opportunity to destroy the Germans in Italy was missed and the slog up Italy would continue for another year.

Italy surrendered to the Allies on 8 September 1943. The British Eighth Army had already crossed the Straits of Messina five days before, and on 9 September the Fifth Army, a mixed US-British force, landed at Salerno. The near successes of the German counterattack against the Salerno beachhead

MONTE CASSINO FACTS

Who: II US Corps and II New Zealand Corps of General Mark Clark's (1896–1984) Fifth Army and subsequently General Oliver Leese's (1884–1978) British Eighth Army under overall command of General Harold Alexander (1891–1969) faced Lieutenant-General Fridolin von Senger und Etterlin's (1891–1963) XIV Panzer Corps.

What: A series of offensives against the Gustav Line, a German defensive line anchored around the imposing position of Monte Cassino.

Where: The area surrounding Monte Cassino and the nearby town, just over 100km (62 miles) south of Rome.

When: 24 January–18 May 1944

Why: Cassino controlled the mouth of the Liri Valley and thus the most straightforward route to Rome.

Outcome: Despite the efforts of Allied forces, the Germans held their position through the first three costly attritional battles, before the Gustav Line was finally broken across the front in May 1944.

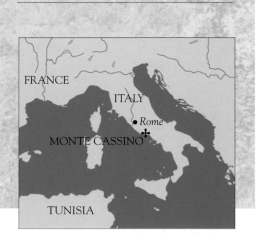

GERMAN PARATROOPERS OF *the 1st Paratroop Division man an MG 42 in the ruins of the monastery. The Allied bombing did little more than create even more defensible positions and legitimize the German occupation of the building.*

convinced Hitler to follow the advice of Field-Marshal Albert Kesselring (1885–1960) and resist the Allied advance as far south as possible. He also issued orders for the construction of the Gustav Line 160km (100 miles) south of Rome. This stretched from the Adriatic to the Tyrrhenian sea.

The key to the position was the entrance of the Liri valley, which offered the most obvious route to Rome. Monte Cassino dominated the approach, overlooking the rivers that crossed the mouth of the valley. The Germans built pillboxes and dugouts across the Liri, established positions in the surrounding mountains, fortified the town of Cassino and flooded the rivers. It was probably the most formidable defensive position in Europe.

ANZIO LANDINGS

Operation *Shingle*, a planned landing at Anzio behind the Gustav Line, forced the Fifth Army to push on to draw the German reserves from the Anzio area. General Mark Clark (1896–1984), the Fifth Army commander, launched the French Expeditionary Corps (FEC) against the German positions north of Cassino while the British X Corps

attempted to cross the river Garigliano to the west in mid-January. Neither operation was wholly successful, although they did draw the Germans south.

Then Clark committed US II Corps against the Cassino position. The 36th Division had two regiments destroyed trying to cross the Gari river between 20 and 22 January. The Anzio landings took place virtually unopposed on 22 January. Clark knew the Germans would throw everything available at the beachhead, so he committed his final division, the 34th Red Bull, north of Cassino to maintain the pressure. The 34th attacked on the night of 24 January. It took them three days to establish themselves in strength across the Rapido river.

On 29 January, the division pushed into the high ground behind the monastery and managed to secure a foothold in the outskirts of the town. It then inched its way across the Cassino massif before the attack petered out on 12 February. Despite the extraordinary efforts of the US infantry, the town and monastery remained in German hands. Aware

THE DOMINATING POSITION of the Monastery at Monte Cassino is clear in this photograph taken prior to the bombing of 15 February 1944. Castle Hill sits in front of the Monastery, while the town of Cassino nestles around its base.

ABOVE: THE ALMOST LUNAR appearance of the monastery after it had endured 309 tons of 227kg (500lb) bombs and incendiary bombs and 126 tons of 454kg (1000lb) bombs. It was the largest use of tactical airpower in the war to date.

that the Germans still intended to counterattack at Anzio, the Allies attacked again using II New Zealand Corps, made up of 2nd New Zealand and 4th Indian Divisions under Lieutenant-General Bernard Freyberg (1889–1963). The 4th Indian took over US 34th Division's positions, finding that the key piece of terrain, Point 593, had been retaken by the Germans. Much to the disgust of the divisional commander, Francis Tuker (1894–1967), Freyberg ordered a direct assault on the monastery.

Despite misgivings, the Allied commander in Italy, General Harold Alexander (1891–1969), authorized the bombing of the monastery. On the morning of 15 February, more than 250 bombers destroyed the abbey. However, due to an appalling lack of coordination, the lead formation of 4th Indian Division was unable to attack until the night of 16/17 February, 36 hours later, by which time German paratroopers had occupied the ruins. Despite strenuous efforts, 4th Indian Division failed to capture either Point 593 or the monastery over the next three days. On 17 February, the New Zealanders attacked the town from the east, managing to seize the railway station, but they were unable to advance further.

GERMAN COUNTERATTACK

Despite the efforts against Cassino, the Germans launched a massive attack on the Anzio beachhead. Still desperate to maintain pressure on the Gustav Line, Alexander ordered Freyberg to attack again. This time 4th Indian Division would attack the monastery on a slightly different axis,

RIGHT: A GERMAN 150MM (5.9IN) S-FH 18 artillery piece in action. Most German artillery at Cassino was located in the Liri Valley. As the Germans held most of the high ground, they could bring observed fire on the whole battlefield.

INDIAN SOLDIER

Soldiers of the British
Commonwealth rendered
outstanding service during
the Italian campaign.

Here, a corporal of the
6th Rajputana Rifles is seen in
characteristic walking out
uniform. Part of the 4th (Indian)
Infantry Division, the unit was
closely involved in the battle for
Monte Cassino, and sustained heavy
casualties. The 6th Rajputana Rifles
had previously served with the
Eighth Army in Syria and throughout
the North African campaign.
Awarded many honours and medals,
the unit still exists today as part of
the modern Indian army.

above the town through Castle Hill, while the New
Zealanders attacked the town from the north. After air raids
and a massive bombardment, the two divisions attacked on
the morning of March 15 and managed to seize the railroad
station, but were unable to advance further.

Again the German paratroopers put up fierce resistance,
and even though the New Zealanders managed to clear most
of the town and 4th Indian Division took Castle and
Hangman's Hills, the Allies were not able to gain complete
control of Cassino or capture the monastery. Having
achieved very little, Freyberg called off the offensive.

EIGHTH ARMY TAKES OVER

As the weather improved, the Allies reorganized their
forces and Cassino became the responsibility of the Eighth
Army. Alexander's chief-of-staff, General John Harding
(1896–1989), was the driving force behind Operation
Diadem, the fourth battle of Cassino. He organized a
coordinated offensive across the front. In the west, US II
Corps would drive up the coastal plain toward Anzio, where
US VI Corps had been reinforced and was ready to break out
from the beachhead.

The FEC would attack through the Aurunci mountains
and break into the Liri valley behind the Gustav Line. The
British XIII Corps would attack up the mouth of the Liri with
Canadian I Corps ready to exploit up the valley. The Polish

*US ARTILLERY MEN demonstrating a massive 240mm (9.5in) M-1 Howitzer
to British troops. The largest piece of field artillery in the US armoury, the
M-1 was also used by the British Eighth Army at Cassino.*

RIGHT: A NORTH AFRICAN GOUMIER *of the 2nd Moroccan Division of the French Expeditionary Corps. The achievements of these formidable troops in the Aurunci mountains were critical to Allied success in the fourth battle.*

II Corps would attack Cassino, while British X Corps would conduct minor operations north of the town.

MONASTERY CAPTURED

Diadem opened at 11.00 p.m. on 11 May. The main thrust up the Liri by XIII Corps made slow progress, as did US II Corps on the coast. The French, however, achieved excellent results, threatening to turn the German flank.

The Poles took terrible losses up on the Cassino massif, but managed to seize Point 593 and the high ground around the monastery by 17 May. The Poles entered the abbey the following day to find it abandoned.

Threatened by Allied success in the valley, the Germans withdrew north. Alexander ordered VI Corps to break out of Anzio and cut off the German retreat. The German Tenth Army faced being trapped and destroyed. However, in an act of gross insubordination and military stupidity, Clark countermanded Alexander's order and turned US VI Corps towards Rome, which fell to him on 4 June. Much to his astonishment, Kesselring was able to extricate his forces and regroup on a defensive line north of Rome. The chance for a decisive victory had been lost.

The conduct of the Allied offensives round Cassino was uninspired and costly, but the vulnerability of the Anzio beachhead and the psychological importance of the monastery necessitated action. The chance to redeem the campaign was lost with Clark's vainglorious decision to capture Rome rather than defeat the enemy.

BELOW: ALLIED TRAFFIC MOVES *through the town of Cassino in the aftermath of the fourth battle. The ravages of four months of bitter fighting are evident.*

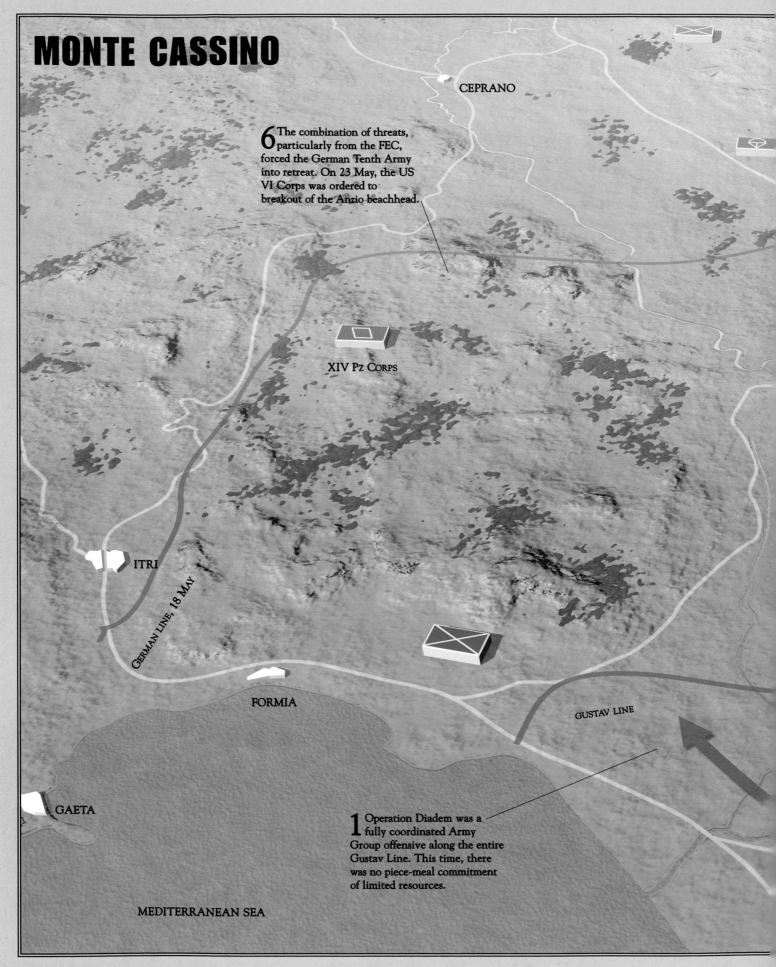

MONTE CASSINO

CEPRANO

6 The combination of threats, particularly from the FEC, forced the German Tenth Army into retreat. On 23 May, the US VI Corps was ordered to breakout of the Anzio beachhead.

XIV Pz Corps

ITRI

GERMAN LINE, 18 MAY

FORMIA

GUSTAV LINE

GAETA

1 Operation Diadem was a fully coordinated Army Group offensive along the entire Gustav Line. This time, there was no piece-meal commitment of limited resources.

MEDITERRANEAN SEA

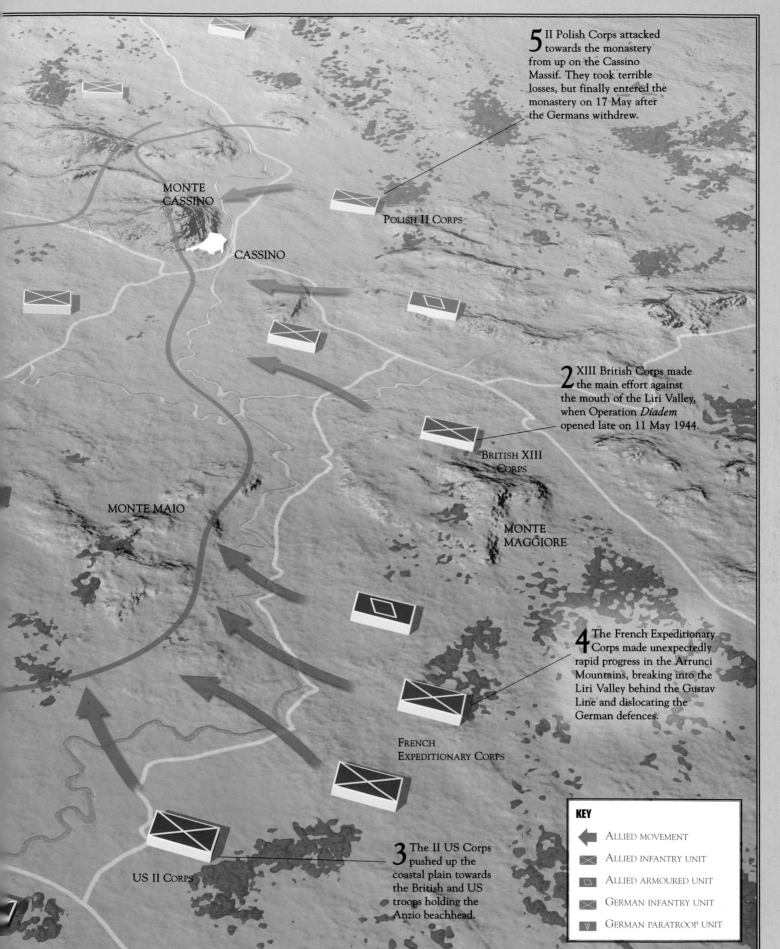

5 II Polish Corps attacked towards the monastery from up on the Cassino Massif. They took terrible losses, but finally entered the monastery on 17 May after the Germans withdrew.

MONTE CASSINO

CASSINO

POLISH II CORPS

2 XIII British Corps made the main effort against the mouth of the Liri Valley, when Operation *Diadem* opened late on 11 May 1944.

BRITISH XIII CORPS

MONTE MAIO

MONTE MAGGIORE

4 The French Expeditionary Corps made unexpectedly rapid progress in the Arrunci Mountains, breaking into the Liri Valley behind the Gustav Line and dislocating the German defences.

FRENCH EXPEDITIONARY CORPS

3 The II US Corps pushed up the coastal plain towards the British and US troops holding the Anzio beachhead.

US II CORPS

KEY

← ALLIED MOVEMENT

⊠ ALLIED INFANTRY UNIT

▭ ALLIED ARMOURED UNIT

⊠ GERMAN INFANTRY UNIT

▽ GERMAN PARATROOP UNIT

ALLIED VICTORY

Despite the tipping of the balance against the Axis countries, the nature of the regimes meant that they would fight to the bitter end. Thus the Allies had to fight their way across Europe and the Pacific towards the heartlands of Germany and Japan.

Although there were great and impressive military achievements from the Allies, such as the Normandy landings in June 1944 and the Soviet summer offensive the same year, the determination and remarkable resilience of the German and Japanese forces meant that the final campaigns would be extremely hard fought. Bitter defensive battles were fought at Monte Cassino and Iwo Jima, and the Allies suffered setbacks with the failed airborne operation at Arnhem in the autumn of 1944 and the surprise German offensive in the Ardennes in December of the same year. The final battles, for the island of Okinawa and the city of Berlin, proved costly outcomes to the most bloody war in world history.

THE END OF THE REICH: *as Soviet IS-2 tanks rumble along a Berlin street, refugees emerge from the cellars of gutted buildings, carrying their belongings with them. This photograph was taken in late April 1945, just days before the surrender of Germany.*

NORMANDY LANDINGS

1944

D-Day – the Allied landings on the Normandy coast of German-occupied France 6 June 1944 – was one of the most climactic days of World War II. Ever since 1943, the Western Allies had prepared for this operation, codenamed Neptune/Overlord. On D-Day, the Allies landed 160,000 US, British and Canadian forces (plus a small French contingent) to establish beachheads in Normandy.

With the 'Second Front' successfully established, the German Reich would subsequently find itself locked into a three-front war of attrition that would eventually overwhelm it. As Supreme Allied Commander, the US General Dwight 'Ike' Eisenhower (1890–1969) exercised overall control over the

NORMANDY LANDINGS FACTS

Who: Supreme Allied Commander General Dwight Eisenhower (1890–1969) commanded the US, British and Canadian forces of General Bernard Montgomery's (1887–1976) Twenty-First Army Group, which faced Field Marshal Erwin Rommel's (1891–1944) Army Group B.

What : The largest amphibious operation in history, marking the Western Allies return to North West Europe.

Where: The Baie de la Seine in Normandy, France.

When: 6 June 1944

Why: The British and Americans had long intended to return to Northern Europe, and

Normandy provided suitable beaches within range of land-based air cover.

Outcome: The Allies successfully established themselves ashore, thus opening the Second Front and marking a crucial turning point in the war.

BRITISH INFANTRY gather on Sword Beach in preparation for the push inland. British troops were meant to push on to the strategically important town of Caen in the first day, and did make significant inroads.

A PRIEST ADMINISTERS a blessing to US sailors and soldiers on 4 June 1944. Operation Overlord was scheduled to begin on 5 June, but was delayed by bad weather.

invasion while below him came the three British service chiefs: Admiral Bertram Ramsay (1883–1945), Air Chief Marshal Trafford Leigh-Mallory (1892–1944), and General Bernard Montgomery (1887–1976). Field-Marshal Erwin Rommel's (1891–1944) Army Group B controlled the German forces that opposed the D-Day landings.

NAVAL ARMADA

The D-Day plan began with the night-time passage across the Channel of a naval armada laden with Allied troops, to anchor opposite the five designated invasion beaches: in the east, the three Anglo-Canadian sectors – 'Sword', 'Juno' and 'Gold' and in the west the two US beaches, 'Omaha' and 'Utah'. Shortly before this, three Allied airborne divisions would land to secure the invasion's eastern and western flanks. Finally, after heavy aerial and naval bombardments, the assault forces would land on these five beaches. After these initial assaults had established small beachheads, follow-up forces would advance inland so that by the end of D-Day Allied forces would have captured Bayeux and consolidated the four eastern beachheads and the British airborne zone into a single salient.

BAD WEATHER

D-Day was slated to begin on 5 June, but bad weather forced Eisenhower to postpone the invasion. It nevertheless went ahead on the 6th despite the continuing rough seas. However, the launching of the invasion in bad weather enabled the Allies to surprise the Germans, whose slow

reactions let slip their best chance of defeating the invaders. On 5 June, 6939 vessels assembled off the coast of southern England and that evening headed south towards the Normandy coast. Next, from 11.30 p.m., 1100 Allied transport planes transported 17,000 airborne troops to Normandy. In the early hours of 6 June, British airborne forces landed northeast of Caen and seized key locations to protect the invasion's eastern flank. Simultaneously two US airborne divisions landed in the marshes behind 'Utah' to delay German ripostes against the invasion's western flank.

While local German forces concluded that these airborne landings were the start of the invasion, higher German authorities remained convinced that they were a diversion prior to the main Allied attack in the Pas de Calais. As these airborne operations unfolded, the naval armada weighed anchor off the Normandy coast. As dawn approached, the Allies commenced naval and aerial bombardments of the German coastal defences.

BEACH ASSAULTS

Next, between 6.30 a.m. and 7.45 a.m, the Allied amphibious assaults commenced on the five designated beaches. At the eastern beach, 'Sword', the British 3rd Division commenced its assault at 7.15 a.m.; here the assault force, as at the other beaches, comprised a combination of infantry, commando and specialized armoured units. Over

SHERMAN 'FLAIL' TANK

The Sherman Crab was one of a number of specialized armoured vehicles used during the D-Day landings. The Crab mounted a flail – a set of heavy chains suspended on a rotating drum in front of the tank – that was used to clear a path through a minefield. The method was first used, aboard a Matilda tank, at El Alamein. The Crab, mounted on the standard Allied medium tank the M4 Sherman, could clear a lane about 3.3m (11 ft) wide at the speed of 2km/h (1.2mph). The chains would need replacing after several detonations.

the next two hours, the British forces fought their way off the beach and captured the fiercely defended German strongpoint at La Brèche. Meanwhile, other Allied units fought their way east into the fringes of Ouistreham and advanced 3.2km (2 miles) inland to capture Hermanville. All morning, follow-up forces landed on 'Sword' beach, which became increasingly narrow as the tide rose. The resulting traffic jam prevented the supporting armour from moving inland, but eventually the British spearheads renewed their drive inland despite this lack of armour.

FOUR PATHFINDER OFFICERS of British 6th Airborne Division synchronize their watches in front of a Dakota C-47, before take-off at RAF Harwell.

LEFT: *AMERICAN TROOPS from the 1ˢᵗ Infantry Division, the 'Big Red One', board landing craft in preparation for Normandy landings.*

Meanwhile, at 7.45 a.m., 3ʳᵈ Canadian Infantry Division commenced its assault on 'Juno'. In the face of fierce enemy resistance, it took over two hours to secure the first exits from the beach. Over the rest of the morning, British and Canadian units advanced through St-Aubin and Courseulles to create a defensive line 6.4km (4 miles) inland. Further west, the British 50th (Northumbrian) Infantry Division had commenced its assault on 'Gold' at 7.30 a.m. Here the preliminary bombardments suppressed German resistance and thus the spearheads established an initial beachhead despite their lack of armour, delayed by the heavy seas.

On the western flank, however, the German strongpoint of le Hamel had escaped much of the recent bombardment. British forces battled for many hours against intense enemy resistance to capture le Hamel. While this action raged, other British units both pushed inland and drove 6.4km (4 miles) west to seize Port-en-Bessin, narrowing the 14.5km (9-mile) gap that existed between 'Gold' and 'Omaha'.

BLOOD BATH AT OMAHA BEACH

The assault of 1ˢᵗ and 29ᵗʰ US Infantry Divisions on 'Omaha' commenced at 6.30 a.m. Even before this time, things had gone awry, with the fire support proving less effective than planned. The heavily loaded infantry that managed to struggle through the neck-high water to the shore then encountered murderous enemy fire that inflicted terrible casualties; Allied intelligence had failed to detect the recent

BELOW: *THE SCALE OF OPERATION OVERLORD is clear here in this picture of beached landing craft and supply ships on Omaha Beach in the aftermath of the fighting.*

ABOVE: WOUNDED MEN OF the US 3rd battalion, 16th Infantry Regiment pause to smoke and eat after capturing Omaha Beach on 6 June 1944.

reinforcement of the German defences here. Throughout the morning, US troops strove to fight their way off the beach and into the bluffs beyond, yet by midday the US foothold on enemy-occupied soil still remained precarious.

THE OTHER BEACHES

This stood in stark contrast to the less costly assault mounted at 'Utah', located along the southeast corner of the Cotentin Peninsula. Here, at 6.30 a.m., the 4th US Infantry Division commenced its assault after accurate naval gunfire had smashed the relatively weak German defences; the enemy believed that the marshes located behind 'Utah' would persuade the Allies not to land there. In the face of moderate resistance, the Americans soon advanced inland to close with the perimeter held by the US airborne forces.

Over the rest of D-Day, the Allies advanced further inland from these seven separate amphibious/airborne assaults, to create four larger beachheads. In the west, British units linked up with the airborne forces located east of the Orne. However, a German armoured counterattack north prevented the forces landed at 'Sword' from linking up with those landed on 'Juno'. Meanwhile, in the latter sector Canadian forces had linked up with British forces landed on 'Gold'. Further west at 'Omaha', US forces had secured a tenuous 1.6km (1-mile) deep foothold on French soil but at

the price of more than 2000 casualties, while at 'Utah' US forces had linked up with their airborne comrades.

By midnight on 6 June 1944, the 159,000 Allied troops ashore had established four sizable beachheads. While the Allied invasion front remained vulnerable to German counterattack, D-Day's success now made it virtually impossible for the enemy to throw the invaders back into the sea. The establishment of the 'Second Front' on 6 June 1944 represented a crucial step forward on the Allied march to victory over Nazi Germany, which was finally realized on 8 May 1945.

RIGHT: A PARATROOPER SERGEANT of US 101st Airborne Division. He carries .30 M1A1 Carbine with a folding stock, a weapon specifically designed for paratroopers.

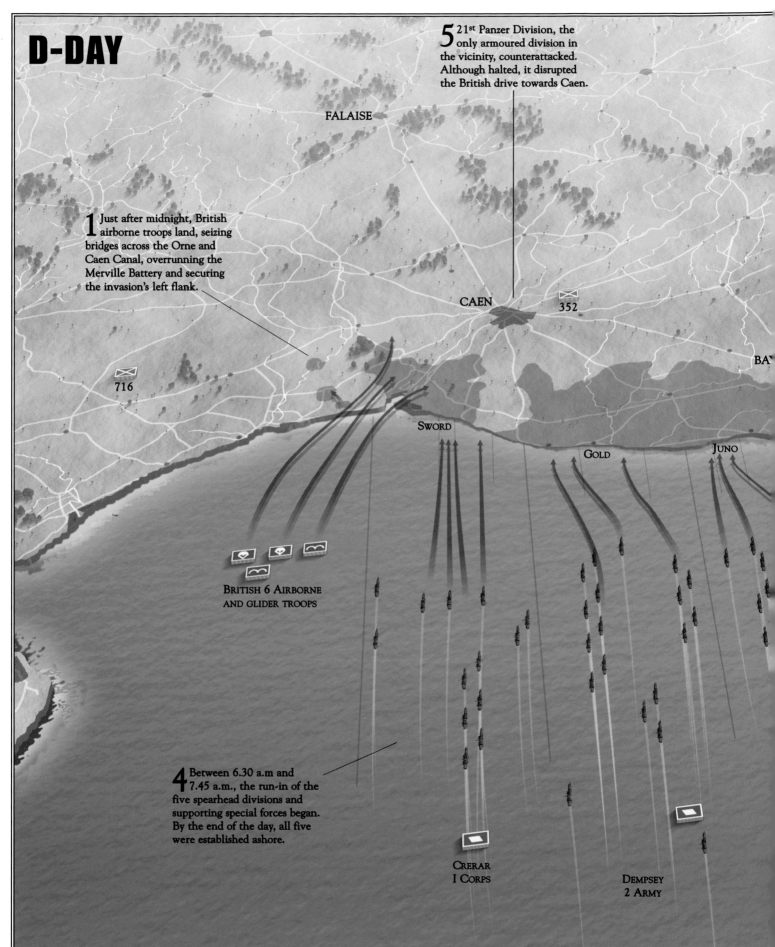

D-DAY

5 21st Panzer Division, the only armoured division in the vicinity, counterattacked. Although halted, it disrupted the British drive towards Caen.

FALAISE

1 Just after midnight, British airborne troops land, seizing bridges across the Orne and Caen Canal, overrunning the Merville Battery and securing the invasion's left flank.

CAEN

716

352

BA

BRITISH 6 AIRBORNE
AND GLIDER TROOPS

SWORD

GOLD

JUNO

4 Between 6.30 a.m and 7.45 a.m., the run-in of the five spearhead divisions and supporting special forces began. By the end of the day, all five were established ashore.

CRERAR
I CORPS

DEMPSEY
2 ARMY

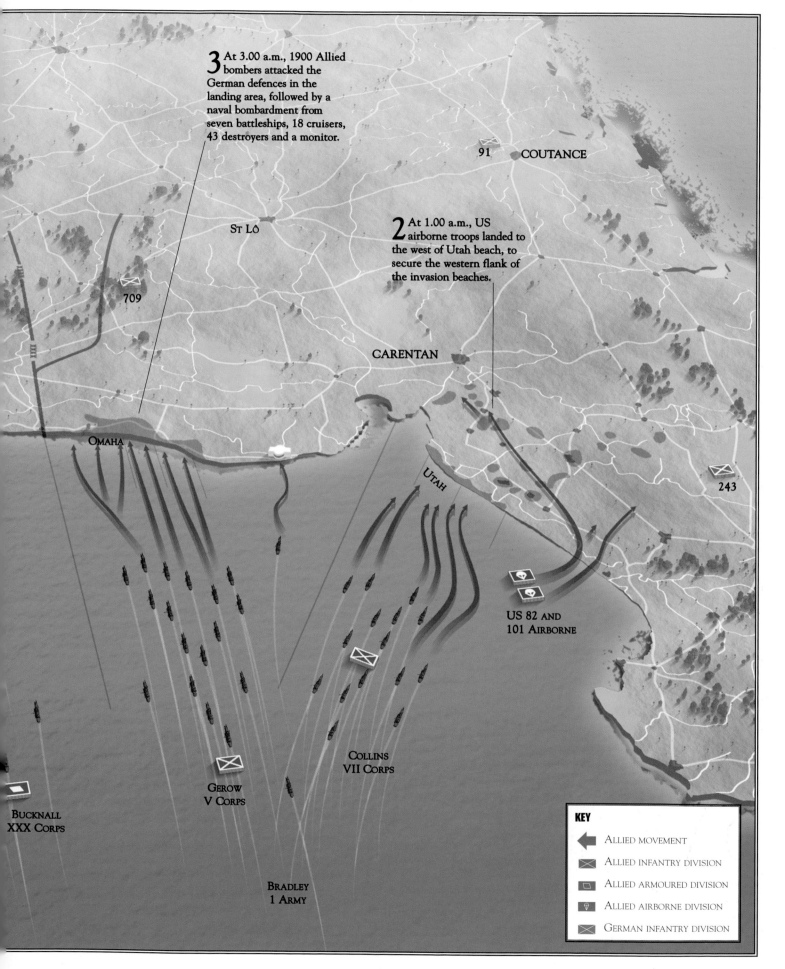

3 At 3.00 a.m., 1900 Allied bombers attacked the German defences in the landing area, followed by a naval bombardment from seven battleships, 18 cruisers, 43 destroyers and a monitor.

2 At 1.00 a.m., US airborne troops landed to the west of Utah beach, to secure the western flank of the invasion beaches.

91 COUTANCE

St Lô

709

CARENTAN

243

Омана

Utah

US 82 AND
101 AIRBORNE

COLLINS
VII CORPS

GEROW
V CORPS

BUCKNALL
XXX CORPS

BRADLEY
1 ARMY

KEY

←	ALLIED MOVEMENT
⊠	ALLIED INFANTRY DIVISION
⬭	ALLIED ARMOURED DIVISION
⬻	ALLIED AIRBORNE DIVISION
⊠	GERMAN INFANTRY DIVISION

BREAKOUT FROM NORMANDY

1944

During late July and August 1944, the Western Allies successfully broke the stalemate that had emerged in the Battle for Normandy and subsequently translated this into a decisive strategic victory that saw the German forces expelled from the region.

The development of such a stalemate was far removed from Allied plans. Their expectations were that once the D-Day landings had established a beachhead subsequent operations would quickly force the Germans to withdraw behind the river Seine, where the decisive battle would ensue. Hitler, however, ordered his forces to prevent the Allies advancing inland, forcing the latter Allies to mount continual attacks against fierce resistance that turned the campaign into a bitter six-week attritional struggle.

BREAKOUT FROM NORMANDY FACTS

Who: Twenty-First Army Group and from 1 August 1944 US Twelfth Army Group commanded by Lieutenant-General Omar Bradley (1893–1981) under land commander General Bernard Montgomery faced Field Marshal Günther von Kluge (1882–1944) until 18 August, then field Marshal Walther Model's (1891–1945) Army Group B.

What: A series of Allied offensives that finally cracked the German line in Normandy and allowed the Allied forces to break out of the bridgehead.

Where: Normandy, France

When: 25 July–30 August 1944

Why: Rather than withdraw to behind the River Seine once the Allies established

their beachhead, German forces were ordered to hold their ground by Hitler, leading to a six-week attritional struggle.

Outcome: The German position in Normandy was broken and the Allies crossed the Seine, liberated Paris on 25 August and embarked on a rapid advance westwards across France towards Germany. It was a decisive strategic victory.

BRITISH MEDICS *recover a wounded comrade and carry him to a Jeep, somewhere in Normandy, July 1944.*

These grinding battles began to bear fruit in mid-July as Allied numerical superiority wore down the Germans. In mid-July, General Bernard Montgomery (1887–1976) launched Operation *Goodwood*, an armoured assault to outflank Caen from the east. While the operation failed to achieve its objectives, it did facilitate the success of the subsequent US offensive – Operation *Cobra* – initiated on 25 July. To sustain their fierce defensive stands against *Goodwood*, the Germans had to divert most of their logistical supplies to the eastern sector of the front. Consequently, the German forces defending the Saint-Lô front were starved of vital logistical supplies just prior to *Cobra*, and their ensuing shortages of fuel and ammunition made it easier for the Americans to secure success.

WAR OF ATTRITION

On 25 July, General Omar Bradley's (1893–1981) First US Army initiated *Cobra*, a massed break-in operation preceded by massive aerial and artillery bombardments. Once these infantry forces had torn a hole in the German line, the Americans aimed to insert three mobile divisions that would advance through the enemy's rear areas to the coast near Coutances, thus cutting off sizable enemy forces. The heavy bombing strike so weakened the defending German forces that VII US Corps drove forwards 3.2km (2 miles) during that first day. Over the

A BRITISH SECTION MOVES up a sunken lane in Normandy. The close nature of the Normandy bocage is well illustrated here.

next 48 hours, US audacity turned this break-in into a decisive breakout by securing a 27.4km (17-mile) advance. By 29 July, the Americans had ripped asunder the German front and so Bradley now widened the scope of *Cobra*. Between 29 and 31 July, US forces crossed the Sélune river at Pontaubault, thus rounding the base of the Cotentin peninsula and opening the gateway for further advances west into Brittany, south towards the Loire and east towards the Seine.

On 30 July, to widen this breach, Montgomery launched an improvised British offensive from Caumont towards Vire, codenamed *Bluecoat*. By 1 August, therefore, the grinding attritional battle of Normandy had been transformed by *Cobra* into a rapid campaign of mobile warfare. The growing US influence on the campaign was now underscored when Bradley's Twelfth US Army Group became operational and assumed command of the First Army and General George Patton's (1885–1945) Third Army.

GERMAN COUNTERATTACK

On 2 August, Hitler reacted to the US breakout by attempting to stuff the genie back into the bottle: he ordered Army Group B to mount a hasty counterattack against the

weak western flank of the breakout. By retaking Avranches, this would isolate the US forces located south of the penetration. During the night 6/7 August, a hastily assembled mobile force attacked down the narrow corridor between the Sée and Sélune rivers towards Mortain. Unsurprisingly, after some initial success this German riposte was halted. This failure now presented the Allies with a strategic opportunity to encircle and destroy the German forces in Normandy, either in the Argentan–Falaise area or via a larger envelopment along the Seine.

In early August, US forces were surging west against feeble enemy resistance, thus outflanking the still cohesive German line against the British around Caen. With this deep US advance into their rear areas, the only feasible German strategy was to withdraw behind the river Seine – but Hitler insisted that his forces stood and fought where they were.

ADVANCE TO FALAISE

By early August, given the scale of recent US success, it had become crucial for the British and Canadian forces bogged down near Caen to advance south towards Falaise. This

LEFT: A TIGER TANK of the SS Schwere Panzerabteilung *101 moves through a Normandy town on 10 June 1944.*

BELOW: A US INFANTRY SECTION *lies prone on the edge of field. The time of year meant that the corn in Normandy was often chest high.*

ABOVE: A MIXTURE OF *jubilant American GIs and French civilians aboard what appears to be a tracked German AFV.*

advance would assist the British attacks being executed further west to widen the breach in the enemy lines created by *Cobra*. Thus between 7 and 8 August General Guy Simonds' (1903–1974) II Canadian Corps commenced Operation *Totalize*, its drive on Falaise. By using a novel night-infiltration attack, supported by strategic bombers, *Totalize* secured significant initial success. However, determined German resistance slowed Simonds' armour and so on 11 August he halted the attack.

Meanwhile, between 8 and 13 August US forces had raced northwest deep into the German rear to reach Alençon, just 32km (20 miles) away from Simonds' spearheads. If the two forces could link up in the Falaise–Argentan area, the German Seventh Army would be caught in a huge pocket. This led Simonds on 14 August to mount an improvised offensive towards Falaise, codenamed *Tractable*. On 15 August, however, bitter German resistance stymied Simonds' advance before it could secure the key high ground north of Falaise.

SEINE BRIDGEHEAD

But by then the Americans had halted their advance north from Alençon, partly due to supply shortages and fears about friendly fire from Simonds' forces. Instead, Bradley divided his forces and directed US V Corps to race eastwards to the Seine. Incredibly, by 19 August, this corps had secured a

bridgehead across the Seine at Mantes-Gassicourt. Despite the US halt at Alençon, the Falaise pocket was nevertheless well-formed by 16 August with the Germans holding just a precarious 16km (10-mile) wide neck around Trun.

FALAISE BREAKOUT

Between 16 and 19 August, Simonds' armour thrust southeast towards Trun and linked up with the Americans to close the pocket. This weak Allied blocking position could not withstand the ensuing German breakout, for as the battered remnants of Seventh Army desperately fought their way out of the pocket through these blocking positions, SS armour also attacked the latter from outside the pocket. These attacks enabled some 40,000 German troops to escape, albeit without their heavy equipment. With Seventh Army no longer cohesive and with the Americans racing into the interior of France, the Germans now had no choice but to withdraw back to the Seine.

Even before the Falaise pocket had been closed, Montgomery had initiated his own offensive towards the Seine, reflecting his desire to enact the 'long' rather than 'short' envelopment. By 21 August, four corps had struck northeast towards the Upper Seine north of Paris, seeking to

ABOVE: A FRENCH RESISTANCE *fighter armed with a sten submachine gun and an American officer crouch behind a car during a gun fight in a French city.*

catch up with the US advance. However, between 21 and 30 August, the battered remnants of Army Group B mounted a controlled withdrawal back to the northern bank of the Seine. At Vernon on 26 August, the first British bridgehead was established across the river. Just four days later, all German resistance south of the Upper Seine had ceased and with this the Normandy campaign ended. By this

On 20 June 1944, US troops pause for a break outside a small French café during their advance inland.

juncture, Paris had fallen and the Americans had raced north beyond the Seine and east into the interior of France. The Allies had won the Battle of Normandy and now their thoughts turned to advancing into the German Reich itself.

TIGERS IN NORMANDY

The PzKpfw VI Tiger Mark I heavy tank entered service in late 1942. The appearance of the Soviet T-34 spurred the production of the Tiger, mounting the formidable 88mm (3.46in) gun and extremely thick armour. It was automotively less impressive.

Nonetheless the Tiger – deployed in heavy tank battalions at the corps and army level – was the scourge of Allied tank crews in Normandy. It could deal with any of the British and US tanks deployed and was virtually invulnerable to the Sherman's 75mm (2.95in) gun from the front. It achieved massive tactical success on occasion, but there were never enough available to make a difference.

179

BREAKOUT FROM NORMANDY

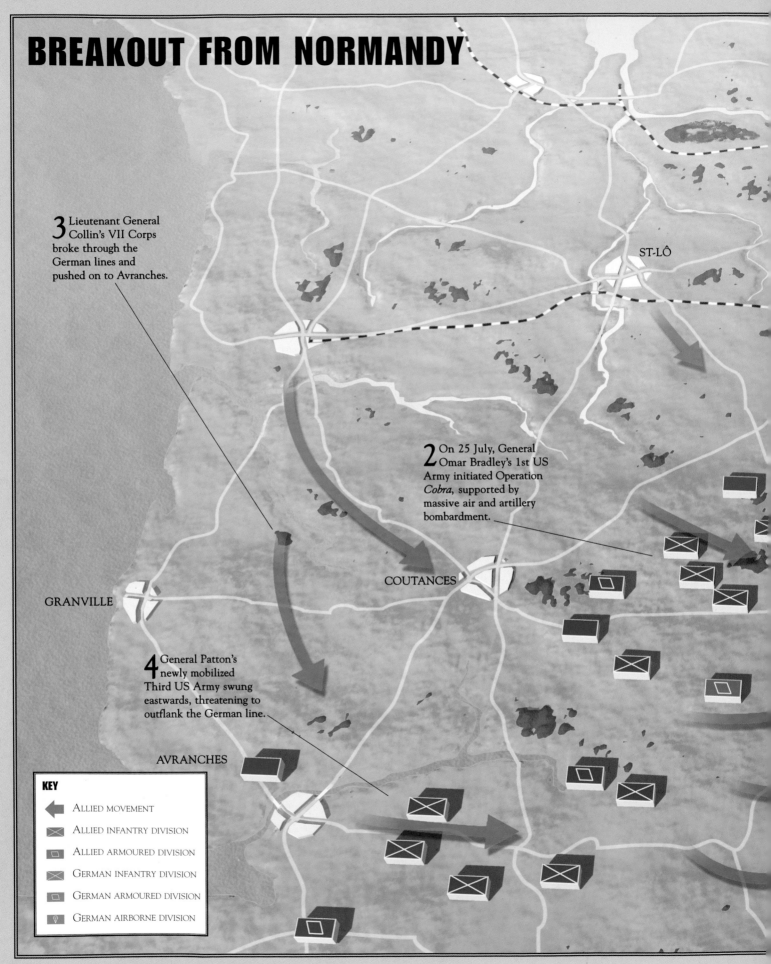

3 Lieutenant General Collin's VII Corps broke through the German lines and pushed on to Avranches.

ST-LÔ

2 On 25 July, General Omar Bradley's 1st US Army initiated Operation *Cobra*, supported by massive air and artillery bombardment.

COUTANCES

GRANVILLE

4 General Patton's newly mobilized Third US Army swung eastwards, threatening to outflank the German line.

AVRANCHES

KEY

⬅ ALLIED MOVEMENT

ALLIED INFANTRY DIVISION

ALLIED ARMOURED DIVISION

GERMAN INFANTRY DIVISION

GERMAN ARMOURED DIVISION

GERMAN AIRBORNE DIVISION

1 On 18 July, Operation *Goodwood* began, sucking in the German reserves. It was followed by *Totalize* on 7 August, fixing the Germans in the area.

BAYEUX

CAEN

FALAISE

5 Hitler ordered a counterattack against Mortain, which opened on 7 August. It did little more than push the remaining German armour deeper into the pocket now forming.

6 The US forces made rapid progress to the south and finally linked up with British and Canadian forces on 19 August, sealing the Falaise pocket at last.

181

PHILIPPINE SEA 1944

Rising like the mythical phoenix from the devastation of Pearl Harbor, the United States Navy had become a veritable juggernaut by the spring of 1944. In support of amphibious operations which had wrested key bases and outposts from the Japanese in the Gilbert and Marshall Islands, the US Pacific Fleet was poised to accomplish another primary mission – the destruction of the Imperial Japanese Navy.

During 30 months of fighting, the grand strategy for victory in the Pacific – Island Hopping – had carried the US armed forces across vast expanses of ocean. On 15 June 1944, amphibious landings were conducted on the island of Saipan in the Marianas, an archipelago that lay in the path of the American advance toward the Philippines. The capture of Saipan, along with the islands of Guam and Tinian, would disrupt Japanese supply efforts to the far reaches of the Empire while providing bases from which long-range US bombers could regularly attack the Japanese home islands.

PHILIPPINE SEA: FACTS

Who: Admiral Soemu Toyoda (1885–1957), commander of the Japanese Combined Fleet, and Admiral Jisaburo Ozawa (1886–1966), commander of the First Mobile Fleet, versus Admiral Raymond Spruance (1886–1969), commander of the US Fifth Fleet and Admiral Marc Mitscher (1887–1947), commander of Task Force 58.

What: The Japanese committed the majority of their air power against the US fleet.

Where: The Philippine Sea in the Central Pacific.

When: 19–20 June 1944

Why: The Japanese hoped to stem the tide of the US advance across the Pacific.

Outcome: A decisive victory for the US Navy resulted in the virtual annihilation of Japanese carrier air power.

A DAMAGED US NAVY Curtiss SB2C Helldiver dive bomber is inspected by officers and crewmen on the flight deck of an aircraft carrier. The Helldiver replaced the ageing Douglas SBD Dauntless.

ABOVE: A TWO-SEAT CARRIER-based dive bomber, the Curtiss SB2C Helldiver proved to be highly successful during the Pacific War. The Helldiver was also heavily armed with machine guns and 20mm (0.78in) cannon.

ABOVE: ADMIRAL CHESTER W. NIMITZ served as the US Navy Commander-in-Chief in the Pacific. Nimitz assumed command days after Pearl Harbor and led the revitalized fighting force to victory.

Anticipating dire consequences if the Americans succeeded, Admiral Soemu Toyoda (1885–1957), Commander-in-Chief of the Japanese Combined Fleet, set in motion operation A-Go, a desperate gambit. Toyoda dispatched Admiral Jisaburo Ozawa (1886–1966) and the First Mobile Fleet to the waters of the Philippine Sea to confront the US naval armada, which was screening the Saipan invasion force and fully expecting such a response from the Japanese.

Ozawa hoped to utilize the one advantage his aircraft still possessed, that of greater range than the American planes, and to leverage land-based air power in the Philippines and surrounding islands to hit the Americans decisively before they could bring their overwhelming superiority to bear. Under his command was a still potentially lethal assemblage of five fleet and four light aircraft carriers, five battleships, 11 heavy cruisers, two light cruisers, 28 destroyers and more than 500 aircraft. The force included the super battleships *Yamato* and *Musashi*, each displacing 71,400 tonnes (78705 tons), the largest warships of their kind ever built.

Admiral Raymond Spruance (1886–1969), commander of the US Fifth Fleet, was in overall command of a striking force built around the core of Task Force 58, led by Admiral Marc Mitscher (1887–1947). Organized into four battle groups, Task Force 58 included a complement of seven large fleet carriers, eight light carriers, seven battleships, 21 cruisers, 69 destroyers and nearly 1000 aircraft.

Although the US naval contingent was quite capable of potent offensive action, Spruance realized that his mission was twofold. Not only was he to engage the Japanese when and where practical but he was also charged with protecting the Saipan invasion beaches and support shipping. Therefore he determined to conduct a defensive operation rather than concentrate wholly on annihilating Ozawa.

In retrospect, Ozawa's effort appears doomed from the start. Warned by Naval Intelligence and a cordon of picket submarines that the Japanese were on the move, Spruance was well prepared for the coming engagement. He did not have long to wait.

TURKEY SHOOT

On the morning of 19 June 1944, Ozawa launched 69 planes against the Americans, 45 of which were soon shot down. A follow-up strike of 127 planes met a similar fate, 98 of them splashing into the sea under the guns of US Grumman F6F Hellcat fighters. During four raids against Task Force 58, the Japanese managed to inflict only slight damage on one US carrier and two battleships. The slaughter of planes and pilots was so thoroughly one-sided that the action came to be known as the 'Great Marianas Turkey Shoot'. In effect, Spruance was allowing what remained of Japan's carrier air power to dash itself against the rocks of his formidable air defences.

Compounding Ozawa's troubles, the newest aircraft carrier in the Japanese fleet and the admiral's flagship, *Taiho*, was struck by a torpedo from the submarine USS *Albacore* on 19 June. The damage had not been fatal, but early in the afternoon a young officer ordered the ship's ventilation system to be turned on to clear fumes from ruptured fuel lines, and the *Taiho* quickly became a floating bomb. A spark ignited the fumes, causing a catastrophic explosion, and the carrier slid beneath the waves within an hour. Furthermore, just after noon the submarine USS *Cavalla* slammed three torpedoes into the aircraft carrier *Shokaku*. Hours later, the ship was shattered by a massive internal explosion and sank.

COME RETRIBUTION

US search planes hunted the Japanese warships throughout the next day, but it was late when Ozawa's force was finally discovered. Mitscher, aware that the enemy ships were steaming at the outermost range of his planes and his returning pilots would probably have to land on decks in gathering darkness, quickly turned his carriers into the wind and launched 240 aircraft.

The sun was low in the West when the US planes found their target. Sweeping in to attack, they seriously damaged the carrier *Zuikaku*, the lone surviving veteran of the Pearl Harbor attack 30 months before. The light carriers *Ryuho* and

A HEAVILY ARMED VERSION of the North American B-25 Mitchell medium bomber, with .50-cal. machine guns mounted in its nose, strafes a Japanese patrol craft off the Philippines in July 1944.

LEFT: STATIONED ABOARD A JAPANESE aircraft carrier, a naval officer keeps track of planes as they take off to attack US Navy ships during the Battle of the Philippine Sea.

Junyo were hit by bombs and the light carrier *Hiyo* was sunk. As combat operations ebbed, the most formidable foe faced by the Americans during the Battle of the Philippine Sea turned out to be darkness. Numerous accidents occurred as planes with nearly empty fuel tanks attempted to land on their carriers. Other pilots were forced to ditch in the open sea and await rescue. Courageously, Mitscher risked attack by enemy submarines in ordering his ships to turn on their lights and fire star shells to assist the returning pilots. Eighty-two planes were lost, but the majority of the downed airmen were plucked from the water the next day.

AIR POWER ON THE WANE

The Battle of the Philippine Sea resulted in the destruction of Japanese carrier air power. When the fighting was over, Ozawa had only 35 aircraft remaining. He had lost three

BELOW: BRACKETED BY BOMBS from US Navy aircraft, a Japanese warship takes evasive action during the Battle of the Philippine Sea. Japanese naval air power was virtually eliminated during the fighting.

AIRCRAFT BURN AS DAMAGE control parties attempt to contain the flames aboard a US aircraft carrier that has been struck by a Japanese kamikaze. Another stricken carrier is visible in the distance.

carriers and more than 400 planes over two disastrous days. More than 200 land-based planes had been shot down or destroyed on the ground as well. The victory had cost the Americans 130 aircraft and relatively few casualties. Some historians have criticized Spruance for failing to completely destroy Ozawa's fleet and deliver the decisive blow against the Japanese navy. However, given his dual responsibilities, it must be concluded that Spruance accomplished both to the best of his ability.

In October, the Battle of Leyte Gulf, the last great naval engagement of the Pacific War, would settle the issue once and for all. After the Philippine Sea, however, the final defeat of Japan was a foregone conclusion.

PHILIPPINE SEA

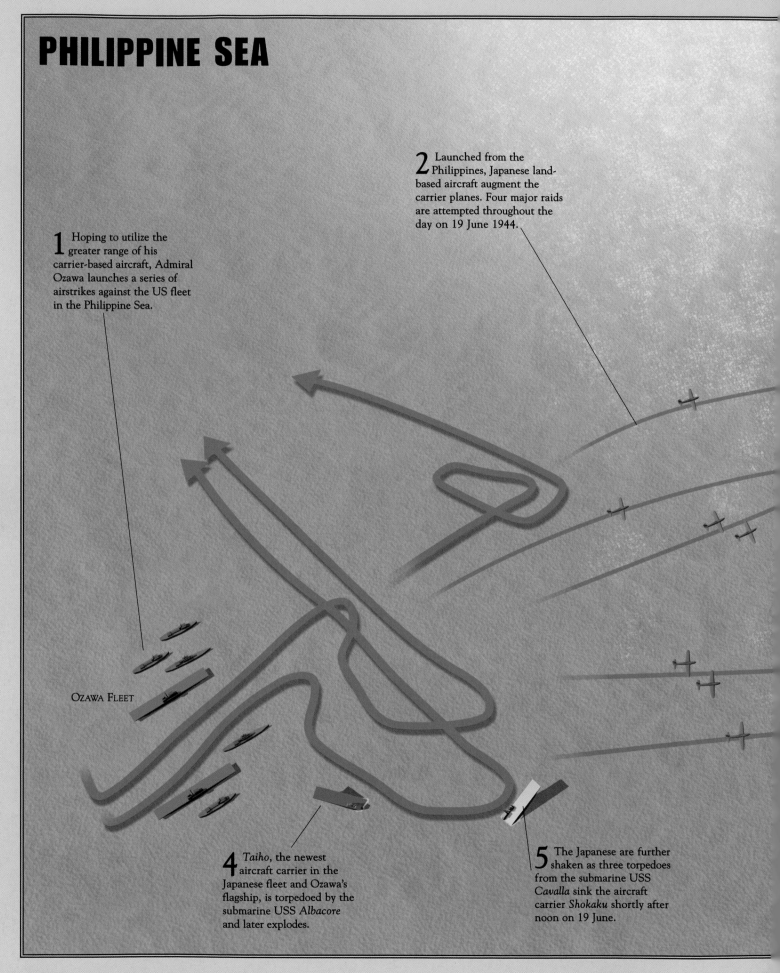

2 Launched from the Philippines, Japanese land-based aircraft augment the carrier planes. Four major raids are attempted throughout the day on 19 June 1944.

1 Hoping to utilize the greater range of his carrier-based aircraft, Admiral Ozawa launches a series of airstrikes against the US fleet in the Philippine Sea.

Ozawa Fleet

4 *Taiho*, the newest aircraft carrier in the Japanese fleet and Ozawa's flagship, is torpedoed by the submarine USS *Albacore* and later explodes.

5 The Japanese are further shaken as three torpedoes from the submarine USS *Cavalla* sink the aircraft carrier *Shokaku* shortly after noon on 19 June.

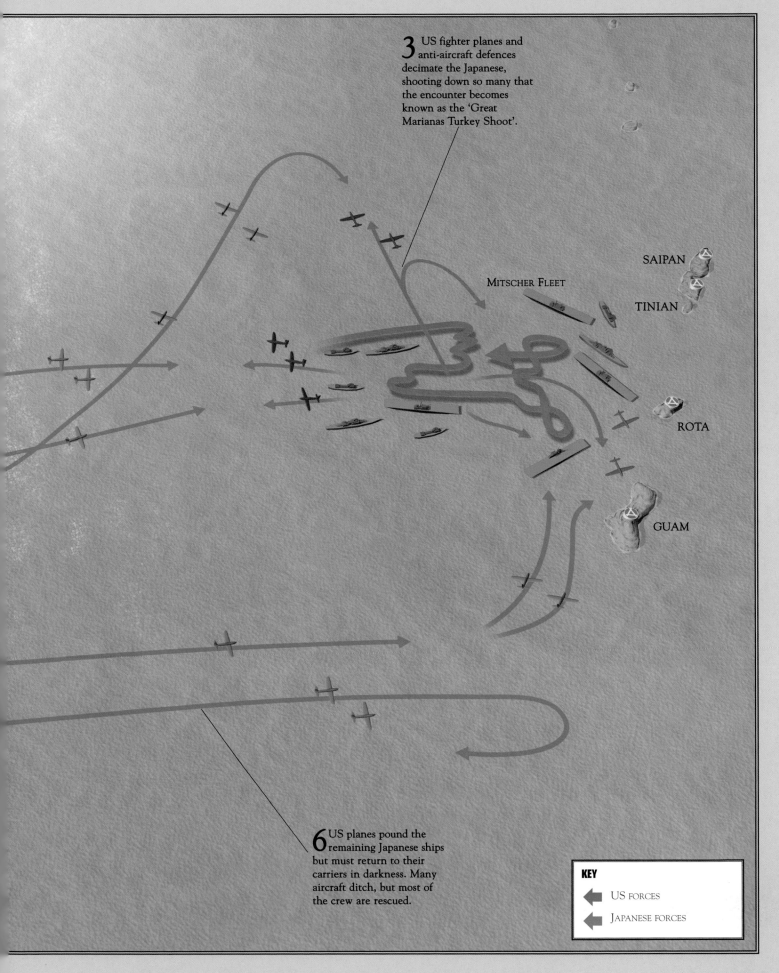

3 US fighter planes and anti-aircraft defences decimate the Japanese, shooting down so many that the encounter becomes known as the 'Great Marianas Turkey Shoot'.

SAIPAN

TINIAN

MITSCHER FLEET

ROTA

GUAM

6 US planes pound the remaining Japanese ships but must return to their carriers in darkness. Many aircraft ditch, but most of the crew are rescued.

KEY

← US FORCES

← JAPANESE FORCES

WARSAW RISING

1944

As the war moved towards its conclusion, the Allies agreed to divide Europe into spheres of influence. This was not acceptable to the Polish people, who wanted once again to be a free and sovereign nation. To demonstrate their independence, the Poles planned an uprising to liberate their capital before the advancing Red Army arrived.

Poland was one of the earliest victims of Nazi aggression, invaded in September 1939. The nation's army resisted as best it could, but defeat was inevitable even before the Soviet invasion from the other direction. However, this was not the end of Polish resistance. Free Polish forces were an important part of the war while resistance networks at home did all they could to further the Allied cause.

WARSAW RISING FACTS

Who: More than 40,000 Polish irregulars versus German occupying forces of roughly 25,000 troops.

What: The Uprising began on 1 August 1944 as part of a nationwide rebellion. It was intended to last for only a few days until the Soviet Army reached the city. However, it developed into a long urban guerrilla campaign against the occupiers.

Where: Warsaw, Poland.

When: August–October 1944.

Why: The Poles sought to re-establish their sovereignty after four years of Nazi-German occupation.

Outcome: The uprising was ultimately put down with great losses on both sides. It is estimated that more than 200,000 civilians died in the fighting, while 700,000 were expelled from the city.

In August 1944, Polish volunteers equipped with whatever weapons they could obtain seized much of Warsaw from the German occupation forces, beginning a long and bitter struggle for the city.

MEN OF THE *Dirlewanger Brigade, a formation supposedly intended to rehabilitate criminals by military service. The brigade's career of atrocities reached its peak during the Warsaw Rising.*

Once the tide of the war had turned and German forces began the long retreat out of Russia, it became obvious that Poland was going to be 'liberated' by the Soviet Union, which meant inevitably falling into its sphere of influence. Indeed a pro-Soviet government was being readied for installation as soon as the Red Army pushed the Germans out. The Poles did not welcome this prospect. They wanted a free and independent state and that meant doing more than waiting for one foreign army to leave and another to arrive. The plan, named Operation *Tempest,* called for orchestrated risings in several cities and a campaign of attacks in various regions of the country.

This would hopefully drive the German occupiers out before the Red Army arrived and also assist the Allied cause by distracting German attention. Once the capital was liberated, members of the Polish government would come out of hiding and assume control.

No one had any illusions that there would not be bloodshed when the rising took place, but the Poles were willing to make the sacrifice. They had been fighting a hidden war for the entire occupation, hampering German efforts in Russia by disrupting the logistics chain running eastwards.

The largest resistance organization was named *Armia Krajowa* (Home Army). It had over 400,000 members, who were armed with weapons dropped by the Allies or obtained from German sources – by theft, capture or sometimes black market purchase. In addition, there were stocks of weaponry concealed in the last days of freedom when it became apparent that the German advance could not be halted.

Thus there was no shortage of willing and experienced fighters available for the operation. The resistance forces had been fighting this kind of guerrilla war for years, albeit on a smaller scale. Now they saw their opportunity to win a decisive victory.

THE RISING

In July 1944, the Red Army was advancing on Warsaw and it seemed obvious that the battle for the city would soon begin if the German garrison did not retreat. This was unlikely as the city was a major logistics and transport centre and was also politically significant.

Plans were made to use Polish labour to construct fortifications around the city and a demand was made for men to come forward to do the work. Suspicious of the motives behind the order, the population largely refused to obey it. This increased tensions between the population and the occupiers even further and prompted the Home Army commanders to move up their timetable. The order was given to launch the rising on 1 August 1944.

The Home Army had about 45,000 members in Warsaw at the time of the rising, under General Antoni Chrusciel (1895–1960). About half of these personnel were equipped for combat, though it was necessary to get weapons to many of them just before the rising started.

ABOVE: FLAMETHROWERS PROVED VERY EFFECTIVE in the urban fighting for Warsaw. Their use was acceptable to a regime that did not care about damage to the city – indeed, much of it was deliberately destroyed.

Organizing such a large-scale operation was difficult, especially within an enemy-held city, and it was not possible to conceal from the occupiers that something was going on. The garrison and internal security forces, including SS troops and secret police, were alerted and able to prepare to an extent. The original plan had been for the first strikes to be made at night and by surprise. Instead, the Home Army had to attack alert troops in daylight. Success was mixed: in some areas, objectives were quickly overwhelmed where in others the attacks were met with intense machine-gun and small-arms fire and repelled.

There were about 11,000 German troops in the city under the overall command of Lieutenant-General Reiner Stahel. About half were regulars; the rest were mostly from the *Luftwaffe*. There were also more than 5000 SS personnel in the area under the command of Colonel Paul Giebel. Cooperation between these units was patchy at times and there was no coherent strategy for dealing with the uprising.

The result was a very confused situation with groups from both sides cut off from their allies by territory held by the enemy. Barricades were erected and control over captured areas consolidated, and gradually the insurgents took

RIGHT: HITLER TOOK A personal interest in the battle for Warsaw, allocating large resources and condoning the harsh measures used to suppress the insurgency.

ABOVE: A GERMAN OFFICER *directs his men during street fighting in Warsaw. In this sort of close-quarters battle, effective junior leadership was of paramount importance; in a fluid situation higher command could not react quickly enough.*

control of more and more of the city. By 4 August, most of Warsaw was under Polish control. All that was necessary was to hang on until the Red Army arrived.

GERMAN COUNTERMEASURES

Even as the Poles were reaching the high watermark of their uprising, an organized response began to unfold. German reinforcements came up, and all forces were placed under a single commander, General Erich von dem Bach (1899–1972), an SS officer who formulated plans to retake the city.

A spearhead of combat troops drove into the city, establishing a line behind which the streets were under firm German control. Here the SS and Gestapo were free to operate as they wished. There was no pretence of justice or justification – civilians were simply rounded up behind the German line and shot.

The massacre was intended to break the will of the population and bring the insurgency to an end without having to dig the Poles out house by house. In this, it failed. Resistance became ever more determined, partly from outrage and partly from the feeling that to surrender was a death sentence anyway.

Once it became apparent that reprisals were not the answer, a different approach was used. Instead of simply executing captured resistance fighters, some were accorded the status of prisoners of war and fairly treated in the hope that this would make it seem that it was worth surrendering. This also had little effect.

STREET FIGHTING

The uprising had been intended as a short campaign to end with the Red Army arriving at the city limits. Yet the Red Army remained strangely inactive, suddenly unable or perhaps unwilling to make much progress in its advance. Thus the Poles were forced to fight on.

The arrival of tanks on 7 August did not shift the balance much. The insurgents had prepared obstacles and barricades, and although some ground was lost the situation had stabilized by 9 August. The fighting reached a climax between 9 and 18 August, with large-scale urban combat raging across wide areas of the city.

By 2 September, the tide had turned. Under air attack and bombardment by distant artillery to which they had no reply, the Poles had to pull out of the old town, using the sewers to avoid detection. The fighting went on elsewhere, the German forces grinding their way through the city in a manner not dissimilar to the urban hell of Stalingrad.

THE SOVIETS APPROACH

By the middle of September, the advance units of the Red Army had almost reached the Vistula and were pushing the Germans back once again. Although Soviet forces seemed unwilling to help the insurgents, Free Polish units fighting with them moved into the city and joined their countrymen. They were not given support by their Soviet comrades in arms, however, and were badly defeated.

The Free Polish commander, General Zygmunt Berling (1896–1980), was relieved of command by his Soviet allies and the remainder of the Soviet army halted short of

LEFT: THE RED ARMY *had significant forces nearby and could perhaps have come to the aid of the insurgents, but did not. Instead, weapons like this Su-152 self-propelled gun stood idle while the battle raged.*

Warsaw and stayed there. There were solid tactical reasons – the Soviets were closely engaged with German armoured battle groups at the time – but there was more to it than this.

Although the Soviets had been calling for a Polish uprising for months, Stalin did not desire the Warsaw insurgency to succeed. He wanted Poland under Soviet control, not independent, and the insurgents had risen in the name of the pro-West government-in-exile based in London. By waiting until the rising was crushed and then moving in, he ensured that Poland would fall under the sway of Moscow.

Stalin also refused to allow the Western Allies to use Soviet airbases to fly supplies in to the insurgents. Some drops were

THESE WOUNDED POLISH insurgents were captured at the end of the uprising, and stood a good chance of being treated as prisoners of war. Earlier on, captured personnel were simply shot.

still made, but they had to fly out of distant bases and were not effective. Soviet troops at times fired on Allied aircraft making supply runs, though a re-supply mission was eventually permitted. By then, it was too late: the insurgents had been ground down to the point where they could no longer resist.

On 2 October 1944, General Tadeusz Bor-Komorowski (1895–1966), Chrusciel's superior in the Home Army, surrendered what was left of the forces in Warsaw after receiving a promise that the insurgents would be treated as regular combatants in accordance with the relevant conventions. The civilian population was also to be spared reprisals.

THE DESTRUCTION OF WARSAW

Some of the insurgents did not turn themselves in but tried to fade out of sight among the population. Of those who did surrender, some were treated as any other prisoners of war and sent west to camps in Germany. Of the remainder, some were sent to concentration camps, some to labour projects and most dispersed and released. None was allowed to remain in the city.

The city was then systematically destroyed by fire and explosives. Some houses escaped but all public and historic buildings were deliberately targeted. The Red Army finally entered Warsaw in mid-January 1945, by which time very little remained of the city.

A CITY DESTROYED

About a quarter of Warsaw was destroyed in the fighting that resulted from the uprising. After the Polish surrender, the population was driven out and an attempt was made to burn or demolish the remainder of the city. In fact, 85 per cent of Warsaw was destroyed in this manner, with special emphasis put on cultural buildings, from churches and schools to monuments and the university.

The city was rebuilt after the war, and considerable effort was put into recreating the historic city centre, which is now a World Heritage Site. In 2004, a ceremony was held to mark the 50th anniversary of the uprising, though it was suggested that the Russian delegation should observe from the far bank of the Vistula.

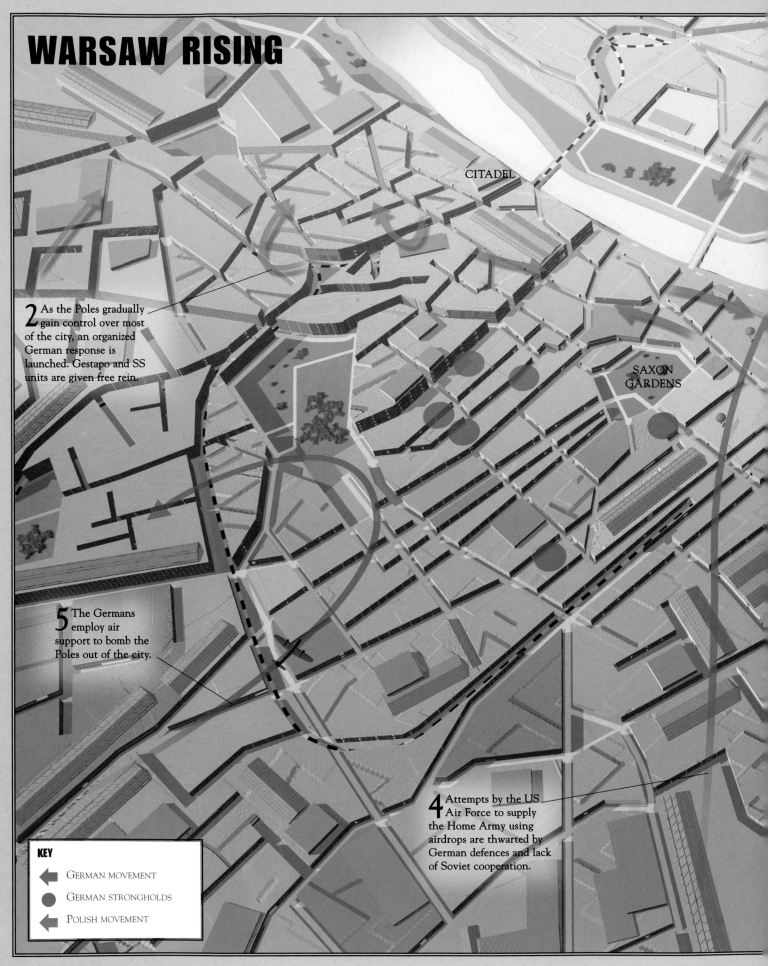

WARSAW RISING

2 As the Poles gradually gain control over most of the city, an organized German response is launched. Gestapo and SS units are given free rein.

CITADEL

SAXON GARDENS

5 The Germans employ air support to bomb the Poles out of the city.

4 Attempts by the US Air Force to supply the Home Army using airdrops are thwarted by German defences and lack of Soviet cooperation.

KEY

◄ GERMAN MOVEMENT

● GERMAN STRONGHOLDS

◄ POLISH MOVEMENT

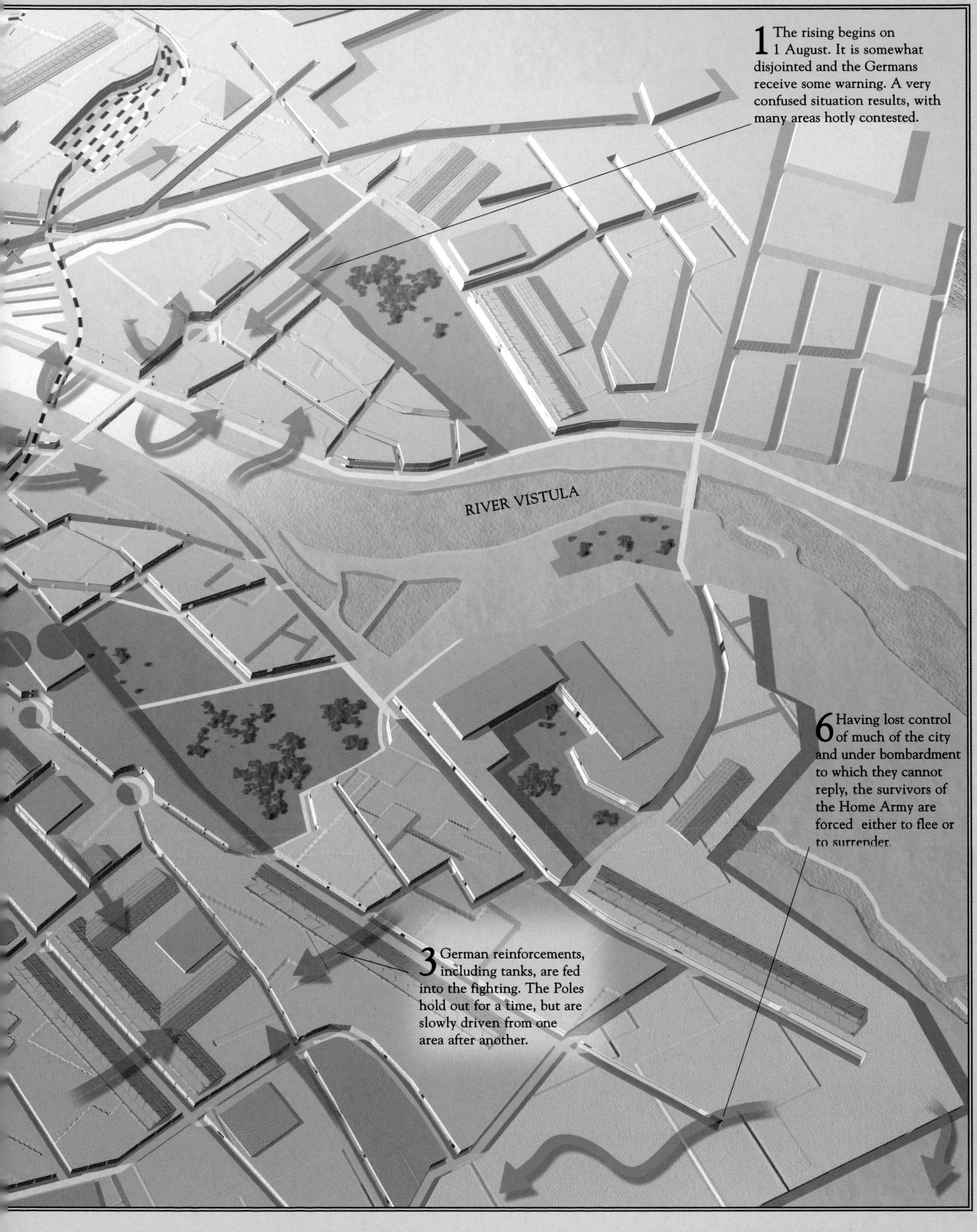

1 The rising begins on 1 August. It is somewhat disjointed and the Germans receive some warning. A very confused situation results, with many areas hotly contested.

RIVER VISTULA

6 Having lost control of much of the city and under bombardment to which they cannot reply, the survivors of the Home Army are forced either to flee or to surrender.

3 German reinforcements, including tanks, are fed into the fighting. The Poles hold out for a time, but are slowly driven from one area after another.

OPERATION 'MARKET GARDEN'
1944

Operations 'Market' and 'Garden' were complementary halves of a daring plan to seize strategic bridges with airborne troops, then rush ground forces up and across them. Had it succeeded, Market Garden might have shortened the war by a year.

The Siegfried Line, or Westwall, was a chain of fortifications facing France, constructed before the war. Rather than a solid line, it was a deeply defended zone covered by minefields, pillboxes, bunkers and antitank obstacles, all covered by artillery in protected emplacements. Entrenched in such positions, even third-line troops could inflict serious casualties.

In the summer of 1944, it was obvious that if the Allies were forced to assault the Siegfried Line they would suffer serious casualties. An alternative line of attack, into the heavily defended Ruhr, would be equally costly. So the Allies

OPERATION 'MARKET GARDEN' FACTS

Who: Allied airborne and ground forces, including the British 1st Airborne Division and Polish Brigade, opposed by German armoured and infantry units.

What: Although at first the advance was a success, German resistance was heavier than expected.

Where: The Netherlands, near the town of Arnhem, on the River Rhine.

When: 17–25 September 1944

Why: The Allies wanted to get across the Rhine quickly, bypassing major German defences and trapping large numbers of German forces in the Netherlands.

Outcome: The operation was a failure, prolonging the war in Northwest Europe by at least a few months.

PARATROOPS AND GLIDERBORNE infantry land at Arnhem. Putting troops in a glider required less training than creating paratroops, though it was scarcely less dangerous. Glider troops were also less prone to being scattered.

sought an alternative and found one that, with luck and daring, might be workable.

The plan was relatively simple. Attacking by surprise, the Allies would seize strategic bridges over the rivers Maas, Waal and Lower Rhine, enabling the establishment of a bridgehead behind the enemy's main defended zone and the most formidable natural obstacles. The only problem was that the first bridge might indeed be taken by *coup de main*, perhaps by light armoured forces racing up to grab it, but by the time the assault force got across and reached the next bridge, they might find it to be blown or strongly held.

The answer was for all the bridges to be captured at the same time, by paratroops and glider-borne infantry who would defend their objective until relieved by the rapidly advancing armoured spearhead. The airborne component was codenamed *Market* and the armoured advance *Garden*, but in reality neither had any point without the other. It was the whole, Operation *Market Garden*, that mattered. It was a bold plan – perhaps a little too bold. One Allied officer, feeling that the Allies were about to overextend themselves remarked, 'I think we're going a bridge too far'. But it was all

BRITISH PARATROOPERS EN ROUTE to Arnhem. Just getting onto the ground was a dangerous business; 'jump casualties' from enemy fire or a bad landing were inevitable on any operation.

or nothing – there was no point in grabbing just some of the bridges. *Market Garden* had to succeed completely or not at all.

The most serious threat to the operation was not the enemy but poor planning. Perhaps as a result of complacency following the success of the Normandy landings, much was taken for granted. As a result, re-supply operations came unstuck and cooperation between units failed. Sometimes this was due to problems with radios but just as often to a lack of good communications procedures.

OPENING MOVES

The operation began with paratroop landings by British, American and Free Polish units. RAF concerns about the air defences in the Arnhem region meant that the paras were dropped at a distance from their objectives, requiring a forced march and giving the enemy time to react to the threat.

This might not have been too serious but for two facts. Firstly, II SS Panzer Corps was in the region, rebuilding its strength after taking a battering in Normandy. This was an experienced and well-equipped unit that retained its offensive spirit. Secondly, Field-Marshal Walter Model (1891–1945) was in the immediate vicinity. Model had gained a well-deserved reputation as an excellent commander on the Eastern Front, where he staved off defeat again and again by scraping a battle group together from whatever was to hand and improvising a brilliant battle plan. Now, that experience came to the fore.

Model gave orders to prevent the paras from reaching their objectives, then went to his headquarters and began organizing a response to the overall situation. By this time, he knew that Allied armour was smashing its way towards him and that paratroops had landed along its projected route. It was not at all difficult to determine what the Allies were attempting.

Model's fast response meant that very few of the paras assigned to take the Arnhem bridges reached the town at all. Elements of 2nd battalion, the Parachute Regiment under Lieutenant-Colonel John Frost (1912–1993), along with an assortment of troops gathered along the way, were able to reach the north end of the bridge and hang on there, but this was the limit of the paras' success. Model assigned part of his force to contain the paras and began gathering everything else he could find to halt the armoured attack coming his way.

THE ALLIES ADVANCE

Although some of the airborne troops were still in England, unable to take off due to fog, the advance went ahead. There were several minor waterways to cross and plans had been laid to set up temporary bridges if necessary, but in the event the Allies were able to overrun what defenders there were and to gain control of the permanent bridges.

However, there were two waterways that could not be bridged: at Nijmegen and Arnhem the Allies had to cross

ABOVE: ALTHOUGH PARATROOPERS jumped in quick succession, a 'stick' could become widely separated if there was much wind. Paradrop operations always began confused, with lost personnel hoping to rejoin their units later.

BELOW: THE SDKFZ 251/22 mounted a heavy antitank gun on a proven half-track truck chassis. These vehicles were effectively used as mobile tank destroyers by SS troops fighting at Arnhem.

arms of the Rhine. There was no way for combat engineers to create a temporary crossing of such wide rivers. Here the bridges would have to be taken and that meant getting there while the paras still had control of the bridges.

Despite this, the ground assault had been delayed, waiting for confirmation that the airborne operation was a success. As a result, resistance along the roads towards the bridges firmed up and the advance fell behind schedule. Nightfall forced a stop and by the time the armoured spearhead reached Nijmegen an organized defence was in place. Attempts to break through were met by fire from 88mm (3.46in) antitank guns and repelled.

The original plan had called for all the bridges to be in Allied hands within 48 hours. However, by this time the ground forces were still trying to get on to the Nijmegen bridge while the airborne forces were fighting sporadic and scattered actions all over the countryside. Some were successful and more paras reached Arnhem, but overall the chances of success were diminishing fast.

Frost's paras were still clinging to the end of the Arnhem bridge, incidentally denying its use to the enemy, but they were under ferocious pressure from artillery and tanks. The Allies had to get across the Waal at Nijmegen and start making some headway before it was too late.

BELOW: A KAMPFGRUPPE OF German infantry advances. In such a confused situation, an attack could come from anywhere and it was not always possible to tell whether a contact was a couple of lost paras or a major force.

ABOVE: THE ROAD BRIDGE at Arnhem. Although the paratroopers were not able to capture the whole bridge, they held one end of it long enough to deny its use to a German counterattack.

The solution was daring and aggressive: US airborne troops would make an assault crossing in small boats and then storm the far end of the bridge. While their attack distracted the defenders' attention, the armoured forces would advance across at full speed.

The crossing was extremely difficult even without the intense enemy fire that came from the bank. Many paddles were missing from the boats so the troops used rifle butts and helmets to crawl slowly across the wide river. Even with assistance from tank guns and aircraft, many boats were riddled, yet somehow the paras got across and launched an attack up the bank.

As the assault boat crews took them back across to pick up more paras, those that had survived the crossing fell on the defenders and drove them from the banks. In a very confused action, where aggression counted for more than anything else, the armoured troops charged on to the bridges from one end while the paras attacked the other.

During the advance, the German commander on the spot tried to detonate previously laid demolition charges, which failed to work. The likely explanation is that a member of the Dutch Resistance cut the wires during the fighting. After the bridge was made safe, the armoured forces were able to advance across it.

The Allies were finally across the Waal and only 18km (11 miles) from where Frost and his paras were holding one end of the Arnhem bridge. A rapid advance might have been in order but the Allied force was tired and disorganized. It was not possible to put together a sufficient force to break through and achieve anything at Arnhem.

A BRIDGE TOO FAR

The situation was still very fluid, with German forces coming in from the flanks and at times cutting the Allied line of communications. Model's forces at Arnhem were gaining strength and Frost had finally been overrun.

It was clear that an assault was very unlikely to succeed. Worse, Model had managed to get some panzers across the river (using an alternate route since Frost's paras denied him the use of the bridge until it was too late) and was advancing down the road to Nijmegen.

An Allied armoured thrust up the Arnhem road was unable to break through and attacks along other axes ran into heavy resistance. The operation had obviously failed and it was time to salvage all they could. As many paras as possible were brought across the river in assault boats during the night of 25/26 September.

AFTERMATH

The goal of getting across the Rhine quickly and without fighting through heavy defences had not been achieved. A combination of mischance, poor planning and the determination of the enemy robbed the operation of success.

ABOVE: MAN-PORTABLE MORTARS *were the only artillery available to the lightly equipped paratroopers. They were effective in close-range urban fighting, but ammunition was limited by what could be carried.*

As a result, the allies were forced to fight their way in 'though the front door' and took heavy casualties as a result. The damage in still-occupied territory caused by the extra months of war was also considerable.

ABOVE: ALTHOUGH GOOD TACTICS *and use of cover could improve the odds, it was also possible to be in the wrong place at the wrong time. This German soldier may have made a mistake or simply been unlucky.*

OPERATION 'MARKET GARDEN'

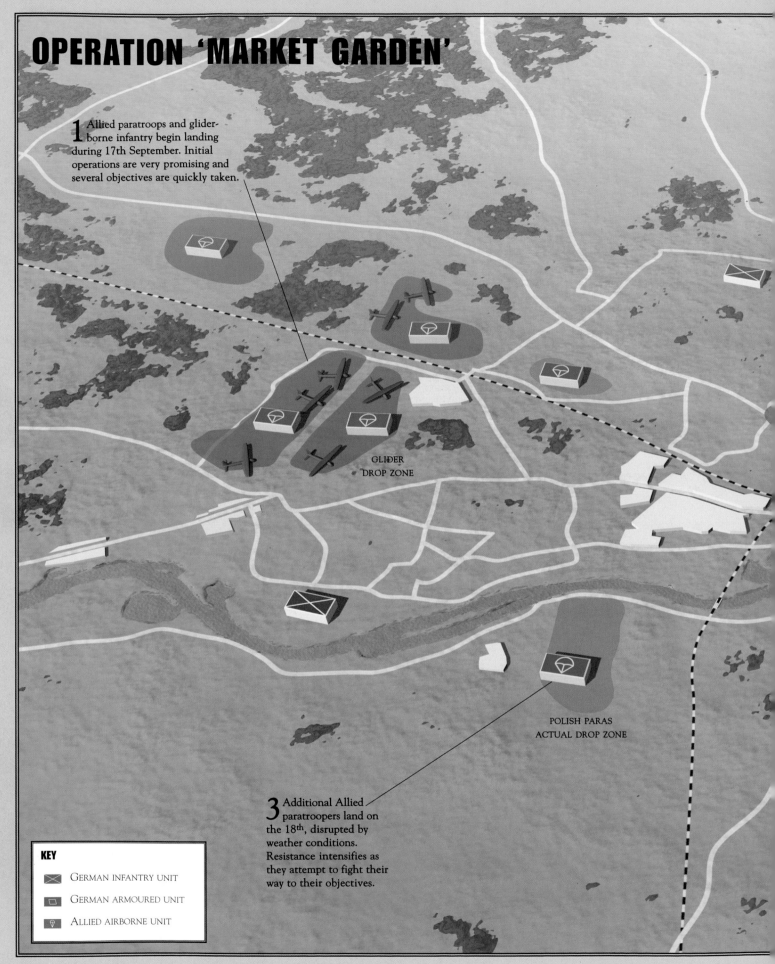

1 Allied paratroops and glider-borne infantry begin landing during 17th September. Initial operations are very promising and several objectives are quickly taken.

GLIDER DROP ZONE

POLISH PARAS ACTUAL DROP ZONE

3 Additional Allied paratroopers land on the 18th, disrupted by weather conditions. Resistance intensifies as they attempt to fight their way to their objectives.

KEY

German infantry unit

German armoured unit

Allied airborne unit

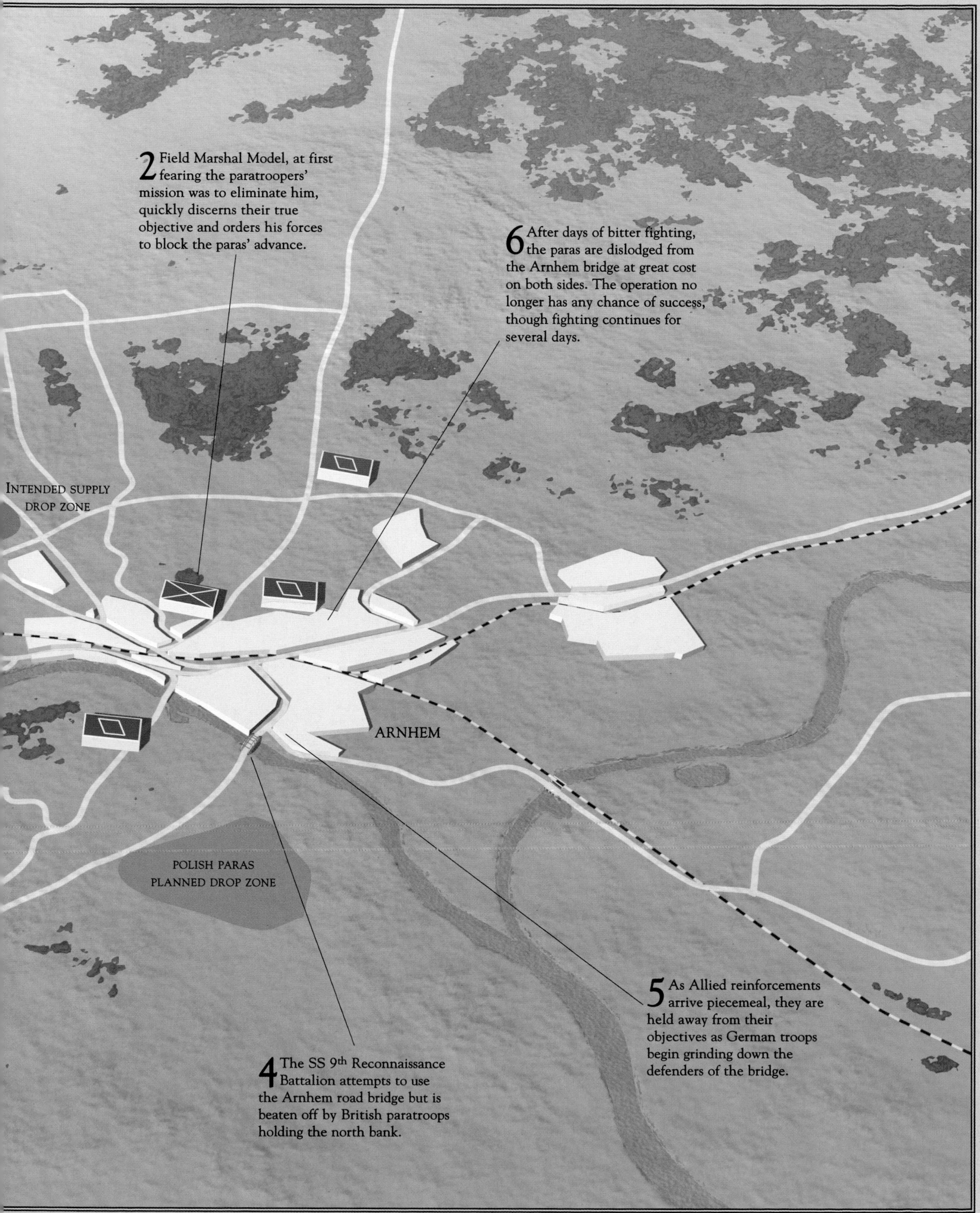

2 Field Marshal Model, at first fearing the paratroopers' mission was to eliminate him, quickly discerns their true objective and orders his forces to block the paras' advance.

6 After days of bitter fighting, the paras are dislodged from the Arnhem bridge at great cost on both sides. The operation no longer has any chance of success, though fighting continues for several days.

INTENDED SUPPLY
DROP ZONE

ARNHEM

POLISH PARAS
PLANNED DROP ZONE

5 As Allied reinforcements arrive piecemeal, they are held away from their objectives as German troops begin grinding down the defenders of the bridge.

4 The SS 9th Reconnaissance Battalion attempts to use the Arnhem road bridge but is beaten off by British paratroops holding the north bank.

BATTLE OF THE BULGE 1944–45

At 5.30 a.m. on the morning of 16 December 1944, the thunder of hundreds of German guns shattered the stillness of the Ardennes, a relatively quiet sector of the Allied lines on the German frontier. It was the beginning of Operation Wacht am Rhein (Watch on the Rhine), a last gamble by Adolf Hitler in the West.

The *Führer's* objective was to force a wedge between the Allied Twelfth and Twenty-First Army Groups with a fast-moving armoured thrust that would drive across the river Meuse and on to the vital Belgian port city of Antwerp. Hitler also hoped subsequently to shift forces to meet a coming offensive in the East, where the Soviet Red Army was poised to strike across the river Vistula into

BATTLE OF THE BULGE FACTS

Who: German forces under the command of *Führer* Adolf Hitler (1889–1945) and his generals versus Allied forces under General Dwight Eisenhower (1890–1969).

What: Hitler hoped to divide Allied army groups in the West, drive to the port of Antwerp and change the course of the war.

Where: The front lines in Belgium, France and Luxembourg.

When: 16 December 1944 to 15 January 1945

Why: Hitler sought to divide the Western Allies and gain time to confront the coming Soviet offensive along the river Vistula in the East.

Outcome: The battle resulted in a disastrous defeat for Nazi Germany. Less than four months later, World War II in Europe was over.

HALTED MOMENTARILY ALONG *an icy road in Belgium, German Panzer V 'Panther' tanks spearhead the German Ardennes offensive. With its large gun, the Panther was one of the best tanks of World War II.*

ABOVE: CAPTURED DURING THE opening phase of the Battle of the Bulge, American prisoners are marched by their German captors toward an uncertain fate. SS soldiers were guilty of atrocities during the fighting.

the heart of Germany. Bypassing Field-Marshal Gerd von Rundstedt (1875–1953), his commander in the West, Hitler instructed three armies – Sixth Panzer under SS General Josef 'Sepp' Dietrich (1892–1966) to the north, Fifth Panzer commanded by General Hasso von Manteuffel (1897–1978) in the centre, and Seventh Army under General Erich

Brandenberger (1892–1955) further south – to strike on a 97km (60-mile) front from Monschau, Germany, to the town of Echternach in Luxembourg.

THE STORM BREAKS

For months, Hitler had mulled over his plan. Finally, with 275,000 troops, hundreds of tanks and nearly 2000 artillery pieces, he launched his attack against a sector of the line that Allied commanders had considered virtually inactive. Warning signs of a pending offensive had been ignored and when the Germans jumped off, numerous American units were taken completely by surprise. However, pockets of stiff resistance formed along Elsenborn Ridge, particularly by troops of the 99th Division.

These determined efforts slowed Dietrich to a crawl until a shift of troops to the south outflanked some defensive positions along the Schnee Eifel, a cluster of hamlets and tree-covered hills in front of the high ground. Thousands of US soldiers were scooped up as prisoners. The untested troops of the 106th Infantry Division found themselves cut off in the Schnee Eifel, and on 19 December two entire regiments surrendered – but the Americans on Elsenborn Ridge stood their ground.

Dietrich's armoured spearhead, commanded by SS Colonel Joachim Peiper (1915–1976), pushed hard for several key bridges over the Meuse and other waterways, which would facilitate rapid crossings. In the process, however, the Germans were held up by groups of US combat engineers, one of which disabled Peiper's lead tank and blocked access to a bridge across the Amblève river at the town of Stavelot. Other bridges were blown up nearly in the Germans' faces by the engineers. Enraged by the delays, Peiper was also plagued by a shortage of fuel. His force, which originally numbered 4000, was eventually surrounded and only around 800 managed to escape. Peiper and his command gained lasting infamy in the fight, which would

BELOW: THE GERMAN TIGER II or King Tiger tank combined a high velocity 88mm (3.46in) cannon and sloped armour in a formidable fighting vehicle. The horizontal lines of anti-mine zimmerit coating are faintly visible.

RIGHT: SOLDIERS FROM KAMPFGRUPPE PEIPER on the road to Malmédy. In the background is a SdKfz 251 half-track armoured personnel carrier.

come to be known as the Battle of the Bulge. One of his units was guilty of murdering 85 captured Americans in a field near Malmedy in one of the most publicized atrocities of World War II.

As Allied troops held Elsenborn Ridge, the north shoulder of the great bulge began to form. Brandenberg's thrust ran into the veteran 9th Armoured and 4th Infantry Divisions of the US Army and made little or no progress along the southern edge of the offensive. In the centre, Manteuffel's tanks came closest to reaching the Meuse near Dinant, roughly 80km (50 miles) from their start line. A heroic stand by elements of the US 7th Armoured Division at the town of St Vith delayed the Germans for six days. The town did not fall until 23 December and British Field-Marshal Bernard Montgomery (1887–1976), placed in command of forces north of the bulge, used the time to consolidate his defences.

BELOW: AS THE TIDE of the fighting in the Ardennes begins to turn in late December 1944, American infantrymen proceed through some abandoned, snow-covered buildings toward German positions.

101ST AIRBORNE DIVISION

The paratroopers of the 101st Airborne Division, activated in 1942, had jumped into Normandy during Operation *Overlord* and into Holland during Operation *Market Garden*; however, their most difficult test of the war may well have been in defence of the key Belgian crossroads town of Bastogne during the Battle of the Bulge. As the tide of German armour and infantry swept around them, the 101st held firm, considerably slowing the advance of the enemy. Refusing to surrender, the Screaming Eagles were eventually relieved by elements of the 4th Armoured Division, the vanguard of the Third Army commanded by General George S. Patton, Jr.

'NUTS!'

Southwest of St Vith, the Belgian crossroads town of Bastogne proved critical to the outcome of the Battle of the Bulge. Continued possession of Bastogne by the Americans would deny the Germans use of a key road network and slow their advance considerably. On 17 December, the vanguard of Manteuffel's forces reached the outskirts of the town. Unable to capture it by direct assault, the Germans bypassed Bastogne, which was defended by the lightly armed 101st Airborne Division and elements of other units.

The encircled paratroopers held on by their fingernails, but when heavy German forces drew the noose tighter on 22 December they were invited to surrender. The ranking US officer in the embattled town was Major-General Anthony McAuliffe (1897–1983), and his famous reply to the German ultimatum was simply, 'Nuts!'.

Although he was in dire straits, McAuliffe did have reason to hope. Foul weather, which had benefited the Germans, had begun to clear the previous day and allowed an airdrop of desperately needed supplies. Of even greater importance, relief for the beleaguered defenders of Bastogne was already on the way.

BARRICADES NOW OPEN, American troops move through a village in Belgium that shows signs of heavy fighting, late December 1944.

LEFT: A P-47 THUNDERBOLT *carries out a ground attack against targets in the Low Countries, late 1944. The Allies' total air superiority played a big part in ensuring the Ardennes offensive would eventually fail. Ground attack aircraft like the P-47 could strafe German columns without fear of interference from the Luftwaffe.*

Americans in the Ardennes, and his gamble had reached the brink of success. In the end, a lack of fuel, unexpectedly stiff resistance and clearing weather had conspired to bring about a crushing defeat.

The offensive had cost the *Führer* dearly. More than 120,000 Germans had been killed, wounded or taken prisoner during a month of hard fighting. Scores of tanks and other armoured vehicles had been destroyed or abandoned. American casualties totalled nearly 80,000, with about 8500 dead, 46,000 wounded and more than 20,000 captured. Both sides had suffered terribly. For the Allies, the losses could be made good. For the Germans, they could not.

PATTON PIVOTS

On 20 December, under orders from the Supreme Allied Commander, General Dwight Eisenhower (1890–1969), elements of General George Patton's (1885–1945) Third Army disengaged from their own offensive in the Saar, wheeled 90° to the north and began slashing towards the surrounded town, which appeared on maps as an American island in a sea of German tanks and troops. Hardly stopping to rest or eat, the men of Third Army penetrated the German perimeter. Patton's spearhead, the 4th Armoured Division, made contact with the 101st Airborne on the day after Christmas.

The relief of Bastogne sealed the fate of the German offensive, while heroic defensive efforts at Elsenborn Ridge, St Vith and elsewhere had contained the German thrust within a week. Soon the great bulge began to resemble a gigantic Allied pincer movement rather than a tremendous German threat. As 1944 ebbed away, so too did Hitler's dream of ultimate victory in the West. By 15 January 1945, Allied forces had converged on the city of Houffalize, Belgium, effectively reducing the German salient.

IRREPLACEABLE LOSSES

With the failure of Operation *Watch* on the Rhine and the commencement of the Red Army winter offensive in the East on 12 January 1945, the endgame of World War II in Europe had begun. In two months, the Allies would be across the Rhine, the last imposing natural barrier to their advance. Soon the Soviets would be fighting in the suburbs of Berlin. Hitler had diverted precious troops and matériel from the Eastern Front for the all-out effort against the

RIGHT: GENERAL ANTHONY MCAULIFFE, *acting commander of the 101st Airborne Division at Bastogne, issued the famous reply of 'NUTS!' to a German demand for surrender during the Battle of the Bulge.*

BATTLE OF THE BULGE

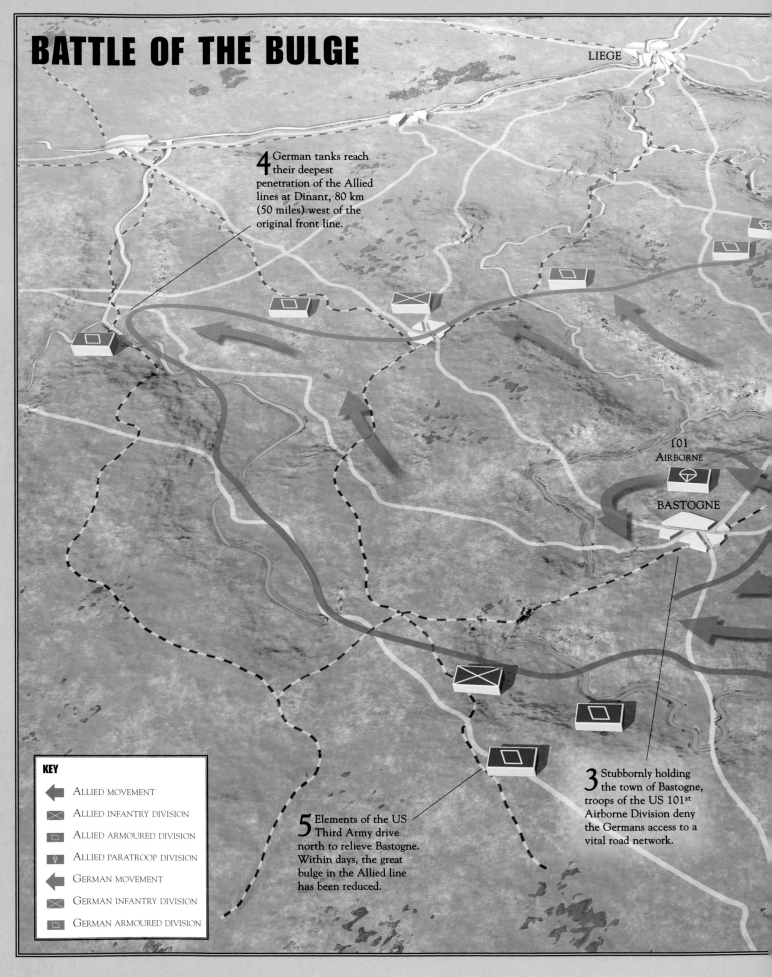

LIEGE

4 German tanks reach their deepest penetration of the Allied lines at Dinant, 80 km (50 miles) west of the original front line.

101 AIRBORNE

BASTOGNE

3 Stubbornly holding the town of Bastogne, troops of the US 101st Airborne Division deny the Germans access to a vital road network.

5 Elements of the US Third Army drive north to relieve Bastogne. Within days, the great bulge in the Allied line has been reduced.

KEY

⬅ ALLIED MOVEMENT

⊠ ALLIED INFANTRY DIVISION

▭ ALLIED ARMOURED DIVISION

▽ ALLIED PARATROOP DIVISION

⬅ GERMAN MOVEMENT

⊠ GERMAN INFANTRY DIVISION

▭ GERMAN ARMOURED DIVISION

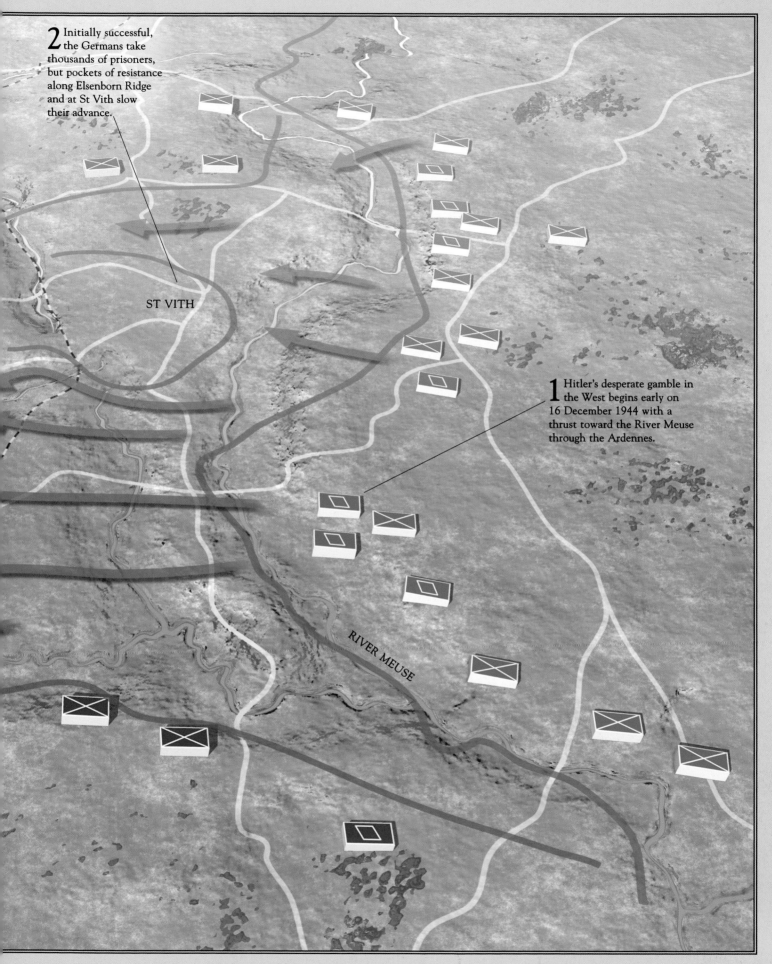

2 Initially successful, the Germans take thousands of prisoners, but pockets of resistance along Elsenborn Ridge and at St Vith slow their advance.

ST VITH

1 Hitler's desperate gamble in the West begins early on 16 December 1944 with a thrust toward the River Meuse through the Ardennes.

RIVER MEUSE

IWO JIMA 1945

The island road to Tokyo was long and bloody for the US military. Although the United States had seized the initiative in the Pacific, it was clear throughout the campaign that the Japanese were resourceful and tenacious foes – willing to fight to the death. As the war entered its fourth year, American planners had become resigned to the fact that final victory would necessitate an invasion of the Japanese home islands.

Such an undertaking would require extensive logistical preparation and suitable staging areas were needed. Already, long-range bombers were being deployed to rain death and destruction on Japanese cities. Crippled bombers returning to distant bases in the Marianas needed a safe haven to land. Aboard each bomber was a crew of 10–14 men.

The island of Iwo Jima in the Volcanoes Group seemed to fill both requirements. Situated only 1062km (660 miles) south of Tokyo, the Japanese had already constructed airfields there. Although taking the island promised to be a

IWO JIMA FACTS

Who: Japanese troops under Lieutenant-General Tadamichi Kuribayashi (1891–1945) versus US Marines under Lieutenant-General Holland M. Smith (1882–1967).

What: US Marines attempted to capture the island in the Volcanoes Group.

Where: The island of Iwo Jima in the Pacific Ocean, less than 1127km (700 miles) from the Japanese home islands.

When: 19 February to 26 March 1945

Why: Iwo Jima could provide a staging area for future operations and a safe haven for crippled bombers returning from raids on Japanese cities.

Outcome: US Marines captured Iwo Jima after more than a month of savage fighting. Over 20,000 Japanese soldiers were killed and just a few hundred captured. American forces suffered almost 7000 killed and 19,000 wounded.

CAPTURED BY PHOTOGRAPHER *Joe Rosenthal, this image of US Marines and a Navy corpsman raising the US flag on Mount Suribachi at Iwo Jima is perhaps the most enduring of World War II. In fact, the flag had been raised earlier that day but the action was restaged for the camera.*

IN THIS AERIAL VIEW of the American landings at Iwo Jima, assault craft approach the black, volcanic sand beaches. The Japanese waited for the landing areas to choke with men and equipment before opening fire.

LVT-4 'WATER BUFFALO'

At the landings on Iwo Jima, the LVT-4 (Landing Vehicle Tracked) was the latest in a series of amphibious assault vehicles deployed in the Pacific during operations against the Japanese. Thousands of LVT variants were produced during the war.

Based upon an initial design by Donald Roebling in 1935, the LVT demonstrated its worth during the landings at Tarawa in November 1943, and was improved with greater armour protection and both .50-cal. and .30-cal. Browning machine guns.

difficult affair, Admiral Chester Nimitz (1885–1966), Commander-in-Chief of the Pacific Fleet, authorized Operation *Detachment* to commence in February 1945, with US Marine Major-General Holland Smith (1882–1967) in command of the offensive against Iwo Jima.

SULPHUR ISLAND

Shaped like a pork chop, Iwo Jima is scarcely 8km (5 miles) long and 7.2km (4½ miles) across at its widest point. At the southern tip, the 170m (550ft) Mount Suribachi rises to dominate most of the island. Despite its relatively diminutive stature, Iwo Jima had been turned into a fortress by more than 25,000 Japanese troops and a large contingent of Korean labourers under the command of Lieutenant-General Tadamichi Kuribayashi (1891–1945).

Across the island the Japanese had constructed a labyrinth of pillboxes, bunkers, machine-gun nests, artillery emplacements and spider holes large enough only for a single soldier. Many of the Japanese guns were positioned with interlocking fields of fire, their positions reinforced with steel, concrete, coconut logs and heaps of sand to absorb the shock waves of American pre-invasion bombardment. The Japanese had also honeycombed Mount Suribachi itself with tunnels and artillery and machine-gun emplacements near the mouths of caves.

The US plan was straightforward: the 4th and 5th Marine Divisions with the 3rd Division in reserve, more than 40,000 strong, were to assault beaches on the southern end of Iwo Jima. From there, they would isolate and capture Mount Suribachi, fight their way across the island, take the airfields and subdue pockets of Japanese resistance.

TO THE SUMMIT OF SURIBACHI

On the morning of 19 February 1945, US Marines hit the beach on Iwo Jima. For 20 minutes, there was virtually no reaction from the Japanese defenders. Kuribayashi, who had instructed his soldiers to kill 10 Americans before sacrificing themselves for the emperor, had also told his men to hold their fire until the invasion beaches were choked with American troops and landing craft. With a thunderous crash, the eerie silence was broken. Japanese bullets and shells rained down on the Americans and inflicted heavy

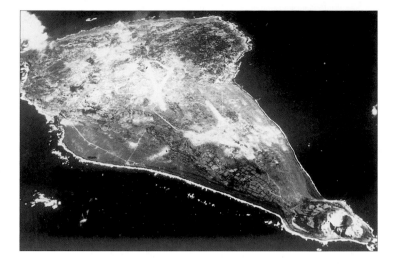

ABOVE: SHAPED LIKE A *pork chop, the island of Iwo Jima is dominated by the 170m (550ft) Mount Suribachi. Control of its airstrips saved the lives of thousands of American airmen.*

BELOW: GRUMMAN F4F WILDCAT *fighter planes prepare to take off on a support mission from the deck of the escort carrier USS Makin. US air superiority was complete by this stage in the war.*

WARY OF JAPANESE SNIPERS and well camouflaged machine gun nests, a US Marine shouts to a comrade. After more than a month of bitter fighting, Iwo Jima was declared secure.

casualties. To make matters worse, the black volcanic sand of the island made footing difficult and impeded the progress of tracked vehicles.

Nevertheless, the Marines braved withering enemy fire and managed to cut off Mount Suribachi on the first day. Subsequently they fought their way to the base of the extinct volcano and began an arduous climb. Although the high ground was far from secure, on 23 February a patrol worked its way to the top of Mount Suribachi and triumphantly raised a small US flag amid exploding Japanese grenades and sniper fire.

Hours later a second, much larger flag was located and carried to the summit. It was the raising of this flag which Associated Press photographer Joe Rosenthal captured on film. At the sight of the banner, Americans fighting and even dying across Iwo Jima lifted a collective cheer. Naval vessels offshore sounded their horns and claxons. Rosenthal's frame became one of the enduring images of the twentieth century and made instant celebrities of the group of six flag raisers, three of whom did not survive the battle for Iwo Jima to learn of their newfound fame. The image became the focus of a war bond tour across the United States and inspired the US Marine Corps Memorial in Washington DC.

YARD BY TERRIBLE YARD

In spite of this great boost to morale, more than a month of difficult fighting lay ahead for the Americans, whose numbers continued to grow on this small spit of land. Tanks were called upon regularly to fire point blank into Japanese fortifications. Individual acts of heroism occurred everywhere, and 26 Marines were awarded the Congressional Medal of Honor for their courage.

Progress was measured in yards, and otherwise nondescript locales earned lasting nicknames such as Bloody Gorge, the Amphitheater, Turkey Knob and the Meat Grinder. Marines crawled forward to fling grenades and satchel charges into the firing slits of Japanese bunkers or the mouths of caves. Flamethrowers burned defenders alive, routing them out of their defensive positions or immolating them where they stood. Some caves were sealed with explosives or bulldozers, burying their enemy occupants alive. Several times, the Japanese hurled themselves against well-entrenched Marines in suicidal banzai charges and died to the last man.

By 27 February, the two completed airstrips were in US hands and a third, which was under construction, had been taken as well. On 4 March, with the battle for the island still raging, the first four-engine Boeing B-29 Superfortress bomber made an emergency landing on Iwo Jima. During the remainder of the war, more than 2200 such landings were made and the estimated number of airmen saved topped 24,000. Fighters soon began flying escort missions with the big bombers as well.

IN THE MOUNTAIN'S SHADOW

Not until 26 March, after 36 days of combat, was Iwo Jima finally declared secure. The Japanese garrison on the island was virtually wiped out during the fighting. The Marines captured only 216 prisoners and some 3000 holdouts were still being eliminated months later. Although Kuribayashi's

body was never found, he was reported either to have committed suicide or to have been killed while leading a final desperate banzai charge. The Americans lost more than 6800 dead and 17,000 wounded at Iwo Jima, but the objectives of Operation *Detachment* had been achieved. Just days after the official end of the Iwo Jima battle, Marines and troops of the US Army landed on the island of Okinawa, moving another step closer to the home islands of Japan.

Iwo Jima stands as an epic of heroism and sacrifice by the men of the US Marine Corps. 'The raising of that flag on Suribachi means a Marine Corps for the next 500 years,' noted Secretary of the Navy James Forrestal (1892–1949). Admiral Nimitz captured the essence of the struggle, stating that at Iwo Jima 'uncommon valour was a common virtue'.

A US MARINE uses a flamethrower to silence a Japanese bunker on Iwo Jima. The island's fanatical defenders usually fought to the death, preferring even suicide to surrender.

IWO JIMA

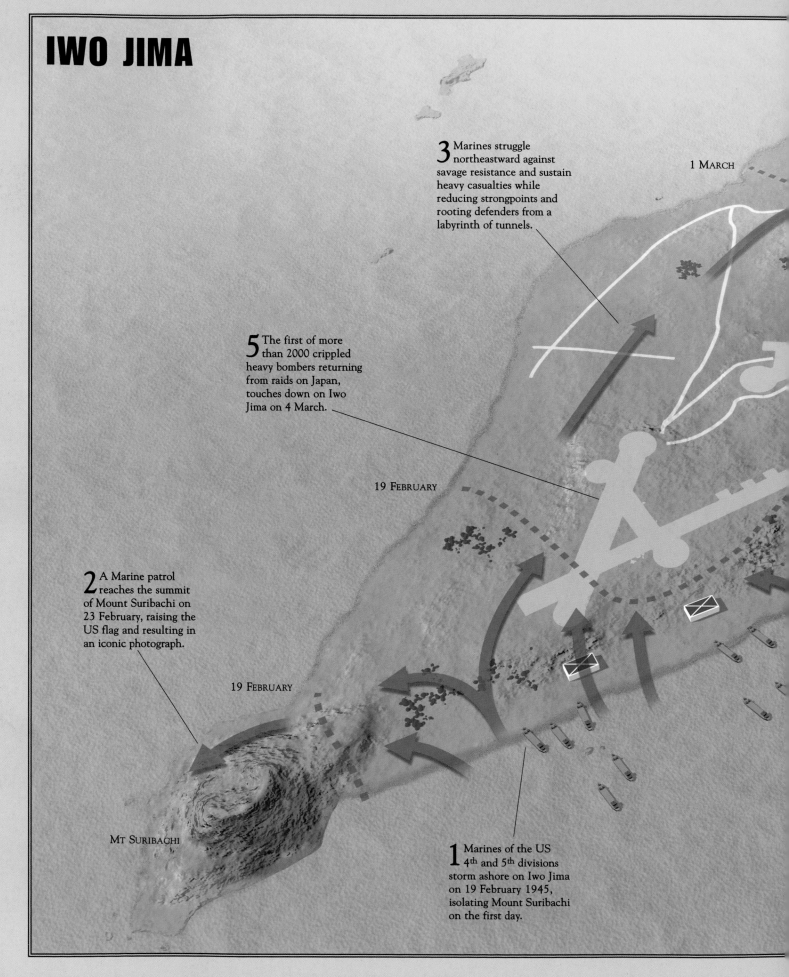

3 Marines struggle northeastward against savage resistance and sustain heavy casualties while reducing strongpoints and rooting defenders from a labyrinth of tunnels.

1 MARCH

5 The first of more than 2000 crippled heavy bombers returning from raids on Japan, touches down on Iwo Jima on 4 March.

19 FEBRUARY

2 A Marine patrol reaches the summit of Mount Suribachi on 23 February, raising the US flag and resulting in an iconic photograph.

19 FEBRUARY

MT SURIBACHI

1 Marines of the US 4th and 5th divisions storm ashore on Iwo Jima on 19 February 1945, isolating Mount Suribachi on the first day.

6 Following 36 days of harrowing combat, Iwo Jima is declared secure on 26 March. US casualties exceed 17,000. The Japanese garrison is virtually annihilated.

9 MARCH

4 Using flamethrowers and explosive charges, the Marines seal some enemy positions with bulldozers. Three airfields constructed by the Japanese are captured by 27 February.

KEY

⬅ US MOVEMENT

✉ US MARINES

✉ JAPANESE FORCES

BATTLE FOR BERLIN

1945

By the end of 1944, it was clear that Germany was losing the war. Two Red Army Fronts, commanded by Marshal Ivan Konev (1897–1973) and Marshal Georgy Zhukov (1896–1974), were advancing rapidly across western Poland. Further north, the 2nd Belorussian Front under Marshal Konstantin Rokossovsky (1896–1968) pushed into the Baltic states.

Here Colonel-General Gotthard Heinrici's (1886–1971) under-equipped Army Group Vistula was the sole barrier between Berlin and the Soviets. On the western front, German forces had smarted from the failed offensive in the Ardennes. By 3 April, Anglo-American forces had completed their encirclement of the Ruhr and prisoners were being taken at the rate of 15,000–20,000 a day.

BATTLE FOR BERLIN FACTS

Who: Red Army forces ordered by Stalin to capture Berlin, led by Marshal Ivan Konev (1897–1973) and Marshal Georgy Zhukov (1896–1974), versus Hitler's designated defender of Berlin, General Karl Weidling (1891–1955)

What: Victory was eventually assured for the Soviet Union as German forces, overwhelmed by sheer weight of men and armour, were encircled by eight Soviet armies smashing their way through Berlin.

Where: The Soviet Army's final offensive broke across the Oder and after vicious street-by-street fighting took the *Reich's* capital itself.

When: Between 16 April 1945 and 2 May 1945.

Why: The Allies believed that only with the successful assault on Berlin and defeat of the forces controlling it could the war be brought to a final, irreversible conclusion.

Outcome: Nazism was effectively defeated, leaving Berliners to count the cost. The daunting task of rebuilding a shattered Europe lay ahead.

LARGE ARTILLERY PIECES such as this tractor-borne 152mm (6.5in) gun formed a significant arm of Red Army forces shattering Berlin, along with assault guns, infantry and support troops.

LEFT: RED ARMY SOLDIERS were involved in a week of street fighting in Berlin before finally destroying any effective German resistance. By 27 April, the capital's garrison was confined to a narrow 16km (10-mile) corridor.

assured that the Red Army would never reach Germany, soon realized that the enemy was edging into the city suburbs. Amid the rumble of Soviet guns, people of all ages were mustered to build fortifications. Houses and blocks of flats were transformed into concrete strong points. On Sunday 15 April, Adolf Hitler, confined to his bunker beneath the Chancellery garden, issued the last of his directives, which was given an optimistic gloss: 'The enemy will be greeted by massive artillery fire. Gaps in our infantry will have been made good by countless new units … The Bolshevik … must and shall bleed to death before the capital of the German *Reich* … ' The prospect of new units was the *Führer*'s delusion. Manpower ranged from 15-year-old Hitler Youth personnel to men in their seventies. So-called 'infantry' consisted of 60,000 untrained, exhausted *Volkssturm* (Home Guardsmen) whose average ammunition supply was around five rounds per rifle and these, along with such machine guns as there were, had largely been salvaged from occupied countries.

At 3 a.m. Berlin time the next day, three red flares shot into the sky and the artillery opened fire. The sky was full of searchlight beams boring into dense smoke and boiling dust. Although many of the pontoon bridges had not been completed, Red Army infantry north and south of the bridgehead situated near the town of Kustrin, who had expected the arrival of assault boats, plunged into the river Oder, their log boats supporting guns and rafts heavy with supplies.

BRIDGEHEAD ATTACK

The troops of Zhukov's First Belorussian Front had been ordered by Stalin to make the attack on Berlin from the bridgehead. At the Seelow Heights, situated some 90km

By then, Berlin was an outnumbered fortress city: one million men were concentrated in the sector with 10,400 guns and mortars, 1500 tanks and assault guns and 3300 aircraft. The Soviets had 2,500,000 men, more than 42,000 guns and mortars, more than 6200 tanks and self-propelled guns and 8300 aircraft. Berliners, who had been

BELOW: THE T34/85, part of the 4000-strong Soviet armada of tanks approaching Berlin, was a later variant on the USSR's highly effective leviathan, armed with enlarged turret and armament. By the war's end, the T-34 was accounting for around 70 per cent of Soviet tank production.

30 April 1945: Soviet infantrymen battle their way into the still defended Reichstag, fixing an improvised flag to one of its columns. The event was later restaged for cameras.

(60 miles) east of Berlin and overlooking the western flood plain of the Oder, reception was fierce and the Soviets were held off until late on 17 April. This was in contrast with Konev, who had crossed the Neisse to the south across open terrain more favourable to tanks and made rapid progress. Stalin ordered Konev to turn two of his tank armies northwards to aid Zhukov. The breakthrough to the Berlin suburbs was achieved on 19 April.

The next day was the *Führer's* birthday, marked by barrages of exploding artillery shells and the deafening howls of multi-barrelled rocket launchers. But still there were forces desperately fighting to hold their positions before the city. Ninth Army under General Theodor Busse had originally been given the task of blocking the Soviets' direct route to Berlin, while General Hasso von Manteuffel's 3rd Panzer Army had been positioned further north. Although von Manteuffel had some success and managed to hang on briefly, it was clear by 21 April that Busse's forces were on the point of total collapse. An appeal went out to Lieutenant General Hans Krebs of the High Command of the Army Chief of Staff, that Busse should

withdraw or face total destruction. The reply was predictable: Ninth Army was to stay where it was and hold on to its positions.

HOPES OF RESCUE

Hitler next seized on the presence of SS *Obergruppenführer* Felix Steiner's III SS *Germanische* Corps, situated in the area of Eberswalde to the north of Berlin. Steiner's Corps was directed to attack forthwith on von Manteuffel's flank, drive south to cut off the Soviet assault and re-establish contact between the Third and Ninth Armies. But there were no experienced troops available to Steiner. What Hitler called Army Group Steiner was mostly sweepings from the *Luftwaffe* personnel, local *Volkssturm* and assorted police. In no way could they challenge the strength of Rokossovsky's and Zhukov's fronts. Von Manteuffel was heard to comment, 'We have an army of ghosts.'

ABOVE: ON 20 APRIL, HIS 56TH BIRTHDAY, Hitler in the Berlin Chancellery garden makes his last photographed appearance, awarding decorations to Hitler Youth, the youngest of whom was 12.

BELOW: RED ARMY ARMOUR passes through the suburbs of Berlin following the surrender of the city, May 1945.

Frantically clutching at straws, Hitler next pinned his hopes on the Twelfth Army of General Walther Wenck, which was to be rushed from the Western Front. Wenck was ordered to disengage from the Americans to his west and attack to the east, linking up with Busse and together attacking the Soviets surrounding Berlin. Sole resources were raw recruits; there were no battle-worthy tanks. On 23 April, Hitler received a blunt report from General Karl Weidling, Battle Commandant of Berlin, that there was only sufficient ammunition for two days' fighting. Nevertheless, Weidling hung on with such forces as he possessed while the Soviet stranglehold grew tight around the city, now a few blocks from the bunker. There Hitler, rapidly declining in health and lost in his delusions, kept saying, "Where is Wenck? Where is Wenck?" But by now Wenck, a realist and severely disillusioned, was seeking to bring remnants of his own army and of Ninth Army, together with as many civilian refugees as possible, safely across the Elbe into US Army-occupied territory. By 30 April, Berlin was a raging inferno throughout. For the Soviets, there was a prime objective: the capture of the iconic *Reichstag*, still heavily defended by its garrison. Even so, by early afternoon the Soviet Red victory banner was flying from the dome.

UNCONDITIONAL SURRENDER

Later that same day Hans Krebs, a Russian speaker, was dispatched under a white flag to meet the Red Army's General Vasily Chuikov to discuss surrender terms and to

MARSHAL GEORGY ZHUKOV

A man of peasant background, Georgy Zhukov emerged as the most outstanding military figure in the Red Army during World War II. He was created First Deputy Supreme Commander-in-Chief Soviet Armed Forces in August 1942, serving in the post throughout the conflict. Responsible for the attack that relieved Stalingrad, he went on to coordinate the First and Second Belorussian Fronts in the 1944 summer offensive, and he commanded the First Belorussian Front in the final assault on Germany and capture of Berlin, becoming Commander-in-Chief of Soviet occupation forces. In 1955–57, he served as Soviet Minister of Defence, but had long incurred Stalin's jealousy, and was dismissed and disgraced for allegedly challenging the Communist Party leadership of the Armed Forces. Partly rehabilitated under Khrushchev, he died in June 1974, his ashes buried in the Kremlin wall with full military honours.

THE BERLIN POPULACE faces the reality of defeat, with hardly a building left intact. Here, women and children pass by the Brandenburg gate.

inform him that Hitler and his new spouse Eva Braun had committed suicide. Chuikov made it clear that the Soviets would not accept anything but unconditional surrender. Meanwhile, Soviet military action would be unremitting. Krebs also killed himself and his body was later found in the bunker. It was left to Weidling, the last commander of the Berlin defence zone, formally to surrender the city to the Soviets at 1.00 p.m. on 2 May. By 4.00 a.m., the fighting was over. Figures for the number of dead during the battle could never be calculated precisely, but it is generally thought that up to 100,000 German troops lost their lives and a likely equal number of civilians. Around the same number of Soviet soldiers died. Berlin, in effect, had to be recreated.

AFTERMATH

Defeat heralded a long period of decline for much of Germany. With the ending of the Nazi dictatorship, East Germany faced years of Communist oppression, economic misery and, for the ordinary citizen, many of the familiar trappings of dictatorship, notably the presence of the Stasi secret police, regarded by many as successors to the Gestapo. Not until 12 September 1990 was Germany formally reunified and many of the inequalities of the poor East and prosperous West consigned to history.

BATTLE FOR BERLIN

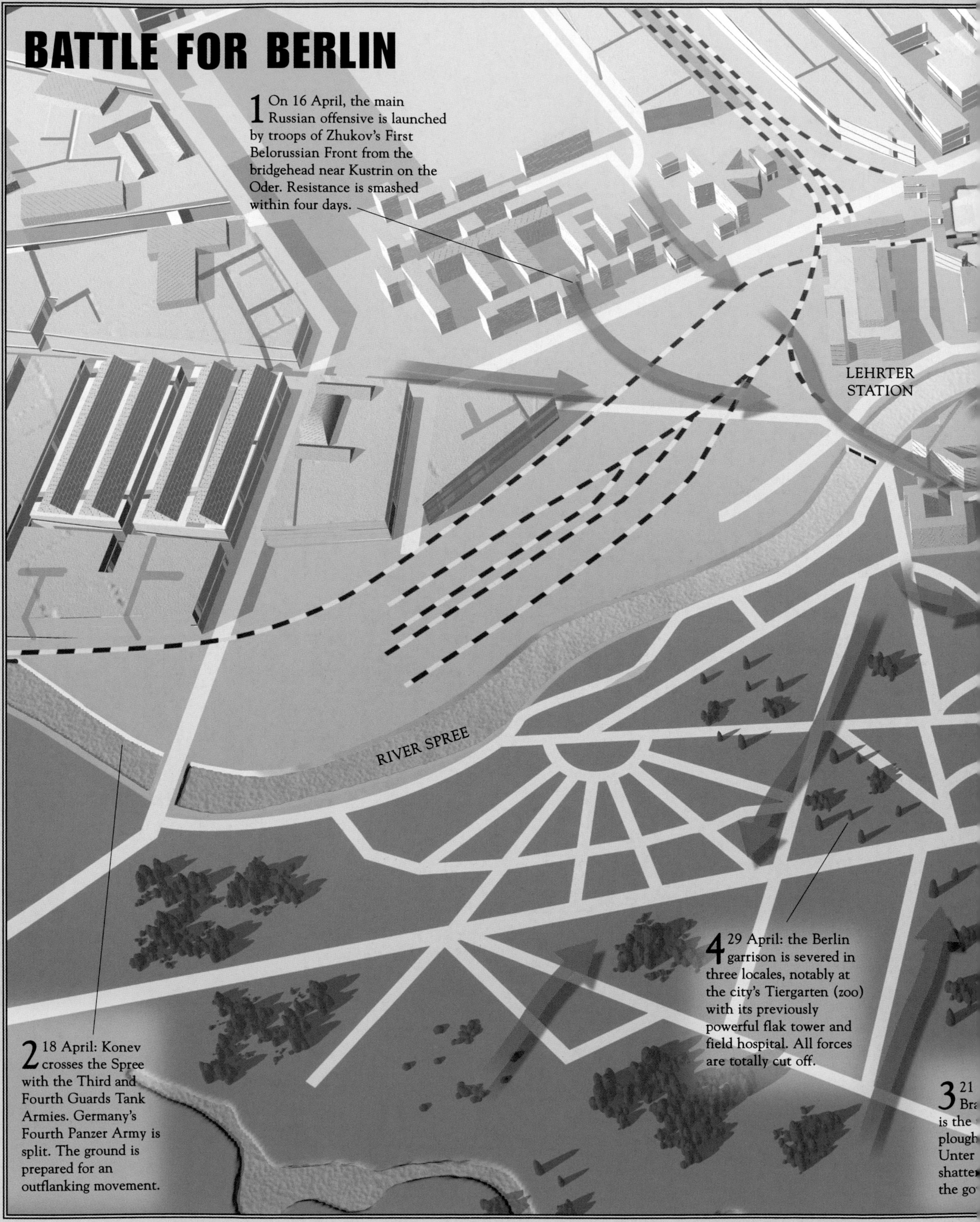

1 On 16 April, the main Russian offensive is launched by troops of Zhukov's First Belorussian Front from the bridgehead near Kustrin on the Oder. Resistance is smashed within four days.

LEHRTER STATION

RIVER SPREE

4 29 April: the Berlin garrison is severed in three locales, notably at the city's Tiergarten (zoo) with its previously powerful flak tower and field hospital. All forces are totally cut off.

2 18 April: Konev crosses the Spree with the Third and Fourth Guards Tank Armies. Germany's Fourth Panzer Army is split. The ground is prepared for an outflanking movement.

3 21 Bra is the plough Unter shatter the go

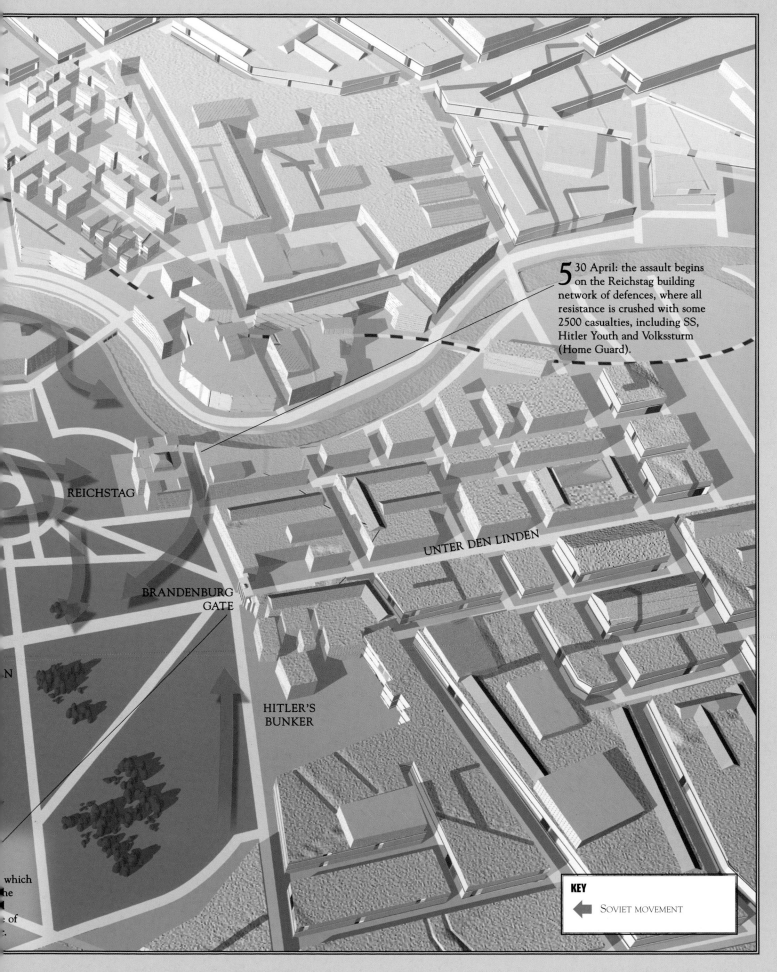

5 30 April: the assault begins on the Reichstag building network of defences, where all resistance is crushed with some 2500 casualties, including SS, Hitler Youth and Volkssturm (Home Guard).

REICHSTAG

UNTER DEN LINDEN

BRANDENBURG GATE

HITLER'S BUNKER

N

which the e of

KEY

SOVIET MOVEMENT

OKINAWA 1945

The Allies' amphibious invasion of Okinawa was a massive undertaking, against heavy and determined resistance. Japanese forces on the island were aware that they faced overwhelming opposition and were determined to exact as high a price as they could from the invaders.

The war in the Pacific was characterized by 'island-hopping' operations, which allowed the Allies to steadily encroach on the Japanese islands. Where possible, garrisons cut off by the Allied advance were bypassed and allowed to wither on the vine. Without amphibious transport, they were no threat and, lacking re-supply, would eventually become incapable of combat.

However, some objectives simply had to be taken. Okinawa was one – it was needed as a staging post for the final assault on Japan. This was obvious to the Japanese as well as the Allies and preparations were put in place well in advance. As the Japanese perimeter out in the Pacific gradually collapsed inwards, fortifications were dug and plans were laid to make the assault on Okinawa as expensive as possible.

OKINAWA FACTS

Who: Allied (mainly US) forces numbering 548,000 soldiers and 1300 ships, versus 100,000 Japanese ground, air and naval forces.

What: The Allies launched the largest amphibious operation of the Pacific campaign.

Where: Okinawa, in the Pacific Ocean

When: 1 April–21 June 1945

Why: The island was to be used as a staging point for the invasion of the Japanese homeland.

Outcome: The Allies captured Okinawa and 90 per cent of the buildings on the island were completely destroyed. Okinawa provided a fleet anchorage, troop staging areas and airfields in close proximity to Japan, allowing the Allies to prepare for the invasion of Japan.

US LANDING CRAFT bring stores ashore on 13 April 1945, during the battle for Okinawa. The packed horizon gives an indication of the size of the naval armada involved in the operation.

ABOVE: AIR SUPPORT FOR THE NAVAL armada and the ground forces fighting on Okinawa was supplied by naval fighters and fighter-bombers, such as these F4U Corsairs, flying from more than 40 Allied aircraft carriers.

With near-total command of the sea, the Allies could land more or less anywhere they pleased. It was not possible to prevent a landing and unlikely that a counterattack could contain one. The Japanese assumed that the Allies would get ashore, though they did what they could to make this costly. The defences of the island were centred on a medieval castle whose position guaranteed that the Allies would have no easy avenue of attack and would have to fight through the well-prepared fortifications.

While some of the islands the Allies assaulted were garrisoned by small forces, often with little artillery or air defence equipment, Okinawa was defended by several divisions with good support and, critically, plenty of artillery. These belonged to the Thirty-Second Army under the command of Lieutenant-General Mitsuru Ushijima (1887–1945), who had his headquarters in the medieval fortress of Shuri Castle in the south of the island. Defence of the northern sector was the responsibility of Colonel Takehido Udo.

The Allied ground commander was Lieutenant-General Simon Buckner Jr (1886–1945), commanding the US Tenth Army. Buckner had a marine and an infantry corps under his command, each of two divisions, plus an additional marine and two more army divisions as a reserve.

THE ALLIES ARRIVE

The first phase of the battle was the Allied effort to establish air and naval supremacy in the vicinity of Okinawa. Forces from Britain, Australia and New Zealand contributed here, though the ground forces were exclusively American.

Marines were landed on nearby islands from 26 March onwards, clearing opposition to create a safe anchorage. Meanwhile carrier-borne aircraft attacked airfields while the Japanese struck back with air attacks including hundreds of kamikaze aircraft. These sank several vessels and damaged others; the US Navy suffered its heaviest battle casualties of the war off Okinawa.

The Allies also faced naval attacks. By this time, the Imperial Japanese Navy was a skeleton of its former power, short of fuel and with few ships remaining. However, the super-battleship *Yamato* was available along with the light cruiser *Yahagi* and eight destroyers. There was only enough fuel for a one-way mission, so the *Yamato* was to attack the Allied fleet while her fuel remained, then beach herself on Okinawa, where her 450mm (18in) guns would join the defence.

RIGHT: THE US INVASION force moors off Okinawa, April 1945. The Americans committed more than half a million men and 1300 ships to capturing this small Japanese island.

Yamato and her escorts sailed on 6 April under the command of Admiral Seiichi Ito (1890–1945), who had originally refused to carry out what he saw as a wasteful and hopeless gesture. Events proved him right.

Yamato was incredibly well protected, but the Allies had total air supremacy with large numbers of dive-bombers and torpedo aircraft available. The Yamato task force was sighted soon after leaving port. On 7 April, it came under intense air attack from more than 400 Allied planes. One by one, the escorts were sunk and the giant ship was hit by several bombs as well as ten torpedoes.

A battleship force was waiting in case Yamato somehow got through, but there was no need. After two hours of

THESE US MARINES' ARMAMENT includes rifles and carbines, which were handier for close-range combat in the jungles of the island. Semi-automatic operation allowed for a high rate of fire.

attack, the last Japanese battleship capsized and exploded, taking most of her crew with her. There was no further naval interference in the invasion.

THE ALLIES ADVANCE

US Marines began going ashore on Okinawa on 31 March 1945, when an advance force was put ashore. The main landings began the next day, assisted by diversionary operations to distract the enemy and slow their response.

USS *INTREPID*

Aircraft carriers were a vital weapon in attacking the islands of the Pacific, which were often out of range of land-based aircraft, and in defending the fleet against air attack. Although the Japanese naval air arm was irretrievably smashed by 1945, kamikaze aircraft and small-scale raids still posed a serious threat.

USS *Intrepid*, an Essex-class carrier, suffered a near miss and a hit from kamikaze aircraft while on station off Okinawa. Good damage control procedures kept her in action. She operated 90-100 fighters, dive bombers and torpedo bombers; her loss or withdrawal for repairs would have dented Allied air superiority, though not badly, as many other carriers were available.

LEFT: THE LANDING VEHICLE (TRACKED) is an armoured fire support variant designated LVT(A)-4. Its 75mm (2.95in) howitzer had a short range but could provide vital fire support for troops assaulting a defended island.

The initial landings went well, largely because the defenders knew they could not be strong everywhere and had concentrated their forces where they would be most effective. Okinawa is a long, narrow island running broadly southwest–northeast with small peninsulas and a number of islands off the coast. The main Japanese force was concentrated in the southern end of the island and took some time to reduce. Defences were lighter to the north, and after clearing the immediate area the Allies were able to push northeast, driving the defenders steadily back.

The Allies made steady progress in the north, reaching the end of the island by 13 April, though the Motobu Peninsula and the island of Ie Shima were stubbornly held and not taken until 21 April. Pushing south was more of a problem: progress was slow and fiercely opposed by well dug-in Japanese troops. High ground, caves and artificial strongpoints had to be cleared by assault, resulting in hand-to-hand combat. Each was hotly contested and the Allies took heavy casualties as they pushed onwards.

After clearing what turned out to be a strong outpost line at Cactus Ridge, the advance became stalled for a time against the main Japanese line of resistance at Kakazu Ridge. Then from 12–14 April the Japanese counterattacked strongly.

Each assault was beaten off with heavy casualties on both sides and after this attempt the Japanese went back on the defensive.

On 19 April, the Allies made a renewed attempt to get the offensive moving. Under cover of diversionary operations and a huge artillery and naval bombardment, a powerful assault went in, supported by heavy air attack. However, the Japanese had ridden out the barrage in strong positions and were in good shape to resist the assault. Tanks – including flamethrowers – were of some assistance, but little headway was made.

Ushijima considered a counterattack but decided against it. His reserves were needed to counter a possible landing behind his lines by US 2nd Marine Division, which was making threatening movements by way of a diversion.

THE FIGHT FOR OKINAWA

The stalemate went on until the end of the month despite fresh US troops rotating into the line. On 4 May, the Japanese again counterattacked. The plan was ambitious and included an attempt to outflank US positions by amphibious operations. Despite determined efforts, the counterattack failed, and on 11 May Buckner went back over to the offensive. On 13 May US forces finally broke the Shuri defensive line. Infantry of the 96th Division and armoured supports ground their way into Japanese positions on Conical Hill as 6th Marine Division took Sugar Loaf Hill. With these key terrain features in US hands, the main Japanese line was compromised, but the monsoon weather made further advances difficult for a time.

The centre of the main line was Shuri Castle. With the flanks turned, the castle was exposed to attack and there was a chance to encircle the defenders. Major-General Pedro del Valle's (1893–1978) 1st Marine Division stormed the castle on 29 May. This not only broke the main defensive line but also greatly disheartened the Japanese forces on Okinawa, though they were able to fall back to a final position on the southern tip of the island.

The costly advance was then resumed, with the marines forced to dig fanatical defenders out of their positions. Many fought to the last or killed themselves to evade capture. Among them were Ushijima and his chief of staff, Lieutenant-General Isamu Cho. The remainder held their final line until 17 June, when the defence finally collapsed. This was a rare occasion on which significant numbers of Japanese troops surrendered. The

LEFT: A US MARINE FIRES his Thompson submachinegun during the fighting on Wana Ridge. Heavy shelling has reduced the vegetation to tree stumps and tangles of fallen branches.

RIGHT: A JAPANESE BOY CARRIES his baby sibling following the surrender of Okinawa. The civilian population suffered terribly, with an estimated 140,000 dying over the course of the three-month battle.

US Marines developed techniques to reduce casualties: for example, one method of clearing a cave involved the mouth being taken under heavy fire, after which a flamethrower tank approached and sprayed burning fuel into the interior, clearing any last defenders. However, despite such measures losses were very severe.

In the last days of the campaign, General Buckner was killed by enemy shellfire, making him the most senior US officer to be killed in action during the war. Heavy shellfire from both sides was a characteristic of the Okinawa campaign, which became known as the Typhoon of Steel.

The last organized resistance on Okinawa was the 24th Infantry Division, which was still fighting on 21 June. After this formation was broken, pockets of Japanese soldiers held out for another 10 days or so, but were mopped up one by one. The most senior Japanese officer captured alive was a major.

Many of those who survived tried to hide among the local population but were revealed by the Okinawans, who had no reason to shelter their enemies. Japanese soldiers had used Okinawan civilians as human shields or sent them to collect water under fire. In the closing stages of the battle, the Japanese encouraged locals to kill themselves rather than submit to the Allies.

AFTERMATH

Okinawa was firmly in Allied hands by the end of June. There was never any chance of the Japanese military holding the island. The defence was intended to delay the Allies as long as possible and to inflict as many casualties as possible. In this, the defence was a success. US forces suffered extremely heavy casualties, in part because of the refusal of Japanese troops to surrender even when surrounded and cut off. Once Okinawa was taken, it could be used as a base for the invasion of Japan itself. The nature of the resistance and the casualties incurred worried the Allies. An attack on the Japanese islands would be extremely costly. However, such a costly assault was made unnecessary by the use of atomic bombs in August 1945, which brought the war to an end.

BELOW: ALTHOUGH THE JAPANESE defence of Okinawa collapsed on 17 June, clearing out the last pockets of resistance took until the end of the month.

OKINAWA

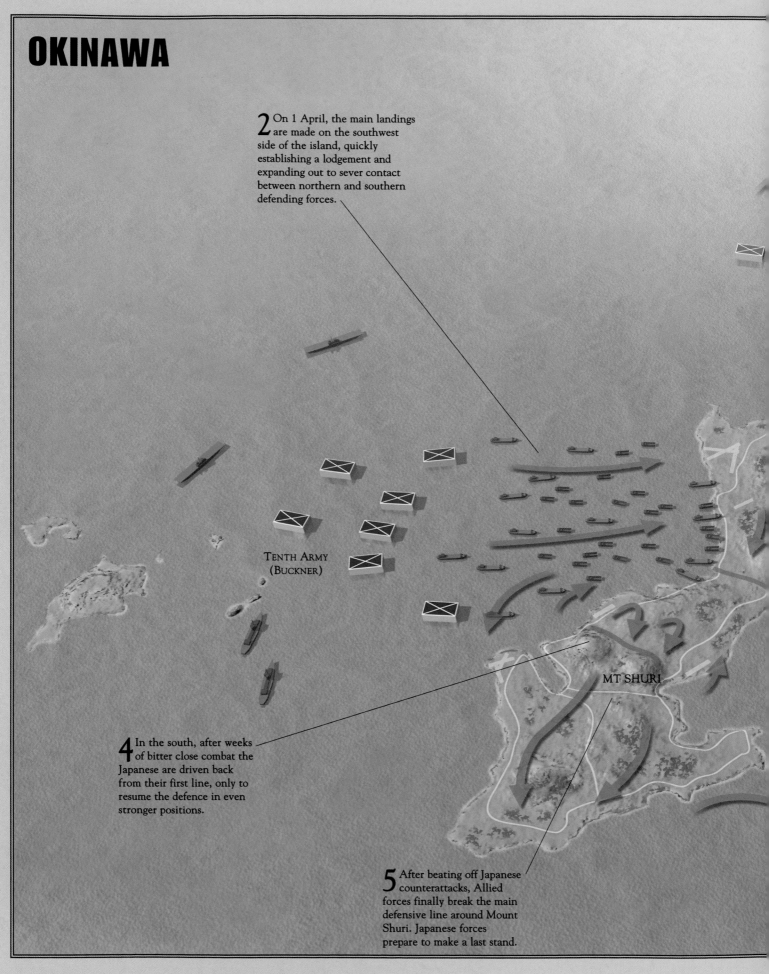

2 On 1 April, the main landings are made on the southwest side of the island, quickly establishing a lodgement and expanding out to sever contact between northern and southern defending forces.

TENTH ARMY
(BUCKNER)

MT SHURI

4 In the south, after weeks of bitter close combat the Japanese are driven back from their first line, only to resume the defence in even stronger positions.

5 After beating off Japanese counterattacks, Allied forces finally break the main defensive line around Mount Shuri. Japanese forces prepare to make a last stand.

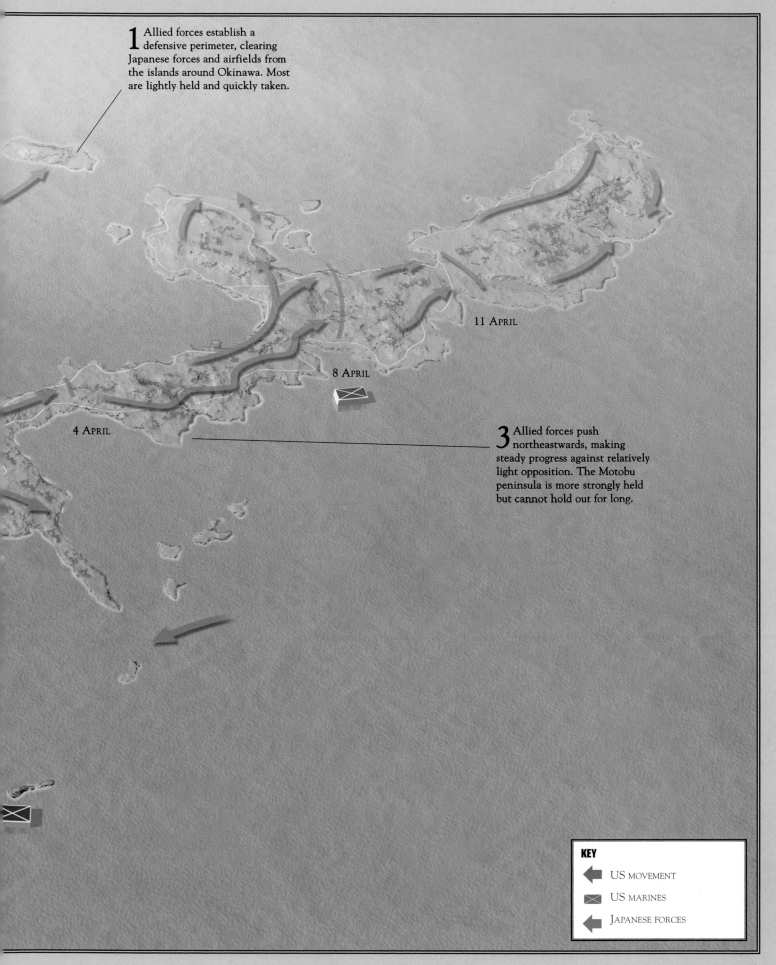

1 Allied forces establish a defensive perimeter, clearing Japanese forces and airfields from the islands around Okinawa. Most are lightly held and quickly taken.

11 APRIL

8 APRIL

4 APRIL

3 Allied forces push northeastwards, making steady progress against relatively light opposition. The Motobu peninsula is more strongly held but cannot hold out for long.

KEY

US MOVEMENT

US MARINES

JAPANESE FORCES

INDEX

Page numbers in *Italics* refer to illustrations: those in **bold** type refer to map illustrations with text.

1942

2 JANUARY British and Commonwealth forces in Malaya retreat in the face of Japanese forces.

8 FEBRUARY Red Army cuts off 90,000 German troops at Demyansk.

15 FEBRUARY Surrender of British and Commonwealth forces to the Japanese at Singapore.

24–29 OCTOBER British launch their big offensive at El Alamein, defeating Rommel's Africa Corps.

8 NOVEMBER Allied forces land unopposed in Vichy French North Africa.

24 DECEMBER German forces are encircled in Stalingrad.

---

1 FEBRUARY New Enigma cipher adopted by U-boat fleet, rendering communications traffic unreadable by British codebreakers.

7 FEBRUARY Supply convoys sail to Malta, carrying Spitfire fighters aboard aircraft carriers.

16 FEBRUARY U-boats launch a major anti-shipping offensive off the US eastern seaboard, sinking 71 ships during the remainder of the month. As a consequence, convoys are introduced.

7–8 MAY Battle of the Coral Sea.

4–5 JUNE Battle of Midway. All four Japanese aircraft carriers are sunk by the end of the 5 June.

12 NOVEMBER Battle for Guadalcanal begins.

---

19 FEBRUARY Japanese bomb Darwin, Australia.

5 APRIL Japanese bomb Colombo, Ceylon.

18 APRIL 'Doolittle raid' on Tokyo by US bombers.

30/31 MAY First 1000 bomber raid against Cologne, planned by new Air Chief Marshal Arthur 'Bomber' Harris.

25/26 JUNE Third and final 1000 bomber raid by RAF against Bremen.

10 AUGUST RAF's area bombing offensive threatened as Germans begin jamming the Gee navigation system.

---

12 JANUARY Japan declares war on Dutch East Indies.

25 JANUARY Siam declares war on Britain and US.

8 MARCH Japanese forces enters Siam, oil-rich Rangoon and land on Australian New Guinea.

9 MARCH Dutch East Indies surrender to Japan.

8 NOVEMBER Marshal Pétain secretly instructs the French High Commissioner in Algiers to open negotiations with the invading Allied forces of French North Africa.

11 NOVEMBER French forces in Morocco and Algeria sign armistice with the Allies; in retaliation, Germans occupy Vichy France.

1943

22 JANUARY German Sixth Army in Stalingrad cut in two: the final phase of the defeat of the Germans at Stalingrad begins.

1/2 FEBRUARY Japanese begin evacuation of Guadalcanal after Allied attack.

7 MAY Tunis falls to Allies.

5–12 JULY Germans launch Operation Citadel at Kursk in an attempt to gain the initiative on the Eastern Front. The operation is a failure.

3 SEPTEMBER Allied landings on mainland Italy begin.

6 NOVEMBER Soviets liberate Kiev.

27 DECEMBER In Italy, Eighth Army captures Ortona after fierce German resistance.

---

18 FEBRUARY US Navy bombards Japanese positions in the Aleutian Islands.

24 MAY Germany withdraws U-boats from North Atlantic after losing 33 U-boats in a month.

1 JULY Allies concentrate on attacking 'Milch Cow' refuelling U-Boats in Bay of Biscay.

10 JULY Allied landings in Sicily begin.

20 SEPTEMBER The Wolfpack U-boat campaign attacking Allied convoys reopens.

26 DECEMBER *Scharnhorst* sunk by British Home Fleet in last major gunnery duel in Royal Navy history.

---

18 FEBRUARY US Navy bombards Japanese positions in the Aleutian Islands.

17 MARCH The Axis powers now outnumbered in North Africa: while Britain and America have 3000 aircraft, the Axis powers have only 500.

13 MAY Sardinia bombarded by Allies from air for 14 days.

16/17 MAY RAF 617 Squadron carries out 'bouncing bomb' raids against German Ruhr dams.

17 AUGUST USAAF raid on Schweinfurt and Regensburg suffers heavy losses.

10 OCTOBER US Flying Fortresses begin attacks on Greece and Romanian oil fields.

---

9 MARCH Due to illness, Rommel is replaced as German commander-in-chief in North Africa.

18 APRIL Admiral Yamamoto, mastermind of the Pearl Harbor attack, is shot down and killed by American fighters.

25 JULY Mussolini arrested and deposed as Italian leader.

8 SEPTEMBER Italian surrender announced.

13 NOVEMBER Allies recognize Italy as a co-belligerent, formally accepting Italy's wish to change sides.

28 NOVEMBER–1 DECEMBER Tehran Summit between Churchill, Roosevelt and Stalin.

THE HORSE

THE COMPLETE GUIDE TO HORSE BREEDS AND BREEDING

JANE KIDD

Exmoor Ponies

Caspian Pony

Above: A Shire mare and foal.

THE HORSE

THE COMPLETE GUIDE TO
HORSE BREEDS AND BREEDING

JANE KIDD

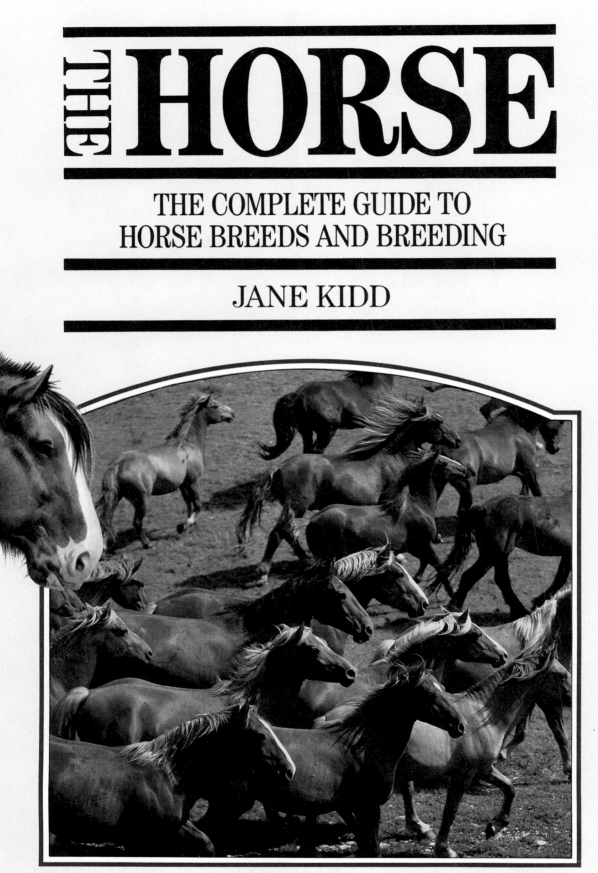

Above: Dülmen Ponies

TIGER BOOKS INTERNATIONAL
LONDON

A Salamander Book

This edition published in 1990 by
Tiger Books International PLC, London

© Salamander Books Ltd 1985

ISBN 1 85501 070 4

This title previously published as
Horse Breeds and Breeding

All rights reserved. Except in a review, no part of this book
may be reproduced, stored in a retrieval system or transmitted
in any form or by any means, electronic, mechanical,
photocopying, recording or otherwise, without the
prior permission of Salamander Books Ltd

Credits

Editor: Jonathan Elphick
Designer: Roger Hyde
Colour Reproductions: Rodney Howe Ltd,
London, England
Filmset: Modern Text Typesetting Ltd,
Essex, England
Printed in Italy by Canale & C.
S.p.A, Turin

Author

Jane Kidd has ridden internationally in show jumping and
dressage and has many books on equestrian subjects to her
credit. Among others, she has written *The Better Horse,
Horsemanship in Europe* and *Festival of Dressage*. For
Salamander Books, she has compiled *The Complete Horse
Encyclopedia, The Horse and Pony Manual* and *An Illustrated
Guide to Horse and Pony Care*. She has also extensively
revised *The New Observer's Book of Horses and Ponies* and
is a regular contributor to leading equestrian magazines,
including *Horse and Hound, Horse and Driving,* and *Riding.*
Jane is Vice Chairman of the British Horse Project, the national
organization which promotes the breeding of competition
horses in Britain, and, when time allows, she helps with the
running of the family's Maple Stud in Surrey, England, which
breeds both Norwegian Fjord Ponies and Hanoverians.

Author's Acknowledgments

Writing this book has involved collecting vast amounts of information.
Various breed societies the world over have been extremely helpful.
Those of many countries have provided detailed literature on all the
native breeds, while for other countries I have had to rely on individuals
—in particular, I should like to thank Professor E Sasimowski from
Poland, and Vivienne Burdon in England, who provided invaluable
advice and authentication for the Russian breeds and who wrote the
entry on the USSR in the Guide to International Breeds. I am also
indebted to the veterinarian Russell Christie who checked my manuscript of the section on Horse Breeding. Finally, I should like to thank
the illustrator, John Francis, for his painstaking artwork, and the chief
photographer, Kit Houghton, who has shown great flair and enterprise
in obtaining so many superb pictures for this beautifully illustrated
book; thanks are also due to the picture agencies and individual
photographers who have supplied the rest of the photographs.

Above: A pure-bred Arab.

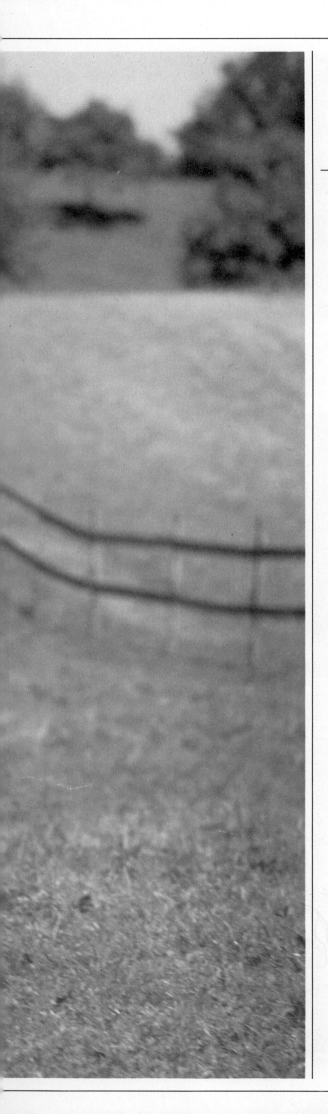

Contents

THE EVOLUTION OF THE HORSE

The numerous breeds of horses and ponies, from the 7-hand-high Falabella pony to the 18-hand Shire, are all members of the same species, *Equus caballus*. There are other species within the larger biological group (or genus) *Equus*: *Equus przewalski* (Asian Wild Horse or Przewalski's Horse) is the only other living horse (see page 42). There are 4 species of wild ass, all rare today: *Equus hemionus* (Mongolian or Asiatic Wild Ass), *Equus kiang* (Tibetan Wild Ass), *Equus onager* (Persian Wild Ass) and *Equus asinus* (African Wild Ass, the ancestor of the donkey).

Three species of zebra exist in Africa today. These are *Equus zebra* (Mountain or Cape Colony Zebra), *Equus grevyi* (Grévy's or Somaliland Zebra) and *Equus burchelli* (Common Zebra of East Africa).

All these species can be traced back to the Eocene epoch, more than 50 million years ago. Their common ancestor is *Eohippus*, the Dawn Horse (also known as *Hyracotherium*, a name derived from the Greek word for hog). Although "Dawn Horse" is a more romantic title, *Hyracotherium* was more apt. The originator of the horses was rather ugly and bore little resemblance to today's handsome creatures. There was so little resemblance that when horse fossils were first discovered they were not considered to be those of horses. It was not until much later that the evolution of *Equus caballus* was pieced together.

Eohippus had four-toed forefeet, three-toed hindfeet, an arched back and higher hindquarters than forehand. It took over 50 million years for this 10-inch (25cm)-high creature to gradually evolve, through many intermediate forms, into the horse Man first began to use around 1,750 BC.

It was a classic evolution—a gradual adaption to the changing environment. Those species that did not adjust died out. *Eohippus'* habitat was the forests and swamps. It was a browser, reaching for lush vegetation that it broke off with its small sharp teeth. It hid, rather than fled, from its enemies and probably had a striped coat that camouflaged it in the dappled light of the forests.

In the Miocene epoch (beginning about 26 million years ago and ending about 7 million years ago), the habitat began to change. The climate became drier, and the rain forests and swamps gradually changed into prairies. The horse's ancestors survived over millions of years by adapting to these changes. There were many species that did not make successful adaptions and died out, but some of the family Eohippae evolved into Mesohippae, then Merychippae, and eventually Pliohippae, gradually changing from forest dwellers into prairie dwellers.

An early adaptation of the primitive horses was to eat the grass instead of tearing off vegetation, so the sharp teeth became large flat molars that provided the grinding power needed for chewing. The muzzle lengthened to accommodate these teeth, as did the neck, allowing the animals to reach food on the ground as the species grew larger.

Another need was to run fast enough to flee from predators across the open grasslands where there was no place to hide. The horses grew larger, which enabled them to take longer strides. Their feet became streamlined, and lost all but the middle toe, which ended in a special nail, called the hoof. The limbs became stronger because of their greater length and the need to absorb the shock created by the small area of the hoof landing on the ground. Ligaments and tendons developed. Although these gave more strength, they also prevented the original lateral movement of the foot.

Another important change was to the senses. From being rather sluggish swamp dwellers, horses gradually became more alert to danger through improvements in hearing and vision. The eyes moved farther apart to give a wider range of vision, which in the modern horse spans about 215°.

The result was that *Pliohippus* of the Pliocene epoch (2 to 7 million years ago) developed into *Equus* by the time Man had evolved into *Homo sapiens*. The new *Equus* horses evolved into a variety of different forms. It seems likely these variations arose largely according to the habitat, depending on whether the animals were adapted to survive in the damp heat of swamps, the dry heat of scrubland or semi desert or the tough, cold conditions of high mountains.

Fossil remains of the original swamp-dwelling Dawn Horse are confined to North America, so this was probably its original home. Extraordinarily, the lack of fossils in America from about 6,000 BC indicates the horse became extinct in its original homelands. Primitive horses migrated from America across the Bering Straits land bridge to Europe, Asia and Africa. This occurred over millions of years, beginning in the Pliocene epoch and ending with the last Ice Age, during the Pleistocene epoch. The period of the migration and

Above: Przewalski's Horse is now extinct in its native Mongolia, but over 600 have been bred in zoos.

Below: This fossil of a primitive 50-million-year-old horse, called

Propalaeotherium, *was found in 1982 in a disused oil-shale mine at Darmstadt, West Germany. It is so well preserved, the ear and tail hair and undigested food in the stomach are visible.*

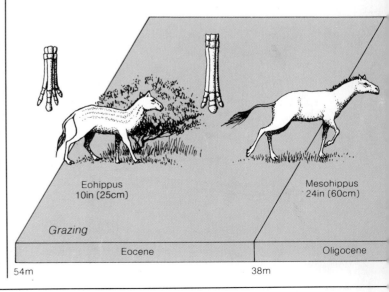

Below: Evolution of the horse through its most important genera (zoological groups), from the tiny Eohippus to today's Equus. *Larger scale drawings of the forefeet of each group show the development of the hoof. Along the bottom

are the geological epochs. Time is shown in millions of years before present-day (m).*

Right: Götland Ponies are among the oldest members of the horse group. They live today in Sweden.

Eohippus 10in (25cm)

Mesohippus 24in (60cm)

Grazing

Eocene

Oligocene

54m   38m

Merychippus
40in (1m)

Pliohippus
50in (1·25m)

Equus
Height varies

Browsing

Miocene

Pliocene

Pleistocene

6m

7m

2m

the climatic conditions of the time were probably the two major influences on the evolution of *Equus* into different species. It seems likely that the earliest migrants, arriving when the climate was still warm and tropical, were the most primitive members of the group, which became the species of zebras and asses.

The next group of migrants were the leggy Pliohippae. They adapted to the warmer climate in America and survived the Ice Age in Eurasia by moving south, where they became the Southern Group of horses.

Of these, one subgroup, the Steppe Horses, roamed a vast area, from the Atlas mountains and Spanish sierras in the west to Turkmenistan in the east. In the arid conditions of this environment, the Steppe Horses had to be tough, lean and fast. They tended to be rangy types with large long heads (the greater surface of mucus membrane in the elongated mouth and nostrils aided breathing in very dry air) and with big ears for acute hearing. Their coats were thin and fine. They appeared to have a capacity to grow tall; some Steppe types have been found that reached as high as 18 hands.

Some experts believe the Steppe Horse is the only Southern Group Horse. But Michael Schafer, a German veterinarian, has put forward a plausible theory that there was also a Proto-Arab sub-group. It is believed these horses migrated from America about the same time as the Steppe Horse but roamed into hill country with a subtropical climate that lay between East Asia and North Africa. With easy grazing, their teeth remained small, and research has proved intelligence is in inverse proportion to the size of teeth. Today's Arabs have a tapering jaw and small teeth and are noted for their intelligence.

At the end of the Ice Age, the

Above: A Common Zebra grazing in Kenya. Three species of zebra live in Africa today.

Proto-Arabs lost their lush habitat, as about 10,000 years ago their homelands gradually turned into deserts. Too short a time has passed for any noticeable further evolution.

Biologists believe the other main group of what was to become *Equus caballus,* the modern horse, migrated much later than the Southern Group, when conditions in America were becoming tougher and colder, and the horses had evolved accordingly. They tended to stay farther north when they reached Asia and Europe, and became the Northern Group. The first subgroup of Northern Group horses are the Primeval Ponies, which spread over a larger area—all over Europe and Asia—than the other three subgroups.

The Primeval Pony seemed able to adapt to many conditions. It could acclimatize to high rainfall, growing a two-layered coat and a long, thick mane. It could also adapt to hotter, dry weather, when its mane remained upright, because it was no longer needed to protect the head and neck from rain. An important feature of these ponies

Below: One of several species of ass, the African Wild Ass was the ancestor of the domestic donkey.

Below: The Persian Wild Ass, or Onager. The asses and zebras are, like the horses, members of the genus (group) Equus.

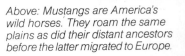

Above: Mustangs are America's wild horses. They roam the same plains as did their distant ancestors before the latter migrated to Europe.

Right: Welsh Mountain Ponies, of ancient ancestry, are tough enough to survive harsh conditions on their native hillsides.

was their short legs and cannon bones, together with a rather restricted action. They did not have the long strides of the Steppe Horses but took short steps instead. They quickened, instead of lengthened, their strides to move faster.

The less mobile subgroup of Northern horses, called the Tundra Horses, is the ancestor of the modern cold-bloods. Some cold-bloods grew very tall. Unlike the Primeval Ponies, which had been quick to migrate seasonally, and to avoid the permanent arctic conditions of the Ice Age, the Tundra Horse was more sluggish, and less agile. Instead of moving, it adapted to life in the subarctic tundra, in marshlands and in the Siberian swamps. At times, it may even have managed to survive on the fringes of the ice-free zone during the last Ice Age. Giant forms of the Tundra Horse (about 18hh) have been excavated in Greece and close to Vienna, although the average size was about 13·2hh (54in). Growing to a large size meant the body surface was smaller in relation to its bulk. It radiated less heat and helped the animal better survive the cold. The Tundra Horse usually had an extra lumbar vertebra in its lower backbone, which allowed the digestive organs more room to accommodate fodder. It also had a big, coarse head with a Roman nose, which must have made breathing in the cold air easier. The feet were very broad, reducing the risk of sinking into the marsh, and the action had a pulling effect from the forehand rather than a pushing from the quarters, which helped the horses move across boggy terrain.

The existence of these four wild types of *Equus;* the Primeval Pony, the Tundra Horse, the Steppe Horse and the Proto-Arab, helps explain the different types of modern horse. Our knowledge of their evolution is based on examination of fossils, cave drawings and evidence from modern horses, but early information is scanty. Zoologists have put forward a number of theories. None can be authenticated because the horse has been domesticated, while the original types died out or were crossbred. Only one wild horse still exists today: *Equus przewalski Poliakoff* (see page 42). Some experts claim all modern breeds come from this single wild form, but with the great variety of domestic horses, the multi-origin school of thought seems more convincing.

The breeds in this book are largely the result of human adaptations of the species for industry, war and pleasure. The natural evolution that took place over 55 million years has been

(see page 42)

Below: Norwegian Fjords are an ancient breed of pony. They have probably survived for so long because they are versatile and tough.

Above: The Arab has had an enormous influence on the development of modern horse breeds.

largely replaced by selective breeding methods. Few of today's breeds have evolved naturally. Most are the result of arranged cross-breeding and improvement of the animal's environment to make the horse faster, taller, stronger, more refined, more athletic, better tempered or a combination of any of these characters.

The breeds do fall into cagetories that are best explained by the theory suggesting the existence of four forms of wild horse. The first group is the ponies—the smallest equines—that also tend to have most primitive features and breed truest to type. Their size has limited their use to human beings, which means there has been less reason to crossbreed and destroy old breeds. However, ponies have

been used for crossbreeding with larger stock and have contributed to the development of other groups.

The second group is the work horses—or cold-bloods—whose ancestors were probably the Tundra Horse, although the Steppe Horse, with its capacity to grow taller, may have played a part. Work horses are the slow, powerful horses that have made a major contribution to the economies of countries for centuries. The name "cold-blood" refers to these horses' placid nature, not to any peculiarity of their circulatory system.

The third group is the largest today. With mechanization, the demand for work horses has fallen. Instead, the horses bred for leisure and sport have become very popular. The progenitor of most of these horses is the Arab, but the Steppe Horse has also made a contribution. The majority of sports horses, however, have had quite a mixture of ancestors, including

Right: Shires were once renowned as outstanding work horses. They continue to flourish as show animals, although there is little work for them.

Below: The Thoroughbred is the finest example of man's development of a breed to suit his purposes, in this case racing.

ponies and work horses. Some breeds of sports horses are very old; others have only been developed over the last decade. All over the world there has been a great increase in the number of breeds of sports horses to supply the growing number of riders and drivers.

Sports horses are divided into two major groups, the hot-bloods (Arab and Thoroughbred) and the warm-bloods (all other sports horses). As with the cold-bloods, the name refers to the animals' temperaments.

Over the last 3,500 years, the human race has been influencing the form and other characteristics of the horse. The results have led many people to become fascinated by the breeding of horses, whether homely Shetland Ponies or valuable racehorses. Breeders can have an effect—they can improve the chances of breeding a talented horse or one that is more true to type to a particular breed. But this influence must be kept in proportion. Evolution has led to much more dramatic changes, over a period of 50 million years.

In the following pages 220 breeds are described. Most of these breeds have been created through crossbreeding to suit our demands. Breeds, such as some ponies and work horses, are always dying out because they are no longer needed, while others, such as the various national Warm-bloods, are created to meet new demands. The breeds that are described in this book reproduce their own distinct form and characteristics with a certain degree of consistency.

PONIES

The official definition of a pony is an animal that is under 14·2hh (58in). However, height is not the only criterion for the definition of a pony. Most have other features that distinguish them from their larger relatives. It's possible for a very small pony, such as a Shetland, to be bred with a very large horse, such as a Shire, because they are all members of the species *Equus caballus*. But most ponies are not considered miniature horses. There are exceptions to this, such as the Caspian (pages 18-19) and Falabella (page 27), which do have horse features. But the majority of breeds described on the following pages are distinguishable from horses.

At birth a pony has the same proportions as the adult. It is not a long-legged animal with higher hindquarters than forehand, as are the foals of horses. Ponies tend to be stronger than horses relative to their size, and can pull greater weights in proportion to their height. They usually have shorter legs in proportion to their bodies, particularly short cannon bones. Their strides are usually shorter and less free than those of horses.

Equestrian experts often use the phrase "pony cunning." This refers to the fact that ponies seem to have great powers of survival and are quick thinkers.

The original members of the equine race would all conform to the official definition of a pony—under 14·2hh. Horses have been developed from ponies, increasing their size largely through selective breeding and favorable environmental conditions. Consequently, pony breeds are much closer to the original equines than are horses. Many of today's breeds, such as Exmoor, Norwegian Fjord, and Mongolian, resemble ancient types.

The extensive range of ponies, from the tiny, fragile Falabella to the strong, broad, muscular Norwegian Fjord, is living proof that ponies have long been used for many purposes. While the Falabella can never be much more than an unusual pet, the Fjord and the many other tough, native breeds have been economically important, working the fields, pulling carts and carrying packs and people. However, the demand for working ponies has diminished, as with the Cold-bloods, while that for children's riding ponies is increasing. The trainable, athletic breeds, created mainly by crossing older, sturdier pony breeds with small Arabs and Thoroughbreds, are multiplying most rapidly.

Right: Dartmoor Ponies grazing wild on their native moorland.
Below: A Hackney Pony trained to be driven.

AUSTRALIAN PONY

Country of origin
Australia.
Height
12-14hh (48-56in).
Color
Any.
Features
Based on Arab and Welsh blood, this is a particularly elegant pony. It has great presence, quality and character which makes it very popular with children.

Like many other countries, Australia discovered that most purebred ponies are rarely ideal for children. Crossbreeding is needed to refine them and make them faster and more athletic.

The most important foundation stock for the elegant Australian Pony has been Arab and Welsh, and in particular the Welsh Mountain Pony stallion Grey Light, which was imported in 1911. Infusions of blood have also come from Timors (one of these ponies was known to have been imported as early as 1803), Shetlands, Exmoors and Thoroughbreds. In the 1920s the Australian Pony began to emerge as a definite type, and in 1929 The Australian Pony Stud Book was formed.

The Australian Pony has a fine, Arab-like head, large dark eyes, a long crested neck, good sloping shoulders, a deep body, short back and powerful hindquarters.

Below: A fine example of an Australian Pony—a relatively new breed, developed this century.

		Hand
		18
		16
		14
		12
		10
		8
		6
		4
		2

Australian Pony (122-142cm) Avelignese (140-142cm) Bashkir (Average 140cm)

Above: The Avelignese is the Italian version of the Austrian breed called the Haflinger. It *has the same flaxen mane and tail, but is a stockier and somewhat heavier animal.*

AVELIGNESE

Country of origin
Northern Italy.
Height
13·3-14hh (55-56in).
Color
Chestnut, with flaxen mane and tail, and white markings.
Features
This stocky pony, with its short thickset neck, long back and short legs, is powerful for its size. It is also renowned for its tractable temperament and longevity, features that have made it an extremely popular breed both for draft and pack work.

In Italy today, one of the most numerous and oldest breeds is the Avelignese Pony. There are about 3,000 mares registered with the breed society. The original territory of the Avelignese was the mountainous area in the province of Bolzano, and it is still bred there, as well as in Tuscany and around Venice. Although there were no official documents for the breed until 1874, its close connections with the Haflinger make it of ancient lineage. Both breeds allegedly descended from the old Roman breed of Avelinum-Haflinger, but the Avelignese is a stockier pony than its Austrian relative. It is capable of carrying heavy weights through rough mountain terrain. Because it is exceptionally sure-footed, it has been an extremely popular pack horse in the Alps and Apennines. Its toughness and strength have also made it useful as a farm horse, particularly on mountain farms where larger horses would have difficulty working.

The Avelignese has an elegant head, which is probably due to its partly Oriental ancestry. The body, however, is powerful, compact, broad and deep through the girth. The cannons are short and there is little feather on the legs. The hooves are largish and very hard, enabling the ponies to pick their way along the stony mountain tracks without becoming footsore.

Above: The head of a Bashkir (or Bashkirsky) Pony, a breed that originated in the USSR, where it is still widely bred. It also has representatives in the USA.

BASHKIR

Country of origin
Urals, USSR.
Height
Around 13·3hh (53in).
Color
Bay, chestnut and light brown are most common.
Features
This tractable, strong pony has been a reliable all-rounder, invaluable to the Bashkiri people. It has a wide range of functions, from serving as a riding horse or a draft animal to pulling sleighs and providing meat, milk and clothing. Recently, the original native pony has been upgraded by adding Budyonny, Don and Orlov Trotter blood.

This ancient breed has lived for centuries in the Ural Mountains where it has been reared by the Bashkiri people. Bashkir Ponies have provided their owners with an important means of livelihood, because they are strong and sensible enough for pack and agricultural work. They can be ridden and when old, they can be used for meat.

The most unusual feature of this breed is that younger mares are milked. They produce such large quantities of milk—as much as 3-6 gals (14-27 litres) each day—that they are often kept in milking herds. The milk is used for cream and butter or drunk. It is also fermented into a medicinal (though intoxicating!) drink called *kumiss* by the Bashkiris.

The Bashkir has the ability to survive freezing temperatures as low as −40°F (−40°C) is based on a thick coat, which may be noticeably curly and up to 6in (15cm) long in winter, so their hides are used for clothing.

Although the Bashkir's homelands are in the USSR, the breed was also discovered living in the United States, in Nevada, at the end of the 19th century. They may have been brought by the Russians to Alaska or by the Mongols via the Bering Straits. However they arrived, they bear a striking resemblance to the Russian breed. The distinctive feature of the American version is a curly coat with a kinky, fine mane and tail that is shed each summer. A register for the American Bashkir Curly was started in 1971.

The Bashkir is a thickset pony with a big head, a short dumpy neck and a straight back with well-rounded hindquarters. The legs are short with good bone. The mane and tail of this breed are long and extremely thick.

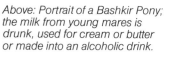

Above: Portrait of a Bashkir Pony; the milk from young mares is drunk, used for cream or butter or made into an alcoholic drink.

BASQUE
(Pottock)

Country of origin
Southwest France.
Height
11·2-13hh (46-52in).
Color
Most.
Features
The tough, small Basque has roamed wild for centuries in France. But it has shown a remarkable ability to adapt to a domestic life and be a good riding pony.

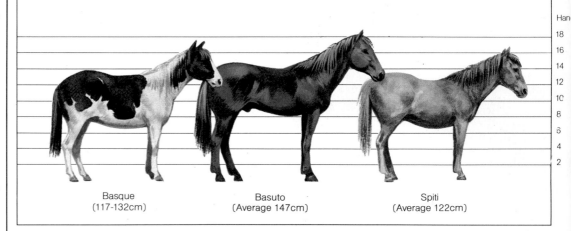

Basque
(117-132cm)

Basuto
(Average 147cm)

Spiti
(Average 122cm)

This ancient breed, which exhibits a number of primitive features, still roams free in the mountains of the Pyrenees and Atlantic cantons of France. Basque Ponies have owners, and they are rounded up periodically, traditionally on the last Wednesday in January, to be branded and released again or sold at the local markets.

To live in these hilly, spartan regions, Basque Ponies must be tough. Survival of foals is aided by rapid growth to maturity: they reach their adult size when only 1 to 2 years old.

Earlier this century, these small ponies were used in French and British mines as pit ponies. Today, they are in demand as children's ponies because they adapt well to domestication. To improve them for this latter purpose, some have had Arab and Welsh blood added. But the French are taking steps to safeguard the continued purity of this ancient breed, which now numbers between about 2,500 and 3,000 purebred Basque Ponies.

The Basque Pony has a small body and a large head, which has a basically rectangular profile with a slight depression at the level of the eyes. The ears are short, and the eyes small and lively. The neck is short, with a thick mane. The back is long. The legs are strong and the feet are small and hard.

Left: The Basque Pony, or Pottock, breeds in the wild, high in the Pyrenees Mountains between France and Spain. Basque Ponies are rounded up periodically and branded, then set free or taken to fairs such as this one to be sold.

Below: Although bred in the wild, Basque Ponies have owners. Here a stallion is being led over the steep terrain typical of their breeding areas.

BASUTO

Country of origin
Basutoland, South Africa.
Height
About 14·2hh (58in).
Color
Chestnut, brown, bay and gray.
Features
This is one of the strongest ponies, and it has great powers of endurance. It gained fame during the Boer Wars when the British bought as many as 32,000 Basutos. This increased the mobility of British forces and helped turn the tables in the war on the Boers who had their own pony—the Boerperd.

The Basuto Pony is named after the area where it is found in South Africa, but it is not indigenous to that region. It developed in the 19th century from the Cape Horses, which were brought to Basutoland after raids and left to fend for themselves in this tough country.

The Cape Horse in its turn had been developed in the southern province of South Africa from imported stock. Importing began in the 17th century with ponies from Java, and they were later upgraded by using Arabs, mainly from Persia. After 1770 a trade developed with India, when the tough, intelligent Cape Horses were sold in large numbers as remounts to the British Army. This success encouraged additional improvements to the ·breed, and 40 Thoroughbred stallions were imported to help the Cape Horse develop into a military horse of world renown.

In 1828, the Sotha (Basuto) Chief, Moshesh, raided the Cape, captured some of its Cape Horses and took them home. After a few generations of unfavorable climate, bad grazing, overexertion and inbreeding, they became smaller and tougher. Those that survived became known as Basuto Ponies, and proved to be exceptionally strong and brave.

Basutos have been used for military purposes, and also for racing and polo. They are extremely tough, with great powers of endurance, and can carry a rider for many miles each day. Not surprisingly, they are very popular for trekking.

The head usually shows the elegance of its Arab and Thoroughbred forebears. The neck is long and thin and often ewe-shaped The shoulder can be rather upright, while the back is long, the legs short and the feet very hard.

Basuto Ponies are also frequently used in various parts of South Africa for general riding.

Above: Spiti Ponies very heavily laden near Manali, India.

BHUTIA AND SPITI

Country of origin
India (the Himalayas).
Height
12-13·2hh (48-54in).
Color
Gray.
Features
Their strength and sure-footedness has enabled them to carry humans or packs around the mountainous regions of the Himalayas.

The Bhutia is a larger version of the Spiti. These two breeds are found in the Himalayas of India and have similar origins to the Tibetan (Nanfan). Both derive from the Mongolian Pony.

The smaller, less stocky Spiti (which averages 12 hands high, as compared to the Bhutia's average height of 13·1 hands) is bred in the high mountains by a tribe of high-caste Hindus called Kanyats. They have practised in-breeding on the Spiti in order to keep it small in size.

The Spiti's homelands are the mountainous regions of the Kangra District. There and in surrounding regions they are in demand as pack ponies. Their small size and sure-footedness enables them to carry loads with safety along the narrow, precipitous mountainous tracks.

In both breeds, the head is intelligent with alert ears, the neck is short and thick, the shoulders rather straight, the back strong and short and the quarters muscular. The limbs are short with good bone and the feet are hard and round.

BOER PONY
(Boerperd)

Country of origin
South Africa.
Height
13·3-15·3hh (55-63in).
Color
Black, brown, bay, chestnut, gray, roan, dun and palomino.
Features
This calm, tough pony is often capable of five gaits: walk, trot, canter, slow gait and rack. It is a slightly larger animal and has more quality than its close relative the Basuto Pony.

This pony has similar origins to the Basuto Pony (page 17). It developed from the Cape Horse in the 19th century. During that time, however, it was influenced by imported stock, such as Flemish, Hackney and Cleveland. The Boers looked after their breed better than did the developers of the Basuto, and it did not have to survive such rough conditions. Consequently, the Boer Pony has become a better-developed animal.

In the Boer Wars, its great mobility and toughness helped the Boers move around and hold out against the British Empire for three years.

Various attempts were made to form a Boerperd Society, and in 1973 the Boerperd Society of South Africa was formed. Today, Boerperds are found in isolated herds in the south-east Transvaal, northern Natal, eastern Free State and north-eastern Cape. They are used as utility horses on farms and for the increasingly popular sport of endurance riding.

BOSNIAN

Country of origin
Yugoslavia.
Height
12·3-15hh (51-60in).
Color
Bay-brown and black are most common, but they are sometimes a light yellowish brown or chestnut.
Features
This mountain breed's intelligence, strength, sure-footedness and powers of endurance mean that even in modern times it is used in large numbers by farmers and transporters in the Balkans.

These ponies are bred in large numbers all over the Balkans, but their homelands are the hilly, mountainous regions of Bosnia and Herzegovina in Yugoslavia. They are selectively bred by the Yugoslavian government because the Bosnian is useful to the economy, both on the farms and in transportation, particularly in the mountains. There are more than 130,000 in Yugoslavia.

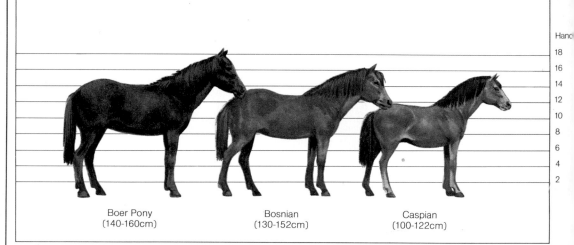

	Hands
	18
	16
	14
	12
	10
	8
	6
	4
	2

Boer Pony (140-160cm)   Bosnian (130-152cm)   Caspian (100-122cm)

In appearance, this breed is similar to the Huçul, the mountain pony of Poland. Both are descendants of the wild breed of Tarpan and have been upgraded with a good deal of Arab stock. With selective breeding at the Borike stud, the Bosnian's size is being increased from that of a small pony to a small horse.

It is a compact, broad pony with a long, slightly sloping croup and very thick long mane and tail. It has great powers of endurance, great strength and all the assets of a mountain breed, and is frequently used in pack trains over the mountains.

Below: Stocky and powerful, the Yugoslav-bred Bosnian is highly valued as a working pony over the whole of the Balkan region.

CASPIAN

Country of origin
Iran.
Height
10-12hh (40-48in).
Color
Bay, gray, chestnut and occasionally black and cream. Some white markings may be found.
Features
This kind, intelligent, narrow pony has been used as a work pony in Iran for centuries but these features also make it ideal as a children's pony. It has a natural floating action, great powers of acceleration and athletic ability over fences. It is also a good harness pony and has been used as such over the past 1,000 years or so.

In 1965 a few lean, scraggy ponies were found on the northern shores of Iran, that border the Caspian

Below: The Caspian is a miniature horse with a very ancient history.

Sea. The importance of this discovery was that they did not have the features of ponies, but looked like miniature Arabs with the same big, bold eyes, prominent jaws, dished face and high-set tail. They were miniature horses that bore a striking resemblance to the equines carved on the ruins of a staircase of the ancient Persian city of Persepolis in the late sixth or early fifth century BC. Some authorities believe the Caspians' forebears could be Iran's native wild horses which were used by the Mesopotamians in the third millenium BC. They were probably the forerunners of most breeds of hot-bloods, including the ancient Arab.

There had been no records of this breed of miniature horse for about a thousand years until 1965, but their authenticity has now been confirmed by scientific research, following archaeological digs on ancient remains in Iran. Identification is helped by the Caspian's unique features, such as its blood hemoglobin construction, the skeletal structure of its small skull, with a broad forehead, and the well-developed parietal and frontal bones of its spine, which make it a much narrower shape than any other pony.

For the missing 1,000 years, these ponies were bred in a very small area and were known locally as Monleki or Ponseki. They never ventured farther from the Caspian shores than the northern slopes of the Elburz mountains, but it meant that this ancient breed was

preserved and not crossbred into oblivion. Since 1965, the importance of the breed has been realized. The Shah of Iran was one of the first to help their promotion. Despite the subsequent political upheavals in Iran, enough Caspians have been exported to Britain, America and Australia to ensure their survival.

The Caspian does not look like any other pony. Its tapering head has a forehead that is wide and vaulted, the cheek bones are deep, and the muzzle is small. The eyes are large and often prominent. The nostrils are low-set and large. The ears are short and set wide apart and often turned in at the tips. The body is narrow with a longish neck, a long sloping shoulder and a deep girth.

Above: For centuries, Caspian Ponies have been pulling carts on the shores of the Caspian Sea. Today they are used for competition driving in Western countries.

The limbs are particularly fine and strong, and the hooves strong and oval.

Below: A portrait of the Caspian Pony shows its unique features.

CONNEMARA

Country of origin
Western Ireland.

Height
13-14·2hh (52-58in).

Color
Gray, black, bay, brown and dun.
Occasionally roan and chestnut.
More than 50% of the registered
ponies are gray. The dun and
palomino were once common
but are now becoming rare.

Features
This ancient inhabitant of the
British Isles is one of the best
breeds of children's ponies.
It is also strong enough to carry
an adult and sensible enough
to work well in harness. It is a
high-class utility breed.

Connemara
(132-147cm)

Dales
(137-147cm)

The Connemara is the first of
the British Mountain and Moorland
ponies to be described in this
book. All nine (Connemara, Dales,
Dartmoor, Exmoor, Fell, Highland,
New Forest, Shetland and Welsh)
are named after the regions
where they have bred and run wild
for centuries. The Connemara is
indigenous to the west of Ireland
in the area of Connaught, a
small part of which is known as
Connemara, bounded on the
west by the Atlantic and on the
south by Galway Bay. This bleak
area consists mainly of mountains
and bogs. There is only rough
grass for food, and the Connemara
has had to be tough to survive.
It has lived there in a wild state for
centuries and is thought to be one
of the oldest equine residents of
the British Isles.

There is no authentic evidence
as to its origins, but it is certainly
a primitive type. Some say it is
based on the same stock as
the Highland, Shetland, Icelandic
and Norwegian Fjord. Certainly,
the Connemara has a touch of
class, an oriental influence. The
typical Connemara is more beautiful
and athletic than an ordinary
mountain pony. One legend claims
it derived from horses shipwrecked
in the Spanish Armada of 1588,
but it is more likely that Galway
merchants, who traded with Spain
during the 16th and 17th centuries,
imported some good Oriental
horses. Some of these must have
managed to break free and bred
with the native pony stock in and
around Connemara.

This combination of primitive
toughness plus Oriental beauty and
athleticism has produced a pony
that is popular today all over
the world.

The Irish Government has taken
steps to preserve its ancient
lineage, and a society was formed
with its assistance in 1928 to
preserve and improve the
Connemara Pony. Crossbreeding
was restricted, and foundation
stock established. The stud book is
now closed to all but full-pedigreed
parents, and the result is a more
uniform type than was found at
the beginning of the 20th century.

There is great temptation to
crossbreed with the Connemara.
When it is put in a better environment
than its bleak homeland, and kept
warm and fed well, it usually

grows larger. This tendency to grow larger is greater in the Connemara than in other native British breeds. Consequently when crossbred with a horse, it tends to produce sizable competition horses.

As purebreds, Connemaras are one of the most popular children's ponies and are capable of all forms of equitation from dressage to hunting. They are also excellent in harness and are becoming very popular for the sport of competition driving. They are agile, fast and athletic, having great stamina and commonsense typical of primitive breeds. They also thrive on poor keep, having had to survive for centuries on rough lands. These qualities have made them reliable utility ponies for the Irish. Today, they also include high class competition ponies for children.

The typical Connemara has a harmonious head and neck with a compact deep body and short legs. The bone is hard and flat and measures about 7-8in below the knee. The great substance this bone gives enables the Connemara to carry adults as well as children. The Connemara is an athletic pony, and its action is free, fluent and true.

Below left: Connemara Ponies have bred in the wild for centuries, in Galway in western Eire.

Below: The Irish have traditionally used the Connemaras as work ponies for pulling heavily laden carts.

Above: This is Tulira Blue Hawaii, who won the ridden Connemara class at the Bath & West Show, England.

DALES

Country of origin
Britain (eastern Pennines).
Height
13·2-14·2hh (54-58in).
Color
Black and brown are most common, but some are gray and bay. The only permissible white markings are a star or snip on the head.
Features
This strong, energetic and intelligent pony has been a major aid for transportation and agriculture in the past. Today it is popular for harness work and trekking, and as an all-around utility pony capable of jumping, endurance racing and general riding.

The Dales Pony is bred on the eastern hills of the Pennines. Its close relative, the Fell, is bred on the west of these hills. The Dales has long been bred as a pack pony, because the moors were famous sources of lead. This heavy metal had to be transported across rough land to the ports on the coast. Pack ponies, until 100 years ago, were the best means of moving it. The ponies worked in groups, with one mounted man herding the loose, heavily laden ▶

▶ ponies. The Dales fulfilled this important function.

Foundation stock for these load carriers was the Scottish Galloway, which in its turn had some Friesian blood (see Fell, page 28). The Galloway was a fast, sturdy pony and was Britain's original racehorse. It was also used as foundation stock for the Thoroughbred, the Norfolk Trotter and the Clydesdale. The Scottish Galloways, which became extinct by the early 19th century, were bred to the native Fells that roamed wild on the moors. Only the tough survived, and only the biggest and most powerful of the offspring were used as pack ponies and for further breeding. It was a rough form of selective breeding.

The Dale Galloway, as it became known, soon earned fame for its strength, intelligence and agility over rough country. Farmers began to use them because they could pull more than a ton in weight. They were ridden, also, and their ability to trot fast led to further crossbreeding. In the 18th and 19th centuries, there were some outside influences. One of these was probably the Clydesdale and the other the Norfolk and Yorkshire Roadsters. The latter were becoming famous as fast trotters. Pulling light vehicles in harness provided a speedy means of transport. Some stallions of these Roadster breeds, notably Merry Driver, Shales Merrylegs, Sir George and Sir Harry, were bred to speed up the Dales.

Another influence was Comet, a

trotting cob believed to be an early Welsh Cob that came to Westmoreland in the 1850s and sired many good Dales. In the 20th century, two steps were taken to preserve and promote the breed. In 1916, the Dales Pony Improvement Society was formed and a stud book opened. Sadly, World War II led to terrible disruptions, so that by 1955 only four ponies were registered. The formation of The Dales Pony Society in 1963 has led to

distinct improvements in quality and quantity and an increasing interest in this tough and adaptable breed of pony.

The Dales Pony should have a neat, ponylike head, with bright alert eyes set well apart. The ears should curve inwards slightly. The neck should be long and strong, the shoulders sloping and the withers fine. The body should be compact and deep, and hind-quarters deep, lengthy and powerful. The limbs should be short

with good bone, measuring about 9in, and set square. The feet are renowned for their strength and are open, large and round in shape—many ponies never need shoeing. There should be a little silky feather on the heels and an abundance of hair in the mane and tail.

The action of the Dales is distinguished, with great flexion of the joints to produce a high knee and hock action. They have tremendous energy, and are cour-ageous, intelligent and kind.

Above: The Dales Pony is a fast and spectacular trotter in harness.

Left: One of the many uses of the tough Dales Pony is for shepherding.

Left: The Dales Pony breeds free on the east side of the Pennine Hills in northern England.

Above: Portrait of a Dales Pony.

DARTMOOR

Country of origin
  Britain (Dartmoor).
Height
  A maximum of 12·2hh (50in).
Color
  Bay, brown, black and gray are most common. Occasionally chestnuts and roans are found, but piebalds and skewbalds are not allowed. White markings are permissible but not in large areas.
Features
  This sturdy pony has particularly good conformation and a kind temperament, which makes it an excellent child's pony and good foundation stock for larger riding ponies. Its ability to survive in its rugged homeland enables it to thrive in most climates.

Hands
18
16
14
12
10
8
6
4
2

Dartmoor
(Maximum 127cm)

Dülmen
(Average 130cm)

The Dartmoor Pony is another of Britain's Mountain and Moorland ponies. Its homelands of Dartmoor are the most southern of any of these nine breeds. Ponies have roamed these austere moors, which stand over 1,000 feet above sea level, for centuries. The earliest reference to this pony is in 1012 in the will of a Saxon bishop named Aelfwold of Crediton. It is also known these ponies were well used in the era of tin, when they carried the metal from the mines on the moor to the Stannary Towns. When the tin mining ended, they were once again let free to roam and breed on the Devonshire moors.

It was at the end of the last century, in 1898, that the first attempts were made to officially define and register the breed. By 1902, the Dartmoor Committee laid down that ponies with more than 25% alien blood could not be entered in the stud book. This rule was ignored a few years later, when in 1920 a stallion named The Leat, which looked like a Dartmoor but was sired by a desert-bred Arab, was allowed to stand. He proved to be a very successful sire, and most of today's Dartmoors trace back to him.

In 1957, the stud book was finally closed to entry by inspection. Soon after there was a great upsurge in interest in the Dartmoor, and many of the ponies were exported.

The Dartmoor has proved to be an excellent first pony for children. It is economical to keep, has a quiet, kind reliable temperament and is a good size for young children. It is a particularly versatile breed, and has the ability to hunt, jump and be driven.

The Dartmoor has a small, elegant head with small, alert ears. The neck is strong but not too heavy, too long or too short. The shoulders are well set back to give the rider a 'good front.' The back is of medium length; the loins and hindquarters are strong and muscular. The tail is full and

Below: Dartmoor Ponies breed wild on the moors in Devon, South-west England, after which they are named.

Above: A typical Dartmoor head: intelligent, with small ears.

Right: Standing square, a Dartmoor Pony shows off its conformation.

set high on the hindquarters. The limbs have a medium amount of bone. The feet are well-shaped and strong. The Dartmoor moves with free, low strides that make it a particularly comfortable ride.

DÜLMEN

Country of origin
Germany (Westfalia).
Height
Around 12·3hh (51in).
Color
Black, brown and dun are most common.
Features
The Dülmen, together with the Senner (now nearly extinct), are Germany's native wild ponies. The Dülmen is said to have played a part in the development of the Hanoverian breed.

The Dülmen is a German breed of wild pony. Its homeland is the reserve of Mierfelder Bruch on the Duke of Croy's estate in the state of Westfalia. It was mentioned as being there as long ago as 1316, but today relatively few are left.

There has been some out-crossing with ponies from Britain and Koniks from Poland, and the resulting animals do not breed particularly true to type.

The Dülmen does not have very good conformation. It has rather weak hindquarters. The head is small with a straight face. The ears are small; the neck and back are short and the shoulders are rather upright.

Crossed with Arabs, Dülmens have sometimes been used to produce children's riding ponies.

Right: The Dülmen Pony from Germany is becoming quite rare.

EXMOOR

Country of origin
Britain (Exmoor).

Height
Mares not exceeding 12·2hh (50in) Stallions and geldings not over 12·3hh (51in).

Color
Bay, brown or dun, with mealy markings on the muzzle, round the eyes and inside the flanks. No white markings anywhere.

Features
This is the oldest breed in Britain, and is thought to be the Celtic pony that pulled the chariots of the Celts. It has unusual features like the "toad" eye and mealy muzzle.

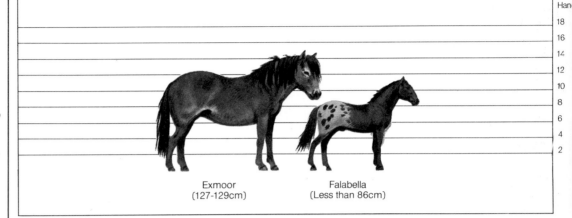

Hands
18
16
14
12
10
8
6
4
2

Exmoor
(127-129cm)

Falabella
(Less than 86cm)

The Exmoor is claimed to be the oldest of Britain's native ponies and is likely to have roamed Exmoor in Somerset since the Bronze Age. Roman carvings of chariots, found in the West Country, are pulled by ponies looking much like today's Exmoor.

The other exciting bit of evidence about their antiquity is that fossils of ponies found in Alaska have the same jaw formation and the same indications of a seventh molar tooth as the Exmoor. It seems the Exmoor has changed little from the time when its ancestors crossed the land bridge of the Bering Straits from the horse's original home in America and spread through Europe.

The Exmoors that remained in the West Country have been isolated and have not been subjected to out-crossing. They are remarkably purebred.

Research into the Exmoor's history has been carried out by Britain's Royal School of Veterinary Studies. This confirms that the Exmoor can be considered England's indigenous pony, and was probably foundation stock for Britain's other breeds.

Records of Exmoor Ponies roaming the moors date back to the Doomsday Book of 1085. Today, they still run wild in herds, but these are privately owned and are registered in a stud book. The earliest pedigree records can be traced to 1820, but a breed society was not formed until 1921. Registration today depends on inspection and pedigree. This happens in autumn, when the ponies are "gathered" and driven down to the farms. If they are accepted as good specimens of the breed, they are branded with an individual number on the near flank together with the Society's star and their herd number on the near shoulder.

Exmoor Ponies have a native cunning that helps them take care of themselves and their riders. They have long been used as pack animals and for herding sheep by the farmers. Some taken straight off the moor appear wild but if well-trained, they make high class children's and harness ponies.

The Exmoor has also been good foundation stock in the past and is still used as such. The Grand National winners, The Colonel and Zeodene, had Exmoor blood in their veins.

The Exmoor is typically "pony" in appearance. The particular features of its head are the short thick ears, the wide forehead and prominent "toad" eyes. The muzzle is an unusual mealy color. The neck is long enough to give a good length of rein. The shoulders are well laid back, the chest is deep and wide, and the back is broad and level as far as the loins. The legs are short and well apart. The hindlegs are nearly perpen-

Below: Probably the oldest native British pony, the Exmoor is likely to have roamed the West Country since Bronze Age times.

dicular from the hock to the fetlock, with the point of the hock in line with the pelvic bone. There is a wide curve from the flank to the hock joint.

The coat is close, hard and springy, which helps insulation. It is hard and bright in the summer but has no shine in the winter.

The Exmoor's action is straight and quite low to the ground.

FALABELLA

Country of origin
Argentina.
Height
Less than 8·2hh (34in).
Color
Any.
Features
Falabellas have the appearance of scaled-down horses rather than that of ponies. They are very rare but are bred in Argentina at Señor Falabella's ranch and in England at the Kilverstone Stud at Thetford, Norfolk.

The Falabella is a miniature horse that stands no higher than 34in (86cm). This extraordinary breed is produced at Señor Falabella's ranch in Argentina and has been since his grandfather's time. During the 19th century, an Irishman named Newton, the maternal grandfather of the present Señor Falabella, settled in Argentina, where he encountered the Indians

living in the region. The Indians watered their horses in a river that ran through Newton's land. One day, a small stallion appeared, which was said to have "the dwarf sickness". Newton was fascinated. He kept it and bred small horses from it for his daughter.

No-one knows anything more

Above: Falabella Ponies were developed in Argentina. They are so small and fragile that they are rarely strong enough to be ridden; they are usually kept as pets.

Below: A portrait of the Falabella Pony.

about this unique stallion, but when put to other stock, it was found his genes for small size were dominant. Mares bred with him produced much smaller foals than themselves, and the result was the gradual development of the breed of Falabellas.

Many breeds have been used to produce Falabellas, in many different colors. Today on the ranch, different-sized ponies can be seen, for it takes a few generations to "shrink" them down to the average Falabella height of less than 34 inches (86cm).

Falabellas have been exported all over the world, and the genes that produce small horses remain dominant.

The Falabella is not a small pony but a miniature horse. It is proportioned like a horse, with fine bone and small feet. It cannot be ridden and cannot be compared with that other small breed, the Shetland, which has a deep girth and short legs and is extraordinarily strong.

Falabellas are delicate and must be looked after like Thoroughbreds. They need to be blanketed when it is cold and fed concentrates, such as oats.

An unusual feature of the Falabella is the gestation period is two months longer than for most horses and ponies—close to 13 months. The foals are tiny—just 16-17in (41-43cm)—but they grow very quickly in their first year.

Falabellas also have two fewer ribs and vertebrae than the normal horse or pony.

These ponies are not strong enough to be ridden, but are used in harness. For their size, they are great jumpers but this can only be seen when they are loose.

FELL

Country of origin
Britain (West Pennines).
Height
13·1-14hh (53-56in)
Color
Black, brown, bay or gray. A small amount of white markings is permissible.
Features
Breeds remarkably true to type, which proves its ancient lineage. It is a tough, hardy, eye-catching pony with great energy and strength.

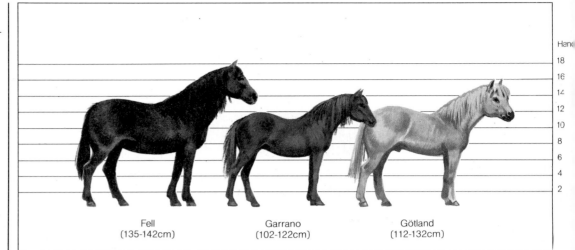

Hand
18
16
14
12
10
8
6
4
2

Fell
(135-142cm)

Garrano
(102-122cm)

Götland
(112-132cm)

The Fell Pony is a close relative of its neighbor, The Dales. It lives on the opposite (western) side of the Pennine Hills in northern England. Although it has roamed wild through Cumbria, Northumberland, and even south Lancashire and north to the Scottish borders, most have been found on the moorland surrounding the Lake District, around Ullswater, Windermere and Derwentwater.

The foundation stock was believed to have been strong alert ponies of less than 13 hands. They were agile enough to move quickly around the moorlands to seek their forage. The first known influence on them was the Friesian Horse. Friesians were brought to the area after the Roman Emperor Hadrian decreed in AD 120 that a huge wall be built across Britain to shut out the warring Picts.

The Romans hired labor from Friesland (now part of Holland and Germany). The Frieslanders brought with them some handsome black horses that stood close to 15 hands. When the Romans left Britain they did not take the horses, which allegedly amounted to about 1,000 Friesian stallions. These were probably foundation stock not only for the Fell and Dales but also for the Shire, and for the extinct Galloway Pony from Scotland.

The Friesian blood, mixed with the local native mares in the Pennines, resulted in a pony very similar to today's Fell. Few other influences reached the Pennines, and the result is a pony that breeds truer to type and is more easily recognizable than any of

Britain's native ponies, except the Exmoor (see page 26).

There was probably some mixing with the Scottish Galloway Pony, but it had similar foundation stock. More importantly, with the industrial revolution and the demand for larger, stronger horses, most of the northern and Scottish horses were bred to the bigger Clydesdale. This had some effect on the Dales, which became a heavier, larger pony, but the fact that the Fell stayed about the same proves that little Clydesdale blood was mixed with it.

Some good trotting blood has been added. The Fells are naturally fast trotters, and with the vogue for racing and using such horses in harness in the late 18th and 19th centuries, this aspect was

developed. Some Norfolk and Yorkshire Roadster stallions were used, and in the 1850s the Welsh Cob stallion, Comet, was stood at stud in the Orton district and put to Fell and Dales mares.

Through the ages this agile, strong, energetic, yet thrifty, pony has been well used. It is perhaps most famous, like the Dales, as a pack pony. From the 13th century, Fells were used in pack-pony droves with one ridden pony guiding groups of heavily laden free ponies. They used to be driven as far as London, but the advent

Below: Fell Ponies have similar origins to those of the Dales and breed close to them on the west of the Pennine Hills in England.

Right: A Fell mare grazes content-edly with her foal by her side. She has bred in captivity.

of railways reduced the demand for their use in transportation. They have also been used extensively by farmers for herding sheep and for general work, as well as between shafts as a speedy means of transport.

As with other British Mountain and Moorland ponies, the first official attempts to organize the breed were made at the end of the 19th century by the National Pony Society.

The Fell Pony Society was formed in 1912, and it has helped to ensure the continuance of this breed. Fells are used extensively for riding, particularly trekking, but it is with the growth of driving that the breed has found a real outlet. They breed so true to type that it is easy to find a matched pair or team. They have tremendous energy but lack the speed needed to excel in top class Combined Driving.

The Fell stands up to 14 hands. The head is ponylike, with a longish neck and well-laid-back shoulders. The quarters are muscular and strong. The hocks are well let-down. The limbs are strong, with good bone, and the hooves are blue, round and open. The feather should be silky on the legs and the mane and tail are long and thick.

The Fells are renowned for their energetic action, which is also free and straight.

GARRANO

(Minho)

Country of origin
North Portugal.
Height
10-12hh (40-48in).
Color
Usually chestnut.
Features
Work pony of ancient lineage.

In northern Portugal, in the provinces of Garrano de Minho and Traz do Montes, the Garrano has been bred for centuries on mountain pastures. It is believed to come from ancient stock, having changed little for thousands of years, although some upgrading has been carried out recently by introducing Arab blood.

It is a small pony, never more than 12hh (48in), yet is strong enough to be used by the army and local people as pack ponies and timber haulers.

In the past, the Garrano was used in trotting races, but these are rarely held today.

This pony has a small, attractive head with large eyes and small ears. The body is light but compact and deep. The legs are quite short. There is an abundance of hair in the mane and tail.

GOTLAND

(Russ)

Country of origin
Sweden (Island of Gotland).
Height
11-13hh (44-52in).
Color
Although bay and black are most common, other colors are found, including dun and palomino. A dorsal stripe along the back is usual.
Features
This ancient breed has changed little since the Stone Age, yet it is still useful in modern times as a child's pony and competitor in trotting races.

The Gotland has been bred since the Stone Age on the Swedish island after which it was named It is also known locally as the Russ. Its island life has left it relatively free from alien blood, although some Arab has been added over the last 100 years.

The Gotland ancestor is believed to be the Tarpan, and such primitive features as a dorsal stripe are found on many ponies.

Today, the Gotland still runs wild in the forests of Lojsta on Gotland, but many are now found on the mainland. The Gotland has proved to be a good children's pony and also such a fast trotter that it was used for races. It was also invaluable to the farmers until mechanization reduced the need for horsepower.

Continuance of this ancient breed is now aided by the government-supported Swedish Pony Association.

Above: The Gotland Pony has bred in the wild on the island of Gotland, Sweden, for centuries, probably since the Stone Age. Most are now bred on the mainland. A few have this eye-catching palomino color, although most are bay or black.

This is a light, elegant pony. The head has a straight face, broad forehead, small alert ears and big eyes. The neck is short and strong, with a long sloping shoulder. The back is long, but the quarters are round and short. The pony does not have great substance; the bone is light, yet strong. The hooves are small, hard and well-shaped.

The movement of the Gotland Pony is good at walk and trot but not in the canter and gallop.

GREEK PONIES
(Skyros, Pindos, Peneia)

SKYROS
Country of origin
Greece (island of Skyros).
Height
9.1-11hh (37-44in).
Color
Usually gray but also bay, brown or dun.
Features
The smallest Greek pony.

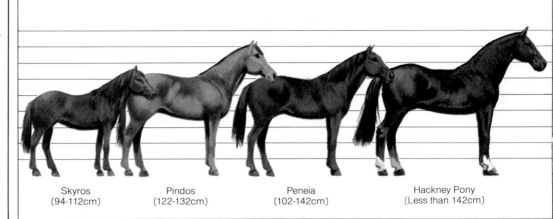

Skyros
(94-112cm)

Pindos
(122-132cm)

Peneia
(102-142cm)

Hackney Pony
(Less than 142cm)

Hand
18
16
14
12
10
8
6
4
2

Greece once had many native breeds of ponies that proved invaluable for transportation and agriculture. With mechanization, the demand for them has decreased, and most of the breeds have died out. The most popular today is the Skyros, which is the smallest of the Greek ponies. It is named after the island on which it originated.

Skyros ponies run wild in the mountains most of the year, but at harvest time some are rounded up and chased over the corn as a primitive, but effective, method of threshing it.

The Skyros has a small, pretty head with small ears, and a short neck. Its body is narrow and its quarters are not very muscular. The limbs are relatively long and there is a tendency to have cow hocks (see Glossary, page 198).

Below: The Skyros is both the best known and the smallest of the Greek ponies. This stallion has the smallish head and small ears typical of the breed, as also are the thick mane and tail.

PINDOS
Country of origin
Greece (Thessaly and Epirus).
Height
12-13hh (48-52in).
Color
Usually gray but also bay or brown.
Features
This eye-catching pony is used for all types of work; the mares are sometimes used for breeding mules.

The Pindos comes from the mountains of northern Greece, from the regions called Thessaly and Epirus. It is a larger, more elegant pony than the Skyros, and is said to have Oriental origins.

Like the Skyros, it is used for pack work and farmwork, but because of its mountainous origin, it is particularly surefooted and agile.

The Pindos is lightframed, with little muscle on the neck and quarters. The limbs are relatively long and the feet are narrow and boxy. The tail is set high.

PENEIA
Country of origin
Greece (Peloponnese).
Height
10-14hh (43-56in).
Color
Most colors but usually brown, bay, chestnut or gray.
Features
Stallions are sometimes crossed with female donkeys to breed hinnies (mules).

The Peneia is less well-known than the other surviving Greek pony breeds. It is named after its homelands in the Peloponnese. Like the Pindos, it shows signs of Oriental ancestry. It varies in size more than the other Greek breeds and can grow as high as 14 hands (56 inches).

Like its close relatives, it is a tough and willing worker and is used for transport and farmwork.

HACKNEY PONY

Country of origin
England.
Height
Under 14hh (56in).
Color
Bay, brown and black are most common.
Features
Its spectacular action makes this an ideal show pony. Spectators love to watch it, but its high spirits mean it needs careful handling. It is rarely a good children's pony.

The Hackney Pony is the small version of the Hackney Horse (see pages 106-107) and shares much of its history. Both are based on Norfolk and Yorkshire Roadsters, breeds that were developed in the 18th century as fast trotters to pull light carriages and provide a speedy means of travel. The Yorkshire version was based on Thoroughbred and Coach Horse crossbreds and the Norfolk one on Trotters, Galloways and Thoroughbreds.

The Norfolk foundation Thoroughbred sire was Shales the Original (foaled in 1755), an offspring of Flying Childers, the son of Darley Arabian. Shales produced such good lines that Yorkshire breeders used some of the Norfolk stock, and this led to the development of the Hackney.

The pony version was started by Christopher Wilson of Westmorland. He used a Roadster stallion, with Yorkshire and Norfolk blood, named Sir George (foaled in 1866). He was put to the very best Fell mares. In the 1870s, Wilson started breeding ponies for use in many activities, including racing. He was so successful that they became known as "Wilson ponies".

Ponies that were from Sir George started a new breed, which became known as the Hackney Pony. Sir George was 14 hands (56in), but most of the Fell mares were only about 13 hands (52in). Wilson kept the height of his new ponies down by turning them out on the moors. This also kept them

tough, so only sound individuals survived. Sir George's assets were his "high class" (Flying Childers was in his pedigree), speed and elegance. The Fell mares' qualities were their high knee action, power and substance. The result was the spectacular, high-stepping Hackney Pony that became so popular that one filly sold for $1,000 (£900) in 1896.

Hackney Ponies were exported the world over; they were, and still are, exhibited at shows and used to deliver goods. They are tough, energetic workers and also great "show-offs", with their flashy appearance and extraordinary movement.

The Hackney Pony should look like a genuine pony with a small, intelligent head. The neck should be long, the shoulders powerful, the body compact and the limbs strong.

The most important aspect of the Hackney is its brilliant action. This should be fluent and spectacular, with the knee raised as high as possible and the feet flung forward in a rounded movement. The hocks should come well under the body and lift so high they nearly touch it.

Above: The Hackney Pony has a spirited nature and is most popular as a harness pony. It is rarely ridden, but is often driven in classes where it is judged for its conformation, action and manners.

Below: The spectacular action of the Hackney Pony makes it a feature item at many major shows.

HAFLINGER

Country of origin
Austria (Southern Tyrol).

Height
13·1-14·2hh (53-58in).

Color
Palomino or chestnut, with a flaxen mane and tail.

Features
This Austrian breed has proved to be one of the best workers in the high mountains. Today, this quality makes them popular as mounts for tourists. In the past, before mechanization, these attractive ponies were a major aid for transport and agriculture.

Haflinger
(135-147cm)

Highland
(132-147cm)

The Haflinger developed high in the mountains of the South Tyrol, in areas between 5,000 and 6,600ft (1,500-2,000m). Isolated from other influences and subject to a rigorous climate, it developed into a robust animal that bred true to type.

Its history cannot be proved, but the main center of breeding was in the valley of Sarn around the village of Hafling. Its inhabitants are believed to be descendants of the Ostrogoths, who settled there after they had been driven out of Italy in the mid-6th century. They brought with them small Arab horses that had been used in the war, and crossed them with the mountain ponies to produce the native foundation stock for the Haflinger.

The first written evidence of the breed was in 1868, when the stallion El Bedavi XXII was described as being used to upgrade the local stock. He was the son of an Arab stallion, from the famous Hungarian stud at Babolna, and an Arab mare. El Bedavi XXII was bred to local stock, and it is to him that today's Haflingers can be traced. His son, 249 Folie, became the foundation sire. Folie had the typical chestnut coat, white mane and white tail. With a considerable amount of inbreeding in the late 19th century, these traits proved to be 99% inherited.

With its sturdy constitution, sure-footedness, docility and strength, the Haflinger has been a valuable aid to the Austrian hill farmers. It was used also for pack work in peace and war. Just before World War II, the Germans promoted the breeding of Haflingers because they wanted to use them for transportation in the mountains.

Today, the Austrian government supports their breeding. The emblem with which they are branded is an "H", combined with Austria's national flower, the eidelweiss.

The Haflinger's head is small and has the same elegance as the Arab's. The eyes are large, and the ears are small and alert. The neck is strong and the shoulder long and sloping. The back is straight and broad; the quarters are muscular and rounded. The legs are quite short with good bone. There is a little feather on the legs and an abundance of hair in the mane and tail.

Right: The Haflingers are the work ponies of their native country of Austria. Strong and sensible, they are ideal for harness work.

Right: A portrait of the Haflinger Pony.

HIGHLAND

Country of origin
Scotland.

Height
13-14·2hh (52-58in).

Color
Various shades of dun, gray, brown or black are most common. Bay and liver chestnut, with silver mane and tail, are occasionally found. Most have a dorsal eel stripe, and many have zebra markings inside the forelegs. White markings, apart from a small star, are disliked.

Features
This intelligent, strong, docile, sure-footed pony is one of the most versatile of Britain's native breeds.

The Highland Pony has been part of Scotland's history for centuries. It has provided its main form of transport for a long time. Although it is one of the oldest breeds of the region, its origins are obscure. It was not isolated, as were the Exmoor and the Fell, and in recent times there have been a number of outside influences. These have included Arab stallions introduced by the MacNeills of Barra and high-class French stallions sent to James IV of Scotland by Louis XII of France.

In the past, the ponies varied from area to area, according to local needs and climate. Those on the islands (known as Western Isles) tended to be smaller and faster than those on the mainland (known as Garrons). Crossbreeding has caused these distinctions to disappear.

For hundreds of years, Highland Ponies have been valued by the Scottish people. In addition to providing transport, they have been used as pack animals, and by sportsmen for hunting and carrying game. In the forests, they are still used for pulling felled trees and are used on farms for carting and sheep herding.

Today, other uses have been found for these versatile ponies.

They carry tourists across Scotland. They are also used for driving competitions, for general riding and as foundation stock for breeding Hunters and Eventers.

Highland ponies are particularly hardy and have an unusual winter coat that consists of a layer of strong, badger-like hair over a soft, dense undercoat. This enables them to live outside all year, even in the worst weather.

The Highland's head is broad in width and short in length, but the muzzle is not pinched. The

Above: The Highland Pony has served Scottish farmers for centuries; today, it is used mainly for general riding and showing.

neck is strong and arched with a clean throat. The shoulder is well-laid-back with a pronounced wither. The back is compact and deep and the quarters are powerful. The legs are short, with well-shaped hard, dark hooves. The bone is flat and hard. There is a little silky feather on the legs.

HUCUL
(Hutsul)

Country of origin
Poland (Carpathian mountains).
Height
13-13·2hh (52-54in).
Color
Bay, black, mouse-gray or occasionally chestnut.
Features
This mountain pony is still used as a work pony in Poland.

The Huçul is a primitive-type pony, which evolved in Poland in the eastern Carpathians. It is known locally as the Hutsul after the Ukrainian mountains which are also called the Hutsuls.

Its origins are fairly directly connected to ancient wild horses. It is believed to be a cross between Tarpan derivatives and Mongolian breeds derived from Przewalski's Horse. Later there have been infusions of lighter horses, notably the Arab.

The small robust Huçul has great powers of endurance and that highly-developed instinct of mountain horses. It has worked in the mountains for centuries where it has been a pack pony and a harness pony, especially for the carting of wood, and it has been used for riding, especially in the very hilly regions. Today it is also used by children.

The ponies are selectively bred at the state stud of Siary. Their breeding is aided by the government as they are still used as work ponies in many parts of Poland and help the economy of the country.

The Huçul resembles Poland's other pony, the Konik, but its legs are shorter.

It also looks like the Tarpan, with its rather long, broad head. The body is compact and strong but there is a tendency for the limbs to be cow hocked.

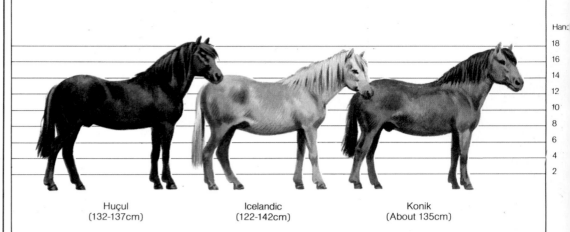

| Huçul (132-137cm) | Icelandic (122-142cm) | Konik (About 135cm) |

Below: The Huçul is a native of Poland and is descended from the Polish Wild Pony, or Tarpan. Both horses share many of the same primitive features, such as the long broad head.

Above: The Icelandic Pony has been a mainstay of the economy of its country, helping with transportation and farmwork for centuries. It is found in many colors, including this pinto type.

ICELANDIC

Country of origin
Iceland.
Height
12-14hh (48-56in).
Color
Most colors are found, but the most popular ones are the various shades of dun and chestnut, including liver chestnut with a flaxen mane and tail.
Features
The tough, docile Icelandic has provided its country's residents with an important aid to the economy. Indeed, it was their sole means of transport for over 1,000 years. Many are now exported, and until recently large numbers were used as pit ponies in British coal mines.

The forbears of the Icelandic Pony were brought to Iceland by settlers in the late 8th and early 9th centuries. The settlers came from Norway, from Scotland and the islands of Orkney and Shetland, and the ponies they brought with them were from their homelands. There must have been some ponies of the Celtic type, because ponies found in south-west Iceland look very like the Exmoor

The foundation stock never completely blended into one breed, and even after hundreds of years of isolated breeding, there is still variety between the ponies found in Iceland, although all are agile and sure-footed. Their traits are not dominant, because if an Icelandic is put to another breed, very few are transmitted.

These ponies are greatly valued as working animals by the Icelandic people, and there are still large numbers of them. They once carried soldiers into battle. They are still bred for their meat, because beef cattle are not tough enough to survive the northern winter. Icelandic farmers have also relied on them to plow, transport goods and to shepherd flocks. They were the main form of transportation, and still remain so today because there are few roads. They are used as pack ponies, as draft animals for pulling carts, and for riding. They are also used for sport, and race meets are held for them throughout the summer.

An unusual feature of these ponies is their homing instinct; it is customary to turn them loose after a long trip, when they will find their own way home. Most provide very comfortable, fast rides. In addition to the usual trot, canter and gallop, they have the gaits of pace and running walk. Although docile by nature, Icelandic Ponies are not particularly tractable. They have a highly independent nature, and shouted commands seem to be the best means of control.

Icelandics are stocky ponies with large heads, intelligent eyes and short, muscular necks, with a thick mane. The body is compact and deep. The quarters are sloping, the limbs short and strong, and the feet well-shaped and strong.

KONIK

Country of origin
  Poland.
Height
  About 13·1hh (53in).
Color
  Mouse gray or dun with a black dorsal stripe and transverse stripes on the forearms and second thighs.
Features
  This primitive-type pony is directly descended from the Wild Tarpans.

Below: A portrait of the Icelandic Pony, which has a mixed origin, and sometimes does not breed true outside it own blood.

These primitive-type ponies are supposed to have developed directly from the Wild Horse, or Tarpan. The name means "small horse" and it was the addition of some Oriental blood that helped to make it horselike. Koniks have been bred throughout Poland for centuries, but today their breeding is concentrated in the northern part of Rzeszow province.

The Koniks are bred and allowed to roam free at the Experimental Stud of the Polish Academy of Science at Popielno in Mazury, at the Racot State Stud and at the Roztocze National Park.

This pony has influenced a large number of other breeds. It was used as foundation stock for regional Polish breeds (most of which are now extinct) and also neighbouring countries' breeds, such as the Viatka from Russia.

Koniks have very good temperaments, and they are strong. They are also frugal feeders. This has made them popular with farmers for draft work and with children for riding.

They are similar to the Huçul in appearance and temperament.

Above: The Konik is similar to Poland's other native pony, the Huçul, shown at the foot of the opposite page. It is used extensively in Poland as a work and riding pony.

They have the same large, rectangularly-shaped head. The body is well proportioned, but the limbs are not always well-set and they tend to have "cow hocks". Although used for riding, they have a very short stride. They have a long life-span but take a long time to reach maturity.

LANDAIS
(Barthais)

Country of origin
France.
Height
Not more than 13·1hh (53in).
Color
Bay, brown, black or chestnut.
Features
A pony with Arab-like features and character that have made it an excellent children's riding pony.

This French pony has ancient origins, but over a period of time it has been strongly influenced by the Arab. The first Arab addition was from the horses left behind after the French victory over the Muslim horsemen at Poitiers in AD 871. Finally, in 1913, an Arab stallion was used on the Landais mares. These additions explain the Arab-like features of the pony, but it is a little more robust than its Oriental ancestors, because it has been subjected to wetter and colder conditions.

The Landais has run wild on the Barthes plains and Landais marshes along the Ardour river for centuries. It is still found there today. This hard life has made it a tough and cunning pony.

During this century, its numbers have dwindled, and the French now use occasional Arab or Welsh Section B stallions to help maintain the breed.

The Landais is used as a children's pony, and for harness work, and it is an excellent trotter.

This breed is not particularly homogenous, but all Landais are fine, elegant, intelligent, robust ponies. They usually have an Arab-like head with the Arab's concave face, large eyes and small pointed ears. The neck is long and the shoulder sloping. The back is short and straight, with the tail set high. The limbs have bone of about 6·5-7in (17-18cm). The coat of the Landais is fine.

Below: The Lokai has long been used as a pack and riding horse by the tribesmen in the USSR after whom it was named.

Landais
(Maximum 135cm)

Lokai
(140-150cm)

Manipur
(112-132cm)

LOKAI

Country of origin
USSR (Uzbekistan).
Height
13·3-14·3hh (55-59in).
Color
Most are bay, gray, chestnut or black. Occasionally they are dun and sometimes they have a golden sheen to the coat.
Features
Its agility and sure-footedness make the Lokai a good worker in its native mountains.

The Lokai is a tall pony from Southern Tadzhikstan in the USSR. Originally a mountain pony, it evolved from Steppe horses and those from Central Asia. It is used by the Lokai tribe of Uzbekistan: hence its name. It has been crossbred with other breeds, including the Iomud, Karabair, Akhal Teke and Arab, to improve its 'class' and increase its height.

It is a sure-footed pony that is still used for work in the mountains, where it can be ridden or used as a pack pony. In the sporting world, it is most famous as the mount of the Tadzhik riders in the game of *kopar,* in which a mounted man carries a goat that others try to take from him by chasing after him.

The Lokai is a light-framed pony. The head has a straight face and sometimes even a Roman

Above: A Lokai being ridden by one of the Lokai tribesmen at Dushanbe, Tadzhikstan, near Afghanistan.

nose. The neck is muscular and set low on the shoulder. The withers are long and not prominent. The body is deep and the loins are straight, but the croup slopes. The forearm is long, but the cannons are short. The feet are hard and strong.

MANIPUR

Country of origin
India (Manipur).
Height
11-13hh (44-52in).
Color
Most.
Features
This tough, maneuverable pony is famous both as a polo pony and as a cavalry mount, but it has also been used extensively as a work pony.

The Manipur has been bred for centuries in the state in India after which it is named. It has gained fame as being one of the earliest breeds to be used as a polo pony. There is a manuscript dating back to the 7th century discussing the introduction of polo to the state and the use of the ponies bred there in the game. Manipurs were certainly the ponies being used to play polo in India when the British discovered the game during the last century. This pony has also been used in wartime. The Manipur cavalry was always noted as being particularly well mounted.

The Manipur is similar to the Burmese (Shan) Pony and is likely to have been derived from the same origins—a basis of the Mongolian Pony, with a little Arab blood to provide speed and a more refined conformation.

This thick-set pony has a fairly long head with a broad muzzle and well dilated nostrils. The body is broad and deep. The tail is set quite high.

Right: The Manipur was the original polo pony, and is so strong that it can carry heavy men or packs for many miles without tiring.

MONGOLIAN

Country of origin
Mongolia.
Height
12·2-14·2hh (50-58in).
Color
Black, bay and dun are most common.
Features
This ancient type of pony is very tough, frugal and fast. It is a working pony in Mongolia and can be used for many other activities, including racing.

Mongolian
(127-147cm)

New Forest
(Maximum 142cm)

Norwegian Fjord
(132-147cm)

Large numbers of this hetero-geneous pony are found in vast areas of the Far East, where it breeds and is used as a general work pony. It is found all over Outer Mongolia, Tibet and China, and it has close relatives in the surrounding countries.

The Mongolian is an ancient type. Its foundation stock was Przewalski's Horse (or Mongolian Wild Horse, page 42). It was thought to be the domesticated version of the Wild Horse, but it is now known that there has been crossbreeding with other horses and ponies. Today there are many types of Mongolian because of differences in ancestors, climate

and feeding. These include the Wuchumutsin Heiling Kiang, Hailar, Sanho, Sanpeitze and Ili. The Ili is larger because it has been crossed with Russian breeds.

Mongolian Ponies are traditionally bred in large herds by the Mongol tribes. In the past, these tribes conquered foreign territory, which led to the spread of the pony to many parts of the world. It has been important foundation stock for breeds such as the Turkoman, the Spiti, the Bhutia, the Manipur the Tibetan and the China Pony.

In its home territory this fast, frugal pony is used by the Mongols for pack work, herding and the few agricultural activities that take place. The mares are often milked; the milk is used for cheese or fermented to make a form of alcohol called *kumiss*.

The Mongolian has a heavy head with small eyes and short, thick ears. Its neck is short and thick, with a full mane. Its shoulders are heavy, its chest deep, its back short and strong and its tail set high, with thick hair at the roots. The legs

are strong with good bone, and the feet are hard and round. This is a description of a typical pony, but Mongolians do not breed true to type, and they vary greatly, particularly between regions.

Below: The Mongolian Pony is the work pony of its vast, bleak homeland in northern Asia. It is remarkably strong and fast-moving. Together with a derivative, the China Pony, it is used for racing and for playing polo.

Above: This chestnut New Forest Pony foal has a small star on its head. It was born in the open in England's New Forest region.

Below: A group of New Forest Ponies photographed in their natural habitat, which consists mainly of heather and grass.

NEW FOREST

Country of origin
Britain (New Forest, Hants.).

Height
Maximum 14hh (56in); although there is no lower limit few are under 12hh (48in).

Color
Bay and brown is most usual, but all colors are acceptable, except piebald, skewbald or blue-eyed cream. White markings on head and legs are permitted.

Features
This breed combines the strength, agility and intelligence of native British ponies with a narrower frame, speed and a tractable temperament. The New Forest is an ideal pony for the entire family. It has been used in most equestrian sports, including driving, and has even been raced. There has been some cross-breeding with Thoroughbreds and Arabs to produce small riding horses.

The New Forest Pony is the second largest of Britain's Mountain and Moorland ponies. It is also the most heterogeneous, showing a large range of types. This is because it has occupied a territory—the 60,000 acres of the New Forest, in Hampshire—that is not as wild or remote as the habitats of Britain's other ponies.

Through the centuries, many different types and breeds of pony were free to roam the area, and at times this has been deliberate policy. In 1852, for example, Queen Victoria allowed an Arab stallion called Zorah to be let loose in the forest for eight years to "improve" the breed. Thoroughbreds have also been used and, during the 20th century, stallions from other native breeds.

The origins of the breed are obscure. The first known fact is that in the 11th century, during the reign of King Canute, there are records of horses running free in the New Forest. The first systematic efforts to improve the breed began at the end of the 19th century.

In 1891, the Society for the Improvement of New Forest Ponies was founded and it offered pre-miums for quality stallions to run in the forest. This was followed in 1905 by the formation of the Burley and District New Forest Pony and Cattle Breeding Society, which started registering mares and their young stock. In 1938, these two societies merged, and during this period it was laid down that no further outside blood could be used. ▶

▶ Like the other native ponies, the New Forest is no longer confined to its natural home but is bred all over the world. It is the closest in conformation and action to a riding pony and is used for riding and driving. This riding type of pony has substance. The head should be ponylike, well set on, with a long sloping shoulder. It should have a good deep body, powerful quarters, good bone, straight legs and hard, round feet. Narrower than other native ponies, the New Forest is a good ride for children. All but the smallest ponies, nevertheless, are stong enough to be ridden by adults. Its movement is free, active and straight but not exaggerated.

NORWEGIAN FJORD

Country of origin
Norway.
Height
13-14·2hh (52-58in); about 14hh (56in) is standard.
Color
Various shades of dun (usually cream or yellow) with a dorsal stripe from tail to forelock. The legs are dark and usually have zebra markings on them. The tail is dark. The mane is dark in the center, with silver hairs on either side.
Features
For centuries, the coarse mane of the Fjord has been clipped in a curve to give the neck a distinctive shape and to allow the dark hairs to be seen just above the silver. These ponies are depicted in Viking runestones. The Fjord's kind nature, sturdy constitution and great strength have made it useful to man for centuries. Once indispensable on farms and in the mountains, today it is used in driving competitions, as a children's pony and for the popular European activity of vaulting.

The Norwegian Fjord, with its pale dun color and dark, clear-cut eel stripe bordered on the mane by lighter hairs, bears the distinct features of the primeval pony. The hairs in the mane are bristly, which makes them stand upright for a few inches. This is similar to the manes of ancient types that did not have to contend with a rainy environment; a mane falling over protects against the wet. The mane does eventually fall over in the Norwegian if it grows very long.

Some theorists claim that all domestic horses are descended from the primeval pony, of which Przewalski's Horse (page 42) is the wild example. The Norwegian Fjord, despite centuries of domestication and use by man, bears a close resemblance to it. This shows there has been little crossbreeding for thousands of years. This remarkable pony breeds very true to type and produces its primitive features generation after generation.

Above: This closeup of a Norwegian Fjord pony shows its concave head and the unusual mane.

Below: A Norwegian Fjord mare and foal. The foals are very tough; they are often born in northern Scandinavia.

Right: The Norwegian Fjord is a strong pony, with endless stamina and a kind, even temperament. This has made it a high-class work pony. It is popular throughout Scandinavia and in Germany. This one is pulling an extremely large cart.

The Norwegian Fjord is still very similar to the pony on which the Vikings waged war and had their playful fights on horseback. It must have been the pony they took to Iceland in AD 871 and acted as foundation stock for the Icelandic Pony. The Vikings' ponies were not used solely for warlike activities because the Vikings were the first people to use the horse to pull the plow. It was through their invasions of other lands that horse plowing became widespread. The ancestors of the Norwegian Fjord probably were the original plow-pullers on the mountainous farmlands of Scandinavia. The breed has since been used in the mountains for pack work, on the farms and as a weight-carrying pony. Its strength, tractable nature and ability to live on relatively little food has made it popular as an all-around work pony both in its homeland and in those countries without a native work pony (all over Scandinavia and in Germany).

This sturdy pony has a small head, with a broad, flat forehead and large eyes set well-apart. The head is refined and the face tends toward being concave rather than convex. The ears are small and well apart. The mane is coarse and stands upright for a few inches. The neck is short and thick and merges into the body without a clear division. The withers are rounded and not distinct. The back is of medium length but muscular and rounded. The hindquarters are strong, the limbs are short and sturdy, with good bone, and there is a little feather on the heels.

Below: A pair of Norwegian Fjord foals. They are usually born with fluffier, lighter-color coats than when they are mature. Their manes tend to become stiffer as they grow older.

PONY OF THE AMERICAS

Country of origin
United States (Iowa).
Height
11·2-13·2hh (46-54in).
Color
Appaloosa coloring.
Features
This miniature spotted horse is eye-catching and well-made, which makes it popular for riding and in the showring.

This new multi-colored breed was created in the 1950s by Leslie Boomhower of Mason City, Iowa. The foundation stock was a Shetland pony stallion and an Appaloosa mare. These spectacularly colored ponies have multiplied and are popular for riding and showing with both children and adults alike.

A Pony of the Americas has the appearance, in miniature, of a cross between a Quarter Horse and an Arab. The head is often slightly concave, with large eyes and pointed ears. The neck is slightly arched. The shoulders slope, and the withers are prominent. The body is well-rounded, short and muscular. The croup is long, level and muscular. The movement is free and easy; the pony takes long, straight strides. In the trot, there is good hock action.

Pony of the Americas (117-137cm)   Przewalski's Horse (122-132cm)   Sable Island (142-152cm)

The chief distinguishing feature of these ponies is their coloring. They should have Appaloosa coloring, including a mottled skin and exposed sclera of the eye (the white circles round the eyes, as in our own). They should be white over the loin and hips with dark, round or egg-shaped spots, and have mud-colored shading around the mouth and nostrils. The hooves are often striped.

Below: The Pony of the Americas is an eye-catching new breed. All have appaloosa coloring, like this multi-spotted pony, and also white sclera (circles round the eyes).

PRZEWALSKI'S HORSE

Country of origin
Western Mongolia.
Height
12-13hh (48-52in).
Color
Yellowish dun with a mealy muzzle and dark mane and tail. There is a dorsal stripe down the back and zebra markings on the legs.
Features
This is the only true wild horse. It is a different species from the domestic horse.

Przewalski's horse, *Equus przewalski poliakoff,* is the only true wild horse. It is unlike other 'wild horses' that have escaped from domestication. It is the only horse that has survived since prehistoric times. It it believed to be a distinct species, different from *Equus caballus* (the domestic horse), although closely related, because *Equus przewalski* and *Equus caballus* can be crossed, and the hybrids are fertile.

This wild horse is believed by some to be the foundation stock for all domestic horses. It *was* probably the foundation stock for the Mongolian and Burmese ponies, ponies from India and some from the USSR, but it seems probable that there were as many as four basic types of wild horse (see page 10). Przewalski's Horse is most likely to be a member of the first subgroup of the Northern Group Horses, known as the Primeval Ponies.

Przewalski's Horse was discovered by the Russian explorer Colonel Przewalski in 1881 in the northwest part of Mongolia. He found a small herd in the Tachin Schara Nuru Mountains, on the edge of the Gobi Desert. The breed was named after him. In an effort to preserve these rare animals, the Chinese and Russians have now forbidden hunting. For centuries, various nomadic tribes killed them for meat.

Although it is planned to re-establish herds of Przewalski's Horse in the wild in western Mongolia, most representatives of the breed are captive. They are kept in zoos all over the world, where they breed and can be studied and observed to help scientific research on equine evolution.

Przewalski's Horse is very wild and timid around humans. It has a massive head with small ears and eyes, a big jaw and very big teeth. The body is broad and short coupled. The neck is short, and the shoulder is straight. The hindquarters are not very strong and lack muscle. The legs are fine-boned, and the cannon bones are rather short. The mane is short and upright, but it can fall over on the neck, particularly in winter when the hair grows. The tail is distinctly tufted at the end.

SABLE ISLAND

Country of origin
  Canada (Sable Island).
Height
  14-15hh (56-60in).
Color
  Mostly chestnut, but some are bay, brown, black or gray.
Features
  These are tough ponies that have to survive rigorous conditions in their natural habitat.

This pony is named after the small island where it still runs wild today. It has to survive bleak conditions; Sable Island lies in the Atlantic 100 hundred miles offshore from Nova Scotia.

Although legends claim that ponies have been on the island since the 16th century, evidence points to their being taken there in the early 18th century. They were believed to be of New England stock.

Sable Island ponies have multiplied in numbers, and today there are 40 or 50 herds on the island. Some of the ponies are caught and used both in harness and under saddle.

They have largish heads with a straight face and large ears. The body is finely built and rather short. The limbs are short and there is some feather on the heels.

Above: A Sable Island mare and foal. They breed in the wild on Sable Island, to the west of Novia Scotia, Canada.

Right: A portrait of Przewalski's Horse, with a foal.

SHETLAND

Country of origin
  Britain (Shetland Isles).
Height
  Not more than 10·2hh (42in).
Color
  Black is the foundation color but ponies may be bay, brown, chestnut, gray or part-colors.
Features
  This tiny pony is the strongest horse in the world relative to its size. This power has enabled it to help the inhabitants of its homelands for centuries. Today it is popular for harness work, as a children's pony or simply as a pet.

Shetland
(Maximum 107cm)

Sorraia
(122-132cm)

The Shetland is the smallest British Mountain and Moorland pony. Its diminutive size is not due to the bitter weather in its northerly homelands of the Shetland Isles, off Scotland: if it is bred in warmer climates, it is still small in size. It is believed to trace back to a dwarf variety of the "Exmoor type" brought to England by some of the first people to cross the seas to Britain. Drawings that date from the Stone Age in caves along the Bay of Biscay in France and Spain show ponies with Shetland features. No existing breeds, other than the Shetland, show these features today—the Shetland is unique.

  Isolated in its bleak islands for nearly 2,000 years, this tough pony was not subject to any outside influences until it began to be taken to the mainland during the 19th century. For hundreds of years, it has helped the people of Shetland; its main work has been to cart peat for fuel (there were no trees), to carry fresh seaweed (used as manure) or burned seaweed (used as fertilizer) to the fields. As a pack pony, it is very strong, and is able to carry more weight in proportion to its size than any other horse or pony in the world.

Right: A Shetland Pony. This famous breed is very tough and capable of surviving in the snow.

Below: A Shetland Pony mare and her foal. Although small, the breed is extremely strong.

In the 19th century the value of this pony was realized, particularly for work in the mines. Many Shetlands were taken from their homelands to be used as pit ponies. They were bred for quantity, and there was a deterioration in quality. Then, in 1870, the Marquess of Londonderry established studs in Bressay and Noss, and through selective breeding, he helped to establish a good type of Shetland. Most of today's best Shetlands can be traced back to Londonderry stock and in particular the stallion Jack.

The Shetland was the first British native pony to have its own society. It was started in 1890 and a stud book was opened. At times, this was open to inspected stock, but in 1969 it was finally closed to all but the progeny of registered parents.

The Shetland has been extensively exported, and many countries now have their own stud book.

The Shetland's head is broad in the forehead, with a fairly straight face. The neck is slightly crested (more so in stallions) and a good length. The shoulder is sloping, and the body is thick-set and deep. The back and loins are short, with strong quarters. The limbs are strong and well-placed. The feet are strong, round and of a good shape. There is an abundance of hair in the mane and tail and some feather on the legs. The action is straight and free with good hock and knee flexion.

An unusual feature of the Shetland is its coat; although smooth in the summer, it grows two layers in the winter.

The American Shetland is a more slender and refined version. It is shown in hand or in harness with high front and rear action.

SORRAIA

Countries of origin
Portugal and Spain (near the Sorraia River).
Height
12-13hh (48-52in).
Color
Usually dun or gray with a dorsal stripe and zebra markings on the legs.
Features
A tough primitive pony that has lived on the Iberian peninsula for centuries.

The Sorraia is similar to its neighbor, the Garrano. Its homelands are along the Sorraia River and between its tributaries, the Sor and the Raia. It is found in western Spain and Portugal and it has lived there from ancient times. Some authorities believe it was one of the first horse breeds to be domesticated. The Sorraia is a primitive pony, bearing certain similarities to Przewalski's Horse and the Tarpan, from which it must have been descended.

It is very tough and able to survive heat and cold, as well as a lack of food. It was formerly used for rounding up cattle and other farm-work. Today, the Sorraia runs wild and one purebred herd has been kept in its natural state by the d'Andrade family.

Above: A Sorraia Pony of the typical dun coloring. The dorsal stripe on the back is also visible.

The head is large but varies in shape. In some individuals it resembles the Tarpan. The ears are long, with black tips. The neck is long, with upright shoulders. The quarters are rather weak. The legs are slender and long.

Below: The Sorraia Pony breeds in Portugal and Spain along the river valley after which it is named.

TARPAN

Countries of origin
  Poland and Russia.
Height
  Average 13hh (52in).
Color
  Ranges from mouse to brown
  dun with a dorsal stripe. There
  are zebra markings on the legs,
  and the mane and tail are dark.
Features
  This ancient strain was hunted
  for its meat. Domestic versions
  were used as work ponies,
  but today the Tarpans run wild
  in reserves, where they are
  studied by scientists.

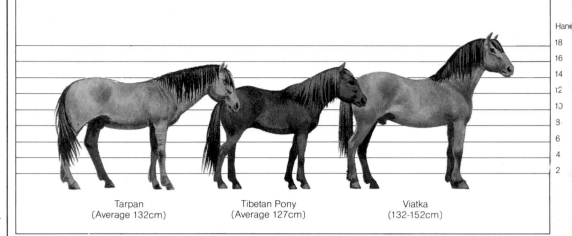

Tarpan
(Average 132cm)

Tibetan Pony
(Average 127cm)

Viatka
(132-152cm)

Tarpan is the Russian word for "wild horse." Some claim that this animal, together with Przewalski's Horse, is one of the original species of wild horses. It has been given the species name *Equus przewalskii gmelini antonus.* But evidence now seems to point instead to the Tarpan being a hybrid of the Proto-Arab group of the Southern Horses and the pony group of Northern Horses. The fact domestic descendants of the Tarpan—the Konik, Huçul and others—are all resistant to extremes of temperature helps support this theory.

The Tarpan of today is an artificially "restored" breed. It was recreated largely by Professor T. Vetulani in the 1930s. All genuine specimens of this wild horse had become extinct. Today, Tarpans live the life of wild horses in the forests of the state reserve at Popiellno, in Poland.

Many original Tarpans ran wild across the steppes of Russia, south of the Ural mountains. Another type, the Forest Tarpan, roamed the forests of central and eastern Europe. These animals were foundation stock for many of the European and Eastern breeds of horses and ponies, but they were hunted for meat. By the end of the 18th century they were close to extinction.

Some Tarpans were gathered into reserves like those of Count Zamoyski of Poland. But most of the ponies escaped, died out or were captured and domesticated by peasants. However, some claim it was the remnants of this Zamoyski stock, together with some from another reserve in the Bialystock forests, that were used to re-create the Tarpan in captivity. Even if today's animals are not purebred Tarpans, careful selective breeding has meant they bear the distinctive features of this ancient breed.

The head is long and broad. The face has a straight or even convex profile. The ears are long. The neck is short and thick, and the shoulder sloping. The back is long, the hindquarters weak and the tail set high. The limbs are long and fine.

Below: The Tarpan Pony became extinct last century, but the breed has been "reconstructed" by Polish scientists.

TIBETAN PONY
(Nanfan)

Country of origin
Tibet (Himalayas).
Height
12·2hh (50in).
Color
A white coat with an unpig-
mented skin is most common.
Features
Sure-footed, strong pony ideal
for mountain packwork.

The Tibetan comes from the
Himalayas. It is similar to the Spiti
and Bhutia from India. Like them,
it is derived from the Mongolian.

This pony is sure-footed and
able to carry heavy packs along
steep mountain trails. On flat
ground it is a fast walker. However,
it is most suited to the colder
climate of the mountains and can
withstand rugged, freezing
conditions better than the heat.

It is a strong, compact pony. The
legs are short, with plenty of bone.
The mane and tail are very thick.

*Right: The Tibetan is a tough
mountain pony, used for centuries
as a sturdy, hard-working pack
horse in the Himalayas.*

VIATKA

Country of origin
USSR (Kirov and Udmurt).
Height
13-15hh (52-60in).
Color
Dun and light brown are most
common. The mane and tail
are black. There is often a
dorsal stripe.
Features
Energetic, tractable and frugal,
with great stamina, these are
useful work ponies in harness
or under saddle.

The Viatka is a primitive type pony.
It seems likely to have evolved
mainly from the Tarpan. However,
there has also been some influence
from the strong cobby types (not
a breed) of working ponies from
Estonia in the USSR. These are
called *Kleppers* (the local word
for 'nag'). They have practically
died out because most were used
for the upgrading needed to establish
the Toric. The Viatka is bred in the
Baltic states of the USSR in Kirov
Province and the Udmurt Republic.
Its original home was along the
River Viatka.

The Viatka has a fast trot and was
used in the past for pulling the
troika sled (three horses pulling
one sleigh). Today, they are used
in harness and under saddle, for
farm work and general transport.
They have inherited many of the
primitive features of their ancestors.
They possess strength, frugality

and stamina. They also grow an
unusually thick coat which, together
with a special subcutaneous
layer of fat, enables them to survive
very cold weather.

They have the plain, long head
typical of Tarpan stock. However,
there is a tendency for the face

to be a little more concave than their
ancestors. The neck is medium
length, very muscular and crested.
The withers are broad. The chest
is deep and strong. The back
is broad, straight and long. The
quarters are rounded. There is
a tendency to have cow hocks.

*Above: The Viatka Pony is bred in
the Baltic states of the USSR.*

The mane and tail are very thick.
The action of the Viatka is energetic, but the strides tend to be
short and quick.

WELSH MOUNTAIN PONY

(Section A)

Country of origin
Britain (Wales).
Height
Not to exceed 12·2hh (50in).
Color
Any solid color.
Features
Beauty, strength and an ancient lineage have made this good foundation stock, as well as a good children's pony.

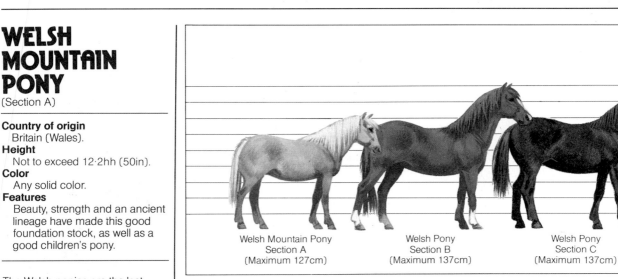

Welsh Mountain Pony
Section A
(Maximum 127cm)

Welsh Pony
Section B
(Maximum 137cm)

Welsh Pony
Section C
(Maximum 137cm)

The Welsh ponies are the last of Britain's Mountain and Moorland ponies to be described. They cover a wide range of types. Because of this, the stud book is divided into four sections. The first (Section A) is for the most beautiful of the native ponies—the Welsh Mountain, not to exceed 12·2hh (50in); the second (Section B) is for the slightly larger riding type—the Welsh pony, not to exceed 13·2hh (54in),

the third (Section C) is for the stockier Welsh pony of Cob type, (not to exceed 13·2hh (54in) and the fourth (Section D) is a horse type. It is covered in the Sports Horse Section of this book; see pages 142-143. Also called the Welsh Cob, it stands over 13·2hh (54in) and has similar features to the Section C pony.

The oldest of these four types is the smallest, the Welsh Mountain.

Some believe it is derived from the Celtic pony and was in the Welsh hills for over 1,000 years. Its beauty, with its elegant head and well-proportioned body, probably comes from infusions of Arab blood (probably in Roman times) and Thoroughbred blood. It is certain the Welsh Mountain Pony itself has been foundation stock for breeds such as the Hackney, Welsh Pony and Cob, as

well as possibly the Thoroughbred. It has also been used for cross-breeding to produce types such as the Polo Pony, the Riding Pony, the Hack and the Hunter.

The Welsh Mountain Pony is not only beautiful but, because it has lived wild for centuries in the Welsh hills, it is also courageous, sound, tough and intelligent.

These assets have been confirmed in today's breed through

Right: The Section A Welsh Mountain Pony. This is one of the prettiest of the native British ponies.

WELSH PONY
(Section B)

Country of origin
Britain (Wales).
Height
Not to exceed 13·2hh (54in).
Color
Any solid colors; not piebald or skewbald.
Features
An eye-catching type of riding pony that is very tough and intelligent.

The Welsh Pony is a larger, more modern version of the Welsh Mountain Pony. It is based on the smaller pony and is similar to it but with a little more substance and greater emphasis on riding qualities.

Welsh Ponies were originally bred by Welsh hill farmers. They provided them with transport and a means of herding their livestock in the mountainous pastures. To do this work they were good tempered, fast, strong, hardy, balanced and agile. These are qualities that stand them in good stead today as children's riding ponies.

At times, the stud book for Welsh Ponies (Section B) has been opened to part-bred Welsh stock but it has always been at least 50% Welsh. The Welsh part-bred stock tends to be lighter and taller than pure Welsh Mountain. The most influential in the 1920s were Craven Cyrus and Tanybwlch and in the 1950s Solway Master Bronze.

Conformation and action are similar to those of the Welsh Mountain.

This is the most common breed in the United States.

careful selective breeding. The Welsh Pony and Cob Society was founded in 1901, and its products have been the most numerous exports of any British pony. They have been sent all over the world, and for good prices, making it worthwhile for breeders to take trouble with breeding.

The Welsh Mountain Pony is an athlete, a good jumper and a good show pony. Consequently it has been in great demand

as a children's pony as well as foundation stock for other breeds and types.

The head should be small, with neat pointed ears, big bold eyes and a broad forehead. The jaw is clean-cut and tapers to a small muzzle. The silhouette of the face is concave or 'dished,' never convex or too straight. The neck is a good length and well carried, with shoulders sloping back to a clearly-defined wither. The limbs

Above: The Section B Welsh Pony is larger than the Welsh Mountain and more of a riding pony.

are set square, with good, flat bone and round, dense hooves. The tail is set high and carried gaily.

The action is straight, quick and free. The hocks and knees flex distinctly.

WELSH PONY
(Section C)

Country of origin
Britain (Wales).
Height
Not to exceed 13·2hh (54in).
Color
Any color except piebald or skewbald.
Features
This is a smaller version of the Welsh Cob and shares its action and conformation. This makes it a highly versatile animal, capable of trekking, riding, jumping, hunting, working and competing in harness.

This Cob-type pony is based on Welsh Mountain blood but with Andalusian and Cob blood added. This has made it into a stocky pony; it is active, strong and sure-footed. It is as versatile as its larger relative, the Welsh Cob, and shares the latter's history, conformation and action. The Welsh Cob is described on pages 142-143.

Left: This is the cobbier Section C Welsh Mountain pony.

WORK HORSES

This is the biggest and strongest group of horses, the horses on which the world once depended for transport and power in agriculture and industry. For centuries, and especially since the improvement of roads and the beginning of the Industrial Revolution, they were a vital part of the economy. However, with the development of the internal combustion engine, demand for them has declined dramatically. As a result, horse populations all over the world have dropped considerably, because work horses (or "heavy horses") made up the largest proportion of the total number.

Today, heavy horses are still used in countries with non-industrialized economies and on farms where mechanization is difficult. They are used in draft work, especially by breweries that benefit from the publicity generated by magnificent teams of horses delivering their beer. The major use today for heavy horses is in demonstrations and shows. Horse lovers do not want to see this vital part of our heritage die out, so various breed societies have been promoted. Each organizes regular events where the general public can admire their particular breed.

A more technical name for the work horses is the cold-bloods. This doesn't mean their body temperatures are lower than those of the hot-bloods and warm-bloods, which are described in the next section. The term 'cold-blood' is derived from the German '*Kaltblütigkeit*', which means calmness and stolidness. Because of their overall size and large muscles, work horses tend to be sluggish and slow to react.

There has been a great deal of disagreement about the evolution of the cold-bloods, but it seems probable that they were developed from the Tundra Horse and the Steppe Horse; both had the tendency to grow larger. These horses tended to increase in size in an environment of marshy lands with good sources of vegetation and a temperate to cold climate. It is an advantage to be bigger in cold weather because larger horses have a relatively smaller surface area from which heat is lost by radiation.

Right: Shires in action at the Royal Show in England.
Below: Ardennes heavy horses ploughing.

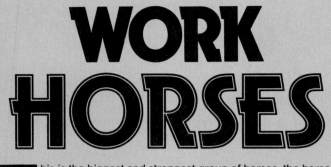

ARDENNES
(Ardennais)

Countries of origin
  Belgium and France (Ardennes), but a version is also bred in Sweden.

Height
  15·1-16·1hh (61-65in).

Color
  Bay or roan, although some are dark or liver chestnut.

Features
  This ancient breed is a willing, powerful worker, used greatly in the past. Today, with mechanization, its numbers are dwindling.

Ardennes
(155-165cm)

Boulonnais
(165-170cm)

The Ardennes breeds take their name from the mountains from which they come. These mountains lie between France and Belgium. This has led to a distinction being made between the French and Belgian Ardennes Horse. To complicate matters still further, there is also a Swedish Ardennes, established when Ardennes were imported in Sweden and crossed with the North Swedish Horse. The Swedish versions are similar to their foundation stock from the mountains, but they are a little smaller and more agile.

The ancestors of this sober, robust horse have allegedly been bred on the plateaus of the Ardennes for more than 2,000 years. The climate and vegetation suited the raising of heavy horses that were particularly well-built and energetic. It is believed they are some of the earliest specimens of cold-bloods. They were mentioned and used by Caesar, who talked about the horses of Gaul (Northern France). Nero was also supposed to have favored them.

It is believed that in the 8th century they were refined into more handsome, agile horses through the introduction of Arab blood. More recently, the other Belgian Heavy Horse—the Brabant—has been crossbred to the Ardennes to increase its size and strength.

In the early 19th century Napoleon valued highly the strength and endurance of the Ardennes, and he used the smaller versions for his armies.

Napoleon was not alone in exploiting the hardworking Ardennes for military purposes. The Dutch Army made extensive use of them in World War I, especially as artillery wheelers.

This breed is renowned for its toughness, its ability to withstand all types of climate, its eagerness to work and its frugal feeding. It is still used for draft work in France, Sweden and Belgium. In Belgium farmers claim it is "the ideal tractor on hilly and forested land."

The head of the Ardennes is distinctive; small with a straight face, prominent eye sockets and pricked ears. It is also thick through the jowl. The body is stocky, broad, deep and compact. The legs are relatively short, so it stands close to the ground. There is a little feather on the limbs.

Below: A pair of handsome Ardennes cold-bloods being driven in their working harness.

BOULONNAIS

Country of origin
France (Boulogne).

Height
Small: 15·1-15·3hh (61-63in).
Large: 15·3-16·3hh (63-67in).

Color
All shades of gray. Sometimes bay, chestnut, roan or black.

Features
This is the most elegant of the heavy horses, but it is sadly facing a falling demand. At present, its major use in France is as meat.

The Boulonnais is bred in northern France in the region of Calais. It is alleged its ancestors were Caesar's horses, which were stationed for some time in this area waiting to cross to England. It is said they brought to the Boulonnais some Oriental influence.

Through the centuries, Arabs continued to be crossed with the Boulonnais, which helps to explain why many consider this to be the most distinguished of the cold-bloods. The breed has been used to upgrade other cold-blood breeds, as the Thoroughbred is used to improve sports horses.

Additional use of the Arab was made by French crusaders who brought back horses from the Levant. Later, infusions of Andalusian blood were another

important element in the mixture.

In the 17th century the breed was named Boulonnais, from the town of Boulogne. Two varieties were, and still are, recognized — one large (the Dunkirk), and the other small (the Mareyeur). The breed was not confined to Boulogne because it was also popular in Picardy, Artois, Haute Normandie and certain areas of Flanders.

The smaller version is particularly agile for a heavy horse. It has good action and stamina, and was used to pull coaches, providing a fast connection between the coast and Paris. It was called the Mareyeur, from the French word for 'fresh fish' because the most important goods carried on the coaches were oysters and other seafood.

Its fame as a speedy, strong horse spread far beyond France, and the Boulonnais was exported to many countries to be used for transportation and breeding to upgrade local stock.

Boulonnais mature quickly. This factor, together with their elegance, means they are still used on farms and for draft work. However, they are now mainly bred for meat in France.

The head of the Boulonnais is short and broad with a straight face, wide flat forehead, large alert eyes, small erect ears and a small mouth. The neck is short, often crested, with a long, thick mane. The back is straight and broad, the body deep and wide, the flanks short and the quarters rounded. The limbs are strong and muscular, the cannon bones are short, and the bone is big and strong. There is no feather. The coat of the Boulonnais is beautifully silky.

Above: A Boulonnais demonstrates how agile a heavy work horse can be. This breed is one of the most elegant of the cold-bloods.

Below: A fine Boulonnais cold-blood stands square to show off its well-proportioned body and handsome appearance.

BRABANT
(Belgian Draft Horse)

Country of origin
  Belgium.
Height
  15·3-16·3hh (63-67in).
Color
  Most are red roans with black points.
Features
  This calm, docile horse is one of the strongest of the heavy horses. In Belgium, it is said to be "the most powerful living tractor in the world." It is still bred in large numbers; 700 foals are entered in the Belgian stud book annually.

Brabant
(160-170cm)

Breton
(152-165cm)

The center for the development of this breed was the fertile plain of the low-lying Brabant region in the middle of Belgium. Belgium has long been famous for her heavy horses. Much has been written about the Flanders Horse as the mount of knights in armor in medieval times. Some Flanders Horses were supposed to have been imported to Britain, where they were used as foundation stock for that country's horses.

The Brabants are direct descendants of the Flanders Horses. There are three slight variations within the Belgian breed, which were recognized as separate breeds until the beginning of the 20th century. They are the Big Horse of the Dendre, the Gray Horse of Nivelles and the colossal horses of Mehaignc. Today they vary little in conformation or color. The distinction was based mainly on different areas and bloodlines.

Belgian farmers have been proud breeders for centuries, using selective methods and—with few exceptions—shunning any outside blood. The result is that the Belgian Draft breeds true to type.

Its strength, good temperament and willingness to work has made it popular all over the world. Many have been exported, particularly

Below: The Belgian Draft Horse, or Brabant, is large, very heavy and extremely powerful.

to the United States. It has also been used to improve or found breeds: the Rhineland or Rhenish-German Cold-Blood from Germany was based on it. The Ardennes' size has been increased through breeding with Brabants.

The head of the Brabant is light and expressive. It is square in shape. The neck is short, thick and crested. The shoulders and quarters are massive. The body is short and deep. The limbs are strong, lean and sound, and carry some feather.

BRETON

Country of origin
France (Brittany).
Height
15-16·1hh (60-65in).
Color
Chestnut, bay roan, strawberry roan, gray and black.
Features
The Breton is a strong, energetic worker that is used to this day in France and other countries for farmwork and, sometimes, for pulling coaches.

Above: Belgian Draft Horses at work, bringing in the harvest. This sight is rarely seen today because mechanized harvesters have replaced horses in Belgium on all but a few farms.

Below: The Breton is one of the most energetic of all breeds of heavy horses.

For centuries, Brittany has bred her own types of heavy horses to suit the local climate and demands of the people. In the Middle Ages, we know there were the Sommier, a robust horse used for agricultural work, light draft and pack transportation, and the Roussin, a lighter version of the Sommier used for riding. The Roussin was well-known for its fourth gait—the 'amble,' a comfortable and fast pace for getting across country.

The Roussin was particularly popular in southern and central Brittany. More recently, Arab and Thoroughbred blood was added to the Roussin to create the Corlay, a Breton used for riding and racing. Today, this breed is almost extinct.

In northern Brittany, a heavier horse was needed for draft work. Outcrosses with the Percheron and Boulonnais were made. Another popular mixture, particularly in mountainous regions, was with the Ardennes. These heavier Bretons were known as the Draft Breton.

Another important subdivision of the Breton was created in the 19th century, when Norfolk Trotters and Hackneys were imported and used for breeding. This mixture created the Postier Breton, a fine horse with active paces.

Today, the last two divisions to the Breton are still recognized—the heavier stronger Draft Breton and the more active, lighter Postier Breton. These horses are registered in a stud book. Two separate books were started in 1909, but they were soon joined together and maintained with two divisions. Since 1920, the use of outside blood has not been allowed, and since 1951 the Breton stud book has been closed.

The Breton has a great ability to adapt to different climates and conditions; it is energetic and robust. It is still in demand as a work horse, particularly in under-developed countries and in the vineyards of the Midi.

The Breton is also quick to mature, a quality that has made it a good animal for the French meat market.

The Postier Breton is popular with farmers in Brittany, and it is also used for coaching.

The head is relatively square, with a straight face, bright eyes and small ears. The neck is strong, slightly crested and a little short. The shoulder slopes but is not very long. The back is short, muscular and broad, with powerful hind-quarters. Limbs are short and muscular with a little feather.

CLYDESDALE

Country of origin
Scotland.

Height
16·3-18hh (67-72in).

Color
Preferably bay or brown, with a white stripe on the face and white stockings on the limbs up to, and over, the knees and hocks.

Features
This close relation of the Shire is one of the world's most popular work horses.

Clydesdale
(170-183cm)

Comtois
(150-160cm)

Døle
(147-157cm)

The Clydesdale was developed in Scotland to meet the demands of the Industrial Revolution. Improved roads meant pack transport could be replaced by more efficient horsedrawn vehicles. A strong animal was needed for hauling, to turn machines and to work the lowland farms.

The first development of Clydesdales was in the late 18th century when local native mares were crossed with larger, stronger imported Flemish stallions. Some believe one of the best of these was named Clyde, and he gave the breed its name. But the concentration of breeding in the area of Clydesdale is the more probable reason.

The major development came in the mid-19 century, particularly in Lanarkshire, when large numbers of Black Horses (later to become Shires) were brought north from the Midlands. Scottish breeders bought some of the very best English stock to establish the Clydesdale. Although local mares were used in this development, the Clydesdale became very similar to the Shire.

The Clydesdale was the first of the British Heavy Horses to have its own society. It was started in 1877 and helped encourage the best possible breeding. The Clydesdale Society was able to promote one of the most successful systems of breeding: stallion hiring. This was started in the 1830s and helped develop successful breeding of carthorses.

Owners of about 100 mares in one neighborhood got together to hire the best stallion available. One hundredth of the fee was an affordable amount for each individual; also the district could change stallions as advisable and ensure the next one chosen was a good mate for the daughters of his predecessor. This system helped establish this excellent breed, which became so much in demand that at a public auction in 1919 the stallion Baron of Buchlyrie was sold for £9,500 (about half a million dollars today).

Today Clydesdales still bring high prices for export, mainly to the United States. The valuable animals are used chiefly for showing and breeding. Poorer quality ones are used for work in the Scottish woodlands. Unlike tractors, they can avoid damaging the remaining trees. They are also used for British deliveries where they are

economically competitive with motorized transport. Another use for the Clydesdale is for crossbreeding. The first cross with a Thoroughbred is a useful, heavy-weight type. The second generation (quarter Clydesdale) has often proved a high-class competition horse.

The Clydesdale's head looks intelligent and is carried high. The forehead and muzzle are broad, and the profile of the face is straight. The eyes are alert and the ears large. The neck is arched and long, springing out of an oblique shoulder with high withers. The back is short and strong, with well-sprung ribs. The quarters are long and muscular, with the tail set quite high. The limbs are long, with an abundance of fine silky feather.

The forelegs are planted well under the shoulder. The hindlegs are set close together, with the hocks turned inward. The second thigh and cannon bones are long.

The feet are large, round and strong.

The Clydesdale moves with great energy. The feet are lifted clear of the ground.

The general appearance of the Clydesdale is of strength, power and activity. These are all valuable assets for a work horse.

Below: A pair of Clydesdales competing in a plowing contest.

COMTOIS

Country of origin
France (in the Jura mountains).
Height
14·3-15·3hh (59-63in).
Color
Bay or chestnut.
Features
This is a light draft animal is still used extensively in France. It is second only to the Breton in numbers.

This mountain work horse has been bred in France's Jura mountains for centuries, but today it is also found in the Massif Central. It was used as far back as 1544 to improve the horses of Bourgogne, but became most famous as an army horse. Louis XIV used Comtois for his cavalry and artillery, and they were taken to Russia in Napoleon's campaign.

The Comtois has not remained pure from the 19th century. Percheron, Anglo-Norman and Boulonnais were used for cross breeding but without good results. At the beginning of this century, breeders found that using the small mountain Ardennes gave a better mix and provided a stronger horse.

This active, robust, long-lived horse is easy to train. It is used for work in the forests or in the vineyards, as well as for pulling sleighs at ski resorts. The Comtois is appreciated also outside France and has been exported to North Africa. Like other French breeds of heavy horses it is also kept for meat production.

Typically the head is square, with lively eyes. The ears are small and mobile. The neck is straight and muscular. The wither is prominent and the body deep and broad. The back is strong, and the hindquarters round and broad. The limbs are strong, with good bone. The feet are strong, and there is a little feather.

DØLE
(Gudbransdal)

Country of origin
Norway (Gudbransdal Valley).
Height
14·2-15·2hh (58-62in).
Color
Usually black, brown or bay.
Features
This small cold-blood is tough, active and has great stamina. It is a high-class, all-round animal.

For centuries this small heavy horse has inhabited the Norwegian Gudbransdal Valley, which connects the Oslo region with the North Sea coast. The Gudbransdal was a major overland route. The Døle is similar in appearance to the Friesian, Dale and Fell. It is questionable whether this is because they were all derived from the same prehistoric stock or because of an interchange of blood lines. The latter theory seems more likely, in view of the fact that during the period AD 400-800 Friesian merchants traded extensively between Norway, Britain and the Rhine Delta. It is highly likely that they took their black Friesian horses to both Norway and Britain.

This breed has an attractive trot and great pulling power. It is used as an all-round general purpose horse.

The Døle varies in size and type. Some are light due to Thoroughbred influence, while others are heavy draft horses. This variety means individuals can be found for many different tasks. The Døle is the most influential, widespread Norwegian breed.

Despite their variability, Døles have important features in common. They all have a small pony head, with a straight face and good width between the eyes. The neck is usually slightly crested. The shoulder tends to be a little upright. The body is strong and deep. The back is long and the quarters muscular and rounded. The limbs are short. There is an abundance of feather on the heavy types.

The Døle is a particularly active heavy horse with a very good trot.

Above: A Clydesdale shows off the white socks and face that are typical of this breed.

Below: A Døle mare. This Norwegian breed is one of the smallest cold-bloods.

DUTCH DRAFT

Country of origin
Holland.
Height
Up to 16·3hh (67in).
Color
Chestnut, bay, gray or black.
Features
This massive animal is docile, willing and active. It matures quickly and lives to a great age. These qualities make it a popular heavy draft animal.

The Dutch Draft is a modern development and was established as a breed in the Netherlands this century. Most foundation stock came from the neighboring country, Belgium, in particular the Ardennes.

These introductions were crossed with native Netherlands stock, and the result is one of the most massive, muscular breeds of heavy horses.

The Royal Dutch Draft Horse Society was founded in 1914. Since 1924 its stud book has been confined to horses with known pedigrees, which has helped to establish the breed. There is also a Preferential Stud Book for breeding stock that has passed conformation tests.

Today, breeding stock is selected on the basis of easy movement, fertility and low cost to keep. The Dutch Draft's major use is as a show horse and for draft work in cities as an aid to advertizing for companies.

The Dutch Draft is a massive horse that is strong and solid. The head has a straight profile and short, lively ears. The neck is short and it has a strong-muscled front. It has good withers, heavily-muscled broad loins and quarters with a sharply sloping croup. The legs are good and well-muscled, with good feet. The movement is free and easy.

Below: The Dutch Draft Horse was developed in the 20th century from Ardennes stock. The similarity can be seen by comparing this picture with that of the Ardennes on page 52. The Dutch Draft is one of the largest cold-bloods.

Dutch Draft
(Maximum 170cm)

Finnhorse Draft
(145-180cm)

FINNHORSE DRAFT

Country of origin
Finland.
Height
Usually around 15·2hh (62in) but can vary from 14.1-17.3hh (57-71in).
Color
Most.
Features
Agile, sure-footed, strong, small cold-blood that is still used extensively in the forests of Finland.

Finnhorses, which have lived for a long time in Finland, are descendants of the North European domestic horse. The basic stock has always been tough enough to withstand the cold climate, but variations have been larger or smaller, heavier or finer, according to the demands of the day. Today there are three types of the Finnhorse—the draft, trotter and riding horse. These vary in the degree of substance and sturdiness of frame, but all are quite similar in conformation. They are muscular, robust, well-proportioned horses. The neck is short and the back long, with a rounded or sloping croup. The limbs are strong. There is an abundance of hair in the mane and tail and light feather on the limbs.

Finnhorses are calm and easily trainable but lively and intelligent. They make particularly good trotters, because selective breeding has produced a specialized type of Finnhorse racing trotters, which are much finer and faster than the Draft Horse.

Since 1907, when the stud book was first established, the principle of pure breeding has been strictly adhered to. About 50 years ago, performance tests were introduced for breeding stock, and the draft test allows only the best workers to breed for this Finnhorse section. Trotting ability is an important performance test for all sections, which ensures the Finnhorse is an all-round performer.

As a draft horse, the Finnhorse is unusually agile and able to move easily over difficult terrain. This is an especially useful asset for its major function of thinning forests. Tree pulling is still better done by horses than tractors because they are less likely to damage remaining trees.

Right: The Finnhorse often pulls sleighs rather than carts.

Below: A portrait of a typical Finnhorse Draft.

FREIBERGER
(Franches Montagne)

Country of origin
Switzerland (Juras).
Height
14·3-15·2hh (59-62in).
Color
Most.
Features
An agile, sure-footed, light draft horse specifically bred to help the Swiss Army and the farmers in the mountains.

			Hand
			18
			16
			14
			12
			10
			8
			6
			4
			2

Freiberger (150-157cm)   Irish Draft (152-173cm)   Italian Heavy Draft (152-163cm)

. The Freiberger originated in the Jura mountains in western Switzerland. It has a mixture of ancestors—some Norman, Thoroughbred and Anglo-Norman, some British Thoroughbred and Draft breeds, and some Belgian draft horses. More recently, outside influences have been restricted to Anglo-Norman and Arab blood. Today all Freiberger breeding stock is controlled and tested by the Swiss National Stud at Avenches. The Swiss are aware of the importance of this light draft breed to their country and take extensive measures to ensure the production of the best animals possible.

The Freiberger's importance relates to the mountainous nature of its native country. The Swiss Army cannot rely on mechanized transport for patrols and carrying artillery—horses are still vital. They are also still used by farmers who live in the high mountains and cannot use tractors on their steeply sloping fields. The Swiss are aware of the increasing costs of energy production and the harmful effects of pollution; they are keen to maintain a good stock of horses as an alternative source of power. For all these reasons, the Freiberger

remains an important national asset, and the government promotes its breeding financially and administratively.

The variety of breeds used in the past means there has been a range of types within the Freiberger breed.

Today, the breed is becoming more uniform because of the controls exercised by the National Stud and the extensive tests used for breeding stock. Nevertheless, as the breeding program is directed more toward producing soundness, character and ability, conformation still varies.

The Freiberger is a compact, sturdy horse with a small head, a harmonious muscular body, strong limbs and little feather. It is energetic, but docile, easily trained, agile and sure-footed for its work in the mountains.

Below: The Freiberger is a Swiss cold-blood used both for farmwork and for transporting army personnel and equipment.

IRISH DRAFT

Country of origin
Ireland.
Height
15-17hh (60-68in).
Color
Bay, brown, chestnut or gray are most common.
Features
This light draft breed is a utility horse capable of working on farms, transporting goods and hunting. Today its major purpose is for crossbreeding with Thoroughbreds to produce hunters and competition horses.

The Irish Draft is almost light and fast enough to be classified as a warm-blood. The aim of breeders was to produce a multi-purpose animal, and it is certainly one of the most versatile of all the cold-bloods. The Irish farmers wanted an animal that could

pull their plows, transport their goods and families in carriages and take them hunting. The Irish Draft has been doing this for centuries, although its size, conformation and type have changed according to the demands of the time.

The original Irish horses were ponies. Some early outside blood was Spanish or Arabian, but the first confirmed history of the Irish Draft was the use of Thoroughbred sires on native Irish mares in the 18th and early 19th centuries.

The Irish Draft flourished until the agricultural recession of 1879 led to a marked decline in their numbers. When the situation improved for farmers, there was a great shortage of horses. Clydesdales and Shires were imported from Britain, but this led to coarser animals and the increase of feather on the legs.

This century, the Irish government has become increasingly aware of the importance of these horses and has taken steps to promote breeding. In 1907, registration plans were introduced for stallions. In 1911, plans were made for mares, and then inspections were started.

In World War I, the Irish Draft made an important contribution. To ensure their continuing production, an Irish Draft Stud Book was started in 1917.

Since World War I, there has been a declining demand for work horses. However, the Irish Draft was found to be an excellent cross with the Thoroughbred in the production of hunters and competition horses. Ireland became an exporter of partbred Irish Drafts but the foundation purebred stock began to disappear. The formation of the Irish Horse Board in the 1970s marked a major attempt to halt this decline, and today there is an effective Irish Draft Society preserving this breed.

The Irish Draft has an intelligent head with a straight face. The neck is short, thick and usually slightly crested. The body is long, and the hindquarters slope sharply but are very powerful. The limbs are strong, with good flat bone and very little feather. The forelegs tend to be straight, and the feet are large and round.

The Irish Draft is an active

horse, and its powerful hindquarters make this handsome breed a good jumper.

ITALIAN HEAVY DRAFT

Country of origin
Italy.
Height
15-16hh (60-64in).
Color
Liver chestnut, with flaxen mane and tail is most common, but some are roan and chestnut.
Features
The Italian Heavy Draft is one of the fastest of the large work horses.

These heavy horses are called *TPR's,* an abbreviation for *Tiro Pesante Rapido,* or quick draft horses, in Italy. The breed originates from the mid-19th century, when Arab, Thoroughbred and Hackney blood was used to breed speedier mares. In the 20th century the most important blood has been from the Breton, to which the Italian Heavy Draft now bears great similarity.

The main breeding areas were in the plains and hills around Verona, Padova, Vicenza, Venice, Treviso and Udine. The Italian Heavy Draft was an important breed for Italian farmers because it is large, docile, strong and fast. But today, the tractor has almost replaced it. The declining numbers of the breed (currently about 1,000 brood mares) are kept mainly for meat.

The head is relatively long but fine and elegant. The neck is short and crested, the body is broad and deep, and the hindquarters are rounded and muscular. The limbs are muscular, the feet are a little boxy and there is some feather.

Above: The champion Irish Draft mare Baultic Rossi. This versatile breed is almost a warm-blood.

Below: The Italian Heavy Draft is a breed based on the Breton.

Right: A close-up shows the Italian Heavy Draft's handsome head.

JUTLAND

Country of origin
Denmark (Jutland).
Height
15·1-16hh (61-64in).
Color
Usually chestnut, but it can be sorrel or roan.
Features
This strong, kind-tempered breed of draft horse has very early origins and has acted as important foundation stock.

This famous Danish breed comes from Jutland, the region after which it was named. It is believed to be very ancient, and types similar to it were taken to Britain by the Vikings in the 9th and 10th centuries. The British breed, the Suffolk·Punch, is very similar, indicating joint origins.

In the Middle Ages Denmark's heavy horses became famous as war horses. Many were exported because their agility and strength made them popular mounts for the heavily-armored knights.

The modern Jutland was strongly influenced by British breeds. Yorkshire Coach horses and Cleveland Bays were imported to

Jutland
(155-163cm)

Latvian
(163-168cm)

Murakoz
(Average 163cm)

Hand
18
16
14
12
10
8
6
4
2

lighten it, but most influential of all was a stallion named Oppenheim LXII, who was imported to Denmark in 1860. He is claimed by some to be a Shire and by others to be a Suffolk; most modern authorities believe he was a cross between the two breeds. He is the ancestor of all important Jutland stock, including Aldrup Munkedal (born in 1893) who set the type for today's Jutlands. There are now two important lines — both traceable to Oppenheim — the Fjandø line

and the Dux line.

Danish farmers have a long tradition of horse breeding. They use selective methods, and the result is a high-class breed of draft horse that has been used to improve other countries' cold-bloods and to act as foundation stock.

The Jutland has tremendous substance for its size. The head is plain, the ears are long and the neck short and thick. The body is broad and deep, and the quarters are round and muscular. The

limbs are short, with tremendous bone and an abundance of soft, smooth feather.

This kind-tempered, strong, medium-sized draft animal is still used on some Danish farms and for transport.

Below: A pair of Jutlands, a Danish heavy horse breed, in harness.

LATVIAN

Country of origin
USSR (Latvia).
Height
16-16·2hh (64-66in).
Color
Normally black, but bay, brown and chestnut are found.
Features
Latvian Horses vary in type to suit different demands, from draft work to competitions.

In Latvia, a Baltic state of the USSR, a local cold-blood has been bred for centuries. In the past, it was used on farms and as transportation. More recently, with the declining demand for work horses, the Latvian has been lightened. Some draft types remain, but two further divisions have developed. One, the Harness Horse, arose originally through introduction of Norfolk Roadster and Anglo-Norman blood, and later with the introduction of Oldenburg and Hanoverian breeds.

Then, even more recently, some of the Harness types have been crossed with Arab, Thoroughbred and Hanoverian stallions. This has produced riding horses that are talented in jumping and eventing.

Latvians vary considerably in type and are the USSR's multi-purpose breed. According to their type and the areas where they are bred, the Latvians do draft work, harness work or are used for riding. They are popular with farmers and riders because they have great powers of endurance, and are very strong.

The substance, amount of bone, frame and height varies but most have large heads with a straight Roman-nosed face and big eyes. The neck is slightly crested and long (longer in the riding type).

The body is thickset, deep and broad. The quarters are round and muscular. The legs are long and have a little feather. The mane and tail have plenty of hair.

MURAKOZ
(Murakozer)

Country of origin
Hungary (South).
Height
Around 16hh (64in).
Color
Usually chestnut with flaxen mane and tail.
Features
A medium-sized draft horse with a kind temperament, strength and a willingness to work.

The Murakoz, Hungary's heavy draft horse, was developed as a breed at the end of the 19th century and the beginning of the 20th on the farms around the Mura River. The foundation stock

was native Hungarian mares (known as Mur-Insulan), Ardennes, Percherons, Norikers (from Austria) and some Hungarian half-bred stallions.

The Murakoz was very popular with farmers and was used extensively by the army in both world wars. Today, it is still used on the land, although its numbers have dwindled.

The Murakoz is a small draft horse, active and strong. It has a large head, and the face tends to be convex. The eyes have a generous outlook, and the ears are large. The neck is short and slightly crested. The withers are barely noticeable. The body is broad but has a pronounced dip to the back. The quarters are rounded and the croup slopes. The legs are short with a little feather and round feet.

Above: The Latvian varies in type from a heavy work horse to a riding horse. This is one of the riding types, but it still shows plenty of strength.

Below: A Murakoz from Hungary. This breed of cold-bloods was very popular as a work horse, but with mechanization, its numbers are dwindling.

NORIKER
(Pinzgauer)

Country of origin
Austria.

Height
16-17hh (64-68in).

Color
Chestnut, bay, black, grey, dun, sometimes spotted with small patches like a Dalmatian dog.

Features
This breed, which has ancient origins, is still used extensively by the Austrian farmers and army, particularly in mountainous areas.

| | | Har |
| Noriker (163-173cm) | North Swedish Horse (155-160cm) | Percheron (157-168cm) |

This cold-blood is of ancient origins. It is named after the Roman province of Noricum, which included most of modern Austria. The horses the Romans bred in this area were well-known to contemporary observers, and were allegedly brought by them from Thessalonika, northern Greece.

The Noriker proved an invaluable worker in mountainous areas, with its good temperament, adaptability and sure-footedness. It was used extensively in agriculture, transport and by the Army. Different strains have developed. The best-known of these is found around Salzburg, which became known as Pinzgauer Norikers. Another well-known strain are those in Bavaria, which were called South German Cold-Bloods (see page 71).

The Pinzgauer Noriker got its name from the Pinzgau district of Austria. This line became renowned as a spotted horse. It was supposed to have developed around the time of the Renaissance, when Andalusian and Neapolitan blood was introduced. Today, spotted horses are rarer, but the Noriker has retained all the assets that make it a high-class, all-round mountain worker. Large numbers are still bred in Austria.

The Noriker has a plain, large head and a straight face. The neck is short and thick. The body is broad and deep, the back is long and the legs are short and have a little feather. The feet are strong and round.

Right: Norikers are often used in the mountains of Austria for pulling logs.

Below: The Pinzgauer Noriker, with its distinctive spotted coat, is rare today.

Above: North Swedish Horses are small work horses that have been used for centuries by Swedish farmers, foresters and the Army.

NORTH SWEDISH HORSE

Country of origin
Sweden.
Height
15·1-15·3hh (61-63in).
Color
Any solid color.
Features
Active, tough horse that trots well and is similar to its near relative, the Døle. It is still used extensively by the Army and for forestry work.

The North Swedish Horse has ancient origins, that are closely connected with those of its neighbor, the Døle from Norway. There has been a lot of cross-breeding, and it was only after a breed society was established at the end of the 19th century that a more uniform type was produced. Døle stallions from Norway were used, and at the ▶

Right: A portrait of a Noriker, an adaptable, sure-footed, all-around Austrian work horse.

► beginning of the 20th century stringent performance tests for breeding stock were introduced.

The North Swedish horse is tractable, robust, economical to feed and very active. Like the Døle, it is a good trotter. It is still used for log-pulling by farmers and by the Swedish Army.

The North Swedish Horse is dumpy, with a big head and long ears. The neck is short and thick. The shoulders are sloping, the body is deep and the back long. The quarters are rounded, with a sloping croup. The limbs are short, with substantial bone. There is an abundance of hair in the mane and tail.

PERCHERON

Country of origin
France (La Perche).
Height
15·2-16.2hh (62-66in).
Color
Gray or black with a fine coat.
Features
This clean-limbed, powerful, free-moving, docile-natured, good-looking horse is one of the most popular cold-blood breeds in the world.

The Percheron is one of the oldest and handsomest breeds of cold-blood. It originated in north-west France, in an area called La Perche. The soil and climate in the area are conducive to breeding good, large horses. The foundation stock were the Oriental horses, left by the Moors after their defeat in 732 AD, and the heavy Flemish horses.

Additional infusions of Arab blood were made when Oriental stock was brought back by the French Crusaders and when the

Above: Percherons are particularly handsome cold-bloods and are often used to pull carriages.

Below: Cold-bloods, like these Percherons, have gentle temperaments and get along well together.

government stud at La Pin used two Arab stallions, Godolphin and Gallipoly, on selected Percheron mares early in the 19th century. This Arab blood has helped make the Percheron an active, elegant draft horse.

The Percheron first earned fame as a war horse, but with the passing of the heavily armored knights it was used for transport and agriculture. The Percheron's heyday was from 1880 to 1920. Today, although its numbers are much smaller, it is used for agricultural work, draft work in cities and for showing all over the world. The breed is very popular in the United States, Argentina, Britain and France.

In its homelands, the Percheron is divided into two types—the Heavy Draft and the Postier. The Postier was developed at the end of the 19th century as a horse to pull the omnibuses in Paris. The Heavy Drafts are the most numerous and are in demand for export. There have been other divisions (such as Draft Maine and Draft Bourbonnais), according to the area bred, but they are all now covered by one stud book. Like

Above: Percherons in a row of stalls. This form of stabling makes it easier to look after large numbers of horses.

Below: The Percheron is a very good-looking heavy horse. Its Arab ancestors have given it more elegance than most work horses.

other breeds of heavy horse in France, the Percheron is in demand by the meat trade.

The head is intelligent, short in length, with a straight face, a deep curved cheek, good breadth between the eyes and erect, medium-sized ears. The neck is slightly crested (well-crested in stallions), muscular and a good length. The chest is wide, and the shoulders well laid back. The back is strong and short. The ribs are wide and deep, and the quarters are wide and long from the hips to the tail. The limbs are strong and muscular. The knees are big, and the hocks are broad. The cannons are short and the feet are a strong, black horn. There should be as little feather as possible—an unusual feature in a heavy horse. It makes the Percheron less likely to develop skin problems in the legs.

The Percheron is a straight, free mover, taking longer, less choppy strides than most heavy horses. The hocks flex well and move close together. Despite its docile nature, it is not sluggish. This action makes it a very showy animal, highly suitable for demonstrations and advertising.

POLISH DRAFT

Country of origin
Poland.

Height
15-16·3hh (60-67in).

Color
Most.

Features
Poland's draft breeds have been developed to suit local demands and environments. They still play an important role on farms.

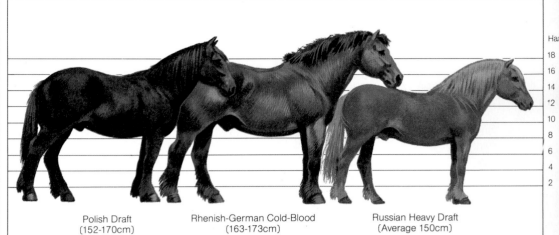

Polish Draft
(152-170cm)

Rhenish-German Cold-Blood
(163-173cm)

Russian Heavy Draft
(Average 150cm)

Ha
18
16
14
·2
10
8
6
4
2

In Poland, there are five regional breeds of heavy draft horses. These vary according to their environment and foundation stock. The most massive is the Sztum, which originated from local stock crossed with Belgian, Rhenish, Jutland, Ardennes and Døle stock. It is usually chestnut but can be bay or roan.

The Løwicz is similar to the Sztum but a little lighter. Its main foundation stock is Ardennes and Belgian stallions. Løwicz are the same colors as the Sztum.

The Sokølka was also founded on Ardennes stock, but there is also some Breton and Døle, which give the breed its good free movement. Sokølkas are frugal feeders. The most common color is chestnut, but there are occasional bays and roans.

The Garvolin is similar to the Sokølka, except that Boulonnais blood was added. This has led to some members of this breed being gray.

A smaller Polish draft horse is the Lidzbark, derived from Oszmian horses. These were primitive horses of West European cold-blood stock and the North Swedish breed.

The smallest of the Polish horses is the Kopczyk Podlaski, whose foundation sire was Kopczyk 20, a stallion born in Podlaska in 1921. He was of unknown origin and was crossed with local mares to produce offspring that are small, stout, active, economical feeders and usually bay or chestnut.

Below: A Rhenish-German Cold-Blood standing loose in a field.

RHENISH-GERMAN COLD-BLOOD

Country of origin
Germany.
Height
16-17hh (64-68in).
Color
Chestnut, red roan with flaxen mane and tail, red roan with black points.
Features
This cold-blood was very popular in its heyday at the beginning of the 20th century, but now there is little use for it.

The Rhenish was developed as a breed in the Rhineland less than 100 years ago. Local heavy

horses from Rhineland, Westphalia and Saxony were used, but the main foundation stock came from Belgium. The Belgian Heavy Draft was imported in large numbers to establish what was to become Germany's most numerous breed of heavy horses. Some Ardennes blood was also used.

The heavy horses of Germany now make up only 2% of its equine population. The Rhenish is one of four German heavy horse breeds (the others are the Black Forest, Schleswig and South German), and its numbers today are very small.

The Rhenish is similar to the Belgian, with a huge muscular body. Its head is plain, and the neck is short and strong. The body is compact, broad and deep, and the hindquarters are very muscular. The limbs are strong and short and have feather.

RUSSIAN HEAVY DRAFT

Country of origin
USSR (Ukraine).
Height
14·3hh (59in).
Color
Chestnut, bay and roan are most common.
Features
This is one of the smallest of the cold-bloods. It is a popular horse and is agile, active and strong.

This clean-legged, small draft horse was developed in the Ukraine about 100 years ago. Originally it was called the Russian Ardennes, because it was based on the

Above: A Russian Heavy Draft cold-blood. During the 20th century the Russians have developed this breed by crossing native with imported stock.

Belgian imports that were crossed with local cart mares. Together with many other Russian breeds, it was reorganized and renamed in the 1950s.

These active, small draft horses have great longevity. They are used for log pulling and agricultural work in western Russia.

This is a very short-coupled, broad and deep horse. The head is medium-sized, and the neck is short and thick. The withers are flat, the back dipped and the croup sloping. The hindquarters are strong and the legs are short, with a little feather. The action is free and light.

SCHLESWIG HOLSTEIN

Country of origin
  West Germany (western area of the province of Schleswig).
Height
  15·1-16hh (61-64in).
Color
  Almost all are chestnut with a flaxen mane and tail, but a few are grey or bay.
Features
  This dumpy cold-blood has a tractable character yet it is strong and energetic and a good mover. This makes an excellent worker.

The Schleswig-Holstein is at the opposite end of the spectrum of cold-blood to the Shire. Compared to the Shire, the Schleswig Holstein is small and dumpy: it stands no more than about 16 hands (64 inches). Indeed, some consider it to be a cob. However, it is derived from distinctive cold-blood ancestors; its neighbor, the Jutland, and its close relation, the Suffolk Punch, have been the strongest influences on the breed. In 1860, the Suffolk Punch Oppenheim LXII was imported from England to become what was probably the most important foundation sire of the breed. His son Munkedal 445 and inbred descendants, Prins of Jylland 1000 and Høvding 1055, were also very important. However, some authorities believe Oppenheim LXII was not a Shire. Because this stallion lived before stud books were introduced, his breed is not absolutely certain.

The Schleswig-Holstein was developed as the breed we know today to meet the demand for horsepower in the 19th century. The Schleswig Breeders' Association was formed at the end of the 19th century to regulate and promote its breeding. A stud book was started in 1891, but it was not until 1938 that the use of the major foundation blood—the Jutland— officially ceased. Other breeds that played a smaller part in its development were the Breton, the Boulonnais, the Thoroughbred and the Yorkshire Coach Horse. These breeds were introduced chiefly to counteract faults such as a too-long back and soft feet. These other breeds also served to lighten the Schleswig Holstein and give it more energy than its cold-blooded ancestors. This enabled it to be useful as an artillery horse and as an animal suitable for heavier draft work on farms and in industry.

The heavy, cob-type Schleswig-Holstein stands low to the ground on short, muscular legs with a little feather. The head is large and plain, with a tendency toward a convex face. The neck is crested, short and thick and merges into the back because there is no distinctive wither. The girth is deep and the front broad, although the body is long and flat.

Schleswig Holstein (155-163cm)   Shire (163-183cm)   South German Cold-Blood (163-168cm)

SHIRE

Country of origin
  Britain (Midlands and Fens).
Height
  Mares can be 16hh (64in) but males should be at least 16·2hh (66in) and the standard height is above 17hh (68in).
Color
  Black is very common. Brown, bay and gray are less common. There should be no large splashes of white.
Features
  This massive horse has a docile nature. It is very strong, and is usually able to pull a load of 5 tons. It is quick to mature and is often worked at 3 years old. Because of these qualities, demand for it was heavy in industry, agriculture and transportation. Today, its practical assets, together with its commanding appearance, make it a popular show horse and draft worker for displays and brewery firms.

Right: Shire mare and foal.

The Shire is the tallest, heaviest breed among the cold-bloods. Stallions and geldings are usually over 17 hands (68in) and are often as high as 18 hands (72in). Weight is between 17 and 22cwt (860-1,120kg).

There is much argument about the history of these massive horses. Some say they are descended from the horses William the Conqueror brought to England. More certainly, they are probably descended from the Great Horses and Old English Black Horses of the Middle Ages on which knights rode into battle. Influential continental ancestors must have been the horses of Flanders and the smaller, black Friesians.

The Shire's history becomes clearer in the 18th century, when the Old Black English Cart Horse was popular for draft work. In the 19th century, the Black Horses of the Midlands and the Fens were well-known as some of the most popular cart horses. They were in great demand as transport in fast-industrializing Britain. Some authorities believe Thoroughbred blood was introduced to these types, which could account for the size of the Shire. There was indiscriminate breeding after Waterloo (1815) to meet this demand, and in 1878, a Society was formed (originally named the Cart-Horse Society but later changed to the Shire Society) to try to raise standards and to breed for quality, not just quantity. The breed flourished until well into the 20th century, when mechanization drastically reduced demand.

In recent years, there has been a revival of the Shire. Today, an increasing number of enthusiasts produce these horses for the show ring and for displays. Since shortly before the Shire Society's centenary in 1978, the breed's numbers and quality have improved considerably.

These magnificent horses have

a long, lean head with a slightly Roman nose. The eyes are large and docile in expression; wall eyes are unacceptable. The ears are long and lean, and the neck is long,

Above: A team of Shires at a show. It is rare to drive them four abreast because they are unwieldy, but they do provide a magnificent spectacle.

slightly arched and well-set. The shoulders should slope well. The Shire is deep and broad in the girth, 6-8ft (2-2·5m) for stallions. The back is short, strong and muscular, and the loins are clearly shaped and not flat. The hindquarters are long, wide, well-muscled and let down toward the thighs. The forelegs should be straight, to the pastern. The hindlegs should be well-apart and set below the hindquarters. Sickle hocks are not of value. There should be some fine feather on all the limbs, but the fashion for very hairy animals (defects of the limbs could thereby be covered up) is past. The bone should be flat and strong and should measure 11in (28cm), although 12½in (31·75cm) has been recorded. The feet are wide, with a large circumference around the coronet. The action should be powerful and straight. Mares usually have shorter legs and cannons than stallions and geldings.

SOUTH GERMAN COLD-BLOOD

Country of origin
  Germany (Bavaria).
Height
  16-16·2hh (64-66in).
Color
  Most.
Features
  This is the lighter German version of the Noriker.

This is the German branch of the Austrian draft horse, the Noriker (page 64). It has been bred in the Bavarian Mountains for a long time, but during the 19th century, Norman, Cleveland, Holstein, Hungarian, Clydesdale and Oldenburg blood was added to establish this distinctive relative of the Noriker. It is lighter and better adapted to work in the mountains than the Noriker.

Today, the center of breeding is the Marbach State Stud in Württemburg. The Baden State Stud also breeds the South German Cold-Blood together with some Rhenish stock.

The South German Cold-Blood has been the main foundation stock for another German draft breed, the Black Forest Chestnut. This is a smaller version of the South German Cold-Blood with added Rhenish blood. It is used on small farms in the region.

The South German Cold-Blood has been used extensively by the Army for carrying packs and artillery in the mountains. Today, some are still used for this purpose, but usually it is the small mountain farmer who makes use of this breed.

The conformation and action of this breed is similar to the Noriker; it is simply a lighter version.

Below: South German Cold-Bloods being driven at Schwarzwald, which is close to their stud at Marbach.

SOVIET HEAVY DRAFT

Country of origin
USSR.
Height
15·2-15·3hh (62-63in).
Color
Chestnut and roan are most common, but can be bay.
Features
A strong, tractable cold-blood breed, which is found in large numbers in the USSR.

This breed was developed, in western Russia, mainly from Belgian Heavy Horses that were imported from 1850 on. Some other breeds were used in smaller quantities; these included the Percheron, Ardennes and Suffolk, together with some native Russian stock. The result was a lighter, smaller, more-energetic version of the Belgian. It was officially recognized as a breed in 1952.

The Soviet is an early maturer and is used extensively for draft work. The head is of medium size, as is the muscular neck. The body is broad, the back is occasionally weak and the loins are straight, while the croup slopes. The legs are tough but do not have great bone.

SUFFOLK HORSE

Country of origin
Britain (Suffolk)
Height
About 16hh (64in).
Color
Chestnut with no white other than a small star on the face or a few silver hairs on the body. Seven shades of chestnut, from dark to bright, are recognized, but by far the most common is the bright chestnut.
Features
Its great width, in front and behind, and the short legs give the Suffolk Horse a low point of draft and great pulling power. This was recognized early because there is a record of an advertisement for pulling contests (the best of twenty pulls) for Suffolks in 1766. It has long been used on the farms of East Anglia, particularly in Suffolk, but it has also been popular with the Army. The horse has been successfully crossbred.

The Suffolk Horse, also called the Suffolk Punch, is the purest British cold-blood. Its genealogy is traceable into the 18th century. Every member of the breed can be traced to a horse foaled in 1760, and descriptions of his progeny indicate a close resem-

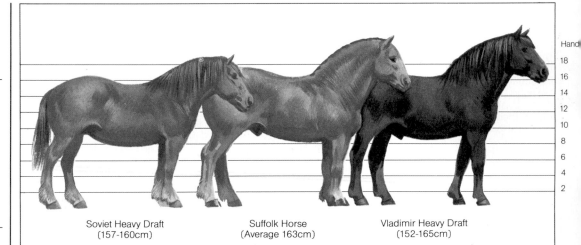

	Hands
	18
	16
	14
	12
	10
	8
	6
	4
	2

Soviet Heavy Draft (157-160cm)   Suffolk Horse (Average 163cm)   Vladimir Heavy Draft (152-165cm)

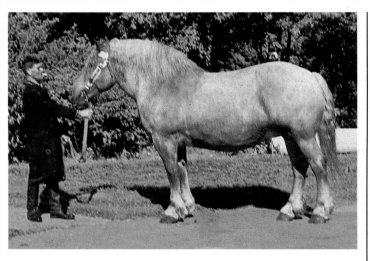

Above: The Soviet Heavy Draft is one of the largest cold-bloods found today in the USSR.

Below: The Suffolk Horse, also called the Suffolk Punch, comes from East Anglia in England.

blance to the modern Suffolk. Camden's *Britannia* claims that the Suffolk Horse dates back to 1506.

There is evidence that during the 19th century the Suffolk was the best of the British breeds. Representatives won the heavy horse class (when it was open to all breeds) at the Royal Show between 1838 and 1860 — 14 times out of 23. The Suffolk breed society was formed in 1877, before the Shire's. By the time the Suffolk Society celebrated its centenary in 1977, the Suffolk was less numerous and valuable as a breed.

The Suffolk has tremendous assets: apart from its ability to breed true to color (it is always

Above right: Suffolk Horses are always chestnut and make a good team for demonstrations.

chestnut), it is able to thrive on less food than most horses and has tremendous longevity. It often works well into its 20s and lives until 30. The purity of the breed is proven by the uniformity of color, but there were attempts in the 18th century to introduce a smarter element. Norfolk Trotter, Cob and even a little Thoroughbred were used.

This compact, well-rounded horse stands about 16 hands (64in). The head should is big with a broad forehead. The neck is thick, deep at the shoulders but tapering gracefully toward the head. The shoulders are muscular, long and well-set-back at the withers. The body is broad, deep and rounded, with a graceful outline to the wide level back, the loins and the muscular hind-quarters. The tail is well-set and high. The legs are straight; the second thigh on the hinds is particularly strong. The knees are big, and the hocks long and clean. The particular feature of the breed is its short cannon bones, which have very little feather for a cold-blood. Elbows should not turn in and pasterns should be fairly sloping. The feet are large and round and the horse moves in an active, balanced manner.

Below: The Vladimir Heavy Draft is a modern Soviet work horse. It was first recognized as a true breed in 1946.

VLADIMIR HEAVY DRAFT

Country of origin
USSR (Vladimir).
Height
15-16·1hh (60-65in).
Color
Bay is most common, but some are black and chestnut.
Features
A strong horse that is an all-around draft horse of medium size.

This horse was developed in the province after which it was named at the turn of the 20th century. Today, its breeding is widespread. The imported foundation stock was mainly British, consisting of Suffolk Punch, Clydesdale and Shire. Some Ardennes and Percherons were also used. In 1946, the Vladimir Heavy Draft was found to be breeding sufficiently true to type to consider it a true breed.

This quick-maturing, strong, heavy horse is popular for draft work. It is also used for pulling Vladimir troika sleighs.

The head is large and long, with a Roman nose. The neck is strong and long. The back, although broad, can be weak. The croup is long, with a definite slope. The limbs are long and feathered.

SPORTS HORSES

This century has seen a dramatic change in the use of horses. For over 2,000 years people have depended on them for transport, agriculture, industry and in war. They have provided vital means of power that is now achieved by the internal combustion engine. Today, there is little demand for the horse in its former roles. The total number of horses bred has dropped drastically, though not in all areas. Mechanization has brought us more leisure time. Equestrian sports are becoming more popular, from simple pleasure riding to the highly professional multibillion dollar industry of showjumping and racing.

The governments of many countries sponsor the breeding and use of horses for sport. They do so not simply because it is prestigious, but because riding as a risk sport is a character-building, health-promoting activity.

The number of sports horses is increasing, and many new breeds have been created to meet the demand for horses that have the even temperaments needed to be trained and ridden, and the athletic ability to jump and move well.

Many old breeds, particularly carriage and cavalry horses such as the Hanoverian, have had fresh blood added to make them more suitable for sports and leisure riding.

Sports horses fall into two categories—hot-bloods and warm-bloods. As with the cold-bloods, this term does not refer to a difference in body temperature but to a difference in pedigree and character. Hot-bloods are the breeds with the purest blood in their veins and they have "class" and great spirit. There are only two hot-bloods, the Arab and the Thoroughbred. These famous breeds are the progenitors of most warm-bloods.

The warm-bloods are not so purebred. They were developed through mixtures of hot-bloods, other warm-bloods and sometimes cold-bloods. They are breeds created by crossbreeding and selective breeding to meet current demands. They are not as slow as the cold-bloods nor as high-spirited as the hot-bloods. They have a character that is trainable and suitable for riding and driving.

Right: Monaco, a brilliant event horse, at Badminton, UK.
Below: A Quarter Horse herding cattle.

ARAB

Country of origin
The Arabian peninsula has developed the most famous lines.

Height
14·1-15hh (57-60in).

Color
The originals were chestnut and bay; now can be most strong solid colors. Many are gray. The skin is dark, and the mane and tail are fine and silky.

Features
Stamina, grace, noble shape and outlook, adaptability, intelligence, soundness, longevity, fertility, prepotency and perceptiveness of the senses all make the Arab one of the world's outstanding breeds. Its promoters breed it for beauty and its affectionate nature. They show it, keep it as a pet, ride it and race it. With the Thoroughbred, it is used most often to upgrade and improve other breeds.

Chestnut   Gray   Bay

Arab
(145-152cm)

The Arab is the oldest purebred horse in the world. It is also the most influential. Its blood has been used to improve nearly every other breed. It is the most widespread, with a national breed society found in almost every country. It is easy to understand how with this popularity, a multitude of tales have been told about the past history and origins of the breed.

The "Lady Wentworth school" claims the Arabian peninsula, and in particular the Yemen region in the south, is the true homeland of the Arab. They believe the breed has been there since 5,000 BC. Another claim, made by the German Carl Raswan, is that Nejd, Saudi Arabia, was the main center. The Iranians have always claimed to be the first to domesticate the Arab.

Despite all these rival claims, there is a great deal of evidence the Arab is derived from the proto-Arab type (see page 8), which came from America at a relatively early stage. It spread across the temperate regions from East Asia to North Africa. The belief that the wild ancestor of the Arab occupied this widespread habitat is supported by the discovery of bones similar to the modern Arab in Japan and Western Iran. In both cases bones date back to before the domestication of the horse; this indicates the bones must have belonged to wild horses.

The discovery too of the Caspian (see page 18-19), with its miniature, Arablike features, indicates it was a descendant of a wild horse of Arab type. Later, a prehistoric rock drawing of a horse with Arablike features and a distinctive, concave face was discovered in southern Fezzan in the Libyan Sahara. The picture dates back more than 8,000 years. It seems the wild ancestor was similar to the modern Arab, emphasizing the purity of the breed. It does

Above: The head of this Arab mare shows the finely chiseled features typical of the breed.

not appear to have been a descendant of Przewalski's horse but had its own separate progenitor to that of the ponies and cold-bloods. Also, it is unlikely it originated in a small area of desert, and may have wandered over a wide area of the Near, Middle and Far East.

Most of the early stories about the Arab originate from the area around the Arabian peninsula. It was allegedly Noah's great great grandson Baz (3,000 BC) who was the first to capture and tame one of the wild ancestors of today's Arab. Solomon, who ruled Israel from 974 BC to about 973 BC, captured Arabs from Egypt and the Arabian deserts. It is believed he had 1,200 riding horses and 40,000 chariot horses in his stables.

The most famous promoter of the Arab was the Prophet Mohammed in 600 AD. The horse became a foundation stone of his campaign to expand the faith of Islam and the Muslim Empire. The horse played a special part in his religion. Allah was said to have created it, and those who looked after their horses were promised a life in paradise after death. The incentives to breed and care for horses helped build a great Muslim cavalry that

conquered all before it as it moved through Egypt, North Africa, across the Mediterranean into Spain and up into France.

Eventually the Muslims were beaten and pushed back to their homelands, but they left many horses behind. This was the start of the Arab influence on the native breeds of Europe. Almost every modern breed has Arab ancestors.

There are many lines within the Arab breed. The most famous is the desert stock, which is known as the Original or Elite Arab. The major breeders of Original Arabs were the Bedouin —the nomadic tribesmen of Nejd. They needed a horse tough enough to survive a rough, hard life, but beautiful enough to be proud of. Rigorously selective methods of breeding were used

Above: Awtash, a Persian Arab belonging to HRH Princess Anne, gallops free at Windsor, England.

Below: This portrait of an Arab shows the breed's lovely, proud prancing action.

for centuries to achieve this.

The courage and stamina of the mares were tested by using them in battles and for hunting. Stallions were chosen for their beauty, conformation and intelligence. No alien blood was permitted, and tribesmen could quote pedigrees of their stock for many generations. Some in-breeding was practised, which led to the prepotency of the most valued assets—stamina, soundness and beauty.

Some claim it was the Bedouin tribesmen, with their rigorous methods of selective breeding, who developed the Arab breed. But from the evidence discussed above, it seems the modern Arab has changed little from prehistoric times. Man has had little influence on its build or shape.

There are many famous lines spread around the world. The Persian is one of the oldest. The discovery of its bones in western Iran indicates it was indigenous long before domestication. The Persian Arab has been carefully maintained in Iran to the present day and has received only a few injections of desert stock.

The Egyptian type is very old because there is a statue of a ridden horse closely resembling the Arab that dates back to 2,000 BC. This national line is one of the most famous, and its best known promoter was Abbas Pasha, Viceroy of Egypt (1848-1850). The horses he collected are the ancestors of some of the best of

the breed today in the United States, the United Kingdom, and Egypt, where most are kept at the El Zahara National Stud.

Poland has an old and pure line. The early stock arrived with the Turks as war booty in the 16th century but in the 19th century, it became fashionable to collect desert stock. A leader of this trend was Count Rzewuski, who started the Sawran Stud in 1828, with 81 stallions and 33 mares that he collected from the desert. Today, the government promotes their breeding because they have become a valuable export. It runs studs at Janow, Michalow, Kurozweki and Biaka.

The Arab in Hungary has a similar history to that in Poland. Early stock came with the Turkish conquerors in the 16th century, but the main foundation for today's stock came from horses collected from the desert during the 19th century. Babolna Stud became the famous center for Arab breeding, with great sires, such as Shagya and the Bedouin stallion, Kuhaylan Zaid.

The other major European Arab line is in the United Kingdom. The earliest stock came after the Crusades. The horses that came at the end of the 16th and the beginning of the 17th centuries ▶

► founded the Thoroughbred. In the sphere of purebred Arab breeding, the stock brought to Britain from Arabia and Egypt at the end of the 19th century was important. The original, highly enterprising collectors were lady Anne and Wilfred Scawen Blunt, who used their imports to begin the famous Crabbet Stud, which was later taken over by their daughter, Lady Wentworth, great Arab authority and promoter.

France has had Arabs for a long time, since the Muslim battles at the end of the 7th century. Two great promoters of the breed were Louis XV, who set up the Pompadeur Stud, and Napoleon, who ordered the import of 221 stallions and 31 Oriental mares.

In Germany, early collectors were the Kings of Württemberg, who founded the Wiel Stud in 1817. Today, the German Central Arab Stud is at Marbach.

Spanish breeds, like the French, were heavily influenced by the Arab and Barb stock left behind by the Muslims in the 7th century. The purebred lines have a more recent origin. Queen Isabella II imported desert stock in the mid-19th century.

In the USSR, too, the Arab has played a vital part in the foundation stock for its breeds. However, purebreds found in Russia can usually be traced back only as far as the 1930s, when Arabs were imported from Babolna, France, the United Kingdom and later as war booty from Poland. After World War II, some Egyptian stallions were added to the purebred stock.

Above: A rider dressed in traditional Bedouin costume poses astride a fine Arab horse.

European countries that bought desert stock today find themselves selling it back to the Middle East. Most of the oil-rich Arab nations are again building up stables of the magnificent Arab horses that were bred for centuries in their deserts.

There is hardly a country in the world that does not have important Arab studs. Those in the United States and Australia are probably developing at the greatest rate. To control the authenticity of pedigrees and to promote the best possible selective breeding, a World Arabian Horse Organization was set up. Today, the Arab is an international breed.

The Arab is often considered the most beautiful of all horses. Its long history of pure breeding is probably responsible for its harmonious proportions and the overall impression of balance.

The head is short, with a prominent forehead, a concave face and a small muzzle. The nostrils are large, and the eyes, set well apart, are large, circular and expressive. The jowl is deep and wide between the branches. The ears are small, alert and curved.

Below: Arabs are popular show horses. This is Prince Mikesha, a winner at The Royal Show at Stoneleigh, UK.

Above: An Arab stallion. The chestnut color with the four white socks is typical.

This is one of the original colors of the breed; today, Arabs can be of various solid colors.

Below: A handsome gray Arab is shown at the trot in a horse show. Many consider this to be

the most beautiful of all horse breeds, with its elegant proportions and free, fast action.

The neck is long and arched. The withers are not too prominent and slope into a strong, level, short back. The shoulder is long and sloping, the chest broad and muscular, and the girth deep. The croup is long and level, the quarters are muscular and the tail is set high.

The limbs have good hard bone and strong, clearly defined tendons. The knees and hocks should also be clearly defined. The pasterns should be relatively long and sloping and the feet hard and round.

With its handsome appearance and action, it is not surprising that this beautiful and aristocratic breed is universally admired and highly valued, both as a purebred and for upgrading other breeds.

The Arab has one less lumbar vertebra in its backbone—five instead of six—than other breeds. It also has one less rib.

This noble breed moves proudly, with its head and tail held high and its ears pricked. In the trot, it takes free, straight strides, but the gallop is its natural pace. It floats across the ground with free, fast strides and has the stamina to maintain speed for exceptionally long periods.

THOROUGHBRED

Country of origin
  Britain.
Height
  Ranges from 14·2-17·2hh (58-70in), but around 16hh (64in) is average.
Color
  Most solid colors.
Features
  This is the fastest, most valuable breed in the world. It is used all over the world as a racehorse. Its speed, "class" and elegance are in demand, and the Thoroughbred is used extensively for breeding to upgrade other breeds. It is also crossbred with more substantial, "lower-class" horses to produce "types," such as the hunter, polo pony and hack.

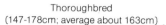

Brown   Chestnut   Gray

Thoroughbred
(147-178cm; average about 163cm)

The Thoroughbred is the fastest horse in the world. It is also the most expensive of all breeds and forms the basis of the multi-billion dollar racing industry. Despite many efforts, no one has been able to develop a faster breed. Over the last 100 years no one has been able to improve the Thoroughbred itself—racing times have not become faster, in the same way as those of human athletes.

Records are rarely broken today, yet from the start of the Thoroughbred's development, after the Restoration of Charles II in 1660, until the mid-19th century, records were consistently broken. It took a little less than 200 years to develop this great breed and maximize its potential as a racehorse.

The beginning of this success story must have involved a certain amount of luck when the foundation stock was collected. But British breeders recognized their chance and built on their good fortune, using rigorously selective breeding.

There is little authentic information about the entire range of Thoroughbred foundation stock. We know that prior to the Restoration, Britain's racehorses were a varied group. The original British racehorse—the Galloway Pony—stood a little over 13 hands. Other racehorses included some Oriental stock and halfbreds. But it was Charles II, with his passion for racing, who was responsible for increasing imports of Oriental horses. We also know that in the hundred years following the Restoration, more than 200 Arabs, Barbs and Turks were imported. Of these, about 75% were stallions, and 25% were mares.

From records that exist, it seems few imports were raced. They must have been bought for breeding purposes—to upgrade and establish a type to Britain's heterogenous collection of racehorses.

The records also prove three imported stallions imported

Above: The head of Secretariat, an outstanding racehorse in the United States and a successful sire.

produced the offspring on which the breed was based. The Byerley Turk, the Darley Arabian and the Godolphin Arabian are the three sires to whom all Thoroughbreds can be traced.

The first to arrive in Britain was the Byerley Turk, who started life as a charger. He was supposed to have helped his owner, Colonel Byerley, to escape at the Battle of the Boyne (1690). The Colonel then sent him to stand at stud in the north of England. He was used on a large cross-section of mares. It is believed they were British racing mares of Galloway, Spanish, Connemara and perhaps Welsh blood, but the number of Oriental mares was gradually increasing.

At this early stage in the development of the Thoroughbred, there was a good deal of crossbreeding. But by 1704, when the next great sire, the Darley Arabian, arrived in England from Syria, there were mares of the developing breed on which he could be used. He stood in the north of England at the Yorkshire stud belonging to Thomas Darley's brother.

The third great foundation sire, the Godolphin Arabian, was foaled in the Yemen and was bought from the King of France by Edward Coke of Derbyshire. His eventual owner, when he was stood at

the stud from the 1720s, was Lord Godolphin: hence the name. This stallion served mares of a better type. The era of crossbreeding was over, and the Thoroughbred was being consolidated as a breed.

Other imported sires played an important part in the foundation of the Thoroughbred. But because all modern Thoroughbreds can be traced back to one or more of these three, they have become established in the history of Thoroughbred horse breeding as

the foundation sires.

The first "great" British racehorse was a son of Darley Arabian. Named Flying Childers, he was born in 1715; he was never beaten in a race. He passed on his racing ability and it was his great great nephew, Eclipse (born 1764), who became even more famous. He remained unbeaten in 18 races. His progeny, in turn, inherited much of his talent.

Racehorses were becoming faster, but this was no longer due to luck. British breeders rigorously

tested their breeding stock. All except the early imports had to prove themselves on the racecourse. Pedigrees became increasingly important. They were kept meticulously, even though they were only private records. Then *An Introduction to a General Stud Book* was published in 1791 and Volume I of the *General Stud Book* in 1808. Any horse entered in these books was entitled to be called a Thoroughbred.

The breeders also changed their aims as they bred faster horses. The original races were over distances ranging from 4 to 12 miles (6·4-19·3km), the weights carried were up to 170 pounds (77kg), and usually finalists had to earn their place by running in a series of heats. To succeed, horses had to be mature and endowed with tremendous courage and stamina. These racehorses were little more than 14·2 hands (58in) and they included the great Eclipse.

At the end of his career, the trend changed. Breeding was becoming big business. Faster returns on investments were needed, and races for younger horses were in demand. With their increasing "class," the developing Thoroughbreds could run faster, but their stamina and weight- ▶

Above: Wajima, from the United States, is a magnificent example of the Thoroughbred breed.

Left: A Thoroughbred mare accompanied by her foal.

► carrying capacity were sacrificed. Races were shortened so young horses could participate, and speed became the all-important asset.

Speed and early development became the prime criteria for breeders. The horses did not need to be as tough, so they were given more warmth and better food. Gradually they became taller and faster. In the 19th century the normal Thoroughbred's height increased by 6 inches to 16 hands (64in) and speeds on the racecourse over the shorter distances improved so rapidly that records were consistently being broken.

By the 1850s, the Thoroughbred had reached its zenith. Between then and the present, there have been few increases in size or speed.

The Thoroughbred was developed as a flat-racehorse, and this remains the main reason for breeding. The largest prices were paid for the horses that had, or appeared to have, the potential to run faster than the others. The most valuable of all are the horses that are at their best as 3-year-olds over 1-1¾ miles. These are called the "classic" distances, and the top races are called "the classics" (such as the Kentucky and British Derby).

Another set of races, the "sprints", cover 5-7 furlongs (1,100-1,590yd, or 1,000-1,450m). The shorter distances suit horses that mature early and have great speed but little stamina. Races that test stamina are for the late-maturing stayers. These are more angular and leggy than the compact sprinters with their powerful quarters. Consequently, there are three categories of flat-race Thoroughbreds: the sprinter, the classic or middle-distance horse and the stayer.

There is a fourth category of Thoroughbred racehorse; those who jump. They race in steeplechase or hurdle races over longer distances, and the horses must have stamina, toughness and an ability to jump well. Horses are specifically bred for each of these four categories because there are obviously distinct differences in the requirements.

In addition, Thoroughbreds are used for other sports, including hunting, jumping, eventing and dressage. The requirements are different for each event. Substance is needed; so is a good temperament, so the horse can work in harmony with its rider. It's difficult to breed these assets into a Thoroughbred because the major criterion for breeders for nearly

Right: The Thoroughbred breed was created as a racehorse. Here Thoroughbreds are racing at Goodwood Course, England.

Below: A Thoroughbred being trained as a racehorse at Chantilly, northern France.

Below right: Thoroughbreds also race over fences. This is a point-to-point for amateurs.

300 years has been speed and the courage necessary to beat other horses. Consequently, the Thoroughbred is often crossbred with calmer, more robust breeds to produce horses for sports other than racing. This has proved to be another major use for the Thoroughbred—upgrading other breeds, adding "class," elegance and speed to more common horses. Like the Arab, the Thoroughbred has been used to improve other breeds for many years.

Most countries have their own national society that organizes the breeding of their Thorough-breds. Despite numerous efforts, no other country has been able to develop a faster breed than the British Thoroughbred. Countries all over the world have imported British stock, and now breed their own. Today, the Thoroughbred is even more international than the Arab.

Particular countries have found their soil and climate conducive to breeding top animals. In the United States, breeders started importing Thoroughbreds at the end of the 19th century. Kentucky proved to be the best breeding area. The "blue-grass", combined with huge financial investments in top horses, such as Mahmoud, Blenheim, Nasrullah and Ribot, has led to the current near-supremacy of the American Thoroughbred.

The French Thoroughbred became an official national breed in the 1830s. It has long been a strong competitor to the British Thoroughbred. The French horses are renowned as stayers.

Influential French Thoroughbred sires included Monarque, Le Sancy (a gray), St Simon, Dollar, Brantôme and Galopin.

In 1863, an international race for Thoroughbreds, the Grand Prix de Paris, was started. Two years later, a French horse, Gladiateur, won the British Triple Crown.

Today, French Thoroughbred breeding is carried on mainly around Paris and in Normandy.

Italy's great era was when Frederic Tesio (who died in 1953) bred such fine horses as Nearco, Donatello II and Ribot.

Australia and New Zealand have gradually improved their reputation as Thoroughbred breeders. Other countries all over the world have become major producers of this extraordinary animal.

It is not surprising that with the many categories of Thoroughbreds their conformation varies con-siderably. However, the best have a refined, intelligent head, an elegant, arched neck, pronounced withers and a sloping shoulder. The back is short, but the body is very deep. The quarters are strong and muscular, and the hock is well let down. The limbs are clean and hard.

The Thoroughbred moves freely, taking long strides with a sweeping, ground-covering action. It can gallop faster than any other horse.

AKHAL-TEKE

Country of origin
USSR (Turkmenistan).

Height
14·3-15.2hh (59-62in).

Color
Pale honey gold, with black points, bay, chestnut, gray and black. Most coats have a metallic bloom.

Features
An ancient breed with endless stamina and an ability to withstand extreme temperatures and lack of food. Originally used as a war horse by the Turkmen warriors, it is now used for racing, competitions and crossbreeding.

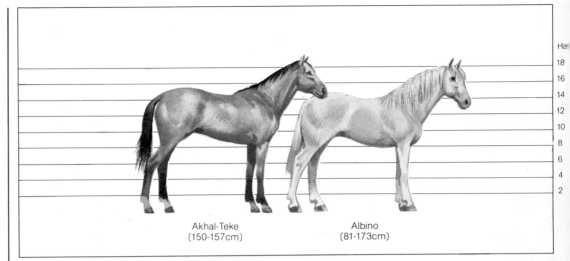

Akhal-Teke
(150-157cm)

Albino
(81-173cm)

The Akhal-Teke is an ancient Russian breed that has been bred in Turkmenistan, Central Asia, for centuries by the Turkmen tribes. This is an isolated area surrounded by mountains and desert. There is substance to the Russian claim that the Akhal-Teke has never been crossed with other breeds; it is a pure breed of ancient lineage (more than 4,000 years) protected by the tribesmen who took great pride in the purity of their horses. On the other hand, some claim it is a descendant of the horses left by the Mongols, who raided the occupied areas in this region during the 13th and 14th centuries. It *is* certain that the Akhal-Teke bears a close resemblance to the Turkoman from Iran, which was said to have originated in this way. But it could be the Turkoman was descended from the Akhal-Teke.

Whatever its origins, this is a unique, eye-catching breed. It has enormous stamina and the ability to withstand great extremes of temperature. This may be due to its adoption for many centuries as the chief mount of the Turkmen warrior. The Akhal-Teke was used as a charger; so weak specimens were not allowed to survive. Food was difficult to come by in the arid Asian desert, and these horses were tethered and fed mixtures of alfalfa and barley by hand, rather than being set free to graze in herds, like most other breeds.

Is is believed the Akhal-Teke had an influence on the development of many breeds — the Byerley Turk (one of the Thoroughbred's foundation sires) probably had Akhal-Teke blood. This can't be authenticated because it is too far in the past, but the Polish and West German Trakehner has some Akhal-Teke blood, as do many of the Russian breeds, such as the Don, Karabakh and Karabair. Today, one of the chief bases of the Akhal-Teke is the Tersk stud in the northern Caucasus, where it is being used to evolve new breeds.

The Akhal-Teke is fast, and has great powers of endurance. It has long been used for racing, and attempts were made at the beginning of the 20th century to make it even faster by crossing it with the Thoroughbred. The Anglo-Teke proved to be very fast over long distances, but it remained smaller than the Thoroughbred and lost its distinctive features. More recently, breeding policies have focused on re-establishing the original type.

The Akhal-Teke's lack of size has restricted its value as a competition horse. However, there have been notable exceptions to this general rule. One of these was the stallion, Absent, who won the individual gold medal in dressage for the USSR at the 1960 Olympic Games. There have been many good show-jumpers, and in 1935 a group of Akhal-Tekes performed an outstanding feat of

Below: The ancient breed of Akhal-Teke is related to the Turkoman Horse. This mare and foal are being shown at the Moscow Exhibition.

endurance when they traveled 2,500 miles (4,000km) from Ashkhabad to Moscow. This epic journey included 3 days spent crossing a desert without water.

The Akhal-Teke is an elegant, narrow, light framed horse. The head is intelligent and beautiful, with a face that is usually straight but can be slightly Roman or concave below the forehead. The eyes are large and expressive, and the ears are long. The neck is straight, long and narrow. The withers are high, and the shoulder has good shape. The body tends to be shallow. The back is long. Often the back and loins lack strength and muscle. The croup is straight to slightly sloping. The tail is set low. The thighs are fine and strong. The forearm is long, the cannons are short and the hindleg is often sickle-shaped. The feet are small and strong. There is little hair in the mane and tail.

ALBINO

Country of origin
Albinos are found all over the world, but as a breed, they originated in the United States.
Height
32in-17hh (32-68in).
Color
Snow-white or cream with pink skin, and light blue, dark blue (nearly black), brown or hazel eyes.
Features
This unusual color may be found in a wide range of types, from miniature ponies to draft horses. The skin is often highly sensitive to the sun.

The Albino is a color but in the United States the American Albino Association has been formed to establish it as a breed. Although the Albino color (a complete absence of pigment from the skin and other tissues) does appear at random amongst many breeds, in this case, the horses breed true to color, and are *consistently* white. The ability to do this over a number of generations establishes membership of the breed.

The foundation sire of the American breed was Old King (1906), which was claimed to be of Arab-Morgan stock. Careful selective breeding of his offspring has led to multiplication of the Albino color.

Albinos come in all shapes and sizes. The criterion is color, not shape. They are used for general riding, but because of their striking appearance they are in demand for demonstrations and ceremonies. They are popular in parades as flag bearers and for circus work.

Above: An Akhal-Teke with the golden sheen to its coat that is typical of the breed.

Below: An Albino foal born to a Lusitano mare. The characteristic colors of the breed can be seen—the snow-white coat and the pink skin that surrounds the muzzle and eyes.

ALTÉR REAL

Country of origin
Portugal.
Height
15-15·3hh (60-63in).
Color
Bay, brown and gray are most common.
Features
Athletic, intelligent horses that are popular for general riding. They are most famous as "high school" horses for demonstrating advanced horsemanship.

The Altér Real is a Portuguese breed based on Andalusian blood from Spain. In the mid-18th century, when high-school demonstrations were so popular amongst the courts of Europe, a royal stud was started in Alentejo Province, Portugal. More than 300 Andalusian mares were imported and used as foundation stock. The progeny were intelligent and athletic, which suited the requirements of the court. They wanted horses on which the nobility could ride and show off their skills as horsemen in exhibitions and carousels. These are similar to those now practiced at the Spanish Riding School in Vienna by the Altér Real's distant relative, the Lipizzaner.

The popularity of high-school work and the Altér Real did not last. With the coming of Napoleon at the beginning of the 19th century,

Right: An Altér Real trotting free to show its paces.

Below: Altér Reals being ridden in a display, showing their springy, collected gaits.

	Han.
	18
	16
	14
	12
	10
	8
	6
	4
	2

Altér Real
(152-160cm)

Andalusian
(155-160cm)

the stud was disbanded and the Altér Real was crossed extensively with other breeds.

By the beginning of the 20th century, the value of the breed began to be appreciated again. Existing Altér Reals were crossed with their original foundation stock, the Andalusian, to re-establish the features of the breed.

The Portuguese government now takes an interest and promotes selective breeding of their national breed. This has led to great improvements, and the Altér Real is again established as a breed famous for high-school work.

The Altér Real is similar to its founder, the Andalusian. It has an intelligent head, with eyes set well-apart, and it can have a convex face. The neck is muscular and crested, the shoulder slopes and the body is short and deep. The quarters are muscular and powerful, and the limbs are strong and well-set.

The action of this intelligent horse is highly valued. It is very athletic, with high knee and hock action. This enables it to take elevated strides, which are so useful in high-school work.

ANDALUSIAN

Country of origin
Spain (Andalucía).
Height
15·1-15·3hh (61-63in).
Color
Gray is most common but this breed can be found in bay, black or roan.
Features
This ancient breed has an eye-catching, high-stepping, athletic movement. It is most famous as a high-school horse but it is also popular for general riding.

The Andalusian is of ancient lineage. Cave drawings in the Iberian Peninsula, dating back 20,000 years to the early part of the last Ice Age, show a very similar type. The Andalusian probably is a direct descendant of the Steppe Horse (see page 8). But experts who believe all horses are descendants of Przewalski's horse claim the Andalusian comes from the Barbs brought over by the Moors in their invasion of the Peninsula in AD 711 and during their long occupation until 1492. It seems possible some of the Muslims' Arabs and Barbs were crossed with the indigenous Iberian horses in Andalucía, a province in southern Spain. But the shape of the Andalusian does not indicate that this breed possesses much Oriental blood.

The Andalusian is important. Its blood is found in the ancestry of many breeds. These include the Kladruber, Nonius, Altér Real, Lusitano, Lipizzaner and many German regional breeds, such as the Hanoverian and Holstein. It

Above: An Andalusian galloping free. This is a very athletic breed as shown by this individual's spectacular stride.

was also the breed that went with the Spanish colonists to North and South America. The Criollo, Paso Fino, Mustang, Peruvian and Appaloosa were based on Andalusian stock.

The major reason for its popularity as a foundation breed was its fame as a high-school horse. From the Renaissance until the French Revolution, the nobility performed high-school work in their courts. All over Europe, carousels and exhibitions became part of court life. The Andalusian, with its tractable temperament, great presence and athletic

Below: Andalusians being ridden in a Pas de Deux in front of a huge crowd. They are extremely skilled performers.

high-stepping paces, was ideal for this demanding work.

The Andalusian's athleticism also made it a good cavalry horse. From the departure of the last Muslims from Spain in the early 15th century until the end of the 18th century, it was in demand all over the world. Its breeding was enthusiastically promoted by the Spanish court.

With the dawn of the French Revolution, European monarchies ran into difficulties. The fashion for high-school was forgotten and, with it, the Andalusian, except by some

of the Spanish monks.

The Carthusian monks in the monasteries of Jerez de la Frontera, Seville and Castello, made an important contribution by selectively breeding the Andalusian for centuries. The Jerez monastery, in particular, maintained these activities when elsewhere the Andalusians' purity was in jeopardy due to crossbreeding to make it heavier. Many were exported, especially during Napoleon's rule. Fortunately, some purebred Andalusians were maintained at the Jerez de la Frontera Stud, and their progeny still live there today.

Today, there are other helpful promoters of the breed. The Spanish government is responsible for a number of studs, run by the army, and it controls private breeding. As a result of this extensive promotion the Andalusian flourishes.

However, the horse is not used extensively. The *Rejonedores (mounted bullfighters)* use them for high-school work in the bullring. They are also used in Spain for demonstrations and for dressage. They are gaining popularity in other countries because of their athleticism, which can make them good jumpers, dressage horses or simply excellent "fun" horses to ride.

The Andalusian's head is large. The forehead is broad, and it has a convex face. The neck is muscular and crested. The shoulder is long and sloping. The wither is prominent and the body is deep and close-coupled. The quarters are broad, muscular and rounded. The tail is set quite low. The limbs are normal length, but the cannons tend to be short. The mane and tail are very long and have an abundance of hair.

ANGLO-ARAB

Country of origin
All over the world, but the French Anglo-Arab is the only well-established breed.

Height
The French Anglo-Arab used to be no more than 15·3hh (63in), but its size has been increased, and some now reach 16·1hh (65in).

Color
Most solid colors, but gray is most common.

Features
A very athletic horse, which has excelled in all types of equestrian sports, from racing to dressage.

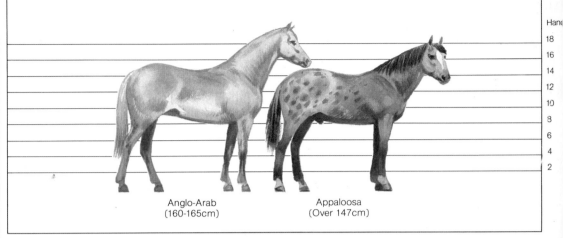

Anglo-Arab
(160-165cm)

Appaloosa
(Over 147cm)

Hand

The Anglo-Arab is found all over the world, but in most countries it is a crossbred animal produced by crossing an Arab and a Thoroughbred. In some countries, it has become so well-established that many Anglo-Arabs are the progeny of Anglo-Arab parents. This is the case in France, where they are one of the most popular breeds.

One reason for their development as a breed in France was the existence of foundation mares in the southwest and in Limousin, in central France. These were light horses that had been bred in these areas for centuries.

They had a very strong Oriental influence and appearance. They were known as the horses of Navarre, Bearn and Gascogne, and they were used to develop the breed of Anglo-Arab after its creation in 1843.

The center for the development of the Anglo-Arab was the Pompadour Stud. There purebred Arabs and Thoroughbreds were used, together with the local and southwestern mares of Oriental type. From the 1920s, the breed was sufficiently established to use Anglo-Arab stallions.

The Anglo-Arab became popular, first as a mount for the cavalry,

then as a general riding horse and a specialist for competitions. It was the first French breed to be created and bred for use in a wide variety of sporting events, including jumping, eventing, dressage and racing. Races especially for Anglo-Arabs were started in 1874.

With this increasing success, two additional studs, Pan and Tarbes in south-west France, began concentrating on breeding the Anglo-Arab.

The two centers for Anglo-Arab breeding—Limousin and the southwest—produced different types. In the southwest, the breeding aim was speed for the racetrack, so the preferred type was light. In the Limousin, on the other hand, the aim was athleticism and power for competitions, so the resulting type was heavier and stronger.

The success of the French Anglo-Arab as a competition horse has led to it being used to breed France's other competition horses, the Selle Français and the Cheval de Selle. Only 31% of the Anglo-Arab stallions' progeny is Anglo-Arab; the remainder of their offspring are either Selle Français or Cheval de Selle.

In France, there are two divisions of the Anglo-Arab – the Anglo-Arab itself and the Anglo-Arab de Complement. This second division has less than 25% pure Arab blood in its veins.

The French Anglo-Arab has a more consistent build and shape than those in other countries, which quite often resemble their Arab or Thoroughbred parents. The French Anglo-Arab has alert eyes, open nostrils, long ears and withers well back. This gives "a good length of rein" to riders. The shoulders slope well, the back is short, the body is deep, the quarters are powerful and hocks are set low.

The outstanding feature of the French Anglo-Arab is its cour-ageous temperament. Sometimes it is spirited. It also has supple, brilliant paces.

Above: The Anglo-Arab has Arab and Thoroughbred blood. This horse shows features of its forebears – the short, tapering head and flattish croup of the Arab and sloping shoulder of the Thoroughbred.

APPALOOSA

Country of origin
The breed was established in the United States, but spotted horses are found all over the world.
Height
Over 14·2hh (58in).
Color
Spotted; for detailed descriptions of the various patterns, see the text immediately on the right; see also the painting of some of them on the left. Gray and pinto are not allowed.
Features
This strong, intelligent, docile breed has great powers of endurance. It is useful for all types of riding. Its unusual coloring makes each horse unique.

The Appaloosa dates back to the ancient spotted horse that is depicted in cave drawings of prehistoric times. One of the most famous is at Lascaux in central France. The first famous spotted horse was Rukash, the mount of Prince Rustam, who led the Persian armies to victory in 400 BC. Today Iranians claim Rukash was the founder of the spotted horse. This isn't easy to prove, but spotted horses became quite common as mounts of nobility. The Spanish and Neopolitan breeds were particularly noted for the beauty of their spots.

It is believed spotted horses came to America from Spain around 1600. The Indians captured some of them, and their most famous promoters, the Nez Perce tribe,

were riding them by 1730. They bred their horses so that they had the strength, speed and stamina to hunt and travel the mountains, yet the horses also possessed the docility to be handled in camps. This tribe's homelands were near the Palouse River and the horses they bred were first called A Palouse by the French. This eventually became "Appaloosa".

In 1877, when the Nez Perce surrendered to the U.S. Army, their horses were dispersed to be sold or left to wander free. Appaloosas were subjected to crossbreeding. The breed was not maintained until Claude Thomson of Oregon began to collect horses from all over the country and selectively breed the Appaloosa. He re-established the quality of the Appaloosa with the help of an injection of Arab blood, and in 1938 the Appaloosa Horse Club of America was established. Today the Appaloosa is one of the foremost American breeds.

The Appaloosa has several distinguishing characteristics. The sclera of the eye is encircled with white, like a human's. The skin is mottled with irregular spots of black and white. These are especially noticeable around the nostrils. Hooves are striped vertically with black and white.

The Appaloosa's coat is variable, and no two horses are identical. There are eight basic patterns:
1. *Spotted blanket:* Dark forehand with a white blanket over loin and hips with spots.
2. *White blanket:* Dark forehand and a blanket that has no, or very few, spots.
3. *Marble:* Base color is dark when born. It eventually fades to nearly white, except for darker "varnish marks" on face and legs.
4. *Leopard:* Base color is pure white, with evenly distributed black spots over the entire body.
5. *Near-leopard:* Has leopard markings at birth, but head and legs and possibly even the shoulders are a darker color. This dark coloring usually fades as the horse matures.
6. *Few spot:* Leopard, with only an odd spot but with some blue or red roan marks. The base color is still white.
7. *Snowflake:* Base color is dark with white spots. It is often born as a solid color, and spots appear later.
8. *Frosted tip:* Dark base color with either frost or white spots on loin and hips.
The Appaloosa's head is straight and lean. Shoulders are long and sloping, with a well-defined wither, deep body and strong limbs. The mane and tail have little hair compared with most horse breeds.

Action is free and smooth, which makes this horse good to ride. The variety of types within the breed mean it is used for many activities, including general riding, trail riding, showing, ranch work, parades and gymkhanas, as well as competitions and racing. Its eye-catching appearance makes it popular for exhibitions and circuses.

Left: Various spotted horses, all of which are representatives of the breed of Appaloosa.

AUSTRALIAN STOCK HORSE

Country of origin
   Australia.
Height
   14·2-16hh (58-64in).
Color
   Most colors.
Features
   An agile, tough, kind horse, it is
   used for cattle and sheep work.
   Its type is varied, but it is gradually
   becoming more uniform.

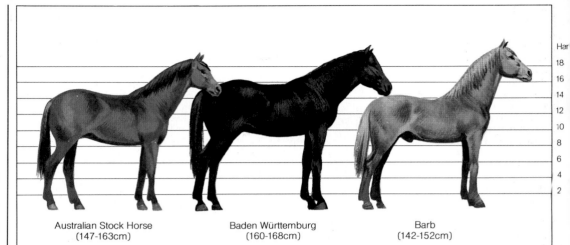

Australian Stock Horse
(147-163cm)

Baden Württemburg
(160-168cm)

Barb
(142-152cm)

The Australian Stock Horse Society
is responsible for the registration
of this group of horses. Its aim
is to make them more uniform,
but as yet they cannot be said to
breed true to type.
   The foundation stock was the
Australian Waler. Although never
a true breed, it was a famous
cavalry horse. It served bravely
as the standard mount of the
Australian cavalry. It was exported
to many countries, particularly
India, from the time of Waterloo
until the 20th century. The Waler
was used also to herd stock, for
riding and for light harness work,
mostly in New South Wales, where
its breeding was concentrated.
   Original foundation horses came
from South Africa and Chile in
1795, and these were of Dutch,
Spanish, Arab and Barb background. Thoroughbred was added
to establish the tough, agile Waler.
   During the 20th century, the
crossbred Waler has had more
Arab and Thoroughbred added,
together with some Percheron and
Quarter Horse. It is now called
the Australian Stock Horse.
   This is a versatile horse and
is used extensively on sheep and
cattle farms and in rodeos. It
is also used for jumping, polo,
eventing, endurance riding and
some racing.
   The Australian Stock Horse is a
robust version of the Thoroughbred.
It has a light forehand, strong back
and quarters and good limbs.

*Above: The most famous Australian
Stock Horse, the World Event
Champion Regal Realm. Bred in*
*Australia, he came to Europe as
one of the Australian event team
and was bought by Lucinda Green.*
*Below: A Baden-Württemburg
horse outside a traditional barn in
its homeland of Bavaria.*

BADEN WÜRTTEMBURG

Country of origin
   Germany (south-west).
Height
   15·3-16·2hh (63-66in).
Color
   Most solid colors.
Features
   This athletic horse is based on the
   Trakehner, and is helping
   to meet the increasing demand
   for sports horses.

Apart from the Trakehner, all
German warm-blooded breeds

are regional breeds. Consequently, these horses are given one of nine regional titles according to the area where they were born. For example, the horses born in Lower Saxony are called *Hanoverians* after the main town of this old region of Germany. Horses from the southwest of Germany are known as *Baden-Württemburgs,* and these form the third largest warm-blood breed in Germany, next to the Hanoverians (page 107) and Westphalians (page 144).

The center of the breeding of Baden-Württemburgs is the Marbach Stud. This is the oldest state stud; it was established in 1573. Through the ages, it has produced regional breeds to meet the demands of the time. Today, there are South German Coldbloods to meet the demand for work-horses and the Baden Württemburg to supply the ever-increasing demand for horses for sporting and leisure activities.

The Baden-Württemburg is a refined version of the older dual-purpose cob type—the Württemburg. This horse was the result of many centuries of crossbreeding between horses from Hungary and Turkey, and later Andalusians and Neopolitans, Barbs and East Friesians, Anglo-Normans and Trakehners. The Baden-Württemburg is, therefore, derived from a variety of sources. In 1895 a stud book was started for the Baden Württemburg.

Today's version of this breed owes much of its athletic movement and elegant good looks to the Trakehner, or East Prussian (page 140). This breed has been used since World War II to give the Baden Württemburg more quality.

Above: A rider from Morocco in traditional dress mounted on a fine-looking Barb.

Below: A Fantasia display in Morocco in which Barb horses are ridden at a gallop.

BARB

Country of origin
Algeria, Morocco, Libya.
Height
14-15hh (56-60in).
Color
Bay, brown, chestnut, black and gray.
Features
An ancient, tough breed with great stamina and the ability to survive on little food. It has acted as important foundation stock for a wide variety of breeds, and is still valued as a purebred in its North African homelands and in other countries, too.

The Barb's original home—and the origin of its name— is the region of North Africa once called Barbary. This area is made up of the modern countries of Morocco, Algeria and Libya. It is likely that Barbs have lived there since prehistoric times, weathering out the cold conditions of the last Ice Age that affected areas as far south as North Africa, even though they were not gripped by ice. The Barb shares many similarities with the Arab, but these could well be due to frequent crossing between the two breeds. Since the time the Muslims invaded Barbary the Arab has been mixed with Barb blood. Yet there are some important distinguishing features between the two breeds.

The Barb has a ramlike head with a straight face and muzzle that is almost as broad as the forehead. This is very different from the small, fine head of the Arab, with its concave face and relatively small muzzle. The hindquarters, too, slope more than those of an Arab, and the tail is set much lower. Finally, the character differs, the Arab being much kinder and more tractable than the quick-tempered Barb.

These distinctions indicate a different background and derivation from the Steppe horse rather than from proto-Arab Oriental stock. Whatever its origins, this tough horse, which is so fast over short distances, has had a great influence on other breeds, most notably the Thoroughbred. Barbs were imported into England in the 17th and 18th centuries and played an important part in the foundation of this great British racehorse.

The Barb cannot be considered a purebred. There has been much crossing in the past with the Arab, and this has continued to the present day, as the crossbred tends to be a more easily trained riding horse.

Today, the Barb is still found in its original homelands. The King of Morocco keeps some of the best examples at his own stud.

The head is long and narrow with a straight face. The neck is crested, the shoulders are flat, the body is rounded and the croup slopes, with a low set tail. The limbs are long, fine and strong. There is an abundance of hair in the mane and tail.

BELGIAN HALF-BLOOD

Country of origin
Belgium.
Height
Minimum of 15·2hh (62in) but the aim is between 16-16·1hh (64-65in).
Color
Most solid colors.
Features
Although this breed originated in the 1920s, it is only since 1975 that these strong, high-quality horses have been bred in sufficient numbers to make an impact in international sports.

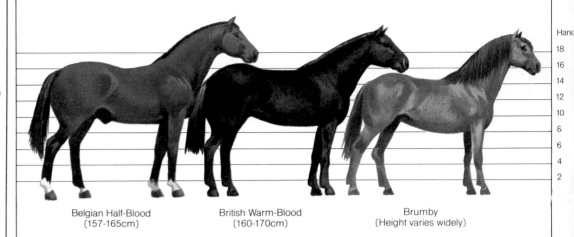

Belgian Half-Blood
(157-165cm)

British Warm-Blood
(160-170cm)

Brumby
(Height varies widely)

Belgium has been famous for work horses for a long time, but until recently it imported many of its horses for general riding and sport. A society for the Belgian Half-Blood has existed since 1920. But it was not until 1967, when it was given the right to add the adjective "Royal" to its title, that it began to make an impression and increase the quality and quantity of Belgium's national breeds of sports horses.

The most numerous and most influential stock has come from France. This has included Arabs, Anglo-Arabs, Thoroughbreds and Selle Français. Together they constitute about 60% of the stallions

Below: The Belgian Half-Blood Cyrano, representing Belgium in the 1982 World Show Jumping Championship, Dublin, Eire.

standing to produce Belgian Half-Bloods. There have also been some German and Dutch imports, but the majority of non-French stallions are home-bred Belgian Half-Bloods.

The Royal Society has followed the policies of most other European countries that have started a national breed of warm-blood. They have encouraged the importation of good stock and aided selective breeding through registration, grading mares, testing stallions and providing both financial incentives and prestigious awards for the producers of good breeding stock.

The aim is to produce an athletic horse that is comfortable when ridden. The head should have a broad forehead and small ears and the neck should be long. The shoulders should slope and the limbs should be straight and muscular, with good feet.

BRITISH WARM-BLOOD

Country of origin
Britain.
Height
15·3-16·3hh (63-67in).
Color
Most solid colors.
Features
This new breed of warm-blood exhibits great variations in type and does not breed true. This is due to the range of breeds among the breeding stock. They tend to be athletic and supple, which helps them excel in jumping and dressage competitions.

Britain has many significant breeds and types, but none are specifically bred to be sports horses as are

warm-bloods in continental Europe. From the end of the 1960s, increasing numbers of British riders began going abroad to find horses for jumping, dressage and driving. Import levels rose, and the British Warm-Blood Society was started at the end of the 1970s to offer the continental imports (mainly Hanoverian, Dutch and Danish, and their offspring by recognized British breeds) the same opportunities for selective breeding as exist in the rest of Europe. The aim of the Society is to gradually establish a recognizable and uniform type of British Warm-Blood.

The British Warm-Blood must have at least 50% of recognized continental warm-blood in its veins; for such horses, there are opportunities to register and for breeding stock to be graded and tested.

The result is the steady growth in Britain of high-quality horses with

athletic paces and the robust conformation needed in competitions.

Most British Warm-Bloods tend
to be more refined than their
European relations. A great deal of
Thoroughbred blood is being used
in the creation of this new breed of
sports horse, which has done well in
dressage and showjumping.

BRUMBY

Country of origin
Australia.
Height
Varies.
Color
Most.
Features
Brumbies are a collection of wild
horses that are now close to
extinction.

This wild Australian pony was
established from imported stock
turned loose after the great
Gold Rush of 1851. The Brumbies
flourished and multiplied, but they
also interbred and had to live
off poor grazing so their quality
deteriorated. Brumbies also
proved to be difficult to train
so no valuable use was found
for them.

Soon, the Brumbies became so
numerous they posed a threat to
agriculture, damaging fences,
grazing land and water holes. For
many years, Brumbies were drastically culled, and today few of these
horses still roam wild in Australia.

Above: The British Warm-Blood is
a new breed type and this horse,
Dutch Gold, was one of the first to
be registered. Ridden by Jennie
Loriston-Clarke, he is a star in
dressage and eventing.

Below: Brumbies have bred and
run wild in Australia for more
than a hundred years.

BUDYONNY

Country of origin
USSR (Rostov region).
Height
15·2-16·1hh (62-65in).
Color
Most are chestnut, but some are
bay or brown. Budyonnys
occasionally have a golden
sheen to their coat that
is typical of the Don and
Chernomor breeds.
Features
This elegant, intelligent horse was
purpose-bred for the cavalry.
With the recent addition of more
Thoroughbred blood, it is proving
to be a high-class sports horse.

Budyonny
(157-165cm)

Calabrese
(160-165cm)

Camargue
(135-145cm)

Hand
18
16
14
12
10
8
6
4
2

The Budyonny is a 20th century
Russian breed. Foundations were
laid in the 1920s. It was largely
encouragement from the Russian
cavalry officer, Marshal Budyonny,
that led to its official recognition
in 1949. He wanted to create the
ideal cavalry horse, and the army
stud in the Rostov region became
the center for the program.

Rigorous selective breeding
methods were applied to develop
the breed. All breeding stock
was thoroughly tested for the
features most needed in a cavalry
horse—speed, endurance and
a tractable character.

The foundation stock used was
the Thoroughbred and the breeds
of the Cossacks—the Don and the
slightly smaller, lighter Chernomor.
By 1948, these "outside" breeds
were rarely used because the
Budyonny had been established and
was breeding relatively true to type.

Today, as the demand increases
for a riding/sports horse, rather
than a cavalry charger, the
Budyonny is being refined by

*Below: A Budyonny horse; this
new breed is becoming very
popular in the USSR.*

*Above: A Calabrese horse. Today,
relatively few are found in their
home country of Italy.*

re-crossing with the Thoroughbred.
This has made it fast enough
to race in steeplechases, and it
has won the fearsome Pardubice
marathon race in Czechoslovakia.
It is also a good mover and is used
in dressage, jumping and eventing.

In appearance, it is an elegant,
muscular, light horse. Its head is
harmoniously shaped, with a
straight face. The neck is long, the
withers prominent and the shoulder
long and sloping. The body is

deep and close coupled. The loins
are muscular, the croup long and
rounded. The legs are long and
fine but with good dense bone
and hard feet.

CALABRESE

Country of origin
Italy.
Height
15·3-16·1hh (63-65in).
Color
Any solid color.
Features
This was a popular saddle horse
in the 19th century. Its numbers
are now dwindling, although it is
a good jumper.

The Calabrese is bred in the south
of Italy and Sicily from a foundation
stock that consisted of Oriental
horses imported from Africa.
During the 19th century, it was a
popular saddle horse, but today
there has been a great deal of
interbreeding with the Salerno and
the Thoroughbred. The result is
there are few purebreds left.

The Calabrese has a fine,
rectangular-shaped head. The
shoulder is long and sloping, the
back is strong and the croup has a
medium slope. Limbs are strong
and muscular. The hooves are
correct and wide.

This is a lively horse but still easy
to train. It is frequently used for
riding and equestrian sport.

CAMARGUE

Country of origin
France (Rhône Delta).
Height
13·1-14·1hh (53-57in).
Color
Gray.
Features
An ancient breed, that still runs
wild in herds in France. When
caught and trained, it is an agile,
tractable riding horse.

These shaggy, wild horses have
roamed the swamplands of the
Rhône Delta in the south of France
for centuries. Their history is
obscure. It is possible they
are descendants of the prehistoric
horses whose fossils were
unearthed at Solutré in southeast

France. It is probable they have been subjected to crossbreeding from the horses brought into the area by Romans, Saracens and Moors. These influences probably included Arab and Barb because features of both are apparent. In the 19th century some attempts were made to introduce Thoroughbred, Arab, Anglo-Arab and Breton blood. But none were effective in changing the rugged, wild features of this breed, which has caught so many people's imagination.

Today, Camargues still run wild on their damp, reedy homelands, which are hot in summer and bleak in winter. They roam in small herds, consisting of one stallion, mares of all ages and colts to 3 years old. There are regular roundups when foals are branded. Three-year-old colts not good enough to remain as stallions are caught and gelded. Stock is selected to be broken and trained. Catching and breaking Camargues is difficult. Initially they are wild creatures, but once they have been trained to accept human commands, they make good rides.

Trained Camargues are used extensively in the Delta. Their long-term use has been as cattle-herding ponies for the *"Gardiens,"* the cowboys of the Camargue.

One of the most important agricultural activities in the Camargue is the breeding of small black bulls; the tamed, wild horses are used for herding, surveying and rounding up the bulls, and taking them to the bullring at local fairs.

The Camargue must be tough, strong and sure-footed to survive on the lonely marshlands. These qualities have made it a good work pony, able to carry heavy packs. It is also an ideal mount for tourists who take guided tours across the wild and beautiful Delta. It is good for this purpose, not only over the rugged area to which it is indigenous but also in other parts of France.

Since 1968, the Camargue has been officially recognized as a breed. Together with the formation of a Breeders Society, this has led to wiser selection of breeding stock. Even though they are allowed to run wild and breed, only the better stallions and mares are allowed to remain free when they reach the age for breeding. This is leading to distinct improvements in the quality of the stock.

The Camargue is robust rather than elegant. Its head is large and rectangular with a straight face. Ears are short with large bases

and are placed more to the side than those of other breeds. The shoulder is straight and short, and the back is short. The quarters are short, with a slightly sloping croup. Limbs are strong and of a good shape. The knees are large, and the feet are hard.

The Camargue is slow to mature, but lives to a great age. It can exist on very poor fare and is exceptionally robust. It is justly famous for its exceptional powers of endurance.

Above: A group of Camargue horses roam free in the wild region of south-eastern France in the Rhône Delta, after which they are named.

Below: A portrait of a typical Camargue horse.

CLEVELAND BAY

Country of origin
Britain (Cleveland).

Height
16-16·2hh (64-66in).

Color
Bay, with black points (black legs, mane and tail). No other color is permissible; only a small white star and gray in the mane and tail are allowed.

Features
This bay horse is the oldest established breed of English horse. It has great substance, stamina and strength, with a fine appearance and a tractable temperament. These characteristics make it suitable for riding and driving.

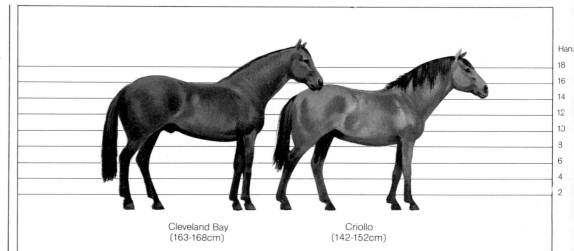

Cleveland Bay
(163-168cm)

Criollo
(142-152cm)

The Cleveland Bay has been bred in Cleveland, northeast England, for centuries. It is believed the original stock dates back to the work horses brought to England by Romans. It is certain that from medieval times a clean-legged bay animal was popular in this area. It was also called the "Chapman Horse" because before the advent of wheeled carriages, horses were ridden or used as pack animals. The chapmen, or traveling salesmen, used Clevelands to carry their wares.

Farmers also used them and valued them as all-purpose animals, for work on the land as well as riding. When wool was Yorkshire's chief export, Clevelands were used as pack animals, carrying huge loads from the farms to the mills. It is thought likely that the pack and riding horses of these times had a little of the Yorkshire racing Galloway blood in them. It is certain two of the original Thoroughbred foundation sires had an influence through Manica (1707), a son of the Darley Arabian, and Jalap (1750s), a grandson of Godolphin Arabian.

Since the time of Jalap in the 1750s, there have been no further injections of Thoroughbred blood into the purebred Clevelands.

However, Thoroughbreds have been crossed with many Clevelands. The progeny became so popular that in the late 19th century, a breed based on additional Thoroughbred blood was established and named the Yorkshire Coach Horse. This "classy" carriage horse became a fashionable means of pulling elegant, light vehicles until the era of carriages ended. The breed passed into extinction in the 1930s.

It is as a carriage horse that the Cleveland excels; its consistent color makes matching pairs and teams easy. Its tractable temperament facilitates training, while its strength enables it to pull large, heavy loads. During the 19th century it was popular for this purpose. By then farmers were using it for general riding, hunting, farm, draft and carriage work. In 1884, a Cleveland Bay Horse Society was started to ensure the continuing purity of this multi-purpose breed.

With the demise of horse power in the face of tractors, trucks and cars, the Cleveland has been put to new uses. As a purebred, it is shown, hunted and driven, but partbreds are earning the most fame. They have made Olympic show jumpers, international dressage and event horses and combined driving champions.

Below: Cleveland Bays are most famous as carriage horses. This team of four is being driven by HRH Prince Philip of Britain.

HRH Prince Philip has successfully driven for Britain with a homebred team (consisting of 4 horses) of partbreds.

The Cleveland has long been important in breeding. It was used extensively in Germany during the 18th and 19th centuries to lighten the native breeds for use as high-class carriage horses. The Holstein, Hanoverian and Oldenburg all benefited from influential injections of Cleveland blood.

The Cleveland's head is large, with a straight face. Eyes are large, ears are long, the neck is long and lean and the shoulder is sloping and deep. The body is wide and deep, the back is muscular and not too long and quarters level, long, and powerful. Limbs are strong, with at least 9in of flat bone below the knee. Arms and thighs are muscular, and knees and hocks large and well-closed. The legs are clean with no superfluous hair. The feet are black in color, and good shape. Those that are shallow or narrow are undesirable.

The Cleveland Bay moves freely with true, straight action. Although the hock and knee flex, strides are sweeping and ground-covering rather than rounded and springy.

CRIOLLO

Country of origin
  Argentina.
Height
  14-15hh (56-60in).
Color
  Dun with dark points, and a dorsal stripe, is most common, but Criollos can be red or blue roan, chestnut, bay or palomino.
Features
  This compact, sturdy breed has great powers of endurance and the ability to withstand temperature extremes. It can survive on very little food.

The Criollo is Argentina's native horse. It was derived from stock brought to the country by the Spanish in the 16th century that was thought to be of Andalusian, Barb and possibly even Arab blood.

Legend has it that this foundation stock came from the cavalry horses that sailed across the Atlantic in a ship in 1535. Buenos Aires was sacked by the Indians soon after their arrival; the horses escaped to run wild on the South American pampas.

For over 300 years, these horses, which were probably joined by other escapees, bred naturally. The tough environment, with its temperature extremes, ensured that only sound individuals survived to continue breeding.

The Criollo developed into a very

tough horse, and it acquired a colored coat that aided its safety by camouflaging it. Dun became the predominant color among Criollos; the color blends in well with the sandy pastures of the Argentinian pampas.

The Argentinians discovered they had a tremendous asset running free in their country. Criollos were captured, tamed and bred as mounts for the Argentinian cowboys, or *gauchos*. The horse proved to be ideal for cattle herding, being quick, agile, maneuverable and intelligent. They also made strong ponies for pack work and were good mounts for those who wanted to ride for pleasure.

The Criollo has found another important use in the 20th century. It is often crossed with the Thoroughbred to produce the famous Argentinian polo pony.

A notable feature of the Criollo is its great powers of endurance. The most famous test of this was when Professor Aimé Tschiffely took two ponies, Mancha, 15 years old and Gato, 16 years old, on a 13,350 miles (21,485km) trek from Buenos Aires to New York, using them alternately as a mount and packhorse. This journey involved crossing some of the world's bleakest deserts and highest mountain ranges. Both horses coped with temperature extremes of well below freezing and higher than 100°F, (38°C) and they endured the thin air at altitudes of almost 20,000ft (6,100m).

The Criollo's head is broad, with

a straight face. Eyes are set well-apart, and the ears are alert. The neck is muscular, the withers clearly defined, the shoulder strong and the chest broad. The body is deep, the back short and loins are muscular. The croup slopes, and the quarters are rounded and muscular. Limbs are strong, with good bone and short cannons, and the feet of this tough breed are small and hard.

Below: this Criollo is being ridden in a demonstration.

Above: Criollos grazing free in their native lands of Argentina.

The Criollo has many close relatives in South America. Breeds were founded in other countries under the same conditions. The horses of the Spaniards and Portuguese were set free to adapt to local conditions and to breed in a wild state. These include a slightly smaller version in Brazil, called the *Crioulo*, and a lighter-framed horse in Venezuela, called the *Llanero*.

DANISH WARM-BLOOD

Country of origin
Denmark.
Height
15·3-17hh (63-68in).
Color
Bay is common, but horses are found in all solid colors.
Features
A new breed of warm-blood that has proved itself to be a top-class competition horse.

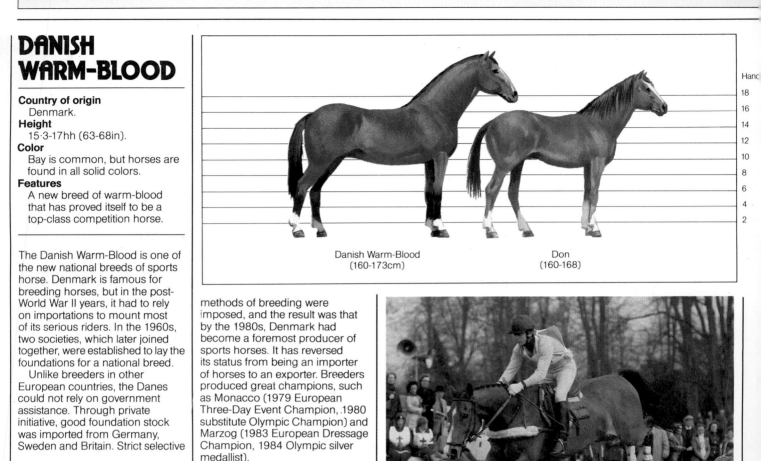

Danish Warm-Blood
(160-173cm)

Don
(160-168)

The Danish Warm-Blood is one of the new national breeds of sports horse. Denmark is famous for breeding horses, but in the post-World War II years, it had to rely on importations to mount most of its serious riders. In the 1960s, two societies, which later joined together, were established to lay the foundations for a national breed.

Unlike breeders in other European countries, the Danes could not rely on government assistance. Through private initiative, good foundation stock was imported from Germany, Sweden and Britain. Strict selective

methods of breeding were imposed, and the result was that by the 1980s, Denmark had become a foremost producer of sports horses. It has reversed its status from being an importer of horses to an exporter. Breeders produced great champions, such as Monacco (1979 European Three-Day Event Champion, .1980 substitute Olympic Champion) and Marzog (1983 European Dressage Champion, 1984 Olympic silver medallist).

Danish horses are famous for their generous, tractable temperaments and their athletic movement. As with most new warm-bloods, a variety of types are registered in the studbook.

Above: The Danish Warm-Blood 3-Day Event champion, Monaco.

Right: Marzog, the Danish Warm-Blood that won the 1984 Olympic Silver medal.

Left: A portrait of the Danish Warm-Blood.

DON

Country of origin
USSR.

Height
15·3-16·2hh (63-66in).

Color
Chestnut and bay are most common, often with a golden sheen.

Features
This Cossack horse has great stamina. It can survive extremes of temperature and live off frugal fare.

The Don is the famous Russian Cossack's horse. The extraordinary toughness and courage of this breed became renowned after Napoleon's Russian campaign. When Napoleon retreated to France in the dreadful winter weather of 1812, he lost many thousands of his French horses. Yet the Russian Cossacks, and their Dons, were tough enough to survive the appalling conditions, and continued to attack the French, driving them all the way back to their homeland, and then made the long return journey to Moscow. This feat is without equal in cavalry history.

At the time of this great achievement, the Don was a comparatively new breed. It had been developed in the steppe country around the rivers Don and Volga. It is still bred there. In this early stage in its development, it was smaller and more robust than it is today. It had been based on the horses of the nomadic steppe tribes but was refined with additions of Turkoman and Karabakh, and later the Thoroughbred and Orlov. In the 20th century, it has been purebred, with no additional outside blood added.

Part of the toughness and stamina of the Don must be attributed to the way it has been bred. Herds of Dons run free on the steppes and must be sound to survive the bleak and extremely harsh winter conditions.

The cavalry no longer needs large quantities of Dons. However, they are still in demand for general riding and endurance riding—a sphere in which they excel. In competitions, their successes have been limited because they are rather short striding.

The Don has been used to improve other breeds, in particular to give them greater stamina. The Don has been particularly influential as foundation stock for the development of the Budyonny, and in the improvement

Above: Don horses pulling a troika. This is a traditional means of driving them in the USSR.

of the Kazakh and Kirghiz.

The Don's head is Thoroughbred-like, with breadth between the eyes. The neck is medium length. The shoulder tends to be upright. The back is straight and broad. Legs are long and strong, but there is a tendency for the pasterns to be upright. Feet are quite large.

DUTCH WARM-BLOOD

Country of origin
The Netherlands.
Height
15·3-16·3hh (63-67in).
Color
Most solid colors.
Features
This new breed of warm-blood is divided into types. This variety ensures there are Dutch horses available to fulfill a wide range of demands from riders and drivers.

Dutch Warm-Blood
(160-170cm)

East Friesian
(157-168cm)

Frederiksborg
(160-163cm)

Har
18
16
14
12
10
8
6
4
2

The Dutch Warm-Blood is a new breed, which like its Danish equivalent, was started in the 1960s to meet the rising demand for sports horses. The Dutch used their heavy mares—the Groningen and Gelderland—as foundation stock. They also brought in Thoroughbreds, Anglo-Arabs and Arabs. In the 1980s seven Lipizzaner stallions were included among the breeding stallions.

The Dutch Warm-Blood Society covers a wide range of horses and aims to breed five types. There is the sport horse, which should be sound with excellent conformation and movement, good character and temperament, and capable of good performance in show jumping, dressage and eventing. The second type is the riding horse, with 25% or more Arabian or Anglo-Arab blood. The carriage horse, which is similar to the old Dutch breeds, with high-stepping gaits, great power and grace, is the third type. The fourth type is the basic horse, which is a heavier horse with the old Gelderland and Groningen lines, and is suitable for riding and driving. Finally, there is the Lipizzaner-bred type, used for riding and driving.

These types have one factor in common—the breeding stock is strictly graded, and rigorous selective methods are imposed.

Dutch horses are famous for their docile, likable characters, athletic, rounded paces and muscular quarters. The breeding aim is a noble, likable horse with an honest character. The constitution should be strong and the average height about 16·1hh (64in). Movement should be easy, supple, strong, balanced and rhythmical, with a natural forward urge.

Dutch horses have excelled in all competitive disciplines. Tjeerd Velstra won the World Driving Championships with a Dutch team. Other notable examples are Calypso, who won the World Cup Show jumping for America, Oran who won the European Three-Day Event Championship for Switzerland, and Limandus, who won the silver and bronze medals for Switzerland in dressage at the 1984 Olympic Games in Los Angeles.

EAST FRIESIAN

Country of origin
East Germany.
Height
15·2-16·2hh (62-66in).
Color
Most solid colors.
Features
A powerful all-around horse, that can be used for riding and driving.

The East Friesian, from East Germany, is based on its neighbor from West Germany, the Oldenburg (page 123). It was developed in the 19th century, and a few other breeds were used to lighten it. These included British, Polish, Hungarian and Spanish horses. Since the partition of Germany, the East Germans have relied on the Arab and Hanoverian for this refining admixture.

The East Friesian is a handsome, strong, all-purpose horse used for riding, competition and harness work.

Left: The famous Warm-Blood, Calypso, being ridden for the USA.

Below: Dutch horses are famous as carriage horses.

Above: A fine example of the all-purpose East Friesian breed.

Below: A typical Frederiksborg, with its flaxen mane and tail.

FREDERIKSBORG

Country of origin
Denmark.
Height
15·3-16hh (63-64in).
Color
Chestnut is most common.
Features
An honest, strong athletic breed that has been used all over Europe as a cavalry, high-school and harness horse. For the last 100 years, it has been close to extinction.

The Frederiksborg was a famous Danish breed during the 17th, 18th and 19th centuries, when it was exported to many countries and used for upgrading and as foundation stock. Today, there is only a small number of purebreds left (about 250 mares), and few are good quality. The breed has been weakened by crossbreeding and attempts to lighten it to meet modern riding demands.

The Frederiksborg was named after the stud where it was bred, north of Copenhagen. It was founded in 1562 by King Frederick II. He was a keen horse breeder and developed this breed to perform the high-school work that had become so popular in the courts of Europe.

Andalusian and Neapolitan horses were used as foundation stock. Later, Oriental and British half-bred stock was introduced. The Frederiksborg became such a high-class horse that it was used all over Europe as a high-school, cavalry and harness horse. During the 18th century, the Frederiksborg was even used to upgrade Lipizzaner stock.

Frederiksborgs were so popular that many were exported. Stock became poor, and in the mid-19th century the Danish stud, which had survived for almost 300 years, was forced to close.

Today, efforts are being made to preserve this breed which has given Denmark so much prestige in the past.

The Frederiksborg is a strong horse, with a large, plain head, a straight face and big ears. It has a powerful shoulder, and a long, strong deep body with a flat croup. Limbs have good bone.

Below: Frederiksborg horses have been used for many purposes, from serving as cavalry mounts to working in harness.

FRENCH TROTTER

Country of origin
France (Normandy).

Height
Varies, but an average is 16·1hh (65in).

Color
Chestnut, bay and brown are most common. Gray is rare, but some are roan.

Features
The French Trotter has competed against the best harness racers in the world. It is a more robust breed, with greater stamina, than other breeds of harness racers. It is used for jumping, general riding and breeding riding horses.

This breed was developed in the 19th century in France, although it was only officially recognized in 1922. The stimulus for its development was the growth of harness racing. The first French Trotting course was opened at Cherbourg in 1836, and it was so popular that within years, five more courses started in and around Normandy.

Horses were needed for this fast-developing sport. British stock was imported to supply speed and trotting ability when crossed with Normandy mares. The most influential examples of the British blood were the Norfolk Trotter called The Norfolk Phenomenon and a Thoroughbred named The Heir of Linne. These gave rise to Anglo-Normans; the foundation lines of the breed were Lavater, James Watt, Phaeton, Cherbourg and, most important, Fuschia. The development of the French Trotter and Anglo-Norman (later to be called the Selle Français) ran along a parallel, overlapping route during the 19th century and only became different breeds in the 20th century.

The sport of harness racing soon spread; courses opened around Paris, beginning in the 1870s. The fastest horses were most desired and some American harness horses, which had been so successfully developed into the Standardbred, were imported. The use of outside Trotter blood was limited, and in 1937 the French stud book was closed.

An unusual form of harness racing is practiced in France, which also helps the breeding of Trotters. In these mounted races, the horses must have the substance, strength and soundness to carry the weight of the rider. Therefore speed is not the only breeding criterion.

Consequently French Trotters are more robust than other national breeds of harness horses. This makes them suitable for a variety of activities. Some are used for general riding and jumping, and many are used to breed riding horses, particularly the Selle Français (see pages 132-133).

The Trotter is bred all over

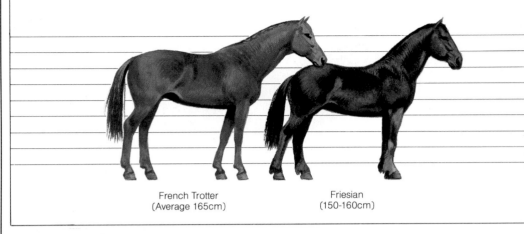

French Trotter
(Average 165cm)

Friesian
(150-160cm)

Above: Close-up view of the head of a French Trotter.

France, but the original area of development of the breed in Normandy remains the most important. Two studs, at Haras du Pin and Haras de Saint-Lo, are still the centers for breeding these impressive horses.

The French Trotter varies in type, from those that closely resemble the Thoroughbred to the more old-fashioned type, which is much sturdier, with straight shoulders and rounded action. The one area they all are strong in is the hindquarters. These tend to be short, with sloping croups and tremendous muscle power. Limbs are well-formed, hard and sound.

Below: The French Trotter is a particularly robust harness horse.

FRIESIAN
(Frisian)

Country of origin
Holland (Friesland).

Height
14·3-15·3hh (59-63in).

Color
Black. A small star is permissible.

Features
This old breed is renowned for its great "presence" and its very fast trot, with showy high-knee action. It is a part of Holland's past and is often used in demonstrations of historical pastimes, as well as in driving competitions and for general riding.

The Friesian cow and horse were developed in northern Holland, in the province of Friesland, which is famous for its rich grasslands. Horses have existed in this

province for a long time—the bones of a heavy horse from thousands of years ago have been unearthed there. The Romans favored and used a horse from Friesland. It is believed they took it with them to England. There the horse influenced many breeds, including the Fell, Dales and Clydesdale (see pages 28-29, 22-23 and 56 respectively).

It is certain the Friesian was very popular in medieval times; there are many pictures of knights mounted on these showy, stocky, black horses.

One of their great assets is a very active, fast trot. They flex their legs very high, which is spectacular to watch. In the 18th and 19th centuries, this speedy trot was valued, providing a fast, fashionable means of travel. The Friesian was used extensively to inject this asset into other breeds. It was exported to Russia to influence the Orlov Trotter (page 124), to England to affect the Norfolk Trotter (page 195) and, through this latter breed, the American Morgan (pages 118-119).

Friesians were used in trotting races, but the development in the 19th century of specialized harness breeds (such as the French Trotter) led to their eclipse.

The demand for the Friesian for crossbreeding led to the adulteration of the purebred stock, so in 1879 a Friesian Herdbook Society was started to ensure the continuance of the breed. It was not an easy task because the demand

for Friesians fell with the approach of the 20th century. Mechanization led to their demise as a speedy means of transportation.

Another important demand for the breed had been from farmers who used them for pasture maintenance. But with the advent of tractors, the Friesian became redundant also in this sphere.

Recently the Friesians' fortunes have taken a turn for the better. Their ability as carriage horses has been put to good use; Tjeerd Velstra won a silver medal in the

European Championships with a Friesian team. They are also used for demonstrations.

Because they are always black, color matching is no problem. Their willing, gentle character means they are easily trained. Their showy action and spirited way of going makes them spectacular to watch. They can be ridden or driven and are often used in circus work.

The Friesian has a fine, long head with alert, expressive eyes and short ears. The neck is crested, shoulders and back are strong,

Above: The black Friesian horses from Holland are famous as circus and driving horses.

quarters are well-rounded and the tail is set quite low. Limbs are strong, with good bone. There is a lot of hair in the mane and tail and feather on the legs.

The legs are sometimes covered with hair right up as far as the knee joint.

Right: A Friesian horse, one of the oldest of all European breeds.

GELDERLAND

Country of origin
  Holland (Gelderland).
Height
  15·2-16·1hh (62-65in).
Color
  Chestnut, bay or gray.
Features
  Bred as a utility farmhorse, the Gelderland is a strong, willing worker. With little demand for it from mechanized farms, very few remain.

The Gelderland is a utility farm horse bred in the Dutch province after which it is named. It was developed from the native breeds of the area and mixed with Thoroughbreds, Norfolk Trotters, Holsteins and Anglo-Normans. The intent was to provide farmers with a horse that could work the land, pull carriages and be ridden, similar to the Irish Draft and Cleveland Bay. The Gelderland was used extensively on the farms during the 19th century. The demand for it has declined, but until the 1950s it was used by many farmers.

As the demand from agriculture declined, the Gelderland was converted into a coach and riding horse. Holstein, Trakehner, Anglo-Norman and Thoroughbred horses were used to refine the breed. In the 1960s, another use was found for the Gelderland—it served as foundation stock for the Dutch Warm-Blood. This crossbreeding, together with the small demand for farm horses, led to near-extinction of the breed. Steps have now been taken to ensure its survival.

The Gelderland forms an important section (basic type) in the Dutch Warm-Blood studbook.

Today, Gelderlands are used for general riding and harness work. They are also popular as show horses in the Netherlands.

The Gelderland has a plain head but an honest, gentle outlook. The face is straight to convex, and ears are long. The neck is strong and crested, the shoulder is deep and sloping, the body is deep and powerful, the croup hardly slopes and the tail is set quite high. Limbs are clean, well-formed and have good bone, so that the Gelderland has the appearance of an animal of substance.

Below: With their quiet temperaments, Gelderlands can make good driving horses, as this splendid team of four shows.

Gelderland
(157-165cm)

Groningen
(160-165cm)

Han
18
16
14
12
10
8
6
4
2

GRONINGEN

Country of origin
The Netherlands.
Height
15·3-16.1hh (63-65in).
Color
Black, bay, brown or dark brown.
Features
This strong utility horse nearly became extinct in the 1970s when only one stallion remained. The Dutch authorities have ensured its preservation.

The Groningen is the Netherland's second utility farmhorse; its breeding areas are in the north of the country. The Groningen is larger and heavier than the Gelderland. It has been based more on the bigger Oldenburg and East Friesian breeds (the East Friesian is the East German version of the Oldenburg). Some British Suffolk blood was used in the 19th century. This made it into a strong

Right: A Groningen mare. This heavy breed of Warm-Blood often has a flat croup (or rump), as shown by this mare.

horse, greatly valued by farmers.
Like the Gelderland, mechanization meant less demand for it, and attempts were made to lighten it into a useful riding and harness horse. It is used for these purposes today. Like the Gelderland, it is used also as foundation stock for

Below: A Gelderland mare and her foal in the field.

the Dutch Warm-Blood. Its powerful quarters are an asset needed in a riding and competition horse.
Groningen numbers declined drastically in the 1970s, but this decline has now been halted. Oldenburgs are being imported and used to ensure against too much inbreeding. Today, the Groningen is being carefully preserved. Like the Gelderland, it is established as a basic type in

the same section of the Dutch Warm-Blood studbook.
The Groningen has a long head, with a straight face, and long ears. The body is deep and powerful. Limbs are a good shape with good flat bone. The feet are round and strong. The tail is set quite high and it is carried gaily. The croup of the Groningen is relatively flat and the quarters are muscular.

HACKNEY HORSE

Country of origin
England (Norfolk, Cambridge and Yorkshire).

Height
14-15·3hh (56-63in).

Color
Bay, dark brown, chestnut or black.

Features
The brilliant action of this elegant, small horse originally made it a fashionable, fast means of transport. Today it is a feature item at many shows.

Hackney Horse
(142-160cm)

Hanoverian
(160-173cm)

"Hackney" may be derived from the Old French word "haquenée" which means "horse for hire". That is how the ancestors of this spectacular high-stepping horse used to work. Harnessed to light vehicles, they were available for hire in London, just as taxi-cabs are today. The original hackneys were rather cobby trotters, and the breed was developed, like the Hackney Pony (see pages 30-31), from the older British regional breeds of trotter, the Yorkshire and Norfolk Roadsters (see page 195).

The Hackney was derived from some of the best of the Norfolk Roadster stock. One of the most famous sires was Shales the Original (1755). Shales could be traced back, via foundation stallions, to the Thoroughbred: he was by Blaze, the son of Flying Childers, who was by Darley Arabian, one of the chief ancestors of the Thoroughbred. Another famous sire was Fireways, whose son, The Norfolk Cob (1829), out of Shales's Mare, is reported to have trotted at 24 miles per hour. This high-class speedy Norfolk blood was crossed with Yorkshire Roadster mares, and the result was the Hackney.

The Hackney, together with the Roadsters, thrived from the early part of the 19th century until the advent of the railways. Horses provided a speedy, elegant means of travel along the newly macadamized roads. However, the railways reduced the demand for horses. The sturdier, less-spectacular breeds of Roadsters died out, but the Hackneys, with their high-stepping action, continued to be fashionable mainly as show animals.

In 1878, serious efforts were made to organize a society. The original meeting was at Downham Market in Norfolk, but it was not until 1883, at Norwich, that it was agreed to start a stud book for Hackneys, Roadsters, Cobs and Ponies. Eminent names were soon involved; the Prince of Wales became Patron to the Hackney Society. This helped to make the breed very fashionable, and the Society an active, prosperous organization.

Hackneys are still exported all over the world. Even after the automobile had superseded them

Below: Hackneys being driven to a carriage called a "unicorn" at the Royal Windsor Show, UK.

Above: The Hackney has great presence, with head held high and brilliant action.

as a means of transport, they were kept for demonstrations and showing. They became known as "the ballerinas of the show ring," with their volcanic personality and brilliant action. Today, they are a feature item in the show ring in many countries.

The Hackney has a small head, with a convex face, large eyes, small ears and a small muzzle. The neck is long and well-formed. The shoulders are powerful, with low withers. The body is compact, with a broad chest. The tail is well set on the quarters and carried high. The forelegs are straight, with gently sloping pasterns and well-shaped feet. The hocks are well let down. The coat is fine and silky.

The action is a striking feature of the breed. The legs must be raised high enough and thrown forward far enough to cover the ground, not just raised up and back. The head should be carried erect but not too high or too low. The ears should be pricked. The whole animal should be a living portrait of elegance and beauty.

HANOVERIAN

Country of origin
Germany (Lower Saxony).
Height
15·3-17hh (63-68in).
Color
Most solid colors.
Features
A strong, powerful breed of sports horse that is very athletic and has excelled as a show jumper and dressage horse.

The Hanoverian is the most famous and numerous of the regional German breeds. It comes from the state of Lower Saxony and dates back to the hefty War Horse of the Middle Ages. Its history is a classic case of adaptation to current needs. The make, shape and character of the Hanoverian have been modified to meet the demands of the time.

The first major step at organizing the breed came in 1735, when George II, Elector of Hanover and King of England, established by royal decree the Celle State Stud. This housed selected stallions that were available, at a nominal fee, to brood mares owned by local farmers. The aim was to upgrade and refine existing Hanoverians and turn them from the heavy, War Horse types into farm horses and carriage horses. The first stallions came from Holstein, but later some came from England (Thoroughbred and Cleveland Bay). Then some Neapolitan, Andalusian, Prussian and Mecklenburg stock was used. By the end of the 18th century, sufficient improvement had been made to use mainly stallions foaled in Hanover. The Hanoverian had become a very famous coach horse.

Celle housed 200 stallions, but many others were privately owned.

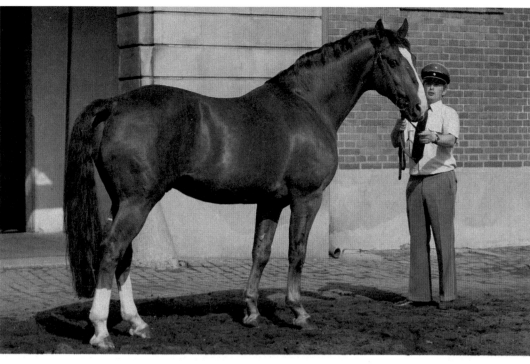

Above: A Hanoverian stallion from the state stud of Celle, in West Germany, which was founded in 1735 by King George II of England.

To raise the general standard of stallions in 1844, a *Kor-Ordnung* (Selection Rule) established that only those stallions passed by a commission could be used for breeding. Today, there is still an annual *Hengst Körung* (Stallion Selection) for 2½-year-old stallions.

In 1867, the private breeders formed a society. They laid down as their breeding aim "the production of a robust, strong horse equally well-suited to serve as a coach and as a military horse." This was followed in 1899 by the establishment of a stud book for mares. The results were impressive, and Hanoverians were used all over Germany as well as in Scandinavia and Switzerland.

After World War I, there was much less need for horses in the army. The breeding aim was restated as "a strong warm-blood capable of doing every kind of farm work, yet possessed of enough blood, nerve and gaits to be usable as a bold riding and coach horse."

To further this aim, a young stallion training and testing station was opened in 1928. All young stallions went through 11 months

Below: The Hanoverian gelding, Aramis, is shown here jumping for Canada at the 1984 Olympics in Los Angeles.

of training. Constitution, character and disposition were recorded before facing tests in endurance, jumping, speed and willingness. Only those that passed could be used for breeding.

World War II and the mechanization of farms changed the need again. A horse bred solely for riding was desired, and the aim became a "noble, correctly built warm-blood capable of superior performance—a horse with natural impulsion and space-gaining elastic movements—a horse which, because of its temperament, its character and willingness, is principally suited as an all-around riding horse."

This gradual conversion of the Hanoverian from a heavy agricultural-coach-military horse into an elegant, athletic, sports horse has been achieved mainly by adding Thoroughbred blood. At present at Celle, about 10% of the 200 stallions are Thoroughbreds. The other refining influences have been Trakehner and Arab. Representatives of these breeds still make up 3% and 1%, respectively, of the stallions at Celle.

With the breeding aim concentrating on its character, movement and soundness, the Hanoverian's make and shape varies. Its distinguishing features are a sensible temperament, powerful, extravagant movement, a muscular, strong body and good substance.

Hanoverians are used for driving and general riding, but they have excelled in competitions. They include Olympic show jumping gold medalist Warwick, the World Dressage Champion Mehmed and the World Show Jumping Champion Simona. With these successes and the existence of pedigrees that make breeding stock traceable for hundreds of years, the Hanoverian has been used for upgrading practically every European breed of warm-blood, also show jumpers and other sports horses in the United States.

HISPANO

Country of origin
   Spain.
Height
   15·3-16·1hh (63-65in).
Color
   Bay, chestnut and gray are most common.
Features
   This brave, intelligent, athletic horse is used for all types of riding.

The Hispano is Spain's Anglo-Arab. Spanish-Arabian mares were crossed with Thoroughbreds, mainly in Estremadura and Andalucia, to produce this all-around riding horse. It is popular with the Army, general riders and competitors in eventing, jumping and dressage. The Hispano is sometimes even seen in the bull-ring.

As a composite breed, the Hispano varies. Sometimes it looks more like a Thoroughbred, and at other times it looks more like an Arab. It usually has an elegant, light-framed body, with a good front. The limbs are long and slender but with dense bone.

Right: A Spanish Hispano performing in a display.

HOLSTEIN

Country of origin
   Germany (Schleswig-Holstein).
Height
   16-17hh (64-68in).
Color
   Most solid colors.
Features
   Over the centuries, this old German breed has played many roles, as a great war horse, as a high-stepping, sturdy carriage horse and as an elegant competition horse.

This is probably the oldest German breed: documents dated 1225 prove Holsteins were bred by the monks in the pastures and marshlands along the River Elbe in the northern German state of Schleswig-Holstein. These lands have been very good breeding grounds for horses and cattle.

In the Middle Ages, a well-known war horse was produced from these regions. In the 16th, 17th and 18th centuries, Holsteins were very popular and were exported all over Europe. They were famous as big, black horses with high action. It is believed some Spanish, Neapolitan and Barb blood was used on native mares.

The Napoleonic wars depleted the Holstein numbers and demand for them fell. They were too heavy to meet a major need by the military for cavalry horses. Breeding stock was imported from England to upgrade and refine existing Holsteins and to increase

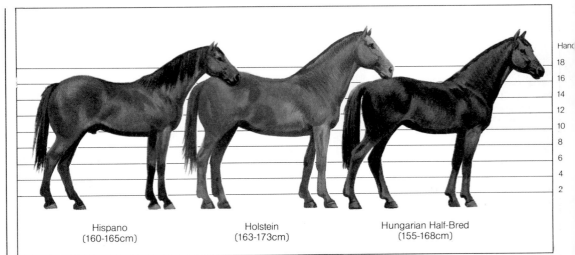

| | | Hand |
| Hispano
(160-165cm) | Holstein
(163-173cm) | Hungarian Half-Bred
(155-168cm) |

numbers. Sixteen horses were imported, but the most important blood came from three Yorkshire Coach Horses—all could be traced back to the Thoroughbred, Eclipse. Some interbreeding was practiced on these three sires, and the resultant carriage horse, featuring a high action to get out of the mud but also the ability to go a long way, became very popular. It was also useful to farmers as well as the Army. By the beginning of the 20th century, with the growth of competitions, the Holstein proved to be a powerful, heavyweight jumper and dressage horse.

After World War II, the demand by farmers for the Holstein fell. Although it was still sometimes required as a carriage horse, many thought it too heavy for

Above: The Holstein Montevideo competing at the 1984 Olympics, when it helped to win a gold medal.

competition. Numbers declined — in 1947 there were 20,000 registered mares, but by 1960 this had fallen to only 1,280. The Holstein Society decided to take steps to modernize and refine the breed. Twenty-five Thoroughbred stallions were imported from Britain. In 1960, the centre for breeding was moved from the Traventhal Stud to Elmshorn Riding School.

Since then, the breed has become increasingly successful. Numbers are still small (it is the smallest numerically of the German breeds), but quality is exceptional. At the 1984 Olympics 70% of the German horses in the dressage, jumping and eventing teams were Holsteins.

The modern Holstein is one of the most elegant of all sports horses. They are tall horses, with long, crested necks, strong, well-shaped backs and quarters, plenty of flat bone and elegant heads, with bold, honest expressions.

Holsteins have proved to possess great stamina and power, which has made them the most successful German breed in eventing. They have also excelled in driving, dressage and jumping.

The forelegs should be set well apart and the elbows should have freedom of movement. The feet should be open at the heel, dense and smooth. The tail should be carried well and not set too high.

Below: Hungarian Half-Breds have been successful in Combined Driving classes, winning many championships.

HUNGARIAN HALF-BREDS
Furioso, Gidran
Kisbér, Mezőhegyes

Country of origin
Hungary.
Height
15·1-16·2hh (61-66in).
Color
Most solid colors.
Features
Athletic, sound sports horse that varies in type from the light Kisbér to the stronger Mezőhegyes and the Anglo-Arab, which is known as the Gidran.

The Hungarians are famous horse breeders. They have bred great Thoroughbreds, such as Kisbér, which won the 1876 British Derby. Today, they are famous for their driving horses, which are exported all over the world. Horses are bred at state studs and stock farms. Each tends to specialize in a particular strain, type or breed of horse.

The officially designated major breed of Hungarian sports horse is produced at the stud at Mezőhegyes, after which it is named. The Mezőhegyes is a crossbred based on the older breeds of Furioso (originally Thoroughbred, Arab and local mares) and North Star (Thoroughbred and local mares). The Furioso and North Star breeds were named after their foundation Thoroughbred sires, which were imported from Britain in the middle of the 19th century. Both breeds are now merged into the Mezőhegyes. Since 1962, some Hanoverian and Holstein blood has been added to improve its sporting ability.

The Kisbér is the lightest Hungarian half-bred. It is produced at the military stud after which it is named. Holsteins and Mecklenburgs were used in its development during the 19th century, but the emphasis has been on adding Thoroughbred blood to make the Kisbér a useful event horse. Guy's Choice and Supreme Court were two recent Thoroughbred imports to Hungary from Britain.

The Gidran is the Arab-based half-bred. It was again developed in the 19th century from the Arab stallion, Gidran Senior, which was imported into the country in 1816. Local mares were used, then Thoroughbreds and some more Arab. The Gidran is the Hungarian Anglo-Arab. It is stockier and more robust than an Arab.

These breeds are used for riding and harness work, but it is an unnamed crossbred that is Hungary's most successful sports horse. It comes from the Kecskemet stud, where Lipizzaner mares are crossed with Trotter stallions (from the USSR and USA) and has become a world famous driving horse.

IOMUD
(Yomud)

Country of origin
USSR (Turkmenistan).
Height
14·3-15·1hh (59-61in).
Color
Gray is most common, but many are bay or chestnut.
Features
A slender, tough breed with the stamina to carry riders over long distances.

The Iomud is similar to the Akhal Teke. Both share the ancestry of the Turkoman, or Turkmen, horse (pages 140-141) and have been bred in Turkmenistan for centuries. The Iomud's homelands are the Turkoman steppes that stretch from Russia into Northern Iran. It is sturdier, smaller, more compact and slower than the Akhal Teke, but it has more stamina. This is probably the result of some mixing with Arab horses and horses belonging to the nomadic steppe tribes.

The homelands of the Iomud are desertlike lands, so the horses have had to have a hardy constitution and an ability to live off frugal fare to survive. They were used as riding horses in the past by the Turkoman tribes and the cavalry. Today they are used for distance riding.

The Iomud has been raced over as great a distance as 30 miles (48km), but today it is usually tested over about 2 miles (3·2km). It has a very fast walk, a short, striding trot and a lightly balanced canter; each of these gaits is comfortable for the rider.

The Iomud's head is thin, with a straight profile, large eyes set far apart, wide nostrils and small, alert ears. The neck is long and straight, the body rather shallow and straight and loins broad, with a slightly sloping croup. Limbs are fine but with dense bone. There is little hair in the mane and tail, and the coat is fine and sleek.

IRISH HORSE

Country of origin
Ireland.
Height
Typically 16-16·3hh (64-67in).
Color
Most.
Features
These sports horses are still being developed as a breed. They are usually tough, and have proved to be outstanding jumpers and eventers.

The Irish Horse is a new addition to the sports horse group. It was formerly classed as a type, like the hunter and hack. It was a cross between a Thoroughbred and (usually) an Irish Draft. The Irish Horse did not have registration

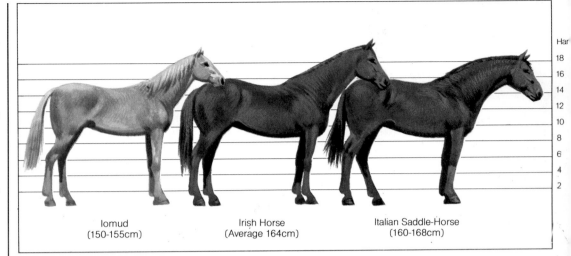

		Har
Iomud
(150-155cm)

Irish Horse
(Average 164cm)

Italian Saddle-Horse
(160-168cm)

papers and few, especially stallions, were ever used for breeding. Since the 1970s, selective breeding of the Irish Horse has been started, under the organization of the Irish Horse Board. Mares and stallions are graded, and stock is registered. More Irish Horses are being used as stallions.

There is still a variety of types among the Irish Horses, depending on the origins of the parents and the percentage of Thoroughbred blood. But most tend to have good heads and plenty of substance. Most are good, careful, sound hunters. Large numbers are talented jumpers, capable of going eventing and performing well in the show-jumping arena. Some have made good dressage horses.

Left: The Irish Horse, Rockbarton, ridden by Gerry Mullins.

Below: Irish horses competing for Switzerland in driving.

ITALIAN SADDLE-HORSES

Anglo-Arab Sardo, Maremanno, Salerno, Sanfrantellano, Siciliano

Country of origin
Italy.
Height
15·3-16·2hh (63-66in).
Color
Most solid colors.
Features
This breed group is in the early stages of its development. The large number of breeds playing a part in its establishment means that there are considerable variations in type.

Like so many European countries, Italy has merged her regional breeds of riding horses and imported stock to upgrade the new breed group into a useful sports horse. Importation has been from France, Ireland and Germany, with a few horses from the Netherlands and Eastern Europe.

The majority of brood mares for the Italian Saddle-Horse (more than 4,000 are now registered) come from the two Anglo-Arab types of Italian-bred horses—the Sicilian Anglo-Arab and the Sardinian Anglo-Arab. Both are based on Arab and Barb stock originally brought from Africa. These have been infused with other Arabs and Thoroughbreds. The Sardinian has some Andalusian

blood added. The two breeds have shown talent in equestrian sports and are good foundation stock for the Italian Saddle-Horse.

In addition, Salernos (Salerni-tanos), were developed in the 16th century in Salerno province, close to Naples. They were infused with Neapolitan and Andalusian blood. The Salernos were popular cavalry horses and are now used mostly for recreation and competitions. Maremannos from the central and western areas of Italy, in and around Tuscany, have also been used in the breeding of the Saddle-Horse. It was originally a tough, frugal, fast horse with little quality. But the mixture of British Thoroughbreds has

Above: A representative of a new breed type in Italy, the Italian Saddle-Horse. It is being developed from a variety of different breeds.

Below: A fine Irish Horse with her foal.

increased its nobility. It is still used for work and riding, so the lighter Maremanno is crossbred to the Thoroughbred to make the best Saddle-Horses.

Sanfrantellanos, from Messina in Sicily, have also been used in breeding Saddle-Horses. The Sanfrantellanos are allowed to run wild in their native lands, but when caught they are used for riding and harness work. Crossing with the Thoroughbred has given a new perspective to the breed. It has enabled them, like the Maremannos, to be used for competitions. Foundation stock includes the Anglo-Normans, which came to Italy as cavalry horses in the 17th century, and Hackneys, Lipizzaners, Maremannos and Nonius, which have been introduced for breeding during more recent times.

This amalgam of different breeds is being used to develop the Italian Saddle-Horse. Numbers of this interesting breed group are steadily increasing in Italy.

KABARDIN

Country of origin
  USSR (Caucasus).
Height
  14·2-15·1hh (58-61in).
Color
  Bay is most common, but they
  can be dark brown, black or
  gray.
Features
  An active, strong, sure-footed
  mountain horse that can be used
  under saddle or in harness.

The Kabardin is a native of the
northern Caucasus mountains
in the USSR. It has all the assets
of a mountain horse—sure-
footedness, docility and intelligence.
It is strong enough to serve as a
pack horse and is good enough
to be ridden.

The Kabardin has been used by
the nomadic tribes of the region
for a long time. They developed
the breed by crossing horses
from the south—Karabakh,
Persian and Turkoman—with their
own steppe horses.

Since the beginning of the 20th
century, some Kabardin have
been crossed with Thoroughbreds
to establish the taller, finer, faster
breed of Anglo-Kabardin.

The typical Kabardin has a long,
thin head with a short muscular
neck, a straight shoulder, a short
straight back and a broad, sloping
croup. The limbs are strong
with dense bone and good feet.

*Below: The Kabardin is bred by
nomadic Caucasus tribesmen.*

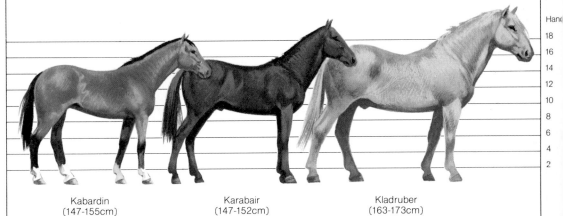

Kabardin
(147-155cm)

Karabair
(147-152cm)

Kladruber
(163-173cm)

*Above: A jet-black Karabair
horse from the USSR.*

*This is an ancient breed with a
sparse mane and tail.*

KARABAIR

Country of origin
  USSR (Uzbekistan).
Height
  14·2-15hh (58-60in).
Color
  Gray, bay and chestnut are
  most common, but other colors
  are found.
Features
  A tough, lean breed adapted
  to hot climates. For centuries
  it has served as a riding horse
  for the tribesmen in Uzbekistan.

The Karabair is a very old breed
based in Uzbekistan. It was
developed from the steppe horses
of the nomadic tribesmen and
from horses that came from the
south—the Turkomans, Persians
and Arabs. It is a dual-purpose

horse and is useful for riding and harness work. The Karabair is also used for sport in local games such as *kokpar*, in which riders fight over a goat. When crossed with Thoroughbreds, Karabairs have proved to be talented at other equestrian competitions, such as jumping or eventing.

The Karabair is a small, thickset riding horse. The head is of average length, with a straight to convex face. The neck is straight and thick, running onto low withers. The body is broad but shallow. The back is short and strong, and the croup is rounded and muscular. The limbs are fine but with dense bone. There is a tendency for the hind legs to have cow or sickle hocks. The feet are tough, with good quality horn. The mane and tail have very little hair. The coat is fine.

Above: The noble-looking Kladruber is one of the largest breeds of sports horses.

KLADRUBER

Country of origin
Czechoslovakia (Bohemia).
Height
16-17hh (64-68in).
Color
Gray or black.
Features
Strong, kind horses with short strides and high knee action. They are famous as coach horses.

The Kladruber is bred at Kladrub, the oldest functioning stud in the world. It lies in the region of Bohemia in Czechoslovakia, close to the steeplechasing course of Pardubice. The stud was started by the Emperor Maximilian II, who imported Spanish stock of Andalusian lines during the 1570s.

Horses from this royal stud were bred to provide coach horses for the royal stables. They are a heavier, taller version of their relations the Lipizzaners, which were developed at the Yugoslavian stud of Lipizza. Today, Lipizzaners are bred in Czechoslovakia at the Topolcianky Stud. There has been some use of Lipizzaners in the breeding of Kladrubers, along with heavy native horses, Barbs, Turks and Neapolitans.

More outside blood was used after World War II, because stock was severely depleted by the fighting. Oldenburgs, Anglo-Normans and Hanoverians were imported to restore the breed, which was in danger of becoming extinct.

The Kladruber is bred in two colors. The most common is gray, but black was also developed in the 19th century. The base for the black Kladrubers was the state stud of Slatinany.

Today, the Kladruber is used for riding and driving but it is more famous as a driving horse. A spectacular attraction at international events is a team of 16 gray Kladrubers pulling a carriage.

The Kladruber's head has a noble look, with a convex face. The neck is muscular and crested, and the shoulder slopes. The body is long and shallow. The hindquarters are rounded and muscular and the limbs are clean.

Below: A team of Kladrubers being driven in a dressage arena.

KNABSTRUP

Country of origin
 Denmark.
Height
 15·1-16hh (61-64in).
Color
 Appaloosa patterns on a roan base.
Features
 A gentle, strong horse that is popular for use in demonstrations and exhibitions.

The Knabstrup is a spectacularly spotted horse from Denmark. Like the Appaloosa, patterns vary, and no two horses are identical.

The breed developed from one mare named Flaebenhoppen. She was allegedly brought to Denmark during the Napoleonic Wars. She eventually fell into the ownership of the proprietor of the Knabstrup estate. This chestnut mare, with a white blanket and white mane and tail, was put to one of the Danish Frederiksborg stallions; he had the palomino colour. The result was the foundation sire of the Knabstrup breed. He was called Flaebehingsten. Although similar in color to his mother, he had many more shades to his coat.

Recently, there has been much crossbreeding. Breeders have concentrated on producing better color patterns rather than consistent conformation. This has led to considerable variation in type.

The Knabstrup, with its spectacular coloring, has been much used as a circus horse, but it is valued also for general riding.

LIPIZZANER

Country of origin
 Austria.
Height
 15-16hh (60-64in).
Color
 Usually gray but can be bay. They are born dark but lighten as they mature.
Features
 For many years, these intelligent, athletic, strong horses have been famous as high-school horses. Today, they are also earning fame as harness horses in Combined Driving.

This famous breed of Austrian high-school horse has Spanish origins—hence the name "Spanish School" for the base in Vienna, where these gray horses demonstrate their gymnastic ability. The foundation stock of nine stallions and 24 mares was brought to the stud of Lipizza (now in Yugoslavia) by Archduke Charles of Austria in 1580.

The vogue for high school was just beginning in the courts of Europe, and the Archduke was determined that the Austrians would have the material to excel.

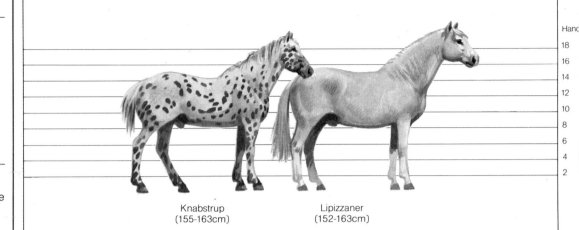

Hand

18
16
14
12
10
8
6
4
2

Knabstrup
(155-163cm)

Lipizzaner
(152-163cm)

Above: A Knabstrup, with its spectacularly spotted coat, galloping free.

Below: Lipizzaners are famous for giving high school demonstrations all over the world.

The Andalusians from the Iberian peninsula were recognized as top-class material for this form of riding, so these must have been the imported stock that was bred to local mares. It is likely that over the ensuing 200 years, more imports were made from Spain, and possibly some from Italy. The Neapolitan, from Italy, was the other fashionable high-school horse.

After the establishment of the school in Vienna, in 1735, the Lipizzaner's breeding began to be recorded. All Lipizzaners today trace back to six stallions imported in the late 18th and early 19th centuries. These are Pluto, a Frederiksborg; Conversano and Neapolitano, both Neapolitans; Maestoso and Favory, both Kladrubers; and Siglavy, an Arab. This was not such a heterogenous collection as it seems: Frederiksborgs, Neapolitans and Kladrubers are based on Andalusian stock, and there had been crossbreeding

before between these three breeds and the Lipizzaner. Attempts were made later to use other blood, such as Thoroughbred and Anglo-Arab, but their stock was not very successful at the Spanish Riding School. The best of the Lipizzaners have not had much outcrossing, because Andalusian lines are the most important.

The breeding of the Lipizzaners suffered great disruption with the break-up of the Austro-Hungarian Empire in 1918. The original stud at Lipizza became Italian territory, and the Italians did not make good use of the stock left there. After World War II, Lipizza became part of Yugoslavia, which has done much to promote the Lipizzaner.

The Yugoslavians collected stock from elsewhere, and today there are about 10,000 Lipizzaners in Yugoslavia. The Yugoslavian dressage team is the only one in the world to be mounted on Lipizzaners.

Lipizzaners are not only used in competitions and demonstrations. The Yugoslavs have discovered that farm mares crossed with Lipizzaner stallions make good

Above: A Lipizzaner being ridden by a member of the Spanish Riding School at a British show.

agricultural workers. These crossbreds are also often used by farmers in parts of Romania and Hungary, where the terrain is similar to that in Yugoslavia.

Hungary promotes her Lipizzaners for another reason. It has found that purebred and crossbred horses, bred with the Trotter, make high-class harness horses for Combined Driving. The Hungarians export these horses all over the world and use them to win major driving championships.

Despite the various uses for these intelligent, athletic, strong

animals, it is as the mounts of the members of the Spanish Riding School that they remain most famous. The stud for these school horses is now at Piber in Austria. The only stallions that can breed at the stud are those that have proved themselves to be outstanding high-school horses in Vienna. Even the mares are put through performance tests before they are allowed to breed. The Austrians still follow the principle that the best basis for selecting Lipizzaners is their performance ability.

Right: The Lipizzaner is one of the most intelligent and athletic of all horse breeds.

LUSITANO

Country of origin
Portugal.
Height
15-15·3hh (60-63in).
Color
Gray is most common, but other solid colors are found.
Features
A courageous, athletic horse which is famous in the bullring. It is also valued by farmers and the Portuguese cavalry.

The Lusitano is a relative of the Lipizzaner because it is believed to be founded on Andalusian stock. There are indications that some Lusitanos went to Austria as foundation stock for the Lipizzaner. The Lusitano's home country is Portugal. Together with the Altér Real, it has been the country's main riding horse for centuries. It is similar to its forbears, the Andalusians, but is thought to have more Arab blood.

The Lusitano was popular with the Portuguese cavalry. It is a very strong horse, and farmers used it for riding and light draft work. The Lusitano is most famous as the horse of the mounted bullfighters (*rejoneadores*). Horses are trained to advanced levels of high school, to make the fight more entertaining and to reduce the risk to horse and rider. Some horses are used in demonstrations

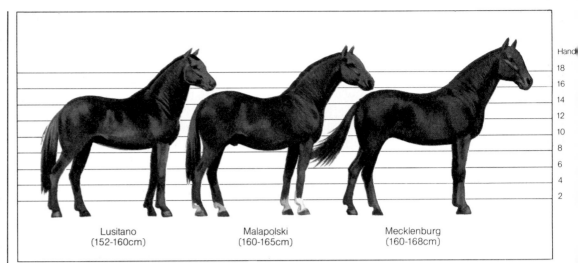

			Hand
			18
			16
			14
			12
			10
			8
			6
			4
			2

Lusitano
(152-160cm)

Malapolski
(160-165cm)

Mecklenburg
(160-168cm)

prior to the appearance of the bull. Others, which are particularly skilled and fast, are used during the actual fight. In Portugal, unlike Spain, the bull is not killed.

The Lusitano has an Andalusian-type head, with a straight-to-convex face. Ears are small but alert. The neck is muscular, the shoulder slopes and the body is compact and deep. Quarters are rounded and very powerful. The mane and

Left: A Lusitano being driven.

Below left: Lusitanos are famous as mounts of bullfighters.

Below: Lusitanos are as popular for hacking as for high school riding.

tail have an abundance of hair.

The Lusitano has great courage. It moves with relatively high, round strides which makes it easy to train for the exacting standards of high-school work that are required for the Portuguese bullring.

MALAPOLSKI

Country of origin
 Poland.
Height
 15·3-16·2hh (63-66in).
Color
 Bay, gray, chestnut and black are most common.
Features
 An honest, willing worker that is useful under saddle and in harness.

This all-around horse is bred in the southeast of Poland. It developed from primitive local horses (of Tarpan origins) that were crossed with Arab and Thoroughbred blood. This was largely through the use of such Hungarian and Austrian horses as the Shagya, Furioso, Gidran and Lipizzaner, as well as Poland's other riding horse, the Wielkopolski.

The Malapolski is an elegant horse with a lean frame. It has great powers of endurance and conserves its fodder. It is used

Above: A Mecklenburg. This horse is based on, and is similar to, the West German Hanoverian.

extensively by farmers as an all-around horse that can be used to tend the land, act as transportation and be ridden. The demand for it is extensive; at the state studs there are 300 stallions. Another 800 or so are privately owned.

The Malapolski has good width between the eyes and a tendency toward a concave face. The body is strong and muscular, but not deep.

MECKLENBURG

Country of origin
 East Germany.
Height
 15·3-16·2hh (63-66in).
Color
 Most solid colors.
Features
 A docile, trainable horse that is athletic and suitable for general riding and competitions.

The Mecklenburg is East Germany's version of the Hanoverian.

Blood lines are similar, and there has been considerable interaction between the two studs at Celle and Mecklenburg.

The Mecklenburg's main use has been as an Army horse. But today it is in demand as a general riding horse.

It has good substance, yet it is also a very athletic and powerful breed.

The head is medium-sized, the neck muscular, the chest broad and the body deep and compact. The hindquarters are muscular and the legs have substantial bone and short cannons.

MISSOURI FOXTROTTER

Country of origin
United States (Missouri).
Height
14-16hh (56-64in).
Color
Any.
Features
A reliable, gentle horse with an unusual shuffling gait called the *fox trot,* which provides a fast, comfortable means of travel.

The Missouri Foxtrotter was developed in the Ozark Hills of Missouri, at the beginning of the 19th century. Pioneers who settled the area brought with them their horses— mainly Arabs, Morgans and Southern Plantation Horses. These were used (later additions were the Saddlebred, Tennessee Walker and Standardbred) to produce a horse that provided a fast and comfortable means of travel. A horse of this type was in great demand from doctors, sheriffs, assessors and stock raisers.

Stallions were used that had shown the ability to perform an ambling gait that became known as the *fox trot.* The horse walked in front and trotted behind. In this type of gait, they could travel at 5 to 8 miles an hour and were very comfortable to ride. Careful selective breeding

Below: The Missouri Foxtrotter is one of the most comfortable rides in the United States.

Above: This Missouri Foxtrotter wears a bridle that is designed for Western riding.

produced the Missouri Foxtrotter.

Besides its distinctive gait, another feature of this breed is its docility. It was often described as "the common man's pleasure horse" because of its gentle disposition, ease of training, handling and feeding.

Today, it is very popular for trail riding because of its comfort, sure-footedness, speed and gentleness. It is also used as a show horse. A breed society, which began in 1948, promotes exhibiting of Missouri Foxtrotting Horses which are judged 40% on the fox trot gait, 20% on the flat foot walk, 20% on the canter and 20% on conformation.

The Missouri Foxtrotter's head is neat and intelligent, with pointed ears, large eyes and a tapering muzzle. The neck is well-shaped, the shoulder slopes and the body is deep. The back is short and strong, and the limbs are strong and distinctly tapered.

Missouri Foxtrotter
(142-163cm)

Morgan
(145-157cm)

Han...
18
16
14
12
10
8
6
4
2

MORGAN

Country of origin
United States (Vermont).
Height
14·1-15·2hh (57-62in.)
Color
Preferably dark with minimal white. Bay is most common.
Features
This is a versatile breed that is easy to handle, and endowed with great presence.

This versatile breed was founded in the 1780s in the United States by a single stallion, believed to be of Arab and Barb descent. It is possible he also had some Welsh Cob or Friesian blood. He took his name from his owner, a Vermont singing teacher named Justin Morgan. The teacher added to his income by using his stallion to pull logs. At only 14·1hh (57in) he was capable of outpulling all his rivals. The stallion was then given a chance at racing, and he beat challengers both in harness and under saddle. His fame spread and so did the demand for his services by the owners of mares in Vermont. Demand grew even greater when, whatever the standard of the mare, he stamped their progeny with his assets. With this demand, and because he lived well into his 20s, he was able to leave a large enough family to found a breed.

Justin Morgan's progeny soon became known simply as "Morgans". Some were used to found other major American breeds, such as the Standardbred and American Saddlebred.

The army quickly adopted the breed. Morgans were the best available breed in terms of ease of training, remaining calm under stress, enduring hard work, living off little food and coping with the demands of parade work.

Today, the Morgan is still popular, because its versatility makes it a high-class family horse. Its kind nature and sturdy physique combined with a relatively short stature enables it to carry a man or a child with equal comfort. It can also be driven and has a tremendous air of importance,

which is very eye-catching. The Morgan is used in dressage and endurance tests. It also is used as a cow pony or a roadster (speed trotter). It is still used for work on the farm.

The breed is divided into Park and Pleasure divisions. Both work in harness and under saddle. The Park takes time to train—about 7 years—and has higher action. The requirements are a combination of balance and light controls with animation and great spirit. The Park Morgan is expected to present a picture of great beauty, brilliance, animation and elegance. It can be shown under English or Western tack. The Pleasure Morgan has a lower action, is easier to train and has very good manners.

The Morgan's head is medium sized, tapering slightly from the jaw to the muzzle. The face is straight or slightly concave. Ears are small, alert and have fine points. The neck is medium length and well-crested. Withers are prominent and slightly higher than the point of the hip. Shoulders slope. The chest is broad and deep, and the

Above: A Morgan Horse pulling a buggy. This is just one of the many uses for this versatile breed, which can also be ridden. Its kind temperament, compact shape and athletic movement makes it valuable for many tasks, from farmwork to dressage.

back is short, broad and muscular. Loins are wide and muscular, the quarters are muscular, and the croup is gently rounded, with a fairly high-set tail. Limbs are set square, with muscular forearms and second thighs. Knees are wide and flat, hocks are wide, deep and clean, cannons are short, wide and flat, and the feet are round, smooth and dense.

The Morgan moves with flat-footed, elastic, rapid, long, straight and free strides at the walk. It moves with square, freegoing, collected and balanced strides at the trot. Smooth, easy, collected straight strides are usual on both leads at the canter.

Right: A portrait of the hard-working Morgan Horse.

MURGHESE

Country of origin
Italy.
Height
14·2-16·1hh (58-65in)
Color
Usually chestnut.
Features
This is a utility type of horse developed since the 1920s in the famous breeding area of Murge.

The Murghese comes from Murge, an area that was famous for its horses in the 15th, 16th and 17th centuries. There were two types: a heavier type used for agricultural

Murghese
(147-165cm)

Mustang
(137-152cm)

Above: The Murghese horse, which is bred in Italy.

work and a smaller type that was used for work in the mountains. The smaller type became extinct and the former type became very rare. In the 1920s, the Italian Ministry of Agriculture took an interest in establishing the breed. Today's Murghese is a utility horse capable of being worked in harness and ridden. It is particularly popular with foresters for pulling trees.

The Murghese is a robust horse. Its head is medium length. The shoulder is muscular and straight, and the hooves are very hard and compact.

Above: Mustangs, feral horses of the United States and the original mounts of the American cowboy, are shown in a demonstration at Lexington, Kentucky.

Left and Above: Mustangs are tough, wiry horses of every known color, with many unusual shades and combinations.

MUSTANG
(Bronco, Cayuse, Chickasaw)

Country of origin
United States.
Height
13·2-15hh (54-60in)
Color
Any.
Features
This is a feral horse with a tough constitution. It isn't elegant, but it has a romantic history, closely allied with that of the United States. It was the original Indian horse and cowpony of the American West.

The Mustang has Spanish origins, based on Andalusian and Barb stock brought to North America by the first Spanish Settlers. Escaped horses ran free and multiplied to form large herds. They were sometimes caught by the North American Indians, and later by cowboys. In California, Texas and New Mexico, these horses became known as 'Mustangs'. Farther north they were often referred to as 'Broncos' and sometimes 'Cayuse'.

Many earlier Mustangs were fine representatives of the Spanish Barb ancestry. The Indians used some of the best Mustangs to chase bison. They were also caught and tamed by the cowboys, and proved to have "cow sense", a valued ability to work livestock.

Many Mustangs were left to breed in the wild. The continuous drainage of the finest stock eventually depleted the wild herds of their best stock quality. The remaining Mustangs, while tough and wiry, lacked the original beauty and quality.

As settlers moved West, they brought carriage, draft and riding horses with them. Often they were taller, heavier horses; they were crossed with Mustangs to increase the size of the native western horses. The most successful of these crosses were the early Quarter Horses, from crosses of imported Thoroughbreds with the fast Chickasaw Horses of the Southeast. The Chickasaw Horses, also Mustangs, were probably survivors of horses lost by early Spanish explorers in the southeast area of the United States.

With their common ancestors and heritage, these Quarter Horses helped increase the size and substance of the Mustangs without diluting the "cow sense" desired in a stock horse. Today, most western American breeds, including the Quarter Horse, Appaloosa, Pinto and Palamino, owe a great deal of their stock-horse qualities to their Mustang heritage.

We can only estimate how many of the original Mustangs remained by the early 1900s, but it was certainly not many. Crossbreeding diluted most of the remaining herds. Because they were considered a nuisance to cattle ranchers, many remaining horses were rounded up and subsequently sold or shot.

Although the true Mustang has been crossbred almost to extinction, several registries have been set up to preserve those of pure Barb type and bloodlines. The term "Spanish Mustang" is used to refer to those animals of obvious Barb descent collected by Robert Brislawn and bred at the Wild Horse Research Farm in Porterville, California. These horses show the Barb characteristics of only five lumbar vertebrae (most horse breeds have six), a slab-shaped body that is narrow and deep, a sloping croup and low set tail. They have small ears, round bone to the limbs and the straight or convex profile typical of the Barb. They come in a variety of colors, including the "Medicine Hat" pinto (nearly all white over pinto, with dark markings over the ears), roans and various duns including grulla (black dun) and claybank (red dun).

Many of these horses are fine examples of the old Spanish Barb and make excellent riding and endurance horses. Another group, the Spanish Barb Mustang Registry, also registers horses with Barb characteristics. No claim is made that they are of pure Barb descent, but horses must prove to have desirable characteristics to achieve permanent registration.

Finally, there is the American Mustang. This is registered by the American Mustang Association, which was formed in 1962.

NONIUS

Country of origin
Hungary.
Height
Large: 15·3-16·2hh (63-66in).
Small: 14·3-15·3hh (59-63).
Color
Bay, brown or black.
Features
A gentle, active horse that can be used for light draft work and riding.

The Nonius is the most numerous and best-established of the Hungarian breeds. It is produced at Hungary's major stud for sports horses, Mezöhegyes. The original stock for this breed was brought back by the Hungarians from France in 1815. They were Normandy horses, and the best one was a stallion named Nonius. He proved to be highly fertile when put to local mares and also possibly some others of Lipizzaner, Arab and Turkish blood. The new breed, to which Nonius gave his name, was used extensively by the Army and farmers.

Toward the end of the 19th century, more Thoroughbreds were used on the Nonius mares. This resulted in a lighter division to the breed. Consequently, there is the heavier light-draft type, now used for driving and for farm work, and the riding horse.

The Nonius is a good-looking horse with an attractive head, a long muscular neck and sloping shoulders. It has a broad back and loins, muscular quarters and strong limbs.

NOVOKIRGHIZ

Country of origin
USSR (Kirghiz).
Height
14·3-15·2 (59-62in).
Color
Usually chestnut or bay, with a gold sheen.
Features
This tough utility breed was developed after the 1930s.

The Kirghiz was the native pony of the mountainous regions of Kirghiz and Kazakstan. It was derived from Mongolian stock and used by the local tribes for many centuries. During the 20th century the demand grew for a larger animal to work the farms, so Kirghiz ponies were crossed with Thoroughbreds and Dons. Through selective breeding, a new breed, called the Novokirghiz, was established, and this was officially recognized in 1954.

The Novokirghiz has proved to be a good horse under saddle and in harness. It is also used for pack work in the mountains.

| | Han |
| Nonius (150-168cm) | Novokirghiz (150-157cm) | Oldenburg (165-178cm) |

Mares continue to fulfill an important traditional function of the old breed by providing *kumis* (fermented milk).

The Novokirghiz type varies from a type close to Thoroughbred to one that is a heavy work horse. All of them have a good-looking head, a straight back, muscular quarters and a short, sloping croup. Limbs are strong and short, although they often have cow or sickle hocks. Feet are hard.

Left: The head of a Nonius with its honest expression.

Below: A Nonius horse stands square to show its conformation.

OLDENBURG

Country of origin
Germany (northwest).
Height
16·1-17·2hh (65-70in).
Color
Bay, brown and black are most common.
Features
An early maturing, even-tempered, strong breed, that has been famous as a coach horse. Now it is being adapted to make a sports horse.

The Oldenburg has been bred in northwest Germany for centuries. It has much in common with its neighbor, the East Friesian, whose breeding grounds are now in East Germany. Both breeds were based on Friesian blood from Holland.

The Oldenburg breed was named after Count Anton von Oldenburg (1603 to 1667). He organized importations of Spanish and Italian stock to improve local mares.

Farmers in the 19th century established today's breed. They organized themselves into a Breeders' Society and imported upgrading stock. These included Thoroughbreds, Cleveland Bays, Yorkshire Coach Horses, Normans, and some Hanoverians from Lower Saxony. The breed they developed was a large warm-blood capable of working fields, pulling coaches and being used by the Army.

Recently, the Oldenburg has

Above: A tall, handsome Oldenburg stallion at stud.

been further lightened with Thoroughbred and French blood to make it less of a coach horse and more of a sports horse.

The Oldenburg's popularity has not been confined to Germany. It is frequently seen in neighboring Denmark and has been used to restore and upgrade other breeds, including the Kladruber.

The Oldenburg is the tallest, heaviest German regional breed, although the recent lightening process is bringing it more into line with the others. Its *métier* in the past has been as a high-class, strong coach horse, but it has adapted to the falling demand in this field and the rising one in equestrian sports.

Its head is plain, with a straight-to-convex face. The neck is long,

the shoulder sloping, and the body is deep and muscular. Quarters are strong, and the limbs are relatively short, with a good amount of bone.

Below: Oldenburgs are big, strong horses that are excellent for driving.

ORLOV TROTTER

Country of origin
USSR.

Height
16hh (64in), but it can grow much taller.

Color
Gray is most common, but black and bay are often seen.

Features
An elegant horse with athletic action and sound conformation. It is used in trotting races and as breeding stock to improve other breeds.

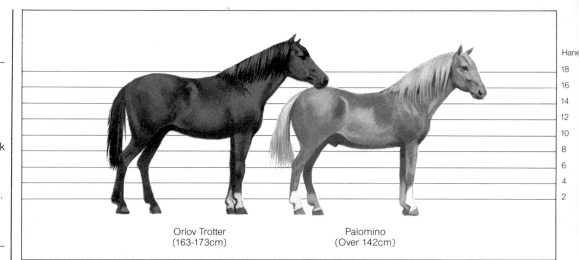

Orlov Trotter
(163-173cm)

Palomino
(Over 142cm)

The Orlov Trotter was the first of today's breeds to be bred for harness racing. It was developed at the instigation of Count Alexius Grigorievich Orlov (1737 to 1808). In 1777, he imported foundation stock and supervised the selective breeding of the progeny.

The first, and most important, stallion to be imported was the Arab, Smetanka. He was put to a Danish mare of Spanish origins to produce the stallion Polkan. When Polkan was put to a Dutch mare, the first important trotter and progenitor of the breed was produced in 1784. He was called Bars First. He was bred with more Arab, Dutch and Danish mares, and to Mecklenburgs and British half breds. There was considerable in-breeding to him, and most of

today's Orlovs have Bars First in their pedigrees.

By the time harness racing was seriously under way, in the 1830s, the Orlov had been developed into a definite type. Use of stock on the race track and culling those with poor performance records led to further improvements in the breed. The Orlov became the world's supreme trotter, and by the end of the 19th century more than 3,000 stud farms in Russia specialized in its breeding.

The Russian Revolution in 1917 disrupted breeding. The Orlov's breeding was restored when peace returned, but it never regained its international supremacy of the 19th century. The American Standard-

bred took its place. To speed up race time, Russians crossed some of their Orlovs with the Standard-bred to produce the faster Russian Trotter (see page 130).

The Orlov is a handsome, tall horse, and it has been used extensively to upgrade other breeds. It passes on its height and its strong light conformation. These are useful qualities for improving other breeds.

The Orlov's head is small, with an Arab influence. The neck is long, and the chest is broad.

Below: The Orlov Trotter was developed as a racehorse, but it is strong and robust enough to be used for general driving purposes.

The back is long and straight and the loins and croup are powerful. The quarters are rounded and muscular, and the legs are fine, with good, dense bone.

PALOMINO

Country of origin
Found all over the world, but America has the longest established breed society.

Height
Over 14hh (56in).

Color
Like a newly minted gold coin, with light mane and tail.

Features
Their beautiful color makes these horses in demand for general riding, showing and parades. Because they are categorized according to color, not shape, there is a great variety of types and an equally varied range of talents.

Palominos have coats the color of untarnished gold, with light manes and tails. They are some of the most eye-catching horses in the world but do not yet breed true to type. They are said to be a "color" rather than a breed. Consequently, there are Palomino Saddlebreds, Quarter Horses, half-breds or ponies. They are very popular.

Palomino societies are being established all over the world. In South Africa and Britain, there are thriving organizations, but it is the Americans who were the first to take an interest. This may be because of the Palomino's association with the cowboys. Palominos were found among the wild herds of Mustang horses that escaped from the first settlers.

The Palomino's origins precede the first settlers. It is believed that golden horses with silver manes and tails were ridden by China's early emperors. Achilles, the Greek warrior, rode Balios and Zanthos, who were "yellow and gold and swifter than storm winds".

For a while Palominos were called Isabellas after their most famous promoter, Queen Isabella of Spain. They were taken to the New World with Columbus or Cortez. Queen Isabella gave some to Count de Palomino, who was said to have named them after himself. However, there is another possible explanation for their name. It may have derived from the luscious golden grape called *Palomino*.

When the Spanish suffered military setbacks in America, most of their horses escaped to become Mustangs. It was from among these that the cowboys chose their Palomino cowponies.

Today, the Palomino has had another surge in popularity. It is much in demand in the show ring, for cutting, Quarter Horse racing, Western classes, pleasure and trail riding.

The Palomino's coat is never more than three shades darker or lighter than a newly-minted gold coin. It has a light mane and tail and should have dark skin, except under white markings. The eyes are dark or hazel. White markings are permitted on the legs to the knees or hocks and on the face. In addition, proof of breeding is required by most Palomino societies. Breeds accepted vary from country to country.

Above: The beautiful color of the Palomino makes it popular in the showring for many classes, such as Western Pleasure.

Below: A portrait of a Palomino. It is a color type rather than a true breed.

PASO FINO

Country of origin
  Puerto Rico.
Height
  13-15hh (42-60in)
Color
  Most.
Features
  A very comfortable riding horse
  with an unusual four-beat gait
  known as the *Paso*. It does
  not trot.

The Paso Fino is supposed to
have been derived from stock
brought to Santo Domingo (now
known as the Dominican Republic)
by Columbus on his second
voyage. Allegedly he had on board
Barbs, Andalusians and Spanish
Jennets. A feature of the Spanish
Jennet was its four-beat gait. It
was a broken pace which was very
fast and comfortable to sit to. This
became known as the *Paso gait*.
  Breeding farms for these horses
were established on several of the
Caribbean islands.Stock from
them was used as remounts for
the Spanish Conquistadores in
their conquest of Mexico, Peru and
other parts of South America.

*Right: A Paso Fino performing the
gait for which it is famous, the
four-beat, lateral Paso gait.*

*Below: This view of a Paso Fino
shows how the lateral pair of the
right fore and right hind leg are
lifted almost together.*

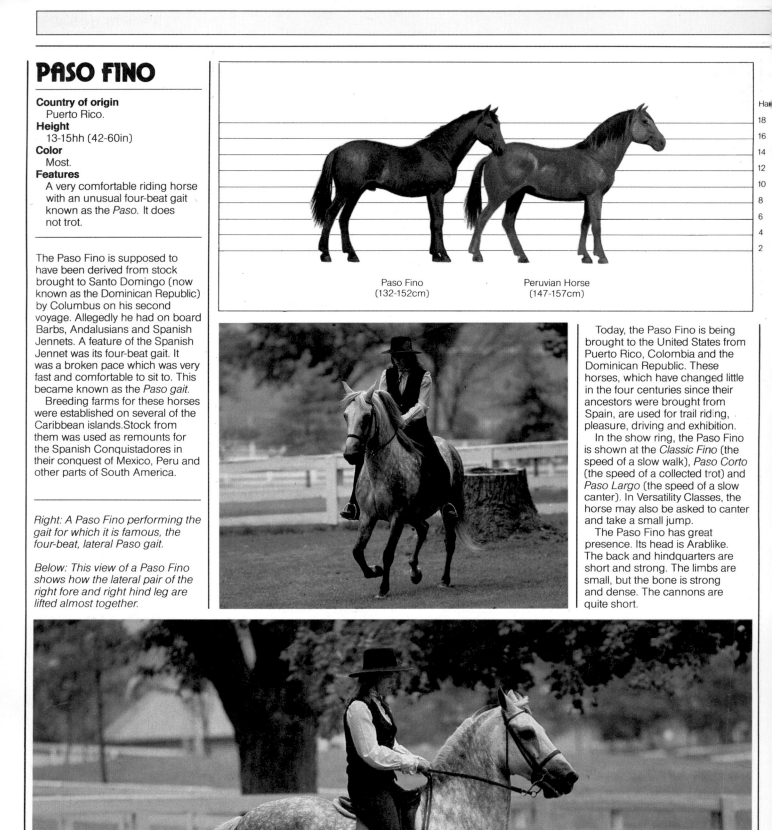

Paso Fino
(132-152cm)

Peruvian Horse
(147-157cm)

Today, the Paso Fino is being
brought to the United States from
Puerto Rico, Colombia and the
Dominican Republic. These
horses, which have changed little
in the four centuries since their
ancestors were brought from
Spain, are used for trail riding,
pleasure, driving and exhibition.
  In the show ring, the Paso Fino
is shown at the *Classic Fino* (the
speed of a slow walk), *Paso Corto*
(the speed of a collected trot) and
Paso Largo (the speed of a slow
canter). In Versatility Classes, the
horse may also be asked to canter
and take a small jump.
  The Paso Fino has great
presence. Its head is Arablike.
The back and hindquarters are
short and strong. The limbs are
small, but the bone is strong
and dense. The cannons are
quite short.

PERUVIAN HORSE
(Peruvian Paso)

Country of origin
Peru.

Height
14·2-15·2hh (58-62in).

Color
Bay, chestnut, brown, black or gray. Roan, once common, is now seen less often. Palomino and various shades of dun are found occasionally.

Features
This breed has flourished in Peru for over 300 years. Its growing popularity in other countries is based on its Paso gait, which is fast and comfortable, and its kind, easily managed disposition.

Above: A Peruvian Horse at a show being ridden in the national costume of the country.

The Peruvian Horse was developed from the same origins as the Paso Fino: Andalusians, Barbs and Spanish Jennets brought to South America by the Spanish Conquistadores. Nearly 400 years of selective breeding have improved its harmonious gaits, fast, smooth ride and gentle disposition that are the unique characteristics of this breed.

In other countries, the development of roads led to the growing popularity of trotting horses. However, in Peru the need was for a smooth traveling ambler that could be used to cover the vast estates. The Peruvian Horse's unique gait is inherited by 100% of purebred foals and often by partbreds. It is called a broken pace.

The Peruvian Horse, with its distinctive Paso gait, swings its forelegs outward in an arc as it moves. The hind legs are very powerful and push forward with long, straight strides. The hindquarters are held low, and the back is straight. The horse can travel over very rough terrain in this gait and can keep up a speed of as much as 15 to 18 miles an hour for a surprisingly long time without tiring. An indispensable breed characteristic, called brio, enables the horse to respond with energy and willingness and gives it great ability to withstand fatigue. The Peruvian is used in parades, endurance riding, pleasure riding and showing. At a show, the Peruvian is always "in gait" and is not allowed to walk or canter in the show ring.

The Peruvian has a stocky conformation of Criollo type, combining strength and elegance. It is broad and deep in the body, with strong loins and hindquarters. Generally larger than the Paso Fino, the Peruvian has long, sloping shoulders to facilitate its longer stride. The bone is strong and dense, and the pasterns are long. The croup slopes, and the tail is set low and carried quietly. The mane and tail are full, and hair is long and fine. The neck is crested, but long, and the head is always carried high.

Below: A fine Peruvian Horse mare and foal feeding in a well-fenced paddock.

PINTO
(Paint)

Country of origin
United States.

Height
Varies widely.

Color
There are two Pinto patterns. In the Overo, white patches start from the belly and extend up. The back, mane and tail tend to be dark, the face white and the eyes "glass" (blue). The limbs are dark and white.

In the Tobiano, white patches have no regular place of origin but often start from the back. Patches are larger than on the Overo and are of solid color. White legs are common, but the white face and glass eyes are rare. Tobiano horses are usually larger than Overos.

Features
Tough, spectacularly colored horses. They were famous as mounts for Indians, but today they are used for general riding.

Like the Palomino, the Pinto was originally registered in the United States as a color rather than a breed. However, today, the name covers four conformation types because the Pinto coloration is prepotent and tends to reproduce itself. The mixture of black and white (called piebald) or of bay or brown and white horses (skewbald) is not found amongst purebreds, such as the Arab and

Pinto
(Height varies widely)

Quarter Horse
(150-163cm)

Above: A Pinto, or Paint as it is often called, standing square.

Below: Portrait of a Pinto horse.

Thoroughbred.

Pinto types are covered by three separate registries in the United States. The American Paint Horse Registry was founded to register horses of Stock Horse type, with Quarter Horse and Thoroughbred breeding and conformation.

The Pinto Registry registers four types—the Stock-Horse type,

Above: Pintos being ridden in Western Gear.

the Hunter type (an English horse of predominantly Arabian or Morgan breeding) and the Saddle type (an English horse of predominantly American Saddlebred breeding with a high head carriage and animated, high action).

The Moroccan Spotted Horse Cooperative Association registers gaited horses and also those of Hackney, Saddlebred, Tennessee Walker, Arabian, Morgan and Thoroughbred ancestry.

The Pinto Registry, started in 1956, now includes over 30,000 horses in the United States, Canada, Europe and Asia, but it is as an American horse that the breed is best known.

QUARTER HORSE
(American Quarter Horse)

Country of origin
United States..
Height
14·3-16hh (59-64in).
Color
Most, however white markings are not allowed. Horses cannot be registered if there are white markings.
Features
A tremendously strong, gentle, agile and versatile breed that is used for everything from racing to rodeos and trail riding. It is the most common breed in the United States.

The American Quarter Horse was developed in the 18th century in the United States by settlers in Virginia and the Carolinas. They wanted a horse to race, but the only easily accessible tracks were main streets and cleared ways through virgin wilderness. About ¼ mile was the usual length of this type of track, hence the name given to the breed when the Society was formed in 1940.

Over this distance, great powers of acceleration were needed. It was discovered that the fastest horses were crossbreds between the British imports of the developing Thoroughbred and the local Chickasaw Indian pony. The Indian pony was wild Mustang stock of Spanish and Barb origins (see page 121) that had been caught by the Indians. Mustangs had tremendous powers of acceleration.

The most famous early Thoroughbred sire was Janus, which stood at stud in Virginia and North Carolina between 1756 and 1780. In England, he had raced over 4 miles, but his progeny won regularly over quarter of a mile sprints in the United States.

With the development of proper courses and the advancement in Thoroughbred breeding, racing down main streets and through clearings became less common. But more organized Quarter Mile Horse Racing continued. Today, the world's richest horse race is the All-American Futurity for 3-year-old Quarter Horses.

It was discovered that the Quarter Horses had talents other than racing. They were strong enough to carry big men and heavy packs all day. With the spread of cattle ranches, these horses became known as *the* best cowponies and, later, rodeo horses. They were agile, fast and tough, which made them very popular with the cowboys for ranching and for rodeo work.

Today, the Quarter Horse is the most numerous breed in the United States, with more than two million horses registered. Their export has resulted in more than 80,000 Quarter Horses being registered in 57 other countries. Their calm temperament, their great powers of acceleration and their strength and agility make them popular in so many spheres.

The Quarter Horse has a short, broad head with small alert ears, wide-set eyes, large, sensitive nostrils and a short muzzle. The head joins the neck at almost a 45° angle, with a distinct space between the jaw bone and neck muscles. The neck is medium length and slightly arched. Shoulders are deep and sloping. Withers are pronounced and medium to high. The chest is deep and broad, and the back and loins are short and very powerful. Quarters are broad, deep and heavy when veiwed from either side or rear. They are very muscular through the thigh and second thigh. Hocks are wide, deep, straight and clean. Cannons are short. Pasterns are medium length. The feet are round and roomy, with a deep, open heel. There is considerable substance to the limbs.

The Quarter Horse possesses great driving power in its hind-quarters and stands with its hindlegs well underneath its body. This use of the hindquarters continues in movement—the hocks are always placed well under the horse. This gives great collection to its action, and it can turn, stop and start with unusual ease and balance.

Below: These Quarter Horses are being ridden out. This is the most popular cowpony in the United States because it is agile, fast and readily trainable.

RUSSIAN TROTTER

Country of origin
  USSR.
Height
  15·3-16hh (63-64in)
Color
  Most are bay, but some are black, chestnut or gray.
Features
  A tough, muscular horse developed from Orlov and Standardbred blood to produce a fast trotter with good, strong conformation.

The USSR led the world in the early stages of harness racing. It was the first to produce a specialized breed, the Orlov Trotter (page 124). This breed sustained its reputation as the finest harness racing horse until the late 19th century. The development of the American Standardbred ended this supremacy, and from 1890 on, American horses were imported and crossbred to the Orlov. A faster trotter was produced.

In the ensuing years, selective breeding with the Orlov and these crossbreds resulted in the official recognition of the Russian Trotter as a breed in 1949. In recent years, small additional infusions of American blood have been introduced.

The Russian Trotter has a light, robust frame. Its head has a straight face. The neck is straight and the shoulder long and sloping. The body is deep, the back muscular, and the croup sloping. The legs of the Russian Trotter are fine and hard.

Har 18 16 14 12 10 8 6 4 2

Russian Trotter
(160-163cm)

Saddlebred
(152-163cm)

Above: A Russian Trotter showing the breed's typical straight face.

Right: The Russian Trotter was produced by crossing Russian Orlov trotters with American Standardbreds.

AMERICAN SADDLEBRED

(Kentucky Saddler)

Country of origin
United States.

Height
15-16hh (60-64in).

Color
Bay, chestnut or gray, but occasionally roan, pinto, or palomino.

Features
An intelligent, versatile breed that can be used for many purposes. It is best known as a show animal with animated gaits. In the case of the Five-Gaited horses, two extra gaits can be taught, which are unique to the breed.

The Saddlebred, originally called the Kentucky Saddler, is the "All American Horse." The breed was developed by Kentucky pioneers as an all-around asset. It was comfortable and fast to ride the trails and plantations, stylish and eye-catching to pull fancy buggies, strong and tractable to pull a plough, and fast and courageous to race against other farmers' horses on special occasions. These were the demands, and the stock used was Thoroughbreds, Morgans, Trotters and the now extinct Narragansett Pacers.

Of the Thoroughbreds, the most famous was Denmark (1839), whose son, Gaines Denmark (1851) is the officially recognized foundation sire. The result was a horse with speed, action, style and stamina, that gained fame as the mounts of many well-known generals in the Civil War.

In 1891, in Louisville, Kentucky, the American Saddle Horse Breeders Association was formed— one of the earliest breed associations to exist in the United States. A register was started, and careful selection of parents with adherence to a recognized type was encouraged.

The American Saddlebred, as it is usually called, is used for many purposes. It is agile, fast, intelligent, responsive, strong and balanced. It is popular for pleasure riding, driving, hunting, jumping, and as a parade horse, but it is best known as a show horse.

The American Saddlebred has three divisions: The Three-Gaited, the Five-Gaited and the Fine Harness Horse. The Three-Gaited Horse is judged on its action, conformation, animation, manners and soundness. It should execute gaits in a slow, collected manner, with high action. The head should be high, with an overall impression of brilliance. The mane of a Three-Gaited Horse is always clipped.

The Five-Gaited Horse has a full mane. It is shown in its three natural gaits, walk, trot and canter, and two man-made gaits, the slow gait and the rack. The ability to learn these two gaits is inherent

in the breed, but it usually takes a good trainer for the horse to perform well. They are both four-beat and very smooth for the rider. The slow gait should be done very slowly with the legs lifted very high, particularly in front. The rack is a much faster version. Speed is desirable if done in form. The knee and hock action should be snappy.

The Fine Harness is shown in two gaits: the animated walk, and an airy part trot, when there should be plenty of action behind and in front. Extreme speed is penalized. The mane is full and the vehicle four-wheeled. Once again performance, conformation, animation, manners and soundness are judged.

These three divisions are sub-divided. In each of them there may be performance classes, where the emphasis is on activity and motion, pleasure classes, where the emphasis is on manners and the provision of a pleasant ride, (in this sub-division even the Three-Gaited have a full mane), and the equitation classes, where riders are judged for their skill in presenting their mounts.

The Saddlebred has great quality and substance. The head is well-shaped, with small alert ears. The large eyes are set well apart. The Saddlebred has a good muzzle and wide nostrils. The neck is long and arched. The withers are sharp, the shoulder is sloping and the back is short. The croup is level with the tail, which is set high. The quarters are muscular. The legs are straight with long sloping pasterns. The hooves are good and sound and they are open at the heels.

Above: A handsome Saddlebred trots out to exercise.

Below: The Saddlebred shows off one of its spectacular gaits, the rack.

SELLE FRANÇAIS

Country of origin
France.
Height
15·3-16·2hh (63-68in)
Color
Chestnut is most common, but all colors are permissible.
Features
This supple, active, robust sports horse was established in 1958 by the amalgamation of the French breeds of half-bloods.

Selle Français
(160-168cm)

Shagya
(147-152cm)

The Selle Français came into existence in 1958. It was a title given to the amalgamation of the French regional breeds of riding horses, other than Arabs, Thoroughbreds, and Anglo-Arabs. These regional breeds had been classed as half-bloods, and they were pedigree breeds with records tracing back many generations. Those with unknown or missing origins are now known as Cheval de Selle.

The most popular of these half-bloods was the Anglo-Norman. It had been bred in Normandy where the soil and climate help to produce horses with good bone and strong muscles. The breed

traces back to the medieval Norman war horse, which was refined in the late 18th and early 19th centuries through the use of Arab, Thoroughbred and Norfolk Trotter blood. These refinements led to two branches— the trotter and the cavalry horse. The cavalry horse became known as the Anglo-Norman, which has proved to be the more influential blood for the Selle Français.

The other major breeding area for half-bloods was in the Limousin, after which the regional breed was

named. The Limousin has had a strong Arab influence, beginning with horses brought to France by the Moors in the 8th century. Thoroughbred blood and Anglo-Norman blood has also been used.

Other regional breeds include the Vendeen Charollais and Angevins. Since the 19th century, they have been based on crossing native mares with Normans, Anglo-Normans, Thoroughbreds, Arabs, Anglo-Arabs and Norfolk Trotters.

With Anglo-Normans used often for crossbreeding, regional breeds

of horses became more alike. The establishment of the Selle Français was a logical step.

The Selle Français remains an amalgamation of breeds, with 33% having a Thoroughbred sire, 20% Anglo-Arab, 45% Selle Français and 2% Trotter.

The Selle Français falls into three divisions. The most valuable are the competition horses. The Selle Français have shown their aptitude for jumping, dressage and eventing with such great horses as I Love You and Galoubet.

The second division is for race

horses. There are many French race meetings for horses which are not Thoroughbreds, known as *A.Q.P.S.A., (Cheveaux) Autres Que Pur Sang Anglais*, or "(Horses) of Other than Pure English Blood." Most of these races are over fences. Horses from this division have also excelled as Eventers.

The third division is for non-specialist horses, which are useful in riding schools and trail riding.

With such a variety of parents and uses, the Selle Français is not uniform. It is divided into middleweights and heavyweights, according to their substance and weight-carrying capacity. Middleweights have more Thoroughbred blood.

The ideal Selle Français is a strong, muscular horse, with a distinguished head, expressive eyes, a long neck and sloping shoulders. It should have a strong muscular body, large hindquarters, strong limbs with muscular forearms, well-defined joints and good bone. Its paces are supple, free and active.

Above right: A Selle Français has muscular, strong conformation.

Below: A team of Selle Français being driven.

SHAGYA

Country of origin
Hungary.
Height
14·2-15hh (58-60in).
Color
Usually gray.
Features
Similar to the Arab, this horse is famous as a cavalry and carriage horse and has proved itself capable of a wide range of activities, from farm work to general riding.

The Shagya is a Hungarian breed that is based on the Arab. It was developed at the Hungarian Arab stud of Babolna, which the state has owned since 1789, and which has specialized in Arabs since 1816. Like other Hungarian breeds, the Shagya is named after its foundation sire, which was born in 1830 and bought from the Bedouins to stand at Babolna. Other desert and Egyptian stock was imported around this time. Some Arab mares, together with local stock which was not always purebred, were put to Shagya to start a special type. Careful selective breeding and some inbreeding was practiced to establish this distinctive breed.

As the breed became established, and its value was realized as a

Above: O'Bajan 1, a beautiful Shagya from Hungary.

light cavalry and carriage horse, it was bred elsewhere in Hungary. It was then exported to Poland, Austria, Romania, the United States and Czechoslovakia.

Today, at Babolna nearly half the stock is original Arab and the remainder are Shagyas. The breed has proved itself as a sports horse and as a good mount for general riding.

In appearance, the Shagya is similar to the Arab but a little more robust. It is a hardy breed and can thrive on poor food. It is a good mover, athletic and energetic.

STANDARDBRED

Country of origin
United States.
Height
14-16hh (56-64in)
Color
Bay is most common, but all colors are found.
Features
This is the fastest breed of trotter. It is used extensively for racing and to upgrade other breeds of harness racers.

The Standardbred is the world's fastest breed for harness racing. It was developed principally from Thoroughbred stock. The most important of these was Messenger (1780), who traces back to all three foundation sires of the Thoroughbred. When he stood at stud in the United States he was put to a variety of local mares. But as the trotting races were held over well-ridden fields and were very amateur affairs, there was little thought of starting a breed of trotters from this sire.

Yet Messenger founded a dynasty of harness racers. He had four sons to which nearly every Standardbred can be traced.

The most important of his descendants was born in the era when the sport was fast gaining popularity and selective breeding

Standardbred
(142-163cm)

Swedish Warm-Blood
(157-170cm)

was being practiced to produce fast harness racers. This great sire was Hambletonian 10 (1849), who is considered to be the father of the modern Standardbred, producing 1,335 offspring.

The other important Thoroughbred sire was Diomed (1777).

Thoroughbreds were put to more robust strains and particularly those with the talent for trotting or pacing. These included Narragansett and Canadian Pacers and Cleveland Bays, but the most important breeds, apart from the Thoroughbred, seemed to be Morgans and Norfolk Trotters. The most

Right: A Standardbred shows its natural ability to pace.

Below; Standardbreds racing in Kentucky.

influential Norfolk Trotter was Bellfounder (1816), who stood in the United States in the 1820s and was the grandsire of Hambletonian 10.

In the 19th century, the informal, ridden trotting races began to be turned into increasingly official harness races. This saw the consequent growth of selective breeding to produce faster horses for the sport. An American Trotting Register was started in 1871 and the National Association of Trotting Horse Breeders laid down the standards for inclusion in 1879. A 1-mile speed standard was set of 2 minutes, 30 seconds for trotters and 2 minutes, 25 seconds for pacers, hence the name Standardbred. Pacers move their legs in lateral pairs rather than in diagonal pairs like trotters. Entry standards were adjusted with the passage of time, and today they relate to blood alone.

Harness racing has flourished in the United States with horses becoming as valuable as flat race horses. The American Standard-bred has become so good at its sport that it has been exported all over the world to improve other breeds of harness racer.

With speed being of primary importance, conformation of the Standardbred varies. It is usually shorter in the legs and stronger in the body than a Thoroughbred. It is more robust in appearance, with powerful quarters, and hind legs behind, not under, the quarters.

SWEDISH WARM-BLOOD

Country of origin
Sweden.
Height
15·2-16·3hh (62-67in).
Color
All solid colors.
Features
A highly intelligent horse, with spirit, yet tractable. It is athletic and has excelled in all Olympic equestrian disciplines, as well as driving.

The Swedish Warm-blood was developed as remounts for the Swedish cavalry. During the 19th century, native stock was crossed with carefully chosen imports, mainly Thoroughbreds, Hanoverians and Trakehners. A stud book was started in 1874, and more rigorous standards were laid down for entry into it. These began with veterinary, conformation and action tests. Temperament, performance and pedigree tests were added at later stages. The stallions must go through extensive tests in dressage, jumping, cross country and harness. Then they are given a full breeding license only after their 3-year-old progeny

has been examined.

This rigorous selection, together with continued importing of breeding stock when it is needed to counteract any weakness in the breed (the studbook is not closed), has led to the Swedish Warm-blood being one of the best breeds of sports horse in the world. Representatives of the breed have won gold medals at the Olympics in all three disciplines and have been very successful in driving.

The Swedish government actively supports the breeding of their Warm-blood. They run a national stud at Flyinge, where most leading stallions stand. Only a few stallions are privately owned.

The Swedes are very particular about the heads of their horses. The breed has an intelligent outlook, big, bold eyes and refined features. The neck is long and slightly crested. The shoulder is deep and sloping. The body and quarters are muscular and strong. Limbs are round, with short cannons. Feet are strong but tend to be narrow.

The Swedish Warm-blood is an athlete, with springy, free, powerful paces. This makes it much in demand as a competition horse.

Left: The Swedish Warm-Blood, Salute, does a pirouette in dressage.

Below: Jan Pahlsson drives his team of Swedish Warm-Bloods.

SWISS WARM-BLOOD
(Swiss Half-Blood)

Country of origin
Switzerland.
Height
15·3-16·2hh (63-66in)
Color
Any.
Features
This is a new breed of sports horse that is being promoted by the Swiss government, and is beginning to make its mark in competitions.

Swiss Warm-Blood
(160-168cm)

Tennessee Walking Horse
(152-163cm)

The Swiss Warm-blood is another post-World War II breed of sports horse. The Swiss are major importers of riding horses. But their national stud at Avenches has been directed by the government to produce riding horses, work horses and Army horses. This is leading to a successful new national breed.

The foundation stock were Swiss mares. Many of these can be traced to foreign origins (usually Holstein and Anglo-Norman). The main Swiss breed used was the Einsiedler, which is now merged with the Warm-blood. Records of the Einsiedler trace back to a stud started at the Benedictine Abbey of Einsiedler in 1064. The breed was a utility type for work, pleasure and the Army. But increasing injections of Anglo-Norman blood led to it becoming more of a sports horse, indistinguishable from the Swiss Warm-blood. In 1967 and 1968, some imported blood from Sweden and Ireland was added to these homebred mares.

Stallions were originally mainly imports, but today more Swiss Warm-bloods are standing at Avenches. The original stock

Above: One of the most successful Swiss Warm-Bloods is the dressage horse, Aristo. Here he is being ridden by the late Clare Koch.

Right: A Swiss Warm-Blood suckling her foal.

was mostly Selle Français, with some Thoroughbred, Hanoverian, Trakehner and Swedish Warm-blood.

Strict selective methods have been imposed. Stallions must go through two performance tests, one at 3½ years of age and another at 5½. Tests for conformation, action, soundness and pedigrees are also given. There are also progeny tests, and mares are strictly examined.

The aim of the Swiss is to produce a noble horse, large and correct, with a tractable temperament and a good character. It should be suitable for general riding, competitions and driving.

TENNESSEE WALKING HORSE

(Plantation Walker, Turn-Row)

Country of origin
United States (Tennessee).

Height
15-16hh (60-64in).

Color
Chestnut, (sometimes with flaxen mane and tail), black, bay and roan are common. Many often have white markings. Occasionally gray.

Features
An exceptionally comfortable and kind breed. This is a popular pleasure and show horse. Its unique "running walk" is a breathtaking spectacle. It once was a utility farm horse used in harness or for riding, but today it is used for showing, pleasure and trail riding.

The Tennessee Walking Horse is known as 'the world's greatest show, pleasure and trail-ride horse'. It was developed as a breed in the 19th century by the Tennessee plantation owners. They wanted a comfortable horse to ride around their properties. The horse needed to be agile to turn in plantation rows without injuring plants. Other names for this breed, *Plantation Walker* and *Turn-Row,* indicate how successful it was at these tasks.

The main foundation stock used were Narraganset Pacers and Canadian Pacers, both popular lateral-gaited horses of colonial times. Thoroughbred, Saddlebred, Standardbred and Morgan were also used in the formation of this unusual breed. The most influential stallion was Black Allan, a Standardbred, foaled in 1886.

The Tennessee Walker is highly versatile. As a pleasure horse, it can be ridden Western, English or plantation style. It can also be driven. It has a docile temperament which makes it highly trainable, and it is suitable both for novice and experienced riders.

One of the outstanding features of this breed is its comfortable

Above: The handsome head of a Tennessee Walking Horse, wearing a Western bridle.

and unusual gaits. These are the *flat-foot walk, running walk* and *rocking-chair canter.* All are natural to the breed, and even the running walk is performed by foals without any training. Yet it is unique to the Walker; no other breed has mastered this gait.

The flat-foot walk is a 1-2-3-4 beat with each foot hitting the ground at regular intervals. With its right hindfoot, the horse glides over the track left by the right front foot, and the same with the left. This is called *overstride.* The horse nods its head in time with its feet.

The running walk is basically the same flat-foot walk but with an increase in speed and overstride. It is a smooth gliding gait in which the horse pulls with the front feet and pushes with the rear. The hindfoot overstrides by 12-20 or more inches, and a speed of 6 to 9 miles per hour is sustained. In the show ring, the running walk is done at an extremely fast speed. Great elevation is obtained by keeping the horse's front hoofs long and having him wear heavily weighted shoes that must be attached with steel bands. Speeds of over 15 miles an hour can be obtained but cannot be maintained for long. Due to the manner of shoeing, a show horse can only be ridden in an arena.

The canter is often called the "rocking-chair canter." It is a high, rolling, collected movement that doesn't jar or jolt the rider.

This horse is used in the United States and abroad. Its success has stemmed largely from the work of the Tennessee Walking Horse Breeders' Association, started in 1935. The Tennessee Walking Horse is close coupled and robust. The head is large and plain, and the neck and back are short. The hindquarters are muscular and strong, and the croup slopes. The tail of the show horse may be artificially set to be carried high. The limbs of the Tennessee Walking Horse are strong, with good bone.

Below: The Tennessee Walking Horse displays its spectacular gaits.

TERSK
(Tersky)

Country of origin
USSR.

Height
14·3-15·1hh (59-61in).

Color
Gray, with a silver sheen, is the most common, but they can be chestnut or bay.

Features
A tough, robust version of the Arab, this horse is capable of a wide range of uses, from circus work to racing.

The Tersk is a new breed developed in the Stavropol region (North Caucasus) of the USSR. The first steps in its creation were taken in the 1920s when some of the few remaining (now extinct) Strelets were collected at the Tersk stud. The Strelets were large Arab types, based on native Ukrainian mares and selected Oriental sires. These Strelets were crossed with Arabs, Arab-Don crossbreds, Strelets-Kabardin crossbreds, and Shagyas from Hungary. Selective breeding was imposed, and the breed was officially recognized in 1948.

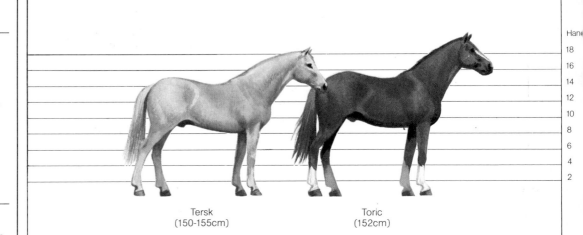

Tersk
(150-155cm)

Toric
(152cm)

The breeding aim was to produce a horse with the features of the Arabs (elegance, movement and endurance), combined with the robustness and toughness of native breeds.

The Tersk has proved to be gentle, intelligent, agile, athletic and capable of endurance. This has made it suitable for many purposes. It is entered in races for non-Thoroughbreds. It is used also for endurance rides and is popular with the Army, both for riding and harness work. It is used in competitions, particularly for dressage, and is popular in the circus. It is also used to improve other breeds, including the Karabakh and Lokai. Recently, there has been some crossing with the Thoroughbred to produce a larger horse.

The Tersk's head is of medium length, and the face is straight or slightly dished. The eyes are large, and the ears are long. The neck and back are medium length, the shoulder is sloping, the body is deep and the quarters are broad and muscular. The tail is set high. The limbs are fine, but the bone is dense. The hooves are strong.

Right: A herd of Tersks roaming free at Stavropol in the USSR.

Below: A Tersk stallion. This breed from the Caucasus in the USSR is based on Arab stock.

TORIC

Country of origin
USSR (Estonia).
Height
15hh (60in).
Color
Most are chestnut or bay.
Features
A high-class utility horse, capable of heavy draft work and general riding. It has great powers of endurance and unusual energy for such a heavy breed.

The Toric is probably the heaviest breed included in this section. It is used extensively for farm work, but lighter versions are used also increasingly for sport and general riding.

The Toric was developed in the late 19th and early 20th centuries from local ponies of Estonia, called Kleppers. These were the working ponies of Estonia, and a very small number still exist today. These dun ponies were prepotent for toughness and hardiness, which made them useful foundation stock. The Viatka (see page 47) also has Klepper blood. The Toric was officially recognized as a breed in 1950.

In the development of the Toric, many breeds were utilized in this upgrading of the Klepper. Arab, Ardennes, Thoroughbred, Orlov, Norfolk Roadster and Breton were used to increase its size and strength. The Norfolk Roadster Hatman seems to have been one of the most influential. Many Torics today trace back to him. Further crossbreeding was practiced in the 20th century with some German breeds, and the end result was a strong horse with unusually good paces and jumping ability.

The Toric's head is medium length. The neck is muscular and crested; this feature is especially noticeable in stallions. The back is long, broad and muscular. The limbs are short and strong.

Below: A strong, powerful Toric from Estonia, in the USSR.

TRAKEHNER
(East Prussian)

Country of origin
West Germany (East Prussia)

Height
16-16·2hh (64-66in).

Color
Any solid color, but they tend to be dark.

Features
Once renowned as cavalry horses, in the 20th century Trakehners have become leading competition horses. The serious depletion of their numbers, due to the destruction of their stud in World War II, has enabled other breeds to compete with them for the leading breed of sports horse.

The Trakehner is one of the oldest, most elegant of the German breeds of warm-bloods. Its breeding was based at the Trakehnen stud, which was founded in 1732 by Frederick William I of Prussia. The stud consisted of a large area of drained marshlands, which proved to be ideal for rearing horses. The foundation stock was the local Schweiken horse, a tough, active, little horse used on the East Prussian farms for centuries. The Schweikens were put mainly to Arabs and later Thoroughbreds, but some Turkoman blood was

Below: The Trakehner Agent shows his handsome head.

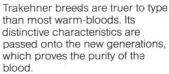

Trakehner
(163-168cm)

Turkoman
(150-155cm)

used through the stallion, Turkmen Atti. This mixture and careful selection soon resulted in a high-class cavalry and coach horse.

The production was extended as the Trakehner's fame spread. Just before World War II there were more than 10,000 breeders and 18,000 registered mares. All the farmers in the area bred Trakehners, because it was profitable and the horses thrived well on their lands.

Breeding was strictly organized. The Trakehnen stud was the center where breeding stock was thoroughly tested. Three-year-olds were trained, and 4-year-olds tested by hunting with hounds and competing in cross-country races. The best stallions were kept at the Trakehnen stud. The second class went to the state studs, the third to private breeders

and the remainder were gelded and used as Army remounts.

The war disrupted the stud, and with the prospect of Russian occupation, a small group of refugees took 600 mares and a few stallions to the West. The majority of the breed was left behind in what became Poland. These formed the basis of the Mazury and Poznan breeds and were later amalgamated into the Wielkopolski breed.

The small nucleus of Trakehners that crossed the River Elbe into West Germany in 1945 was carefully built up. The Trakehner is the one national breed of warm-blood in Germany with bases all over the country. Neumünster in the northwest is used as the auction and training center.

Care was taken in this multiplication of the breed, and today's

Trakehner breeds are truer to type than most warm-bloods. Its distinctive characteristics are passed onto the new generations, which proves the purity of the blood.

The Trakehner features of elegance, courage and stamina are in demand, and it has been used to upgrade stock in Germany (particularly the Hanoverian and Baden Württemburg) and abroad in the United States and Sweden.

The Trakehner has an elegant head, which is broad between large eyes and narrows toward the muzzle. The neck is long and crested, the shoulder slopes and the withers are prominent. The back is strong and medium length, and the quarters are muscular and gently rounded.

The Trakehner's supple paces and its tractable but spirited temperament make it a good competition and riding horse.

TURKOMAN
(Turkmen, Turkmene)

Country of origin
Turkmenistan (Afghanistan/ Iran/USSR).

Height
14·3-15·1hh (59-61in).

Color
Gray, bay, chestnut or dun.

Features
This is an ancient horse that has tremendous stamina and speed over long distances. It was used for racing more than 2,000 years ago.

The Turkoman is not a breed in the strict sense of the word. It has no breed society. It is a horse that has been bred for centuries in Turkmenistan, an area of mainly desertlike land, that now forms the southeast corner of the USSR. It is bordered by the Caspian Sea on the west, Afghanistan to the southeast and Iran to the south. Today, the Turkoman is represented by the Russian breeds of Akhal-Teke and Iomud, which were established from the horses of Turkmenistan.

The Turkoman is a legendary

horse, which was supposed to have been used in Persia in ancient times by the great leaders Darius and Alexander. It was then called the Bactrian or Turanian horse. Darius was believed to have had 10,000 horsemen mounted on them. It also became known as the "heavenly" horse of Chinese legend. In 126 B.C., the Chinese attacked the Bactrian Kingdom (made up of the northern slopes of Afghanistan, which had formerly been part of the Persian Empire) to collect these extraordinary "blood-sweating heavenly horses"; such was their reputation.

The origins of the Turkoman are controversial. Some authorities, such as R. S. Summerhays, claim it is a mixture of Mongolian and Arab blood (mainly Persian). Others, such as Michael Schafer, believe it descended from the wild horses of the Steppe type and it is this group of Steppe Horses which settled in Asia. The other horses went to the Iberian Peninsula and are represented today by the Andalusian (page 87).

The Turkoman was said to have been similar to the mount of the Scythians in the first century A.D. It was certainly the horse of the Turkoman tribesmen. Descriptions of the Turkoman tribes' horses from the 16th century on say it was larger and longer striding than the Arab. It is also said it had a rather big head, was lean, angular and fast, and did not have the beauty of the Arab.

These Turkoman horses were important foundation stock for other breeds, particularly in the USSR. Turkomans were also used in the founding of the Trakehner. Turkmen Atti was an important early sire of Turkoman descent. Turkish horses were definitely used in the development of the Thoroughbred, and these must have had some Turkoman blood.

J. Osborne, in *Horsebreeders' Notebook*, claims there were 32 Eastern sires of Turkoman origin used in the founding of the Thoroughbred. However, it is questionable whether the most famous one, Byerley Turk, was pure Turkoman. He was believed to have a large proportion of Arab blood. However, the Turkoman has founded breeds that are based on its stock. The Akhal-Teke (pages 84-85) and Iomud (page 110) from Turkmenistan in the USSR have been developed from it.

One of the Turkoman's original homes was Persia. It is still being bred on the Turkoman Steppes in northern Iran that border the USSR.

Below: A portrait of a Turkoman.

Above: The most successful Trakehner stallion, Abdullah. Conrad Hornfeld rode him in 1984 to win the Olympic Silver medal.

UKRAINIAN RIDING HORSE

Country of origin
USSR.
Height
Around 16hh (64in).
Color
Most are bay, chestnut or black.
Features
This is a new breed group of purpose-bred horses for general riding and sport. They have been developed since the last war, and nearly 50,000 are registered today.

The Ukrainian Riding Horse is a new type of sports horse that was developed by the Russians to provide them with a high-class horse for competitions, riding and driving. The foundations were laid after World War II, and the

Below: A Ukrainian Riding Horse is one of the new breed groups in the USSR. This brood mare is at the Moscow Exhibition.

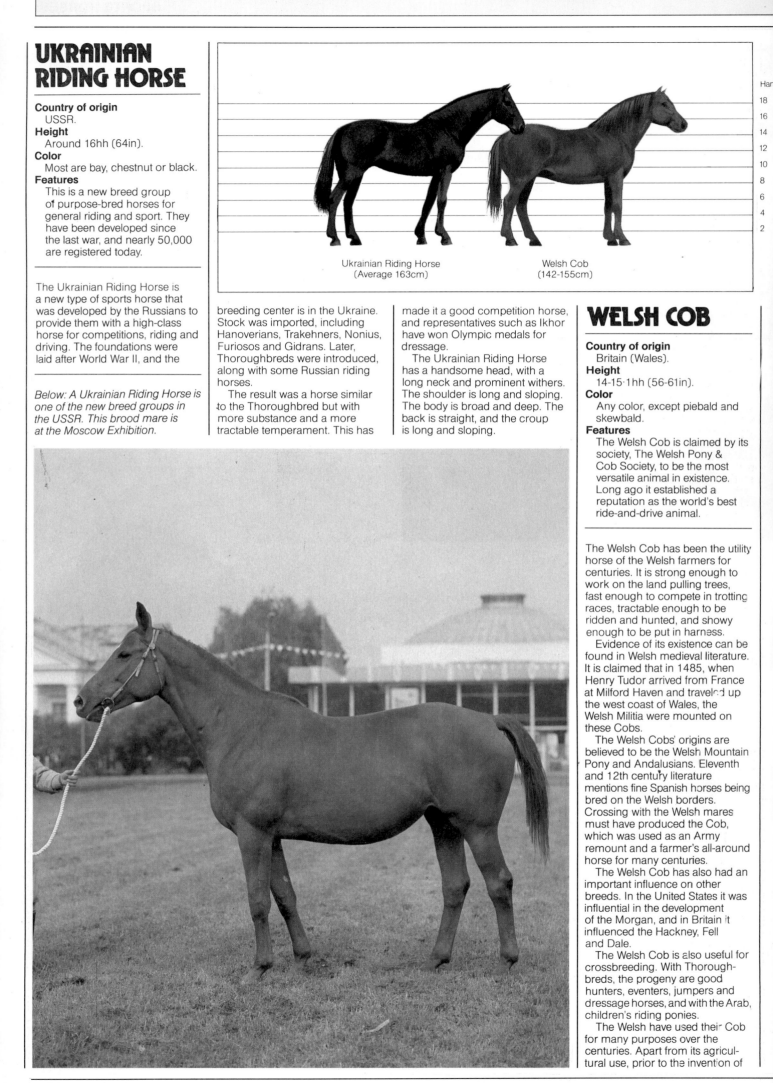

Ukrainian Riding Horse
(Average 163cm)

Welsh Cob
(142-155cm)

breeding center is in the Ukraine. Stock was imported, including Hanoverians, Trakehners, Nonius, Furiosos and Gidrans. Later, Thoroughbreds were introduced, along with some Russian riding horses.

The result was a horse similar to the Thoroughbred but with more substance and a more tractable temperament. This has made it a good competition horse, and representatives such as Ikhor have won Olympic medals for dressage.

The Ukrainian Riding Horse has a handsome head, with a long neck and prominent withers. The shoulder is long and sloping. The body is broad and deep. The back is straight, and the croup is long and sloping.

WELSH COB

Country of origin
Britain (Wales).
Height
14-15·1hh (56-61in).
Color
Any color, except piebald and skewbald.
Features
The Welsh Cob is claimed by its society, The Welsh Pony & Cob Society, to be the most versatile animal in existence. Long ago it established a reputation as the world's best ride-and-drive animal.

The Welsh Cob has been the utility horse of the Welsh farmers for centuries. It is strong enough to work on the land pulling trees, fast enough to compete in trotting races, tractable enough to be ridden and hunted, and showy enough to be put in harness.

Evidence of its existence can be found in Welsh medieval literature. It is claimed that in 1485, when Henry Tudor arrived from France at Milford Haven and traveled up the west coast of Wales, the Welsh Militia were mounted on these Cobs.

The Welsh Cobs' origins are believed to be the Welsh Mountain Pony and Andalusians. Eleventh and 12th century literature mentions fine Spanish horses being bred on the Welsh borders. Crossing with the Welsh mares must have produced the Cob, which was used as an Army remount and a farmer's all-around horse for many centuries.

The Welsh Cob has also had an important influence on other breeds. In the United States it was influential in the development of the Morgan, and in Britain it influenced the Hackney, Fell and Dale.

The Welsh Cob is also useful for crossbreeding. With Thoroughbreds, the progeny are good hunters, eventers, jumpers and dressage horses, and with the Arab, children's riding ponies.

The Welsh have used their Cob for many purposes over the centuries. Apart from its agricultural use, prior to the invention of the automobile, businessmen and tradesmen found the Cob to be the speediest means of transportation. In the Army it was considered so valuable for mounted infantry and for pulling guns and equipment over rough terrain, that the government paid premiums for the best stallions.

Today, these handsome Cobs, with their spirited nature, are popular for driving. Welsh Cob teams have been very successful in international events. They are also used for trail riding. At shows, particularly in Wales, classes for Welsh Cobs are very popular. They are shown in hand, and their handlers have to run very fast to demonstrate their spectacular high-stepping trot.

The Cob's head is ponylike and full of quality. The eyes are bold, prominent and set well apart. The ears are neat and well-set. The neck is lengthy and well-crested in stallions. The shoulders are strong and laid back. The body is deep. The back and loins are muscular and strong, and the quarters are lengthy and strong. The limbs are muscular, with well-defined joints and good bone. The feet are well-shaped and dense. The hind leg should not be too bent nor the hock set behind a line falling from the point of the quarter to the fetlock joint. There is a moderate amount of fine silky feather on the limbs.

The Welsh Cob's action is free, true and forcible. The knee should bend, and the whole foreleg should extend straight from the shoulder as far forward as possible in the trot. The hocks should flex under the body, with straight, powerful leverage.

Above: The Welsh Cob, Llanarth Flying Comet, galloping free.

Below: Llanarth Flying Comet is from Section D of the stud book.

Here, he shows off his stocky, strong conformation.

WESTPHALIAN
(Westfalian)

Country of origin
Germany (Westphalia).
Height
15·2-16·2hh (62-66in).
Color
All solid colors.
Features
An athletic, strong breed of sports horse that has excelled at show jumping and dressage. It has also done well in eventing and driving.

Westphalian.
(157-168cm)

Wielkopolski
(163-165cm)

The Westphalian is Germany's second most numerous regional breed after the Hanoverian. Like the other German warm-bloods, it is not purebred. The stud book is not closed. At the state stud of Warendorf, there are Thoroughbred and Hanoverian stallions and Westphalians. The neighboring Hanoverian breed has played a major part in the West-phalian's 20th century development and its adaption from a farm and army horse into a sports horse.

Today, Westphalians are one of

Below: A handsome example of the Westphalian breed.

the world's leading breeds of competition horses. Roman was their first major victor when he won the 1978 World Show Jumping title. In 1982, Fire won for them the same title. At the 1984 Olympics, Ahlerich took the individual gold medal and team gold medal in dressage.

The success of the breed is due to the rigorous methods of selection that were applied to a large number of horses. The Breeders Association was formed in 1826. At the Warendorf state

stallion depot, horses are only permitted to stand after they have been through pedigree, confor-mation, character and riding tests. Stallions are tested for tractive power at 3½ years, for riding ability and jumping without a rider at 4 years, and for jumping and dressage with rider, plus veterinary examination, at 4½ years. These tests include observation of temperament, character, consti-tution, feed utilization, willingness to work, riding ability, jumping ability, working style and general

efficiency. Each horse is given a "training score" for these factors. Only the best are allowed to stand at Warendorf.

The Westphalian is a heavier, more substantial version of the Hanoverian. The head has an intelligent outlook, with good width between the eyes. The neck is well-shaped and harmoniously attached to a well-proportioned, deep, muscular body. The quarters are strong, but the croup can be straight. The Westphalian's limbs have good bone.

Above: The Westphalian show jumper, Fire, won the individual title for Germany at the 1982 World Championships in Dublin, Eire.

Below: Poland's riding horse, the Wielkopolski, standing square.

WIELKOPOLSKI

Country of origin
Poland.
Height
16-16·1hh (64-65in).
Color
Chestnut is most common but it can be bay, black or gray.
Features
This breed is based on the Trakehner stock left after the original stud was destroyed in World War II. The breed makes good riding, competition and draft horses.

This breed was established after the amalgamation of the Mazury (Masuren) and Poznan. Both these breeds were based on Trakehner/East Prussian stock. (The original, but now destroyed, stud of Trakehnen lies today in Poland.) With this common foundation and because they have been crossbred, it was logical to put them in one stud book.

The Wielkopolski is a utility breed and it is a good riding horse. Many have done well in competition. They are also used on the farms for draft work, particularly in western and central Poland.

Selective breeding of the Wielkopolski is practiced at 13 Polish state studs, and five of these concentrate on horses for sports purposes. Through this selective breeding, the height of the Wielkopolskis has been increased.

The Wielkopolski is a gentle horse, with a well-proportioned conformation. It is a muscular and strong middle- to heavyweight horse. Limbs have good bone.

TYPES

COB·HACK HUNTER POLO PONY RIDING PONY

Types differ from breeds because there are no stud books and no authenticated pedigrees. Also, because it is normal for the colts to be gelded, they are not used for breeding. Mare types are bred from, but rarely stallions. Types are produced by crossbreeding and there is no breeding true to type.

Types originated in the English-speaking world in response to a particular demand for horses or ponies. Most have a Thoroughbred or Arab as one of their parents. The abundant supply of Thoroughbreds that have relatively disappointing track performances and are therefore not in demand for breeding racehorses has meant crossbreeding is an economical way of producing the types of horses needed. There has been little incentive to turn them into a breed, as is usually done on the European continent.

The most important types produced today are the Cob, Hack, Hunter, Polo Pony and Riding Pony. In the United States, the Hunter is called a Jumper when it is used purely for jumping fences in an arena.

These types are used mainly in Britain, the United States, South Africa, Australia and New Zealand—countries that have not been so concerned with selective breeding and organizing societies (other than for racehorses and established purebreds) as in Europe.

Right: This Hunter is being exercised by the Master of the Taunton Vale Foxhounds, Somerset, England.
Below: Polo Ponies in action in Spain.

146

COB

Country of origin
Britain.
Height
14·2-15·2hh (58-62in).
Color
Any.
Features
A dumpy, strong, gentle horse that is popular for hunting, showing and general riding.

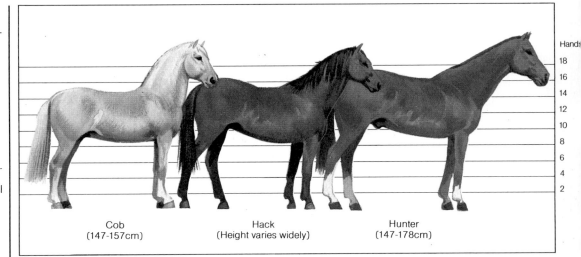

| | Hands |
| Cob (147-157cm) | Hack (Height varies widely) | Hunter (147-178cm) |

Cobs are compact, muscular, small horses, with tremendous bone. Although the term did not come into use until the 18th century, the type was used long ago in feudal times when squires rode them in battle and estate stewards rode them in peace time. They were called "rouncies".

Apart from the Welsh Cob, they are not a breed and are produced usually by chance. They are quite often the by-product of Hunter breeding. They did not grow large but had great substance. The breeding stock for Cobs is highly varied, but some examples are a Highland and a small Thoroughbred, a Suffolk Punch and an Arab, or a Hunter mare and an Arab. (See also Welsh Cob, pages 142-143.)

The Cob has a ponylike head on a muscular crested neck and a strong sloping shoulder. It should also have a deep, broad body, a short back, rounded quarters, short limbs with plenty of bone and very short cannons. Feet are hard and round.

The other feature of the Cob is its temperament. It is supposed to be very tractable and have high-class manners. This makes it a good ride for older and nervous people. It is also used by race-horse trainers to watch their horses work. It is an excellent hunter over rough country or for heavy riders who do not want to go too fast.

Its other use is as a show horse. Classes are held for Cobs at most major British shows.

HACK

Country of origin
Britain.
Height
Varies from country to country.
Color
Any.
Features
A refined, elegant horse that is a pleasure to ride and has great "presence".

"Hack" is a term that has been used to describe a variety of horses. It once meant a horse for hire. Then it came to mean the horse ridden to the meets (covert hack) before transferring to the hunter that was brought by the groom. Later, it was the name given to the elegant, refined horse ridden by fashionable people. Today, it covers different types of

Above: The head of a Cob, which is small and of good quality.

horses in different countries. In the United States, "Hack" usually refers to a riding horse. It can also refer to a pleasure-type American Saddlebred or Hunter. A Bridle-path Hack is usually a Saddlebred type; a Hunter Hack is typically a Thoroughbred and a Road Hack can be a Morgan, Saddlebred or any good-trotting English pleasure horse. In Australia it is a Thoroughbred, and in Britain it is a smaller horse, occasionally a Thoroughbred, but usually a crossbred.

Today's Hacks are showy animals, which are well trained, responsive to the aids (means of controlling the horse) and very easy to ride. They are supposed

Below: A prize-winning Cob at the 1984 Royal Show, Stoneleigh, UK.

to be horses which give pleasure to riders who like non-competitive activities, such as hacking, but who also like to look good. To be an enjoyable ride, the Hack should have impeccable manners and light, easy gaits.

Classes are held for Hacks in various English-speaking countries. Although terms of reference vary (height, work required, etc.), all are for lightweight, elegant riding horses.

The principle criteria for judging Hacks is conformation, "presence", action, training, manners and ride. Contestants are required to give a short demonstration of their correct training.

The head should have great quality and be small. The neck should be elegant and crested, the body deep, quarters rounded and limbs correct and fine. Action should be light, straight and true.

HUNTER

Country of origin
Britain.
Height
14·2-17·2hh (58-70in).
Color
Any.
Features
A courageous type, bold enough to get across country, yet clever enough to stay out of trouble. The Hunter must also have great stamina and provide the rider with a comfortable, smooth means of following hounds. In addition, Show Hunters need to have correct, harmonious conformation, "presence" and good free paces.

The Hunter carries a rider behind hounds. It will vary greatly according to the requirements, i.e. the weight of the rider, the type of quarry being chased, and the type of terrain over which the hunting takes place. All Hunters have some features in common; these include intelligence, "handiness" (the ability to get out of trouble when going across country), stamina, jumping ability good temperament, good con-

Above: The champion show Hack, Tenterk, ridden by Robert Oliver. This fine horse has the elegant action of a true Hack.

Below: When young, Hunters are also shown in hand. This is Celtic Gold, which was champion young Hunter at The Royal Show, Stoneleigh, UK, in 1982.

In Britain there are classes for Small Hunters, which are 14·2-15·2hh (58-62in); Lightweight Hunters, typically capable of carrying up to 175lb (79kg); Middle-weight Hunters, typically capable of carrying over 195lb (88kg); and Lady's Hunters which are horses suitable for carrying a lady side-saddle. In all of these classes the Hunters are judged upon how they perform on the flat. They should show free, straight, correct paces, particularly in the gallop. They should also have good manners, give a good ride to the judges, be sound and have a conformation that is likely to keep them this way, with harmonious proportions to the body, correct limbs and sufficient bone.

In the United States and in Britain's Working Hunter classes they are also required to jump. In the United States style is very important, and it is essential to maintain a constant rhythm into the fences.

The American classes are also split into divisions, some according to weight-carrying capacity, others according to the experience and previous successes of the horses. A Green Hunter is one in its first or second year of showing. A Working Hunter is one regularly hunted to hounds, and a Heavyweight Hunter one capable of carrying 200lb (91kg) or more.

The Hunter often turns out to be a good showjumper and, with the growth of this sport, the Jumper has become an important subdivision of the Hunter type.

formation and soundness.

In grassy country where there are plenty of fences to jump, a fast horse is needed, and the Thoroughbred or near Thoroughbred is considered the best.

In country where the going is deep and holding, a short-legged and powerful animal is more suitable. In hilly country, a balanced sure-footed horse with the stamina

for the hard work of climbing up inclines is needed. In rough country, where there are many obstacles and little open land, a clever, handy horse of Cob type is suitable. Consequently, there are various subdivisions within the Hunter type. In addition, there are many other separate classes of Hunters that are used in the show ring.

POLO PONY

Country of origin
Argentina is the most successful producer.

Height
14·2-15·3hh (58-63in).

Color
Any.

Features
Courageous, spirited, tough, agile, fast types, that are usually almost Thoroughbred.

Some of the original Polo Ponies, such as the Manipurs from India, were true breeds. Over the last century, when the game was introduced to Europe and North and South America, the height of these ponies has increased. They now usually range from 14·2hh (58in) to 15·3hh (63in). Although they have become horses, they are still referred to as ponies.

No single breed has been established as *the* Polo Pony. A number

Below: Polo Ponies in action on the unusual surface of snow.

Polo Pony
(147-160cm)

Riding Pony
(Maximum 147cm)

of small Thoroughbreds are used, but it is the crossbred which has excelled. Argentina's Polo Pony is generally recognized as the best in the world. It is produced by crossing tough Criollos with Thoroughbreds.

In the 1890s, efforts were made in Britain to establish a good Polo Pony by using pony blood from some of Britain's native Mountain and Moorland ponies, and the Thoroughbred. World War I disrupted this program, and it was never re-established. Instead, most countries have used imported Argentinian mares that have been crossbred to the Thoroughbred.

The Polo Pony is judged by its performance on the field. It must be able to gallop, to accelerate and stop very quickly, and to turn on a dime or sixpence. It must be bold and strong enough to ride off the opposition. Polo Ponies do not need to be beautiful, but they must be tough and athletic, with a robust conformation.

Most Polo Ponies tend to have long thin necks, angular bodies with very strong quarters, correct sound limbs and quite upright pasterns.

RIDING PONY

Country of origin
  Britain.
Height
  Up to 14·2hh (58in).
Color
  Any.
Features
  Types with good conformation, action and manners, that are suitable for children to ride.

Most pony breeds evolved in the wild over the centuries. They had to be tough to survive and usually have a touch of native cunning, which makes them less tractable and trainable. Their robust bodies tend to be broad, which makes it difficult for children to get their legs around them. They are not ideal children's ponies.

A more athletic, gentle, elegant pony is required, and this has led to crossbreeding between native ponies and Thoroughbreds and Arabs. The Thoroughbred and Arab added the "class," elegance, athleticism and harmonious conformation.

Above: One of the many uses of the Riding Pony is showing. These are the prizewinners in a riding class at a major show.

Below: Most of the world's Riding Ponies are used for hacking out and general riding, and do not ever enter shows.

Many countries have followed this procedure. Some have followed the principles of selective breeding and have started a stud book such as those for the Australian Pony and German Riding Pony. In other countries, the process has been left to individual efforts. These ponies remain types, not breeds.

A riding pony has a good temperament, with the manners needed to give children confidence. Its conformation is harmonious and correct, and its paces are free, straight and true.

Most countries hold show classes for riding ponies. These are usually divided up to 12·2hh (50in), 12·2-13·2hh (50-54in), and 13·2-14·2hh (54-58in). Ponies that do well in these classes tend to be elegant, near-Thoroughbred types. In addition, most countries hold classes for working ponies. They are required to jump, when style and way of going is important. These working ponies do not need to be pretty as long as they are good performers and often these good performers have more substance and less Thoroughbred blood.

GUIDE TO HORSE BREEDING

This chapter deals with all aspects of the fascinating and rewarding subject of horse breeding, and gives sound practical advice on how best to go about it.

It opens with a guide to the selection of suitable parents, then goes on to the specific tasks of choosing a stallion and a mare. There follows an account of planning a stud, from the design of buildings to the choice of grass, and then a concise account of the biology of horse reproduction.

The next sections deal with stallion management and mare management, and these are followed by a comprehensive account of the all-important processes of trying and covering.

Proper treatment of the pregnant mare is vital for successful breeding, and this is fully explained. The process of foaling is described in detail, with the help of step-by-step pictures, and possible complications are covered, too.

Finally, there is a full account of the care of youngstock, from the newborn foal to the two-year-old.

SELECTION OF PARENTS

Facing the Facts

Breeding is one of the most rewarding of equestrian activities, and it has the advantage that it can be done at all levels from multimillion dollar investments in a Thoroughbred stud to having a pony in a backyard paddock. Breeders have the satisfaction of watching the youngsters grow from fragile, fluffy creatures into animals they can ride and drive, or at least whose progress can be followed, especially if it is a racehorse, competition horse or show horse.

To those contemplating these romantic-sounding activities, there are some hard facts to be faced. Although native breeds of pony that have long bred in the wild can be left very much on their own, most of the more-refined breeds need regular attention, adequate facilities, occasional veterinary treatment, feed and knowledgeable handling. Although a pony may involve little expense, the higher the quality of the horse, the greater the expense involved in breeding. It is vital that the type of horse you choose to breed is one you have the knowledge, experience, facilities and finances to cope with.

The breeding of most horses involves considerable time and expense. It is worth making the best possible preparations and, in particular, taking careful consideration over selection. The higher the quality and ability of the horse bred, the greater the returns in terms of pleasure and finance when it is old enough to be shown or ridden.

The selection of parents is a fascinating study and one that has intrigued breeders of quality stock, especially racehorse breeders. The major requirements are common sense, a clear idea of the type of horse or pony to be bred and the application to gather and use data about the parents.

It is surprising how many people go into breeding simply because they take pity on some mare. They think of the joys of seeing her with a foal. They don't bother too much about the selection of a stallion and are happy to use one nearby. They think little about the future of the foal or what purpose it will serve. It often ends up valueless, rather a nuisance to its breeders, and the only person who will buy it is the meat man. Apart from the unhappy ending, the breeder has missed out on one of the most fascinating aspects of breeding— the selection of parents that are complementary so the breeder has the greatest possible chance of producing a horse that is both sound and talented.

The Goal

It is much more fun and interesting to start from another angle, and to decide what type of horse or pony it would be interesting to breed. Establish a clear goal, whether it is to be a racehorse, a show jumper, riding pony or a

purebred to be shown. List the qualities needed to achieve this goal, such as athletic ability, substance, power, courage, trainability, good temperament, good looks, elegance, good conformation, correct size or pretty movement. See which of these qualities are necessary for the breeding of a chosen type of horse or pony.

The only common feature to all goals is soundness, otherwise the requirements needed to achieve the goal vary considerably. The important factor is to clarify the assets needed.

Breeding Criteria
The next stage is to find parents that will reproduce these assets. There are four sources of data to help breeders ascertain if a horse or pony is likely to do so. These are the appearance of the parents, their records when performing, the pedigrees of ancestors and their progeny records.

When searching for suitable parents, it's important to realize the perfect horse or pony is *never* found. There will always be defects, but as long as the defect is not serious and the other parent does not suffer from it, then it can be accepted. Consequently, if a mare has a long back, look for a short backed stallion and one that passed on this particular feature to its progeny (offspring). The matings should be complementary.

Appearance
The appearance is the easiest criterion to investigate. The conformation, temperament and action of prospective parents can be examined to see if they behave, move and look like the type of animal you are aiming for. If one has a weakness, such as stiff movement, the other should be a particularly athletic mover and known to be prepotent for it. (*Prepotency* is the tendency in a horse to pass on its features to its offspring.)

Pedigree
Appearance is important but it cannot be taken as the sole criterion. It does not reflect the ▶

Left: Ben Faerie, the stallion that proved himself through such progeny as Priceless (Olympic Silver Medal) and Night Cap.

Above: This mare's progeny is too young to be judged on anything other than its conformation, but in less than 2 years it should race.

Below: The long-backed stallion (left) would be more suitable for the short-backed mare (center) than the long-backed mare (right).

Above: The most successful purpose-bred purebred is the Thoroughbred. It is a breed that was developed to race.

▶genetic makeup of a horse and it can be affected by the environment and feed. A tall mare may produce only small offspring because the genes for being tall were present in her parents only in minute quantities. For example, both parents were small but by some fluke the tall genes happened to be dominant and they produced a tall daughter. The few tall genes in her makeup were ineffective, and her progeny were small.

It's important that the genetic material of the parents has a high concentration of the required assets. This is best ascertained by consideration of two further criteria—the pedigree and the progeny. If the parents' ancestors and any offspring have the required traits, there must be a high

concentration of them in their genetic material.

A study of the pedigree for the above-mentioned tall mare might have revealed that her parents were small, and she was carrying a diluted quantity of genes for height. It is important to study the pedigree and determine if the ancestors possess the required assets.

Type of Breeding

The type of breeding (inbreeding, linebreeding or crossbreeding) is also important. If it is found that the potential parent is inbred (such as mother and son or brother and sister matings) or linebred (relations mated but a larger generation gap), and that the ancestor which consequently appears two or more times in the pedigree is prepotent for specific assets, there will be a high concentration of those traits. However, it is important to ensure that the stock to which it is inbred or linebred is prepotent for desirable, not undesirable, traits. Inbreeding can consolidate weaknesses and strengths. Also inbreeding leads to a loss of vigor, so this effect must be considered. If both parents have an asset in large amounts, and so do all their ancestors, then the offspring is likely to inherit that asset. The problem arises when one wants to breed a number of assets into a horse, and no purebred exists that possesses them all. Such has been the case this century in the escalating production of competition horses. The breeding goals are athleticism, suppleness, a tractable temperament, good size and substance. No single breed fulfills all these requirements, so crossbreeding (the mating of two entirely different breeds or types) becomes necessary.

When crossbreeding, it is important to select fairly similar types. A cross between a Shire and a Thoroughbred, if unlucky, might produce a huge-bodied horse on fine legs, or, if lucky, a good heavyweight with the required features of each in the right proportions. When the genes are such opposites the make, shape and ability of an offspring cannot be forecast and breeding with such extremes can be dangerous.

It is wiser to crossbreed fairly similar types, such as a small Thoroughbred with a Connemara. This crossbred (which should be bigger than the Connemara) can be put to a larger Thoroughbred, and a good-sized competition horse will be the likely progeny. Crossbreeding of similar types can help you forecast the make and shape of the offspring more accurately. And when that offspring is used as breeding stock itself, a lack of extreme genes means its genetic material is reasonably

Left: Connemara foals. This breed is good foundation stock with Thoroughbreds for producing competition horses.

Above: Overton Amanda, an Olympic team silver medalist for Britain in 1984 and an ideal mare with which to breed.

well-concentrated.

Consequently, pedigrees must be examined carefully to see if there has been any outcrossing, and if so, how extreme, because this affects the ability of parents to pass on their own traits.

Crossbreeding has another advantage; it restores vigor, so if there has been a great deal of inbreeding, then an outside cross gives an invigorating effect.

Progeny

The progeny are the best indicators of a parent's ability to pass on its traits. Unfortunately, this criterion cannot be used until the parents have produced many offspring. For mares with a maximum of one foal a year (and most mares fail to get in foal every 3 or 4 years), it takes many years before a fair assessment can be made. With stallions, particularly those that are popular and have many mares in a season, an assessment can be made earlier, when the

stallions are still young.

Making a serious analysis of a stallion's progeny is the best means of finding out which assets he will pass on, although this is easier for racehorses who run at 2 years than it is for competition horses.

Performance

The final criterion for breeding is performance. Like appearance, this is usually a good indicator. But, on occasion, it can be misleading. There are always freak horses or ponies that are brilliant in themselves but which do not have a concentration of the genetic material to pass on to their progeny. Making allowances for these exceptions, in most cases examination of performance records is an aid and does increase the chances of achieving the breeding goal. The likelihood is a horse that jumps in great style is more likely to produce a talented jumper than one that jumps poorly.

The important factor when making a selection is to remember none of the four criteria are reliable on their own. It is only by studying all of them—appearance, performance, pedigree and progeny—that a reasonable assessment can be made as to the type of progeny a mare will produce if put to a similarly studied stallion. There are bound to be exceptions to the predicted results, but by making a careful selection you are shortening the odds in favor of producing the breeding goal, and increasing the chances of breeding a talented horse or pony. This makes the effort worthwhile, and the process involves fascinating studies. No breeder should ever rely on haphazard selection of parents.

CHOOSING A MARE

A brood mare is selected on the basis of her appearance, performance and pedigree, as well as progeny, if she has any. There has been less emphasis on performance for mares than for stallions, usually because a mare's performance is considerably affected when she comes into season. For this reason, many mares never realize their full potential. Also the effects of a mare's breeding are less widespread. The average mare produces about five foals in her lifetime, while a stallion may sire as many as a thousand.

When judging appearance, there are the specialist factors to be considered, such as a springy, elastic trot for a dressage horse, a free sweeping walk for a race horse, black color for a Friesian or a spotted coat for a Knabstrup. But there are also many general qualities that every brood mare should possess. The first of these is soundness. If the mare has a physical problem, it should not be an inherited one. Many people breed from an old mare they can no longer ride because she has

Below: This brood mare has a deep body and an air of femininity. She has a harmonious, well-proportioned body, an elegant head and a convex curve to the neck that smoothly joins the withers and the deep sloping shoulders. The withers are defined, the back gently curved, the hindquarters strong and the hind legs neither too straight nor too bent.

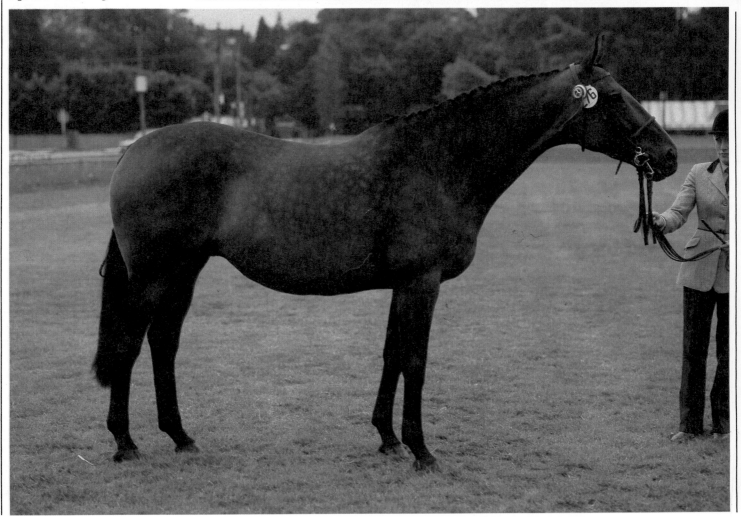

navicular or has gone in the wind, but she is likely to pass on these same defects to her progeny.

The next consideration is conformation—the make and shape of the horse. For a purebred, there will be specialist features the breeder tries to ensure are passed on to the progeny, such as the flat croup of the Arab. But generally there are certain factors everybody would like to see in their foals. A horse with good conformation is more likely to stay sound and work better than one with weak points. Such a horse will also be more valuable.

Despite this, it is worth remembering that weaknesses in conformation, as well as defici- encies in movement and tempera- ment, can be accepted in a mare if she is put to a stallion that is particularly strong in these points and will therefore offset these defects. A weakness is more acceptable if surrounded by strong points, so a relatively straight hind leg is more permissible if the hock is broad and has a good shape, and the quarters are powerful.

A mare must have particular features if she is to be a good breeder. Her heart and lung capacity is important when she is feeding her foal, so she should be deep and broad in the chest and body. It is also important to have her breeding organs checked by a vet if she has not produced a foal, to ensure she is capable of doing so.

The last factor that can be judged simply by a horse's appearance is an air of femininity and grace. Sturdy masculine mares tend to be much more difficult to get in foal. It is also

vital for a mare to have a good temperament. If she is unreason- able, she will be difficult to look after, and it is likely to make the progeny difficult to handle and train. Allowances can be made for mares being more flighty and unpredictable than geldings, but their general approach should still be bold, generous and gentle. The movement is also important, but it is more of a specialist's

Above: This brood mare has proved her fertility by producing a foal; its good looks give confidence in her as a brood mare.

feature. A work horse might be wanted with short strides, a Hackney with high strides, a race- horse with long strides or a dressage horse with free, supple, rounded strides.

Above: Brood mares graze in a well- fenced field, Ballykisteen stud, Eire

Below: A well-proportioned mare by the Cleveland Bay, Forest Superman.

CHOOSING A STALLION

The stallion, also called an *entire* or *stud,* is selected using the same criteria as the mare—appearance, performance, pedigree and progeny. In his case, there usually are performance records, either on the race track or in specific performance tests. If he is old enough, the most reliable test of all can be used—looking at the appearance and performance of his progeny. The ideal stallion is prepotent in the aims of the breeding goal, so he stamps his stock with the desired traits. Seek out his progeny, find out what they have done, and see what their appearance is like.

It is important to look at the appearance of the stallion, and when putting a mare to him, ensure that his conformation, temperament and movement are complementary to hers. It does not matter so much as in the mare if he is deep through his body, but this is still an asset. In contrast to the mare, he should give an impression of masculinity and an air of precociousness and pride.

There is an additional criterion for the selection of stallions—fertility. There is no point in choosing a stallion that rarely gets his mares in foal because he will not be commercially viable if you buy him. He may prove to be an expensive waste of time if

Below: A Thoroughbred Stallion that has a precious, masculine air. He is a compact horse with a bold, intelligent outlook, and the stallion's typical crested neck.

you send your mare to him. It is important to check fertility rates before making a final choice.

Most breeders will select stallions for use with their mares, not for purchase. Stallions need more skillful handling than mares, as discussed in a later section on stallion management. For those embarking on breeding horses, begin with mares or employ an experienced stud groom who

knows how to deal with stallions.

Paying for the Stallion
The services of a stallion must be paid for, and the amount varies from nominal sums for pony stallions to hundreds of thousands of dollars for a top Thoroughbred. Payment can be made in many ways. A syndicate share can be bought in a stallion and up to 40 are issued, entitling owners to

Above: A handsome stallion with its vital air of precociousness.

one service per year. Alternatively, there are nominations, which are usually sold at special auctions, entitling the purchaser to send his mare for service that year. Shares and nominations are the usual procedure for top racehorses, but for the less valuable, stud fees are

normally paid. This can be a straight fee that is due after the service. "No foal, no fee" is payable a few months after the season ends, unless a veterinary certificate is produced stating the mare is not in foal. "Live-foal guarantee" or "no foal free return", as it is known in the UK, means that the fee is due after service but the mare can return to the stallion for a free return if she is barren or has a dead foal.

The size of the fee affects selection, but breeders should remember that the costs of breeding are high (feed, vets, livery fees when at stud). A little more paid for a good stallion is small compared with these costs, yet it is likely to yield much higher returns in terms of talent and value of progeny. The price paid for youngstock is determined largely by the sire.

The final factor in selection of a stallion depends on where he stands. High-class management is important if the mare is to get in foal and return in good shape. Complaints are all too common about poor attention given to mares, so careful investigation of the stud facilities is absolutely necessary for good results.

Right: A handsome Welsh Section B stallion, a winner in his class.

Below: These stallions' stables have been built separately from the stables for other horses.

161

Grassland

The facilities at studs vary from a few fields in which two or three mares run free all year to luxurious, double-fenced paddocks, stables, barns and covering facilities. Studs that house stallions as a commercial business must give a good impression to mare owners, but all stud owners need serviceable facilities for the well-being of their horses. One vital facility is sufficient grassland. As a rough guide, 1 acre should provide enough pasture and space for two to three ponies, or 2 acres should be enough for three horses.

It is not enough to let grass grow naturally. Horses do a lot of damage to grass. If this damage is not taken care of, the grass will turn sour, or it will lead to excessive growth of weeds so the land becomes "horse sick" (see opposite page).

Grassland management is an important, but often neglected, part of stud work. Good grazing makes healthy stock.

The most productive types of grasses for a stud are bluegrass (ryegrass) and timothy. The ideal type of land has a limestone subsoil, that is rich in the phosphorus and calcium needed for the growth of healthy horses. The soil can be analyzed for any elements that are lacking. These can be added easily. Lime should be at a pH level of 6 to 6.5, and the phosphorus should be at ADAS Index 2. There must also be adequate potash (usually deficient in sandy soils) and nitrogen in the soil. Additions of lime or other fertilizers can correct the chemical composition of the soil, but it is also advisable to spread farmyard manure on the land. This helps the humus level and provides extra phosphate and potash.

Applications of specific additions to the land should be done at specific times. Lime is best spread in November, usually about every 5 years. Apply phosphates, which stimulate growth of the nutritious clover, in the spring. The potash salts are most effective if administered after a hay crop but *never* with a nitrogen application in the spring or before the autumn growth. Apply nitrogen, which will be most effective if phosphate-lime and potash levels are correct, 3-6 weeks before growth of the grass is required. When spreading manure, which must be stored for at least 6 weeks, don't graze the field for another 6 weeks.

To ensure the highest productivity of grass, a soil analysis is advisable every 4 to 5 years. This can be done by contacting your local agricultural agent.

Grass cannot grow efficiently in waterlogged fields, so drainage must be considered. Sand, chalk or gravel-type soils may drain naturally. But for clay lands, in particular, a drainage system is needed. This can be expensive, but it is a long term economy in terms of fertility and consequent yield. If

Above: A collection of mares and foals grazing on green grass. There are few weeds and no clumps of tough grass in this field.

a field remains ungrazed for such a period of time, due to waterlogging, it isn't an asset at all.

Drainage and adding correct elements are basic requirements, but there is other work involved in grassland management that needs to be done more frequently.

The first of these is harrowing. This drags out dead moss and grass and prevents a mat from forming. For this purpose, the spokes of the harrow must be long, and heavy enough, to dig into the grass. Harrowing also helps scatter droppings. Do it often because droppings sour the ground; only tough grass, which the horses will not eat, grows in their vicinity. Scattering droppings also reduces worm infestation because worms which thrive in damp piles of droppings tend to dry out and die in the sun and air. However, no matter how frequently you harrow, it will not totally eradicate worm infestation. Most high-class studs pursue the time-consuming but effective work of picking up droppings daily to ensure against

Left: Picking up droppings is the only way to stop worm infestation when acreage is limited and there is no crop rotation.

the worm hazard.

Rolling is another activity best done with a tractor (although both activities can be done with a pony or work horse in harness). This is not as essential to maintaining or increasing productivity, but it helps improve damaged pasture, and consolidates topsoil after frequent frosts, thaws or floods.

Understocking a field can be damaging. If the grass grows too quickly for the horses to keep it grazed, they won't eat the long grass. If this occurs, the higher, unpalatable grass needs to be cut.

Topping the grass is often necessary, even in fields that have been well grazed, because horses tend to leave patches of long grass. To make these areas more palatable requires regular cutting.

Efforts should be made to keep weeds down. Among the most common weeds are buttercups and thistles, which can be sprayed in late spring. Cut

Below: A foal grazing on what appears to be poor grassland. There is little length to the grass; the foal is eating thistles.

Above: This lush, green pasture should provide the good keep that is so important for the mare and foal.

burdocks (docks) in July after flowering, but before seeding. Spray ragwort in late spring. Other than chemical prevention, some weed control can be achieved by maintaining a correct stocking rate, good drainage and a rotation of land use. Where all else fails, reseeding may become necessary.

The alternate use of good pasture is vital. If the grass is used only for horses it is difficult to avoid "horse sickness". This occurs when the pasture is infested with worms and they are eaten by the horses. In large numbers the worms can greatly affect the horses' health causing loss of condition, colic and even death.

As mentioned above, horses are bad grazers, concentrating on certain areas and not touching others, so the grass length becomes very uneven, with "rings" of long coarse grass. The ideal solution to these problems is to rotate horse grazing with cattle grazing. Cattle reduce the worm count by eating the horse worms, and they will graze patches of grass left by the horses. It's better if the horses graze the land first and the cattle follow. Don't keep them both in the same field at the same time.

Sheep can also be used as alternate grazers, but, although better than nothing, they are not as effective as cattle.

Alternating a hay crop with horse grazing is another beneficial rotation method worth trying. ▶

▶ Fencing

Good fencing is necessary to minimize accidents. Horses, particularly youngstock, have an unfortunate tendency to gallop or slip into things that hurt them, so all sources of danger must be removed. Use common sense to ensure that there are no sharp-angled corners into which horses can gallop. Smooth the edges of troughs, stakes and old trees. Gates should be solid; never use barbed wire.

Ideally a paddock fence should be high, strong and solid. Wood rails are the most suitable material for fencing, but they are expensive. There is some special wire available, designed specifically for stud fences, that seems safe. Chain wire, as long as it is pulled taut between strong posts, is relatively safe. Natural, thick hedges are also usually an effective barrier as well as making the paddock look attractive.

The ideal size for an enclosed paddock is about 6 acres. It is best to have smaller areas rather than huge fields because it's easier to catch stock and inspect it. The availability of a number of paddocks makes alternate use easier as well as the safe division of horses.

It is best to separate barren mares and mares with foals. Geldings should be kept well apart from mares and foals, and only one gelding should be allowed to graze with barren mares: two or more tend to fight. Separate young horses from older horses; colts and fillies can usually run together until they are 18 months old, then they need to be separated. Stallions must always be kept away from all other stock.

Shelter

Another facility needed in a field is shelter. The type depends on the weather and stock. Native breeds in most weather and refined breeds in summer need only a few trees and perhaps a high hedge or wall to protect them against strong winds and rain or flies. For horses out the year round, a hut is advisable. One that is provided with a wide entrance is best, so horses can move freely in and out.

Water

There should be an abundant supply of fresh water at *all* times. Stagnant pools are dangerous. If there is no running stream in the field, a piped supply to a trough with an automatic filling device is necessary.

The Buildings

The quality and quantity of buildings depends on the type and size of the stock. Studs for Thoroughbred stallions have the most luxurious facilities, because investments are high, and these are delicate creatures. For native ponies, little is needed other than storage facilities for food, a tack room and some stables for veterinary care. Even a foaling box is rarely essential because ponies are usually best left to follow their natural instincts,

Above: These Thoroughbred yearlings are enclosed by sturdy wood posts and rails; this is expensive but safe fencing.

Below: A mare and foal in front of a good shelter that has a broad entrance and an adequate amount of space inside.

Below: The well-designed stables for stallions at the Irish National Stud.

Above: Cold-blood stallions have equitable temperaments and are kept in stalls at Le Pin State Stud, France.

Right: Baron Blackeney, a Thoroughbred stallion, being ridden for exercise.

and foal out in the field.

Storage facilities for feed must be designed so hay can be kept under cover and grain is protected from the damp and from vermin, such as rats or mice.

Stables need to be large enough to house the horses but designs vary considerably, from barns where all the stalls are inside, looking onto a central passage, to yards where all the horses look out. It's advisable to have some isolation boxes in case of diseases or contagious skin infections. Most studs have one or more foaling boxes that are larger, approximately 12 x 16ft (3·7 x 4·9m) in area, and easily observable.

For expensive stock, it's advisable to have a peep hole through to an adjoining room where stud hands can keep watch. Some studs now use closed-circuit television to provide this observation facility.

At a stallion stud, a covering yard is necessary where mares can be tried and covered with optimum ease and safety. Stallion studs should always have special exercising areas. An indoor school or outdoor school with a high fence is best. Horses can then be set free, lunged or ridden. For highly-strung stallions that cannot be turned out in a field, a small paddock with a special high fence is advisable.

THE BIOLOGY OF REPRODUCTION

Physiology of the Mare

To be able to give the mare the best possible care and opportunity to get in foal, it helps to know a little about her physiology and anatomy. The amount of knowledge needed will vary. If native ponies are the breeding stock they can be left to run free and little assistance is needed. But the more refined the stock, the closer it is to being Thoroughbred, the more knowledge of breeding is required.

The important organs are the two ovaries that are connected to the Fallopian tubes. This is where fertilization occurs. These tubes lead to the uterus, which is able to expand and house the foal. Beyond the uterus is the cervix, the vagina and the vulva, which together make up the birth canal. At the lower end of the vulva is the small, round clitoris, which may sometimes harbor venereal microbes. Sex hormones are produced by the anterior pituitary gland, the ovaries and the uterus.

The Estrus Cycle

When a mare matures to achieve puberty—usually between 15 and 24 months, although she can be as old as 4 years—cyclical changes start to occur in these organs. The correct terminology for this is the *estrus cycle*. The estrus cycle is also referred to as being "in heat," "in season," "on," "in use" or "showing," and it usually lasts for 5 days. During this time, the mare will accept the stallion, but for the following 15 days she will not. She is then said to be in *diestrus,* "out of season," or "not showing." The cycle lasts for about 20 days.

This cycle is controlled by hormones. A *follicle stimulating hormone* (FSH) produced by the growth of follicles (fluid sacs that form around the eggs just below the surface of the ovary). These follicles produce estrogen that affects the mare's behavior. She will then come into season and accept the stallion.

Signs of Estrus

There are several distinct signs that a mare is in season. The tail goes up, the cervix relaxes, the

genital track becomes moist and "winking" occurs: this is when the vulval lips open and close. The mare also passes urine frequently. Stretching her neck up and out and raising her upper lip is another sign a mare is in season and ready to be covered.

Usually on the fifth day of being in season, one follicle that has grown larger than the others (about 1-1¼ in) ruptures from the stimulation of another pituitary hormone called the *luteinizing hormone (LH)*. The egg is released, and the ruptured follicle becomes a yellow body that secretes the hormone *progesterone*. This hormone then induces the typical behavior of a mare "out of season". The cervix closes, the genital track becomes dry and she is likely to kick the stallion if he gets too close. The egg passes into the Fallopian tubes where fertilization can occur.

If it is fertilized, it moves into the uterus. There the uterus starts preparations for pregnancy, but if the egg is not fertile, these will be

stopped about the 15th day of the cycle. The hormone that stops these activities is *prostaglandin,* which is secreted by the uterus and stops the yellow body on the ovary from producing progesterone. About the same time, there is a switch in secretion from LH to FSH by the pituitary. Another cycle is then started.

Changing the Cycle

It is possible for veterinarians, to use hormones to control the cycle and increase the chances of difficult mares becoming pregnant.

The estrus cycle does not occur normally all year round. Native mares running free tend to come into season in late spring and summer only. They produce their foal at the best possible time, when the grass is growing and the climate is most conducive to the foal's well-being. More-refined breeds, in particular racehorses and show horses, have been encouraged to come into season earlier so they can produce foals that will be more

Above: A veterinarian irrigating a mare's uterus.

Below: Equipment used by vets to facilitate mare examinations.

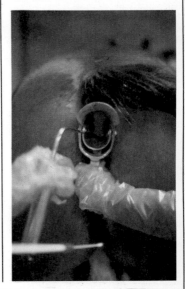

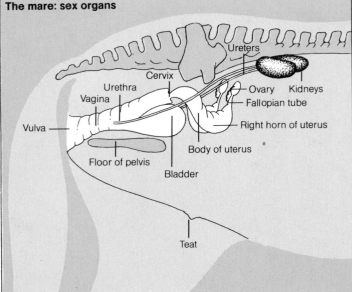

The mare: sex organs

Ureters
Cervix
Urethra
Vagina
Vulva
Ovary   Kidneys
Fallopian tube
Right horn of uterus
Body of uterus
Floor of pelvis
Bladder
Teat

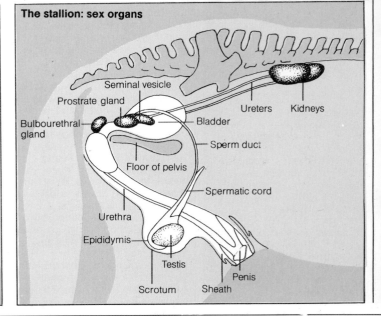

The stallion: sex organs

Seminal vesicle
Prostrate gland
Bulbourethral gland
Ureters   Kidneys
Bladder
Sperm duct
Floor of pelvis
Spermatic cord
Urethra
Epididymis
Testis
Penis
Scrotum   Sheath

mature when they are needed to race or show.

The artificial life of horses who are stabled and are given an abundance of feed has been proved to have led to an earlier annual start to the estrus cycle. The use of artificial aids, such as light and hormones, can be used to induce an estrus cycle even in winter.

Variations in the Cycle
Most mares come into season every 3 weeks for 3 to 4 months every year, but there are many variations. Ovulation may not occur the first few times the mare comes into season each year, or ovulation can occur when the mare is not in season. A mare can be out of season for more than 15 days, which usually means she did not ovulate in the previous season. Alternatively, she may come into season and ovulate without showing any of the behavioral signs. Then there is the "normal" variation, when the mare with a new foal comes into season about 9 days after foaling. She is considered to be exceptionally fertile during that season. Pregnant mares will not come into season, although they have been known to accept the stallion, but then they usually lose their foal.

Length of Pregnancy
Pregnancy last about 11 months (336 days), but smaller breeds tend to have a shorter gestation. There are considerable variations; 10 days either way is not unusual, and there can be normal births 2 weeks early and 3 or 4 weeks late.

Fertilization and Development
Pregnancy occurs when the egg is fertilized by the sperm in the Fallopian tubes. Eggs die within 24 hours and are at their most fertile when they first enter the tubes. It is best for the mare to be served by the stallion *before,* not after, ovulation. The fertilized egg passes into the uterus or womb. The egg grows by dividing into an increasing number of cells and becoming loosely attached to the lining of the uterus. Differentiation of the cells occurs so the embryo gradually changes from a one-celled fertilized egg into a miniature horse. About 60 days after fertilization it is called the fetus.

Embryo and Fetus
Membranes form around the embryo as it develops into the fetus. The outer one is referred to as the "bag of waters" at birth. The placenta is the membrane through which the embryo receives oxygen, nourishment and removes its waste material. It is also where the fetal blood comes into close contact, but does not actually mix, with the mother's. The placenta is loosely attached to the uterine wall, and to the embryo by the umbilical cord, but it is not part of the foal's body so it can be discarded at birth.

The umbilical cord contains two major arteries and a vein, together with a duct connected to the foal's

Above: A mare grazing peacefully with her foal. It is important to give mares as natural an existence as possible.

bladder. The placenta contains the allantoic fluid which escapes at birth with the rupture of the placenta and the "breaking of waters". It consists partly of waste material not yet removed through the placental-uterine contact, and it is kept separate from the embryo by another membrane called the "amnion". This membrane protects the foal during pregnancy from the allantoic fluid. During birth, its slippery surface helps delivery through the birth canal. The amnion contains the amniotic fluid that bathes the airways of the fetus' head, neck, eyes, skin and ears. The fetus also swallows it to lubricate the stomach and intestine. Both the allantoic and the amniotic fluids act as shock absorbers to the fetus. Both the amniotic and placental membranes make up what is known in the foaling as the 'afterbirth'.

Development of the Fetus
As the embryo grows into the fetus, the walls of the uterus stretch, but the uterus walls are sealed from the outside by the cervix. The organs develop, and all internal ones are present after 1 month gestation but most do not function until birth. The exception to this is the heart, which provides blood circulation and nourishment. There is clearly some activity in the intestines because these contain waste material at birth.

The embryo

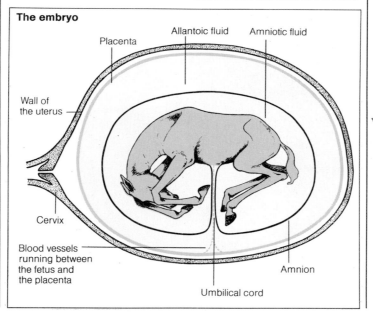

Placenta
Allantoic fluid
Amniotic fluid
Wall of the uterus
Cervix
Blood vessels running between the fetus and the placenta
Amnion
Umbilical cord

STALLION MANAGEMENT

Handling

A high-quality stallion is the most majestic and noble of horses. In his natural habitat he is the custodian of a herd of mares and youngstock. For this he needs courage and intelligence to ward off competitors and predators, and pride, strength and high spirits to establish and maintain his supremacy. These features, retained even by those breeds of stallion that have experienced centuries of domestication, make him the most admired and eye-catching type of horse and one which is quick to learn—both to obey and to disobey. If handled by someone who understands these traits, who is confident and who only makes reasonable demands, a stallion can be a very co-operative partner. Equally, he soon realizes who is frightened of him: a timorous pat, or a hesitant or unreasonable command, and he is quick to display his high spirits and courage in willful disobedience. Stallions need handlers who are relaxed, confident, positive and sympathetic in their work; they must grow to trust their handlers, who must never show fear.

This handling is relatively easy in the case of ponies which are small and affable in character, and it is

Right: Stallions, particularly Thoroughbreds, are high-spirited animals, as this horse shows at the St Lô Stud in France.

not too difficult even for the huge but gentle work horses, and for Arabs and warm-bloods which are specifically bred to have a good temperament. But for the most valuable breed of stallion—the Thoroughbred—it can take great skill. In the past, many high-spirited stallions were cooped up in boxes away from other horses, never ridden, and controlled with a big stick. They were treated as savages and usually became so. Now the trend is to treat all stallions, even Thoroughbreds, as normally as possible, so they are ridden, turned out to grass and kept in stable yards with other horses.

Housing

Where the stallion is kept will depend on his breed and character. There are breeds which still roam wild. They need little help from man because they have acres of land to graze and have never been softened by domestication. Today, most of these wild breeds are also bred in captivity, and as long as they are sturdy, tough types, then a stallion can be left at grass with his herd of mares. Attention needs to be paid to the fencing to ensure it is not likely

Below left: The stallion barn at Airdrie Stud in Kentucky, USA.

Below: A stallion in his stable at a Kentucky stud. The hot weather makes a fan (on right) advisable.

to cause injury or be broken down, and there should be no other ponies or horses in adjoining fields. A stallion is likely to treat these as competitors and try to fight them. Stallions should always have sufficient fodder (hay if necessary). Stock should be regularly transferred to other fields under a rotation system, to avoid horse-sick grass (see page 163). There must be

frequent checks to ensure that there are no injuries or illness.

Pony stallions can be allowed to run free with their mares, because they are tough, virile and not too valuable. Other types of stallions may also be let free with their mares, but if the breed is more refined, is one which has never (or has not for centuries) run wild in herds and is valuable, it is usual

Above: Hardy breeds like these New Forest Ponies can breed in the wild.

to let them out with only one mare at a time. Most horse breeding is now practiced in a very controlled and artificial manner to reduce the risk of injury, to maximize the chances of problem mares getting in foal and to ensure the ▶

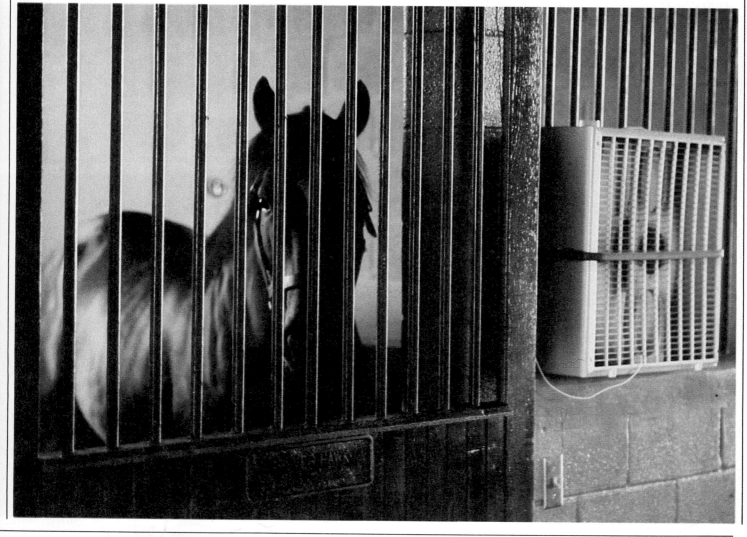

►well-being of horses which after domestication no longer thrive when exposed to a rigorous outdoor life.

Stallions' stables should be strongly built because the animals tend to be more excitable and stronger than other types of horse and can easily demolish fragile buildings. A top door, or a grille for a top door (so that the horse can still see out), is needed: this can be closed in an emergency to stop him trying to jump free. The stable should be at least 12ft x 14ft (3·7 x 4·3m) for a 16h (64in) horse, because stallions like to move around. They like, too, equine company, so most are happiest in yards with other horses. It is important, however, that they cannot smell other horses and that mares in season are not put in an adjacent box.

Exercise

Stable-kept stallions need exercise. Their more fiery natures make it vital that they do not become frustrated through boredom and excess energy, or they will be extremely difficult to handle. The more placid pony and warm-blood stallions are often exercised in the same manner as mares or geldings and are hacked out, hunted and competed. Thoroughbred stallions tend to be more difficult, and only skillful horsemen can use them as riding horses, especially as they grow older. For stallions that are very high-spirited, exceptionally precocious and unmanageable in the company of other horses, or where a rider good enough to control them is unavailable, there are alternative means of exercise. All of these methods can be used for the ridable stallions too.

The first is to turn them out to grass. A small paddock of not more than 2 acres (0·8ha) is generally advisable so they cannot gallop around too wildly. It is essential that the fencing is sturdy and at least 5ft (1·5m) high, since most stallions are prone to jump or crash through fences if they see or hear other horses. There should be no horses in an adjoining paddock, but it often settles the stallion if he can be turned out with a pony, a gelding or a donkey, as long as the latter has been tested to ensure that it has no lung worm. It is also advisable to pick up droppings (see page 163).

Turning the stallion out is good for him psychologically, helping him to loosen up, but is not a means of getting him fit; consequently, although this may be the only form of exercise during and after the covering season, fittening work is needed beforehand. In order to ensure the highest possible fertility, stallions *must* be fit—some cover 100 or more mares in a season. The traditional means of getting a more refined breed fit was for the stallion man to lead the animal out at a walk for 1 to 1½ hours, but this method is time consuming. These days, lunging is a more common method of fittening. Ideally lunging is done in an indoor school or an enclosed outdoor arena. This helps to keep the stallion's concentration

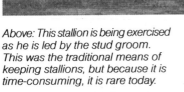

Above: This stallion is being exercised as he is led by the stud groom. This was the traditional means of keeping stallions, but because it is time-consuming, it is rare today.

Right: Lunging is another way to exercise a stallion.

Below: This handsome Andalusian stallion runs free in a field.

and also serves as a place to turn him loose before or after his work.

The stallion starts his fittening work about 2 months before the season begins. The actual dates of the season vary according to the hemisphere (Australia's are in the opposite part of the year to Britain's), the breed, and the planned use of progeny. The racehorse season in the Northern hemisphere starts in February, because early foals are needed to enable maximum maturity for 2- and 3-year-olds. Similarily, sires used to produce in-hand show horses (Thorough-breds and Warm-bloods) have an early start, as a yearling born in March or April will be bigger than one born in June. For those breeders who allow their progeny to mature before use (as in the case of competition horses), the foals are best born when the grass is growing and it is warm enough to turn them out between April and June. In this case, the stallion's season is much later, from May to July.

Feeding

As for exercise, energizing feed should be increased when the season approaches and reduced when the stallion rests in the fall (autumn). Health, well-being and fertility depend on skillful feeding. The stallion must be given the proteins to enable him to muscle up; the energizing foodstuffs to enable him to carry out his work (but not so much that he becomes stupid); enough fattening foods to make him look healthy (but not so much that he becomes fat); the necessary vitamins, salts and additives to maximize his well-being.

Other vital duties for the owner of a stallion are worming, teeth filing and foot trimming, which must be carried out at regular intervals: any pain or indigestion will make a stallion reluctant to serve mares.

Right: Stallions need skillfull care. One annual or biannual duty is to file the teeth so that none have any rough edges.

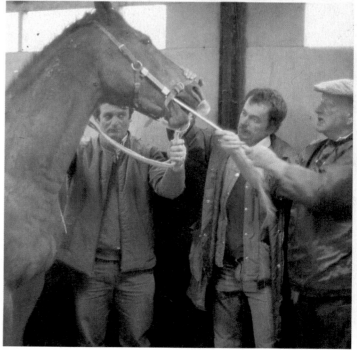

MARE MANAGEMENT

The skill, time and expense needed for mare management depends on the refinement of the breed. Ponies can be left on their own, but Thoroughbreds usually need a great deal of attention. The more we have interfered with a breed's environment, providing warm stables and hard feed, the less able the horses have been to look after themselves.

Condition

The more-refined breeds tend to be more difficult to get in foal and need to be well-prepared. The first concern is the condition of the mare. She is best when left in a natural condition, either having been turned out or, at the least, exercised a little. Fit mares, which are lean and muscular, are hard to get in foal and so are fat mares who have gorged themselves on the spring grass.

Cultures

Most studs today require mares to be swabbed, to ensure they are "clean"—free from contagious infections—and fit for service. A small piece of sterilized cotton is used to collect material that can be studied in the laboratory to check for infectious microbes. The outbreak of contagious equine metritis in 1977 led to much more stringent regulations about checking for infections. Cultures can be taken by the vet from the clitoris at any time or from the cervix when it is relaxed and the mare is in season. It is important to check with the stud whether culturing is required and if so, of which kind. This is then completed before the mare goes away to the stud.

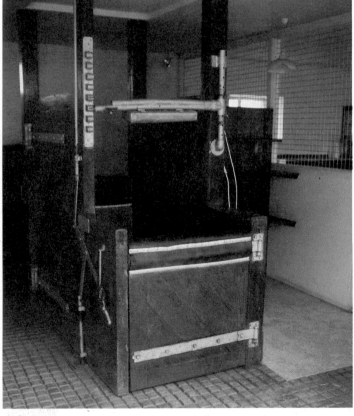

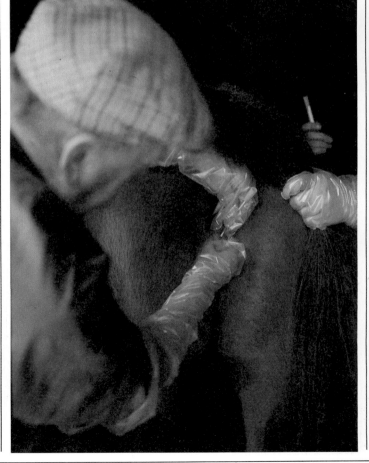

Above: This mare examination box is part of the sophisticated equipment at Ballykisteen stud, Eire.

Right: A vet takes a swab for examination from a mare at the Ballykisteen stud.

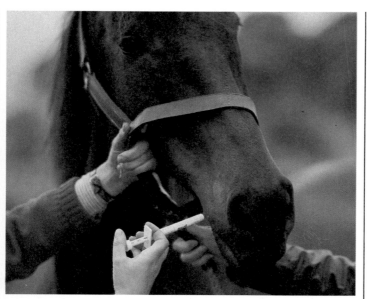

Worming

Studs where many horses graze the land are always liable to worm infestation. It is important, to help prevent this and for the sake of the mare herself, to ensure she is regularly wormed.

Removing Shoes

Prior to service, the mare's back shoes are always removed for safety. Front shoes can be left on.

The Cycle

For barren mares that have had a foal but are not at present in foal, and for maiden mares, which have never had a foal, it helps to establish a clear, regular cycle. Often these mares will not ovulate for their first and maybe second season and will not be fertile. It is wise to ensure a definite cycle before going to the stallion and to keep a record of the dates she comes into season. If an April, May or June foal is desired, and this is the most advantageous timing because grass and climate

Above: Worming tablets can be given in the feed but are often left untouched; oral application is the most foolproof method, and need not be difficult if done calmly.

are best, starting a cycle can usually be left to Nature. However, some mares are required to produce early foals so they will be sufficiently mature to run on the racetrack early in their second year or be shown as young stock. For these mares, artificial aid may be given to encourage an early start to the cycle.

The cycle is affected by season, nutrition and climate. It starts in late spring when the days get longer and the grass gets richer. If the mare is given a good protein diet, if she is kept warm, and if a light of 200 watts is left on in her box for about 6 hours after it gets dark, (so her day is lengthened progressively over about 2 months), her system

should tell her it is spring when it is still winter. This should ensure she comes into season early.

The veterinarian can provide help. He can prescribe a hormone treatment to encourage the start of the cycle. He can also examine her and check the functioning of her organs if she does not start to cycle or if there is any doubt about her fertility. Time and money can be saved if problems are corrected *before* she goes to the stallion. It is less expensive to incur some vet fees than to have the expense of a barren mare, which will involve paying her stud fees, living and keep for the year.

Deciding the Timing

Deciding when she goes to stud depends on when the foal is needed, except in the case of the mare due to foal. In this case, the mare should go to the stud about a month before foaling to be foaled there, or on the 5th day after foaling to catch the foal heat that usually occurs after the 8th day.

With the maiden or barren mare, it is less expensive, in terms of stabling and feed, and best for the foal to be born when Nature prescribed in April, May or June. This means going to stud in May, June or July. But, as in the case of racehorses and show horses, there may be other priorities.

The Stud

Once the cycle of the maiden or barren mare has been established, it's best to send her to stud about 5 days before she comes into season. Otherwise, the journey might upset the cycle. When she goes to stud, send her with a halter that has her or the owner's name on it for identification purposes. If she needs a culture certificate from the vet this should go, together with other details of the mare, such as age, breeding, previous foals, maiden, if in foal, the service dates, vices and idiosyncrasies.

For a mare that is difficult to get in foal, it's helpful to have full details of past veterinary treatment and the regularity of her cycle.

It should also be clarified how long the mare is to stay at the stud. It's a false economy to make her stay too short as this makes it more difficult to ensure the mare is in foal. The normal minimum is 3½ weeks, but it is wisest to allow 6½ or 9½ weeks and have 2 or 3 tests done.

The stud is responsible for keeping the owners informed. They should let them know when their mare has been served and when she has been tested. Owners have the right to enquire about this if not informed, but telephoning should be kept to a minimum because studs are busy places during the breeding season. Those in charge must work very long hours with many foalings in the middle of the night and a tremendous concentration of work. The stallion's quota of mares tends to come over a very short period of the year, and the stud hands have to work exceptionally hard at this time.

Above: A brood mare grazes contentedly on good pastureland.

Below: A laboratory technician examines swabs from mares.

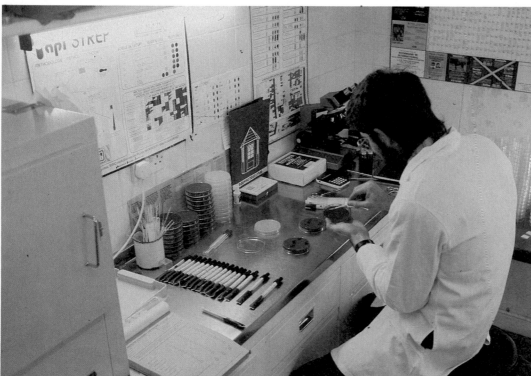

TRYING AND COVERING

Trying (testing whether a mare is ready for covering) and covering can be done naturally when a stallion runs with his herd of mares. No human interference is necessary because there is a well-developed natural system. Mares in season show distinctive signs (see page 166). The stallion smells and notices this and will approach such a mare. She will stand quietly. But a mare out of season will put her ears back and kick at the stallion if he makes any advances; he soon learns the difference.

Running a stallion with a mare is most effective when the breed is tough enough to stand up to the climate, does not require large quantities of hard feed and is not so valuable that the odd kick or accident will be expensive. Herds still need frequent checking for injuries. They need good fencing, and care must be taken that no geldings or stallions are put in adjoining fields, because it could lead to fights.

Trying

With the increasing value of horses, today mares are kept separate from stallions. Most of the trying is done in a more controlled fashion. It is best to keep it as natural as possible; one of the best methods is to lead or ride the stallion close to the mares' paddock. To avoid any kicking it is important not to go beside the fence. The mare's behavior must be carefully observed. Those that take no notice are out of season, those that follow him are likely to be coming in, and those that are 'in' will show the signs. This is a useful method but is not entirely reliable in the case of timid, nervous mares.

One reliable method is to use a trying board that is usually in a yard but can be within a fenced paddock. Ideally, this should be about 8ft 3in (2·5m) long and 6 feet (1·8m) high, padded on the top and on the side where the mare will stand. The ground should be firm and not slippery. Chalk or rough concrete is best. There should be plenty of room on both sides of the board. Alternatively, the stallion can be put into a large stable with a high door looking out onto a yard where the mare will be led.

Any arrangement is feasible, as long as you remember if the mare is not ready, she may react with strenuous kicking. It is important for her not to be able to hurt herself against a rough surface. There must be enough room for her handler to keep clear. The stallion may get excited, so there must be room to keep him safely under control.

The mare is led up to the stallion, head to head with the board or door between them, and reactions are noted. A mare that is strongly "in" will stand quietly. A mare that is pregnant or not in season will be aggressive, putting her ears back and striking out. Occasionally, a mare in season takes time to accept the stallion, and sometimes his attention helps bring her into

Above: A mare being tried. She stands behind trying boards to protect the stallion.

Below: When herds run free, like these Shetlands, trying and covering is naturally accomplished.

Right: Some modern equipment used in the examination of a mare by a veterinarian.

season. The mare should be broadside along the board; if she leans against it and generally inclines towards the stallion, she is ready.

Using a "Teaser"
If a single stallion is used too many times in one day for trying he will become tired; the over-exertion can reduce his fertility. Consequently, when a stallion is popular and valuable, a second, less-valuable stallion, called a *teaser,* is used for the task of finding out when mares are ready for covering.

Trying is a vital task, because it determines the optimum period for fertilization. If the covering is done too early or too late in the cycle, the mare will react aggressively, which can be very dangerous to the handlers and the stallion. Trying also minimizes the number of coverings needed and cuts down the risks of infection. It avoids tiring out the stallion and reducing his fertility.

Another method of trying is used at some studs. A teaser, which can be a pony, is kept in a paddock that is fenced well enough to prevent escape but permits contact between him and the mares in an adjoining paddock or paddocks. The behavior of the mares towards the stallion can then be observed and acted upon.

The Importance of Observation
Observation is a vital part of successful stud work, because cycles can be irregular in timing and intensity. Experienced stud hands have an instinct for when a mare is ready. All changes in behavior are carefully noted.

Maximizing the fertility of the stallions depends on the ability of those running the stud to catch the mares when they are fully in season and to cover them on the optimum day for fertilization.

Optimal Timing
The optimal time for covering is 24 to 6 hours before ovulation (see pages 166-167). There are only 24 hours during which the egg is fertilizable. There are no outward signs to indicate ovulation other than the mare being "very well in season". The only positive sign she has ovulated is when she goes out of season 24 to 28 hours later.

It is important to notice when a mare first comes into season. The covering then takes place when she is "well in"—2 to 3 days after the start. Some people advocate a second covering 24 to 48 hours later, but most experts feel this is unnecessary unless the first covering did not go well. Frequent coverings will tire the stallion, lower his fertility and increase the risk of infection. They are of doubtful value, especially if they are carried out after ovulation.

Veterinary Aid
A veterinary examination is the best way of finding out when there is a chance of conception and when covering will be as effective as possible. It can also determine when a mare is close to ovulation and whether a horse is free from any infections that might hinder fertilization. At many Thoroughbred breeding studs, where for mare owners expenses are minimal relative to the costs of not getting a mare in foal, veterinary examinations are the norm. By feeling the ovaries and the size, position and tension of the follicles, the vet can ascertain whether and when one (or two in the case of twins) of them is likely to rupture. The vet can then advise as to the best possible covering day. Also internal massage of the ovaries can help weak or cystic ovaries.

Another aid is the use of an instrument called a *speculum,* through which the veterinarian can see the condition of the vagina and cervix and forecast when ovulation is likely. He can also check for infections that could inhibit fertilization. Some discharges destroy sperm or a fertilized egg.

Veterinary aid can also help optimal timing by prescribing hormones that will hasten or delay ovulation or help bring a mare into season.

All these techniques help to increase a mare's fertility, so that there is no need for a stallion to cover the mare many times. This is such an important aspect of breeding at major Thoroughbred studs, they may employ a team of veterinarians full-time.

In-foal Mares
In-foal mares are normally easier subjects for optimal timing. They usually show around the ninth day after foaling, and this tends to be a strong season unless they have had twins, a bad foaling or they are so preoccupied with ▶

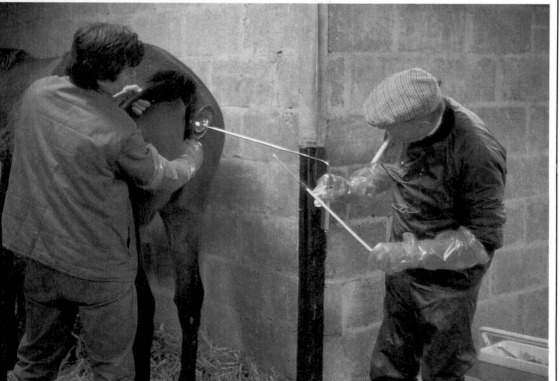

▶ their foal they do not come into season at all. Some mares only produce foals every other year. The mare with foal is normally most fertile in her first season, but if this is missed, the mare should return to the normal cycle, showing every 20 to 21 days.

The Covering
Stallions may be very valuable and must be protected from any cantankerous behavior by the mare. There once was a practice of tying two legs of a mare together with straps called *hobbles* to prevent her kicking or moving. But the realization that if a mare is "covered" (mated) at her optimal time she will be ready and willing to accept the stallion has meant hobbles are almost unnecessary. The normal precaution is to fit felt-and-leather-covered boots over the hind feet of the mare to minimize the effects of any kicks.

The mare is led to the trying board by a bridle, wearing a tail badge. At the board, she is tested with the stallion to make sure that she is "well in". She is then taken to the covering yard. The leader of the mare should have an assistant who can help keep the mare steady and position her.

A maiden mare or a nervous one needs plenty of reassurance. If she has a foal at foot during the service, some studs shut it away in a stable, but most have the foal held at a safe distance from the mare and stallion in the covering yard. In this way the mare is not disturbed by its absence. It's best to lead the stallion around a nervous mare so she can adjust to the situation. On the rare occasion when she is still difficult and may hurt the stallion or helper, yet she is definitely close to ovulation, a *twitch* (a device used to hold the attention of the horse) can be used.

The stallion is led on a bridle or halter with a lead rein 9 or 10 feet, to be positioned behind and to one side of the mare. He is allowed to touch the mare's quarters but not bite or mount her before he has dropped. This preparatory stage may take some time, but as soon as he shows the signs, the rein is loosened so he can mount the mare, still slightly to one side. When the service is finished, he is allowed to dismount and is taken back to his box where his sheath and hindlegs can be washed down with a mild solution of non-irritating disinfectant. The mare should be led around for 10 to 15 minutes after covering.

The key to successful covering is a calm, relaxed, disciplined handling of the mare and stallion. Everybody involved (usually three people) must know exactly what their role is. They must be experienced enough to know when to be firm and when to be gentle, when direction is needed and when to keep clear of flying hooves.

Artificial Insemination
The alternative to covering is artificial insemination (AI). This has many opponents, particularly in the Thoroughbred world, because it is believed it could lead to malpractice and overuse of popular stock. However, it is used on Standard-breds in the United States, where a single collection of semen from one stallion may be split into as many as 20 portions and inseminated daily into mares on the stud. This makes

Above left: The covering of two Percherons. The mare wears hobbles, to stop her kicking.

Below left: Hobbles are rarely used today; instead protective boots are put on, as this mare shows.

Below: Covering being done in a yard with the recommended number of three helpers.

Above: This covering is being done in the open. Only two helpers are necessary in this case.

it possible for more mares to receive semen, and the daily administration close to ovulation helps relatively infertile mares to conceive. It is also an aid when mares are very difficult to serve, and it reduces the risk of spreading contagious diseases, which infected mares can pass on.

Frozen Sperm
Semen can also be frozen; this method is being used for international matings, particularly for competition horses.

Advantages and Disadvantages
Artificial insemination does have the undeniable advantages of containing disease, increasing the chances of an infertile mare having a foal, increasing the numbers of mares to any one stallion and making international matings less expensive. However, it also has problems of control, and these are realized by the most valuable breeding market of all, the Thoroughbred industry. It is for these reasons that no Thoroughbred conceived by artificial insemination is allowed to be registered.

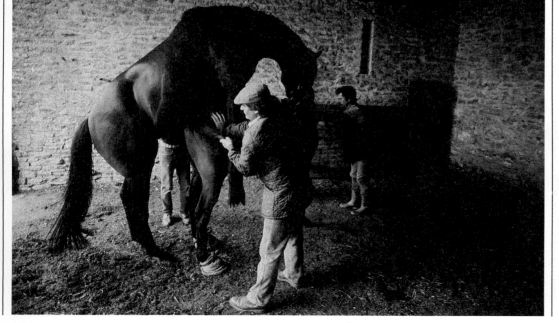

THE PREGNANT/IN-FOAL MARE

The Tests

The first test of pregnancy is when the mare does not come into season when tried. She is said then to have "held" to the stallion. Procedure varies as to how often she is tried. Some advocate she be tried on the 9th, 15th, 21st, 28th, 31st and 42nd day after service. Others simply try on the 21st, 42nd and 63rd day. It is important not to assume she is in foal the first time she "holds" because mares can be 8 weeks between seasons. It is also easy for a mare to "slip" (abort) her foal in the early stages without anybody noticing because the fetus is so small.

On the other hand, less-frequent testing is not only labor-saving, but it is also less disturbing to the mare. It is advisable to make the tests as short as possible if the mare is believed to be in foal, because it is all too easy for her to abort if she gets very upset. Take her away from the trying board as soon as she shows any aggressive reactions.

Trying is the first means of checking pregnancy. It is not an infallible system because infertile mares may not come into season. Other methods are usually used in addition because it is important to know the state of the mare.

The more traditional methods are rectal palpation, blood tests and urine tests. A manual examination, 19 to 21 days after the last service, can determine whether pregnancy is or is not likely. At 30 to 35 days, it is more reliable, also the vet can feel if there are twins. At 39 to 42 days it can be considered an accurate diagnosis and at 60 days a check is carried out to make absolutely sure

there has been no abortion.

There are anxieties that this manual examination can lead to an abortion. Evidence points to this only being the case if the mare is particularly susceptible to abortion.

Besides the manual examination, other traditional methods of determining pregnancy are blood and urine tests. The blood test, which should be done between 45 to 90 days from the service, is not 100% reliable. About 10% of those mares diagnosed as pregnant turn out not to be so. The urine test is more reliable and can be taken any time after the 120th day after service.

The newest, most reliable method of pregnancy testing is by ultrasound scan.

If a mare is barren, then veterinary assistance is probably advisable to help fertility. If she is pregnant, then her feeding, work and environment need to be monitored to promote healthy growth and ensure against the loss of the foal.

Most in-foal mares change in appearance about 6 months after service. Their bellies start to drop, and they swing slightly when they move. This is not an absolute rule for all mares. Those with their first foal may change little, and some barren mares carry a typical "in-foal" belly.

Abortion

Abortion, which is the expulsion of the fetus before the 300th day, is a disappointing and depressing occurrence. After this time, the foal is said to be premature.

When a mare aborts, it may lead to other fertility problems in the following season and then the advice of the veterinarian is advisable.

Some say abortion can be caused by stress, such as a disturbing experience or a sudden

Above: A head-on view of a Thoroughbred mare, heavy in-foal. Pregnancy usually lasts about 336 days (11 months).

change in circumstances. This is why journeys must be undertaken with care and not too close to the expected date of the birth.

The diet should not be changed too dramatically, and the mare should not be deprived of water. Her food should never be musty, frozen or fermented. Take every precaution that she does not develop colic or a chill. She should not be subjected to frights or made to overexert herself.

Twins are often aborted; this usually occurs in the 6th to 9th month of pregnancy. The mare's uterus doesn't have the capacity to house and nourish twins, and as a consequence she aborts. Only about 20% of twins that are conceived are born and those that do last the full term rarely survive the first few days. If one does, it is usually weak and small. Great efforts are therefore made to avoid twins. Only about 2% of Thoroughbreds conceive twins.

Veterinary examinations can be carried out before service to see if two follicles, rather than one, are developing. Diagnosed twins are often washed out (artificially aborted) in the early stages, but they still occur in large numbers.

Abortion also occurs due to problems that can arise in the womb, causing death of the fetus. There can be a shortage of oxygen, the

Below: Thoroughbred mares being fed hard feed. This is needed by nearly all Thoroughbred horses.

Above: This mare, heavy in-foal, is viewed from the side to show the distinct drop in her belly.

umbilical cord can twist and cut off supplies, blood pressure and heart problems in the mare can result in under-nourishment of the fetus, there may be a hormonal imbalance or the fetus may be deformed.

Nutrition can also be a cause of abortion. It is vital for the mare to receive sufficient protein and amino acids in the early stages of pregnancy. Some drugs, such as cortisone and prostaglandins, can have serious effects in the first 6 weeks of pregnancy. Avoid the use of drugs during this period if possible. Some plants, such as ragwort, horsetails, bracken, poppy, flax, locoweed, oleander, jimson weed and bryony can be toxic to horses and may indirectly cause abortion.

Then there are infectious causes. The most serious of these is viral abortion, also called *equine herpes virus* and *rhinopneumonitis*. In young horses, it simply results in a runny nose, but in mares it will result in abortion in the 7th to 9th month of pregnancy. Vaccines have been developed to combat this

serious disease for mares. Bacteria living in the uterus are another cause of abortion and infertility. There is also a fungus that enters the uterus through the vagina after foaling or when a mare is in season. It grows on the placenta, adversely affecting the nourishment of the fetus.

The vet can prescribe preventative measures to reduce the chances of abortion. If a mare has previously aborted, or if it is believed she was exposed to any virus, bacteria or fungi associated with abortions, it is wise to seek consultation.

Health
The other concern during pregnancy is the healthy development of the fetus. It is believed the healthy development of the fetus depends on freedom from stress factors, such as sudden changes in the environment. Dramatic changes seem to radically affect the mother's ability to nourish her foal. A more direct effect on the fetus' healthy growth is the mare's food supply, although the mare's body will sacrifice itself for the foal, growing emaciated, rather than depriving the fetus.

The essential factor is to keep her looking healthy. Her coat should be in good condition and her body shouldn't be too lean or too fat. Too much bulk food, resulting in

too fat a mare, is as serious as too little food. For most mares, summer grass will keep them in good condition, but if the pasture is not too good or if the mare is a poor "doer" (one that does not develop well) then some oats and bran should be given to her. The protein content is particularly important. A mineral supplement is advisable from an early stage in the mare's pregnancy.

Winter Treatment
As fall (autumn) approaches, most mares need feeding with hay, hard feed and supplements, but the amount varies according to the type of mare and the pasture. Whatever the foodstuff, it must be good quality. The vital criterion of good health remains in the mare's appearance.

Winter necessitates, for most types, some form of shelter and an increase of feed. Hardier types are happy with a makeshift shelter in the field, but the more refined mares may need proper stabling at night.

The Last Stages of Pregnancy
As the foaling approaches, the foal's growth increases. In the last third of pregnancy, it increases three times in weight so the mare

will need help from extra feed to nourish herself and the fast-growing fetus, particularly when the grass is at its poorest. Protein is important for the foal's correct development and for the mare's milk production. Some dried milk can also be helpful.

As foaling time approaches, the diet is gradually changed. About 3 weeks from the date the foal is due, bulk food is gradually reduced to half of what the mare has previously been receiving. Oats are also reduced. To avoid the tendency for the mare to become constipated, give her plenty of grass, and a bran mash at least twice a week. Boiled linseed can be given with the mash. Mineral supplements are important at this stage.

Keep the environment of the mare as natural as possible, and encourage natural movement. She can be kept in work for up to 5 months after the start of the pregnancy, but this should progressively involve less exertion and strain. Some people continue to give hardy types of mares light work for even longer, but it is advisable to let them run free in the fields to get their exercise. Movement is important up to the time of foaling, so if paddocks are waterlogged or icebound, allow the mare to wander around some enclosed area.

THE FOALING

It is important to make the foaling as natural as possible. The less human interference there is, the more relaxed the mare will remain. It will be better for the mare and foal, unless there are complications. Problems do not often occur and most foalings are uneventful, but it is advisable for someone to be present who is experienced in the foaling down of mares, especially if the mare is valuable or a refined type.

Preparation

As foaling time approaches, it's important to keep the mare under frequent observation. Because disturbances should be kept to a minimum, it is best to be able to observe the mare without going into the stable. Most studs have a peephole in the door or wall through which assistants can watch. The natural time for foaling is when everything is quiet, between about 11p.m. and 4a.m. Foaling native ponies left out in the field does not require nightly vigilance. The more refined the mare, the more human assistance she is likely to need. She should be housed in a stable where there is room to foal down and where it's easy to make frequent checks without disturbing her.

The foaling box for ponies should be at least 12feet (3·7m) square but for horses 12x16ft (3·7x4·8m) is acceptable. It should be bedded down deeply, with straw banked up along the sides and against the door for protection and to prevent drafts. Keep the temperature at about 59°F (15°C).

Cleanliness is very important, and the foal and mare are particu-

Above: View through a peephole into a foaling box.

larly liable to infections after birth. Before the mare is put into the box, it should be thoroughly disinfected, washed down and dried out. A previous foaling in the box can leave infectious material, and every precaution must be taken to ensure its removal. Assistants should also be completely clean before the actual foaling: they should wash their hands with carbolic soap and disinfectant in lukewarm water, and then dry them.

When preparing for the foaling, note the telephone number of your veterinarian. Collect the equipment that may be needed during foaling. This should include a pair of sterilized scissors, cotton or gauze, some antiseptic powder or lotion for the stump of the foal's cord, a bucket and a supply of warm water. Equipment needed for aftercare of the mare and the foal must also be ready for immediate use. This includes an enema syringe, liquid

Below: This mare produced her foal in the open, without aid.

paraffin, a baby's feeding bottle with a large nipple, petroleum jelly, disinfectant and the means to make a warm bran mash.

Indications of Foaling
The earliest indication the foaling is not far away is when the mare begins to "bag up". This is when the udder starts to grow stiffer, rounder and larger, due to enlargement of the mammary glands and the collection of milk. This milk has a very high level of protein, including globulin that helps protect the foal against disease and infection when it is born. Bagging up is not a reliable indication of foaling, because this enlargement of the udder can occur up to 2 weeks before the birth, and it is not unheard of for a mare to only "bag up" after birth.

Closer to the birth, usually 24 hours before but up to 10 days before, drops of honey-like secretion form at the end of the mare's teats. This occurrence is known as "waxing up."

Another sign is the "softening of the bones". Usually about 2 weeks before foaling, the pelvic ligaments start to soften. The muscles begin to relax to ease the passage for the foal. There are external signs of a gradual deepening of the vagina, and grooves appear on either side of the tail. The points of the hip become more prominent. Muscles around the anus and vagina also slacken, and as the time for the birth approaches, the lips of the vulva swell.

The mare's behavior also tends to change. She becomes more tense and antisocial and shows obvious signs of increasing discomfort as the time for foaling approaches.

Above: The deeply dropped belly of this mare suggests foaling may occur very soon.

Below: Shortly before birth, the teats exude drops of honeylike secretion; this is called "waxing-up".

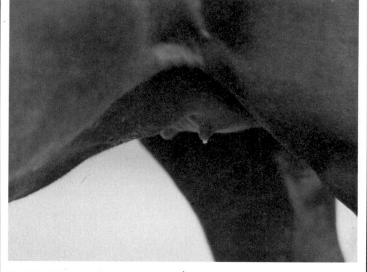

The First Contractions
Early contractions may not be noticed because they start by being light and infrequent. An indication foaling is about to commence is when the mare begins to show signs of pain. She may also sweat, paw the ground and look around at her flank at this early stage in the process.

The intensity of these actions varies. Some mares sweat profusely, others remain docile and unperturbed during this time. In some cases, the interval between contractions can be long, with the mare sweating, then cooling off again. It's more normal for the contractions to become gradually more frequent and intense, quickening from one every 5 or 10 minutes to one approximately every 30 seconds.

Usually it takes up to an hour from the first signs of pain and contractions to the appearance of the gray water bag and its rupture, called "the breaking of the waters." The allantoic fluid released is yellow brown and may gush through the vulva. Or it may be so small in quantity that there is only a trickle. It can even pass unnoticed.

Timetable
A timetable is only a guide, and the most important indication of a healthy foaling is that there is regular progress at all stages.

From the breaking of the waters to the birth of the foal usually takes less than an hour. For a mare that has had foals before, it is usually about 20 minutes. But maiden mares often take a little longer. In a smooth delivery, the yellow membrane of the amnion (also known as the caul) should appear about 5 minutes after the "breaking of waters". The foal should be delivered in 20 minutes, the cord broken within another 30 minutes, the foal suckling in 2 hours and the afterbirth (placenta) freed within 10 hours. If this timetable is not met, or if there is no progress, then veterinary assistance is advisable.

The Stages
Most mares lie down after the breaking of the waters. It is quite normal for a mare to change her position and even to get up and lie down again. But if it happens too frequently, this indicates she is having difficulties and the foal's position needs checking by an experienced person.

Once the foaling starts, the mare normally remains lying down. Usually only nervous mares, disturbed by humans, stand up. The contractions, which at this stage may be quite vigorous, are a healthy sign. A mare that is straining often indicates that the foal is incorrectly positioned, and then experienced help is needed.

Before checking the position of a foal, the hands of the experienced assistant and the anus of the mare must be washed with disinfectant and lubricated with paraffin. Then the assistant's hand slides into the birth passage, feels the foal and, if necessary, manipulates it into the correct position.

For a smooth delivery, one foreleg should slightly lead the other, with the foal in a diving position. The head should be straight and slightly behind the forelegs. If it is sideways or one or more of the forelegs are bent, skillful manipulation can correct this. If the hocks are ▶

visible or felt, it is a breech presentation, and this will require veterinary assistance by all but the most experienced breeders. The foaling is more difficult in the breech position because the broader quarters of the foal come first. Also, the cord is very easily broken in a breech birth. If this happens too early in the foaling, it can cause suffocation.

Although it's best to do as little as possible during foaling, there are occasions, such as when the mare is obviously exhausted and the periods between her straining are lengthening, when skillful assistance is needed to help the foal come through the birth canal. Before this is done, check the foal's position to ensure it is possible for the foal to get through the birth canal. Nature provides for pushing the foal through the birth passage but humans can only pull it through. Force should be exerted *only* as the mare strains and *never* when she stops. If excessive force is used, the foal's forelegs tend to damage its chest. It is only through experience that a person can learn when and where to assist the mare and foal, and how much help to give.

A common problem is when the foal's elbows stick behind the mare's pelvic brim. The head is another area that can get into the wrong position and cause problems. The broadest section of all is the shoulders and withers, so it is not surprising that they, too, can easily become stuck.

After delivery, the foal should be on its side in an arc, with its hind legs in the vagina. By this time the amnion should have broken but if it has not, it should be split by applying pressure between the foal's feet. If necessary, lift the foal's head out of the amniotic fluid. If the amnion is left intact, the foal can suffocate.

The Cord
It is best for the mare to remain lying down for a further half an hour. This gives time for her womb

Below: It is vital to check that the foal is in the normal position. A breech birth requires veterinary help.

and birth passage to contract. The foal's cord should break when the mare gets up or if the foal struggles away from her. The cord breaks naturally close to its belly and the stump can be dressed with antibiotic powder. The practice of cutting and tying the cord has been stopped because it was discovered if it is broken before the foal is breathing, the young animal does not receive all its circulatory blood.

In some cases, after breaking, the cord will bleed. This can usually be stopped by pinching it between the thumb and finger, or tape can be applied if necessary. On the rare occasion when a cord does not break naturally, it can be cut through with sterilized scissors, about 4 inches from the foal's belly. The stump is not tied, but it is dressed as described above.

The Afterbirth
The afterbirth (placenta) takes longer to be delivered. It is attached to the uterine walls during pregnancy, and it takes time to separate from it. Normally it does so about an hour after completion of the birth, but it can take longer. The afterbirth can be tied with twine so it hangs about the level of the hocks. When it falls off, check it out to see if it is complete and be sure no placenta is retained in the two arms of the uterus. A retention of placenta can cause serious infection.

The foal is born with a wet coat, soaked in amniotic fluid. If the weather is cold, or if the foal seems to be very weak, dry the coat to reduce heat loss and to stimulate breathing and movement. In most cases, this is unnecessary, and mare and foal can be left to themselves.

The Newborn Foal
A strong foal is on its feet and searching for milk within about half an hour of delivery. It is likely to be unbalanced and poorly coordinated at first, but it rapidly gains strength. If it has not suckled within 2 hours, or cannot stand without falling over within 3 hours, then there is a problem and veterinary advice is needed.

Some assistance can be given, but try not to frighten the newborn animal. Help it stand and direct it

The sequence of pictures on this page shows various stages in foaling.
Left: The mare is still standing as the water bag appears.
Right: The mare is now lying down; the front legs of the foal are visible. The front feet are clearly pointing down, so it is not a breech birth.
Far right: The foal has now broken through the water bag.
Below: Practically all of the foal's body has now emerged.
Below right: The foal is now completely free.
Below, far right: The foal is being rubbed down to stimulate its blood circulation and help dry its coat.
Bottom: At last—the wonderful moment of the first encounter between the mare and her foal.

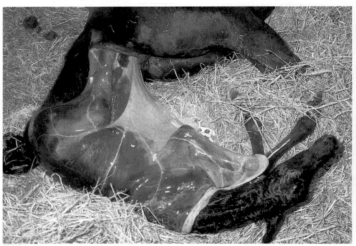

toward its mother's udder. If the mare is ticklish or maiden, it may be necessary to hold her while the foal learns to suck. Leave the mare alone as much as possible until she has licked the foal. Then she can be given bran mash with linseed.

The foal must pass meconium, which is a dark rubbery type of dung collected in the rectum, colon and cecum during its time in the womb. Foals often have a problem in passing meconium, particularly colts.

If the colt is standing with its tail up and straining 4 to 5 hours after birth, an enema is advisable. Use 1¾ to 3½ pints of lukewarm soapy water, and inject it into the rectum. But first the rectum must be cleared of any pellets by carefully inserting a gloved

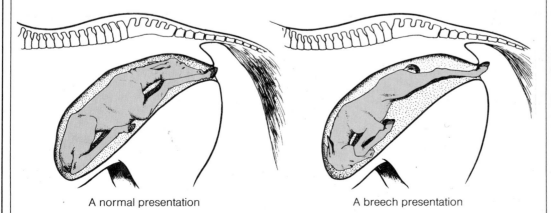

A normal presentation   A breech presentation

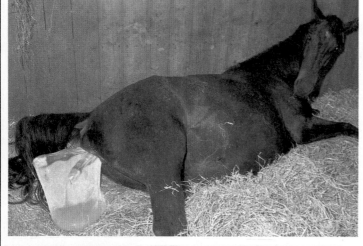

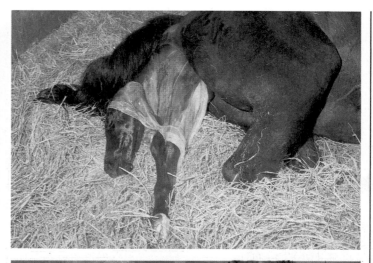

forefinger, lubricated with paraffin, into the anus. When giving a newborn foal an enema, use a rubber tube that is soft and has no sharp edges. As an alternative, liquid paraffin can be injected into the rectum. Only small quantities must be used. Be careful not to damage the foal. If this is ineffective, oil can be administered by mouth or through a stomach tube; in these cases, it is advisable to call a vet.

Dealing with Problems

Most foalings occur smoothly, but vigilance is necessary to make sure there are no serious problems. Close adherence to the timetable is important. If there are any delays, call an expert immediately. However straightforward it might appear, checking a foal's position and giving assistance during delivery should be done by an experienced person.

The most common problem during the birth is incorrect positioning of the foal. This is the most necessary point to check. After foaling it is important to look for weaknesses in the foal: any signs of a blockage or inability to behave normally.

Recording of events and their timing is a great help to a veterinarian if one has to be called in. Hopefully this will not be necessary, but if things start going wrong, speed is important. As long as the foaling progresses smoothly the mare, and when it is born, the foal, are best left to themselves.

CARE OF YOUNGSTOCK

Mare and Foal

For the first few days, keep the mare and foal (except those of hardy breeds) in the stable. The mare can be given boiled feed and mashes, and some fresh grass if it is available. This helps avoid constipation and encourage the flow of milk.

Watch the foal during these early days. The most common problem is a stoppage if there are any signs of straining and the tail going up, then the action described on the previous page is needed. If colic develops, or the foal has diarrhea with dark-colored manure, call the veterinarian. If the foal emits loose, yellow feces, the problem is not so serious, but the foal should be kept clean under the tail.

Depending on the weather and the strength of the foal, the mare and foal can be let out to graze for a few hours about 2 days after the birth. If they continue to do well and the weather remains mild, they can be left for longer each day, until they are eventually in the field all the time. Only very valuable, refined types need to be brought in at night when the foals are strong and the weather is good in the summer. Most stock is better off when allowed to remain in its natural environment.

The Importance of Play

When turned out into the field, the foal will almost immediately start skipping around and playing. It is wonderful to watch a youngster discovering the joys of being alive and being able to use its body to leap and gallop. After a few weeks, it will start to play with other foals if they are in the field. Play is believed to be important for a youngster's development, just as it is considered important for a stallion to play with other colts. It can appear quite rough, with plenty of rearing and biting, but it rarely results in any harm.

Feeding

During the first few days, a laxative type of feed may be advisable. When the mare and foal go out to grass, whether feed is necessary depends on the type of mare, the condition of the mare and foal and the quality of the grass. Thoroughbreds usually need oats or stud nuts, and from 5-15lb (2·3-6·8kg) can be given, together with an occasional addition of boiled linseed. The foal will gradually learn to eat oats by copying its mother and eating some of her ration. As the summer progresses and the grass becomes more scarce and less nourishing, hay may have to be provided. Mares that have been coming in at night should be given hay while they are in the stable.

Some mares may not produce sufficient feed for their offspring. Continual attempts by the foal to suck are a sign of inadequate milk production. If this occurs, give the mare more protein (clover,

Above: A mare and foal loose in an indoor school. In this type of place, they can exercise, even in winter.

alfalfa [lucerne], bran and linseed). If this doesn't help, call your veterinarian immediately.

Worming

Worms are a major hazard to youngstock and their dams. Worm infestation can cause colic and even death. Precautions to keep paddocks from becoming "horse sick" (infested with worms) are discussed on page 163. In addition, regularly worm all stock. Worm the mare 3 weeks to a month *before* foaling, then not again until she has been covered. The foal can be wormed at 8 weeks, then every month thereafter. The veterinarian will provide a special dosage appropriate for the foal.

Handling

Patient handling establishes respect and trust and will pay dividends in the future. Foals coming in at night can have daily handling sessions of 5 to 15 minutes. Those at grass can be left until they are weaned.

The basic concept in handling a foal is that it will stop struggling and resisting as soon as it realizes a human being is more powerful, that it can't get away and that there is no need to get away, because no harm is intended. In this way, it will learn that it can trust its handlers.

One of the first tasks is to fit a head collar. This is most easily accomplished in a stable. One person approaches the foal from the nearside, putting a left arm around the foal's chest and holding the tail at the root with the right arm. While the foal is being securely held, a second person puts on the head collar. If the foal is not weaned, a helper is needed to hold the mare.

The foal can be taught to lead by being pushed from behind — never pull it by the head collar. In the first few lessons, put a stable rubber around the foal's neck (this is soft and won't hurt) while holding the hindquarters with the other hand. This can be used to push the foal forward. The mare is led in front of the foal, which will encourage it to follow. Gradually, over a period of days, the pushing will become less necessary and the foal can be led more from the stable rubber. Eventually, as it relaxes, it can be led off the headcollar.

The other vital aspect of handling is getting the foal used to its feet being picked up. It's important to take care of the feet, and they should be regularly cleaned out with a hoof pick. From about 2 months of age, regular trimming is advisable. If there are any deformities of the feet, corrections can often by made by the farrier. Success is more likely when the bone is still soft.

Weaning
Weaning is the separation of the foal from its mother. Do not do this until the 4th month, at the earliest. Thoroughbreds (except those that are weak or slow to develop) are usually weaned at 5 to 6 months, and other breeds at 6 months. If the mare is not in foal, weaning can be delayed until about 8 months, as long as the mare is keeping good condition.

Some breeders wean the offspring of mares in foal later than 6 months. The argument against this is that the foal is taking food from the fetus, but there is little veterinary evidence for this.

There are two main methods of weaning. The first is the more artificial, but it is safer and easier to manage, and is practiced at most studs. If the mare has been given grain (such as oats), this is cut down to reduce her milk production. Mares out at grass are brought in (at least at night) 7 to 10 days before weaning so the foal can learn to eat grain and hay. Feed mare and foal from separate containers.

Put them in a stable that is thickly bedded. For the last few days do not muck them out. The mare's smell ▶

Bottom left: First stages in teaching a foal to lead using a stable rubber around its neck and pushing, not pulling, it along.

Below: A foal being turned out for the first time. The mare is held so she will not gallop off until her youngster is used to the outdoors.

▶ will remain in the box. The mare is led out quickly and taken far enough away to ensure that neither the mare nor the foal will hear each other's whinnies.

The foal is happier if left with other youngsters. It can then be turned out to grass with them after 2 or 3 days. This sudden separation is very stressful for the foal, and at this time it may lose weight and become particularly liable to picking up nervous habits, such as weaving, crib biting and walking the box.

The alternative, more-natural method is to turn a group of mares and foals out in a paddock and keep them together for several weeks so social bonds develop. To start weaning, two mares are taken out and their foals left. The youngsters don't usually become so upset because they have the herd to return to. After 2 or 3 days, two further mares are taken away; the process continues until only the foals remain. If the foals are stabled at night, the weaning is done when they are first turned out in the morning. In the evenings, pairs of weanlings are put in a stable together.

The mares must dry off, and their milk production must stop.

Above: A foal being handled when it is out in the field under the watchful eye of its mother.

Below: It is important for youngstock to play. Nibbling is usually considered a sign of friendship.

Right: Two yearlings gallop free. This will help to develop their athleticism and character.

Above: A mare and foal being led in from the field to avoid the midday sun in Kentucky.

Less grain helps this. It is inadvisable to touch the udder, and the mares should only be milked if they are very full, because milking encourages further milk production.

Feeding
Diet is an important part of healthy growth. The first major growth period occurs directly after foaling. In the first month the foal's height increases by about 30%. The second growth period is from 6 to 9 months, when most foals are weaned. The third is after puberty. Good feed is vital to maximize growth and to ensure healthy development of the best possible individual.

The important factor is to keep the youngstock in good condition—not too thin or too fat. Overweight can have as serious an effect on bone development as undernourishment. Overfeeding leads to limb troubles (too much weight to carry), and underfeeding restricts growth, so it is important that a balance between the two is reached.

The amount of feed to give depends on the type of youngstock. Native ponies need very little, while Thoroughbreds need a good deal. Also important are the quality and quantity of the grass (in winter its nourishment value falls), the time spent in the stable and the future use of the youngstock. Those that need to mature quickly, such

as racehorses and show stock, should be given more grain.

The important factor, whatever the quantity given, is that the food is good quality. Particularly important is the hay, which if musty and dusty can easily cause wind problems with the lungs in the future.

Although the quantity of hard feed varies, a typical diet for a freshly weaned riding-horse foal would be 5lb (2·25kg) of crushed oats, and 1lb (0·5kg) bran. It is very important that youngstock eat sufficient calcium and phosphorus, so give supplements containing these. Small amounts of linseed (once or twice weekly), carrots, cod liver oil (daily in one feed) and sugar beet can be added.

Shelter
All but the hardy breeds need shelter in winter. This can be a shed with a wide opening to the field or a closed barn with a good bedding of straw. It's best to give youngstock a bigger area than a stable when they come in so they can be kept together and get some exercise. Any youngstock kept in a stable must be given regular opportunities to run free in a field or school. It is natural for them to want to gallop and play. Exercise is important for their mental and physical development.

Yearlings and two-year-olds
Much the same treatment is given to the youngstock as they grow up. In the spring, any stabled stock can be turned out. If the grass is rich when they are first allowed out, it's important to start with only a few hours of freedom and progressively extend the time, so they do not gorge themselves and develop colic. They should be turned out first by day, then all the time.

The feed given to the stock depends on their condition. Usually no hay or grain is necessary during late spring and early summer. Throughout their development, youngstock should be handled, regularly wormed and their feet trimmed. In the early months, colts and fillies can run together, but by 18 months, they should be separated.

Good feeding and handling establishes the basis for future training and work. The success of the youngstocks' life as adults depends greatly on their correct treatment, which should maximize healthy growth and establish a confident, respectful approach toward humans.

Breaking In
For most ponies and horses, work begins with the breaking in at 3 years old. Many racehorses are broken before they are 2 and some early maturing breeds begin their training at 2½ years, but these are exceptions. Leaving the youngstock long enough to become strong ensures the care and attention put into their breeding and upbringing yields the best possible results.

GUIDE TO INTERNATIONAL BREEDS

Each country has developed its own particular breeds of horses. Some, like the Arab and Thoroughbred, have become so international that they are found all over the world, but for the majority of breeds, the greatest numbers are still based in their country of origin.

This section lists all the breeds country by country, and aims to provide a clear, useful cross-reference to the descriptions of the breeds that appear in alphabetical order in the main section of the book, where they are divided into the three main groups of modern horses: ponies, work-horses and sports-horses. It also includes breeds that are rare or even extinct, and that were, therefore, not included in the main section.

The introductions to the breeds of each country give a concise and up-to-date outline of national horse-breeding activities. It is interesting to see how the different breeds have arisen according to the needs and character of each country's inhabitants, whether they favor spirited or docile horses, large breeds or small ones.

Algeria

Originally part of Barbary, together with Morocco and Libya, Algeria forms a major section of the homelands of the Barb. Horses used in this country are mainly of Arab and Barb descent.

Barb ▶91

Argentina

Although most famous for its Criollo horse and Polo Ponies, Thoroughbreds are produced in large numbers for the country's 400 racetracks.

Criollo ▶97
Falabella ▶27

Australia

There are no horses indigenous to Australia, so early settlers began importing them toward the end of the 18th century. The land in Australia and New Zealand proved conducive to rearing horses, and both countries became exporters of horses.

The first famous Australian horse was the Waler. Developed as a stock horse from Arab, Anglo-Arab and Thoroughbred stallions, it became very popular as a cavalry horse. "Country-bred" Walers were foundation stock for the Australian Stock Horse.

Australian Pony ▶14
Australian Stock Horse ▶90
Brumby ▶93
Waler ▶90

Austria

Austria is most famous as the country where the Lipizzaner was developed. Two other well-known and widespread native breeds are the Haflinger Pony and the Noriker Cold-Blood. Government-controlled studs also produce the Austrian Warm-Blood (based on European-Warm Blood imports), which is used in competition and leisure riding.

Austrian Warm-Blood
Haflinger ▶32
Lipizzaner ▶114-115
Noriker Pinzgauer ▶64

Belgium

Belgium is famous for its horses. Its Flemish horses date from Roman times. Today its cold-bloods, the Ardennes and Brabant, are known all over the world, but Belgium is developing a reputation for its new breed of sports horse.

Ardennes ▶52
Belgian Half-Blood ▶92
Brabant/Belgian ▶54-55

Brazil

With its 9 million horses, Brazil boasts one of the largest equine populations in the world. There are many imported breeds, but the native horse is the Crioulo, a smaller version of Argentina's Criollo.

Some Crioulo stock has been improved by crossbreeding. This includes the Mangalarga, a small riding horse developed at the beginning of the 19th century in the state of Minas Gerais. The important foundation stock was Altér Real and Andalusian stallions, put to Crioulo types. The result

was a strong, fast horse useful for ranch work. An unusual feature of the Mangalarga is its extra gait, the "march", which is a fast but comfortable rocking movement for the rider.

Another variation of the Crioulo is the Campolino, first bred in the late 19th century in Brazil by Señor Cassiano Campolino. It is an all-around type used for light draft work and riding.

The Campolino is heavier than the Mangalarga, with a deeper, broader body and shorter legs. The main foundation stock were the Criollo, Crioulo, Andalusian, Thoroughbred and Percheron.

Campolino
Crioulo
Mangalarga

Bulgaria
Horses are systematically bred at the Bulgarian State Studs controlled by the Ministry of Agriculture. During this century, three breeds have been developed

---

Left: Austria's most famous horses are the Lipizzaners, here seen performing a quadrille.
Below: Kladrubers from Czechoslovakia are famous as driving horses.

from local stock and Hungarian and Russian imports.

The Pleven is Bulgaria's version of the Anglo-Arab. The stock used was mainly Russian Anglo-Arabs and local Arab-type mares, with some Hungarian Arabs, Gidrans and Thoroughbreds. Established as a breed before World War II, the Pleven is a robust type of horse, with the beauty of an Arab, and is used on farms and in competitions. The Danubian is based on two Hungarian breeds, the Nonius and Gidran. It is a stocky horse used for draft work and riding.

The East Bulgarian is the most refined of the three new Bulgarian breeds. It was based on Thoroughbred, Arab, Anglo-Arab and English half-breeds. It is very fast and has won the tough Pardubice steeplechase in Czechoslovakia.

Danubian
East Bulgarian
Pleven

Burma
Burma's ponies are closely related to those of northern India. The best known is the Burmese or Shan, which has been used by the hill tribes of the Shan states as a general work pony for a

long time. It is a larger version of the Manipur Pony from India. Both have Mongolian ancestors, but the Burmese has had more Arab added. It is very strong and compact.

Burmese/Shan

Canada
The number of horses in Canada is growing fast but they are all imported breeds. After a few generations of breeding, some, such as the Canadian Quarter Horse and the Canadian Pacer gain the title "Canadian". The only native breed is the Sable Island Pony, developed on Sable Island off Nova Scotia.

Sable Island ▶43

China
Ponies have long been the work animals in China. The greatest concentration is in Mongolia, with its various native types of pony. In south China, Mongolian Ponies have been crossed with Arab and Thoroughbred imports to produce the faster China Pony, used for racing.

China Pony
Mongolian Pony ▶38
Przewalski's Horse/Asian Wild Horse/Mongolian Wild Horse ▶42

Czechoslovakia
Czechoslovakia has the oldest active stud in the world, at Kladruber, which has given its name to the native breed of warm-blood. There are also many other fine State studs. The breeds produced at these studs are mainly Arabs, Kladrubers and Lipizzaners.

Kladruber ▶113

Denmark
Although the numbers of its traditionally famous breeds, the Frederiksborg and Jutland, are declining, Denmark is gaining a great reputation for its native warm-blood, called the Danish Warm-Blood. Farmers are the main breeders, and there is little state aid for breeding.

Danish Warm Blood ▶98
Frederiksborg ▶101
Jutland ▶62
Knabstrup ▶114

Finland
Finland's native cold-blood still plays an important role in this heavily forested country, where it is used to pull logs. The riding horses, usually referred to as the Finnish Universals, are used for racing and sport and leisure riding. Their numbers are increasing.

Finnhorse Draft ▶58-59
Finnish Universal

France
For centuries, the state has played an important part in French horse-breeding. It has been responsible for the maintenance of stallion depots in the various regions. Horses are produced for racing, competitions, leisure riding, draft and meat (for human and animal consumption).

Several varieties of large French breeds are declining in numbers.

These include the Poitevine, Cob, Auxois and Ariègoise. The Poitevine is an unusual horse that is bred in the Poitou region of France. It was based on Dutch stock that was imported to help drain the marshes of La Vendée and Poitou. But since the 19th century it has been used mainly for crossing with asses to produce high-quality mules. In their heyday, mules had great substance and earned a worldwide reputation.

The Ariègoise is a work horse of ancient origins, dating back to the Romans and Julius Caesar. Although their numbers are small today, Ariègoises are still used for work, particularly in the mountains of the Pyrenees and the Alps.

Cobs are bred in Normandy: these are not true breeds and have no stud book. Their development started at the beginning of the 19th century, when a distinction was made between warm-bloods produced for riding and the Army, and those for work. Horses for work were called Cobs. Sometimes called Normandy Cobs, these horses are similar to the cobs of the British Isles.

The French Pony, a result of crossbreeding, has no stud book. Its increasing numbers and popularity as a children's riding pony make it likely it will have one in the future.

Anglo-Arab ▶88-89
Ardennes ▶52
Ariègoise
Basque/Pottock ▶16
Boulonnais ▶53
Breton ▶55
Camargue ▶94-95
Cob/Normandy Cob
Comtois ▶57
French Pony
French Trotter ▶102
Landais/Barthais ▶36
Percheron ▶66-67
Poitevine
Selle Français ▶132-133

German Democratic Republic (East Germany)
East Germany has not been as active as neighboring countries in breeding horses. Its two main breeds are offshoots of West German breeds. The Mecklenburg is based on the Hanoverian, and the East Friesian is based on the Oldenburg.

East Friesian ▶100
Mecklenburg ▶117

Federal Republic of Germany (West Germany)
In West Germany the breeds of sports-horses the country is most famous for are localized in the different regional States. An exception is the Trakehner, which is found nationwide, because it was a refugee breed from the east. The Federal Government promotes and finances regional breeding. Each State has its own breed, although the Pfalz-Saar and Rheinland-Nassau were amalgamated in 1977.

The brand mark given to a horse is determined by its birthplace, not the breeds of its parents. There is a considerable interchange of ▶

Above: Germany's best known breed is the Hanoverian and this jumper, Tigre, is a famous example.

▶ breeds — the Hanoverian is found in the pedigrees of most regional breeds.

Some lesser-known regional breeds not included in the main section of this book are the Bavarian, which is a more angular, longer-legged version of the Hanoverian. It has Westphalian, Trakehner and Thoroughbred blood. The Hessen, bred at the state stud of Dillenburg, is based on, and very similar to, its neighbor the Hanoverian. The Rhineland shares its state stud of Warendorf with the more-famous Westphalian, upon which it is based. The Rhineland Pfalz-Saar inhabits a region that was once part of France and has been influenced by French breeds.

Baden-Württemberg ▶90-91
Bavarian
Black Forest Chestnut, see South German Cold-Blood ▶71
Dülmen ▶25
Hanoverian ▶107
Hessen
Holstein ▶108-109
Oldenburg ▶123
Rhenish-German Cold-Blood ▶69
Rhineland
Rhineland-Pfalz-Saar
Schleswig Holstein ▶70
South German Cold-Blood ▶71
Trakehner/East Prussian ▶140
Westphalian ▶144

Greece
Once the home of classical riding, Greece now has only a few breeds of ponies.
Peneia ▶30
Pindos ▶30
Skyros ▶30

Hungary
Hungary has excellent soil and climate for breeding horses. It is famous for its horsemanship. Today, horses are bred at huge State stud farms. The major influences are the Arab, which has been used since the Turkish invasion, and the Thoroughbred.
Furioso ▶109
Gidran ▶109
Hungarian Half-bred ▶109
Kisber ▶109
Mezohegyes ▶109
Murakoz/Murakosi ▶63
Nonius ▶122
Shagya ▶133

Iceland
The climate in Iceland is not conducive to horse breeding, but ponies brought there centuries ago have prospered and developed into the breed known as the Icelandic Pony.
Icelandic Pony ▶34-35

India
Horses in India are mainly "country-breds," such as cross-breds of imported breeds (usually Arabs and Walers) and native stock. Typical of these are the Kathiawari and Marwari from

northwest India. Some believe they developed from a shipload of Arab horses that escaped and cross-bred with local ponies. The older native breeds of ponies are the Manipur, Spiti and Bhutia.

Bhutia ▶17
Kathiawari
Manipur ▶37
Marwari
Spiti ▶17

Indonesia

With its thousands of roadless islands and primitive economy, Indonesia has discovered ponies make a major contribution to the economy. The government supports the breeding of some breeds, in particular the Batak on the island of Sumatra. This breed has had a great deal of Arab blood added.

Breeds vary from island to island and are primitive types based on Mongolian or Tarpan stock or a mixture of them both. Probably the fastest Indonesian pony is the Sandalwood. Like the Batak, it has had infusions of Arab blood. It is used for racing, but riders are usually bareback and have bitless bridles. The Java is famous for pulling two-wheeled taxis, called *sados,* on the island after which it is named. The Timor is the smallest of the ponies. Because its home-lands are close to Australia, it has been exported there to act as foundation stock for the Australian Pony. The Bali is primitive in appearance, with its upright mane and dorsal stripe. The Sumba, another breed which is dun with a dorsal stripe, has become most famous as a dancer. It performs without saddle or bridle, with bells attached to its knees. A person on foot controls the pony as it moves to a tom-tom rhythm.

Bali
Batak
Java
Sandalwood
Sumba
Timor

Iran

Iran is the home of several ancient lines of horses. The Caspian Pony, the Persian Arab and the Turkoman come from the northern steppes. The Turkoman is differentiated into the Akhal-Teke and Iomud from Russia. The Iranian strain, known as the Tchenaran, has more substance and is more compact. Apart from these famous breeds, Iran also produced the Plateau Persian, which was an amalgamation of the Arablike strains known as the Fars, Basseri, Darashuri and Qashqai. The Pahlavan, which was a mixture of Plateau Persian with Arab and Thoroughbred, and the Jaf, a robust Arab-type horse, are also products of Iran.

These breeds were promoted by the Royal Horse Society, founded during the Shah's reign in 1971. But since the change in government, there has been little

Left: Hungarian horses are now best known as driving horses.

information about horse breeding.

Caspian ▶18-19
Jaf/Kurd
Persian Arab ▶77
Plateau Persian
Turkoman (see also Akhal-Teke and Iomud, under USSR) ▶140-141

Republic of Ireland (Eire)

Ireland is a country with a climate and soil conducive to horse breeding. The government-backed Irish Horse Board gives financial and administrative aid to horse breeders.

Connemara ▶20-21
Irish Draft ▶60-61
Irish Horse ▶110

Italy

About 400 years ago, Italy produced her most famous horse, the Neapolitan. It came from Arab, Barb and Spanish stock. During the 16th and 17th centuries, the courts of Europe used the Neapolitan for High-School per-formances and as foundation stock for their own breeds. This superb breed is now extinct, and none of the present breeds have attained its stature, although most breeds are based on it.

Avelignese ▶14
Anglo-Arab Sardo ▶111
Calabrese ▶94
Italian Heavy Draft ▶61
Italian Saddle Horse ▶111

Below: The Irish horse Ballylusky ridden by Fiona Wentgis in the 1984 Olympics Three Day Event.

Maremmano ▶111
Murghese ▶120
Neapolitan
Salerno ▶111
Sanfrantellano ▶111
Siciliano ▶111

Japan

Japan is becoming more involved in horse breeding. It has imported many high-class Thoroughbreds and sports-horses. Its own breeds are ponies based on Mongolian stock. The best known of these is the Hokkaido, which is usually dun, with a dorsal stripe and dark points. Also native to Japan are the Kiso Pony, from the central part of the mainland, and the Wild Horse of southern Kyushu.

Hokkaido
Kiso
Kyushu

Mexico

Mexico's horses are based on Spanish and Portuguese stock, brought to the country in the 16th century, and on imported American breeds. The chief native breed is the Galiceño, a pony based on two Spanish and Portuguese ponies, the Garrano and Sorraia. The Galiceño is a fast, strong pony, with a running walk. It is used for draft and pack work and riding.

Galiceño

Morocco

Like Algeria, Morocco was once part of ancient Barbary, the home of the Barb.

Barb ▶91

Netherlands

The Netherlands is famous for its horses. The oldest existing breed is the Friesian, which dates back to Roman Times.

Dutch Draft ▶58
Dutch Warm-Blood ▶100
Friesian/Frisian ▶102-103
Gelderland ▶104
Groningen ▶105

New Zealand See under Australia.

Norway

Norway is the home of two important old breeds, the Norwegian Fjord and Døle. Both have been utility animals for centuries. A modern breed version of the Døle is called the Døle Trotter. It was developed by introducing Thoroughbred blood to produce a faster horse to pull light vehicles and, later, to race.

Døle Gudbrandsdal ▶57
Døle Trotter ▶57
Norwegian Fjord ▶40-41

Peru

Peru was one of the main bases for the Spanish *Conquistadores* during the 16th century. Its most famous breed, the Peruvian Horse, was developed during that time. The local "criollo" was developed from Argentinian imports.

Peruvian Horse/Peruvian Paso ▶127

Poland

Poland has 42 major studs, which produce the largest horse popula-tion in Europe. There is a great ▶

▶range of breeds, from work ponies, based on the ancient Tarpan, to Thoroughbreds. A horse that falls between these categories is the Silesian, a breed intermediate between warm-blood and cold-blood. Its most important foundation stock is the Oldenburg, which it resembles, but Hanoverians, East Friesians, and Rhinelands have also been used.

Garvolin ▶68
Huçul/Hutsul ▶34
Konik ▶35
Kopczyk Podlaski ▶68
Lidzbark ▶68
Lowicz ▶68
Malapolski ▶117
Polish Arab ▶77
Polish Draft ▶68
Silesian
Sokolsky ▶68
Sztum ▶68
Tarpan ▶ 46
Wielkopolski ▶145

Portugal
The horses and ponies of Portugal have similar origins to those of Spain.
Altér Real ▶86-87
Garrano/Minho ▶29
Lusitano ▶116-117
Sorraia ▶45

Puerto Rico
Racing is popular in Puerto Rico, so the Thoroughbred is, economically speaking, the most important breed. The native breed is the Paso Fino.
Paso Fino ▶126

South Africa
All types of equestrian activities are becoming more popular in South Africa, with the consequent growth of horse numbers. The Thoroughbred is the most important breed, but many others are represented. The native breeds are the Basuto and Boerperd.
Basuto ▶17
Boer Pony/Boerperd ▶18

Spain
Horse breeding in Spain is on the increase, and it is promoted by the government, which runs regional studs. One of the rarest breeds, the Balearic Pony, is based in Majorca. It has primitive features and an upright mane and occurs in various shades of brown.
Andalusian ▶87
Balearic
Hispano ▶108

Sweden
The government supports horse breeding in Sweden and runs a National Stud at Flyinge.
Götland/Russ ▶29
North Swedish ▶65-66
Swedish Ardennes ▶52
Swedish Warm-Blood ▶135

Switzerland
Switzerland's national stud is at Avenches, where the emphasis is on breeding riding horses. Important breeds are the Swiss Warm-Blood and a dual-purpose Army and agricultural workhorse, the Freiberger (also called the

Franches Montagnes). The old Swiss breed of Einseidler, developed by monks at Einsiedl in the 11th century, has now been merged with the Swiss Warm-Blood.
Einsiedler
Freiberger/Franches Montagnes ▶60
Swiss Warm-Blood ▶136-136

Tibet
Various work ponies are found in Tibet. They are closely related to those from northern India.
Tibetan/Nanfan ▶47

Turkey
Turkish horses are famous, but they have been types rather than breeds. The Arabs, Turkomans and, more recently, Thoroughbreds are most important. With the establishment of the Republic of Turkey, efforts have been made by the government to improve the Arabs and Thoroughbreds and to upgrade local stock to establish the Karacabey. This is a purpose-bred riding and harness horse produced from Arab, Thoroughbred, Nonius and local stock.
Karacabey

United Kingdom
Britain has more breeds for its size than any other country in the world. Most of its ancient breeds are still flourishing, though some have become extinct.

The most influential of these was probably the Galloway, a term that has been used to describe a variety of ponies but more specifically refers to dark-colored ponies bred in the region of Galloway, Scotland. They were very fast and were Britain's original racehorses. They had an influence on many breeds, including the Fell, the Dales and even the Clydesdale,

Above: Portugal is well known for its breeds of High School horses, such as this Lusitano.

but became extinct by the end of the 19th century.

The Norfolk Trotter was the fast strong trotting horse of the 18th century. Although now extinct, it had a major influence on the Hackney and the Standardbred of the United States. The Norfolk Trotter started as a breed by crossing Thoroughbreds with native mares; famous progeny include Bellfounder, who was exported to the United States to become one of the strongest influences on the development of the Standardbred. Another name for the Norfolk Trotter was the "New English Road Horse."

A breed with a shorter history than the Norfolk Trotter was the Yorkshire Coach Horse. It was developed in the 19th century in an attempt to speed up the Cleveland Bay by crossing it with the Thoroughbred. With the advent of automobiles, the purebred Cleveland survived, but its offshoot, the Yorkshire Coach Horse, became extinct.
British Warm Blood ▶92-93
Cleveland Bay ▶96-97
Clydesdale ▶56
Dales ▶21-23
Dartmoor ▶24-25
Exmoor ▶26-27
Fell ▶28-29
Galloway
Hackney Pony ▶30-31
Hackney Horse ▶106-107
Highland ▶33
New Forest ▶39-40
Norfolk Trotter
Shetland ▶44-45
Shire ▶70-71
Suffolk ▶72-73
Thoroughbred ▶80-83

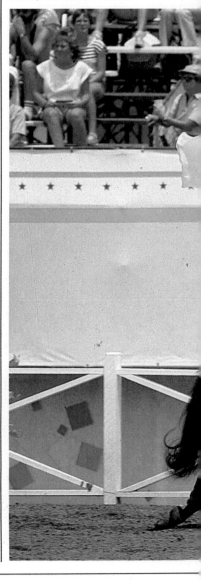

Right: The Appaloosa is a breed developed by the American Indians. Below: The USA's most numerous breed, the Quarter Horse.

United States
The United States has no indigenous breeds. The wild horses that ran across its prairies emigrated or died out. For centuries, until the arrival of the Spanish and Portuguese, there were no horses. The early conquerors and settlers brought their horses, which led to the development of many new breeds.

Most breeds still exist today, but one important one became extinct—the Narragansett Pacer. It was named after Narragansett Bay, Rhode Island. This fast, riding horse was famous for its pacing gait. It probably developed from English and Spanish Amblers and the Indian ponies. Pacers were used for riding across the rough country and for racing. Although no longer in existence, this breed played an important part in the development of the American Saddlebred, the Tennessee Walker and the Standardbred.

USSR

Horse breeding in the Soviet Union is controlled by the Central Board of Horse Breeding of the Ministry of Agriculture, with affiliated bodies responsible for the Russian Federation, the Ukraine and Kazakhstan. All matters relating to selective breeding policies, equestrian husbandry, certain aspects of veterinary care and training at both practical and theoretical level come under the aegis of the All-Union Scientific Research Institute of Horse Breeding, which maintains a close working relationship with the State studs.

State studs, which date back to the 18th century when they existed alongside private breeding establishments, were reorganized in 1930 as part of the policy of collectivization. The 106 studs now spread over 14 Union Republics operate in conjunction with 780 stud centers on State and collective farms, 65 stud stables and 5 stud stations.

The first priority was to increase the number of horses used in agriculture and improve their quality. Although the traditional role of the heavy draft has been usurped by the tractor and the combine harvester, horse power is still more efficient and economical for peripheral farm work.

To keep pace with the rapid growth of the industries producing meat and *kumiss* (a drink of fermented horse milk) it has been recommended that the number of indigenous horses bred specifically for these markets, such as the Kazakh and the Bashkir, should be increased and improved.

The Central Government also recognized the need to improve further the quality of pedigree horses for the classical equestrian sports, racing and export. They wanted to provide larger numbers of suitable animals for the country's up-and-coming leisure activity of hacking and trail riding.

The native breeds

The many local breeds of horses distributed over the vast territory of the Soviet Union are normally classified as native steppe, native mountain and native northern forest types. But within these ecological groupings, there are numerous geographical subdivisions. Traditionally reared in herds as multipurpose saddle, pack and harness horses, many of these small indigenous breeds have been improved since the 1930s by the introduction of Thoroughbred, Don and Trotter blood. They also have been crossed with the Soviet Heavy Draft, a strong cold-blood developed in western Russia in the latter half of the 19th century mainly from Belgian heavy horses. This produces larger, heavier animals suitable for the meat trade. The breeds that are reared specifically for meat and *kumiss* exist in healthy numbers, but certain lesser-known breeds are in danger of becoming extinct and their survival is currently a matter of official concern.

Steppe breeds

The native steppe breeds, which include the Buryat, the Minusin and the Kazakh, are characteristically short legged, with long barrels and light, but dense, bone.

Like all Siberian breeds, the Buryat is a hardy animal, well-adapted to withstand the severe winters of its homeland. Buryats that have been improved with Thoroughbred, Don and Trotter blood are called Transbaikal and Amur horses.

The Minusin, from the Khakassk region of Siberia, comes from the ancient Khakassk breed. But its evolution, like the Buryat's, has been influenced by the Mongolian Horse.

The Kazakh, whose history goes back more than 2,000 years, evolved as a part of the life of the nomadic tribes who inhabited the vast area of present-day Kazakhstan. Two types are recognized within the breed—the Adaev, which as a result of cross-breeding possesses a more-pronounced riding-horse type of conformation, and the smaller, coarser Dzhabe, which is bred primarily for meat.

Mountain breeds

Horses have always played an important part in the life of the tribesman and nomads inhabiting the mountainous regions of the Altai, the Tien Shan, the Caucasus and the Carpathians. For work at high altitudes, the mountain breeds must possess strong hearts, lungs, muscles and tendons and flint-hard feet. To negotiate steep mountain paths cut in the rock, to cross narrow bridges over rushing torrents and to ford fast-flowing rivers, they must also be sure-footed, react quickly in moments of danger and have a temperament that can cope with hazardous situations.

The natural habitat of alpine and subalpine meadows, with excellent grazing most of the year, provides ideal conditions for herd rearing. There is a greater variety of mountain breeds than of the steppe and forest types. To this group belong the Altai, which for centuries has been bred in the Altai Mountains and has common origins with the Mongolian, the Huçul (Hutsul) and the breeds of Transcaucasia—the Tushin and the Megrel (now almost extinct), which are indigenous to the Georgian Republic, and the Deliboz and the Karabakh, both breeds of the light, riding-horse type native to Azerbaidzhan. The Karabakh no longer exists in its purebred form. Work to restore some of the

Above: The Latvian is one of the many breeds from the USSR.

characteristics of the original breed is now being carried out at the Akdam Stud.

Northern forest breeds
The northern forest breeds are divided into an eastern group (the Yakut, the Narym and the Priob) and a western group (the Estonian, the Viatka, the Mezen, the Zhmud (Zemaituka), the Pechora, the Polessk, the Tavda and others). They are all uniquely adapted to the harsh climatic conditions of the northern regions of the country—subzero temperatures in winter and wet summers with swarms of mosquitoes. They possess considerable stamina, are able to exist on a minimum of food, have obedient and placid temperaments, do well in harness and show good paces at the walk and trot.

The northern forest breeds are small animals, with massive, long barrels, short legs and strong feet. A characteristic feature is the thickness of the coat, which grows to a length of 3-6 inches (7·5-15cm) in the coldest areas. The farther west they live, the larger their size and the more-pronounced their harness horse conformation. A number of western types, such as the Zhmud, Obva, Vyatka and Mezen, have been

Below: Quite a number of the older Russian breeds pull troikas.

improved by crossing with Estonian and Finnish horses.

Most forest breeds are named after the region to which they belong or a place or river wihin that region.

The Yakut comes from the Yakut Autonomous Republic, the Priob from around the River Ob, in the Khanty-Mansiisk region of Siberia, the Estonian from the Estonian Republic, the Pechora from around the River Pechora, in the Komi Autonomous Republic, the Mezen from around the River Mezen, in the Archangel region, the Tavda from around the River Tavda, in the Sverdlovsk region, the Polessk from the Belorussian Republic and the Zhmud from the Lithuanian Republic (it is sometimes referred to by its Lithuanian name Zemaituka).

New breeds
The policy of creating new breeds of horses is one that has been actively pursued in the Soviet Union since the 1920s.

In many cases, the formula of using three breeds of stallions with the foundation mares in various permutations at different stages of the breeding program has proved a successful one.

The Kushum, a breed developed primarily for meat and officially recognized in 1976, was evolved by crossing Kazakh mares with Thoroughbred half-bred Russian and Orlov Trotter stallions and at a later stage with Don stallions.

Kazakh mares crossed with Don, Strelets (an extinct breed from the 19th century based on the Arab) and Thoroughbred stallions were also the foundation stock of the multipurpose Kustanair horse, officially recognized as a breed in 1951.

The Lithuanian Heavy Horse is a strong, powerful horse that is used for draft work, for meat, and for crossing with other breeds to make them heavier and meatier. First recognized as a breed in 1963, it is the result of crosses between the Lithuanian Zhmud (or Zemaituka) and imported Swedish Ardennes.

The Latvian Riding Horse, still in the process of development, is based on Latvian mares of the lighter harness type crossed with Arab, Hanoverian and Thorough-bred stallions.

The Lithuanian Heavy Draft breed was registered in 1963 and has flourished since then. It was developed in Lithuania during the early 1900s mainly by crossing imported Swedish Ardennes with Zhmuds.

Local harness breeds
The Voronezh Harness Horse is based on the Bityug, a local breed from the Voronezh Province that lost its identity during the 19th century as a result of repeated crossings with English Heavy Draft Horses. In the 1930s, work began to re-establish the Bityug by mating local improved mares with the heavier type of Orlov Trotter. The desired type that was eventually

created became known as the Voronezh Harness Horse.

The Kuznets, the largest Siberian breed found in the Novosibirsk and Kemerovo Provinces, was evolved by crossing local breeds with Orlov Trotters, English Thoroughbred and English Heavy Draft Horses.

Venezuela
Like most South American countries, Venezuela developed a "criollo" from imported Iberian stock that was turned loose on its hot, dry plains. The Venezuelian version is known as the Llañero.

Yugoslavia
Yugoslavia has many State studs. The government promotes horse breeding because the animals are of great value in this predominantly agricultural country. Many farms are on steep hillsides, and it is difficult to mechanize. Most horses bred at these studs are imported breeds, but Yugoslavia has a native pony, the Bosnian, which is produced in very large numbers. The stud of Lipizza, the original home of the Lipizzaner, is also in Yugoslavia (it was in Austria when the breed was developed).

Aged is an older horse, usually over 10 years.

Ambler Old English word for a Pacer (see **Pacer**).

Ankle is an alternative term for the fetlock joint.

Back at the knee Foreleg that tends towards a concave shape when looked at from the side. Particularly obvious at the knee.

Barrel Term used to describe that part of the horse's body which is enclosed by the ribs.

Bone Measurement of circumference of the foreleg just below the knee. "Good bone" means the measurement is large.

Boxy Feet When viewed from the front, feet are narrow and not round in shape.

Cold Bloods Heavy draft breeds used in industry, agriculture and transportation.

Colic Equine pain in the stomach. A horse with colic shows signs of being in pain, tends to try and roll, and sweats.

Colt Male horse that has not been gelded (castrated), up to the age of 4 years.

Conformation The make and shape of a a horse. A horse with "good conformation" is stronger and more likely to stay sound than one with a weak conformation.

Country breds Horses or ponies that have been bred unselectively. They have no stud book, and their parents have usually been crossbred.

Cow hocks Hocks that turn inward at the point, like those of a cow.

Crossbreeding Breeding from a mare and stallion that are of different breeds.

Deep Horse is deep through the girth if the measurement is considerable from the withers to the elbow. Horse has "heartroom", especially if its chest is broad.

Dishing When forelegs do not move straight forward and back but swing to the side in an outward, circular movement.

Dorsal stripe Stripe found in primitive breeds that runs down the neck along the back to the top of the tail.

Ewe neck Top line of the neck, from the poll to the withers, is concave instead of convex or straight. It is also called an "upside-down neck."

Face markings These are shown on the page 201.

Face Front of the head; in outline it can be concave (dished), straight or convex.

Feather Long hair above, on and below the fetlock joints. It is usually found on Cold Bloods, rarely on Warm Bloods and never on Hot Bloods.

Filly Female horse or pony under the age of 4 years.

Foal Young horse or pony, male or female, up to the age of 12 months.

Forehand Front section of a horse—the forelegs, shoulder, neck and head. A horse is on its forehand when it is carrying a relatively high proportion of its weight with its forehand rather than hindquarters. This makes it less mobile and less able to spring

into the air.

Frog is a V-shaped area on the underside of the hoof. It consists of a horny substance that acts as a shock absorber.

Gait Also called **Pace.** Most breeds' gaits consist of the walk, trot, canter and gallop, but some special breeds have different or additional gaits, such as the five gaited Saddlebred and the Paso Fino.

Gaited horse One that is trained in artificial and natural gaits.

Gelding A castrated male horse.

Goose rump refers to a horse with hind quarters that slope very sharply from the point of croup to the tail. It is

a weak aspect of the conformation.

Hand Unit measurement (4in, 10.2cm) of the height of the horse. A horse is so many hands high, abbreviated "hh."

Heart room is used to describe a horse that is deep (q.v.) through the girth and broad through the chest so there is plenty of room for the heart and lungs. Such a horse usually has good stamina.

Height Taken from the highest part of the withers in a perpendicular line to the ground. It can be measured in hands or centimeters or inches.

High school horse One trained in Classical Riding and able to

perform classical or High-School airs, which are movements above the ground.

Hollow back Natural concave line of the horse is exaggerated and unnatural.

Hot Bloods Pure breeds, such as the Thoroughbred and the Arab.

Inbreeding Mating of brother and sister, sire (father) and daughter, son and dam (mother).

Limb markings illustrated on page 201.

Line breeding Mating of horses that have one or more common ancestors, but are some generations removed.

Lunging Method of exercising

Points of the horse

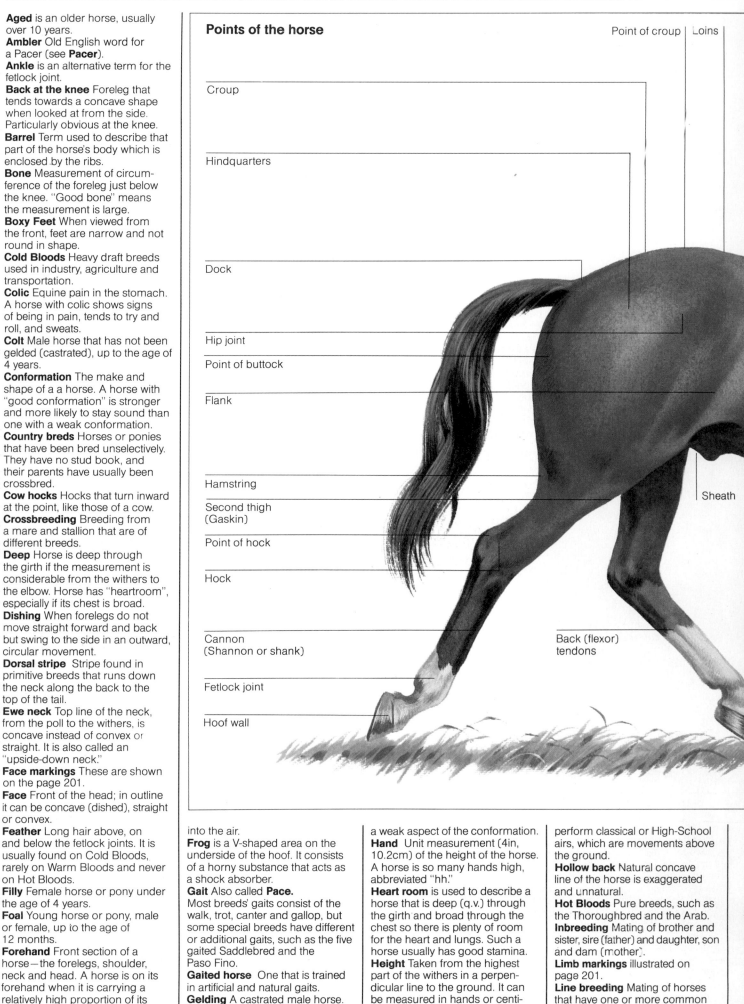

Point of croup | Loins

Croup

Hindquarters

Dock

Hip joint

Point of buttock

Flank

Hamstring

Second thigh (Gaskin)

Point of hock

Hock

Cannon (Shannon or shank)

Fetlock joint

Hoof wall

Sheath

Back (flexor) tendons

Back · Withers · Crest · Mane · Poll · Forelock

Forehead

Face

Nostril

Jowl (Jaw)

Muzzle

Throat

Chin groove

Jugular groove

Windpipe

Shoulder

Breast

Point of elbow

Forearm

Chestnut

Knee

Measurement of height in hands (hh); 1 hand = 4in (10·16cm)

Circumference taken at this point to measure the "bone"

Cannon

Ergot

Fetlock joint

Bulb of heel

Pastern

Coronet

a horse using a long rein (lunge rein) that is attached to a cavesson (a padded, tightly fitting form of halter) or to the bit of the bridle. The horse performs circles around the trainer, who stands in the center holding this rein.

Mare Female equine animal.

Mealy nose or muzzle Oatmeal color that runs up the muzzle. There are no white markings.

Near The left side or left limbs of a horse.

Odd colored Coat with patches of two or more different colors.

Off The right side or right limbs of a horse.

Oriental Name used to describe breeds from the Orient, including the Arab and breeds based on the Arab.

Over at the knee When the foreleg viewed from the side is convex in shape, particularly at the knee.

Outcrossing Use of outside blood in breeding.

Pacer Horse that trots using its legs in lateral pairs, such as near foreleg and near hindleg together. The normal trot uses diagonal pairs, such as near foreleg and off hindleg together. A pacer once was known as an **Ambler.**

Pace Another term for **Gait;** also a variation of the two time gait

(trot) when the horse's legs move in lateral pairs.

Parrot mouth When the upper jaw overhangs the lower jaw so there is no true contact between the upper and lower incisor teeth. In bad cases, grazing is difficult, and the horse often has digestive problems. It is also called an "undershot" mouth.

Pigeon toes Toes that turn inward.

Points Term used to describe colors; refers to the mane, tail and lower limbs.

Prepotent When the sire or dam tends to pass on his or her characteristics to their progeny.

Rack Four beat gait with each foot

moving rapidly, with short, equal intervals between each hoof beat, as in the American Saddlebred.

Roach back Conformation weakness; the back is convex.

Roman nose Describes a horse with a convex face.

Sloping shoulders The line of the shoulders runs obliquely from the withers to the point of the shoulders.

Straight shoulders Line of the shoulders is upright.

Sequence of gaits or paces For each gait, there is a correct sequence of footfalls. At the walk, four hoofbeats should be heard with equal intervals between them. They should fall in the order of right hind leg, right foreleg, left hindleg and left foreleg. At the trot, there are two hoofbeats, with legs moving in diagonal pairs separated by a moment of suspension. At the canter, there are three hoof beats followed by a moment of suspension. The canter can be on the left lead or right lead. On the left lead, the first hoofbeat is the right hind followed by the left hind and right foreleg together and finally the leading leg, the left foreleg. On the right lead, the left hind is first. In the gallop, four hoof beats are heard followed by a moment of suspension. On the left lead, the sequence is right hind leg, left hind leg, right foreleg, left foreleg. On the right lead, the left hindleg starts a similar sequence.

Sickle hocks Weak hocks that when viewed from the side are bent to form shapes similar to a sickle.

Stallion Also called a "stud" or "entire." It is an ungelded horse that should be capable of reproducing the species.

Standing square refers to a horse standing in balance with its legs lined up in pairs.

Tied-in is an expression used to describe the front legs of a horse whose circumference measured just below the knee is less than that measured a little lower and nearer to the fetlock joint.

Toad eye Mealy rim on both eyelids; it almost encircles the eye that is prominent. Found in the Exmoor Pony.

Wall eye Eye with a partial or total lack of pigment in the iris; it is pink or blue-white in appearance.

Warm Bloods Breeds that are not as pure and refined as the Hot Bloods or as large and slow as Cold Bloods. These breeds are used for riding, competitions and driving.

Worms Parasites harbored by horses. If present in large numbers, they can cause serious damage, such as colic, loss of condition and even death. There are many types of worms, but regular dosing of worm medicine and care of grassland usually prevents serious infestation.

Yearling Colt or filly that is over 1 year and under 2 years. For Thoroughbreds, the first birthday is taken as the 1st January.

Zebra marks Stripes on the limbs, neck, withers and/or hindquarters of horses.

COLORS AND MARKINGS

COLORS
There are many colors; if there is any doubt as to which color a horse is, the muzzle and eyelids are examined and are used as the deciding factors. The most common colors are black, brown, bay, chestnut and gray, although the gray is not a color but a failure of the pigment cells in the hair roots to produce color.

Bay
This is a brown color with shades ranging from red and yellow to very close to brown. Points are black.

Black
The coat, limbs, mane and tail are black; any markings are white.

Blue roan
There are various shades of roan; the blue roan has a basic color of black or brown and a sprinkling of white.

Brown
Dark brown or nearly black, with brown-to-black points.

Chestnut
Also called *sorrel*, this is a ginger, yellow or red color to the coat. The mane and tail are the same color as the coat or lighter.

Claybank
A reddish-yellow dun color with a slightly darker mane and tail.

Cream
Cream-colored hairs on an unpigmented skin. The eyes often have a pink appearance.

Dapple gray
The white and black hairs of a gray horse are not uniform, and in this case darker circles form dapples which are separated by lighter areas.

Dun
The more common variation of the dun is the *yellow dun,* usually referred to simply as *dun*. The hairs are yellow on a black skin. Points are normally black, and there may be a dorsal stripe and zebra markings on the limbs.

Flea-bitten gray
This is a gray in which the coat is flecked with hairs of a darker color.

Gray
Hairs are white and black on a black skin. There are many shades, from light to dark gray, and variations, such as the *Flea-bitten* and *dapple grays.*

Liver chestnut
This is the darkest shade of chestnut.

Palomino
Various shades of gold, with a flaxen or white mane and tail.

Piebald
This is one variation of the *pinto* or *calico.* The large, irregular patches are black and white.

Skewbald
Large patches in the coat are white and any color but black; usually brown.

Above: An Appaloosa mare and foal. This breed has a white coat with various patterns of spots. It is not the only breed of spotted horse; others include the Knabstrup (see page 114) and the Pinzgauer, a line within the breed of Noriker (see page 64).

Strawberry roan
This variation of roan (an admixture of white hairs with another color) is white and chestnut, which gives a pink-red appearance to the coat.

Bay

Black

Chestnut (Sorrel)

Claybank (Red roan/Red dun)

Blue roan

Brown

Cream

Dapple gray

MARKINGS

Markings are areas of white on the head, body and limbs. The other type of marking used for identification is a whorl, which is a pattern formed by hairs around a small central spot.

On the head

Star is white on the forehead.
Stripe is a narrow white mark down the face.
Blaze is a broad white mark down the face, usually extending from the eyes to the muzzle.
White face is a white forehead, eyes, nose and parts of the muzzle.
Snip is a small area of white around the nostrils.
Wall eye is white or blue-white coloring in the eye.

On the legs

Stocking is white on the leg from coronet to knee or hock.
Sock is white covering the fetlock and part of the cannon bone.
Other markings on the leg are described by the area they cover.

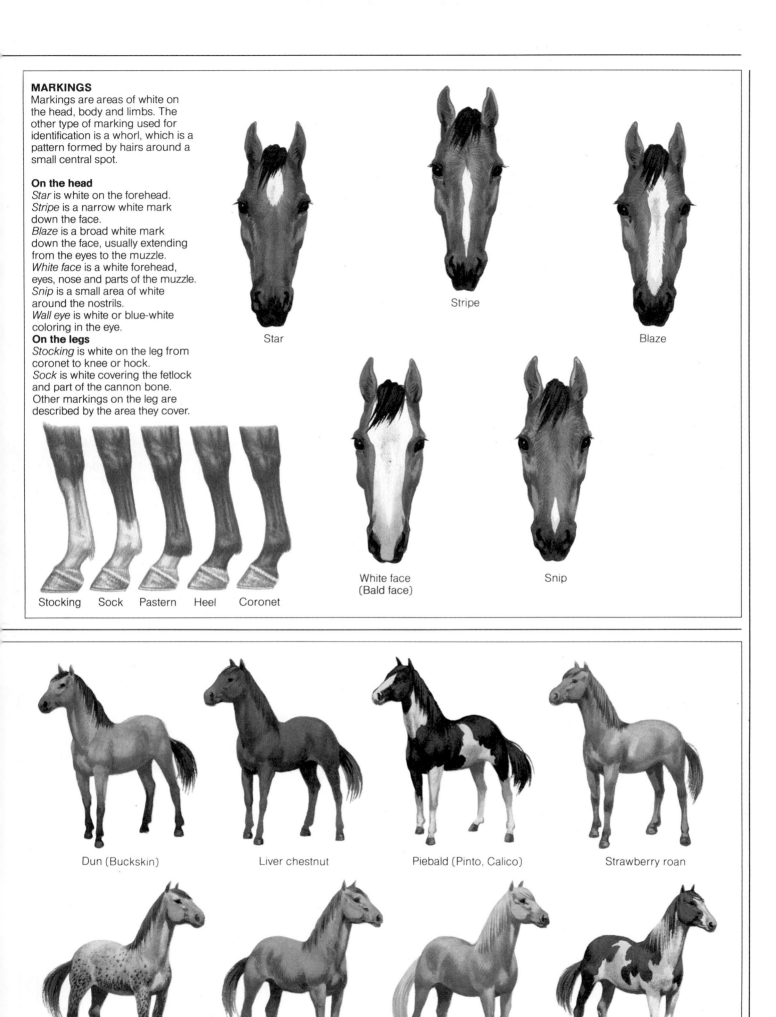

Star

Stripe

Blaze

White face (Bald face)

Snip

Stocking   Sock   Pastern   Heel   Coronet

Dun (Buckskin)

Liver chestnut

Piebald (Pinto, Calico)

Strawberry roan

Flea-bitten gray

Gray

Palomino

Skewbald (Pinto, Calico)

INDEX

PICTURE CREDITS

Photographs
Photographs are credited by page number and by their position on the page, as follows: T (Top); C (Centre); B (Bottom); BL (Bottom Left); FL (Far Left), etc.
Robin Adshead: 37(B), 47(T).
Animal Photography: Sally Anne Thompson, 19, 23, 25(B), 29(T), 29(B), 30, 34(T), 34(B), 35, 37(T), 40(T), 40-41, 47(B), 49(T), 49(B), 55(T), 55(B), 56, 57(T), 57(B), 58, 59, 60, 62, 63(T), 63(B), 64(T), 64(B), 65, 69, 71(B), 72(T), 73(T), 73(B), 76, 79(T), 81, 84, 85(T), 89, 94(B), 95, 99(T), 101(T), 101(C), 101(B), 103, 105(T), 105(B), 107(T), 107(B), 112(T), 112(B), 112-113, 113(T), 114(T), 122(T), 122(B), 123(T), 124, 128, 130(T), 133(B), 138, 139(T), 139(B), 140, 142, 144, 156(T), 156(B), 196-7(T), 200; Zofia Raczkowska, 145(B); R Willbie, 8-9, 71(T), 100(B), 123(B), 135(B), 148(T).
Ardea: Jean-Paul Ferrero, 14(B), 16,

16-17, 87(T), 93(B), 164-165(T), 168(T), 170(B), 176(T), 180(B); Clem Haagner, 97(T).
Vivienne Burdon: 36
Bruce Coleman: Mark Boulton, 8(C); Jane Burton, 46; Eric Crichton, 6(T), 8(B); World Wildlife Fund/F. P. Jansen, 8(T).
Kit Houghton Photography:
Endpapers, 9, 10(T), 10(B), 10-11, 11(T), 12, 12-13, 14(T), 15, 18(B), 20, 21(T), 21(B), 22, 22-3, 24, 25(TL), 25(TR), 26, 27(T), 28, 31(T), 31(B), 33(T), 33(B), 39(T), 39(B), 41(B), 42, 44(T), 44(B), 45(T), 45(B), 50, 50-51, 52, 53(T), 53(B), 61(T), 61(C), 61(B), 66(B), 66-7, 67(T), 67(B), 72(B), 74(B), 74-5, 77, 78(T), 78(B), 79(B), 80, 82(B), 82-3, 83(B), 85(B), 86(T), 86(B), 87(B), 90(T), 91(T), 91(B), 92, 93(T), 94(T), 96, 97(B), 98, 99(B), 100(T), 102(T), 102(B), 106(T), 106(B), 108-9, 109(T), 110(T), 111, 114(B), 115, 116(T), 116(B), 116-7, 118(T), 118(B), 119, 120, 121, 125,

126(T), 126(B), 127(T), 127 (B), 129(T), 129(B), 131(T), 131(B), 132-3, 133(T), 133(T), 134(T), 134(B), 135(T), 136(T), 137(T), 137(B), 141, 143(T), 143(B), 145(T), 146-7, 148(B), 149(T), 149(B), 150, 150-1, 151(T), 152-3, 154(B), 154-5, 157, 158(B), 158-9, 159(T), 159(B), 160(T), 160(B), 161(T), 161(B), 162(B), 162-3, 163(T), 163(B), 164(T), 164(C), 164-5(B), 165(B), 166(T), 166(B), 167(T), 168(B), 169(T), 169(B), 170(T), 170-1, 171, 172 (BL), 172(BR), 172-3, 173(T), 173(B), 174(B), 174-5, 175(B), 176(B), 176-7, 177(B), 178(T), 178(B), 179, 180(T), 181(T), 181(B), 182(T), 182(C), 182-3, 183(TL), 183(TR), 183(CL), 183(CR), 184(B), 184-5, 185(B), 186(B), 186-7, 187(T), 187(B), 190(T), 190-1, 192(T), 192(B), 193, 194(T), 194-5, 195(T), Back Jkt.
Nova Scotia, Canada, Department of Tourism: 43(T).

Senckenberg Museum, Frankfurt, Dr. Jens Franzen: 6(C).
Victoria Settipassi: 38.
Vision International: Robert Maier, 68; Elisabeth Weiland, Contents page, 7, 17(T), 90(B), 104-5, 108, 110(B), 117(T), 146(B), 188-9, 196-7(B).

Artwork
All artwork is by John Francis, except for that of Leg Markings, page 201(C), which is by Eric Tenney. Copyright of all artwork is the property of Salamander Books Ltd.

EDITOR'S ACKNOWLEDGEMENTS
I would like to thank Vickie Walters and Suzanne Willcock for help with picture research; Louise Egerton and Beverley le Blanc for copy-editing and proofreading, and Isobel McLean for preparing the index.

Jonathan Elphick

Above: Mares and foals, Kladruby Stud, Czechoslovakia.